CW01096048

Theory and Practice of Harmonisation

Dedicated to the memory of Gerrit Betlem, who sadly passed away before the completion of this book. A great scholar and friend, he will be missed.

Theory and Practice of Harmonisation

Edited by

Mads Andenas

University of Oslo, Norway, former Director, British Institute of International and Comparative Law, London and Centre of European Law, King's College, University of London, UK

Camilla Baasch Andersen

University of Leicester, UK and Institute of Commercial Law at Pace University Law School, New York, USA, formerly of the Centre for Commercial Law Studies, Queen Mary College, University of London, UK and University of Copenhagen, Denmark

Edward Elgar
Cheltenham, UK • Northampton, MA, USA

Published by
Edward Elgar Publishing Limited
The Lypiatts
15 Lansdown Road
Cheltenham
Glos GL50 2JA
UK

Edward Elgar Publishing, Inc.
William Pratt House
9 Dewey Court
Northampton
Massachusetts 01060
USA

A catalogue record for this book
is available from the British Library

Library of Congress Control Number: 2009941259

ISBN 978 1 84980 001 3

Typeset by Manton Typesetters, Louth, Lincolnshire, UK
Printed and bound by MPG Books Group, UK

Contents

Contributors

Orkun Akseli, Durham University, UK

Mads Andenas, University of Oslo, Norway; Institute of Advanced Legal Studies, School of Advanced Study, University of London, UK

Camilla Baasch Andersen, University of Leicester, UK

Stelios Andreadakis, Oxford Brookes University, UK

Yutaka Arai-Takahashi, University of Kent, UK

Ross Ashcroft, Charles Darwin University, Australia

Hugh Beale, University of Warwick, UK

Gerrit Betlem, Formerly of University of Southampton, UK (Deceased)

Louis F. Del Duca, Penn State – Dickinson School of Law, USA

James Devenney, University of Exeter, UK

Miriam Goldby, George Washington University, USA

Sandeep Gopalan, National University of Ireland, Maynooth

Maren Heidemann, Institute of Advanced Legal Studies, School of Advanced Study, University of London, UK

Rene Franz Henschel, Aarhus School of Business, University of Aarhus, Denmark

Irini Katsirea, Middlesex University, UK

Mel Kenny, University of Leicester, UK

Jimmy Kodo, University of Hertfordshire, UK

Albert H. Kritzer, Formerly of Pace University Law School, USA (Deceased)

Eva J. Lohse, Friedrich-Alexander-University, Erlangen-Nürnberg, Germany

Isidora Maletić, King's College, London, UK

Jurgita Malinauskaite, Brunel University, UK

Gerard McCormack, University of Leeds, UK

Daniel Nagel, BRP Renaud & Partner

Adaora Okwor, Formerly of University of Liverpool, UK

Ricardo Pereira, Imperial College, UK

Dagmar Schiek, University of Leeds, UK

Phil Syrpis, University of Bristol, UK

Christian Twigg-Flesner, University of Hull, UK

Qianlan Wu, University of Nottingham, UK

Helen Xanthaki, Institute of Advanced Legal Studies, School of Advanced Study, University of London, UK

Bruno Zeller, Victoria University, Australia

Preface: Theory and practice of harmonisation

The topic of this book is the theory and practice of harmonisation. This is an ambitious topic, and this book can only make a limited contribution. The contributors come from different fields of law, and develop a number of common themes.

Harmonisation is an important feature of the modern legal system. Harmonisation of the laws of the Member States is a core instrument of the European Union. Many international treaty obligations entail duties to adopt conform legislation and ensure conform application. International and regional human rights treaties provide important examples of this. There is a considerable scholarly literature on different harmonisation issues, but not bringing together the outcome of this scholarship in a comparative analysis or in developing more general theory on the harmonisation process or different aspects of it. There is a further need for bringing together scholars of a range of legal, social science and humanities disciplines, including from within the law, general legal theory or jurisprudence, constitutional law, comparative law, international law, human rights law and EU law, and the different national and international legal areas most affected by harmonisation. Contributions are made in integration studies, international relations, European studies, and political theory. Moving freely over the boundaries that divide the law, and the fragmented scholarly disciplines, may usefully combine perspectives in interdisciplinary and multidisciplinary scholarship. In this way one may provide models for, and improve, the understanding of the harmonisation process. This book is mainly by legal scholars and the wider perspectives and the combination of perspectives from interdisciplinary and multidisciplinary scholarship is left outstanding. The following points will demonstrate how rich and demanding scholarship in one discipline, the legal, can be.

The procedures for adopting the harmonising instrument, and for subsequent amendments to it, are under rapid development. In the EU, the legislative procedures are a central constitutional concern, and are subject to continuous reform. Different treaty regimes offer new and alternative mechanisms.

The forms of the harmonising instrument offer much variety and innovation. International treaties and conventions do not follow universal models. In the EU, there is an important difference between directives and regulations, but also the regulation, which has direct effect without any legislative transposition, often requires different implementation measures to have its effect in national law. Some main types of directives are minimum standards directives, maximum standards directives, framework directives, and directives in the process of open method of coordination. The relationship to the fundamental freedoms in the EC Treaty is another issue. For international treaties and conventions, there is the relationship to customary international law and other treaties and conventions.

The role of international financial institutions, such as the World Bank and the IMF, in legal harmonisation across a wide field, is controversial and requires further analysis to be fully understood. Harmonisation, aid and development bring up many related issues.

Informal harmonisation processes, outside the intergovernmental fora, are of increasing importance. The role of model codes, principles and other outcomes of such processes is another field of study. Their interaction with the intergovernmental organs, and their reception in contract practice or directly by national legislators or courts merits further attention. Important examples here are *Principles, Definitions and Model Rules of European Private Law. Draft Common Frame of Reference (DCFR)*, 2009 (see also the *Interim Outline Edition*, 2009), the research carried out by the Study Group on a European Civil Code (the von Bar Group) and the Research Group on EC Private Law (Acquis Group) and other academic and scholarly projects and their relationship with more formal EU procedures: see for instance the European Commission's 2003 *Action Plan on a More Coherent European Contract Law* which merits study.

Transposition in national law takes different forms in national legislation, and the procedures vary as well. Harmonisation has affected the form of national legislation, and the sources of law in the national legal system. Court practice in the application of harmonised law follows yet other principles and patterns. The response in case law to the new sources of law that can assist in promoting uniformity, or in some fields the ways in which the lack of such sources are compensated for, is of particular interest. The use of judgments from other international or national jurisdictions is one current issue. Informal networks of judges cooperate across jurisdictional boundaries in the application of international instruments, assisting one another in finding sources and practical solutions to the uniformity problems.

Amendment and monitoring of the transposition and subsequent practice under national law is another area where there in some areas are highly developed regimes, and in others practically nothing following the adoption of a convention. There are models involving an independent international monitoring body, or more judicialised institutions, or combinations of supranational monitoring and court institutions. Novel forms of institutionalised peer review have developed over the last couple of decades.

Enforcement and sanctioning provide other challenges, closely related to monitoring and amendment.

The experiences with harmonised regimes provide extensive material which is well suited for research. In the EU, there is an emerging scholarship comparing the transposition of directives in different national laws. This provides a basis for the Review of the Consumer Acquis, which is another of the harmonisation projects of the European Commission, currently limited to eight directives, including the Consumer Sales Directive and the Unfair Terms Directive, leaving aside other directives in the consumer field such as the Consumer Credit Directive, the Unfair Commercial Practices Directive and the Product Liability Directive. Maximum harmonisation and the use of mandatory rules in the directives may have had a profound effect on the private law of the Member States, which if it has had such an effect, remains underexplored.

The international conventions in the long established tradition for harmonisation of commercial law provide another field of emerging scholarship: see for instance, the United Nations Convention on Contracts for the International Sale of Goods, 1980, the UNCITRAL Model Law on International Commercial Arbitration 1985, UNIDROIT's Principles of International Commercial Contracts, the EBRD's Secured Transactions Project, and the ICC's Uniform Customs and Practice for Documentary Credits.

In comparative law there is a current discourse about legal transplants. There is also a challenge to the idea of convergence between national legal systems and traditions. One issue here is to link the theoretical models that have emerged here with the scholarship on harmonisation in different fields.

Most of the chapters in this book are based on the 2008 WG Hart Workshop where they were presented and discussed. 'The theory and practice of harmonisation' was the topic of that year's workshop (which is organised annually at the Institute of Advanced Legal Studies, the University of London). Since then, there have been many important developments that the authors have had scarce opportunity to include in their papers over the period of development of this book. In the field of EU regulation this has especially been true for the finalisation of the DCFR in 2009, the Directive on Consumer Rights in 2011, and the newly proposed Regulation on a common EU Sales Law in October 2011. In transnational commercial law, UNCITRAL have finalised their bid for a convention on carriage of goods by sea. In English Law, the BIS are developing a new registration of company charge regime and there is a new Secured Transactions Law Reform project founded by Professor Sir Roy Goode; both fuelled by inspiration from other legal regimes. Harmonisation is difficult to keep up with, and we ask that readers keep this in mind when reading the individual chapters.

The editors offer their thanks to the contributors to the book, who continue to work in this complex field, undaunted by these rapid developments. We would also like to thank Belinda Crothers, who organised the 2008 WG Hart Workshop with her usual great skill and patience, and Sir Francis Jacobs who was the source of generous advice, as on so many previous occasions, and who graciously opened and chaired the first day of the workshop. Finally, we would like to thank Nick Foster who originally conceived the bid for the 2008 WG Hart Conference, but then had to leave it to us for health reasons. Had it not been for Nick's concept, braving the treacherous depths of the theory of harmonisation, this book would not be here today.

Mads Andenas and Camilla Baasch Andersen

1. Harmonising and regulating financial markets[1]

Mads Andenas[2]

INTRODUCTION

This chapter discusses problems of harmonisation and regulation of the European Internal Financial Market. The argument is that the current division of powers between the EU and Member States is not achieving sufficient harmonisation to develop an internal market. The obstacles to the Internal Financial Market presented by national regulatory and supervisory regimes remain too high, and the EU minimum standards and mutual recognition regime have failed to lower these barriers sufficiently. There is a need for broader based regulatory and supervisory institutions, undertaking at a European level what cannot effectively be done at a national level, including providing a system for preventing and dealing with systemic crises and risks of such crises. The European Central Bank may develop a response to the latter, but the establishment of an EU financial market regulator is the better solution. The chapter also addresses some of the agency problems of the decision making process, and the crisis driven nature of regulatory reform.

1. PROBLEMS OF HARMONISATION AND REGULATION

The subject of this chapter is problems of European financial market harmonisation and regulation. The creation of a European Financial Market has encountered problems of two kinds. The first is that market integration has not been very effective. The markets are divided by national borders as many

[1] An earlier version of this chapter was delivered as the Annual Guido Carli Lecture at the University of LUISS Guido Carli, Rome, in 2006.
[2] MA, DPhil(Oxon.); PhD(Cambridge); Professor, University of Oslo, Norway. Former Director, British Institute of International and Comparative Law, London and Centre of European Law, King's College, University of London. Senior Research Fellow, IALS, University of London, UK. Research was undertaken with support from the Norwegian Finance Market Fund.

financial services and most financial institutions are still limited to one country. The second is that the market integration that has taken place, and other features of modern financial markets working in the same direction, renders national regulators less effective. In one perspective, financial markets are becoming markets without a state. Whereas national authorities' effectiveness in regulation is questioned, in another perspective national regulations still impede market access and make cross-border establishment and provision of services too expensive for it to take off in many parts of the market.

Effectiveness in regulation has many aspects, one of which is to handle financial crises. Another aspect is that regulation is crisis driven, and has always been so. While national regulators today cannot be expected to handle a major financial crisis, the formal powers nonetheless firmly remain at the national level. While the European level may be able to develop the tools to handle such crises, EU institutions are not given the required powers to do so. This may suit both the Member State and the EU level well. Neither can in a real sense be held responsible for a breakdown, should it ever occur. So any more fundamental reform is postponed until the next crisis. Not that the solution with stronger Euro-regulators is a given consequence or outcome of a major financial crisis in Europe. But stronger Euro-regulators, or even a single European financial market regulator, seem the more effective solution for reasons just discussed, and which we will develop further in this chapter. It may seem surprising that it is not considered, or considered as a realistic alternative, in advance of the crisis, with the large welfare costs a crisis would bring with it.

In this chapter, we will first look at the foundations for financial market regulation, its harmonisation in Europe and the institutional dimension. We will discuss the framework of the EU and the different policy options it leaves. The chapter builds on the author's previous work on the problems of handling banking crises in Europe with central banking at a European level and financial market supervision at a national level,[3] complicated further by EU state aid rules,[4] his analysis of the problems of lack of enforcement of

---

[3] See M Andenas and L E Panourgias, 'Applied Monetary Policy and Bank Supervision by the ECB' in J J Norton and M Andenas (eds), *International Monetary and Financial Law Upon Entering the New Millennium. A Tribute to Sir Joseph and Ruth Gold* (BIICL, London, 2002) 119; M Andenas and C Hadjiemmanuil, 'Banking Supervision, The Internal Market and European Monetary Union' in M Andenas (ed.), *European Economic and Monetary Union: the institutional framework* (Kluwer Law International, London, Doordrecht 1997) 373, and also Lazaros E. Panourgias and Mads Andenas, 'The euro, EMU and UK law', in Jean-Victor Louis (ed.), *The euro in the National Context* (BIICL, London 2002).

[4] See M Andenas, 'Who is Going to Supervise Europe's Financial Markets', in M Andenas and Y Avgerinos (eds), *Financial Markets in Europe: Towards a Single Regulator*, with a Foreword by Charles Goodhart (Kluwer Law International, London, The Hague, New York, 2003), xv–xxvi.

financial market regulation,[5] and his work on general services issues in the EU and the WTO.[6]

2. WHY DO WE REGULATE?

We now turn to the different aims of financial market regulation. The stability of the financial system, consumer protection and deterrence of fraud are acknowledged as the three core aims. They are accorded different weight in different sectors of the financial market. Legislators, regulators and academics disagree not only about the weight but also the content of these three aims.[7] Systemic stability is however becoming the more important aim of financial market regulation but remains the most uncertain: we cannot agree on what can lead to systemic breakdown (or what can be done to deter or limit the risks).[8]

Why did 2008 seem a good time to revisit the different aims of financial market regulation? The first is the problems with Lamfalussy process for harmonising the EU Internal Financial Market. It has not delivered the integration which was expected. The second is the lack of a lender of last resort function in Europe which can tackle the issues that national authorities no longer can. The third is the evidence of the many problems in cooperation between national regulators. One simply cannot assume that it would stand the test that a major financial crisis would be.[9]

---

[5] See for instance the article by M Andenas and D Fairgrieve, 'Misfeasance in Public Office, Governmental Liability and European Influences' (2002) 51 *ICLQ* 757–80. They argue in favour of an extended liability for lack of effective banking supervision, and that banking regulators should be liable where there is a sufficient breach of the duty to supervise and enforce banking regulation.

[6] See for instance M Andenas and K Alexander (eds), *WTO and Trade in Services* (Nijhoff, Brill, Leiden 2008) and M Andenas and W H Roth (eds), *The Right to Provide Services in EC Law* (Oxford University Press, Oxford, 2002).

[7] There is often a conflict between the statutory aims and objectives and the aims formulated by the regulators: see M Andenas and D Fairgrieve, 'Misfeasance in Public Office, Governmental Liability and European Influences' (2002) 51 *ICLQ* 757–80. In the UK, the Financial Services Authority (FSA) emphasises systemic stability as the primary aim of banking supervision. The FSA is an independent non-governmental body, given statutory powers by the Financial Services and Markets Act 2000, and the Act lists these aims: market confidence, public awareness, consumer protection and reduction of financial crime.

[8] Recent studies continue to challenge the basis for modern banking regulation. See for instance, J R Barth, G Caprio and R Levine, *Rethinking Bank Regulation. Till Angels Govern* (Cambridge University Press, New York, 2006).

[9] See the discussion in CAE Goodhart and D Schoenmaker, 'Burden sharing in a banking crisis in Europe', Special Paper No 164, LSE Financial Markets Group (FMG)

A financial crisis would most likely open the window for reform. Financial marked regulation can only be understood on the background of the reactive nature of regulation. It develops in response to the crisis or the scandal. In Europe another kind of window was the proposal of the Delors Report which led to the creation of the European Central Bank (ECB) and introduction of the euro. There was strong support for an independent European central bank, for many also the only way of getting an independent monetary policy in their country.[10] The Delors Report proposed to move banking supervision to the ECB, but this proposal was in the end rejected. Since then we have had an expansion of national regulatory institutions, which may work against any European solution. A further window came after the introduction of the Euro and when French and German domestic needs made a European regulator attractive to those two countries. This too, closed rapidly.

What is the scholarly challenge in this? First we have the nature of applied research: analysing and bringing order into a practically important field. Research on financial market regulation often has policy implications and can appear to be mostly about rationalising and justifying policy choices. The level of scholarly ambition in the legal and economic contributions is usually rather low. There is a need to go beyond this. More ambitious contributions are required. And in particular at a point in time, such as today, where scholarship may influence policy choices which are in the process of being made. One can begin with the flawed tools at our disposal in this field, and with the different meanings of concepts that we use as if they had one meaning and were universally applicable. The prudential is a good example of a core concept which is flawed in the way it is used in scholarship and in policy. 'Prudential supervision' is a term used in the EU. Here 'prudential' denotes matters that are subject to home country control, and it also is used as a delimitation of ECB competence, which we will discuss below. The prudential is also used in international regulatory cooperation in the BIS, and here it has a similar but not identical meaning to that it has in the EU. In the WTO the 'prudential carve-out' appears, and here 'prudential'

Special Paper Series (London, March 2006) on who should bear the burden of any proposed recapitalisation should failures occur in large cross-border banks, and also S Osterloo and D Schoenmaker, 'Financial Supervision in an Integrating Europe: Measuring Cross-Border Externalities', LSE FMG Special Papers 156 (London, April, 2004).

[10] The growing realisation of the benefits of an independent monetary policy still met with strong opposition. Some of those responsible for monetary policy in national institutions such as ministries of finance and central banks saw the ECB as the opportunity for gaining central bank independence, which may not have been possible at a national level. They had to accept that this implied that monetary policy moved up to the EU level, a move some of them otherwise might have resisted. See the discussion in Lazaros E. Panourgias and Mads Andenas, 'The euro, EMU and UK law', in Jean-Victor Louis (ed.), *The euro in the National Context* (BIICL, London, 2002).

indicates that something is subject to host country jurisdiction. You find it in different national jurisdictions, again with different meanings, and in US law it is the basis for federal jurisdiction in banking legislation.

The list of tools that are flawed due to the vagueness of concepts continues. The lender of last resort function of central banks is central in the handling of bank crises. Various authors will use the concept as if it only had one and a most precise meaning. The only problem is that they will ascribe different meanings to it. There are historical reasons for the particular degree of vagueness in financial market supervision and central banking. Vagueness may deter distortions and reduce perverse incentives, and hold market actors from placing reliance on state intervention. Vagueness can serve a purpose.

The discussion of the flawed tools could also take account of the rapid growth of financial marked regulation, and the arrested development of many of the concepts used. Regulation has expanded considerably. The meaning of prudential regulation, of conduct of business and consumer or investor protection, and of home country control therefore changes. Home country control, even if the different meanings of the prudential are taken into account, is used in different ways, for instance in the EU and BIS. One has to enquire whether the historical reasons for particular vagueness in financial market supervision and central banking hold up. With the changing nature of the field and its regulation there is every reason to take the enquiry further and to ask whether the concepts underpinning regulation remain adequate.

There is also limited scholarship on the national traditions and approaches. Let us pick two examples. The first is the 1994 IMF study on the effectiveness of banking supervision and handling of banking crises. It gave the highest score to the UK as there had been no regulatory interventions in the relevant period. In another study from 2006 the highest score went to regulators that most actively used administrative measures/interventions.[11] The 2006 study stated that there are methodological problems, which the 1994 IMF study did not.

The tools do not become less flawed with the impact of different national traditions and differences between financial markets. To start with the methods of banking supervision and the UK. The BCCI and Baring inquiries from the 1990s show the difference from other European and from the US regulatory tradition. Then there is the difference between regulation in banking, insurance and investment services. One also has to note the rapid change. There is for instance not much in terms of traditions for investment services regulation. And with the rapid change which now is taking place, national traditions may be less relevant in this sector.

---

[11]   J R Barth, G Caprio and R Levine, *Rethinking Bank Regulation. Till Angels Govern* (Cambridge University Press, New York, 2006).

The core concepts are not wholly belonging to the sphere of law or that of economics. Inter-disciplinarity can be a reason for vagueness with the need to rely on concepts partially based in another discipline. The outcome could be that they are based in no discipline. One ends up with sociological ideal-types built on different models. They are lacking the rigour needed for empirical or legal/normative research. This goes back to the need for going beyond the current state of scholarship, and that more ambitious contributions are required, at a point in time when scholarship may influence policy choices.

3.   SEPARATING MONEY AND BANKING SUPERVISION

Monetary policy and supervision of financial institutions or markets were until recently an unchallenged competence of the national state; some would regard it as being at the very core of the modern state. All the European Community could offer was a low level of coordination of economic and monetary policy and a severely restricted free movement of financial services with a limited harmonisation of supervisory rules. European economic and monetary union introduced a geographical separation between money and supervision of financial institutions and markets. In the euro area, with a single currency, it is still the many different national authorities that are regulating or supervising banks and other financial institutions. The European Central Bank defines and implements a single monetary policy as one of its basic tasks. But within a harmonised legislative framework in the directives, national authorities (in many countries they are more than one) remain responsible for banking supervision. The European Central Bank's complementary supervision role in relation to banks and payment systems adds to the complication.[12]

One of the major obstacles to the development of an Internal Financial Market was the economic policies pursued by Member States. The old quantitative regime regulated the supply of credit. It did this through the fixing of interest rates, loan terms and quotas for credit, both on the total lending by different financial institutions and on what sectors of the economy they could lend to. It restricted the access to the bond market. There were numerous other regulatory techniques applied. This kind of credit policy as well as monetary policy was a matter for Member States. And it could not be effective unless capital flows between Member States were kept to a minimum. Money and banking

---

[12]   See the discussion in M Andenas and C Hadjiemmanuil, 'Banking Supervision, The Internal Market and European Monetary Union' in M Andenas (ed.), *European Economic and Monetary Union: the institutional framework* (Kluwer Law International, London, Doordrecht, 1997) 373.

supervision had to be united in the Member States. This has changed, partly as a consequence of the new economic and monetary policies that have taken over. There are a number of issues that need to be resolved when money and supervision are separated. There is first the question of the lender of last resort and the wider handling of banking crises. The central bank acts as the banks' lender of last resort, providing liquidity when the market does not do so. This will often extend to a more extensive responsibility for the handling of banking crises, and crises of other financial institutions or markets. This leads to the issues of regulation and supervision of institutions and markets generally. Are there problems in separating the handling of crises and the preventative regulation and supervision? Does this lead to any distortions or perverse incentives on the side of regulators or regulated? There are also the questions of efficiency and of transparency and democratic control. It is not clear that the present uncertain and complex situation scores highly on either of these boards.

What is then the optimal institutional outcome? What should remain at a national level, and how would the tasks at a European level best be organised? One major problem here is that financial market regulation has rarely come about as a consequence of rational deliberation. Historically regulatory reform has taken the form of panic stricken short term responses to the crisis that has just passed.

One also has the situation that authorities in this field are generally not too concerned with acquiring the formal responsibility. We have already discussed certain aspects of how, increasingly formalised though detailed rulemaking, the regulatory competences nevertheless remain broad and widely discretionary. Sanctions and enforcement remain uncertain. Certain central bank or regulatory functions, such as the lender of last resort, are traditionally left open-ended in order not to affect market behaviour. It is assumed that clear rules could lead to distortions and perverse incentives. A situation where responsibility is not clearly allocated can have its further advantages for a regulator. Financial market crises will continue to occur, and not having the formal responsibility (the European Central Bank) or not having the tools (national regulators) for handling them may disperse the institutional repercussions of flawed supervision.

The relationship between financial market regulation and economic policy is a complex one. Major changes in the established policies and the abolition of capital controls have been necessary for the development of the Internal Financial Market. The euro will bring it further and will also entail further challenges. Let us go back to the Commission's 1985 White Paper *Completing the Internal Market*.[13] The White Paper set out the legislative programme for the creation of a single market by the end of 1992. Free movement of capital and financial

---

[13]   COM(85)310 final.

services stood out as an area where little had been achieved and as to which the Commission proposed many ambitious measures. One reason for the slow progress of the internal market in financial services was that it depended on capital liberalisation, that is, on the abolition of restrictions and administrative controls on cross-border financial transactions. Capital liberalisation would, in fact, inevitably have two consequences. First, deregulation of financial markets, and, second, the abolition or easing of rules with respect to the participation in domestic financial markets of foreign institutions.

Capital restrictions were a necessary precondition for the effectiveness of the direct instruments of monetary and credit control. Credit control imposed limitations on the growth of clearing banks' assets (in some cases also their liabilities). It usually extended to other financial institutions' assets and to markets such as those in corporate bonds. With the help of such instruments, monetary objectives could be achieved at a lower interest rate than would otherwise be possible. Capital restrictions made it possible to pursue relatively autonomous monetary and credit policies. Such policies depended on the possibility of maintaining an interest rate different from that of neighbouring countries. Capital restrictions were instruments to limit capital inflows and outflows. Their importance would depend on the trends in other financial markets. Restrictions on capital outflows – so that savers and investors could not go abroad – allowed, in the short term, the preservation of low interest rates. The restrictions impeded downward pressures on the currency's exchange rate. In the long term, they protected domestic savings and domestic capital markets. Particularly strict restrictions on pension funds and life-assurance companies, affecting their ability to diversify their investments by investing abroad, could have both such short-term and long-term effects.

Restrictions on capital inflows – for instance, so that lenders could not go to banks or securities markets abroad to raise capital – preserved, in the short term, price stability and avoided upward pressure on the exchange rate. In the long term, restrictions on foreign investors contributed to the protection of the domestic control of key industries, which in several countries was considered to be an important matter of national sovereignty. The national interest in domestic control of business enterprises was thought to be particularly strong in the area of financial institutions, such as banks, pension funds and insurance companies. Strong partnerships would be established between the authorities in charge of banking supervision and the quantitative restrictions, providing an effective shield against foreign establishment or direct competition. Similar intensity partnerships were established in the other financial industry sectors.

Capital controls have been applied by all countries, in different ways and to different degrees. There is a tidal quality to capital controls, which rise and subside with some regularity. In the late 1980s and early 1990s they had subsided to a lower ebb than ever before in modern history. Economic policy in the 1980s became increasingly based on a doctrine of greater market orientation. Indirect instruments, seeking to influence credit expansion through price mechanisms, gradually replaced the direct instruments of monetary control. This is what is usually described as liberalisation in domestic economic policy and in domestic financial markets. The final conversion to liberalisation came after the experiences of the late 1970s and early 1980s. Sceptics had had to accept that the existing controls were characterised by a low degree of effectiveness and high costs. There were costs of an administrative nature. More importantly there was a macroeconomic cost in that distortions in asset prices and interest rates could lead to a sub-optimal allocation of capital resources. Financial markets became less effective. There were also problems following from shielding financial markets from foreign competition. Temporary advantages could be outweighed by the cost of postponing the economic policy and private sector adaptation to changes in international economic circumstances.

The direct instruments of monetary and credit control had created a close relationship between the major players. They were the financial institutions, in particular large clearing banks, and the monetary authorities, ministries of finance and central banks. Banking supervision became subordinated to this relationship, and played a limited role. Prudential rules – for instance, liquidity requirements – were turned into instruments of monetary policy, with a view to influencing interest rates. Competition polices were not developed, or at least not enforced with any rigour. In many countries the banking supervisory authorities managed to keep their sector out of the remit of the general competition authorities. All the parties to those close relationships had a strong interest in retaining them. Eventually, the gradual deregulation in domestic credit and monetary policy, with the abolition of direct controls, spurred a strengthening of prudential requirements and supervision and of competition policies. Some degree of internationalisation of financial markets and institutions took place under the capital controls in spite of the restrictions of national monetary and credit policies. This clearly undermined the effectiveness of these quantitative policies. There was no immediate link between, on the one hand, domestic deregulation and, on the other hand, the opening-up of domestic markets for financial institutions from other Member States or the development of an internal financial market in other ways. The financial services industry continued to enjoy a close relationship to the authorities. In some countries, the state would even directly own the major clearing banks. For most Member States, retaining domestic control over the financial services industry was considered to be of vital importance; financial institutions and markets should remain in the hands of their own nationals. The prospect of clearing banks, pension-fund managers or life-assurance companies being bought up by nationals of other countries appeared distant. Any other direct access to markets for foreign institutions was seriously curtailed. Gradually, however, deregulation in domestic monetary and credit policy did lead to the implementation of free movement of capital from 1990, on the basis of the Capital Liberalisation Directive,[14] which was adopted in 1988. This was the first time that all Member States agreed that the escape clause in Article 67 of the Treaty (abolishing capital-movement restrictions 'necessary to ensure the proper functioning of the common market') implied a full liberalisation.

With the lifting of capital controls, an internal financial market was now possible – and even necessary for ensuring that financial business would not drift to the Member State that would offer the least intensive regulatory environment and the best financial and tax incentives. The economic policies of Member States no longer depended on domestic markets. Most of the other obstacles just mentioned were still in place. The attempt to resolve them, guaranteeing unrestricted market access, was made in a series of financial market directives, the most important of which has been the Second Banking Directive of 1989.[15] Abolishing capital controls was an easy step in terms of execution when the economic polices allowed it. It was mainly a question of abolishing some rather simple regulation. Making free movement work was much more complicated.

Before the 1992 deadline of the Commission's 1985 White Paper, the major directives in this area of financial services and financial institutions were either adopted or going through the late stages of the legislative process, with a common position having been reached, guaranteeing their adoption.[16] The 1992 deadline was extremely tight in an area where so little had been achieved, placing considerable pressure on both the Member States and the Commission. This

---

[14]   Council Directive 88/361/EEC of 24.6.88 for the implementation of Article 67 of the Treaty.

[15]   Second Council Directive 89/646/EEC of 15.12.89 on the co-ordination of laws, regulations and administrative provisions relating to the taking up and pursuit of the business of credit institutions and amending Directive 77/780/EEC.

[16]   In addition to the Second Banking Directive, one must refer here to the following instruments: First Council Directive 77/780/EEC of 12.12.77 on the co-ordination of laws, regulations and administrative provisions relating to the taking up and pursuit of the business of credit institutions (the 'First Banking Directive'); Council Directive 89/299/EEC of 17.4.89 on the own funds of credit institutions (the 'Own Funds Directive'); Council Directive 89/647/EEC of 18.12.89 on a solvency ratio for credit institutions (the 'Solvency Ratio Directive'); Council Directive 92/30/EEC of 6.4.92 on the supervision of credit institutions on a consolidated basis (the 'Second Consolidated Supervision Directive'); Council Directive 92/121/EEC of 21.12.92 on the monitoring and control of large exposures of credit institutions (the 'Large Exposures Directive'); Council Directive 93/6/EEC of 15.3.93 on the capital adequacy of investment firms and credit institutions (the 'Capital Adequacy Directive'); and Directive 94/19/EC of the European Parliament and of the Council of 30.5.94 on deposit-guarantee schemes (the 'Deposit-Guarantee Directive').

was bound to have some impact on the form of the solutions that were found, and certain issues could not be explicitly resolved in the directives.

Making free movement work required more than abolishing capital controls and the supervision of financial institutions and the regulation of financial services. A large number of further issues have had to be addressed. The cost of cross-border payments has become a concern. The euro contributes to making the right to free movement of capital more effective; it could even be seen as the ultimate harmonisation measure! The introduction of the euro harmonises the currency or capital itself and takes care of mutual recognition in a way one could not in practical terms have done if the different national currencies were to be maintained.

We now turn to capital, services and establishment in the EC Treaty. The original provisions of the free movement of capital in the Treaty of Rome (Article 67–73) were more conditional than those concerning the other Treaty freedoms, such as those on the right to provide services and the right of establishment which have provided the basis for review of national financial market regulation. The obligation to abolish progressively restrictions on capital applied only to the extent necessary to ensure the proper functioning of the common market. One consequence of this was that the European Court held that the Treaty freedom was not directly effective. With the revisions of the Maastricht Treaty the free movement of capital was formulated in a broader and less conditional way than any other Treaty freedom. But even before those amendments entered into force, the European Court, held in *Sanz de Lera* [1995] ECR I-4821, that the Treaty freedom was directly effective. The Court argued that the Treaty provisions had to be read in the context of secondary Community legislation giving effect to the freedom, in particular the Directive abolishing the Member States' right to restrict capital movements.

The free movement of capital has been further strengthened by the unconditional and wide formulation in the Treaty. One issue which has been discussed in the legal literature is that of horizontal direct effect. In *Sanz de Lera* the action was against the state and the Court only had to address vertical direct effect. Horizontal direct effect, where a private party invokes the Treaty freedom against another private party, has not yet been addressed by the Court. Treaty provisions are normally capable of both horizontal and vertical direct effect. *Sanz de Lera* does not in any way indicate the contrary in relation to Article 56. Article 56 itself does not depend on implementing measures and is widely formulated. Argument to the contrary may be derived from Article 28 (ex Article 30) on the free movement of goods which is limited to actions against the state, and there are certain parallels between the provisions.

The Treaty freedoms provide a powerful tool for review of national regulation. Most of the field is now also based on EC directives, and harmonisation should reduce the restrictive nature of traditional financial market regulation.

But there remain several issues in relation to the institutional solutions, in particular concerning the level of regulation at EU and national level, and beyond harmonisation which is based on national legislation and actual supervision. The most pressing is to what extent a European supervisor has to be established, and what should be the relationship with the supervisory functions that remain at the Member State level.

4.   SYSTEMIC RISK AND INTERNAL MARKET ISSUES

We now return to the reasons we give for regulation. We have already discussed how the stability of the financial system, consumer protection and deterrence of fraud are acknowledged as the core aims. They are accorded different weight in different sectors of the financial market and there is disagreement also about the content of these three aims. Systemic stability is becoming the most important aim of financial market regulation[17] but remains the most uncertain: we cannot agree on what can lead to systemic breakdown (or what can be done to deter or limit the risks).[18] It has a whiff of the religious about it.

Systemic risk and systemic stability are like sin and redemption, and are based on revelation and tradition. The empirical support is weak, to say the least, for setting it top of the aims of financial market regulation. Pascal's Wager[19] offers a parallel from the religious world. Applied here it would go as follows: even if we cannot know if it exists, as long as we do not know with certainty that it does not, the consequences of being wrong are too terrible to neglect it. Vagueness and uncertainty as we know it from the regulatory sector apply in particular to the systemic issues. This is rarely openly acknowledged by the regulators, and also scholarship and academic teaching will rarely take this into account. So the important question is what consequences one can draw from this vagueness and uncertainty. If systemic risk is what justifies regulation, it must be taken seriously. It may have consequences for the solutions, including whether the national level remains effective.

The problem of coordinating financial market regulation is brought on by several developments. The first may be a convergence in supervisory aims and

---

[17]   In areas other than banking (insurance and investment services), investor protection and market organisation have traditionally been the primary aims but the systemic stability concerns are increasingly central.

[18]   Recent studies continue to challenge the basis for modern banking regulation. See for instance, J R Barth, G Caprio and R Levine, *Rethinking Bank Regulation. Till Angels Govern* (Cambridge University Press, New York, 2006).

[19]   Blaise Pascal, *Pensées* (1669). 'Pascal's Wager' is one of three arguments that Pascal presents for believing, or for at least taking steps to believe, in God.

also in methods. Another is in the integration of markets on the product side, and a third in the integration on the ownership side. The Scandinavian model of a unified financial market regulator has been taken up in the United Kingdom with the establishment of the Financial Services Authority in 1997. Similar developments have taken place in France, Germany and Austria, and most recently in Italy.[20]

We will in this chapter rehearse the arguments for and against a unified financial market regulation. We will also address the issue of whether the European Central Bank and the removal of monetary policy discretion from the national to the European level in the euro area have any impact on the argument. The institutional consolidation of financial market regulation leaves other issues, for instance the material regulation, and also the relationship to European regulation and coordination which remains fragmented. We will also consider the alternative model of 'regulation by objective', as advocated by Giorgio Di Giorgio and others.[21] Among the several questions about this model in a domestic perspective is whether the recent financial crises or scandals demonstrate that different regulators can cooperate in resolving the problems.

Much of the discussion about financial markets and institutions would focus on one kind of institution or market. Traditionally regulation and supervision have developed in very different ways. Banking supervision has focused on banks and their solidity or their supporting role in the traditional credit policies described above. Life insurance and pension fund regulation has had its focus on securing the interests of the insured, and the contractual terms have been regulated often in great detail. Securities markets have been regulated with investor protection as the focus, and fraud legislation an integral part of the regulatory model. The regulators have been based in different ministries and they have championed 'their' industry against the others. Not only the content or character regulation but also the intensity of regulation have varied between these three main sectors.

Similar products are now offered by institutions that are primarily based in any of these three main sectors. Cross-ownership requires new consolidated supervision. And there is an increasing interdependency between financial

---

[20]   See for instance Part III in M Andenas and Y Avgerinos (eds), *Financial Markets in Europe. Towards a Single Regulator?* (Kluwer Law International, London, The Hague, New York, 2003).

[21]   G Di Giorgio and C Di Noia, 'Financial Market Regulation and Supervision: How Many Peaks for the Euro Area?' (2002–2003) 28 *Brooklyn Journal of International Law* 463. See also G Di Giorgio, C Di Noia and L Piatti, 'Financial Market Regulation: The Case of Italy and a Proposal for the Euro Area' in M Andenas and Y Avgerinos (eds), *Financial Markets in Europe. Towards a Single Regulator?* (Kluwer Law International, London, The Hague, New York, 2003) 397.

markets going beyond what can be explained by these features of the development. If sectoral supervision is to be maintained it must be heavily coordinated. In many countries new models of a universal regulator have been developed. In the Scandinavian countries this took place in the 1980s, in the UK in the late 1990s.

Banking supervision is increasingly influential as the emerging paradigm of financial market regulation. The basic regulation relates to capital adequacy and in matching the financial exposures. Risk is priced correctly and the systemic risks of a meltdown of a financial sector or the whole financial market are reduced.

Basically, banking supervision was created to provide solutions for domestic markets. That remains as a limitation even in its modern form. If anything this applies with even greater force to other sectors of financial market regulation. To some extent regulation and the actual supervisory functions undertaken have developed to restrict capital flows from other countries or to protect against competition from foreign institutions or markets. Globalisation creates a new role for financial market regulation which has had to become increasingly European and international.

The process of internationalisation of domestic financial market regulation has created problems to both national authorities and to institutions and markets that have an international dimension in their activities.

Other important surrounding areas of law with important impact in this field, such as contract law and company law, remain even more traditionally national. This leads to problems that are becoming increasingly more pressing. Banks and other financial institutions are authorised in one jurisdiction and it remains very difficult to move that authorisation to another Member State. That can in practice only be done by establishing a branch in the other country which will remain supervised primarily by the authorities of the first country of authorisation. Establishment though a branch is not covered by the authorisation by the home country supervisor. Moving to another jurisdiction is also still impossible as a matter of company law. One cannot move a company from one jurisdiction to another: it remains a foreign company in the new jurisdiction. There are of course techniques that alleviate this. Establishing a subsidiary in the new jurisdiction, and then transferring assets and activities. But a full recognition of a foreign company, so that it can reincorporate or register in the new jurisdiction (acquire a new nationality or citizenship so to speak) is still not possible in the national company laws of the world. The *Centros* decision[22] of the European Court of Justice has limited, as a matter of EU company law, the possibility to withhold the recognition of foreign companies or their branches. For the pur-

---

[22]   Case C–212/97 *Centros Ltd v Erhvervs- og Selskabsstyrelsen* [1999] ECR I–1459.

poses of financial market regulation, financial institutions had already achieved this. Authorities cannot discriminate on the grounds that the authorisation has been granted in another Member State. But the company law restrictions remained as for all other companies. The European Commission has drafted a proposal for a new directive on the ultimate free movement issue: how can a company register (or re-register) in a new jurisdiction. But this proposal still has a long way to go.

The separation of money and financial market supervision provides an opportunity to revisit the obstacles to the development of the Internal Financial Market. The old model under the quantitative regime did more than keep money and supervision together. It created regulatory systems which had as one of their primary aims to limit capital flows. The present level of harmonisation through the directives in the sector has not done away with this.

Even a very high degree of harmonisation will still lead to the double burden of having to follow more than one set of national rules. The proposed mechanism to limit double regulation in the directives – home country control – is not sufficiently effective. Its extent is not clear enough, there are too many and too wide exceptions, and the reporting even when it applies has proven too burdensome.

The recent proposals from the European Commission are still based on the home country control principle.[23] The otherwise very timely proposals deal with the programme of developing and modernising the harmonised regulatory rules. The new model for the adoption of these rules comes from the proposals from the Lamfalussy Committee. The Lamfalussy proposals included the adoption of a new legislative procedure and the use of regulations instead of directives. This has a huge potential when it comes to making the regulatory procedures more rapid and the adopted rules more effective.

It does however not resolve the basic problem of double burden that remains if there are all these different national regulators that remain in charge of the actual supervision. The intensity and extent of regulation of financial institutions are such that this burden is higher than in other sectors.

The Lamfalussy proposals included as mentioned the adoption of a new legislative procedure and the use of regulations instead of directives. This is now adopted for both investment services and (from 2002) for banking. The regulatory procedures become quicker and the adopted rules more effective. But can national regulators deliver a sufficient level of efficiency? They may not only provide restrictions on the free movement which is necessary to get the internal market to function. It is questionable whether they provide the level of effective

---

[23] Financial Services: Implementing the framework for financial markets: Action Plan. Communication of the Commission, COM(1999)232, 11.05.99.

regulation that is required for the market to function? The European Commission has continued its adherence to home country control. The remedy is seen to be in an elaborate structure of bodies to promote cooperation and coordination between the national regulators. There is no doubt that coordination is necessary and that much can be achieved this way. But it is very uncertain if it can achieve the sufficient level of efficiency. Where there are different national interests of sufficient strength, one would expect the agreement to be lasting less.

The aim of systemic stability is now at the core of modern financial market regulation. Financial stability cannot be achieved at a national level with the present level of market integration, even when it is supported by an extensive body of harmonised EU legalisation in directives and regulations. Here there will often be strong diverging national views, and the different fora for cooperation and coordination cannot mediate effectively between these interests.

The handling of financial crises is one area where the lack of a European institutional solution seems particularly critical. The existing lender of last resort (LOLR) arrangements are not adequate to deal with liquidity issues in the context of a European banking system. This is the case for both systemic and individual liquidity crises. In case of a systemic problem, the ECB lacks the supervisory information needed to judge on the systemic effect of liquidity problems and decide quickly on the collateral issues. In case of liquidity problems at individual financial institutions, the national central banks along with the national supervisory authorities will act and undertake the LOLR costs only when the liquidity crisis poses systemic risks for their own banking system. Even if they are concerned with the implications for the European market, they may lack both the necessary resources and the ability to assess the severity of the liquidity problems. Neither is it clear whether authorisation by the ECB is also required.[24] Finally, cooperation on the basis of Memoranda of Understanding (MOU) does not secure the necessary real-time information sharing and action, while availability of resources is questionable.

A centralised LOLR competence at the ECB level will deal more effectively with most of the inadequacies of the current decentralised framework. The ECB will be able to intervene effectively and timely when the emerging pan-European financial institutions face liquidity problems. It will avoid coordination problems – present in a decentralised system involving discussions between the interested central banks and consultations at the ECB level – and it will be able to decide quickly. It will have the capital resources required and will ensure a proper allocation of the LOLR costs across the Community. It will also reduce

---

[24]   The ECB may prohibit or restrict LOLR functions by the national central banks: ESCB Statute Art. 14(4). Neither is it clear whether authorisation by the ECB is also required.

the anti-competitive effect of national central bank policies and decisions on eligible collateral, and of interventions in support of insolvent institutions.[25] Still, the precondition for a successful LOLR role by the ECB will be the establishment of information-sharing arrangements. Such information-sharing arrangements are needed to provide the real-time information necessary for an accurate assessment of the systemic effect of liquidity problems, a decision on the adequate collateral, and a real-time intervention.

Two major arguments may be added for the ECB's handling the LOLR situations. The first argument is that national authorities may act counter to the requirements of monetary policy. It may be preferred that the balancing of financial stability and monetary policy is undertaken by one institution. This runs counter to some of the arguments brought up by others on this point that seems to build on an ordo–liberal division of functions to secure the uncorrupted exercise of monetary policy powers. The second argument in favour is that national authorities would easily run counter to the rules on state aid. ECB could not be restricted under these rules. Time pressures and other factors in this kind of financial crisis will make it less realistic that a solution may be achieved at the national level

At this stage it may be useful to sum up some points relating to regulators' jurisdiction. Regulators should follow markets. This seems an obvious starting point when one deals with regulation aiming at increasing market efficiency or counteracting market failure. Regulators do not follow markets. They follow national jurisdictions and state organisation that less and less often coincide with markets. New economic policies and market conditions should have removed obstacles so regulators now could follow markets. The way they presently divide them up applies also within domestic markets and not only in relation to foreign markets and institutions. National jurisdictions divide markets up. National regulation tends to obstruct market integration. It also makes regulation less effective. Any form of cooperation between regulators will provide less than optimal efficiency, both in terms of costs to business (in the EU, one still has to submit to twelve different regulatory regimes) and in achieving the primary goals of financial market regulation (increased financial stability, effective competition, market surveillance and sanctions against transgressors). In the financial markets regulators have traditionally divided markets up, making borders between countries effective barriers protecting their 'own' financial institutions against competition and also making economic policies effective. Today the EU and also broader forms of international cooperation, WTO/GATS, limit the power of regulators to achieve this. Most will be critical of this at a wholesale level: good reasons

---

[25] It should be mentioned that the ECB can already affect these policies as under Art.14(4) it may restrict national policies that interfere with the ECB's objectives and tasks.

also to challenge in relation to consumer or investor protection. A discussion of national regulation as a barrier leads to the following question. How can so many obstacles remain that are that much against the interests of the financial services industry that wishes to establish itself or sell its products in other Member States? Partly the answer must be that there are other interests that are served by most of the regulatory regimes. There are client relationships where the regulators protect 'their industry' against foreign competition. The other is the inertia that is displayed by many of the main players. It is not so that the interests are carefully balanced and the best solutions automatically solved. The story of the Merger Regulation and the 'one stop shop' is indicative. Only when the EU regulation was a fact that could not be avoided did business involve itself, in spite of the obvious benefits of EU level regulation. Business did not move to make merger control an EU competence. Only when this had come about did business take steps to avoid having an EU and a national level dealing with the individual cases. Conversely, for the international financial institution the independence of the regulator can be of importance. There is a problem of independence in a national context. Regulators are too closely involved with the political process. National business interests forms too close relationships with the regulator (regulatory capture). These problems are still there at EU level but there is less scope for capture than in the more limited national political and business environment. There is a case for saying that financial market regulation and supervision cannot be effectively developed and exercised at a national level: it is too vulnerable to pressure and form too many and too close client relationships. National lobbying at EU level is also a problem, but not as great a problem as at the national level.

One important question is the extent to which financial market regulation acts as a barrier to the Internal Financial Market. This is the justification for harmonisation of national regulation at the EU level. It can also provide grounds for review of existing national legislation, which may be set aside and cause liability for breach of EU law. The Internal Financial Market is far from realised. Nationally based financial market regulation remains the primary barrier. This chapter sets out the stages of the development of the Internal Financial Market, and points to some of the present problems. For instance the problems with the Lamfalussy process and that much EU legislation and Member State practice is not giving effect to free movement.

We have to go back to the fundamental freedoms of the treaty, the free movement rights, and they require financial market regulation (in particular in pro-hibiting double regulation).[26] The concepts of home country control, EC passport,

---

[26]   The process of financial market harmonisation was set on its path by the judgment of the Court of Justice in Case 205/84 *Commission v Germany* (*Re-insurance*) [1986] ECR, 03755.

minimum standards and mutual recognition are discussed.[27] Free movement is leaving little room for special exclusions for banking and other financial services: see for instance the European Court of Justice in the case of *Caixa Bank France*.[28]

When we are assessing the EU legislation on financial market regulation, Lamfalussy's challenge to the lack of effectiveness and to the over-complication of the European regulatory system provides an important background. The different reviews of the Financial Services Action Plan of 1999 add to this.[29] Lamfalussy's ultimatum was that the home country control system had to be made effective or be replaced by 'a European SEC'. Where do we now stand? The Internal Financial Market is about a market in services that functions without national borders and can realise economies of scale, increased competition, etc. Recently focus has been moving towards establishing a functioning regulatory regime with a European level of rules and a national level of transposition and supervision. The question is the weight which free movement is given in this. This chapter argues that the process of eating into home country control by developing conduct of business rules under host country control reduces the effectiveness of the regime.

Regulating and supervising the Internal Financial Market is not only a question of giving effect to the Internal Market or developing a normative regulatory framework. It is also a question of the effectiveness of the present supervisory system. Can the national supervisory authorities undertake their tasks with a sufficient level of effectiveness? This is a typical Internal Market problem (the one in the preceding discussion of national regulation as a barrier is another): is the task better undertaken at an EU level?[30] The handling of banking crises is

---

[27] The European Court of Justice has made clear that these concepts are ways of giving effect to free movement but remain concepts of secondary legislation (directives) and do not have any 'constitutional' character: see Case 233/94 *Germany v European Parliament and Council* (*Deposit guarantee directive*) [1997] ECR I–2405.

[28] In Case 442/02 *Caixa Bank France* [2004] ECR I–89615 the Court held that the prohibition of paying interest on current accounts was a breach of the right to establishment of the French subsidiaries of Spanish banks. It constituted an 'obstacle to the pursuit of their activities via a subsidiary in France, affecting their access to the market'. Such a prohibition restricts, in particular, the activities of subsidiaries of foreign banks in raising capital from the public. The judgment applies in the banking sector the very broad freedom of establishment approach adopted by the Court in *Gebhard*. See Case C–55/94 *Gebhard* [1995] ECR I-4165.

[29] See the critical analysis in J Dalhuisen, *Dalhuisen on International Commercial, Financial and Trade Law* (2nd edn, Hart Publishing, Oxford, 2004) 1102–10.

[30] See S Osterloo and D Schoenmaker, 'Financial Supervision in an Integrating Europe: Measuring Cross-Border Externalities', LSE FMG Special Papers 156 (London, April 2004). The need for European arrangements ultimately depends on the intensity of cross-border spill-over effects or externalities within the EU, and the authors attempted to measure these cross-border externalities. They found that cross-border penetration

one pressing issue which has been discussed. The formal responsibility remains at the national level. The necessary coordination at European level is expected to be undertaken through committee meetings between regulators.[31]

Tommaso Padoa-Schioppa, who ended his distinguished central banking career as member of the Executive Board of the European Central Bank (ECB), developed in a series of lectures an analysis which could be read in this manner: that if the present coordination of national responsibilities is insufficient, only an actual crisis demonstrating this would lead to new arrangements. Only the failure in handling a crisis will provide sufficient momentum to consider a European solution, and, if so, the failure will prove the point about the crisis-driven nature of the regulation of financial market.

Monetary and competition policy is already based at a European level. The European powers are starting to have an effect in relation to financial markets. The EU Commission has gradually stepped up its review of competition and merger cases in the financial services sector (as a matter of competition policy), and a recent initiative proposes to take discretionary control with mergers in the financial sector away from Member State supervisory and political authorities (as an Internal Market/free movement measure).

The European Central Bank has a limited express mandate in relation to banking and other financial services. On the one hand there is monetary policy, the traditional central banking responsibilities for payments and payments systems, and financial stability. This is firmly within the mandate of the ECB. On the other hand there is regulation and supervision at a macro and intermediate level, which there is no clear provision for at the EU level. However, the way is short between monetary policy and regulation at the macro level. There is no clear demarcation of the responsibilities of the ECB in relation to banking supervision. There is a growing feeling of regulatory competition between the European Commission and the ECB (and it is as ever there between the national and the EU level).

We will argue that an expansion of the ECB's supervision powers may be based on the ECB's monetary competence and the Treaty provisions for prudential

---

within the EU is currently limited: only seven banks out of the sample of 30 large EU banking groups are considered to be 'European' banks that have the potential to pose significant cross-border externalities. However, aggregate data show a gradual, though statistically significant, increase of cross-border penetration in the EU. Their conclusion is that policy-makers may in the near future face the challenge of designing European structures for financial supervision and stability.

[31]   The unresolved issues are many. See the discussion of one of them in CAE Goodhart and D Schoenmaker, 'Burden sharing in a banking crisis in Europe', Special Paper No 164, LSE FMG Special Paper Series (London, March 2006): who should bear the burden of any proposed recapitalisation should failures occur in large cross-border banks.

supervision. Monetary policy is strictly defined only in relation to its primary objective and its tools, and the interdependence of banking soundness and price stability establishes the link between monetary policy and prudential supervision. The Community law doctrine of implied powers applies here. The implied powers doctrine provides that when the Community only has competence which is conferred upon it, this may either follow directly from an express Treaty provisions or it may be implied from them. The implied powers doctrine also applies to the ECB, which is 'in the constellation of the EC legal order'[32] and 'fully subject to the principles of primary Community law and to the jurisdiction of the ECJ'.[33]

Article 105(5) of the Treaty (Article 3(3) ESCB Statute) states that the ECB has a responsibility to contribute to the smooth conduct of national policies relating to prudential supervision and financial stability. The ambiguity of the terms used and the importance of prudential supervision for monetary policy suggest against reading any restrictions on possible ECB supervision functions. Article 18(1) of the ESCB Statute does not confine open market and credit operations to monetary policy. Although it is placed under Chapter IV on monetary functions and operations of the ESCB, it is expressly stated that open market and credit operations are to be undertaken for the attainment of the objectives and tasks of the ESCB (European System of Central Banks with the ECB at the summit).

The concept of 'macro-prudential supervision', explained as 'supervision with a view of safeguarding systemic stability', may prove useful here. The concept was introduced in a study I co-authored with Lazaros E. Panourgias in 2002.[34] We argued for a solution where micro-prudential supervision should remain with the bank regulator (national central banks, NCBs, or NCBs as part of the ESCB) and the ECB should intervene only when there is a compelling financial stability or internal market consideration. Prudential supervision in the UK provides an interesting example. First line prudential supervision (micro-) has been transferred to the Financial Services Authority (FSA)[35] while the Bank of England (BoE)

---

[32]   Jean-Victor Louis, *Banking Supervision in the European Community: Institutional Aspects*, Report under the Chairmanship of Jean-Victor Louis (1995), at 73.

[33]   Chiara Zilioli and Martin Selmayr, *The European Central Bank, its System and its Law (first part)*, 2 *Euredia* 187, 203 (1999), at 623.

[34]   See Mads Andenas and Lazaros E. Panourgias, 'Applied Monetary Policy and Bank Supervision by the ECB' in J J Norton and M Andenas (eds), *International Monetary Law and Financial Law in the New Millenium* (British Institute of International and Comparative Law, London, 2002) 119–70 at 130 in a section under the heading 'Default Supervision of Central Banks'.

[35]   The Bank of England Act 1998 transferred banking supervision to the Financial Services Authority (FSA). The 1998 Act did not provide for detailed rules but instead envisaged the enactment of a new Act. The Financial Services and Markets Act (FSMA) was adopted in June 2000 providing for the legislative framework of the FSA as a single financial regulator with regulation and supervision responsibility for the entire financial

remains the primary macro-prudential supervisor. Although the UK model has its own ambiguities, it does provide for a macro-prudential role of the central bank (BoE) on a clearer basis than in most other countries. The BoE has the responsibility for overseeing the payment systems,[36] and it does have a lender of last resort role for both individual and systemic liquidity crises, [37] which it can exercise in the context of its standing cooperation with the Treasury and the FSA, as provided for in the relevant Memorandum of Understanding.[38] The BoE also has the infrastructure to perform its macro-prudential supervision function. In 2010, the UK government outlined plans for reform of the UK regulatory framework, including the creation of an independent Financial Policy Committee at the Bank of England and a new prudential regulator as a susidiary of the Bank.[39]

Community law does not provide for any clear allocation of lender of last resort (LOLR) competences. We argue that this is redressed by attributing LOLR competence to the European Central Bank on the basis that this is applied

---

services industry. For a report on the current supervisory framework in the UK see Lazaros E. Panourgias and Mads Andenas, 'The euro, EMU and UK law' in Jean-Victor Louis (ed.), *The euro in the National Context* (BIICL, London, 2002).

[36] The oversight responsibility of the BoE is provided in the Memorandum of Understanding agreed with the FSA and the Treasury: '[t]he Bank will be responsible for the overall stability of the financial system as a whole which will involve: ... ii. financial system infrastructure, in particular payments systems at home and abroad. As the bankers' bank, the Bank will stand at the heart of the system. It will fall to the Bank to advise the Chancellor, and answer for its advice, on any major problem inherent in the payments systems. The Bank will also be closely involved in developing and improving the infrastructure, and strengthening the system to help reduce systemic risk'. See Bank of England, *The Bank of England's Oversight of Payment Systems*, at 169 (Dec. 2000); David Clementi, Deputy Governor of the Bank of England, 'UK Financial Services following the Launch of the Euro', Speech at the Economist Conferences (23 Apr. 1999), www.bankofengland.co.uk/speeches/subject.htm. Its oversight responsibility covers the CHAPS Euro (Clearing House Automated Payment System for Euro), a Real-Time-Gross-Settlement-System (RTGS) payments system for payments in Euro: *Bank of England, The Bank of England and Payment and Settlement Systems*, www.bankofengland.co.uk/markets/payments/index.htm.

[37] See section 2 of the Bank of England, 'Memorandum of Understanding between HM Treasury, the Bank of England and the Financial Services Authority', www.bankofengland.co.uk/financialstability/mou.htm.

[38] The Memorandum provides also for information gathering and sharing arrangements between the Bank of England and the Financial Services Authority as well as for cross-representation in their decision-making bodies. Apart from continuous contacts and a programme of secondments, the Memorandum provides that the Deputy Governor of the Bank of England, in charge of financial stability, will be a member of the FSA Board, and the Chairman of the FSA will represent the FSA in the Court of the Bank of England.

[39] Such vague powers as we discuss here may not provide sufficiently clear responsibility for the BoE. Some may say the BoE is run more as a monetary policy seminar than as an institution concerned with systemic stability.

monetary policy. There is an inseparable link of LOLR with monetary policy and the commonality of the tools used for both tasks. On the other hand, national central banks, as autonomous national entities, appear to have exclusive competence to exercise LOLR functions. The ECB is entrusted only with an advisory and coordinating role regarding prudential regulation and supervision in general, and this could limit its involvement for LOLR purposes. It seems clear that if financial stability or internal market considerations requires centralization of micro-prudential supervision, and the case for a Community bank regulator or a Community single regulator may be made, then Treaty amendment would be necessary. Our argument is that this is not necessary in relation to the LOLR issues, and we support the general argument that LOLR can constitute applied monetary policy on the system of the Treaty.

There are two exceptions to what may seem to be an exclusive LOLR competence of the national central banks. First, in case of a systemic, pan-European, liquidity crisis the ECB has the power to intervene on the basis of its responsibility for the smooth conduct of national prudential policies pertaining to financial stability.[40] Its competence to intervene will also be supported by the interdependence of the systemic aspects of the liquidity risks with the effectiveness of the monetary policy. Again, this is applied monetary policy with an implied power of the ECB to intervene due to the strong link[41] of systemic liquidity problems with monetary policy. The monetary policy tools, open market operations and credit operations, already available to the ECB,[42] will enable its intervention.[43] The second exception is that in case of a liquidity crisis generated in the payments system the ECB will share the LOLR competence with national central banks, as the Treaty provides for the ECB's competence to oversee the payment systems: '[t]he basic tasks to be carried out through the ESCB shall be…to promote the smooth operation of payment systems'.[44] The ECB can provide liquidity through intra-day credit on the basis of adequate collateral[45] and open market operations.[46]

---

[40]   EC Treaty Art. 105(5) EC; ESCB Statute Art. 3(3).

[41]   See also Johannes Priesemann, 'Policy Options for Prudential Supervision in Stage Three of Monetary Union' in Paul J J Welfens and Holger C Wolf (eds), *Banking, International Capital Flows and Growth in Europe* (Springer, Berlin, New York 1997) 81, at 82–83. Priesemann goes further to support the inseparability of LOLR from monetary policy *both* in case of system and individual institutions crises.

[42]   ESCB Statute Arts 17, 18.

[43]   Of course, the monetary policy tools exclusively entrusted to the ECB will allow it an LOLR role even without any legal basis. Identifying the LOLR function and establishing a legal basis may serve both efficiency and accountability purposes.

[44]   Art. 105(2) of the EC Treaty; ESCB Statute Art. 3(1).

[45]   Art. 18(1) ESCB Statute.

[46]   There is every reason to expect that the ECB will accept non-eligible collateral in case of liquidity crisis. The Governing Council will be able to change the characteristics

The situation becomes more blurred in the case of liquidity problems of individual financial institutions. Are national central banks solely competent for prudential supervision, including as LOLR for individual liquidity crises? There is the view that this form of a decentralised LOLR complemented by other liquidity mechanisms is an effective arrangement. Our argument in this chapter is that the current LOLR framework is inadequate. The existing LOLR arrangements, modelled on a market approach, are not adequate to deal with liquidity issues in the context of a Europeanised banking system. This is the case for both systemic and individual liquidity crises. In case of a systemic problem, the ECB lacks the supervisory information needed to assess the systemic effect of liquidity problems and to make quick decisions on the eligible collateral. In case of liquidity problems of individual financial institutions, the national central banks are expected to act and undertake the LOLR costs only when the liquidity crisis poses systemic risks for their constituent banking system. Even if they are concerned with the implications for the European market, they may lack both the necessary resources and the ability to assess the severity of the liquidity problems. Their ability to act can be further limited due to the ECB's power to prohibit or restrict the LOLR role of the NCBs, and other EU law, in particular state aid rules. Real-time cooperation and information sharing is not guaranteed, neither is the availability of resources. The ECB in turn will not have the necessary information to assess the systemic impact of the liquidity crisis.

Minor reforms and improvements on a system where the competences remain at the national level cannot take the place of a centralised and European LOLR. First, some argue that market operations can deal effectively with liquidity problems and prevent bank runs spreading through contagion. The LTCM rescue orchestrated by the Fed in the 1990s is presented as an example of successful management of a major threatening liquidity crisis through the joint action of private banks. The ECB will face no regulatory impediment in coordinating market forces in a similar fashion to prevent a financial institution from becoming insolvent. However, this argument ignores that market operations are not guaranteed to be effective in a highly competitive environment.[47]

---

of eligible collateral since Art. 18(1) ESCB Statute only requires that the collateral is 'adequate' without determining the characteristics of 'adequate' collateral. This contrasts with the Bundesbank arrangements where the 'eligibility' characteristics are determined, and a legislative act is required in order to accept non-eligible collateral.

[47] The LTCM rescue through coordinated private action took place in a very competitive environment. However, in that case the intervention by the Federal Reserve and its chairman Alan Greenspan was a critical factor. For weaknesses of coordinated private sector lending in the context of a competitive environment see Xavier Freixas *et al.*, 'Lender of Last Resort: a review of the literature', *Fin. Stability Rev.* 151, 162 (November 1999), where a reference is made to related problems in the rescue of Johnson Matthey Bankers Ltd.

Even if feasible, they will often be time-consuming, expensive and subject to free-rider problems.

A centralisation of the LOLR competence for both systemic and individual liquidity crises can be effected without any major reform. A European level institutional solution is available in the ECB. The legal basis for such centralisation would be in the applied monetary policy concept. An activation of the enabling clause of Article 105(6) of the Treaty (Article 25(2) of the ESCB Statute) is one way of allocating LOLR power to the ECB. It is not required if one relies on the applied monetary policy concept. This provides the basis for the ECB's LOLR competence without recourse to the enabling clause. The interdependence of banking soundness and LOLR with stable money growth establishes the link of LOLR with monetary policy.[48] The ECB's responsibility for the smooth conduct of national prudential policies further enhances the legality of the ECB's LOLR role.[49] The ECB's monetary tools make this LOLR role practicable. Open market and credit operations with individual banks allow the ECB both to evaluate their financial situation and when necessary inject liquidity against adequate collateral.[50] There is still a need for effective access to information. Such reforms can proceed alone, or in the context of a further centralisation of macro-prudential functions which moves up to the EU level.

5. SO WHO IS GOING TO REGULATE FINANCIAL MARKETS?

The European system of financial market regulation is continuing to evolve towards a functional multiple peak model.[51] The scholarly argument at the moment seems to have turned against a more comprehensive institutional solution at the European level.[52]

---

[48] It is in this context that we agree with Paddoa Schioppa on the (lack of) adequacy of the existing system operating under 'constructive ambiguity'.

[49] EC Treaty Art. 105(5); ESCB Statute Art. 3(3).

[50] ESCB Statute Arts 17, 18. The ECB's Governing Council has a high degree of flexibility in determining what adequate collateral is.

[51] Since the publication of G Di Giorgio and C Di Noia, 'Financial Market Regulation and Supervision: How Many Peaks for the Euro Area?' (2002–2003) 28 *Brooklyn Journal of International Law* 463 this development has continued. These authors propose the establishment of a European System of Financial Regulators (similar to the ESCB) comprising a European Central Authority, a European Financial Supervision Authority and European Authority for Market Transparency.

[52] E Wymeersch, 'The future of financial regulation and supervision in Europe' (2005) 42 *Common Market Law Review* 987 and Rosa Maria Lastra, 'The Governance

There is still a case to be made for the EU solution, and we will now rehearse some of the arguments that the discussion has brought up, concluding and complementing those in the preceding sections of the chapter.[53] The main support is in the following two points: (1) the obstacles to the Internal Financial Market presented by national regulatory and supervisory regimes, and the failure of the minimum standards and mutual recognition regime to lower these barriers; (2) the need for broader based regulatory and supervisory institutions, undertaking at a European level what cannot effectively be done at a national level, including providing a system for preventing and dealing with systemic crises and risks of such crises.

The choice between regulatory models may not be obvious. There is need for a further sorting out of the arguments which seem partially to be based on national paradigms and usually also based on outdated models of regulation and not taking account of the present state of development of the financial markets. The most radical solution would be an integrated consolidated single regulator for Europe's financial markets and intermediaries. We conclude that the arguments against a consolidated regulator have less weight at a European level. There is a European trend towards a universal regulator. The last decade has seen an emerging European model of a domestic universal financial market regulator in a rather tight European framework responding quickly to international developments. The recent developments include the establishment of the British Financial Services Authority and the German reforms. Their consequences for Europe are still not clear. Here we return to the question whether home country control does achieve the primary internal market aims. The answer remains that very limited financial integration has been achieved. This does, on the other hand, not exclude the increased interdependence and

---

Structure for Financial Supervision and Regulation in Europe' (2003) 10 *Columbia Journal of European Law* 49–68; see also her articles on 'Cross-Border Bank Insolvency: Legal Implications in the Case of Banks Operating in Different Jurisdictions in Latin America' (2003) 6 *Journal of International Economic Law* 79–110, and 'Regulating European Securities Markets: Beyond the Lamfalussy Report' in M Andenas and Y Avgerinos (eds), *Financial Markets in Europe. Towards a Single Regulator?* (Kluwer Law International, London, The Hague, New York, 2003) 211. See the arguments the other way in S Osterloo and D Schoenmaker, 'Financial Supervision in an Integrating Europe: Measuring Cross-Border Externalities', LSE FMG Special Papers 156 (London, April 2004) and CAE Goodhart and D Schoenmaker, 'Burden sharing in a banking crisis in Europe', Special Paper No 164, LSE FMG Special Paper Series (London, March 2006).

[53] And developing the argument in M Andenas, 'Who is Going to Supervise Europe's Financial Markets' in M Andenas and Y Avgerinos (eds), *Financial Markets in Europe. Towards a Single Regulator?* (Kluwer Law International, London, The Hague, New York, 2003) xv.

systemic risk. The introduction of the euro has not in itself changed this situation. But it shows, even more clearly than before, the costs and inefficiencies of existing market divisions. It also leads to increased integration, which in turn increases systemic risk. Cooperation between national authorities is not enough to handle crises. Although certain steps have been made in the field of capital adequacy, arrangements for regulation and monitoring are inadequate in today's markets. Consolidation of financial services calls for consolidation of supervision at EU level. It is not easy today to distinguish between market risk and the risk of financial institutions. A single supervisor could better function as coordinator of national regulatory authorities and lender of last resort. A single regulator with lender of last resort responsibilities could also respond better to a financial crisis, which would need immediate and resolute action. Negotiations and compromise between national regulators may not provide the optimal process. A constant challenge of other EU policies, e.g. on state aid, will remain.

On the other hand, we have the ECB's role: is it the most realistic prospect that it will gradually be filling the void? Its present role is limited but is increasing. It may provide the only realistic alternative for a European macro-prudential regulator and LOLR. We concluded that the argument against central bank involvement in financial market regulation, if rigorously tested, is less than convincing. There is a need for analysis and further sorting out of the issues to provide the basis for rational policy discourse. The ECB must be discussed as a model in relation to the sectoral regulators or the European super regulator. In itself the ECB may provide an organisational model for the development of a European super regulator.

The decision making process concerning financial market regulation and its reform is flawed, also at the EU level. There are several agency issues which distort the decision making process and which will effectively block the integrated consolidated single regulator. That financial market regulation traditionally is crisis driven means that it develops in response to financial crises or scandals and not as the outcome of a process of rational deliberation. There may be a window of opportunity following a financial crisis where the present system is seen to fail. The present coordination of national responsibilities is insufficient, and the risks involved with the current system are considerable. Waiting for such a window to open is not a satisfactory situation, but it seems that only an actual crisis demonstrating this can lead to new arrangements. Furthermore, authorities in this field are generally not too concerned with extending their formal responsibility but a crisis may force them to.

We now come to the discussion of some models for transfers of power to the European level. One is the euro and the ECB. The trade-off for ministries of finance and central banks was monetary policy and institutional independence which they were strongly ideologically committed to and could not achieve otherwise.[54] Trying to identify trade-offs that can create windows of opportunity for moving financial market supervision to a European level, one finds there are several candidates. The needs of the Internal Financial Market, spurred on by the introduction of the euro, should be the most realistic platform. The trade-off should be straightforward: more efficient home financial markets with benefits for investors, savers and society at large, and opportunities for expansion across borders for the financial institutions. Another form of trade-off lies in how a European solution may seem a radical solution. Historically regulatory reform has taken the form of panic stricken short term responses to the crisis that has just passed, and here the European solution may also offer a clean break with discredited national institutions.[55]

There is also a global financial policy challenge. The major issue here is that there is no viable political structure to support an international regulator, universal or sectoral. International financial liberalisation results in a major increase in risk in both the national and international real economies. An effective policy towards financial markets must be international in character. Already the financial instabilities in the 1990s, such as the Asian crisis, as well as collapses of financial institutions such as BCCI and Barings Bank, called for more efficient regulation for an effective lender of last resort. Demand for international financial regulation cannot be coped with by traditional forms of international cooperation between regulators. We need a tighter organisation; an IMF for financial market supervision, not only one that deals with such questions as a sideline to currency issues. The IMF, OECD and World Bank have been concerned with financial systems in the developing countries. There are further legitimacy concerns with the present international standard setting. They cannot be remedied by civil society participation through consultation.

We can conclude with the identification of a set of issues that require further research. There is a clear role for scholarship, institutional economics, legal and interdisciplinary scholarship. The law and the legal and economic concepts remain unclear, and their interrelationship is treated in a way that usually is confusing. We return to Pascal and the need to avoid taking the smallest risk when the risk is eternal damnation and our parallel is systemic risk and regulatory

---

[54] Compare the situation in the United Kingdom where today still the Bank of England and the Treasury strongly oppose joining the euro. The window has closed: the Bank of England has been granted independence. See Lazaros E. Panourgias and Mads Andenas, 'The euro, EMU and UK law' in Jean-Victor Louis (ed.), *The Euro in the National Context* (BIICL, London, 2002).

[55] In the scenario where a crisis just has taken place. There may be diminishing returns from games of musical chairs with consolidations and break ups and further reorganisation of regulators and central banks at the national level. Cynically speaking, the European level offers a fresh start.

models. Systemic risk and regulatory models, whether we base them on revelation or tradition, require rigorous analysis. Also the Internal Market process and what makes it effective require further analysis. We do not know enough about the mechanics of free movement deregulation or its costs and benefits, or for that matter about depositor or investor protection and its effects.

2. Applied uniformity of a uniform commercial law: ensuring functional harmonisation of uniform texts through a global jurisconsultorium of the CISG*

Camilla Baasch Andersen**

DEFINING UNIFORMITY

This book, and the conference which inspired it, focuses on the theory and practice of harmonisation. The concluding chapter grapples with the concept of the taxonomy of harmonised law. One of the key questions here is the determination of what we mean by 'harmonisation' and the closely related term 'unification' of law.

Defining the concept of 'uniformity' in the context of commercial law is a complex task, as it is a term which has been used with a certain element of obscurity.[1] Any attempt to clarify it involves terminological deliberations and a comparative analysis of the preambles to uniform laws and their aims.[2] The present chapter argues that:

1. Uniformity in law is different from a dictionary definition, as no laws are

---

* 1980 Convention on Contracts for the International Sale of Goods [CISG].

** Cand.Jur. (Copenhagen), PhD (Aarhus School of Business). Fellow, Institute of International Commercial Law, Pace University Law School, New York, USA and Senior Lecturer in Law, University of Leicester, UK.

[1] See Michael Bridge's humorous remarks in 'Uniformity and Diversity in the Law of International Sale' in 15 *Pace International Law Review* (Spring 2003) 55–89: '[u] niform law represents a part of that phenomenon that we call globalisation, a word that means so many different things to so many different people and ought on that account to be used sparingly, perhaps with a modest financial forfeit that upon sufficient accumulation will be paid over to charitable purposes. Those of us participating in one or more of the incremental efforts to bring about uniform law are, fortunately, sufficiently obscure to be spared the attentions of anti-globalisation protestors'.

[2] For such an analysis see C Baasch Andersen, 'Defining Uniformity in Law' in (XII) *Uniform Law Review*, 2007–1, 5–57.

ever applied 'always the same',[3] but it is concerned with establishing similarity, and a definition is therefore very result based.

2. The major promulgators of legal uniformity strongly suggest that the concept of unification of law rests on the bringing together of legal systems,[4]
so the result in question is the establishing of similar rules across divides
of legal cultures.

3. Uniform law is a new form of lawmaking, with a different *origin* and a different *focus*,[5] and it usually arises in a transnational context – or at least in
a trans-jurisdictional context (the United States, for instance, being multi-
jurisdictional as far as state law is concerned, applies uniform laws within
the national boundaries).

4. It is not relevant whether a given set of uniform regulations can be classified
as law in a given jurisdiction – the extremely difficult taxonomy of defining
law is irrelevant in this context.[6] One of the most successful instruments
of so-called 'uniform law' is a banking regulation (the ICC UCP 600 on
Letters of Credit). What matters is that the result is a similar governing of
a legal phenomenon.

5. The many different contexts, forms and political goals of law will affect
the realistic level of similarity which the proposed form of uniformity
may reach. It is important to note that uniformity is not an absolute but a
variable, so we see that our intermediary definition has to encompass the
concept of *varying degrees*.

---

[3] According to the *American Heritage Dictionary of the English Language*, New
College Edition, uniform is defined as: **1.a.** *Always the same*; unchanging; unvarying.
b. Without fluctuation or variation; consistent; regular **2.** *Being the same* as another;
identical; consonant.

[4] UNCITRAL defines uniformity as *that which removes barriers in international
trade* (see the preamble to the CISG: 'contribute to the removal of legal barriers in international trade and promote the development of international trade') and UNIDROIT is an
institute *for unification of law, seeking to co-ordinate national private laws* (taken from the
descriptor of the www.unidroit.org homepage: 'Unidroit seeks to harmonize and co-ordinate national private laws and to prepare for int'l adoption of uniform rules of private law').

[5] See Niklas Luhmann, who defines the process of law in globalisation as a process
of law where 'functional criteria increasingly replace geographic ones, with nation-
states' traditional law-generating organs diminishing in importance in determining legal
significance, regulation and evolution', in Niklas Luhmann, *Das Recht der Gesellschaft*
(1993), as translated by Vivian Curran.

[6] For the purposes of this chapter, the concept of law will be considered a broad one,
and borderline cases of what constitutes law will not be resolved, but sidestepped by the
inclusion of the terms 'rules' and 'legal phenomena'. Specifying a general criterion for the
definition of 'law' is not beneficial in the present context of trans-jurisdictional unification.
Suffice it to say that a broad conception of law is needed to encompass the various definitions across the board of different legal families. For more on definitions of law, see W
Twining, 'A Post-Westphalian Concept of Law' in 37 *Law and Society Review*, 199–257.

6.   Modern unification of laws is a political *voluntary* process whereby differ-
     ent jurisdictions elect to share a set of rules – not where it is imposed upon
     them, as opposed to historical uniformity (like Roman law,[7] Common Law,[8]
     or other colonial laws.) The element of voluntarily *sharing* is essential and
     defining; and
7.   It is not in the creation of texts which call themselves 'uniform' that any
     actual uniformity in law is created, but in the successful application of such
     texts, where the success is determined by the degree of similarity attained.

Summing up on the above:

> We can define 'uniformity' as the varying degree of similar effects
> on a phenomenon across boundaries of different jurisdictions re-
> sulting from the application of deliberate efforts to create specific
> shared rules in some form.

It follows from this that if we focus on the effects of law, then it is the degree
of applied uniformity, and not the creation of uniform texts themselves, which
defines the uniform law. The practice of its application sums up its actual uniformity. This means that rules or laws labelled 'uniform' are not technically
uniform at all according to our definition above, until they have been *applied*
cross-jurisdictionally and created similarity on the intended legal phenomenon.

There is a necessary distinction here to be made between applied uniformity, which is the true meaning or goal of unification efforts, and the apparent
uniformity of texts. The late Prof. Schlechtriem distinguished a 'unity achieved
at a verbal level' (the rules as provided by the drafters) from the 'uniform understanding' and 'uniform interpretation' (the commentary and application of
these rules).[9] Building on this distinction between uniform *texts* as opposed to a
uniform *application* of these texts, we can label the former a *textual uniformity*,[10]

---

[7]   See Cicero, *De Republica*, 3.22.33: '[t]here shall not be one law at Rome, another
at Athens, one now, another hereafter, but one everlasting and unalterable law shall
govern all nations for all time ...'.

[8]   De Cruz argues that James I, King of England and Scotland, introduced uniformity to England and Scotland when proposing to unify them under a single legal system
in the early 16th century: see *Comparative Law in a Changing World*, 2nd ed. 1999, 23.

[9]   See Schlechtriem in the introduction to Schlechtriem au Schwenzer (eds), *Commentary on the UN Convention on the International Sale of Goods (CISG)* (OUP, 2005) at 6.

[10]   This term also accords with the way in which Harry Flechtner talks of 'textual
non-uniformity' when comparing the different texts of the six official languages of the
CISG and their meanings, but Flechtner uses it to indicate the level of similarity between

while labelling the latter *applied uniformity*. Textual uniformity, like applied uniformity, is also a question of degrees of similarity and not an absolute. The textual uniformity of legal instruments setting out uniform laws or approaches can vary immensely. The similarity in the legal documents created can vary, the quality of any translations can vary, and style of promulgation of the uniform law in question can vary (i.e. Model Law vs Convention, etc.). For instance, where different translations or texts of the same document with equal official status exist, nuances of difference in meaning in these texts are bound to exist, as language is not a precise science. Flechtner labels this a 'textual non-uniformity', using uniformity as a word of total similarity in this context.[11] Such differences may, naturally, have an effect on the way scholars and practitioners working in these different languages interpret and use given provisions, so the degree of *textual uniformity* affects the degree of actual uniformity.

While it is thus true that the textual uniformity has a profound effect on the applied uniformity, even the most diligently created piece of textually uniform legislation will not suffice. As pointed out by Honnold, 'uniform words do not create uniform results'.[12] Textual uniformity is an expressed goal towards actual uniformity. Only the application of textually uniform instruments will reveal whether similar results are reached and whether the goal of uniformity, of varying degrees, is reached and the textual uniformity thus becomes actual and *applied*.

UNIFORMITY AND THE CISG

The CISG is currently in force in 77 different countries across the world,[13] and often labelled a successful uniform law. But studies of the CISG show that while it is textually uniform, at least to some extent, it is often more successful in creating a uniform text than a uniform result, and the applied uniformity suffers in case law.

---

the texts in question. By inference, if they did have the same meanings linguistically then these texts would (together) represent a textual uniformity. An instrument with only one official text will thus, by definition, always represent a single *textual uniformity*. See H Flechtner, 'The Several Texts of the CISG in a Decentralized System: Observations on Translations, Reservations and other Challenges to the Uniformity Principle in Article 7(1)' in (1998) 17 *Journal of Law and Commerce* 187–217, available online at: http://cisgw3.law.pace.edu/cisg/biblio/flecht1.html.

[11]   *Ibid.*

[12]   See J O Honnold, 'Uniform Words and Uniform Application. The 1980 Sales Convention and International Juridicial Practice', in Schlechtriem (ed.), *Einheitliches Kaufrecht und Nationales Obligationenrecht* (1987) 115–46, at 146–7.

[13]   As of 1 August 2011, UNCITRAL reports that 77 states have adopted the CISG. See http://www.uncitral.org/uncitral/en/uncitral_texts/sale_goods/1980CISG_status.html.

For instance, in the determination of what constitutes 'reasonable time' for notice giving in Article 39 CISG, various interpretations from various CISG states run from four days being untimely to four months being timely.[14] And given that the failure to comply with this notice requirement means a complete lack of remedies, with few exceptions,[15] this is a very serious provision for a buyer suffering from a non-conformity of goods. Such divergences in considering notice reasonable do not create a nice, predictable environment for transnational business. So the question is: is this divergence acceptable or does it lie outside accepted divergences for uniform application?

The CISG finds its basis for uniformity in its preamble, and in Article 7(1) CISG, which provides:

> In the interpretation of this Convention, regard is to be had to its international character and to the need to promote uniformity in its application ...

The determination of 'how uniform is uniform' in the context of uniform CISG application is not a question easily answered. A detailed analysis of the CISG, its *travaux préparatoires* (including a Secretariat's Commentary and antecedents) and its current practice would seem to indicate that different provisions aim for different degrees of applied uniformity, as many have various opportunities for flexibility built into them. However, given the genesis of the convention and the aim to create a level playing field in commercial law and remove barriers to international trade, a certain minimum level of uniformity in application of the convention must be assumed.[16]

For the example of Article 39 and the determination of 'reasonable time' above, the divergences found are too significant[17] as well as too predictable, as they are based on a homeward trend interpretation which reflects domestic law and have nothing to do with the shared law of the CISG.[18]

---

[14] See the CISG Advisory opinion no. 2, with case annex, available at: www.cisg. law.pace.edu/cisg/CISG-AC-op2.html, and for an earlier study see C Baasch Andersen, 'Reasonable time in the CISG' in Pace (ed) *1998 Review of the CISG* (1998) 63–177.

[15] Exceptions are found in Art. 40 (for the seller in bad faith or quasi-bad faith) and Art. 44 (for the buyer who has a reasonable excuse). For more on these exceptions see C Baasch Andersen, 'Exceptions to the Notification Rule – are they uniformly interpreted?' in (2005) 9 *Vindobona Journal* 17–42.

[16] For an in-depth analysis of the uniformity of the CISG see C Baasch Andersen, *Uniform Application of the International Sales Law* (2007), esp. at chapter 2.

[17] See C Baasch Andersen, 'Reasonable time in the CISG' in Pace (ed) *1998 Review of the CISG* (1998), 63–177, and for recent support of this see D Girsberger, 'The Time Limits of Article 39 CISG' in (2005–06) 25 *Journal of Law and Commerce* 241–51.

[18] For more on the homeward trend and how it undermines uniformity, see F Ferrari, 'Have the Dragons of Uniform Sales Law Been Tamed?' in C Baasch Andersen and U G Shroeter, *Sharing International Commercial Law across National Boundaries*

It seems there is a significant problem with the practice of uniform application here, which is caused by problems of failing to obtain a measure of uniform interpretation. If these homeward trends are left to run unchecked, there is a real risk that the CISG will become a deceptive semblance of uniform international law which holds real pitfalls for international trade.[19]

So what can be done? How can courts be influenced to move away from homeward trends in interpretation of concepts which should be shared, and embrace a more uniform and transnational shared approach?

THE GLOBAL JURISCONSULTORIUM OF THE CISG – THE 'LEGAL' ARGUMENTS

Over the last decade, a specific concept regarding this Convention has been growing in momentum to ensure more uniformity in application. The notion that shared law needs to share its global scholarship and global precedents is winning favour with courts in different national jurisdictions. Collectively, this can be described as the *global jurisconsultorium* of the CISG.[20] It can be defined as a concept of sharing and consultation across borders and legal systems in the aim of producing autonomous interpretation and application of a given uniform law.

We can label this tool a shared interpretational sphere – or a *jurisconsultorium*, because jurists consult with one another, either in scholarly contexts or by referring to each others' precedents across jurisdictional boundaries. This jurisconsultorium can be divided in two major groups; the scholarly jurisconsultorium (the cooperation and consultation with transnational scholars rather than single jurisdiction scholarship) and the practical jurisconsultorium (the use

---

– Festschrift for Albert H. Kritzer on the Occasion of his 80ᵗʰ Birthday, April 2008, at 134–67.

[19]   See some of the points made by J Bailey, 'Facing the truth: Seeing the Convention on Contracts for the International Sale of Goods as an Obstacle to a Uniform Law of International Sales', (1999) 32 *Cornell International Law Journal* 282.

[20]   In the context of the CISG, this term was first employed by Rogers and Kritzer: '[a] global jurisconsultorium on uniform international sales law is the proper setting for the analysis of foreign jurisprudence on terminology of international sales': see V Rogers and A Kritzer, 'A Uniform International Sales Law Terminology' in I Schwenzer and G Hager (eds), *Festschrift für Peter Schlechtriem zum 70. Geburtstag* (2003) at 223–53. The term has since been used in varied scholarship. For more information on the global jurisconsultorium of the CISG see C Baasch Andersen, *Uniform Application of the International Sales Law – Understanding Uniformity, the Global Jurisconsultorium and Examination and Notification Provisions of the CISG* (2007) C Baasch Andersen, 'The Uniform International Sales Law and the Global Jurisconsultorium' (2005) 24 *Journal of Law and Commerce* 159–79.

of transnational shared case law in solving disputes before domestic courts). The latter concept is akin to the body of case law of the UCC in the US across the borders of the states applying a shared rule. It can also be compared with the shared body of persuasive precedents of the Common Law throughout the Commonwealth where pieces of legislation of common principles are shared.

It is not a leap to imagine sharing sources where a law is shared, as is the case with the CISG. In the words of Honnold:

> ... tribunals construing an international convention will appreciate that they are col-
> leagues of a world-wide body of jurists with a common goal.[21]

The judges and counsel who apply an international uniform convention must recognise that they are sharing it with colleagues in other jurisdictions, and that its development is a communal evolution requiring a unique approach very different from the (differing) applications of domestic law in varying jurisdictions. It requires it to be shared.

Most scholars would argue that Article 7(1) CISG holds the legal basis for a duty to aim for a uniform interpretation by taking an international vantage point. Prof. Lookofsky paraphrases the duty in the provision thus: 'Article 7(1) commands national courts also to have (some measure of) 'regard' to the international view'.[22] This is a logical conclusion based on the "regard" requirement toward internationality and uniformity in Article 7(1). But it does not support a duty for uniform application – merely a uniform interpretation (which may well aid a uniform application, but does not help to tell us much in the way of how uniform the CISG should aim to be).

There is a basic comity argument present here as well. In undertaking to share a legal text like the CISG, which strives for uniform interpretation, states are also undertaking to pursue the goal of uniformity in unison. The legal basis for this duty to share sources of law when sharing law is one of comity; of recognising the unique nature of shared international laws, and allowing the influences for the interpretation of these laws to be as diverse as the systems which share them.

In short, there can be no questioning the duty to consider alien sources or precedents. This cannot lead to anything other than a duty to refer and consider, and anything by way of binding precedent will never be applicable, but there must be a duty to take them into account. This duty has been supported in legal

---

[21] J O Honnold, 'Uniform Laws for International Trade: Early "Care and Feed-ing" for Uniform Growth' in (1995) 1 *International Trade and Business Law Journal (Australia)*, 1–10.

[22] J Lookofsky, *Understanding the CISG* (2008), 34. Lookofsky also points out the problematic issue of just how much 'regard' must be had at 35.

scholarship in many guises by numerous other CISG experts, including Di Matteo,[23] Ferrari,[24] Zeller,[25] Flechtner[26] and Schlechtriem.[27]

A Tale of Two Jurisconsultoria – the UCC and the CISG

There are a number of similarities between uniform international law and uniform domestic law where the domestic law covers multiple jurisdictions. In the words of Harry Flechtner, the CISG:

> Requires … an approach not unlike the treatment U.S. courts accord decisions of other jurisdictions when applying our Uniform Commercial Code.[28]

The UCC conforms with the above definition of 'uniform'; it is the result of a deliberate effort to create similar results on a legal phenomenon across boundaries of legal jurisdictions, and the only difference is its domestic nature as opposed to transgovernmental. It is not surprising that scholars like Flechtner accustomed to applying uniform *domestic* law draw parallels to the application of uniform *international* law. Those who are familiar with a *jurisconsultorium* of the UCC may find it easier to embrace that of the CISG – but they MUST remember that

---

[23]   See especially DiMatteo, 'The CISG and the Presumption of Enforceability: Unintended Contractual Liability in International Business Dealings' in (1997) 22 *Yale International Law Journal*, at 111 and DiMatteo *et al.*, 'The Interpretive Turn in International Sales Law: An Analysis of Fifteen Years of CISG Jurisprudence' in (2004) 34 *Northwestern Journal of International Law and Business* 299–440.

[24]   F Ferrari, 'CISG Case Law: A New Challenge for Interpreters?' in (1999) 17 *Journal of Law and Commerce*, 246: '[a]s many legal writers have pointed out, this means, above all, that one should not read the Convention through the lenses of domestic law, but rather in an autonomous manner'.

[25]   B Zeller, 'Traversing international waters: With the growth of international trade, lawyers must become familiar with the terms of the Convention on Contracts for the International Sale of Goods', in (2004) 78 *Law Institute Journal* 52 et seq.

[26]   H Flechtner, 'The Several Texts of the CISG in a Decentralized System: Observations on Translations, Reservations and other Challenges to the Uniformity Principle in Article 7(1)' in (1998) 17 *Journal of Law and Commerce* 187–217, available online at: http://cisgw3.law.pace.edu/cisg/biblio/flecht1.html.

[27]   See specially P Schlechtriem, 'Uniform Sales Law – the Experience with Uniform Sales Laws in the Federal Republic of Germany', in (1991/1992) 2 *Juridisk Tidskrift* 1–28, available online at: http://cisgw3.law.pace.edu/cisg/biblio/schlech2.html, where he explains how consideration and critique of case law in other jurisdictions, as well as help from scholars and comparative law centres, smoothes any divergent interpretations of uniform law.

[28]   H M Flechtner, 'Several Texts of the CISG in a Decentralized System: Observations on Translations, Reservations and Other Challenges to the Uniformity Principle in Article 7(1)' (1998) 17 *Journal of Law and Commerce* 187–217, available online at: http://cisgw3.law.pace.edu/cisg/biblio/flecht1.html.

the two are different and determined by the legal community which shares the rules.[29] The UCC must never be used to interpret the CISG, merely because they are both uniform laws – they are different and have different jurisconsultoria.[30] One is found amongst 49 US states sharing the UCC – the other is found amongst 67 nations including all the US states which share the CISG. The latter is an even larger and more complex sphere with completely different concepts and terminologies. The only shared aspect is that there **is** a jurisconsultorium.

Interestingly, another parallel between the CISG and the UCC is the absence of a court to monitor uniformity. Consider the following:

> Many who are not specialists in the US federal system are dismayed to learn that our 'Supreme' Court has no jurisdiction to correct conflicting interpretations of the many uniform laws of our 50 states, for example, the Uniform Commercial Code (UCC). Divergent interpretations have, of course, developed. The important point, however, is that they have not significantly detracted from the great value of our uniform state laws; the 'saving grace' is the shared conviction by our courts of the need to preserve uniformity by giving weight to decisions in other states. As a result, a generally satisfactory uniformity of result has been achieved.[31]

It would seem that the quests for a court to monitor the application of international commercial laws may not be as required for the development of uniformity as some scholars believe. Admittedly, the divergences between international jurisdictions and domestic states are not the same, and thus the arguments in favour of monitoring on an international plane have more merit. Nevertheless, the experience of the American uniform laws is interesting to note, especially as it illustrates a 'generally satisfactory' uniformity – a flexible and relative term of function, much like the relative functional uniformity of the CISG. Moreover, the above statement confirms the significant role of the practical jurisconsultorium and use of precedents.

This parallel between the UCC and the CISG is also drawn by another scholar, Philip Hackney, who states:

> [W]hen interpreting the Convention, a court should look to other court's interpretations of the Convention, including the interpretations of courts from other countries.

---

[29]   See also Ferrari in 'The Relationship Between the UCC and the CISG and the Construction of Uniform Law' (1996) 29 *Loyola of Los Angeles Law Review* (1996) 1021–33.

[30]   See, for example, the humorous and justifiably harsh criticism given by Lookofsky and Flechtner in awarding a 'razzie' for the worst CISG case to the Federal District Court of Illinois which did just this, in the *Raw Materials v Manfred Forberecht* case, in 'Nominating Manfred Forberich: The Worst CISG Decision in 25 Years?' in (2005) 9 *Vindobona Journal of International Commercial Law and Arbitration* 199–208.

[31]   J O Honnold, 'Uniform Laws for International Trade: Early "Care and Feeding" for Uniform Growth' in (1995) 1 *International Trade and Business Law Journal* 1–10.

... The use in the U.S. of case law to interpret the Uniform Commercial Code (UCC) can serve as a model for courts using case law to interpret the Convention. No state within the U.S. is bound by an interpretation of the UCC from another state, but the interpretations of the UCC from other jurisdictions are extremely persuasive. While this method does not achieve exact uniformity, the U.S. has achieved a level of uniformity in sales law that is useful to companies transacting business in many states.[32]

This statement is interesting, because it not only highlights the parallels between two regimes with non-binding precedents, but also places in focus the fact that uniformity is not an absolute, but functions on different levels. A level of uniformity useful to business (as it promotes trade, in accordance with the convention's preamble based on predictability) is a realistic aim for the CISG, and in the interests of the practitioners, as shown below.

THE GLOBAL JURISCONSULTORIUM OF THE CISG – THE 'POLICY' ARGUMENTS

A global jurisconsultorium is not unique to the CISG. See, for example, the classic example of the House of Lords in *Fothergill v. Monarch Airlines* on the interpretation of the Warsaw Convention on the Liability of Air Carriers, wherein the Lords clearly set out that uniform international law is unique and must be treated uniquely.[33] And on the other side of the Atlantic Ocean, the US Supreme Court decided in the *Air France v. Saks* case, concerning the meaning of the term 'accident' under the Warsaw Convention, that judicial decisions from other countries interpreting a treaty term are 'entitled to considerable weight'.[34] This premise was restated more recently in another case on the same convention by the US Supreme Court, the *El Al* case.[35]

However, the awareness in application of uniform law is especially needed in the area of international commercial law, because there are such immediate economic benefits to be had by removing barriers to trade, and because there is no instance of monitoring. There is no International Commercial Court to monitor the application of shared global instruments like the CISG, despite many suggestions for this to be created ranging back to 1911 and to 2003.[36] So, in the

---

[32] P T Hackney, 'Is the United Nations Convention on the International Sale of Goods Achieving Uniformity?', (2001) 61 *Louisiana Law Review*, 473–86, at 479.

[33] House of Lords in *Fothergill v. Monarch Airlines* [1980] 2 All ER 696.

[34] *Air France v. Saks*, 470 US 392, 404 (1985).

[35] *El Al Israel Airlines, Ltd. v. Tsui Yuan Tseng*, 525 US 155, 176 (1999).

[36] Hans Wehberg seems to have been the first to suggest such a tribunal: see H Wehberg, *Ein Internationaler Gerichtshof für Privatklagen* (1911), 23. Another suggestion

application of uniform international commercial law like the CISG, it is up to the judges to realise that the law being applied is a shared multi-jurisdictional law which should be applied with a high degree of uniformity, and therefore must be treated as a unique phenomenon and not follow the path of domestic law. Using a jurisconsultorium ensures a common approach to similar problems, and a shared development of the shared uniform law.

Moreover, it is directly in the interest of legal counsel using the CISG in the interest of clients to 'shop' for precedents as widely as possible. What legal counsel would not welcome a wide array of possible cases which may support his client's position? And why should a case not be cited merely because the commercial court deciding a dispute does not stem from the same hierarchical domestic judicial system? If courts share common commercial values, as we seem to assume in international commercial law,[37] and share the same text, then it would seem most sensible – and in line with the duty laid out above – to cite it to the judge and let him/her decide how persuasive it is. The benefit of having a wealth of potential persuasive case law is self-evident for the commercial lawyer. Moreover, it should also be considered a benefit for judges. As Koch puts it, 'Only a fool would refuse to seek guidance in the work of other judges confronted with similar problems'.[38]

THE GLOBAL JURISCONSULTORIUM APPLIED – THE PROBLEM OF PRECEDENTS

There have been a number of CISG cases following the shared path to uniform application. The first reported one was in 1996, from an Italian District Court in Cuneo, where the judge looked at German and Swiss case law in the determination of Articles 38 and 39.[39] Over the past 12 years, many have followed

---

was made in 1992: see L Sohn, 'Uniform Laws Require Uniform Application: Proposals for an International Tribunal to Interpret Uniform Legal Texts', *Uniform Commercial Law in the Twenty-First Century: Proceedings of the Congress of the United Nations Commission on International Trade Law, 18–22 May 1992* (1992), 50–54, and the latest official suggestion seems to have been made by Filip de Ly. See de Ly, 'Uniform Interpretation: What is Being Done? Official Efforts', in Ferrari (ed.), *The 1980 Uniform Sales Law* (2003) 346.

[37] This view has prevailed since Otto Kahn-Freund, the noted comparativist, first dared to state his point that Commercial law is comparatively culture free: see 'On Uses and Misuses of Comparative Law' in January 1974, 37 *Modern Law Review* 1–27.

[38] C H Koch, Jr., 'Envisioning a Global Legal Culture', 25 *Michigan Journal of International Law* 51.

[39] Trib. Civile of Cuneo, Italian judgment of 31 January 1996, available at http://cisgw3.law.pace.edu/cases/960131i3.html. Ten years ago, in F Ferrari, *Remarks on the*

suit.[40] Some have shown remarkable attention to the multijurisdictional nature of the CISG by looking at cases from many different sister states and weighing scholarship from many legal systems interpreting the shared rule. Yet, even despite the obvious advantages to those working with the CISG as outlined above, there are disproportionately few instances where the global jurisconsultorium can be seen applied.

Why?

Certainly, any practical problems obstructing the access to foreign cases and sources are now all but removed. This sort of multijurisdictional work is now facilitated by the internet, where CISG databases can be found, containing full

---

Autonomy and the Uniform Application of the CISG on the Occasion of its Tenth Anniversary, International Contract Advisor Series, 41 n. 33, Professor Ferrari reported that the decision from the Trib. Civile of Cuneo was the only one of 300 cases reported by Michael Will to comply with the duty to look to foreign case law.

[40] *Scea. Gaec des Beauches B. Bruno v. Société Teso Ten Elsen GmbH & Co KG*, CA Grenoble, 23 Oct. 1996 [94/3859], available at http://cisgw3.law.pace.edu/cases/961023f1.html; *MCC-Marble Ceramic Ctr., Inc. v. Ceramica Nuova D'Agostino S.p.A.*, 134 F3d 1384 (llth Cir. 1998); United States 17 May 1999 Federal District Court [Louisiana] (*Medical Mktg. Int'l, Inc. v. Internazionale Medico Scientifica*) available at http://cisgw3.law.pace.edu/cases.990517u. No. 1990 WL 311945 at *2 (E.D. La. May 17, 1999); Bundesgerichtshof, 13 Nov. 2001, 4C. 198/2003 SRI (Switzerland), available at http://cisg3.law.pace.edu/cases/031113s1.html; Obergericht des Kantons Luzern, 8 Jan. 1997,11 95 123/357, (Switzerland) available at http://cisgw3.law.pace.edu/cases/970108s1.html; Bundesgerichtshof, 24 Mar. 1999, BGH VIII ZR 121/98 (German); *Scatolificio La Perla S.n.c. di Addrigo Stefano e Giuliano v. Martin Frischdienst GmbH*, Trib. di Padova, 31 Mar. 2004, n. 40466 of Rig 2002 (Italy), available at http://cisgw3.law.pace.edu/cases/040331i3.html and *SO. M. AGRI s.a.s. di Ardina Alessandro & C. v. Erzeugerorganisation Marchfeldgemüse GmbH & Co. KG*, Trib. di Padova, 25 Feb. 2004, n. 40522 (Italy), available at http://cisgw3.law.pace.edu/cases/040225i3.html; *Al Palazzo S.r.l. v. Bernardaud di Limoges S.A.*, 26 Nov. 2002, n. 3095 (Italy), available at http://cisgw3.law.pace.edu/cases/021126i3.html; *Usinor Industeel v. Leeco Steel Prod.*, 209 F Supp 2d 880,886 (E.D. Ill. 2002); *Chi. Prime Packers v. Northam Food Trading*, 320 F Supp 2d 702 (E.D. Ill. 2004); *Cherubino Valsangiacomo, S.A. v. American Juice Import, Inc.*, Audiencia Provincial de Valencia, 7 June 2003, 142/2003 (Spain), available at http://cisgw3.law.pace.edu/cases/030607s4.html; LG Trier, 8 Jan. 2004, 7 HKO 134/03 (Germany), available at http://cisgw3.law.pace.edu/cases/040108g1.html; *Chateau des Charmes Wines Ltd. v. Sabaté USA, Sabaté S.A.*, 328 F3d 528 (9th Cir. 2003); BGH, 30 June 2004, VIII ZR 321/03 (Germany), available at http://cisgw3.law.pace.edu/cases/040630g1.html.; *Isocab France S.A. v. Indus Projektbouw B.V.*, 4 Feb. 2005, LJN: AR 6187; CO/007HR (Netherlands), available at http://cisgw3.law.pace.edu/cases/050204n1.html; Italy, 11 December 2008, Tribunale di Forli (District Court) (*Mitias v. Solidea S.r.l.*) available at http://cisgw3.law.pace.edu/cases/081211i3.html; Australia 24 October 2008 Federal Court (South Australia District) (*Hannaford v Australian Farmlink Pty Ltd*) available at http://cisgw3.law.pace.edu/cases/081024a2.html; OLG Stuttgart 31 March 2008, available at http://cisgw3.law.pace.edu/cases/080331g1.html.

text translations of CISG cases to ensure their availability for all.[41] So there is no 'excuse' in claiming it is too difficult to find or translate foreign cases.

So: why do counsel not delve deep in the international goldmine of possible influential reasoning for judges, and why are judges not using them as guidance?

Any form of resistance is either a 'cannot' or a 'will not'. There seem to be very few reasons why any judge or practitioner should not be able to make good use of the CISG case law. There must be a 'will not' at play. And the best guess is, it centres round very traditional values for case law. Counsel suffer from a significant homeward trend in the domestic traditions for what can be considered a correct citation before a domestic judge. And judges suffer from significant restrictions, formed by habit and tradition, in citing foreign sources in their judgments. The notion of a foreign precedent is – simply put – uncomfortable.

An example which may illustrate this is the Danish 'holy mackerel' case.[42] In this case, involving the sale of fish from Russia to Denmark, the fish was frozen and the buyer did not discover that the fish suffered from any deficiency in quality as he did not thaw and sample it. Counsel for the buyer bought in specialist consultation and cited a well-known CISG case on 'Maggots in Mozzarella' from the Dutch District Court of Roermond[43] to support the fact that the examination duty under Article 38 CISG requires the buyer to defrost goods in order to examine them properly. The Dutch case is clearly convincing to the Danish judge in the case, who paraphrases it in the Danish decision. BUT the Danish judge does not refer to the Dutch case. In the case transcript, it appears as a supporting authority as cited by counsel. In the reasoning of the court, the judge does not cite this authority.

Of course, strictly speaking, in the interest of uniform application the Danish mackerel case is a 'good case' as it does follow a uniform line laid down in international (Dutch) case law. But the reluctance to refer directly to the foreign cases may be symptomatic of a larger problem.

It is tempting to assume that traditional Danish jurisprudential values are the reason why the Danish judge is happy to borrow reasoning from a Dutch case cited to him by counsel, but does not refer to the Dutch case as influential or persuasive. In all honesty, the failure of judges to indicate legal sources and authority in Danish cases is a well known predicament in a jurisdiction where findings are traditionally short and unsupported; the reasoning of the court in

---

[41]   See the database at www.cisg.law.pace.edu and all the mirror sites in different languages and countries.

[42]   Denmark, 31 January 200,2 Copenhagen Maritime Commercial Court (*Dr. S. Sergueev Handelsagentur v. DAT-SCHAUB A/S*) available at http://cisgw3.law.pace.edu/cases/020131d1.html.

[43]   Netherlands, 19 December 1991, District Court Roermond (*Fallini Stefano v. Foodik*) available at http://cisgw3.law.pace.edu/cases/911219n1.html.

the mackerel case does not cite ANY authority. But it does seem strange that the judge paraphrases the 'Maggots in Mozzarella' case and adopts its reasoning without referring to it.

It stands to reason that many jurisdictions cannot accommodate the notion of foreign precedent in domestic courts comfortably. So, to win over this resistance, it seems imperative to clarify the nature of these foreign cases, to prevent any resistance to their usage; not just by judges (who, as seen in the mackerel case above, may well be swayed by reasoning even if they do not cite the case), but to persuade counsel that it is worth the research to find them as they have a defined value which not only should, but will, be persuasive to courts.

Ideally, it would be nice to do away with the stigmatised label 'precedent' in this context. But can there be another word for 'precedent'? This is unlikely. Moreover, even if someone were to labour to come up with a carefully constructed terminologically neutral term for a CISG precedent, it can safely be assumed that this carefully constructed concept will merely be equated with its real meaning and be thought of as a 'precedent' by those who work with these terms in practice. So, in the absence of a new product name for this potentially unpopular product, the following strains to clarify the exact nature of the product on the label – to define the non-committing nature of the CISG precedent.

THE NATURE OF A PRECEDENT IN SHARED INTERNATIONAL LAW

An analysis of judicial precedent is a complex affair in any legal jurisdiction, especially in Common Law jurisdiction where it is at the core of lawmaking.[44] And if we attempt to analyse the concept across the boundaries of CISG states, it becomes a comparative study of gargantuan proportion, involving hierarchies of courts, values of precedent and complex issues of determining 'law' from 'fact'.

Simply put: there is no global definition for judicial precedents. And the definitions from different legal systems vary tremendously.

Terminological Caution

Generally speaking, in traditional Common Law systems, the doctrine of precedent forms the very basis of the establishment of law and is the primary source of legal rules, in Equity as well as the judge made law of Common Law:

---

[44]   For more information on the doctrine of precedent in common law see the leading textbook on precedent J W Harris and R Cross, *Precedent in English Law* (1991).

> Our common-law system consists in the applying to new combinations of cir-
> cumstances those rules of law which we derive from legal principles and judicial
> precedent; and for the sake of attaining uniformity, consistency and certainty, we
> must apply those rules, where they are not plainly unreasonable and inconvenient,
> to all cases which arise; and we are not at liberty to reject them, and to abandon all
> analogy to them, in those to which they have not yet been judicially applied, because
> we think that the rules are not as convenient and reasonable as we ourselves could
> have devised.[45]

The terminology of this important discipline in law is very significant in England
and other Common Law jurisdictions, and we civil lawyers need to be very
careful when we address any discussions of precedent to an audience including
English lawyers.

Moreover, even among jurisdictions of law labelled Common Law, the study
of precedents will not yield the same results. In one mixed jurisdiction, South
Africa, the notion of precedent is primarily one of persuasive authority, even
when employing a term which, for the English lawyer, is the very definition of
a binding one.[46]

In civil law, which is based upon statutes and corresponding legal theories, judicial decisions are not technically sources of legal rules, but the extent to which
judges may form judicial doctrine varies considerably between the jurisdictions,
and precedent is of considerable persuasive value and can be of great significance in the development of law.[47] Consequently, as there is no consensus on
the terminology of judicial precedent, an attempt to define the nature of a CISG
precedent has carefully to establish an attempt at terminological neutrality. In the
understanding that the discipline of uniform laws, and the study of precedents
in the context of the CISG, is unique, we can ask scholars and practitioners to
divorce themselves from domestic or regional notions of law. But we cannot
expect them to release basis notions of fundamental importance.[48] This is what
lies at the heart of 13 years of diplomatic drafting and an aim at terminological
neutrality of the CISG. And we have to accept that Common Lawyers attach
particular importance to the study of the doctrine of precedent.

If we look at scholarly contributions to the nature of the CISG precedent, we
find some contributions to the understanding of the degree to which courts and
tribunals should consider case law from other jurisdictions.

---

[45] Justice Parke, in 1833, in *Mirehouse v. Rennell* (1833) 1 Cl. & F. 527, at 546.

[46] See Dolezalek, in *'Stare Decisis': Persuasive Force of Precedent and Old Authority (12th–20th Century)* (1989).

[47] See David and Brierly, *Major Legal Systems of the World Today* (3rd Ed. 1985)
133–49.

[48] Cf Reivic and the notion that the speediest bird cannot fly from itself, *Ibid.* fn 110.

Definitely Not Binding – Not Even in Hinting Terms

The notion of binding CISG precedent is rejected by courts[49] and most scholars[50] alike, and rightly so. It would be impossible to impose such a duty without a hierarchical structure of international courts[51] and tribunals, and such a structure is a political task which would require mandates from constitutional courts or similar institutions or bodies throughout the CISG states.[52]

This is a generally accepted position. But the use of selected taxonomical terms in describing CISG precedents can cloud the issue. For instance, although he explained the context of the quotation in his subsequent book, following criticism by other scholars, a phrase used by Prof. DiMatteo in describing CISG precedent is symptomatic of the termoniological care which needs to be taken. In an article from 1997, Prof. DiMatteo labelled the CISG precedents 'informal *supranational stare decisis*'.[53] To all legal thinkers of the EU, there is a glaring problem with the use of the term 'supranational' in this context. The term supranational does not lend itself to the CISG in any way, informally or not.[54] The fact that this term may be a *faux amis*, and used as a synonym for 'transanational' in the USA explains why a distinguished American colleague like Prof. DiMatteo uses it at all. But it solicits a strong reaction from EU scholars.[55]

---

[49] See Tribunale di Vigevano, Italian judgment of 12 July 2000 [n 405], CLOUT 378, also available at http://cisgw3.law.pace.edu/cases/000712i3.html and Tribunale di Pavia, Italian judgment of 29 December 1999, available at http://cisgw3.law.pace.edu/cases/991229i3.html, where the court expressly states that 'foreign case law merely has persuasive value'.

[50] See Herber in Schlechtriem, *Commentary on the UN Convention for the International Sale of Goods* (1998), 63 and Enderlein and Maskow, *International Sales Law* (1992) 348, available online at http://cisgw3.law.pace.edu/cisg/biblio/enderlein.html, emphasising that 'the only force foreign decisions have is their persuasive effect'.

[51] Ferrari, 'Applying the CISG in a Truly Uniform Manner' in (2001–1) *Uniform Law Review* 209, available online at http://cisgw3.law.pace.edu/cisg/biblio/ferrari4.html: '[t]he court correctly rejected the minority view which attributes binding force to foreign case law … this fails to take into account the rigid hierarchical structure of the court system presupposed by the "stare decisis" doctrine and which is lacking on an international level'.

[52] The attempt to pursue such a mandate has been rejected by UNCITRAL on several occasions in the 1970s. See C Baasch Andersen *The Uniformity of the CISG and its Juris consultonium*, Kluwer 2007, 12–13 esp. fn. 33–35 explaining the developments of the concept of an international commercial court.

[53] See L DiMatteo, 'The CISG and the Presumption of Enforceability: Unintended Contractual Liability in International Business Dealings' in (1997) 22 *Yale International Law Journal* 111, available online at http://cisgw3.law.pace.edu/cisg/biblio/dimatteo.html.

[54] See C Baasch Andersen *The Uniformity of the CISG and its Juris consultonium*, Kluwer 2007, 93–8.

[55] For more on the *faux amis* status of this term 'supranational' and its non-application to the CISG, including the reaction to the use of the term in CISG contexts see *ibid.*, 93–8.

But Prof. DiMatteo's term carries an even greater problem in using the term *stare decisis*. He is not alone, however. René Henschel has joined Prof. DiMatteos in this inadvertent unfortunate use of the term,[56] by referring to an '*ipso facto stare decisis*' which some cases have obtained through regular reference to them by courts and tribunals in other countries, using the (in)famous case of the cadmium-infested *New Zealand Mussels* as an example.[57] While it may be argued rightly that certain cases have gained a strong precedential status by their use before some courts, any *stare decisis* nature of leading CISG cases is not, in actual fact, *ipso facto* everywhere – as one might hope if the uniformity of the CISG is be safeguarded by the evolution of autonomous interpretation.

The use of the term *stare decisis* has a literal meaning for the English Common lawyer, indicating that the decision *must stand*. The term – for the Commonwealth lawyer – is by definition one of binding precedent, and it is oxymoronic to consider any informal notion of *stare decisis*. If we are to strike terminological neutrality, and hope to include the UK into a CISG community of shared international sales law, we would be wise to avoid this terminology completely.[58]

Probably Not Persuasive – Definitely Inspirational

The concept of a 'precedent', especially in legal regimes shaped by a sometimes rigid *stare decisis*, is not limited to the binding precedent, but also encompasses

---

[56]   R Henschel, 'Conformity of Goods in International Sales Governed by CISG Article 35: Caveat venditor, caveat emptor and contract law as background law and as a competing set of rules', [2004/1] *Nordic Journal of Commercial Law*, available online at http://www.njcl.fi.

[57]   This case is the German Supreme Court case BGH of 8 March 1995 [VIII ZR 159/94], available online at http://cisgw3.law.pace.edu/cases/950308g3.html.

[58]   The – possibly – imminent ratification of the CISG by the UK is now hoped to take place in 2012. The CISG and the UK have a turbulent history. The first consideration was in 1989; although there was a majority in favour of accession. See Dep't of Trade and Indus., Doc. No. U.R.N. 97–875. With the arrival of a new Government in May 1997, however, the new Ministry of Trade felt – in the light of the popularity of the Convention, especially amongst EU Member States – that the UK was out of step with international trade law, and new consultations for a UK accession to the CISG are currently in progress; after a long time on the back burner a committee was finally formed in November of 2004. The work of the committee is, at the time of writing, delayed due to illness of one of its most prominent members. This trend regarding the Consultation Document leans slightly towards the favouring of ratification, but the proposal to the legislature is not (yet) a reality. The UK has never embraced uniform international sales law extensively – it is worth noting that the UK has ratified the antecedents to the CISG (ULF and ULIS), but with reservations which render them almost inapplicable, as they require the active incorporation of the provisions by the parties in choice-of-law clauses for them to apply.

precedents which are of persuasive value. For the purposes of the CISG, we can bend the notion even further, to a precedent which is inspirational. There is no need to fear use of the term 'precedent' in a context where it cannot mean binding precedent.

Misgivings on the use of the word 'precedent' in the CISG regime are evidenced often, based on the comprehension that it indicates a binding precedent. An example is illustrated where Franco Ferrari, one of the leading advocates for promoting the use of foreign recourse in the CISG realms, recants the use of the word:

> In my opinion, which, I have to admit, has changed since the CISG case law has begun to arise, foreign case law should always be considered as having merely persuasive value ... Foreign case law should be used as a source from which to draw either arguments or counter-arguments.[59]

As opposed to his earlier statement:

> The interpreter must consider 'what others have already done,' i.e., he must consider the decisions rendered by judicial bodies of other Contracting States, since it is possible that the same or analogous question has already been examined by other States' courts, in which case such decisions can have either the value of precedent – '[i]f there is already a body of international case law,' or a persuasive value.[60]

This clearly demonstrates a great reluctance to use the word 'precedent' in the context of the CISG. However, regardless of such sensitivity associated with the term precedent, it is a fact that some CISG cases do now consider case law from other jurisdictions and do appear to feel bound by a duty towards the principles of uniform law, the CISG community and sister states to take some leading cases into consideration.

In the Civil lawyers' vocabulary, that would seem to be the definition of a persuasive precedent. But while I do not share Prof. Ferrari's reluctance to use the term 'precedent' – simply for want of a viable alternative – I believe we do need to be wary of the use of the term 'persuasive' as the doctrine of persuasive precedent also has an element of *faux amis* for the Common lawyer. The Common law vocabulary of the judicial doctrine encompasses both binding and persuasive precedents which have an established place in a given hierarchy of laws, primarily applied for decisions from other countries within the Common

---

[59] In 'CISG Case Law: A New Challenge for Interpreters?' in (1999) 17 *Journal of Law and Commerce* 260, available online at http://cisgw3.law.pace.edu/cisg/biblio/ferrari3.html.

[60] From 'Uniform Interpretation of The 1980 Uniform Sales Law' in (1994–5) 24 *Georgia Journal of International and Comparative Law* 204–5, available online at http://cisgw3.law.pace.edu/cisg/biblio/franco.html.

law jurisdiction.[61] While I, a Civil lawyer, see no problem with defining CISG precedents as persuasive and equating the way in which Common lawyers look to decisions from other Common law states when sharing Common law to the way they should be using the CISG's precedents by using this term, it will not necessarily be palatable to the Common lawyers who have specific associations with this concept. Even though I would like to say that the CISG should have the same status among the courts of its states as Common law has in this legal family, this will be overreaching from the perspective of the Common lawyer. Moreover, the *extent* of persuasiveness is not a given.

Lookofsky softens the concept of a persuasive precedent by referring to this as a maximum degree of 'regard' that courts/tribunals can give a foreign decision, borrowing the term from Article 7(1) CISG.[62] In the interest of striking a more terminologically neutral balance, I would suggest that we adopt instead a concept of 'inspirational precedent' to apply to the CISG.

Criteria for CISG Precedents

Flechtner makes the point that those in pursuit of uniformity should beware not to pursue it at any price. The first and foremost goal is sound judgement, and we must set out criteria for the weighing application of foreign precedents:[63]

1. The authority of the court rendering a decision;
2. The extent of agreement on the issue amongst other tribunals;
3. The level of experience the court has with trade; and
4. The extent to which the foreign precedent complied with the interpretational guidelines of the CISG (internationality, good faith and uniformity).

Given that the primary goals of UNCITRAL are 'modernity', 'flexibility', 'clarity' and 'fairness', there is more than a common-sense basis for the pursuit of

---

[61] See P Darbyshire, *Darbyshire on the English Legal System* (8th Ed, 2005), at paras 2-030 and 2-037.

[62] J Lookofsky in 'CISG Foreign Case Law: How Much Regard Should We Have?' in Ferrari, Flechtner and Brand (eds) *The Draft UNCITRAL Digest and Beyond* (2004) 218: 'I would nonetheless suggest that foreign court decisions *at most* have "persuasive" (non-binding) value. The fact that (*e.g.*) an Italian court must have regard to the need to promote uniform CISG application ... – means only that the Italian court must "take [them] into account".'

[63] H M Flechtner in 'Recovering Attorneys' Fees as Damages under the U.N. Sales Convention: A Case Study on the New International Commercial Practice and the Role of Case Law in CISG Jurisprudence, with Comments on *Zapata Hermanos Sucesores, S.A. v. Hearthside Baking Co.*' in (2002) 22 *Northwestern Journal of International Law & Business* 121–59 available online at http://cisgw3.law.pace.edu/cisg/biblio/flechtner4.html#iv.

sound judgments as a priority above uniform application, and in this Flechtner is absolutely right. But while his criteria of selection are sound and simple, I nevertheless see no reason why a court should not take foreign judgments into account, even if they do not fulfil Flechtner's criteria – either for the lack of other cases on the subject or because others have already been considered and discarded. As long as we establish that they are only looking at these cases for inspiration, in the interest of the possible creation of an autonomous approach to a given issue, and inspiration for a fair result, where is the harm?

On the more general topic of the use of foreign judgments by judges, Sir Basil Markesinis recently made an interesting biblical parallel, saying that the task of the comparative lawyer is to 'probe everything and keep the best'[64] to find cases which can lend inspiration to a given problem.[65] This kind of general freedom to explore available CISG case law and find the most just parallels and apply them is apt here as well, without the restriction of any fixed criteria. Juergen Schwarze, while explaining the role of the European Court of Justice, suggests another way to screen precedents, which is similarly broad and based on individual applicability, dependant on the 'reasoning which the decisions ... bring to bear on the problem at hand'.[66]

Other CISG scholars have agreed that foreign case law, while not binding, should be considered so that the provision can be considered in the light of all relevant decisions in the spirit of uniform law.[67] Moreover, a body of congruent, established case law from different CISG states on an issue is something which

---

[64]   In the words of Paul in his first letter to the Christians in Thessalonika.

[65]   See Basil Markesinis, 'Judicial Mentality: Mental Disposition or Outlook as a Factor Impeding Recourse to Foreign Law' (2006) 80, *Tulane Law Review*, Issue 4, April, 1325–75.

[66]   In 'The Role of the European Court of Justice (ECJ) in the Interpretation of Uniform Law Among the Member States of the European Communities (EC)', in UNIDROIT (ed.), *International Uniform Law in Practice/Le droit uniforme international dans la pratique* (Acts and Proceedings of the 3rd Congress on Private Law held by the International Institute for the Unification of Private Law (Rome 7–10 September 1987)) (1988) 193–227.

[67]   One of the first to point this out was P Schlechtriem, 'Uniform Sales Law – the Experience with Uniform Sales Laws in the Federal Republic of Germany', in (1991/92) 2 *Juridisk Tidskrift* 1–28, available online at http://cisgw3.law.pace.edu/cisg/biblio/schlech2.html, where he explains how consideration and critique of case law in other jurisdictions, as well as help from scholars and comparative law centres, smooth any divergent interpretations of uniform law. See also J Lookofsky, 'At fremme en ensartet anvendelse af CISG' [1996] *Ugeskrift for Retsvaesen* 139 at 14. '[m]an skal tage hensyn til den internationale præcedens, til hvad de forskellige domstole har sagt' ['Consideration must be had to international precedents, to what the different Courts have said' (author's translation)] and Herber in Schlechtriem, *Commentary on the UN Convention for the International Sale of Goods* (1998) 62.

a practitioner should be strongly criticised for overlooking,[68] rendering the body of case law binding on a more abstract level. On that note, I think we should abstain from laying down even the simplest criteria for the consideration of CISG precedents, and instead leave this to counsel and the judges to find and consider where applicable or helpful, much like Schwartze suggests above for the ECJ. Judges will apply their own common sense in determining how inspirational a precedent is to the case at hand – and where there is a congruent body of cases from different jurisdictions presented to them on an issue, this common sense will indicate the degree of consideration this issue should be given.

Precedents and Procedure

Another interesting issue is the difference in procedural approaches to considering precedents as a whole. Some courts in some states (for example Denmark) will have an *ex officio* duty to find the correct influencing precedent in states where a *jura noscit curia* ('the judge knows the law') principle prevails; others will be subject to a more limited review, based very firmly on the pleadings of the parties (for example Australia). While this does not change the theory of the CISG precedent, it very firmly includes legal counsel in the group of 'practitioners' who now own the CISG and should look to global case law in its interpretation. The reality is, of course, that even in the *jura noscit curia* regimes the judges often, for practical reasons, limit themselves to the material presented by counsel. But the inclusion of lawyers, solicitors and barristers, in the 'practitioners' category for the theory of CISG precedents means that although counsel is, understandably, a subjective force as he/she is presenting an argument, the duty is also on him or her to look to international case law. This is true in all jurisdictions, but primarily in those where the arguments for looking to or applying foreign law are the responsibilities of the parties. The need for inclusion of the CISG precedent extends to the parties presenting their arguments.

Filip de Ly, very cleverly, distinguishes between *foreign law* and *uniform law* in the discussion of precedents, and makes the point that 'uniform law is the law of the land' where it is applied through Article 1(1)(a) or it is a CISG state applying its own International Sales law via Article 1(1)(b).[69] However, procedurally, courts are likely to consider the interpretations of uniform law from a foreign source to be foreign law, regardless of the fact that Prof De Ly is right.

---

[68]   See Bonell in C M Bianca and M J Bonell (eds) *Commentary on the International Sales Law*, (1991: Giuffre) 91.
[69]   See Filip de Ly, 'Uniform Interpretation: What is Being Done? Official Efforts' in Ferrari (ed.), *The 1980 Uniform Sales Law*, (2003) 357.

'Shared Uniform Case Law' – a Comfortable Label?

Personally, this author is very happy with de Ly's label of 'uniform case law', and the distinction from foreign law may make it less uncomfortable for the domestic court steeped in traditional habits of not referring to foreign law to consider the rationale of a case from abroad. Moreover, by not using the label of 'precedent' the notion may be easier to sell to traditional Commonwealth benches. If an emphasis is placed on the notion of this case law being *shared*, it may even further accentuate the need to consider it at all domestic courts. So, for the lack of anything better, the notion of 'shared uniform case law' to label the body of CISG cases from 73 states and arbitration may present a nice solution.

But, at the end of the day, the mere substitution of one uncomfortable label with another is not likely to make much headway.

Until uniform law is acknowledged universally in courts as a separate discipline, and this idea embraced by the application of a duty to look to uniform precedents, will we ever really be making progress in this field? The theory of the need to use CISG precedents is one thing. What the courts, tribunals and counsel actually choose to do is another issue entirely. This chapter has argued the fact that the jurisconsultorium is a tool which it is in everyone's interest to apply – only time will tell whether this notion will become more widespread.

3. Regulatory competition or harmonisation: the dilemma, the alternatives and the prospect of reflexive harmonisation

Stelios Andreadakis[1]

The ultimate goal of the European Community is the establishment of an internal market. A common market will be achieved when all obstacles for cross-border activities of business in Europe are eliminated and when the frontiers between the European countries are nothing more than signboards by the road.[2] Assuming that a free internal market is becoming a reality, the next challenge is to ensure that this market is well-organized, stable and efficient. To that end, an important focus of the EU policy is to develop and implement mechanisms that enhance the efficiency and competitiveness of business across Europe. In order to do so, it will have to be able efficiently to restructure and move across borders, adapt its capital structures to changing needs and attract investors from many Member States and other countries.[3]

In the quest for the best path towards the achievement of economic and political integration and for the best mechanism for the creation of an efficient regulatory environment, a number of alternatives to conventional territorially-based regulation are taken into consideration. These alternatives fall somewhere along a spectrum of models of international securities regulation, with the concept of regulatory competition at one end and harmonisation at the other.[4] Thus, the main subject of this chapter is the interaction between regulatory competition and its main conflicting theory, harmonisation. Do any of these seem

---

[1] Senior Lecturer in Law, School of Law, Oxford Brookes University, UK.
[2] Davis G., (2003), *European Union-Internal Market Law* (2nd ed.), Cavendish Publishing at 2.
[3] Report of the High Level Group of Company Law Experts on a Modern Regulatory Framework for Company Law in Europe, Brussels, 4 November 2002, Chapter II at 30, available at http://www.ecgi.org/publications/documents/report_en.pdf.
[4] Wei, T., (2007), 'The Equivalence Approach to Securities Regulation', 27 *Northwestern Journal of International Law & Business* at 255, 255–6.

to be the missing link in the chain of optimal regulation or is there a third way? In an attempt to shed some light between the two extremes in the regulatory debate, mention will be made of convergence as a third pole in the regulatory debate. Reflexive harmonisation will also be an essential part of the forthcoming analysis, in view of the fact that it is presented as the most promising regime, which seeks to put an end to the polarization between regulatory competition and harmonisation.

In order to address all these themes, this chapter will first of all outline the characteristics of regulatory competition, as they are emphasized by both its supporters and opponents. It will then touch upon harmonisation, which is based less on competition and more on incorporating different legal systems under a basic framework. The conflict between regulatory competition and harmonisation has monopolized the discussion on the ideal regulatory regime so far, but it is worth examining alternative solutions. At this point, convergence will first be examined as an alternative option, before the focus moves towards the issue of reflexive harmonisation, which is considered to represent the future of regulation in the European Union. The chapter concludes by reflecting on the future of the regulatory models in Europe and by assessing the effectiveness of reflexive harmonisation.

(I) REGULATORY COMPETITION

After a close historical analysis, it appears that regulatory competition is not a result of globalization or a side-effect of the modern trend for no barriers in commercial transactions. Regulatory competition came about unintentionally, in the sense that no legislator or judge had it in mind as one of the potential future developments. What can be argued is that it was underpinned by the EU's strategy of removing barriers to inter-state trade and defending against institutional pressures. In consequence, only the fact that it was not an intended and planned development rather than a methodical result of systematic planning has increased its importance.

Regulatory competition is the result of the combination of the words regulation and competition. It is useful to focus on this combination for a while. Nowadays, literately every single economic activity is subject to regulation. Regulation is about politics, as it has to deal with the interaction between the players of the game. In this context, regulation is more than a legal restriction, as it always involves the art of judgement as well as the science of understanding.[5]

---

[5]   Murphy D., (2004), *The Structure of Regulatory Competition: Corporations and Public Policies in A Global Economy*, Oxford University Press at 254.

Effective regulation is that which finds the balance between conflicting interests and which resists pressures from the interested parties. The need for regulation does not indicate a need for a sole regulator, who will take full responsibility for creating the ideal regulatory environment. Such person would be the protagonist, a 'monopolist regulator' as Roberta Romano characterizes him,[6] but there is no viable political structure to support an international regulator.[7] Since monopolistic regulation is not the answer, competition enters the discussion.

Competition between legal and social systems contributes to the evolution of society. This happens not only from a Darwinian perspective, but also because, without competition, laws will sooner or later become less company-friendly and less efficient. As a result, the legal framework will not be the ideal one to promote economic growth and wealth creation. The most considerable counter-argument is that without harmonisation there will be a 'race to the bottom'. The country with the lowest standards will become the cheapest place to operate, so businesses will rush there. After that development, the other countries will have to lower their standards to survive.

At this point, an attempt at an initial definition can be made. Regulatory competition can be defined as a process involving the selection and de-selection of laws in a context where jurisdictions compete to attract and retain scarce economic resources:[8] a process where regulators deliberately set out to provide a more favourable regulatory environment, in order either to promote the competitiveness of domestic industries or to attract more business activity from abroad.[9]

This definition can be used as a basis for the further analysis of regulatory competition. In an attempt to extend it, the following comments are extremely useful. The regulatory approach will be constantly improved through incessant filtering and distilling, in order to meet the preferences, needs and expectations of citizens. In this way, the result will be a set of efficient and up-to-date laws. In that sense, regulatory competition exists by definition in every country. The competing parties are the federal authorities and the state, which basically co-exist and struggle to win the battle of competition. This regulatory co-existence brings together two autonomous 'governments' operating at two different but parallel levels.

---

[6]   Romano R., (1998), 'Empowering Investors: A Market Approach to Securities Regulation', 107 *Yale Law Journal* at 2367.

[7]   Andenas, M., 'Who is Going to Supervise Europe's Financial Markets' in Andenas, M., and Avgerinos, Y., (eds) (2003), *Financial Markets in Europe: Towards a Single Regulator?*, Kluwer Law International at xxv.

[8]   Deakin, S., (2006), 'Is regulatory competition the future for European integration?', *Swedish Economic Policy Review* 13 at 74.

[9]   Gatsios K and Holmes P., (1997), 'Regulatory Competition and International Harmonization', *Global Economic Institutions Working Paper Series*, No. 36, London at 2.

From the above analysis, it can be argued that an important function of regulatory competition is to remove inefficient legal rules. It is also evident that such competition needs to be carried out within a certain framework, because unregulated competition offers no guarantee that the set of legal rules which will prevail will be the most efficient solution. That is why deregulation seems to be an attractive option, not only because the 'laissez-faire, laissez-passer' ideology has always had passionate supporters, but also because everyone nowadays strives for more autonomy and more independence. Chang, after a general review of the economics and politics of regulation, has argued for the division of the last fifty years into three periods. The first period is between 1945 and 1970 and is characterized by regulation. The second period covered the decade between 1970 and 1980 and was a 'transition' period. Finally, the third period started in 1980 and has not finished yet. It is the 'deregulation' period.[10]

But how close to reality is this perception? In reality, we have not experienced and are not experiencing an era of deregulation so much as an era of regulatory flux – an era when dramatic regulatory, deregulatory and re-regulatory shifts are occurring simultaneously. So far nobody can claim a win in the regulation game.[11]

This division illustrates the essence of regulatory competition. Regulatory competition looks like a dilemma. Regulation or deregulation? Market forces or strict rules? Moreover, the two poles of regulatory competition can be described by two phrases which are commonly used: 'the race to the top', where the policy framework consists of a set of rules and 'the race to the bottom', where the market will create the right balance between the conduct of all actors within global economic. The Delaware effect represents the deregulatory dynamic and is considered to be the winner of the race to the bottom in the field of chartering requirements for companies. A good example of race to the top is the state of California. In California, environmental regulation has always been a hot issue and the levels of protection become progressively higher and higher. The Californian market is large enough to make other states raise their own levels of regulation in order not to lose market access. This strategy involves significant risks, but large market power comes with confidence that, in the long-term, the new high standard regulations will be adopted not only throughout the United States, but in other markets around the world. This is the so-called 'Californian effect'.[12]

---

[10]   Chang, H., (1997), 'The Economics and Politics of Regulation', 21 *Cambridge Journal of Economics* at 724.

[11]   Ayres, I. and Braithwaite, J., (1992), *Responsive Regulation: Transcending the Deregulation Debate*, Oxford Socio-Legal Studies, Oxford University Press at 7.

[12]   Genschel P and Plumper T., (1997), 'Regulatory Competition and International Cooperation', MPIfG Working Paper 97/4 at 2, available at: http://mpifg.de/pu/workpap/wp97-4/wp97-4.html.

Although regulatory competition is a new hot topic in Europe, on the other side of the Atlantic it has a full history. Scholars have been dealing with this issue for about 30 years in order to determine whether corporate law is indeed on a race to the top, to the bottom or to nowhere[13] in particular, as William Bratton suggested. The reason Europe did not participate in the discussion about regulatory competition was simply because the regulatory environment in the European Union was not convenient enough until recently. It was only after 1999 and the well-known 'triangle' of ECJ landmark cases[14] that European companies obtained the right to incorporate in any EU Member State regardless of where their business is actually run.

Despite that development Europe still has a long way to go before it becomes similar to the US. But even if our view is expanded away from the EU and US only, it is a fact that all governments approach a regulatory problem in substantially different manners. Such different approaches can easily create tensions between governments and different societies, mostly because the problem involves economic activity. For example, the adoption of strict rules is the choice of one government as the most appropriate means against repression of economic power, whereas another government would choose a more laid-back approach, under the concept that excessive regulation can potentially restrain economic progress.

The role of a government as regulatory authority is totally different from its role as executive organ. Governments all around the world try to create a free and liberal environment for trading. At the same time, the world trends promote – or at least point to – the direction of a completely open world market, integrated, independent and as deregulated as possible. Regulatory competition theorists note that governmental intervention often creates its own burdens and inefficiencies. Nobody denies that such intervention may be welfare-enhancing, but, at the same time, there is always the question whether or not the cure is more harmful than the disease.[15] Excessive regulation or excessive strictness creates protectionism, which can early become a hard-to-overcome obstacle in a free trade orientated world. Pressure can sometimes have adverse results, i.e.

---

[13]   Bratton W., (1994), 'Corporate Law's Race to Nowhere in Particular', 44 *University of Toronto Law Journal* at 401.

[14]   Case C–212/97 *Centros Ltd v. Erhvervs- og Selkabsstryrelsen* [1999] ECR I–1459, Case C–208/00 *Überseering B.V. v. Nordic Construction Company Baumanagement GmbH (NCC), (2002) ECR I-09919, decision* of 11/5/2002, referred to the ECJ by the German *Bundesgerichtshof* (BGH), Resolution of 3/30/2000 and Case C–167/01 *Kamer van Koophandel en Fabrieken voor Amsterdam v. Inspire Art Ltd.* (2003) ECR I-10155, decision of 9/30/2003.

[15]   Esty D. and Geradin D., 'Introduction' in Esty D. and Geradin D. (eds) (2001), *Regulatory Competition and Economic Integration: Comparative Perspectives*, Oxford University Press, at xxii and xxiii.

instead of being welfare-enhancing it may prove welfare-reducing. Negative outcomes are always likely to emerge.

Therefore, there are some voices saying that perhaps competition is not the only pathway leading to 'the land of optimal regulation'. As Esty and Geradin conclude, 'regulatory systems should be set up with enough interjurisdictional co-operation (or harmonisation) to ensure that transboundary externalities and other market failures are addressed, but with a sufficient degree of regulatory competition to prevent the resulting governmental structure from becoming an untamed, over-reaching, or inefficient Leviathan'.[16]

As a result, there was a quest for a new theory that could promise to minimize interjurisdictional conflicts. The catchphrase which was chosen for the new theory was harmonisation.

(II)   HARMONISATION

Harmonisation derives from the Greek word ἁρμονία (harmonía), which means synchronization, concurrence and accord. The verb ἁρμόζω (*harmozo*) has the meaning of fitting together, combining. Harmony was initially used in Ancient Greek as a musical term, in order to describe the combination of contrasted elements: a higher and lower note.[17] Harmonisation, nowadays, means minimizing the degree of variation and reducing the number of significant underlying differences in order to achieve similarity between systems. As far as law is concerned, harmonisation implies that different legal provisions or systems are coordinated and the outcome is a set of minimum requirements or standards. In other words, the essence of harmonisation is the creation of a single, uniform, international regulatory standard.[18] Such a standard offers more certainty, efficiency, consistency and more effective control. An example of a harmonised system would be the Financial Services Authority in the United Kingdom, which replaced 18 other UK regulators when it was formed under the Financial Services Act in 1986.[19] The same concept can be found within the European Union, where the aim is to create a set of common standards across the internal market.

The antagonists of harmonisation compare it to monopoly, implying excessive regulation, lack of diversity, a higher degree of complexity and uncertainty and,

---

[16]   Ibid. at xxv.

[17]   Dahlhaus, C., 'Harmony', *Grove Music Online*, ed. L. Macy, available at: www.grovemusic.com.

[18]   Scott, H., (2000), 'The Future Content of U.S. Securities Laws: Internationalization of Primary Public Securities Markets', 63 *Law & Contemporary Problems* at 71, 78.

[19]   Harvey, B., (2007), 'Exchange Consolidation and Models of International Securities Regulation', 18 *Duke Journal of Company & International Law* at 161.

finally, no flexibility in adapting to the new developments. Nonetheless, they seem to forget that harmonisation does not mean uniformity. Harmonisation recognizes the existence of differences. Differences do not necessarily pose any threat to coexistence and co-operation. When different cultures, nationalities and traditions manage to co-exist and create a harmonised legal system, such system combines all the virtues and the values of them.

Unlike unification of law, harmony does not presuppose a system of similar or identical laws, as harmonisation does not mean 100% uniformity. The goal is the creation of a framework within which laws will be put together and will operate efficiently without creating inequality and inconsistencies. Such framework can be created through the introduction of a set of basic standards, the flexibility of which must be agreed in advance, in order to avoid problems if these standards need any kind of alteration. In other words, it can ensure stability and predictability against externalities. Externalities occur when an activity regulated in one jurisdiction affects the well-being of people in other jurisdictions.[20]

Harmonisation also has an element of centralization. A single regulator is required, who will organize, co-ordinate and enforce harmonisation. The minimum harmonisation requires a set of minimum standards in certain areas and gives countries the privilege and the opportunity to complete the framework by setting all the higher standards themselves. In this respect, minimum harmonisation does not rule out regulatory competition. Harmonisation aims at minimizing the possibilities of future market failures and preventing, to a reasonable extent, the race to the bottom, whereas regulatory competition aims at putting pressure on governments to perform efficiently and effectively.[21] That is why it is mistaken to treat harmonisation and regulatory competition as contradicting theories. It is better to consider them as substitutes rather than complements.[22]

The advocates of the harmonisation theory were extensively using the example of the USA. In the USA, regulatory authority is located to the states more than the federal government. The method adopted is based on a common standard, which is applied to all states and is used as a yardstick and reference point. Of course, if each country were free to adopt or develop any regulatory regime without taking into account the options of the neighbouring countries, this would sooner or later affect any attempt at harmonisation. Governments need a strong incentive in order to produce an optimal degree of harmonisation. Once again, a bell rings that reminds everybody that the USA is not identical, not even similar, to the EU. Romano, summarizing the US experience regarding

---

[20]   Hauser, H. and Hosli, M. (1991), 'Harmonization or Regulatory Competition in the EC (and the EEA)?', 46 *Aussenwirthschraft* at 497, 501–502.

[21]   See above, note 15, at xxiii.

[22]   Sun, J.M and Pelkmons J., (1995), 'Regulatory Competition in the Single Market', 33 *Journal of Common Market Studies* at 67.

regulatory competition in company law, argues that it leads, over time, to a fairly high level of convergence between states, with the dominant model one in which mandatory rules are the exception: 'state charter competition has ... produced substantial uniformity across state codes, preserving variety in it enabling approach to rules, an approach that permits firms to customize their charters'.[23] In the USA, harmonisation means that the federal government frequently takes on the character of a 'monopoly regulator', occupying the field to the exclusion of state initiative. The description of a 'monopoly regulator' which US critics use to attack federal intervention is entirely appropriate in a system which tends to react to extreme failures in the market for regulation by shutting down competition entirely.[24]

Unharmonised national laws could be characterized as restrictions and may act as impediments. Harmonisation is a process that promises, if not guarantees, successfully to fulfil certain conditions. The achievement of uniformity is patently obvious, because a single set of rules is the first goal irrespective of the content and the philosophy of these rules. To put it differently, a common level playing field for all players is created, following the approximation of all local provisions. In reality, harmonisation underscores the autonomy of national legal systems, limits competition and gives priority to a process of evolutionary adaptation of values of the state level.[25] Teubner borrows the term 'co-evolution' from the science of biology in order to characterize this process. Co-evolution implies the co-existence of diverse systems in an environment where each one retains its viability.[26] As a new methodology, it combines self-regulation and external regulatory interference. Self-regulation is always an appealing choice, but regulatory intervention should not *a priori* be rejected as long as it does not have the characteristics of inducement and provided that is does not aim at undermining the quest for a deregulated environment.

Harmonisation at a pan-European level should not be treated as a clone of US regulation. US federal legislation is closer to the stereotype of a single convergent regime. To be more precise, there is not a race to the top or to the bottom, but a race to converge. It is a race to converge through unregulated competition. In company law, for example, the result was more or less predictable: the creation of a near-monopoly supplier, i.e. Delaware.[27] The European perspective,

---

[23]   Romano, above note 6, at 2394.

[24]   Deakin, above note 8, at 13–14.

[25]   Deakin S., (2001), 'Regulatory Competition versus Harmonization in European Corporate Law', in Esty D. and Geradin D. (eds) (2001), *Regulatory Competition and Economic Integration: Comparative Perspectives*, Oxford University Press at 194.

[26]   Teubner, G., (1993), *Law as an Autopoetic System*, Oxford, Blackwell at 52.

[27]   Deakin, S., (2006), 'Legal Diversity and Regulatory Competition: Which model for Europe?', 12 *European Law Journal* at 453–4.

on the other hand, is based more on diversity. Nobody can guarantee in advance that the European market can become the same as the American without any functional and operational problems. There is also no clear indication that this is the objective of EU regulators.

It would be simple and effortless to argue that 'unregulated competition between jurisdictions could well eliminate the most significant differences between them, but without any guarantee that the system, that eventually prevailed, would be the most efficient'.[28] Similarly, we could argue that setting minimum standards as a 'floor of rights'[29] can implicitly initiate a race to the top by encouraging states to set superior standards. Unfortunately, these are the main drawbacks of harmonisation. Namely, there are no guarantees that the most efficient regulatory system will be implemented, and also the harmonised standards require 'each nation to forswear its customary territorial jurisdictional activity'.[30]

(III) ALTERNATIVES

Following the examination of regulatory competition and harmonisation, it is obvious that neither of the two theories is 100% satisfactory, in the sense that it cannot guarantee the most efficient, if not the optimal, regulatory regime. As was highlighted before, regulatory competition and harmonisation stand at the two far ends of the regulatory field. Two other theories will be put under the microscope as alternative options: convergence, which is situated somewhere in the middle between the two extremes, and reflexive harmonisation, which aims at combining the two abovementioned theories.

(a) Convergence

Convergence is based on a process of coordination. In biology, convergence means the development of similarities in unrelated organisms living in similar environments.[31] This definition uncovers the underlying principle of convergence. It is basically a process which achieves a common result, despite the existence of dissimilarities, variations or obstacles. The focus is on the

---

[28] Movsesyan V., (2006), 'Regulatory Competition Puzzle: The European Design', Laboratory of Economics and Management, Working Paper Series 2006/30 at 24.

[29] Deakin, above note 25, at 210.

[30] Tung, F., (2002), 'From Monopolists to Markets?: A Political Economy of Issuer Choice in International Securities Regulation', (2002)6 *Wisconsin Law Review* 1363 at 1368.

[31] See http://www.yourdictionary.com/convergence.

outcome, not on the procedure. When convergence is achieved, regulatory standards are roughly close enough to be functionally substitutable, such that the policy objectives of each nation are adequately fulfilled.[32] Apart from the conclusion, which is not always easy to be achieved, convergence has one more significant advantage. As Bo Harvey explains, convergence is better suited to balance the local with the global by considering the benefits of an international regulatory regime while accommodating important differences of economies, cultures, and legal environments.[33] It is more likely to achieve convergence on an international scale compared to a regime of regulatory competition or harmonisation,[34] for the reason that convergence combines the enforceability of a convergent (international) regime with the distinctiveness of the national legal systems.

The creation of the European Union common market can be used as a good example of a convergence process. Instead of applying the theory of harmonisation or regulatory competition, EU intention was to create a regulatory environment without legal barriers by removing all restrictions on the free movement of persons, goods, services and capital within its territory. The lessons from the EU single market experience can be used as 'a model as to how regulation might be formulated and implemented in the international system at large'.[35]

Despite the positive contribution that the theory of convergence seems to have in the regulatory debate, it has not been unanimously accepted as the best or the most promising solution. The second thoughts which have been expressed do not concern the principal idea of having shared standards, but once again the issue of giving up the sovereign control. For example, the EU does not react positively to the possibility of having standards imposed by the United States and vice versa. Neither of them is willing to accept the authority of a non-domestic body or organization. Unfortunately, convergence seems to be destined to meet a dead end like regulatory competition and harmonisation and it is rather disappointing that this happens essentially for the same reasons.

Facing dead ends and implementation problems, the need for an alternative solution was once again underlined. Deakin came up with a conclusion that was criticized for being paradoxical. According to that conclusion, harmonisation represents the best solution within the framework of the single market as it isolates the positive characteristics of regulatory competition and combines them with evolutionary adaptation of law. Actually, Deakin puts forward 'reflexive

---

[32] Wei, above note 4, at 257–8.
[33] Harvey, above note 19, at 165.
[34] Ibid., at 164.
[35] Scott, H., (2005), 'An Overview of International Finance: Law and Regulation', at 8, available at SSRN: http://ssrn.com/abstract=800627.

harmonisation' as the best choice for the EU and illustrates it as 'the best guarantor of diversity between national systems, and hence of experimentation in
regulatory design'.[36]

(b)   Reflexive Harmonisation

Reflexive harmonisation aspires to strike the right balance between strict
regulation and deregulation and has its source on the theories of reflexive law.
Reflexive law aims at joining successfully self-regulation and external regulation. It involves a regulatory process which seeks to be effective and successful
not by directly imposing certain measures or by stipulating certain outcomes. It
seeks to intervene by showing the ends or by pointing to the right direction without any kind of inducement and persuasion. To put it simply, it has a procedural
orientation.[37] This means that the law underpins and encourages autonomous
processes of adjustment. It simply gives emphasis to the importance of self-
regulation processes by awarding them with law-making powers.[38]

Another distinctive feature of reflexive law is that it does not seek to create a perfect market or to describe the best possible solution, even though it
is doubtful whether it is possible to achieve it in practice. In fact, priority is
given to the method and the process of achieving optimal results, and not so
much to the results themselves. In this context, harmonisation has a different
rationale. It is not on target for creating a monopoly, by occupying the field as
a monopoly regulation instead of state-level regulation.[39] It can be said that
reflexive harmonisation promotes, if not initiates, a 'race to the top', which the
participating Member States would not have otherwise entered into, as there
was no motivation in that direction. At the same time, reflexive harmonisation
promotes a 'race to the bottom' as well, by making Member States compete on
the basis of the withdrawal of protective standards. In both cases, innovation and
independent solutions are promoted, while Member States have the freedom of
choice among a number of available options.

Fundamentally, reflexive harmonisation is about putting a stop to state intervention against imperfections that – are thought to – spoil the side view of the
desired optimal market. These imperfections should not be cured as they are
simply the differences between systems. One of the fundamental prerequisites of
reflexive harmonisation is the preservation of local-level diversity, since without
diversity the stock of knowledge and experience on which the learning process

---

[36]   Ibid., at 22.
[37]   Deakin, above note 25, at 211.
[38]   Ibid.
[39]   Ibid.

depends is necessarily limited in scope. In this sense, diversity of national systems is an objective in its own right.[40]

In a nutshell, the model of reflexive harmonisation holds that the principal objectives of judicial intervention and legislative harmonisation alike are two-fold: firstly, to protect the autonomy and diversity of national or local rule-making systems, while, secondly, seeking to 'steer' or channel the process of adaptation of rules at state level away from 'spontaneous' solutions which would lock in suboptimal outcomes, such as a 'race to the bottom'.[41]

The European Works Council Directive (94/95/EC) can be used as an example of a reflexive harmonisation process, as it has been clearly influenced by the philosophy of reflexive law. The Directive does not impose any specific measures, but it promotes them by giving incentives to companies to make use of its provisions even as the last available choice. In essence, the Directive seeks to achieve its ends, even by giving to companies and employees the opportunity to avoid its application. It sounds an oxymoron but the underlying principle is that the Directive does not directly impose a uniform solution, but it shows the path to the Member States – and to companies – and gives them an incentive to co-ordinate and work out a solution at a state level.

The process of reflexive harmonisation, although it still carries the label of being a controversial method, has been elevated to a higher level among other less suitable solutions. Its 'supremacy' is justified by the fact that it does not prevent solutions based on innovation, nor does it go against diversity in the laws of the Member States. Thus, co-evolution is singled out as being a more efficient solution compared to a single monopoly regime because, as was mentioned before, it combines autonomy and diversity with interdependence.

(IV) CONCLUSION

On the whole, harmonisation did not limit nor affected negatively the diversity of national laws within the European Union; on the contrary, diversity was preserved. As a result, a new type of harmonisation was developed. It was given the name 'reflexive harmonisation' and it represents a modern answer to the dilemma between regulatory competition and harmonisation. Such approach can be characterized as unique and idiosyncratic because, unlike the American experience, it emphasizes the importance of self-regulation and gives priority to

---

[40] Deakin, above note 27, at 445.
[41] Deakin, S., (1999), 'Two types of regulatory competition: competitive federalism versus reflexive harmonization. A law and economics perspective on *Centros*', 2 *Cambridge Yearbook of European Legal Studies* at 244.

the safeguarding of local diversity. In essence, it makes use of central regulation, not in order to impose solutions directly, but to preserve a space for independent governance at lower levels of government. Reflexive harmonisation has the potential to become the missing piece in the puzzle of regulation in many different legal systems, as they operate, for example, within the EU.

Recently, some policymakers have suggested that linking the European Company Statute to a European corporate governance code could provide a more efficient way to induce convergence of best practice norms within the EU.[42] This strategy may prove to be really useful and beneficial, because through linkage the Member States' codes would be left untouched and thereby divergence would be respected, while, at the same time, the prospect of regulatory competition by means of the European Company would be substantially diminished.[43]

It is still too early to determine whether reflexive harmonisation will prove to be an efficient solution. It looks promising due to its flexibility that derives from the evolutionary adaptation of diverse systems to the constantly changing external conditions. The jury may still be out on the long-term prospects for rival systems of corporate governance in a globalizing economy. However, there is much to be said in favour of further developing it, since it would seem to combine the values of local autonomy with system-wide adaptability.[44]

---

[42]   See High Level Group of Company Law Experts, above, note 3 at 67.

[43]   McCahery, J.A. and Vermeulen, E., (2005), 'Does the European Company Prevent the 'Delaware-effect'?', TILEC Discussion Papers, DP 2005-010 at 22.

[44]   Deakin, above note 41, at 259.

4. Harmonisation of substantive legal principles and structures: lessons from environmental laws in a federal legal system (Australia)

Ross Ashcroft[1]

Throughout history, there have been shifts between a harmonised legal system and fragmented legal system.[2] Cultural wars led to a fragmentation of states, and thus the complexity of the 'law of nations' arose. The notion of sovereignty by princes, and later governments, took precedence.[3] In recent centuries, and even more so since the forming of the European Union (and its predecessors), Europe is once again trying to harmonise the legal systems. However, Europe is not alone in this quest. Harmonisation of laws, both within and between legal systems, is a goal of many nations and regions.

Federal states, such as Australia, too have seen the pressing need to harmonise areas of law. The advantages of harmonisation are obvious – decrease the economic costs involved in management of resources and it can increase the ease of trade.[4] The advantages of a single system of law have long been recognised

[1]   BA/LLB (Hons) (*Griffith*), GDLP (*Griffith*) MCL (*Adelaide/Mannheim*), LLM (*Griffith*), Grad. Cert. Arts (*UNE*), Law Lecturer, Charles Darwin University, Australia. The author would like acknowledge Professors Douglas E. Fisher, Sharon Christensen, Bill Duncan of Queensland University of Technology and Professor Pamela O'Connor of Monash University for their helpful comments and Dr Jackie Mapulanga-Hulston of Queensland University of Technology for editorial comments. The author acknowledges the financial assistance from the Australian Research Council, DP0771825. All errors remain solely mine.

[2]   Wiener, J (1999), *Globalization and the Harmonization of Law*, Pinter Press at vii.
[3]   Donlan, SP (2008), '"Our laws are as mixed as our language": Commentaries on the Laws of England and Ireland, 1704–1804', 12 *Electronic Journal of Comparative Law* 1 at 8; see also Jacobson, S (2002), 'Law and Nationalism in Nineteenth-Century Europe: The Case of Catalonia in Comparative Perspective', 20 (2) *Law and History Review* 307–47.
[4]   Zeller, B (2007), *CISG and the Unification of International Trade Law*, Taylor & Francis at 3.

in modern legal systems. In Australia, we can look at least as far back as the introduction of the Torrens system of property registration, which aimed at trying to minimise the costs involved in transferring real property and management of a particular resource, namely land. Today, in Australia like other parts of the world, the context of ecologically sustainable development is much the same as the rationale for creating the Torrens system – trying to regulate resources in an economically efficient manner. However, the twentieth century saw the proliferation of treaties, legislation and policy. Especially since the *information age* and into the twenty-first century, the proliferation problem has grown at a more rapid pace, adding further complications not existing at the time of introducing, and directly following the introduction, of the Torrens system.

The present chapter will take the example of problems encountered in environmental regulation in Australia's development, specifically in relation to sustainable development and resource regulation within property[5] law. This issue has reached a heightened significance in recent times, as several appellate courts in Australian jurisdictions have handed down judgments which permit overriding interests relating to environmental or planning issues in land, many of which may not be notified on the register. Furthermore, there has been significant confusion caused by leading members of the judiciary disagreeing on fundamental issues of property law, including the notion of indefeasibility. In addition to these problems faced, other issues experienced include: a divergence in key vocabulary in environmental legislation and the application of such provisions; differences in the enforcement mechanisms adopted and information problems relating to inability effectively to trade across borders. The analysis will also attempt to suggest possible solutions based on comparative examples.

There are several considerations of harmonisation of property law and environmental considerations. The chapter will proceed as follows. First, the chapter will examine general concerns of harmonisation, where major considerations often relate to establishing jurisdictional competencies. Part 2 of the chapter will then look at the problem of different terminology, with examples given predominantly in the field of environmental law. The third part of the chapter will examine issues of property or resource registers, as this is a fundamental consideration relating to institutional arrangements and mechanisms relating

---

[5] For the purposes of this chapter, it is more precise to refer to the notion of resource than property *per se*. A property right differs between disciplines. For example, lawyers will see the extent of a property right in terms of the extent of limitations of rights placed upon it by the law, whilst economists will view property rights as an unlimited right, creating rights such as trade. For more details see Fisher, DE and Bartley, M (2004), *Trading in Water Rights – Towards a National Legal Framework*, DLA Phillips Fox at 2; see also Fisher, DE (2004), 'Rights of Property in Water: Confusion or Clarity', 21 (3) *Environmental and Planning Law Journal* 200 at 201–3.

to harmonisation between the two key fields of law, namely resource management and the environment. Part 4 will follow on, suggesting the methodology to harmonisation, with key considerations between the two areas of law.

At the conclusion of the chapter, the suggested solution will focus on trying to harmonise the terminology, both conceptually and practically, within both property law and environmental law. The second part of the solution will be determining which area of law should be provided a greater weight within the harmonisation process. Finally, the chapter will suggest a concise framework which may provide not only the way forward for resource management, but also sustainable development in a practical manner. This will include, among others:

- Terminology adopted – both between and within each area;
- Which area of law is given greater weight;
- Institutions and mechanisms necessary for harmonisation and integration.

1.   GENERAL CONCERNS RELATING TO HARMONISATION IN A FEDERALISED LEGAL STRUCTURE

Australia has a federal legal structure. In a federalised legal system, harmonisation not only is required between the international and domestic legal spheres, but also between the federal government (in Australia, referred to as the Commonwealth) and the regional governments (called 'states' in Australia, but other nations may refer to these regions as provinces), and between the states and local government. The benefits of harmonised legal structures have long been recognised in Australia. For example, the Constitution aimed at providing for free trade and commerce between States. This is similar to a key pillar of the European legal framework.

The Constitution provides for specific heads of power to the Commonwealth government[6] and concurrent powers which are shared between the Commonwealth government and the governments of the States or Territories (hereinafter referred to only as States).[7] The Constitution also provides a pathway for the adoption of international law into Australian law, known as the *external affairs*

---

[6]   *Constitution*, s 52 has the majority of such powers.
[7]   Winterton, G, Lee, HP, Glass, A, Thomson, J and Gerangelos, PA (2nd ed., 2007), *Australian Federal Constitutional Law Commentary and Materials*, Thomson Legal and Regulatory at 11–13. Specifically, the concurrent powers are not addressed, but are widely accepted as such. See also Blackshield, A, and Williams, G (2nd ed., 1998), *Australian Constitutional Law and Theory: Commentary and Materials*, Federation Press at 7–10.

power.[8] As such, a major concern in undertaking such a process is the regulatory framework which is adopted – whether it is indeed constitutionally legitimate to do so, especially in light of our 'dualist' legal system and whether such harmonisation will create a democratic deficit in the process. A secondary, but equally identifiable issue is the necessity of effectuating not only institutional changes, but also policy and substantive provisions within the law. If it is clear there is a sole power for one tier of government to proceed, reforms will obviously be much faster and easier to undertake.[9]

To add to the formal constitutional problems, a great difficulty of harmonisation in Australia relates to the fact that jurisdictions each have their own legislative drafting requirements and techniques. Thus, harmonisation requires more than merely adopting formal structural or policy change, but also changes in processes driving the law. This is heavily reliant on politics and a hurdle to overcome in any jurisdictions considering such processes.

Each of these jurisdictions has advanced its own policy and legislative considerations. This is necessary to minimise the proliferation of legislative changes, which can have detrimental consequences for society and business, to increases of economic costs involved with obtaining advice or compliance with the law, and inability to keep track of what the law is. Proliferation of law may also have detrimental effects on legal education – requiring greater need for specialisations rather than general practitioners.

There are some problems which are difficult to overcome in the process of harmonisation, no matter how hard one works. As such, it is important to bear in mind issues may not fall as easily as one may hope. The greatest concern is lack of political will[10] or political recalcitrance. Politicians are driven by short term goals,[11] thus although they may discuss long term *policy*, they may be less willing to undertake formal legal changes. Australia has had several recent examples of this, including the Victorian government essentially holding other jurisdictions to ransom over the proposed National Water Initiative and the possibility of collapse of a national e-conveyancing system. A related concern is that

---

[8]   *Constitution*, s 51 (xxix); see also Winterton, G, Lee, HP, Glass, A, Thomson, J and Gerangelos, PA (2nd ed., 2007), *Australian Federal Constitutional Law Commentary and Materials*, Thomson Legal and Regulatory at 307–75.

[9]   Steven, AJM (2002), 'Scottish Land Law in a State of Reform', 2 *Journal of Business Law* 177 at 180.

[10]   Fisher, DE and Bartley, M (2004), *Trading in Water Rights – Towards a National Legal Framework*, DLA Phillips Fox at 93.

[11]   See for example, Rajamani, L (2008), 'The Indian Way: Exploring the Synergies Between Development, Energy and Climate Goals', in Zillman, D; Redgwell, C; Omorogbe, YO and Barrera-Hernandez, LK (eds), *Beyond the Carbon Economy: Energy Law in Transition*, Oxford University Press at 419–40, where the author describes as 'apathetic ... politicians [who] are largely opportunistic demagogues rather than visionary leaders'.

of democratic deficit. In Australia, governments have sometimes attempted to institute reforms at the Council of Australian Governments (COAG), although this has come under criticism from the High Court of Australia.[12] This is because COAG, as a vehicle to drive 'cooperative federalism'[13] is viewed not as a constitutionally permitted organ, but rather political sloganeering.[14] Similar concerns have been expressed in regard to reform processes in the European Union.

Whilst many more problems may exist, the final one I will highlight is the issue of population education and understanding. The choice of terminology, as well as the rationale for undertaking reforms, may not easily be understood by the general population. These difficulties would arise in the European Union much more obviously,[15] as there are many jurisdictions, many of which have their own languages. The terminology issue is problematic even in a federal state with a single language, but not as much as faced in contexts of harmonisation such as the European Union.[16] As such, one must tread carefully to ensure that whatever changes are advocated in terms of harmonisation, the basis for change is capable of being explained to the citizens.

2. ECOLOGICAL SUSTAINABLE DEVELOPMENT, ITS ROLE IN RESOURCE MANAGEMENT AND THE RECTIFYING OF DIFFERENCES IN TERMINOLOGY

A key issue for harmonisation between jurisdictions is trying to harmonise the *terminology* adopted. Linguistic precision is necessary in creating enforceable and effective legal regimes, whilst avoiding confusion which can occur with imprecise adoption of language,[17] although it has been noted that 'uniform

---

[12]   *Re Wakim – Ex Parte McNally* (1999) 198 CLR 511 at [550]–[557]; Lyster, R and Bradbrook, A (2006), *Energy Law and the Environment*, Cambridge University Press at 120–21; also *Mowbray v Thomas* [2007] HCA 33, at [210]–[219] per Kirby, J (minority).
[13]   Winterton, G, Lee, HP, Glass, A, Thomson, J and Gerangelos, PA (2nd ed., 2007), *Australian Federal Constitutional Law Commentary and Materials*, Thomson Legal and Regulatory at 863–70.
[14]   *Re Wakim – Ex Parte McNally* (1999) 198 CLR 511 at [556] per McHugh, J.
[15]   Castiglione, D and Longman, C (eds) (2007), *The Language Question in Europe and Diverse Societies: Political, Legal and Social Perspectives*, Hart Publishing; see also Ristikivi, M (2005), 'Latin: The Common Legal Language of Europe', X *Juridica International* at 199–202.
[16]   Glanert, S (2008), 'Speaking the Language of Law: The Case of Europe', 28(2) *Legal Studies*, 161–71; see also Berridge, GR (3rd ed, 2005), *Diplomacy: Theory and Practice*, Palgrave at 50 and 78–80.
[17]   Fisher, DE (2004), 'Rights of Property in Water: Confusion or Clarity?', 21(3) *Environmental and Planning Law Journal* 200; see also Gamper, A (2005), 'A 'Global

words do not always ensure uniform results'.[18] In the present context of finding a framework for sustainable resource management, the issue of harmonisation of terminology occurs predominantly within environmental law, but this is in addition to trying to harmonise environmental concerns with resource management and property law. This section will give an overview of the differing language adopted across several jurisdictions in relation to environmental law, including the vertical integration of international treaties and policy into domestic jurisprudence and practice.

International Perspective

The term 'sustainable development', since it was first used in the *Brundtland Report*, is commonly defined as 'development that meets the needs of the present without compromising the ability of future generations to meet their own needs'.[19] Whilst the *Brundtland Report* is the initiation of the term 'sustainable development',[20] the issues of environment and development were previously linked by the earlier *Founex Report* of 1971.[21] There are however statements which date back much further, including a speech given by Theodore Roosevelt, who said in 1900:

> I recognize the right and duty of this generation to develop and use our natural resources, but I do not recognize the right to waste them, or to rob by wasteful use, the generations that come after us.[22]

The term 'sustainable development' has also been defined as 'the procedural and substantive requirement to accommodate, reconcile or integrate economic growth, human rights and environmental protection, for participatory, equitable

Theory of Federalism': The Nature and Challenges of a Federal State', 6(10) *German Law Journal* 1297.

[18]   Baasch Andersen, C (1998), 'Furthering the Uniform Application of the CISG, Sources of Law on the Internet', 10 *Pace International Law Review* 403 at 404.

[19]   World Conference on Environment and Development (1987), *Our Common Future*, Oxford University Press at 44.

[20]   For further discussion of this principle see Ball, S and McGillivray, D (6th ed, 2006), *Environmental Law*, Oxford University Press at 60–70.

[21]   Thatcher, PS (1992), 'The Role of the United Nations' in Hurrell, A and Kingsbury, B (eds), *International Politics of the Environment*, Oxford University Press at 188.

[22]   Theodore Roosevelt, 'The New Nationalism', speech delivered in Osawatomie, Kansas, 31 August 1910, available at: http://www.theodoreroosevelt.org/life/quotes. htm; see also Department of Sustainability and Environment (Victoria), *Government Leadership*, (2008). available at: www.dse.vic.gov.au/ourenvironment-ourfuture/govt. htm. Unfortunately there are conflicting dates of this speech, although he may have repeated it.

improvements in our collective quality of life that can last over the long term'.[23] This term is consistently adopted in international political and legal discourse. Sustainable development has achieved a greater stakehold in this discourse since the 1990s, being set down as a key principle adopted at the United Nations Conference on Environment and Development (the Rio Conference) and repeated subsequently on numerous occasions.[24] Several international and environmental law scholars have suggested that whilst 'sustainable development' as a term has acquired a 'very wide currency',[25] the exact ambit of the phrase remains unclear today, although indicators do exist to guide our understanding.[26]

The international framework of governance has also seen the adoption by some organisations of the term 'environmentally sustainable development', namely the ILO (International Labour Organisation)[27] and the World Bank.[28] The inclusion of the term 'environmentally' preceding sustainable development has wide implications. Environment can refer to man-made and built environment, cultural environment or natural environment. As such, it is much wider than 'ecologically' or 'ecological' as adopted in Australia, which shall be dealt

---

[23]   Cordonier Segger, MC and Weeramantry, CG (eds) (2005), *Sustainable Justice: Reconciling Economic, Social and Environmental Law*, Martinus Nijhoff Publishers at 590.

[24]   The main documents which refer to sustainable development are *Agenda 21*, *United Nations Framework Convention on Climate Change* (1992) 31 ILM 849, Arts 3 & 4; United Nations Convention on Biological Diversity (1992) 31 ILM 822, Arts 8 & 10. Following the Rio Conference, sustainable development was again considered at the World Summit on Sustainable Development in Johannesburg, 2002. However, no formal treaty was concluded with respect to sustainable development at this conference. See Sands, P (2nd ed., 2003), *Principles of International Environmental Law*, Cambridge University Press at 66–7. The Johannesburg Plan of Action was however adopted: see Omorogbe, YO (2008), 'Promoting Sustainable Development through the Use of Renewable Energy: The Role of Law' in Zillman, D, Redgwell, C, Omorogbe, YO and Barrera-Hernandez, LK (eds), *Beyond the Carbon Economy: Energy Law in Transition*, Oxford University Press at 39, 47–9; see also *New Delhi Declaration of Principles Relating to the Law of Sustainable Development*, ILA Resolution 3/2002.

[25]   Hurrell, A and Kingsbury, B (1992), 'The International Politics of the Environment: An Introduction', in Hurrell, A and Kingsbury, B (eds), *International Politics of the Environment*, Oxford University Press at 42.

[26]   United Kingdom Government, *Sustainable Development Indicators in Your Pocket* (2008), available at: www.sustainable-development.gov.uk/progress/international/index.htm.

[27]   International Labour Organisation, *Trade Unions and Sustainable Development*, available at: www.ilo.org/public/english/dialogue/actrav/enviro/index.htm (viewed 21 May 2008).

[28]   World Bank Group, *Environmentally Sustainable Development*, available at: www.worldbank.org/html/dec/Publications/Workpapers/envsusdev.html (viewed 21 May 2008).

with shortly. The term does however not necessarily have consequences for the notion of sustainable development, although does provide a context point from which we can draw a reference.

Australian Domestic Perspective

Australia offers a unique insight when we consider the concept of ecologically sustainable development (ESD) and the diverging terminologies which have developed since. The terminology adopted in this field in Australia is diverse. The restatement of ESD in Australia is not reflective of the four goals or principles of sustainable development which are accepted in international law.[29] Expressions which are often used interchangeably, in legislation, judicial decisions and in commentaries, include for example: 'sustainable development', 'ecologically sustainable development' (ESD) and 'environmentally sustainable development', 'environmental sustainability', 'sustainable management',[30] 'ecologically sustainable use'[31] and 'ecological sustainability'.[32] Each of these terms has its own individual nuances. This creates an intellectual and semantic maze for people trying to understand, implement and enforce the law.

To add to the differing terminology at the international level, Australia has adopted a diverse domestic discourse, creating confusion from what was initially a uniformly accepted term or policy among the Commonwealth, State and local governments. The expression 'ecologically sustainable development' (ESD) was initially adopted in Australian governmental policy in 1992 by the National Strategy on Ecologically Sustainable Development (NSESD). Similarly, the Intergovernmental Agreement on the Environment[33] (IGAE) was adopted by all governments in Australia, including representatives of the local governments, in 1992, and incorporated ESD as the principle terminology. As a legal basis, ESD has been incorporated into a range of Commonwealth[34] and State legislation across jurisdictions.

ESD as normally used in Australia comprises three interrelated concepts – development, sustainability and ecological values.[35] As Professor Douglas Fisher

[29]   Bates, G (6th ed., 2006), *Environmental Law in Australia*, LexisNexis Butterworths at 125.

[30]   *Water Act 2000* (Qld), s10.

[31]   Dawson, F (2004), 'Analysing the Goals of Biodiversity Conservation: Scientific, Policy and Legal Perspectives', 21 *Environmental and Planning Law Journal* 6 at 19.

[32]   *Integrated Planning Act 1997* (Qld), s1.3.3.

[33]   Australian Government, *Intergovernmental Agreement on the Environment*, available at: www.environment.gov.au/esd/national/igae/index.html (viewed 21 May 2008).

[34]   *Environment Protection and Biodiversity Conservation Act 1999, Water Act 2007* (Cth).

[35]   Fisher, D (2003), *Australian Environmental Law*, Law Book Co at 349–50.

has noted, development, by its very nature, connotes action to move forward or create change.[36] Development usually also envisages economic growth and use of natural resources (land, minerals, water) for human consumption. As such, development is undoubtedly anthropological in nature, although there can be environmental values incorporated within this concept.[37]

Another varying term adopted in Australia, most specifically in Queensland, is 'ecological sustainability', which has been incorporated into the *Integrated Planning Act 1997* of Queensland ('IPA'). 'Ecological sustainability' is defined as a 'balance that integrates protection of ecological processes, economic development and maintenance of the cultural, economic, physical and social well being of the people and communities'.[38] Dr Phillipa England has suggested that the focal point of 'ecological sustainability' is contextual – that of ensuring environmental development and protection in the context of planning and development legislation.[39] Thus, 'ecological sustainability' has direct practical implications for the administration of land and resource rights, especially in relation to the determination of development applications.[40]

Problems of Differing Terminology and Suggestions for Harmonisation

There are both theoretical[41] and practical implications (for example, increased dispute and litigation[42]) in failing to ensure consistent terminology amongst and within jurisdictions. First, courts are required to analyse, interpret and apply the relevant legislation question as it has been enacted by Parliament or the relevant jurisdiction. Any inconsistencies can make it impossible, or highly improbable, to be able to work the nuances together. As Salmond J. once lamented, in dissent, the Torrens Statutes were 'so badly drafted ... that it is difficult ... to extract from them the principle intended by the Legislature'.[43] The nuances may cause

---

[36]   Fisher, D (2003), *Australian Environmental Law*, Law Book Co at 349.

[37]   Fisher, D (2003), *Australian Environmental Law*, Law Book Co at 349.

[38]   *Integrated Planning Act 1997* (Qld), s1.3.3.

[39]   England, P (2nd ed., 2004), *Integrated Planning in Queensland*, Federation Press at 23.

[40]   England, P (2nd ed., 2004), *Integrated Planning in Queensland*, Federation Press at 23.

[41]   Gamper, A (2005), 'A "Global Theory of Federalism": The Nature and Challenges of a Federal State', 6(10) *German Law Journal*.

[42]   Lord Slynn of Hedley (2006) [2004], 'Some Thoughts on Language and Law in Europe' in Lundmark, T and Wallow, A (eds) *Law and Language – Recht und Sprache: Rechtswissenshaftliches Symposium*, LIT Verlag Berlin-Hamburg-Münster at 45.

[43]   *Boyd v Mayor of Wellington* [1924] NZLR 1174, 1211; Whalan, DJ (1982), *The Torrens System in Australia*, Law Book Co at 293. For a more general analysis of drawing legal principles see also Gamper, A (2005), 'A "Global Theory of Federalism":

difficulties not only in finding the principles, but may also affect the function of statutory rights, such as enforceability, or just their characteristics. Similar issues have been stated in international cases involving the same principles.[44] Similarly, failing to ensure a consistent use of language may lead to a state of normative anarchy within a principle, thus condemning the principle[45] to a place of irrelevance and uselessness.

Second, by having different definitions, law and policy tend to identify resources as discrete, which is contradictory to the concept of integration of resource management in a holistic manner.[46] Third, different terminology leads to greater problems for the general public,[47] who may not have the ability to understand specific uses as lawyers or politicians do.[48] From the perspective of public participation, a key point for ESD, confusion amongst the terms may mean that there is little chance or little will for the public to put submissions for policy development and thus frustrate the implementation of processes which will effectively and efficiently achieve the goals of policy and/or legislation.[49] This is important not only from the perspective of public participation, but rather the participation of stakeholders more generally.

That these problems exist can create a bleak picture of the viability of harmonising the terminology between and within jurisdictions. However, this need not be the case. The harmonisation of these terms can be achieved by looking at the fundamental pillars or principles which each seeks to achieve. By taking this approach, one notices that there is indeed a great deal of commonality between each of the terms. For example, it is generally agreed that the common thread includes:

- The precautionary principle;
- Intergenerational equity;

The Nature and Challenges of a Federal State', 6(10) *German Law Journal* 1297. Cf nuances in language, Baasch-Anderson, C, (1998), 'Furthering the Uniform Application of the CISG, Sources of Law on the Internet', 10 *Pace International Law Review* 403.

[44]   *Gabcikovo-Nagymaros Project* [1997] ICJ Rep 7 ('Danube Dam case'), per Separate Opinion of Weeramantry J, at 90.

[45]   *Gabcikovo-Nagymaros Project* [1997] ICJ Rep 7 ('Danube Dam case'), per Separate Opinion of Weeramantry J, at 90.

[46]   Dawson, F (2004), 'Analysing the Goals of Biodiversity Conservation: Scientific, Policy and Legal Perspectives', 21 *Environmental and Planning Law Journal* 6 at 26.

[47]   See for the importance of public participation Ball, S and McGillivray, D (6th ed., 2006), *Environmental Law*, Oxford University Press at 316–56.

[48]   Steven, AJM (2002), 'Scottish Land Law in a State of Reform', 2 *Journal of Business Law* 177 at 178.

[49]   Dawson, F (2004), 'Analysing the Goals of Biodiversity Conservation: Scientific, Policy and Legal Perspectives', 21 *Environmental and Planning Law Journal* 6 at 26.

- The polluter pays principle;
- Integration;[50] and
- Intragenerational equity and community participation.

In the context of Australia, it would be politically and legally wise to adopt just one term. The term which was initially adopted – ecologically sustainable development – seems to be the wisest choice. There are several reasons for this. First, this term was widely accepted by several tiers of government – Commonwealth, State and local government. Second, there is the aspect of minimising democratic deficit.[51] There was substantial public participation when the NSESD was first adopted, and as such, is likely to take into consideration the views of a wider cross-section of society.[52] As such, the democratic deficit is arguably less likely to occur.

As to whether the term ecological or environmental should be the key term adopted is up for a somewhat semantic debate.[53] Ecological has the advantage that it recognises a non-anthropological perspective since it considers the manner in which living organisms interact with their environment. This is important for inclusion of animals, as anthropological considerations are already inherent in the definition which includes economic and social considerations. Furthermore, taking the word ecological back to its linguistic roots makes clear that it relates to resource, a word which is far more fitting than environment, and could also include cultural and manmade resources.

However, a significant problem still remains, regardless of the terminology adopted. Under the terms of the IGAE, each jurisdiction remains responsible for the land inside its respective control, together with its related living and non-living resources.[54] There is however an express agreement that jurisdictions will work together to achieve the goals and obligations from international law.[55] As

---

[50]   Fisher, DE (2006), 'Water Resources Governance and the Law', 11(1) *Australasian Journal of Natural Resources Law and Policy* 2.

[51]   Barde, JP and Mountford, H (2001), 'Institutions and Decision Making' in OECD, *Sustainable Development: Critical Issues*, in OECD 99 at 103.

[52]   Australian Government, *National Strategy for Ecologically Sustainable Development*, available at: www.environment.gov.au/esd/national/nsesd/strategy/intro.html (viewed 21 May 2008).

[53]   Hunter, D; Salzman, J and Zaelke, D (2nd ed, 2002), *International Environmental Law and Policy*, Foundation Press at 205–16.

[54]   Australian Government, *Intergovernmental Agreement on the Environment*, available at: www.environment.gov.au/esd/national/igae/index.html, Section 2.2.3 and section 2.3.2 (viewed 21 May 2008).

[55]   Australian Government, *Intergovernmental Agreement on the Environment*, available at: www.environment.gov.au/esd/national/igae/index.html, Section 2.3.3 and section 2.5.2 and schedule 9 (viewed 21 May 2008).

such, reference within all jurisdictions should maintain a watchful eye on the developments at the international level.

3. RESOURCE USE AND THE REGISTRATION OF INTERESTS ON RESOURCE/PROPERTY REGISTERS

Having discussed issues of terminology, the focus of the chapter shall now shift toward resource[56] use and property registers.[57] As has been noted already, most land comes within the jurisdiction of the States and not the Commonwealth. However, it must also be noted that certain resources fall within the Commonwealth jurisdiction, or concurrent jurisdiction, and resource management itself has become an issue of both national and global concern.[58] There is an added level of complexity when we start to consider the issue of onshore and offshore resources and access to such resources. As such, there are already competing interests between governments in the resources which may be registrable, even before the issue of competing interests between public and private rights may arise.

Land and resource registers are not new per se, and date back at least to the seventeenth century in Scotland.[59] There are even early examples of water registers in the Islamic world, with the introduction of a water rights register in the Civil Code Mejelle during the Ottoman Empire during the period of 1870 to 1876.[60] Of the systems of property registration in common law jurisdictions, the Torrens registration system is well known and regarded, although there was a push to introduce complete registration systems at least as far back as the sixteenth century.[61]

During the 1850s the Torrens system of land registration was introduced in South Australia.[62] In subsequent decades, other Australian jurisdictions adopted

---

[56]   A problem with the word resource may also arise, as it implies 'economic' commodity, rather than a natural species for protection.

[57]   In European countries, property registers are also known by the term *cadastre*. See Stoter, JE, van Oosterom, P, Johannes, P, and van Oosterom, M (eds) (2006), *3D Cadastre in an International Context: Legal, Organizational, and Technological Aspects*, CRC Press. For an extensive list of articles with regard to European cadastre systems see also the Permanent Committee on Cadastre in the European Union available at: www. eurocadastre.org/eng/documentseng.html (viewed 20 August 2008).

[58]   Fisher DE (2004), 'Rights of Property in Water: Confusion or Clarity?', 21(3) *Environmental and Planning Law Journal* 200 at 214–15.

[59]   Smith, TB and Sheridan, LA (1955), *The United Kingdom: The Development of its Laws and Constitutions*, Stevens & Sons at 920.

[60]   Caponera, DA (1992), *Principles of Water Law and Administration: National and International*, AA Balkema at 71.

[61]   Whalan, DJ (1982), *The Torrens System in Australia*, Law Book Co at 2.

[62]   For detailed discussion of the Torrens System see Butt, P (5th ed., 2006), *Land Law*, Law Book Co at 717–816; Bradbrook, AJ, MacCallum, SV and Moore, AP (4th

legislation which was either directly, or indirectly, modelled on and influenced by the Torrens system from South Australia.[63] Governors of the time thought that it was 'desirable to have, as far as practicable, uniformity in the Statutes which introduced the new system in the different jurisdictions'.[64] Another rationale for introduction of the Torrens system was to remove problems associated with the fragmentation of the legal system generally and, in particular, the 'dissatisfaction with the system of legal and equitable estates and with the conveyancing complexities to which that division gave rise'.[65]

This system effectively saw the 'commodity concept' approach adopted as the overriding feature of land holding.[66] The reason registers were viewed as a commodity concept is that it was obvious from even the early days that a conclusive resource register would lower transaction costs, give greater protection to interests in resources as they would be more easily enforced,[67] increasing security of title and reducing the conflicts between parties.[68]

Despite the desirability of uniformity across Australian jurisdictions,[69] Hogg's treatises makes it abundantly clear that little harmony existed even in its earli-

---

ed., 2007), *Australian Real Property Law*, Law Book Co at 115–221; Edgeworth, BJ, Rossiter, CJ, Stone, MA and O'Connor, PA (8th ed., 2008), *Sackville and Neave Australian Real Property Law*, LexisNexis Butterworths at 460–65.

[63] *Real Property Act* 1860 (SA); *Real Property Act* 1861 (Qld); *Transfer of Land Act* 1862 (Vic); *Real Property Act* 1862 (Tas); *Real Property Act* 1862 (NSW). The title *Transfer of Land Act* was named after the English model of laws, whilst others relied on the Torrens' naming system *Real Property Act*. The substantive provisions were not affected by these names. This has led to much confusion for many early practitioners, who have thus failed to draw comparisons between the different pieces of legislation.

[64] Hogg, JE (1905), *The Australian Torrens System*, W Clowes at 45–6.

[65] Gummow, WMC, 'Equity and the Torrens System Register', presented at *Taking Torrens Into the 21st Century: A Conference to Mark the 50th Anniversary of the Land Transfer Act 1952*, at the Faculty of Law, University of Auckland, 19–21 March 2003 at 7.

[66] Whalan, DJ (1982), *The Torrens System in Australia*, Law Book Co at 7; see also re commodification of resources Cole, DH. (2000) 'New form of private property: property rights in environmental goods: 1910' in Bouckaert, B and Geest, GD (eds), *Encyclopedia of Law and Economics*, Edward Elgar at 274, 275–6; see also Morgan, OJ (1995), 'The Crown's Right to Gold and Silver in New Zealand', in 1 *Australian Journal of Legal History* 51 at 54–5 in relation to commodification of resources.

[67] O'Connor, PA (2003), 'Information, Automation and the Conclusive Land Register', paper presented at the *Taking Torrens into the 21st Century Conference* held at the Faculty of Law, University of Auckland (19–21 March 2003) at 11.

[68] O'Connor, PA (2003), 'Information, Automation and the Conclusive Land Register', paper presented at the *Taking Torrens into the 21st Century Conference* held at the Faculty of Law, University of Auckland (19–21 March 2003) at 34.

[69] Butt, P (2nd ed., 1988), *Land Law*, Law Book Co, 6 notes that the desire of early judges in Australia for uniformity led to the High Court of Australia overruling their own judgments in favour of decisions from the English courts, as these decisions were seen

est days, and generally the respective colonial systems became more complex with each individual amendment and consolidation,[70] creating a complexity of what otherwise could have remained a remarkable 'creation' for the legal world. Similar criticisms have also been made by Duncan Kerr in the first half of the twentieth century.[71]

Since the inception of the Torrens system, the world has undergone great changes. Planning laws have rapidly spread throughout many jurisdictions around the world, and within Australia these planning laws have taken shape at the State and local levels of government.[72] In addition, we have seen the 'discovery' of a greater amount of resources and become more heavily reliant on a diverse choice of resources, including water, land, minerals and hydro-carbons. Most jurisdictions have replaced common law principles towards resource management with legislation. This legislation, whilst similar, is by no means identical, [73] and thus faces similar criticisms to those aimed at the Torrens legislation in earlier eras. In addition, we have seen the rise of concern for environmental issues such as sustainable development of resources and climate change, particularly since the 1960s. The fear that we may run out of resources has played a big part in this, and the shift towards greater regulation of resources and creation of new interests in resources. This has resulted in a glut of legislation and the issue of overriding statutes, as well as people bringing litigation challenging this legislation overriding what they perceive to be their inherent 'right' based on the indefeasibility.[74]

There are several issues which need to be considered relating to resource or property registers: first, what is the function of the register? Second, what

---

as more authoritative. In times of necessity, the HCA did however depart from English jurisprudence: see also Green, K (1989), *Land Law*, Macmillan at 46–7.

[70] Hogg, JE (1905), *The Australian Torrens System*, W Clowes. The chapter on 'bringing land under system' provides a perfect example, with some colonies relying heavily on statutory provisions, whilst some have rules clarified more through judicial intervention.

[71] Kerr, D (1927), *Principles of the Australian Land Titles (Torrens) Systems*, Law Book Co of Australasia.

[72] Edgeworth, BJ, Rossiter, CJ, Stone, MA and O'Connor, PA (8th ed., 2008), *Sackville and Neave Australian Real Property Law*, LexisNexis Butterworths at 879–973.

[73] Fisher DE (2004), 'Rights of Property in Water: Confusion or Clarity?', 21(3) *Environmental and Planning Law Journal* 200 at 215.

[74] *Spencer v. ACT* (2007) 13 BPR 24, 307, [2007] NSWSC 303; *Dore & Others v. Penny* [2006] QSC 125; *Glasgow v. Hull* [2007] QCA 19; *Bone v. Mothershaw* [2003] Qd R 600; *Wilson v. Raddatz* [2006] QCA 392; *Burns v. Queensland* [2006] QCA 235; for discussion and introduction to indefeasibility see Edgeworth, BJ, Rossiter, CJ, Stone, MA and O'Connor, PA (8th ed., 2008), *Sackville and Neave Australian Real Property Law*, LexisNexis Butterworths at 466–8; also Bradbrook, AJ, MacCallum, SV and Moore, AP (4th ed., 2007), *Australian Real Property Law*, Law Book Co at 131–44.

resources can or should appear on registers and how should these appear? Whether there are any technological impediments stopping a fully integrated registration system?

Possible Resources for Registration and Sources of Conflict

Worldwide, many countries are struggling with the conceptual difficulties which arise from the use of resource registers.[75] As has been alluded to already, many different resources could possibly be entered into a register, including competing titles or uses from the same parcel of land. That competing interests in a resource, such as land, may exist is not new. However, the exact ambit has been greatly increased due to technology and methods of governance generally. For example, person A may be the registered proprietor in a parcel of land. Person B may hold interests to the non-fugacious minerals below that piece of land, whilst person C maintains interests in fugacious resources, such as oils, gases and hydrocarbons. In the future, there may also be interests below the land caused by carbon capture and storage, although this at present is currently under review. Person D may hold a forestry right or interest in the land, whilst person E holds a right to the carbon in those trees. If this parcel of land was by the ocean or a watercourse, or subject to native title and indigenous cultural issues, even more rights would be applicable. Each of these may have one, or more, possible legislative instruments which need to be examined.

A diagram may assist in understanding this a little better. See Figure 4.1.

Despite all these different possible interests of rights, not all of these rights are registered in a manner which makes them easily discernable for interest holders. Furthermore, the resources may be administered by different institutions, making sustainable resource management and sustainable development in any harmonious manner practically impossible. For example, in the realm of transferring and conveyancing between jurisdictions we have seen major hurdles rise, although much of this appears to relate to the politics involved more than possible legal consequences.[76] As such, even more so than in the times when Hogg and Kerr openly criticised the lack of uniformity of legislation between jurisdictions, it is necessary to harmonise not only the legislation but also registers both within and between registers.

---

[75]   Steven, AJM (2002), 'Scottish Land Law in a State of Reform', 2 *Journal of Business Law* 177 at 193.

[76]   Merritt, C (2008), 'States Reject Victoria's E-Conveyancing Plan', *The Australian* (23 May), 34.

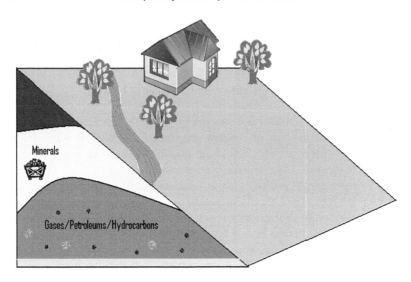

Figure 4.1   Separation of Legal Interests in Landed Resources

Functions of Resource Registers

Registers of title

The Torrens land register is, by its very nature, a register of title and not use. According to *Breskvar v Wall*,[77] the 'Torrens System of registered title ... is not a system of registration but a system of title by registration ... The title it certifies is not historical or derivative. That which the certificate of title describes is not the title which the registered proprietor formerly had, or which but for registration would have had. It is the title which registration itself has vested in the proprietor.'[78] This represents what has been termed the 'affirmative function' of a register system.[79]

Title to resources as a legal concept can be a basic issue, yet, concurrently, a very difficult concept to grapple with.[80] Title can have two distinct meanings in law. Most importantly for this context, title relates specifically to that which is held or 'owned' as much as can be consistent with the feudal notion of owner-

---

[77]   (1971) 126 CLR 376.

[78]   (1971) 126 CLR 376 at [15] per Barwick CJ.

[79]   O'Connor, PA (2003), 'Information, Automation and the Conclusive Land Register', paper presented at the *Taking Torrens into the 21st Century Conference* held at the Faculty of Law, University of Auckland (19–21 March 2003) at 3.

[80]   Edgeworth, BJ, Rossiter, CJ, Stone, MA and O'Connor, PA (8th ed., 2008), *Sackville and Neave Australian Real Property Law*, LexisNexis Butterworths at 139.

ship, by the registered proprietor.[81] A common feature of most registers of title is the notion of indefeasibility,[82] which means that a registered proprietor is subject only to interests or estates recorded on the register. The register has three guiding principles: the *mirror principle*, the *curtain principle* and the *insurance principle*. A register of title is descriptive in nature. The register will indicate a parcel of land and the nature and extent of interests held. These details are deemed 'folios'. [83] There will also be 'dealings', which is information about any instrument which may be registered against the land, and ideally also contains any information which protects the land from being dealt with by a third party without notice. It will also indicate the person who holds the parcel of land.[84] More generally, the register could be described as detailing the following information about a resource: what is owned; where is the resource owned; who owns the resource; and possibly, in the case of leases, for how long is the resource 'owned'.

Whilst the register of title remains descriptive, the principles just described are subject to problems. There are recognised exceptions to the notion of indefeasibility, including statutory exceptions such as fraud, public easements and covenants.[85] There are also private exceptions to indefeasibility, such as the registration of a mortgage, although a mortgage appears on a register. Additionally, we are finding more and more that interests which affect a resource, particularly land, are no longer detailed on the actual register. Many of these interests are 'public' in nature, such as planning laws or native title interests. These cases are thus asked to determine where the balance lies between the competing rights and interests.[86] Moreover, at least one recent decision of several leading judges in Australia[87] has created what could only be described as a debacle of the issue of indefeasibility – a principle which is ultimately central

---

[81]　Butt, P (5th ed., 2006), *Land Law*, Law Book Co at 670. Title may also relate to the process of proving ownership, although this is not so important for the current context. Butt provides a good overview of the processes involved, both historically and contemporarily.

[82]　A note should also be made that, even here, there is no harmony between the terminology. Some jurisdictions in Australia refer to 'indefeasibility', whilst other jurisdictions refer to 'paramountcy'. For discussion see Butt, P (5th ed., 2006), *Land Law*, Law Book Co at 724–5; see also Bradbrook, AJ, MacCallum, SV and Moore, AP (4th ed., 2007), *Australian Real Property Law*, Law Book Co at 131–44.

[83]　Butt, P (5th ed., 2006), *Land Law*, Law Book Co at 722.

[84]　Whalan, DJ (1982), *The Torrens System in Australia*, Law Book Co at 18.

[85]　Bradbrook, AJ, MacCallum, SV and Moore, AP (4th ed., 2007), *Australian Real Property Law*, Law Book Co, 131–44.

[86]　*Ulan Coal Mines Ltd v. Minister for Mineral Resources & Anor* [2007] NSWSC 1299.

[87]　*Hillpalm Pty Ltd v. Heaven's Door Pty Ltd* [2004] HCA 59, 220 CLR 472.

to the registration system. This could possibly be compared to what appeared problematic in Scottish land law only a few years back, where it was noted that a registrar had to note burdens on the title of the land which was affected by that burden, but did not have to note the same information on the title of the property receiving the benefit of that same interest.[88]

Overriding interests   Statutes which have the unambiguous intent of overriding provisions of Torrens legislation have long been regarded by Australian courts as permissible exceptions to indefeasibility in Australian law.[89] Unfortunately, the pieces of legislation which attach the notions of indefeasibility on a land register have become far too numerous. In one jurisdiction, Victoria, alone in the 1980s, there were well over 250 pieces of legislation.[90] With nine different jurisdictions within Australia, this means there could be well over 1,000 pieces of legislation which have consequences for landholders, which are not explicitly appearing on the different registers.

It is common that such overriding legislation has planning or environmental objectives[91] – that is, public policy objectives. But, as Brendan Edgeworth has examined, the public are not necessarily aware of the legislation which has an overriding effect on land since the legislation does not appear on the registers – not even as a short notation bringing one's attention to it. In an era where ESD has become a catchcry of governments around the country, and indeed the world, this could be detrimental to many resource owners. This issue of overriding statutes is going to become only more apparent in years to come as the challenges to the provisions are litigated within the appellate courts of different jurisdictions.[92]

As such, registers of title are losing some of their key advantages in creating security of title and confidence in ownership one feels they may have.

---

[88]   Steven, AJM (2002), 'Scottish Land Law in a State of Reform', 2 *Journal of Business Law* 177 at 187.

[89]   Edgeworth, B (2008), 'Planning law v Property law: Overriding Statutes and the Torrens System After *Hillpalm v Heaven's Door* and *Kogarah v Golden Paradise*', 25 *Environmental and Planning Law Journal* 82.

[90]   Edgeworth, B (2008), 'Planning law v Property law: Overriding Statutes and the Torrens System After *Hillpalm v Heaven's Door* and *Kogarah v Golden Paradise*', 25 *Environmental and Planning Law Journal* 82 at 83; see also O'Connor, PA (1994), 'Public Rights and Overriding Statutes as Exceptions to Indefeasibility of Title', 19 *Melbourne University Law Review* 649 at 652.

[91]   Edgeworth, B (2008), 'Planning law v property law: Overriding Statutes and the Torrens System After *Hillpalm v Heaven's Door* and *Kogarah v Golden Paradise*', 25 *Environmental and Planning Law Journal* 82.

[92]   *Hillpalm Pty Ltd v. Heaven's Door Pty Ltd* [2004] HCA 59, 220 CLR 472; *Bone v. Mothershaw* [2002] QCA 120; *Spencer v. ACT & Ors* [2007] NSWSC 303.

Registers of use

Aside from the registers of title, it is also possible to have registers of use as a means of managing diverse resources in a sustainable manner. The concept of *use* has different meanings for lawyers from colloquial usage. *Use* can be separated into three distinct categories: *prescribed use*; *prohibited* (*proscribed use*); or *permitted use*. The final concept of use relates to common law's notion of a 'bundle of rights'. Under the common law conception, all use was permitted unless otherwise *proscribed*. As such, it could be possible to have a register of each type of use, or merely one category of use. Thus, one must question whether and how these registers operate in a practical situation. Here too, jurisdictions within Australia have initiated a response in relation to water registration, although again, there are problems with what has been adopted. To understand the registers of use, an overview will be provided in regard to the registration of use under the Commonwealth *Water Act 2007* and then I shall move on to the Queensland legislation.

Commonwealth Water Act   The Commonwealth *Water Act 2007* (hereinafter the CWA) has provisions permitting the registration of water rights from the Murray–Darling Basin. Whilst the CWA does create the plans for a register, it is the States/Territories which must grant title. The jurisdictions to which this applies, known as Basin States for the purpose of the legislation, are predominantly on the eastern seaboard of Australia and include: New South Wales, Queensland, Victoria, the Australian Capital Territory and South Australia. Section 101(1) of the CWA provides several types of registrable rights in relation to water:

(a) *water access rights* in relation to Basin water resources;
(b) *water delivery rights* in relation to Basin water resources;
(c) *irrigation rights* in relation to Basin water resources;
(d) rights that:

  (i) relate to access to, or the use of, Basin water resources; and
  (ii) are of a kind prescribed by the regulations for the purposes of this paragraph (*emphasis added*).

Water access rights are further defined as rights to take or hold water from a water resource. A *delivery right* is superfluously defined as the right to have water *delivered* by an infrastructure operator, whilst an irrigation right is defined as rights a right holder may have against an infrastructure operator which do not otherwise fall within the ambit of the previously defined subparagraphs.[93] As such, it is clear that such rights are use or, more specifically, *prescribed use* rights.

---

[93] *Water Act 2007*, s4 'Definitions'.

However, the registration of use rights under the CWA is not as simple as it first appears. There is no single register for these rights. Rather, each jurisdiction, an agency of each jurisdiction or an infrastructure operator[94] or other prescribed person can maintain a register of water rights.[95] Information *may* be accessed from the *Murray–Darling Basin Water Rights Information Service*,[96] although there is no necessity that information provided by different jurisdictions be consistent or uniform. The legislation envisages that the different registers will be interoperable[97] – which would allow access between different jurisdictions. However, no guideline is provided as to how this is to be done, which in practical terms could lead to incompatible registers across the jurisdictions.

An advantage of the envisaged system however is that there is flexibility in the institutional set up of registers between the jurisdictions. This means jurisdictions which may have already maintained water registers need not create yet another institution or mechanism to facilitate the requirements of the *Water Act 2007*. But, of course, with flexibility come problems. A member of the general public does not necessarily know where to look for information in regard to water rights, and where legal advice is sought, there is a greater chance of prices increasing due to the extra work involved for lawyers in information gathering.

A further notable omission of the use register as envisaged by the *Water Act 2007* is the lack of liability or compensation for errors on the *Murray–Darling Basin Water Rights Information Service*.[98] This defies the initial conception of the entire Torrens system, which included as a key pillar the *insurance principle*.

Is it possible to integrate a register of use and a register of title?

As the preceding discussion indicates, neither register is entirely satisfactory for resource management. A register of use details how a resource may or may not be used, but does not necessarily indicate the details of a registered proprietor or third party interests. A register of title on the other hand has party details, the manner in which the interest is held (which may include duration) but does not necessarily indicate other third party interests, such as public interests, or legislative requirements which may override the interests of the registered proprietor. However, a model coming close to an integrated resource management register does exist in Queensland under the state-based *Water Act 2000*.

---

[94]   *Water Act 2007*, s7(2) 'Infrastructure Operators etc'. It is curious that the phrase 'etc' appears in the title of a piece of legislation.

[95]   *Water Act 2007*, s102.

[96]   *Water Act 2007*, s103.

[97]   *Water Act 2007*, s103(2)(h).

[98]   *Water Act 2007*, s103(3).

Queensland Water Act   The Queensland *Water Act 2000* was instrumental in
loosing the traditional nexus between water and land rights. It is the Queensland legislation which implements the plans and grants title to water, which
complements the Commonwealth legislation creating the plans for the register.
Queensland initiated a water register of its own, under the *Water Act 2000*
(hereinafter QWA). Section 127 of the QWA provides:

(1)   The entry on the water allocations register for a water allocation must state the
following –

(a)   details of the person who holds, and how the person holds, the allocation;
(b)   a nominal volume for the allocation;
(c)   the location from which the water may be taken;
(d)   the purpose, including, for example, agricultural, industrial or urban, for
which the water may be taken;
(e)   any conditions required by the chief executive to be entered on the register;
(f)   the resource operations plan under which the water allocation is
managed;[99]
(g)   other matters prescribed under a regulation.

(2)   If the water allocation is managed under a resource operations licence, the entry
on the water allocations register for the allocation must also state the following –

(a)   the resource operations licence under which the allocation is managed;
(b)   the priority group to which the allocation belongs.

(3)   If the water allocation is not managed under a resource operations licence, the
entry on the water allocations register for the allocation must also state the following –

(a)   the maximum rate for taking water;
(b)   the flow conditions under which the water may be taken;
(c)   the volumetric limit;
(d)   the water allocation group to which the allocation belongs;
(e)   the water management area that includes the location from which the water
may be taken.

As we can see from this example, section 127(1) provides for the registration
of both title information as well as use information. Section 127(1)(a) and (b)
indicates to the searcher of the register who the register proprietor of the interest
is, how the interest is held (whether licence or permit)[100] and the 'size' of the
resource held. These indications are merely descriptive in nature. Section 127(1)
(c)–(g) on the other hand prescribe as to the conditions of use of the resource.

---

[99]   At the date of authorship, there were 21 regional water plans to consider, although
normally different plans would not affect the same allocation.
[100]   *Water Act 2000* (Qld), s204.

This appears to be suitable for the recording of public interest requirements, as well as legislative limitations on the register.

There are however several problems with the QWA. The first relates to sustainable development, the second to the register. Section 10 of the QWA provides that the purpose of the Act is to 'advance sustainable management' and 'efficient use' of the resource, namely water.[101] The sustainable management and efficient use include, *inter alia*, protecting the physical, economic and social well-being of the population,[102] protecting biodiversity and natural ecosystems,[103]promoting 'the economic development of Queensland in accordance with the principles of ecologically sustainable development',[104] providing fair and efficient use of water resources[105] and integrating the management of this Act with other legislation.[106] Section 11 of the QWA goes into more detail about what the principles of ESD are. Although spelling ESD out in more detail is useful, the fact that section 10 provides that it is economic development which is to occur in accordance with ESD principles shows the legislative draftsmen were clearly focused on economic considerations before other considerations, which appears contradictory to the other purposes of the Act. As such, ESD is not the principal objective or concern of the Act.

The second issue relates to the register. A major problem which is obvious from this register however is that is does not correspond with the land title register. As such, individuals must undertake separate searches for land and water. The same may occur in the future if other *ad hoc* resource registers are created. As such, it is important that there is not only an integration of the type of information on the register – title and use – but also integration between the differing resources themselves. Furthermore, there is also a necessity to ensure information integration or harmony is achieved.

Technological Considerations

As has been noted previously, integration is a key concept for sustainable development, and it is arguable that this relates not only to the resources managed, but also information about the resources and development. We must now consider whether technology can assist in the management and *information integration*. In short, the answer is yes.

---

[101]   *Water Act 2000* (Qld), s10 (1).
[102]   *Water Act 2000* (Qld), s10 (2)(a).
[103]   *Water Act 2000* (Qld), s10 (2)(b).
[104]   *Water Act 2000* (Qld), s10 (2)(c)(ii).
[105]   *Water Act 2000* (Qld), s10 (2)(c)(vi).
[106]   *Water Act 2000* (Qld), s10 (2)(c)(ix).

As has been highlighted above, one pillar of ESD is integration. The exact ambit is still under consideration, but it can mean: resource integration, institutional integration and arguably more importantly, information integration.

Technological advances since the introduction of the first resource registers present the current generation great opportunities to achieve information integration. In IT terms, a register is what would be called a database. One method which could be adopted is a *feed-in register*. Specifically, in IT terminology, the database would be a portal – a gateway to different databases which store information.

This could be achieved by having one central administrative register, which is able to bring up information stored on other types of registers. The central register could indicate whether there are specific interests in a resource.

Figure 4.2   Central Administrative Register: Is this the Technical Solution for Achieving a Practical Link of Registers?

A consideration of how interests appear on the register must also be taken into account. Do we merely have an oblique reference to the interest, and, as such, meeting the basic requirement of the mirror principle reflecting the title, or do we need a more detailed description of the other interests?[107] According

---

[107]   Price, R and Griggs, L (2005), *Property Law in Principle*, Law Book Co at 108.

to at least one High Court case in Australia,[108] an oblique reference is sufficient to bind a registered proprietor. This would make sense. The register is not necessarily there to provide all conceivable details to the registered proprietor or potentially interested party. The register should instead be viewed as a guide – to direct people to the sources of information which are appropriate and affect the resource in question. As such, a similar concept to the water register in Queensland, whereby there are notations as to the plan which affects the interest, rather than the actual plan itself, is very effective. However effective this may be, one must question whether it is really harmonisation of information.

4.   WHAT IS THE WAY FORWARD FOR HARMONISATION GENERALLY?

A question thus arises. How do we move forward and promote harmonisation between conflicting ideologies and principles, between the issues of practical resource management and the modern requirements of ecologically sustainable development? There are many considerations, which shall be discussed below, with examples provided in diagrammatic form based on the present chapter.

An early consideration (Stage One in Figure 4.3) which needs to be sorted out, for pragmatic reasons, is the jurisdictional issue. For example, one must question whether there are constitutional limitations which may hinder a certain jurisdiction being given power over a particular resource. It is quite necessary to ensure the smooth operation of the law, as well as to ensure that the formal institutions and mechanisms adopted are appropriate. Concurrent to this determination is the asking of the questions about whether a principle is meant to be merely an overarching or guiding principle, or whether it is going to be applicable to determinations or decisions made by relevant agents in charge of implementing, and enforcing, the legislation. For example, does a term become an overarching principle of the entire legal system, such as the manner in which environmental concerns have been addressed in the Spanish Constitution[109] and German Constitution[110] or just a term which is

---

[108]   *Bursill Enterprises Pty Ltd v. Berger Bros Trading Co* (1971) 124 CLR 83.

[109]   Art 45.2 establishes '[t]he public powers should maintain a rational use of natural resources, with a view to protecting and improving quality of life and restore the environment, based on essential collective solidarity'. See Villar Rojas, F (2002), 'Environmental Protection and Land Ownership Regimen in Canary Islands' in Sánchez Jordán, ME and Gambaro, A (eds) (2002), *Land Law in Comparative Perspective*, Kluwer Law International 17 at 20.

[110]   *Grundgesetz für die Bundesrepublik Deutschland*, s20a 'Umweltschutz' (Protection of the Environment).

an overriding goal of the particular legislation?[111] If it is to be the former, the practical consideration from the legal perspective is how does the legislature make the principle, such as sustainable development, become a binding obligation on the society as a whole?[112] Diagrammatically this is represented in Figure 4.3.

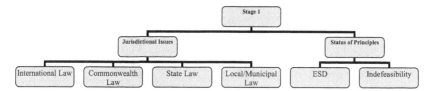

Figure 4.3   Stage One Considerations

Following from this (not represented diagrammatically), it is necessary to consider the manner in which we harmonise the theory and the practice. Many in the profession may consider the history and theory irrelevant to their day-to-day lives, but the reality is that this is what the judiciary will be taking into consideration, especially in a common law jurisdiction. For example, when recent land law reforms were undertaken in Scotland, there was a clear reference to the removal of the notion of a vassal holding land of a superior[113] – this has practical implications for the practitioner and brings the law more into line with the lay person's understanding of property than a common law lawyer's perception. Another example is in relation to water; the common law has historically viewed water as an access right, whereas now legislation is being interpreted to the point of recognising water as a proprietary right.[114] In undertaking this form of analysis, one would also need to consider terminological issues, to ensure that the terminology adopted is consistent. Furthermore, one would have to make certain that there is a level of awareness of the shifts in language over time, to make sure one does not leave historical shifts behind. There are several other related problems which would need to be addressed in searching for the solution to tensions in terminology. For example, it is important to consider that there are, at least, three possible ways in which key terminology may be used:

---

[111]   *Water Management Act 2000* (NSW), in particular ss3(a) and 3(f).

[112]   Fisher, DE (2006), 'Water Resources Governance and the Law', 11(1) *Australasian Journal of Natural Resources Law and Policy* 2 at 5.

[113]   Steven, AJM (2002), 'Scottish Land Law in a State of Reform', 2 *Journal of Business Law* 177 at 182.

[114]   Fisher, DE (2006), 'Water Resources Governance and the Law', 11(1) *Australasian Journal of Natural Resources Law and Policy*, 2 at 14.

- As a goal or objective of the legislation in question;
- Whether the terminology adopted creates a specific duty, and thus the individual sub-duties which may flow from this; and
- Whether the key terms adopted are a criteria for the decision making process.

One however must be careful when undertaking such analysis, as even though we are now able to review changes from other regions of the world with ease, we must still be wary of the context within which the changes have occurred, for otherwise we incorporate changes without necessarily considering the implications or factors which led to the change in the first place.[115]

Once the theoretical aspects have been covered, it is necessary to focus on structural aspects of the harmonisation process (stage three represented in Figures 4.4 and 4.5). This process will require us to determine whether priority is to be given to one area of the law, or whether we indeed decide to have them as equal counterparts. An example of the former can clearly be found in the New South Wales water legislation, where ecological sustainability is given a greater weight than the individual landholder's rights.[116] The structure would include, for the purpose of harmonisation of property law, resource management and ESD, the different institutional arrangements which would be employed to facilitate and manage the resources, as well as the mechanisms which would be adopted to carry out this task with ease. For example, at present, there are differences between the structures of indefeasibility in Australia,[117] but there are common elements, such as similar exceptions to indefeasibility. The most

---

[115]   For example, the rationale for passing the 19th Century prohibitions on commercial use of residential land was probably to stop coal trading. This today is said also to possibly prohibit an online company being set up from the same premises. For discussion see Steven, AJM (2002), 'Scottish Land Law in a State of Reform', 2 *Journal of Business Law* 177 at 187–8. Lynch, A (2008), *From Blair's Britain with Love: Control Orders in Australia*, presentation given to the Griffith University Socio-Legal Research Centre on 10 March 2008, provides another example which is highly relevant to consider the context in which introduced. For example, the context of introducing the laws permitting 'control orders' in Australia had to be examined in light of Australia's lack of a Bill of Rights, or with the exception of one state and one territory, any human rights Act. See also Jaggers, B (2007), *Anti-Terrorism Control Orders in Australia and the United Kingdom: A Comparison*, available at: www.aph.gov.au/library/pubs/rp/2007-08/08rp28.pdf (viewed 5 June 2008).
[116]   Foerster, A (2008), 'Managing and Protecting Environmental Water: Lessons from the Gwydir for Ecologically Sustainable Water Management in the Murray Darling Basin', 25(1) *Environmental and Planning Law Journal* 130 at 131; see also *Nature Conservation Council of New South Wales Inc v. Minister for Sustainable Natural Resources* [2004] NSWLEC 33 at [10] per Talbot J.
[117]   Price, R and Griggs, L (2005), *Property Law in Principle*, Law Book Co at 105.

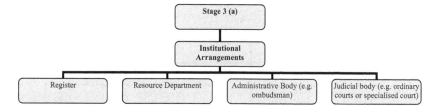

Figure 4.4   What Institutional Arrangements Facilitate Harmonisation?

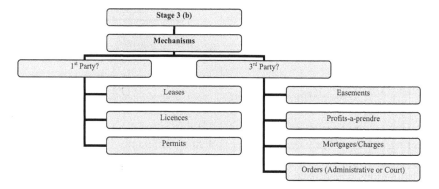

Figure 4.5   What Mechanisms do we Consider Usable? For example, the Possible Use for ESD and Resource Management

prudent methodological approach which should be adopted to formulate structural change would be a comparative analysis of the present institutions which exist amongst the jurisdictions which one seeks to harmonise. Institutional arrangements would include: judicial or administrative oversight; managing agencies or departments; and the type of registers to be adopted.

Mechanisms which are necessary to consider would be the actual legal instruments used for regulation, such as licences, permits, easements and similar such mechanisms. Mechanisms may also be market based, which again could be regulated through legislative requirements. By undertaking an analysis of common institutions and mechanisms, one is able to find common characteristics among them. From here, best practice is potentially discoverable and also limits the possibility of trying 'to reinvent the wheel'.

A further, but by no means final, issue to be considered is what the actual resources are which are sought to be regulated (Figure 4.6). As such, consideration must be given to whether integration of man-made, cultural and natural resources are to be jointly governed. If so, how do we manage this? Or does one aspect or another fall outside the jurisdiction, thus impairing true harmonisation?

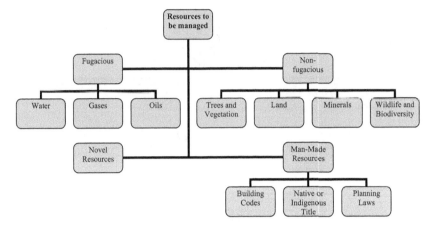

*Figure 4.6   Considerations at Stage 4 – What do we Seek to Regulate
through Harmonisation?*

Again, a comparative analysis would assist this, as well as a check on different terminology. For example, water is defined differently by the legislatures
in South Australia, Tasmania and Queensland.[118] Other examples relate to
jurisdictions which have already attempted to implement integrated resource
management strategies and legislation, such as the *Resource Management Act
1991* (NZ) and *Natural Resources Management Act 2004* (SA).

Figures 4.3–4.6 each indicate a practical step-by-step example of the process
of harmonisation of environmental and property law. However, it would be
simplistic to consider that each step is discrete and entirely separate. Instead,
harmonisation of laws would require a holistic approach to be taken, and thus
at each step, multiple considerations will need to be made. This is represented
in Figure 4.7, with the arrows indicating that, at considering each stage, the
previous stage must be considered and taken into account.

CONCLUSION

It is noteworthy that historically the benefits of uniformity or, as we are discussing now, harmonisation were discussed by leading lawyers, yet were not
acted upon. Whilst uniformity of laws existed centuries ago, historical events
led to fragmentation. This chapter has focused on resource management and

---

[118]   Fisher DE (2004), 'Rights of Property in Water: Confusion or Clarity?', 21(3)
Environmental and Planning Law Journal 200 at 218.

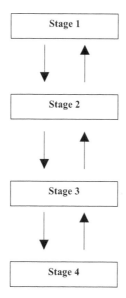

Figure 4.7   Non-linear Considerations at Decision-making Stages

the environment, where there are further layers which add complication to these matters, primarily socio-economic matters. These lie beyond the scope of this chapter, but the additional considerations of socio-economic consequences do add an additional layer of complexity in the decision-making processes faced with a fragmented approach to resource management. Socio-economic considerations will also be a factor in many other areas of law, such as consumer protection.

The lesson for failing to act has become a common reference point of contemporary environmental jurisprudence – our failure to act now will lead to insurmountable costs for the future – readily refined in the 'precautionary principle'. The benefits of harmonisation are of contemporary relevance in sustainable development, resource use, and access to resources more generally, especially in terms of ease of trade of commodities. Sustainable development is about taking a holistic approach to dealing with problems,[119] yet it is often these economic factors and trading considerations which remain at the forefront of the minds of most people in society, but especially politicians and the corporate sector. As such, a push towards legal harmonisation must be undertaken in a politically strategic manner, which would also mean taking into account socio-economic

---

[119]   Lang, W. (ed.) (1995), *Sustainable Development and International Law*, Graham & Trotman Publishers at 5.

considerations. Indeed, in the words of Weeramantry J. of the International Court of Justice, the

> problem of steering a course between the needs of development and the necessity to protect the environment is a problem alike of the law of development and of the law of the environment. Both these vital and developing areas of law require, and indeed assume, the existence of a principle which harmonizes both needs.[120]

Furthermore, we need to harmonise not only among lawyers, but other sectors of society. This chapter highlights that just a slight shift in the language we adopt could assist in bringing together professionals from the field of information technology to assist in resource management, thus advancing the promotion and ultimate achievement of the goals of sustainable development.

Within the law itself, harmonisation requires taking a cross-sectional approach and not merely viewing issues in terms of discrete practice areas which are in competition for all-or-nothing, such as property law or environmental law. Rather, harmonisation should be viewed concurrently from a 'top-down' as well as 'bottom-up' approach. This would lead to the holistic approach which is repeated consistently throughout environmental jurisprudence.

This chapter has provided examples of how Australia is, at present, trying to grapple with similar problems to those being experienced around the world, and in particular Europe – across different jurisdictions and different practices of law. Luckily, we have the benefit of a single language to work with, although this should not necessarily be viewed as problematic, as the richness language can bring may assist us in our theoretical approaches. From an antipodean perspective, by taking a multi-disciplined approach, including both theoretical and practical considerations, we may be able to achieve harmonisation both within, and between, jurisdictions.

---

[120] *Gabcikovo-Nagymaros Project* [1997] ICJ Rep 7 ('Danube Dam case'), per Separate Opinion of Weeramantry J, at 90.

5. Disharmony in the process of harmonisation? – The analytical account of the Strasbourg Court's variable geometry of decision-making policy based on the margin of appreciation doctrine

Yutaka Arai-Takahashi*

1. INTRODUCTION

This chapter seeks to provide an analytical account of the margin of appreciation doctrine in the specific context of the harmonisation of the European Convention on Human Rights (ECHR or Convention). It draws on the affinities between the arguments concerning the margin of appreciation and theories on judicial discretion while duly taking into account the structural difference between the roles and remits of international and national judges. Its aim is to provide a coherent theoretical explanation for the questions whether and if so, how, this doctrine can be said to facilitate the harmonisation of the standards of the ECHR in the enriched jurisprudence of the European Court of Human Rights (the Strasbourg Court).

The chapter firstly undertakes a thorough dissection of the intrinsic nature and underlying rationales of the margin of appreciation within the ECHR's 'constitutional' framework. Secondly, it seeks to identify distinct methodologies leaning toward harmonisation, which can be distilled and culled from the Strasbourg Court's reasoning processes. Thirdly, it analyses the role of the margin of appreciation as an antidote to a smooth process of harmonisation in the ECHR's legal order in which the two opposing rationales of integration and diversification come to the fore in different forms.

* Kent Law School, University of Kent, UK.

2. THE MARGIN OF APPRECIATION AS A 'POLICY STANDARD'

The concept of margin of appreciation, which has been developed in the jurisprudence of the ECHR, suggests discretion given to national authorities in assessing appropriate standards of the Convention rights, taking into account particular values and other distinct factors woven into the fabric of local laws and practice. This concept is more than a mere rhetorical device for window-dressing. Yet, unlike the concept of proportionality, there are certain obstacles to claiming that it is a fully-fledged 'principle'. First, the margin of appreciation does not entail any binding force upon the Strasbourg judges or the national authorities. This makes it somewhat hard to be reconciled with the suggestion that principles and other standards can be binding upon judges.[1] Second, it is not considered equipped with the capacity consistently to predict certain normative outcomes, the capability often associated with a 'principle'. Third, its role in assisting the appraisal of the overall balance in 'a constellation of principles'[2] is hardly evident.

Principles or polices are not part of the law but are treated more as 'extra-legal standards'.[3] As part of his criticism of positivism, Dworkin stresses that many standards other than 'rules' are operative within the legal order, including 'principles, policies and other sorts of standards'. At times he employs the term 'principles' generically to refer to the whole gamut of those standards other than rules.[4] Nevertheless, *stricto sensu*, principles are differentiated from policies. On one hand, a 'policy' is defined as a 'kind of standard that sets out a goal to be reached, generally an improvement in some economic, political, or social feature of the community'. On the other hand, a principle is described as 'a standard that is to be observed, not because it will advance or secure an economic, political, or social situation deemed desirable, but because it is a requirement of justice or fairness or some other dimension of morality'.[5] The distinction between principles and policies can nonetheless be collapsed if a principle is read as stating a social objective, or by interpreting a policy as stating a principle.[6] With regard to the differentiation of principles from rules, Dworkin contends that the former 'states a reason that argues in one direction, but does not necessitate a

---

[1]   Dworkin, R (1977), *Taking Rights Seriously*, Duckworth at 37. In this context, Dworkin attempts to refute the argument that a positivist might submit, according to which principles are not laws and hence not binding.

[2]   Dworkin, R (1977), *Taking Rights Seriously*, Duckworth at 35.

[3]   Dworkin, R (1977), *Taking Rights Seriously*, Duckworth at 35.

[4]   Ibid., at 22.

[5]   Ibid., at 22.

[6]   Ibid., at 22–3.

particular decision'. In contrast, a rule tends to stipulate a discrete resolution because of its specificity and concrete character.[7] Further, principles or policy standards are deemed to have the dimension of weight or importance, so that competing principles or policy standards are susceptible to evaluations in terms of their relative weight. In contrast, rules operate in an all-or-nothing manner, so that the conflict of rules is resolved by allowing one to supersede the other.[8] A policy standard has an advantage over a rule in terms of its resilience. Rules may be changed, or fall into desuetude, when they drastically fail to dictate their normative outcomes, such as in the case where a contrary result continues to be yielded. In contrast, a policy standard is able to survive intact, even in cases where it cannot prevailingly or consistently provide a basis for a certain, normative outcome.[9]

The concept of the margin of appreciation assists the prognosis of the latitudes of discretion accorded to the member states. It may well be that this concept assists the Court's complex, adjudicative role by determining the interaction of rules and principles (such as the principle of proportionality and evolutive interpretation) in specific cases. By setting concrete decisions in an overall balance of competing values, the margin of appreciation helps pinpoint the Strasbourg Court's shifting policy rationales underlying the 'constitutional'[10] structure of the ECHR's legal order.[11] In that sense, if placed in the spectrum from purely descriptive to purely evaluative, it is geared toward the evaluative pole.[12] It can also serve as a vital, analytical tool in such a dialectic of value-pluralism. These lead to the upshot that the margin of appreciation can be considered a *policy standard* that emanates from the decisional choice of the Strasbourg Court. That

---

[7]   Ibid., at 26.

[8]   Ibid., at 24, and 26–7.

[9]   Ibid., at 35–6.

[10]   The erstwhile European Commission of Human Rights expressly recognized that the Convention is the 'constitutional' instrument in the context of European human rights law: *Chrysostomos, Papachrysostomou and Loizidou v. Turkey, Nos. 15299/89, 15300/89 and 15318/89*, Decision of 4 March 1991, 68 *Decisions and Reports of the European Commission of Human Rights* 216 at 242.

[11]   Letsas argues that '[w]hether or not interference with individual freedoms is justified by and large turns on the much broader issue of the role of human rights as a matter of political morality, rather than the concepts of the margin of appreciation or deference': Letsas, G (2006), 'Two Concepts of the Margin of Appreciation', 26 *Oxford Journal of Legal Studies* 705, at 709. Nevertheless, the present writer stresses the role of the margin of appreciation in helping to identify the Strasbourg Court's policy rationales and convictions on political morality.

[12]   It is in that respect that the margin of appreciation is often compared to the European or German law concept of proportionality or to the English law notion of reasonableness. For the analytical account of the notion of reasonableness see, for instance, MacCormick, *supra* n. 2 at 162.

this notion entails a fraction of the result-predicting or result-dictating capacity, the property with which a rule is generally equipped, does not furnish a scintilla of evidence against its functional role as a policy standard.

3.   IS THE MARGIN OF APPRECIATION A GENERAL PRINCIPLE OF THE ECHR?

It may be questioned whether the notion of margin of appreciation is part of the nascent body of 'general principles' of the ECHR. *Prima facie*, in the legal order of the ECHR, the existence of 'general principles' is unfathomable. When discussing general principles within the framework of EC law, continental EC lawyers classify three categories of general principles on the basis of their nature and rational underpinnings: (i) *'principes axiomatiques'*, which are regarded as immanent in the foundation of any legal system and even anchored in natural law, but remain amorphous in nature; (ii) *'principes structurels'*, which are derived from the distinct characteristics of a specific legal system, such as the principle of direct effect developed in the *sui generis* legal order of EC law; and (iii) *'principes communs'*, which are distinct in supra-national legal systems, but are comprised of principles common to the constituent laws (namely, the laws of the member states) of the legal systems.[13] A salient example of the third genre is manifested in the controversial phrase 'the general principles of law recognised by *civilised nations*' within the meaning of Article 38(1)(c) of the Statute of the International Court of Justice.[14] In the context of international law, the term 'general principles of international law' is frequently used. Yet, this must be clearly distinguished from general principles of law derived from national laws. The former is 'sweeping and loose standards of conduct' that can be deduced from customary rules and treaty rules by way of extraction, distillation and generalization of some of their most significant common denominators.[15] It bears close resemblance to the *'principes axiomatiques'* in EC legal order. Tridimas employs the term 'general principles' of EC law to refer to 'funda-mental unwritten principles of law which underlie the Community law edifice'. Such general principles are non-written principles derived from the rule of law. They may take on constitutional or quasi-constitutional importance in EC law.[16]

---

[13]   Tridimas, T (1999), *The General Principles of EC Law*, Oxford University Press at 2.

[14]   Emphasis added. This Eurocentric wording is controversial, given that both this provision and its progenitor in the Statute of the Permanent Court of International Justice manifest the exclusive club of the western states and the supremacy of their legal systems.

[15]   Cassese, A (2005), *International Law*, (2nd ed.) Oxford University Press at 188.

[16]   Tridimas, *supra* n. 13 at 3–4.

To characterize certain principles and policy standards developed by the Strasbourg Court as 'general principles of ECHR' along the lines suggested in the EC law context requires special caution. This is particularly the case for the margin of appreciation. Several reasons can be put forward. First, there is a marked, systemic difference between EC law and the ECHR, in that the EC legal order can be characterized as a 'self-contained' and *sui generis* legal system. Second, in view of the innately indefinite nature of its minimum substantive content, it is hard to see the margin of appreciation doctrine guide judicial inquiries, without the aid of more specific standards that can be identified by disaggregated analyses of this doctrine. Third, it is not immediately clear, even though not excluded, that the margin of appreciation can be said to be equipped with the capacity to resolve the conflict of two clashing Convention rights. Indeed, even the principle of proportionality, which is probably the most eligible for the general principles of the ECHR, remains crude and rudimentary,[17] as compared with the equivalent notion in EC law that has been given considerable elaboration and refinement.[18] It must, however, be stated that these considerations in no way entail a denial that particular rationales must also exist for the decision to apply the varying scope of margin of appreciation. Indeed, as will be examined below, such underlying rationales can be considered to capture the 'constitutional' dimensions of the margin of appreciation.

4. THE ANALYSIS OF THE PROCESSES IN WHICH THE MARGIN OF APPRECIATION IS APPLIED

Functionally speaking, the margin of appreciation doctrine, if taken out of context, would be meaningless.[19] Its operational effectiveness depends largely

---

[17]   See, for instance, Arai-Takahashi, Y (2002), *The Margin of Appreciation Doctrine and the Principle of Proportionality in the Jurisprudence of the ECHR*, Intersentia/Hart at 193–205; and Eissen, M-A (1993), 'The Principle of Proportionality in the Case-Law of the European Court of Human Rights' in Macdonald, R, Matscher, F and Petzold, H (eds), *The European System for the Protection of Human Rights*, Martinus Nijhoff at 125.

[18]   See, for instance, de Búrca, G (1993), 'The Principle of Proportionality and its Application in EC Law', 13 *Yearbook of European Law* 105; Emiliou, N (1996), *The Principle of Proportionality in European Law – A Comparative Study*, Kluwer; and Tridimas, T (1999), *The General Principles of EC Law*, Oxford University Press at 89–162.

[19]   With respect to the concept of reasonableness, MacCormick considers that this concept taken out of context is an example of what Julius Stone describes as 'legal categories of illusory or indeterminate reference': MacCormick, *supra* n. 2 at 165. See Stone, J (1964), *Legal System and Lawyers' Reasonings*, Stevens & Sons, Chapters 7 and 8; and Twining, W (2000), 'The Province of Jurisprudence Re-examined

upon a variety of evaluative standards and interpretive principles, such as the proportionality principle and evolutive interpretation. Analytically, the process in which the margin of appreciation is applied as a policy standard can consist of three phases: (i) the phase of fact-finding and ascertainment of fact; (ii) the phase of evaluating the normative scope; and (iii) the phase of assessing the means to achieve desired social ends.[20]

The first phase concerns 'fact-intensive' determination and the empirical evaluation of 'relatively ideology-neutral criteria'.[21] In essence, this is what Greer terms the 'implementation discretion'.[22] The most salient examples would be the evaluation of the state of emergency that can authorize a member state to invoke the derogation clause under Article 15 to suspend much of the Convention rights, or the assessment of appropriate evidence for criminal convictions. Clearly, the assertion that this phase is 'value-free' is relative. For instance, assessing the obscenity of art work depends largely on subjective grounds.[23] In this phase, the comparative advantage of local administrative authorities in fact-finding corroborates the subsidiarity principle based on utilitarian calculation.[24]

The second phase on which the margin of appreciation operates relates to the determination of the meaning and contents of a specific norm. A human rights norm which is drafted in a general, open-ended, or ambiguous manner may remain unsettled,[25] with limited 'conduct-guidance'.[26] Such a norm can be either: (i) an inherently indefinite norm;[27] or (ii) an inherently discretion-

---

– Problems of Generalization in a Global Context', Julius Stone Memorial Lecture, available at www.ucl.ac.uk/laws/jurisprudence/docs/twi_jstone.pdf (last visited on 22 October 2008).

[20]   Shany, Y (2005), 'Toward a General Margin of Appreciation Doctrine in International Law?', 16 *European Journal of International Law* 907 at 917 and 935.

[21]   Ibid., at 937.

[22]   Greer, S (2003), 'Constitutionalising Adjudication under the European Convention on Human Rights', 23 *Oxford Journal of Legal Studies* 405 at 423.

[23]   Compare, for instance, the European Court of Human Rights, *Müller and Others v. Switzerland*, Judgment of 24 May 1988, Series A, No. 133; and *Vereinigung Bildender Künstler v. Austria*, Judgment of 25 April 2007.

[24]   Shany, *supra* n. 20 at 927.

[25]   Ibid., at 910. See the European Court of Human Rights, *Odièvre v. France*, Judgment of 13 February 2003, at para. 40.

[26]   Shany, *supra* n. 20 at 910. See the European Court of Human Rights, *VO v. France*, Judgment of 8 July 2004, para. 82 (recognizing that 'the issue of when the right to life begins comes within the margin of appreciation which the Court generally considers that States should enjoy in this sphere, notwithstanding an evolutive interpretation of the Convention').

[27]   For instance, see the notion of 'protection of … morals' under Article 8(2) ECHR. For the discussions on the German public law doctrine on indefinite norms (*unbestimmte*

given norm, namely what Shany describes as a 'result-oriented norm'.[28] With respect to the first genre, let it be remarked that all rules of law are, when chosen as standards of behaviour, vulnerable to indeterminacy in their application. They inherently have what Hart refers to as an 'open texture'.[29] Indeed, the Strasbourg Court's law-making policy has been shaped by the need to fill in gaps left by existing legal frameworks in 'unregulated disputes', which result from indeterminacy of both the language of the provisions and the intention of the drafters.[30] Legal standards epitomise a relatively specific subset of social values. Yet, the determinacy of specific legal terms (or the determinacy of the normative values anchored in those legal terms) ineluctably varies. What MacCormick calls the 'degree of localization of values' hinges on an evaluation of a plurality of relevant, competing, and 'value-laden factors' that are 'highly context-dependent'.[31]

After undergoing the first and second phases, the national authorities' discretionary power turns to the third phase. This phase involves the ascertainment of the means (types, suitability, proportionality etc) to attain social objectives in a particular factual circumstance.[32]

Begriffe) see Arai-Takahashi, Y (2000), 'Administrative Discretion in German Law: Doctrinal Discourse Revisited', 6 *European Public Law* 69.

[28]   Shany, *supra* n. 20 at 917. When analysing the theory of the margin of appreciation in the *general* context of international law, Shany argues that special features of the result-oriented norms are that: (i) these norms are indifferent to the manner in which a desired legal end is attained, insofar as its attainment is guaranteed; (ii) state authorities are given discretion over choice of means and manner of implementing such norms; and (iii) the path to the desired social/public end is uncertain: ibid. Examples of each of those 'result-oriented norms' include: (i) most economic, social and cultural rights (International Covenant on Economic, Social and Cultural Rights, Article 2(1), etc.); (ii) environmental law norms, such as the Kyoto Protocol to the Framework Convention on Climate Change, Art 3(1); and (iii) EC directives – a procedure for promulgating result-oriented norms. See, for instance, Case C–6/90, *Francovich v. Italy*, [1991] ECR I–5357, at 5412.

[29]   Hart, HLA (1994) [1961], *The Concept of Law* (2nd ed), Oxford University Press at 127–8.

[30]   For the discussions on discretion left to judges in the domestic, common law context see Raz, J (1979), *The Authority of Law – Essays on Law and Morality* at 193 and 200.

[31]   MacCormick, *supra* n. 2 at 173.

[32]   Shany, *supra* n. 20 at 917 and 935. In this phase, for instance, the proportionality of incriminating measure (penalty) may be assessed.

5. THE CIRCUMSTANCES WHERE THE APPLICATION OF THE MARGIN OF APPRECIATION OUGHT TO BE EXCLUDED

Mahoney limits the application of the margin of appreciation only to the circumstances where restrictions on human rights are made in good faith (even though disproportionately in many cases), as a result of interest-balancing.[33] In those circumstances, 'the preliminary conditions of normal democratic governance have been shown to exist'.[34] The scope of application *ratione materiae* of the doctrine excludes the cases where 'naked, bad faith abuse of power' is committed. Apart from those cases, the doctrine should be deemed impermeable to the cases where violations of human rights are derived from a 'skewed' majority-minority relationship in democracy.[35] Further, moral relativism must not be admitted in such a manner as to call into question the secular and pluralist premises of democracy. In *Refah partisi (The Welfare Party) and Others v. Turkey*, the Strasbourg Court decisively ruled that the Shari'a is incompatible with 'the fundamental principles of democracy', which underpins the Convention.[36]

6. PROBLEMS OF THE MARGIN OF APPRECIATION DOCTRINE

The margin of appreciation doctrine has stirred much controversy among publicists. The thrust of objections that are closely related to the 'constitutional' structure of the Convention's legal system can be three-fold. First, the proponents of the certainty of legal rules problematize the doctrine's application, because it is considered to weaken the conduct-regulating quality of rules.[37] In other words, this may result in eroding the normative guidance of the Convention provisions and fostering normative ambiguity. In a more overarching context of the rule of law, vagueness in normative meaning and the 'evils of

---

[33] Mahoney, P (1998), 'Marvellous Richness of Diversity or Invidious Cultural Relativism', 19 *Human Rights Law Journal* 1, at 4.

[34] Ibid.

[35] Benvenisti, E (1999), 'Margin of Appreciation, Consensus and Universal Values', 31 *New York University Journal of International Law and Politics* 843, at 847 and 849–50.

[36] The European Court of Human Rights, *Refah partisi (The Welfare Party) and Others v. Turkey*, Judgment of 13 February 2003, paras 72 and 123 (Grand Chamber). The Court added that 'there can be no democracy without pluralism': ibid., para. 89.

[37] Shany, *supra* n. 20 at 937.

frustrated expectations' may undermine the dignity of individual persons by failing to respect their autonomy.[38] In contrast, one can counter that too much sacrifice to certainty would risk making judicial interpretation too formal.[39]

Second, the application of the doctrine may be criticized for introducing subjective, and relativist, standards of international law. Such a tendency would entail the risk of judicial double standard,[40] unfairness[41] or bias.[42] The Convention standards may be inconsistently applied in the seemingly similar cases,[43] leading to the asymmetrical standards of human rights. This tendency has an even more profound implication, as it runs counter to the universal claim of human rights.[44]

Third, excessive reliance on the judicial self-restraint rationale would risk fostering a habit of non-accountability,[45] and abdicating the supervisory role of the Strasbourg Court. As a consequence, the continued application of the margin of appreciation may entail corrosive effects on the rule of law and the principle of non-discrimination,[46] two of the cardinal principles that shape the constitutional edifice of the ECHR. Even so, it may be countered that contrary to the initial fear, the reliance on the doctrine has not led to compromising the *acquis* in respect of new member states.[47]

It is often unnoticed that when the Strasbourg judges apply the concept of margin of appreciation and give the national authorities an ambit of discretion, they are exercising their own discretionary power. In other words, the operation of the margin of appreciation hinges on the vertical structure in which different forms of discretion are exercised at two levels (duality of discretion). Is the

---

[38]   See Raz, *supra* n 30 at 222.

[39]   Compare the discussion on indeterminacies of legal rules in a domestic context: see Hart, *supra* n. 29 at 131.

[40]   Benvenisti, *supra* n. 35 at 844. See also Ni Aolain, F (1995–96), 'The Emergence of Diversity: Differences in Human Rights Jurisprudence', 19 *Fordham International Law Journal* 101, at 114, 119 (suggesting that states that adhere to democratic principles can be subject to less exacting scrutiny).

[41]   Shany, *supra* n. 20 at 912.

[42]   Benvenisti, *supra* n. 35 at 850; and Shany, *supra* n. 20 at 923–4.

[43]   Benvenisti, *supra* n. 35 at 844. See also Ni Aolain, *supra* n. 40 at 114, 119.

[44]   Benvenisti, *supra* n. 35.

[45]   Compare the discussions on the Framework Convention for the Protection of National Minorities in Furtado, C (2003), 'Guess Who's Coming to Dinner? Protection for National Minorities in Eastern and Central Europe under the Council of Europe', 34 *Columbia Human Rights Law Review* 333, at 364–5.

[46]   Compare Macklem, P (2006), 'Militant Democracy, Legal Pluralism, and the Paradox of Self-Determination', 4 *International Journal of Constitutional Law* 488.

[47]   See, for instance, Sweeney, JA (2005), 'Margins of Appreciation: Cultural Relativity and the European Court of Human Rights in the Post-Cold War Era', 54 *International and Comparative Law Quarterly* 459 at 468.

Strasbourg Court allowed to exercise such discretion over the extent to which the margin of appreciation is to be given to the national authorities, even when a rule in point is clear? The application of the margin of appreciation doctrine may handicap the development of judge-made law, constituting an obstacle to elaborating international human rights norms.[48] The fact that the doctrine lacks an explicit legal basis in the Convention text reinforces the fear that the Strasbourg Court is jibing at its own power of review in favour of the national authorities' discretion. Surely, the application of the margin of appreciation does not signify that the Strasbourg Court fails to regard itself as a final arbiter of the Convention rights, which is equipped with the capacity to make a non-reviewable decision and judgment.[49]

7. THE 'CONSTITUTIONAL' DIMENSIONS OF THE MARGIN OF APPRECIATION

In the context of harmonisation of the ECHR standards, the margin of appreciation doctrine can serve diverse functions to rationalize the vertical relationship between the international judges in Strasbourg and the national authorities. Four salient functions of this doctrine, which are closely related to the 'constitutional' edifice of the Convention, can be explored here. In the first place, the doctrine is considered to manifest the institutional dimension of subsidiarity.[50] It is purported to demarcate the boundaries in the vertical relationship between the responsibilities of the supranational judicial organ and the sovereignty of the member states (the function of the division of labour). It is in this context that the margin of appreciation can be deemed a 'natural product' of the distribution of powers between the supranational organs and national authorities.[51] It assures the national authorities that their sovereignty is safeguarded from 'unfounded' judicial activism. Indeed, the application of the doctrine signifies what Shany calls 'inter-institutional comity'[52] in that it exhibits the Court's willingness to hold joint 'ownership' of the juridical tasks with the national authorities.[53] Such

---

[48]   Shany, *supra* n. 20 at 922–3.

[49]   See Dworkin's second 'weak sense' of discretion: Dworkin (1977), *supra* n. 1 at 31–4, 68–71 and 327–30. See also Lucy, W (2002), 'Adjudication', in Coleman, J and Shapiro, S (eds), *The Oxford Handbook of Jurisprudence & Philosophy of Law*, Oxford University Press 206, at 215.

[50]   Sweeney, *supra* n. 47 at 474.

[51]   Petzold, H (1993), 'The Convention and the Principle of Subsidiarity' in Mac-Donald, R, Matscher, F and Petzold, H (eds), *The European System for the Protection of Human Rights*, Martinus Nijhoff 41 at 49.

[52]   Shany, *supra* n. 20 at 922.

[53]   Shany, *supra* n. 20 at 922.

'joint responsibility'[54] facilitates the process of 'normative internalization' by domestic courts,[55] which retain confidence in the international adjudication.

The concept of subsidiarity is also linked to the idea of distributive justice. Confronted with a long swath of individual applications and backlog of cases, the Court may take due account of the consideration of judicial economy based on utilitarian calculation, so that its limited judicial resources can be equitably allocated. In the light of a 'resource gap'[56] in collecting and analysing evidence or other empirical data, the international judges in Strasbourg feel the need to endorse the fact-finding by the national authorities. This rationale bolsters the margin of appreciation in assessing the existence of state of emergency[57] or policy choices in socio-economic matters.

In the second place, the margin of appreciation can be considered instrumental in consolidating the operative effectiveness of the Convention when it is in infancy, or when new member states from Central and Eastern Europe (and some former constituent republics of the USSR, including Russia) are undergoing a drastic degree of political transitions from communist dictatorial regimes to liberal democracies. In other words, the doctrine accords 'a face-saving leeway'[58] in the process of integration and harmonisation, giving states in the transition a grace period in which they can calibrate their national standards to the Convention's requirements. Admittedly, whether this 'deferral' rationale of the margin of appreciation can be considered to subsist beyond a transitional period may be questionable. On this matter, Sweeney argues that the Court's deferential stance towards new member states at the outset was quickly shifted to an overwhelming trend to find against them.[59] Indeed, even when the margin of appreciation is applied, the Strasbourg Court's harmonisation policy remains latent so that it can forestall a markedly restrained review of the kind that would undermine the '*acquis*' and internal consistency of the Convention's legal order.[60]

In the third place, the application of the margin of appreciation can be deemed the recognition that the Strasbourg Court lacks democratic accountability so that

---

[54]   Ibid.

[55]   Koh, HH (1998), 'Bringing International Law Home', 35 *Houston Law Review* 623 at 648–50.

[56]   Shany, *supra* n. 20 at 918.

[57]   The European Court of Human Rights, *Ireland v. UK*, Judgment of 28 January 1978, Series A, No. 25, para. 214 (asserting that the Court's evaluation must be made not with the advantage of hindsight but from the standpoint of the conditions prevailing at the time of emergency). Shany argues that the *ex post facto* nature of attributing state responsibility for violations of vague, primary norms might be perceived as a manifestation of 'dubious legitimacy': Shany, *supra* n. 20 at 918.

[58]   Ibid., at 922. Compare Benvenisti, *supra* n. 35 at 846 and 849.

[59]   Sweeney, *supra* n. 47 at 468.

[60]   Ibid., at 468–9.

it ought to defer to national or local legitimacy.[61] This is coterminous with what Letsas calls the 'structural concept of the margin of appreciation',[62] which is derived from a systemic relationship between the supranational judicial organ and the national constitutional apparatuses.[63] In this regard, it ought to be noted that authoritarian regimes epitomise inherent democratic deficit, leaving little scope for the margin of appreciation.[64]

In the fourth place, the concept of margin of appreciation can be deployed to deal with those human rights norms which touch on sensitive, cultural or traditional values of a specific society. It signals the international judiciary's due recognition that a normative objective envisaged in each of the Convention rights can be attained without having resort to strict uniform standards. The member states may reach different, yet lawful, decisions or act differently, while being perfectly consistent with the Convention requirements.[65] The transmission of such a message is predicated on the Court's overall, policy-oriented rationales that are embedded in the ideas of value-pluralism and cultural diversity. In other words, the application of the margin of appreciation manifests the 'moral choice' of the Strasbourg Court in preserving value-pluralism against the conformist trend.[66] This explanatory hypothesis chimes with the moral and ethical understanding of subsidiarity. Sweeney argues that one of the central roles of the margin of appreciation is to give effect to and consolidate the universalizing attempt of human rights in a local society imbued with distinct culture and morality, thereby fostering 'ethical decentralization'.[67]

[61]   Arai-Takahashi, *supra* n. 17 at 239–41.

[62]   The gist of this concept is that 'the Court's power to review decisions taken by domestic authorities should be more limited than the powers of a national constitutional court or other national bodies that monitor or review compliance with an entrenched bill of rights': Letsas (2006), *supra* n. 11 at 721.

[63]   Ibid., at 720. Judicial deference is understood as the exclusion of *de novo* examinations by international judges and the judicial restraint; international judges refrain from second-guessing the decisions made by national authorities: ibid., at 722.

[64]   Greer, *supra* n. 22 at 420; and Shany, *supra* n. 20 at 921.

[65]   Arai-Takahashi, *supra* n. 17 at 242–9; Greer, *supra* n. 22 at 409; and Shany, *supra* n. 20.

[66]   See, for instance, Arai-Takahashi, *supra* n. 17; Mahoney, *supra* n. 33; and Sweeney *supra* n. 47.

[67]   Ibid., at 472–4.

8. METHODOLOGIES FOR HARMONISING STANDARDS OF THE ECHR

8.1. Overview

In the context of the ECHR, the process of the harmonisation of standards is driven by policy rationales of the Strasbourg judges. This process may take shape through: (i) the application of the teleological interpretation that is designed to construe the meaning of the Convention text in line with evolving societal values (evolutive interpretation);[68] (ii) the identification of emerging European consensus among the practice of the majority of the member states in relation to what has hitherto been deemed a controversial issue (the European consensus approach);[69] and (iii) the development and implementation of European autonomous standards,[70] which may deviate from national standards (the European autonomous standard approach).[71]

8.2. The Evolutive Interpretation

The evolutive interpretation is premised upon the characterization of the ECHR as a 'living instrument which must be interpreted in the light of present-day conditions'.[72] In essence, the standard of Convention rules is adjusted, not to social opinions that are prevailing in a particular national or local society, but to what Lord Roger calls '*Völkergeist*' of the Convention's member states.[73]

---

[68]   For assessment of this interpretive methodology see Mahoney, P (1990), 'Judicial Activism and Judicial Self-Restraint in the European Court of Human Rights: Two Sides of the Same Coin', 11 *Human Rights Law Journal* 57.

[69]   See Arai-Takahashi, *supra* n. 17 at 215–16.

[70]   For explorations of this issue see Kastanas, E (1996), *Unité et Divesité – notions autonomes et marge d'appréciation des Etats dans la jurisprudence de la Cour européenne des droits de l'homme*, Bruylant; and Letsas, G (2004), 'The Truth in Autonomous Concepts: How to Interpret the ECHR', 15 *European Journal of International Law* 279.

[71]   For instance, the term 'criminal charge' in Article 6 has an autonomous, European standard, independent of the categorization applied under domestic law: the European Court of Human Rights, *Benham v. United Kingdom*, Judgment of 10 June 1996, para. 56. Similarly, the concept of 'possessions' in the first sentence of Article 1 of the First Protocol to the ECHR bears an autonomous meaning which is not confined to the ownership of physical goods and is independent of the formal classification in national law: the European Court of Human Rights, *Gasus Dosier- und Fördertechnik GmbH v. Netherlands*, Judgment of 23 February 1995, Series A, No. 306-B, para. 53.

[72]   See, *inter alia*, European Court of Human Rights, *Tyrer v. United Kingdom*, Judgment of 25 April 1978, Series A no. 26, para. 31; and *VO v. France*, Judgment of 8 July 2004, para. 82.

[73]   Rodger, A (2005), 'A Time for Everything under the Law: Some Reflections on Retrospectivity', 121 *Law Quarterly Review* 57 at 76.

This interpretive methodology operates within a schema of the 'diachronic variability' of the margin of appreciation doctrine.[74] It allows fine-tuning and tweaking of the Convention rules to accommodate societal trends, while shrinking the ambit of margin left to the national authorities. In that sense, this approach inclines toward the robust review predicated on the rigorous standard of proportionality. Due to the law-making nature,[75] the human rights treaties in general are considered amenable to adjustments of their standards of protection in tune with changing social conditions and attitudes.[76] Indeed, what may be termed 'law-making decisions' by the Strasbourg judges are designed to adjust existing doctrines to changing technological, social or economic conditions to avoid undesirable and iniquitous consequences of applying laws to circumstances that are not foreseen.[77]

The integrationist ethos ingrained in the evolutive interpretation can be discerned in two respects. First, the policy-oriented, value-laden decision-making of the Strasbourg judges may even induce a clear departure from the 'legislative intent'[78] of the drafters of the Convention. Second, the application of the evolutive interpretation may be facilitated by indefinite concepts used in the Convention text. The Strasbourg Court may tap into those concepts to funnel new meaning and interpretations into the normative scope of certain rules without stultifying the bulk of their rationales.[79]

---

[74] Delmas-Marty, M (ed.) (1992), *The European Convention for the Protection of Human Rights – International Protection versus National Restrictions*, Martinus Nijhoff at 338.

[75] For the Court's recognition of the ECHR as a law-marking treaty see, for instance, *Wemhoff v. Germany*, Judgment of 27 June 1968, Series A, No. 7, para. 8; *Golder v. UK*, Judgment of 21 February 1975, Series A, No. 18, para. 36; and *Leyla Şahin v. Turkey*, Judgment of 10 November 2005, para. 141. One of the major implications of a treaty characterized as a law-making treaty is that it is designed to create and safeguard rights of individual persons, which are not dependent upon the notion of reciprocity among the member states: *Austria v. Italy, No. 788/60*, (1961) 4 *Yearbook of the European Convention on Human Rights* 116, at 138. See also the Inter-American Court of Human Rights, *The Effects of Reservations on the Entry into Force of the American Convention on Human Rights (Arts 74 and 75)*, Advisory Opinion OC-2/82, 24 September 1982, Series A, No. 2 (1982), para. 29.

[76] McCormick, *supra* n. 2 at 179. For discussions in the English law context see Rodger, *supra* n. 73 at 75–7 (examining the shift in the case-law on rights of homosexuals and transsexuals).

[77] For discussions on the role of national judges see Raz, *supra* n. 30 at 200.

[78] Compare Wellington, HH and Albert, LA (1963), 'Statutory Interpretation and the Political Process: A Comment on Sinclair v. Atkinson', 72 *Yale Law Journal* 1547.

[79] Compare analyses of domestic laws see Raz, *supra* n. 30 at 193 and 200.

8.3. Two Patterns of Harmonisation Based on the European Consensus Approach

One can contemplate two patterns of harmonising the ECHR standards based on European consensus. The first pattern is to identify European standards from a minimum common denominator among the member states. This inductive approach, along the line proposed by positivists, focuses on empirical data to extrapolate a general norm.[80] It has an advantage that the results of the induction are consistent with verifiable facts, empirically corroborated, capturing what Dworkin calls the dimension of 'fit' in the process of interpretation.[81] It also involves a low risk of unfounded judicial law-making and 'adventurism'.[82] On the other hand, this approach is handicapped by some disadvantages. First, it entails the risk of muddling facts (descriptions of reality in domestic societies) and laws (the normative projection of future behaviour).[83] Second, as is true with any inductive methodology, this approach may prioritize empirical and descriptive accuracy at the expense of rational coherence and integrity. The consequences of these would be that the Strasbourg Court's judicial policy may be criticized for a 'conservative' leaning with deference to national decisions and polices.

The second pattern is a top-down (downward) harmonisation method, which often goes in tandem with the application of the evolutive interpretation. It is harnessed by the Strasbourg Court's policy rationales. It has the benefit of achieving the relatively rapid expansion of autonomous ECHR standards. It is *generally* geared towards the optimization of individual persons' rights. It is innately value-laden in that it is spurred on by the overarching, subjective decisions or 'higher convictions' of the Strasbourg Court about how moral and political ideas should be prioritized at the pan-European level.[84] Nevertheless,

---

[80]   In the context of ascertaining customary law among raw data see Simma, B and Alston, P (1988–89), 'The Sources of Human Rights Law: Custom, *Jus Cogens*, and General Principles', *Australian Yearbook of International Law* 82 at 88–9.

[81]   Dworkin argues that in the process of interpretation (the 'dimension of fit'), a threshold requirement comes into play, so that the interpretation can be accepted as eligible only if the raw data of legal practice adequately support it: Dworkin, R (1986), *Law's Empire*, Hart at 65–8, and 255.

[82]   Benvenisti is opposed to such a conservative tendency, suggesting his favour for teleological construction: Benvenisti, *supra* n. 35 at 852–3.

[83]   Compare Kammerhofer, J (2004), 'The Uncertainty in the Formal Sources of International Law: Customary International Law and Some of its Problems', 15 *European Journal of International Law* 523, at 537.

[84]   Compare the discourse presented by Dworkin in domestic judges' post-interpretative or 'reforming' stage. This stage is what he calls the 'dimension of substance', which becomes relevant only in 'hard cases' (namely where multiple, eligible interpretations are open to judges): Dworkin, *supra* n. 81 at 65–6 and 256.

one of its drawbacks is the risk of judicial arbitrariness and unreliable moral intuitions.[85] Another pitfall is seen in the dimension of legitimacy. To what extent would it be defensible for the judges in Strasbourg to impose their values by overriding decisions reached by the constituent organs (legislative and executive) of the member states, which are democratically accountable?

With respect to the second pattern, two notable features are discernible. First, the Court may assert the existence of European consensus and an autonomous European standard, even though the empirical data are either flimsy[86] or not rigorously tested.[87] With respect to the structure of rationality behind this policy-driven consensus approach, one can recall that search for an outcome of a legal dispute may be contingent on 'an accidental and unstable social consensus'.[88] Second, the Court may insist on an autonomous European standard, even though this may disallow local legitimacy. For instance, in *Tyrer v. UK*,[89] the majority's will among the local Manx population favouring the retention of judicial corporal punishment was decisively overridden by the European abolitionist trend against such punishment. Setting aside local legitimacy may be a special feature of what Letsas refers to as the 'substantive concept of the margin of appreciation', namely, the dimension of the margin of appreciation that serves to rationalize the relationship between the rights of individual persons and the collective interests.[90] In this dimension, the moralistic preferences of the majority in a specific society are abstracted to become a common European position,[91] which may then be imposed in another society as an external preference.[92]

---

[85]   Compare Dworkin, *supra* n. 81 at 66.

[86]   Such a pattern may risk crossing the boundary between interpretation and invention of a rule and becoming arbitrary: Dworkin, *supra* n. 81 at 66.

[87]   This has been seen in cases of discrimination against illegitimate children. See, for instance, *Marckx v. Belgium*, in which the Court noted that the existence of the European treaties aimed at removing discrimination against 'illegitimate' children was 'a clear measure of common ground', despite the small number of states parties to those treaties: judgment of 13 June 1979, Series A, No. 31, para. 41.

[88]   Kennedy, D (1975–76), 'Form and Substance in Private Law Adjudication', 89 *Harvard Law Review* 1685 at 1765.

[89]   *Tyrer v. UK*, Judgment of 25 April 1978, Series A, No. 26.

[90]   Letsas, *supra* n. 11 at 709.

[91]   This can be saliently seen in relation to the notion of obscenity, blasphemy, and the extent of equal rights between heterosexuals and homosexuals.

[92]   Letsas, *supra* n. 11 at 729.

9. VALUE-PLURALISM, HARMONISATION AND THE MARGIN OF APPRECIATION

The idea of value-pluralism suggests the plurality, conflict and incomparability (or incommensurability) of claims.[93] The ECHR's 'constitutional' edifice is value-pluralist rather than value-monist. This has been confirmed in a number of cases where the Court has highlighted the principle of pluralism, tolerance and broadmindedness.[94] Similarly, the Court has consistently stressed the closely intertwined nature of religious pluralism and democracy in the legal system of the ECHR.[95]

The attempt to establish European autonomous and harmonised standards may encounter obstacles stemming from manifestations of distinct cultural values. The Court may be required to clarify the meaning of indeterminate words such as the concept of public morals, or to make its '*Stellungnahme*' in relation to a highly sensitive and intractable issue, including priority to be given to one of the two competing rights. Discernible in such cases are two salient judicial methodologies: (i) the reliance on the margin of appreciation doctrine; (ii) the assertion that no conflict has actually arisen, with the Court sidestepping the sensitive question of a conflict of rights (the evasive or deflective tactic). In essence, the second approach is to narrow down the focus of analysis, and to deflect the focus of concern from the alleged conflict of rights by stating that this is not a central question.[96] It adroitly allows the Court to eschew altogether

---

[93]   Lucy, *supra* n. 49 at 234.

[94]   In the *Handyside* case, the Court stated that:

'Subject to paragraph 2 of Article 10, it [freedom of expression] is applicable not only to information or ideas that are favourably received or regarded as inoffensive or as a matter of indifference, but also to those that offend, shock or disturb the State or any sector of the population. Such are the demands of that pluralism, tolerance and broadmindedness without which there is no democratic society.'

The European Court of Human Rights, *Handyside v. UK*, Judgment of 7 December 1976, Series A, No. 24, para. 49. See also *Refah partisi (The Welfare Party) and Others v. Turkey*, Judgment of 13 February 2003 (Grand Chamber), para. 89; and *United Communist Party of Turkey and Others* v. Turkey, Judgment of 30 January 1998 (Grand Chamber), paras 42–3.

[95]   The European Court of Human Rights, *Refah partisi (The Welfare Party) and Others v. Turkey*, Judgment of 13 February 2003, para. 90. See also *Kokkinakis v. Greece*, judgment of 25 May 1993, Series A No. 260-A, para. 31; and *Buscarini and Others v. San Marino*, Judgment of 18 February 1999, para. 34.

[96]   See, for instance, the European Court of Human Rights, *Open Door Counselling and Dublin Well Woman v Ireland*, Judgment of 29 October 1992, Series A, No. 246, para. 66 (evading the sensitive question whether the ECHR guaranteed the right to abortion

the question which bundle of reasons is the weightiest in cases involving the choice of 'incommensurability'.[97] Yet, in terms of intellectual integrity, the Court could admit that value conflicts are insoluble because the values are simply incapable of or beyond comparison.[98] Further, in view of its *ad hoc* nature and specific context-dependency, the evasive technique can hardly be considered a *general* approach contributing to the formation of European-wide autonomous and harmonised standards.

In contrast, the Strasbourg Court may decisively assert its own value-choice for the purpose of accomplishing a specific public end indispensable for the ECHR legal order.[99] In so doing, the Court may not be inhibited by any element of arbitrariness or inefficiency associated with an uneven pattern of its decisions.[100] The Strasbourg judges may confidently claim that certain societal values are capable of 'reasoned elaboration' and worthy of attainment at the pan-European level.

The fourth constitutional dimension of the margin of appreciation analysed above corroborates the argument that law is 'a form of congealed politics',[101] the proposition that resonates even beyond the realm of critical legal studies. As Jackson notes, moral and political ideals are divisive and varying among states or along the civilizational fault lines.[102] In this light, it is crucial to contemplate the 'nuanced' application of the margin of appreciation, with its varying scope dependent on specific circumstance of different countries.[103]

---

or whether the scope of application of the right to life under Article 2 was broad enough to encompass a foetus, and focusing on the question of restrictions on imparting and receiving information on abortion facilities abroad under Article 10).

[97]   See Lucy's theory on adjudication in relation to value-pluralism: Lucy, *supra* n. 49 at 246.

[98]   This is what Lucy calls 'the incomparability claim': ibid., at 234. He considers the term incomparable as synonymous to the term 'incommensurable': ibid., at 235.

[99]   This can be most saliently seen in cases of discrimination and fundamental aspects of privacy. See, for instance, the European Court of Human Rights, *Marckx v. Belgium*, Judgment of 13 June 1979, Series A, No. 31 (children born out of wedlock); *Dudgeon v. UK*, Judgment of 22 October 1981, Series A, No. 45 (homosexuals); and *Christine Goodwin v. UK* (transsexuals), Judgment of 11 July 2002 (transsexuals).

[100]   For discussions on the role of judges in the domestic, common law context see Kennedy, *supra* n. 88 at 1765.

[101]   Asmal, K (2000), 'Truth Reconciliation and Justice: The South African Perspective', 63 *Modern Law Review* 1 at 15, n. 72.

[102]   Jackson, KT (1993), 'Global Rights and Regional Jurisprudence', 12 *Law and Philosophy* 157 at 158–9.

[103]   Shany, *supra* n. 20 at 914.

10. CONCLUSION

The margin of appreciation gives a semblance of objective authority to the international judges' decisions when they are, in fact, heavily charged with adjudicative subjectivity in discrete patterns. Subjectivity of the Court's decisions may be seen in the spectrum ranging from a robust and conscientious decision of value-choice, through deliberate reticence, to a highly restrained or sloppy approach.[104] This policy standard is context-sensitive and variable.[105]

The margin of appreciation doctrine may be considered an inevitable spin-off of the supranational judicial body's piecemeal but conscientious *law-making* process that is predicated on evaluations (a balance of reasons) of appropriate value-factors. Especially, the essence of the margin of appreciation doctrine is to finesse the confrontation of the two opposing, dynamic forces immanent in the value-laden decision-making policy of the Strasbourg Court: the harmonising or integrationist trend; and the centrifugal force pulling towards distinct local and regional values. In other words, the doctrine acts as an intermediary of those contrasting forces.

When elaborating the pluralist idea of distributive justice, Michael Walzer argues that social goods ought to be distributed for different reasons through varying procedures and by diverse agents. Such differences emanate from various understandings of the social goods themselves, which are 'the inevitable product of historical and cultural particularism'.[106] Each society has its own internal distributive arrangements, and is engaging itself in the ongoing process of developing and revising shared social meaning and cultural identity. Individual persons can obtain identity and wellbeing through their participation in this process, which can be dubbed a 'cultural project'.[107] This furnishes a cogent argument against cultural insensitivity and callosity. The Court should avoid hasting to carry out a top-down harmonisation in a manner that would run counter to a local community's shared consciousness and inveterate attachment to certain traditional values.[108] It is worth recalling Dworkin's caveat that 'the interpretive attitude cannot survive unless members of the same interpretive community share at least roughly the same assumptions about this [what counts

---

[104]   Arai-Takahashi, *supra* n. 17 at 206–30.
[105]   For discussions on this aspect of the notion of reasonableness see MacCormick, *supra* n. 2 at 164.
[106]   Walzer, M (1983), *Spheres of Justice – A Defence of Pluralism and Equality*, Basil Blackwell at 6.
[107]   Buchanan, A and Golove, D (2002), 'Philosophy of International Law' in Coleman, J and Shapiro, S (eds), *The Oxford Handbook of Jurisprudence and Philosophy of Law*, Oxford University Press 868 at 900.
[108]   Compare ibid., at 901.

as part of the practice]'.[109] The dislocation of harmonised European standards of human rights from the majority views in a national or local community may lead to alienating the Court from such municipal or regional authorities, jeopardizing the enforcement of its decisions (for instance, delay in the necessary reforms of national laws etc.). Viewed against such a backdrop, the margin of appreciation can be rationalized as a viable policy standard that enables the Court to engage in an incremental, consciousness-building process in the direction of harmonising human rights standards in Europe.[110]

It ought to be noted that the rationales for applying the margin of appreciation are not limited to the context of harmonising standards of international human rights law across the member states of the Council of Europe. Indeed, even after the integration of the former communist states into the Convention's *acquis* is accomplished, the margin of appreciation is likely to come into play. This is because the Strasbourg Court is obliged to furnish a reasoned judgment (rather than a one-off flash of intuitions) that can rationalize particular outcomes of weighing the rights of individual persons against public goods essential to the Convention's 'constitutional' order.[111] The weight of the Strasbourg Court's authoritatively reasoned responses in concrete cases gives a common metric that makes intelligible how the Court's balancing works in tandem with the varying scope of margin of appreciation.

---

[109]   Dworkin, *supra* n. 81 at 67. He also adds that it is impossible to determine how much difference is excessive with regard to the degree of disparity in the convictions about fit among the citizens): ibid.

[110]   In this respect see the dialectic discourse proposed by Philip Allott. At the time of integration of nation states, he stresses the importance of recognizing a dynamic and value-laden process of consciousness-formation: Allott, P (1990), *Eunomia – New Order for a New World*, Oxford University Press.

[111]   This approximates to what Letsas describes as the 'substantive concept of margin of appreciation': Letsas, *supra* n. at 709. In the *Refah partisi* case, the Strasbourg Court affirmed that '[p]luralism and democracy are based on a compromise that requires various concessions by individuals or groups of individuals, who must sometimes agree to limit some of the freedoms they enjoy in order to guarantee greater stability of the country as a whole': The European Court of Human Rights, *Refah partisi (The Welfare Party) and Others v. Turkey*, Judgment of 13 February 2003, para. 99.

6. The draft academic common frame of reference and the 'toolbox'*[1]

Hugh Beale[2]

In October 2009 the Draft Common Frame of Reference[3] (DCFR) was published. This was prepared as part of the European Commission's Action Plan on European Contract Law.[4] A much shorter 'Outline Edition' had been published in February 2009. In this chapter I comment on the form, coverage, structure and language of the DCFR. I aim to explain that in part the characteristics are the result of the way in which it has been produced, drawing on earlier drafts, but I will argue that with the adaptations that have been made, the DCFR is appropriate for its intended purposes as a 'toolbox'.

THE FORM OF THE DCFR

The shorter book is described as 'Outline' because, for the most part, the work contains only one element of the full academic CFR: that is, the series of articles or model rules, together with a list of definitions. The full version also contains an extensive commentary and comparative notes.

---

* Editor's note: This contribution has been affected by rapid developments in the field, see the Preface on p. xi for details.
[1] This chapter draws on earlier published papers: Beale, H (2007), 'The Purposes of a Common Frame of Reference', 1 *Internationaler Rechtsverkehr* 25–30 and Beale, H (2007), 'The Structure and the Legal Values of the CFR' in 3 *ERCL* 257, 269–72.
[2] Professor of Law, University of Warwick. I was a member of the Commission on European Contract law 1987–2000, a member of the Co-ordinating Committee of the Study Group on a European Civil Code and a member of the Compilation and Redaction Team of the Network of Excellence. The views expressed here are purely personal. Contact address: Hugh.Beale@warwick.ac.uk
[3] Von Bar, C, Clive, E and Schulte-Nölke, H (eds) (2009), *Principles, Definitions and Model Rules of European Private Law, Draft Common Frame of Reference*, (Sellier).
[4] See *Action Plan on A More Coherent European Contract Law*, COM(2003)final, OJ C 63/1 and *European Contract Law and the revision of the acquis: the way forward*, COM(2004)651 final, 11 October 2004 (referred to below as WF).

The Outline Edition also contains an Introduction to the underlying principles. I will return to this later.

In part, the form of the Academic DCFR is the result of its origins. In the European Commission's *Action Plan* it made it clear that to produce the CFR, it would draw on existing research projects. They encouraged many of the existing groups working on European contract law, and particularly those which were drafting 'restatements' of common principles, to form themselves into a joint network and apply to be funded by a grant from a different Directorate General under the Sixth Framework Programme. This Programme listed European contract law as one of its priority areas.

Of the groups who were drafting principles, the Study Group on the European Civil Code (SGECC), the Insurance Group and the Acquis Group joined the network. In addition there were a number of 'evaluative' groups. For example, the group dealing with economic analysis did, as its name suggests, while the *Association Henri Capitant* and the *Société de Législation Comparée* considered questions of terminology[5] and also the philosophy underlying PECL.[6] There were also two supporting groups which provide a database[7] and conferences.[8]

The SGECC is in many ways the successor to the (Lando) Commission on European Contract Law, which produced the Principles of European Contract Law (PECL).[9] The work of the SGECC was intended to build on PECL, and nearly all the volumes which the SGECC produced independently of the CFR project[10] treated their rules as subject to (or supplements to) PECL, just as PECL form the basis of Books II and III of the DCFR. Since PECL contain articles, comments and notes, so do the books produced by the SGECC, and so it comes as no surprise that this is also to be the form of the full version of the DCFR.

However, the CFR is not in the same form as PECL and the SGECC's books just because that was the form of the existing work. The form also reflects the functions of the CFR as a legislator's guide or 'toolbox' as set out in the Commission's various documents on the Action Plan.

---

[5]   See *Terminologie Contractuelle Commune*, Droit Privé Comparé et Européen, vol 6 (2008).

[6]   See *Principes Contractuels Communs*, Droit Privé Comparé et Européen, vol 7 (2008), Titre I ('principes directeurs'). For an English version of the two works see Association Henri Capitant and Société de législation comparée (ed) (2008), *European Contract Law: Materials for a Common Frame of Reference: Terminology, Guiding Principles, Model Rules*, Sellier.

[7]   The Database Group of the Institut Charles Dumoulin.

[8]   The Academy of European Law (ERA) in Trier.

[9]   See Lando, O and Beale, H (eds) (2000), *Principles of European Contract Law, Parts I and II*, Kluwer; Lando, O, Clive, E, Prüm, A and Zimmermann, R (eds) (2003), *Principles of European Contract Law Part III*, Kluwer.

[10]   See the series of volumes on Principles of European Law (PEL) published by Sellier.

The *Way Forward* document stated that the CFR would set out

1. common fundamental principles of contract law, including guidance on when exceptions to such fundamental principles could be required;
2. definitions of key concepts; and
3. model rules, which would form the bulk of the CFR.[11]

It is not clear that the Commission thought that the three elements were different from each other. It may be that it intended the phrase 'principles, definitions and model rules' as a composite notion covering whatever the ultimate document was to contain. However, I believe that the three elements are directly related to different functions of the 'toolbox'. I will argue that the CFR needs to provide definitions, model rules and fundamental principles. I will argue that it should also give the legislator what I call 'essential background information'. To perform these functions, the DCFR must contain all three elements: Articles, Comments and Notes.

Articles

The CFR most obviously contains a series of articles. These provide definitions and model rules. (I will leave the question of fundamental principles to discuss later.)

Definitions

We are all aware of the problem that directives often refer to legal concepts and institutions without defining them. There would be no problem if the word used or the concept referred to meant the same thing in every legal system, but frequently it does not. The classic example, referred to in the Commission's papers, is the *Simone Leitner* case.[12] The ECJ had to decide whether the damages to which a consumer was entitled under the provisions of the Package Travel Directive must include compensation for non-pecuniary loss suffered when the holiday was not as promised. This head of damage is recognised by many national laws but was not recognised by Austrian law. The ECJ held that 'damage' in the Directive must be given an autonomous, 'European', legal meaning – and in this context 'damage' is to be interpreted as including non-pecuniary loss. Another example, also mentioned in the Commission's documents, is 'the conclusion of a contract'.

---

[11]   WF, para. 3.1.3, p. 11.
[12]   Case C–168/00 *Simone Leitner v. TUI Deutschland* [2002] ECR I–2631.

So a CFR which contained a set of agreed definitions would be useful for questions of interpretation of European legislation, particularly if the definitions were adopted explicitly by the European institutions as a guideline for legislative drafting. It could then be presumed that the word or concept contained in a directive was used in the sense in which it is used in the CFR unless the directive or regulation stated otherwise. (This could be achieved by an inter-institutional agreement or simply by stating in the recitals to a directive that it should be interpreted in accordance with the CFR.) The legislators could then employ the words and concepts contained in the CFR with confidence that the meaning would be clear, without it having to be defined in the directive. Alternatively, if the legislators so chose, they could vary or exclude the 'CFR meaning' by particular provisions in the legislation. National legislators seeking to implement the directive and national courts would be able to consult the CFR to see what was meant.

Thus the draft CFR contains an Annex of definitions, covering words and phrases used throughout the CFR, where it is possible to produce a short definition. But it is not always possible to produce a concise definition. For example, I do not know how it is possible to define 'when a contract is concluded' other than by a series of rules – principally, the rules on offer and acceptance to be found in Book II. In this sense, there is no clear distinction between definitions and model rules.

Model rules

The CFR needs to contain model rules in another sense, however. The Commission has reviewed a number of consumer directives, and a new Consumer Rights Directive has been adopted.[13] One change is from 'minimum harmonisation' to 'full harmonisation'. Minimum harmonisation provisions are thought to have hindered achievement of the aim of eliminating internal market barriers caused by differences between the laws of the Member States.[14] But the review is also concerned with the coherence and substance of the consumer *acquis*.

When directives are to be revised, the Commission will find it useful to have 'model' rules which it can use or adapt to replace the existing articles of the various directives. The CFR may contain model rules that are more coherent than the existing *acquis*, for example dealing with rights of withdrawal in a more uniform manner. It may show how principles that underlie the various sectoral provisions can be given a wider application, so as to eliminate current gaps and overlaps. This would be a more 'horizontal approach'.

---

[13]   Directive on Consumer Rights, 2011/83/EU of 25 October 2011.
[14]   WF, para. 2.1.1, p 3; and see Schulte-Nölke, H, Twigg-Flesner, C and Ebers, M (eds) (2008), *EC Consumer Law Compendium*, Sellier.

In addition, the *Action Plan* seems to envisage that the proposed rules in the CFR should go beyond the existing consumer *acquis*, either in terms of sectors that are not yet harmonised (insurance contracts are one example mentioned) or simply in terms of giving consumers stronger protection than they have under the current directives. The CFR may include what the authors of the CFR think are (and I quote the *Way Forward* document) the 'best solutions' found in Member States' legal orders.[15] This might well reflect what is to be found in those Member States that give consumers more than the minimum protection required by current directives.

Thus the CFR should contain 'model rules' that are essentially first proposals for future EC directives.[16] I say 'first proposals' because the researchers are not legislators; they have no democratic mandate. But it is perfectly proper for them to put forward what they consider to be the 'best solutions' for consideration by the Commission and the other EU institutions.

In 2010 the Commission issued a consultation paper[17] which, among other options, suggested that the CFR should be used as the basis for a different kind of instrument, the 'Optional Instrument' also mentioned in the Commission's document. Clearly an optional instrument, if it is to provide a set of rules to govern the parties' contractual relations in place of a national law, would require a full set of rules dealing with all issues within the scope of application of the Optional Instrument. The Commission has since proposed a Regulation on a Common European Sales Law[18] to cover cross-border sales both between businesses and between businesses and consumers. It includes not only specific provisions on sales but also the relevant parts of general contract law.[19] Unfortunately, space does not permit a discussion of this development here.

It will be seen that a particular article of the 'toolbox' CFR may function as either a definition or a model rule, depending on what the legislator wishes to do. Suppose it were decided to clarify the consumer's right to damages under the Package Travel Directive,[20] or to introduce a right to damages under a revised

---

[15]   'The research preparing the CFR will aim to identify best solutions, taking into account national contract laws (both case law and established practice), the EC *acquis* and relevant international instruments, particularly the UN Convention on Contracts for the International Sale of Goods of 1980': WF, para. 3.1.3.

[16]   See Outline Edition Introduction, para. 63.

[17]   Green Paper from the Commission on policy options for progress towards a European Contract Law for consumers and businesses, Brussels, 1 July 2010, COM(2010)348 final.

[18]   11 October 2011, COM(2011)635 final.

[19]   The CESL is based on a *Feasibility Study on a European Contract law for consumers and business* prepared by an Expert Group (May 2011).

[20]   90/314/EEC of 13 June 1990.

Directive on Consumer Sales.[21] The legislator might decide simply to provide that the consumer should have a right to damages, stating that 'damages' is to be interpreted as meaning damages in the sense provided for in the CFR. Then the CFR would be providing a definition. Alternatively it might be decided to include detailed rules on damages in the Directive. In that case the CFR would provide model rules which the legislator could adopt, either as they stand or with changes.[22]

Comments

Whether the CFR is providing definitions or model rules, the Comments are an essential element. It is very helpful to the reader to have an explanation of how the various articles fit together, preferably with examples. But the Comments are even more important for a different reason. The provisions of the CFR have been developed on the basis of a detailed comparative study of the national laws or, in the case of many of the consumer provisions, the national laws and the existing *acquis*. Sometimes the articles represent a rule which is found in all Member States, albeit couched in different terminology or using different concepts. In other cases, however, they do not. Rather they represent what the researchers consider to be the 'best solution' found in the national orders or, perhaps, in international instruments or other legal sources. It is imperative that the Comments explain which, for each article, is the case. Further, if the article represents the 'best solution', the Comments must explain that the researchers have made a choice and *why* they consider rule X to be better than the alternatives. Otherwise the CFR might be misleading and the researchers might justly be accused of silently assuming the task of the legislator. To put it simply, the Comments must flag up any policy choices made.[23]

Notes

Sources
The Notes are also an essential part of the CFR. First, good academic practice demands that researchers indicate, at least briefly, the sources on which they have relied. This is so even if the different laws reach pretty much the same result. It is even more important if the researchers have adopted one solution

---

[21]   1999/44/EC of 25 May 1999.

[22]   The Commission's proposed Consumer Rights Directive (COM(2008)614, 8 October 2008) contained a provision for the consumer to recover damages for non-conformity (art 27(2)), but this provision was dropped from the final CRD.

[23]   See *First Annual Progress Report on European Contract Law and the Acquis Review*, COM(2005)456 final, p 5.

out of several as the 'best solution'. But I think the legislator needs to be given
the comparative information for another reason which is not mentioned as such
in the Commission documents but which is of considerable practical importance. This to provide the legislator, and those preparing draft legislation, with
what I term 'essential background information' about the laws of the different
Member States.

'Essential background information'

European legislators need to know what is a problem in terms of national laws
and what is not. Let me take an example, the question of the duty to disclose
information before a contract is made. If every Member State already had a
rule that a party must disclose to the other any information that is reasonably
necessary in order for the other to make an informed decision about whether
to contract, then European legislation on pre-contract disclosure in consumer
contracts might not be needed. The fact is that very few Member States have
such principles, except as the result of the consumer *acquis*. Conversely, there is
probably no need to legislate on remedies for fraudulent misrepresentation, since
(in one form or another) all Member States seem to provide broadly comparable
remedies. This is all essential background which legislators must have in order
to decide what European legislation is needed.

Moreover, if the CFR were not to include comparative information, the CFR
would itself cause a real problem. This problem is that where the CFR includes
definitions or 'model rules' that do not represent the outcome in every Member
State, the legislator must be told this – or the legislator's guide may be danger-
ously misleading. Let us take as an example the principle of good faith. The
principle of good faith is not known in the laws of all the Member States – in
particular, it is not known in the common law jurisdictions. It is true that even
the common law systems contain many particular rules that seem to be functionally equivalent to good faith, in the sense that they are aimed at requiring
the parties to act in good faith,[24] but there is no *general* rule. So the legislator
cannot assume that whatever requirements it chooses to impose on consumer
contracts in order to protect consumers will, in each Member State, be supplemented by a general requirement that the parties act in good faith. If it wants
a general requirement to apply in the particular context, even in the common
law jurisdictions, the legislator will have to incorporate the requirement into
the directive in express words – as of course it did with the Directive on Unfair
Terms in Consumer Contracts.[25] Alternatively, it will need to insert into the
directive specific provisions to achieve the results in the common law systems

---

[24]   See the Notes to PECL Art. 1:201.
[25]   Council Directive 93/13/EEC, Art. 3(1).

that in other jurisdictions would be reached by the application of the principle of good faith.

In other words, simply to include in the CFR principles that do not reflect the law in every Member State would by itself be highly misleading. To get an accurate picture, the legislator needs to have information about the different laws in the various Member States.

Providing the essential background information is the function of the comparative notes which will be included in the final version of the draft CFR. The Notes are essential.

COVERAGE OF THE DCFR

The range of subjects covered by the DCFR is very broad, and also in part related to the way in which the DCFR was produced. The list of contents shows that in addition to the General Provisions of Book I, Book II on Contracts and Book III on Obligations and Corresponding Rights, there are Books on seven specific types of contracts:

Sales
Leases
Services
Mandate
Long-term contracts (commercial agency, franchise and distributorship)
Loans
Personal security

Further Books deal with non-contractual obligations: Benevolent Intervention in Another's Affairs, Non-contractual Liability arising out of Damage to Another (tort) and Unjust Enrichment. Lastly, three books deal with proprietary issues: Acquisition and Loss of Ownership of Goods, Proprietary Security Rights in Moveable Assets and Trusts.

It has often been asked why all this material is included in the DCFR when there is no likelihood of European legislation in these areas. There are two simple answers.

The first is that the DCFR represents what the academics were working on and which, when the researchers applied for a research grant, the FP6 Programme agreed to fund. It is thus the 'academic' CFR. We all recognise that any final, 'political' CFR may be narrower.

The second is, however, that if the DCFR is to fulfil its 'toolbox' functions of providing definitions of terms referred to in European legislation, and of providing 'essential background information', it needs to include a large amount of this material. Why? Because while the EU may not seek to legislate directly in these fields, it is frequently the case that even existing directives use words and concepts from these fields.

Moreover, directives often leave matters that fall within these topics to be governed by national law – apparently assuming that the national laws already cover them in a sufficiently harmonised way. For example, the Consumer Sales Directive leaves the consumer's entitlement to damages to Member States' laws. The legislator needs to know what the law on these topics is in the various Member States, and to know the meaning that the law of each Member State gives to any terms of concepts the Directive might employ. They also need to have explained how definitions and rules from one topic relate to more general rules or to rules found in another topic. The scheme should include definitions, terminology and concepts that are coherent across the whole range of the law of obligations.

Let me take some topics by way of example.

Consumer Contract Legislation

Definitions and model rules for consumer law clearly must be included if the CFR is to be helpful for a review of the existing *acquis*. PECL had deliberately avoided dealing with consumer contracts. It merely incorporated some principles from directives – for example, the rules on unfair terms in PECL article 4:110 were taken from the directive – but applied them to all contracts. Some of the Study Group Teams necessarily took into account sector-specific regulations (such as the Directive on Sale of Consumer Goods) but no one in the Study Group was working on more general requirements such as Distance Selling.[26] Fortunately the Acquis Group were well able to fill this gap.

General Contract Law

Annex I to the Commission's *Way Forward* document made it clear that at the core of the CFR should be definitions and model rules of general contract law – the Annex reads like a list of the contents of PECL Books I and II and parts of Book III. This is not because the CFR is meant to be a toolbox with which to harmonise general contract law. Nor is it, I think, because ultimately the CFR may be used as the basis for an Optional Instrument, which would presumably need to include general principles of contract law. Rather, it is because it is precisely the terms and concepts of general contract law – concepts such as 'damages' or 'the conclusion of the contract' – which so frequently are used in directives without being defined.

---

[26] See Directive 97/7/EC.

Specific Contracts

Some of the Books on specific contracts are needed simply because these are topics which are covered by the existing *acquis* (sales, commercial agency and to some extent loans and personal security) or which may well be tackled in the future (leases, services). True, the existing *acquis* touches only consumer sales, but consumer sales contracts are governed by general sales concepts which are mentioned in the directive without being defined, such as risk and delivery. Books on other specific contracts may equally be useful to provide definitions, or at least may be useful to provide background information (e.g. mandate, which is largely just the internal relationship between principal and agent).

Unjust Enrichment

The existing *acquis* already assumes the existence of rules on unjust enrichment. Questions of unjust enrichment may arise when a consumer withdraws from a distance contract after having used the goods for a period. The CFR should provide information about this field, and possibly definitions or even model rules.

Tort

I would argue that the same is true for tort law. Not only is the Product Liability Directive clearly concerned with tort, but remedies relating to the formation of contracts, like fraud and misrepresentation, are in many systems tortious in nature.

THE STRUCTURE OF THE DCFR

The deliberate choice to create a DCFR of such width has meant some changes in approach. PECL Books I and II dealt only with general contract law. Incorporating not only consumer contracts and specific contracts but also tort and unjust enrichment has led to a number of problems. These have had to be tackled by the Compilation and Redaction team, very ably led by Professor Dr (h.c.) Eric Clive.

First, PECL did not even have any detailed provisions on other kinds of juridical act often associated with contracts. The term juridical act is not one that is familiar to most English lawyers, but in fact we have them without recognising them. Giving a contractual notice e.g. of avoidance or termination, alters the legal position of the parties, but it is not itself a contract: it is a unilateral juridical act. So is the delivery of a deed or the notification to a seller of an irrevocable credit in its favour. Under PECL and the DCFR there are more examples still:

for example, they recognise that an offer that is to be kept open for a period of time is binding in the sense that it cannot be revoked.

PECL treated these in a rather causal manner. PECL merely recognised that a promise which is intended to be legally binding without acceptance is binding[27] and then provided:

Article 1:107: Application of the Principles by Way of Analogy
These Principles apply with appropriate modifications to agreements to modify or end a contract, to unilateral promises and to other statements and conduct indicating intention.

In practice this is not very helpful. Unilateral acts such as contractual notices frequently give rise to problems, for example as to how they should be interpreted. It is not quite clear how the rules for interpretation of contracts should be applied to them. Particularly in a guide for legislators it seems important to give a full explanation of how they work. So juridical acts that are not agreements have been treated in rather more detail in the DCFR.

Secondly, PECL Book III provided rules which can be applied not only to contractual obligations but to obligations of all kinds – assignment, set-off, prescription, etc. Were these meant to apply to non-contractual obligations also? And if they were, what about the rules on obligations in Books I and II? These were drafted in terms of contracts only, but the underlying principles seemed to be more general.

So the DCFR has taken a different structure. Book II deals with the creation of obligations created by contracts and then, in a separate section, with other juridical acts. The Book goes on to covers issues such as formation, validity, interpretation and contents and effects, where necessary giving separate rules for contracts and other juridical acts.[28] Book III is wider. Its rules apply, by and large, to the performance and non-performance of obligations of all kinds.

This has meant that the DCFR has become more complicated than PECL were. In particular there are a number of provisions that have to be applied to more than just contracts. There was some debate over this. Was it better to state generally applicable provisions just once; or would it be better to state them each time they were relevant; or should they be stated just for contracts and then made applicable 'with appropriate adaptations' to other contexts? It was ultimately decided to state them just once. That does mean that the reader may have to consult a number of different books to find the answer to his/her enquiry. But we are all used to that. It is not much different from consulting Volume I of *Chitty on Contracts* even though you are dealing with a specific type of contract that is covered in Volume II.

---

[27] Art. 2:107.
[28] E.g. Arts II-8:201 and II-8:202.

THE LANGUAGE OF THE DCFR

This has necessitated some change in terminology. For instance, whereas PECL Article 7:101 governed the place of performance of 'contractual obligations', its replacement, DCFR III-2:101, applies to the place of performance of any obligation.

Some changes have been made even where the rules apply only to contracts, for example the rules on termination. This is because of the intended audience. PECL was drafted in simple language, aiming to be understandable to business people without legal qualifications. For example, it used the word 'contract' in two different senses. When it spoke of formation of a contract it mean contract in the sense of agreement. But it also spoke of 'termination of a contract':

Article 9:301: Right to Terminate the Contract
(1)   A party may terminate the contract if the other party's non-performance is fundamental.

Here it meant not termination of the agreement but termination of the contractual relationship or of the contractual obligation.

This seems understandable but it is not wholly accurate and can in fact lead to misunderstanding. After some discussion it was decided that if the DCFR is to be a good guide to legislative drafting, it may need to be more precise, more scientifically accurate. So the DCFR provides:

III. – 3:502: Termination for fundamental non-performance
(1)   A creditor may terminate if the debtor's non-performance of a contractual obligation is fundamental....

III. – 3:509: Effect on obligations under the contract
(1)   On termination under this Section, the outstanding obligations or relevant part of the outstanding obligations of the parties under the contract come to an end...

Some of us may regret that the DCFR is less readily understandable by the layperson than was PECL, but we accept that in this case scientific accuracy is more important.

'FUNDAMENTAL PRINCIPLES' IN THE DCFR

The Way Forward called for the DCFR to include 'fundamental principles'. It is less clear what these would be. In one sense, all the provisions of the DCFR are 'principles', and it may be that the Commission used 'principles' and 'model rules' simply to mean the same thing. Or possibly it had in mind the more general articles, such as the presumption of freedom of contract (i.e. that unless stated otherwise the parties should be free to agree the terms of their contract, so that the rules of the DCFR are mainly 'default rules' only), or the requirement of good faith (if one is to be included!).

However there is a third possibility. This would give a different meaning to 'fundamental principles' and treat them as serving a different purpose. On this approach, 'principles' might mean not a series of rules but a statement of the notions that underlie the DCFR, or of the policy considerations that the legislator should bear in mind when deciding whether or not European legislation is needed and what form it should take. It might be useful to begin the DCFR with a short summary of its underlying assumptions (such as that freedom of contract is the starting point, and of the other values the law seeks to protect) – and with reminders to the legislator, for example that values like freedom of contract should be qualified (for example, by adopting mandatory rules for consumer protection) only when the case for such protection has been clearly made out.

In the Introduction to the Interim Outline Edition,[29] we gave a sample of what such an Introduction might look like. The purpose of doing this was to ask readers whether they thought such a statement would be useful. Such feedback as we received led us to work on a fuller statement for the final version of the DCFR.

The *Association Henri Capitant* has very helpfully provided an evaluation of the guiding principles, *les principes directeurs*, which they believe underlie PECL.[30] These are in the form of a series of articles. We debated whether to incorporate these articles into the DCFR as an initial statement of aims, as opposed to the definitions and model rules which form the bulk of the DCFR. After much debate we have decided not to take this approach, for two basic reasons. First, the *principes directeurs* are in fact only a partial statement – being based on an analysis of PECL, they do not take into account the rules of consumer protection built into the DCFR, let alone the books dealing with special contracts or non-contractual obligations. Secondly, we found it very difficult to formulate an adequate set of aims in the form of a series of articles. Many of the aims that underlie a legal system conflict with each other. Thus freedom of contract and protection of the weaker party are both aims within the DCFR, but they point in opposite directions. What the legislator needs is not just to be told that there are these two aims, but to have some suggestions as to how to strike an appropriate balance between the two. We found it very difficult to express this in terms of articles. A discursive essay is easier to write and understand, and this is the approach adopted in the DCFR.

---

[29]   The Outline Edition of the DCFR was published in an 'interim' Edition in 2008 (Sellier).

[30]   See note 6 above.

CONCLUSION

I hope I have shown how the form, the coverage, the structure and the language of the DCFR are directly related to what we understand to be its functions as a 'toolbox' for the European legislator. However, it has not always been easy to be sure just what it is that the Commission wants, or to decide what would be useful. The feedback we have received suggests that the general form of the DCFR is at least reasonably fit for purpose. We will have to wait to see what use the European institutions make of it.

7.   *Francovich* liability for breach of European *Union* law

Gerrit Betlem*

UN PEU D'HISTOIRE

After a brief historical introduction, this chapter will argue the case for extending the liability of the European Community and its Member States for breach of *Community* law to breach of European *Union* law. A number of developments and analogies will be explored – liability for lawful acts, liability of EFTA Member States for breach of EEA law – and their potential as building blocks for the recognition of such an extended EU liability regime will be assessed. Then there is an examination of the current unavailability of direct damages claims before the Community Courts laid down in Articles 35 and 41 TEU and confirmed by the CFI and ECJ in the *Gestoras* and *Segi* judgments, as well as the overhaul of this position by the Treaty of Lisbon and the potential relevance of the EU Charter of Fundamental Rights.

The rules governing non-contractual liability of Member States of the European Union may be divided in chronological terms into before and after 1991, the year the ECJ handed down one of its most seminal cases: *Francovich*.[1] Before that case, the availability of damages claims against Member States where they were in breach of Community law was discussed in the literature and considered indirectly in the Court's case law e.g. in the context of infringement actions.[2] For many years, it was unclear what legal system should decide not only the actual liability requirements but even whether there should be

---

*   Formerly of University of Southampton, UK (Deceased). This article builds on Betlem, G (2007), 'Beyond *Francovich*: Completing the Unified Member State and EU Liability Regime. A Comment on the Jan Jans Contribution' in Obradovic, D and Lavranos, N (eds) (2007), *Interface between EU Law and National Law*, Europa Law Publishing at 299.

[1]   Cases C–6/90 and 9/90 *Francovich and Bonifaci v. Italy* [1991] I–ECR 5357; [1993] 2 CMLR 66. See the Website '*Francovich* Follow-Up' by Granger et al., available at: www.francovich.eu.

[2]   Arnull, A (2006), *The European Union and its Court of Justice* (2nd ed), OUP at 274.

liability at all;[3] however, it would seem that the Court insisted that liability should exist, but in the absence of any clear pronouncement that Community law should govern such claims it was a matter for national law to provide this remedy. Such an approach was of course entirely consistent with the complete lack of any textual anchor for state liability in the Treaties – Article 288 EC refers to liability of the Community only whereas there is no reference to any liability at all in the EU Treaty – and the well-established principle of national procedural autonomy. However, as noted, this changed in 1991 when the ECJ created a partly autonomous remedy in the cited *Francovich* judgment by defining certain key aspects of a damages claim as a matter of Community law.[4] This chapter is not focusing on the *Francovich* ruling and its aftermath as such; standard textbooks on EU law and the vast literature commenting on the case are covering that ground. Suffice it here to highlight a few key developments as a stepping stone for considering the possibility of extending the well-established rules from the Community pillar to the other pillars making up EU law since the Maastricht Treaty.

There have now been some 20 years of post-*Francovich* jurisprudence about the possibility of Member State liability for breach of Community law. Perhaps the most significant development is the alignment of the liability requirements for both state and Community liability into a single overarching framework. As most cases concern liability for legislative acts, a key factor in setting the benchmark for liability to be triggered is the level of discretion the public authority in question has been granted.[5] The result is a system of a sliding scale of liability with a form of strict liability, i.e. the mere breach of a norm of EC law suffices to establish liability, linked to a situation where there is no or very little discretion,[6] to a very high liability threshold in situations of wide discretion and limited obligations imposed on the relevant authority.[7]

The next section revisits *Francovich* itself to consider not the liability requirements claimants must satisfy to trigger the state's or the Community's liability

---

[3]   Ibid., at 275.

[4]   Ibid., at 295 and 308; Craig, P and De Búrca, G (2008), *EU Law. Text, Cases and Materials* (4th ed), OUP at Chapter 9.

[5]   See Hilson, C (2005), 'The role of discretion in EC non-contractual liability', 42 *Common Market Law Review* 677; the leading cases include Joined Cases C–46/93 and 48/93 *Brasserie du Pêcheur and Factortame III* [1996] ECR I–1029, [1997] 1 CMLR 971 and Case C–352/98 P *Bergaderm* [2000] ECR I–5291.

[6]   See in particular Case C–5/94 *Hedley Lomas* [1996] ECR I–2553, [1996] 2 CMLR 391 and Joined Cases C–178, 179 & 188-90/94 *Dillenkofer* [1996] ECR I–4845, [1996] 3 CMLR 469.

[7]   Key cases concern the liability of the European Ombudsman: Case C–234/02 P *Médiateur Européen v. Lamberts* [2004] ECR I–2803 and state liability for breach of EC law by the highest courts: Case C–224/01 *Köbler* [2003] ECR I–10239, [2003] 3 CMLR 28.

in damages, but the grounds on which the ECJ founded the since then to be called *Francovich* liability as a matter of Community law.

LEGAL BASES OF *FRANCOVICH*

The Court refers to two links with the EC Treaty to anchor state liability into the system and to provide a legal basis for the existence of state liability as a matter of Community law. In my view, the dominant factor founding EC Member State liability for breach of Community law is the principle of effectiveness rather than the notion of loyal cooperation of Article 10 EC. In paragraph 31–4 of *Francovich*, the ECJ only talks about the need for effective protection of individual rights, culminating in the conclusion ('it follows'; paragraph 35) that there is such a thing as the EC law principle of state liability. The Court could have left it at that, namely the announcement of the Community law basis for state liability. Almost as an afterthought did it then refer to the duty of loyal cooperation (currently Article 10 EC) in paragraph 36: '[a] further basis for ...'. Indeed, I agree with Ross who analyses the ruling in no uncertain terms: '[the Court] invoked effectiveness as a rationale for the invention of [a] new EC law principle. ... Here the effectiveness of the Treaty as a whole was presented as a justification for a novel principle that patently had no textual anchor in the Treaty. The demands of effectiveness transmuted an absent requirement into an inherent one'.[8]

Note in particular that the principle of state liability is inherent in the Treaty. In fact, this particular passage of *Francovich* remains of great importance even after 17 years of post-*Francovich* case law, which has now made redundant some parts of the original *Francovich* ruling. The specific liability requirements for the specific breach in question (non-transposition of a directive) have been replaced with the *Brasserie du Pêcheur* requirements of conferment of rights, sufficiently serious breach and direct causal link,[9] which apply to all breaches of Community law. What the Court calls the principle of state liability is quite simply the core rule of any non-contractual liability regime – such as those laid down in Civil Codes[10] – while leaving it for subsequent decision making

---

[8]   Ross, M (2006), 'Effectiveness in the European Legal Order(s): Beyond Supremacy to Constitutional Proportionality', 31 *European Law Review* 476 at 481.

[9]   Joined Cases C–46 and 48/93 *Brasserie du Pêcheur & Factortame III* [1996] ECR I–1029, [1996] 1 CMLR 889 at para. 51.

[10]   Para. 35 of *Francovich* is very similar to Dutch and French tort law as laid down in Art. 6:162(1) *Burgerlijk Wetboek* (Dutch Civil code): '1. A person who commits an unlawful act toward another which can be imputed to him, must repair the damage which the other person suffers as a consequence thereof', and the *Code Civil*: Art. 1382:'Any

which specific liability requirements apply to various situations. The concept of 'inherent in the Treaty' is particularly fertile for the further development of state liability both under EC law and beyond the EC Treaty.

LIABILITY OF THE EC IN THE ABSENCE OF UNLAWFULNESS

Regarding Community law, since *Bergaderm*,[11] the merger of the formerly separate regimes for state and EC law has now been firmly established in the case law of the ECJ and the CFI.[12] It follows that any new law accepted under one line of liability will also be available under the other. A striking consequence must therefore be that state liability for lawful acts – where the state is acting within the scope of Community law – now applies because the CFI has recognised the existence of this principle in the context of liability of the Community under Article 288(2) EC.[13] The CFI ruled as follows:

157   Where, as in the present case, it has *not been established* that conduct attributed to the Community institutions is *unlawful*, that does *not* mean that undertakings which, as a category of economic operators, are required to *bear a disproportionate part* of the burden resulting from a restriction of access to export markets can in no circumstances obtain compensation by virtue of the Community's non-contractual liability ...

158   The second paragraph of Article 288 EC bases the obligation which it imposes on the Community to make good any damage caused by its institutions on the 'general principles common to the laws of the Member States' and therefore *does not restrict* the ambit of those principles solely to the rules governing non-contractual Community liability for *un*lawful conduct of those institutions ...

160   When damage is caused by conduct of the Community institution not shown to be unlawful, the Community can incur non-contractual liability if the conditions as to sustaining actual damage, to the causal link between that damage and the conduct of the Community institution and to the *unusual* and *special* nature of the damage in question are all met ...

202   In the case of damage which economic operators may sustain as a result of the activities of the Community institutions, damage is, first, *unusual* when it exceeds the

---

act whatever of man, which causes damage to another, obliges the one by whose fault it occurred, to compensate it', available in English at: www.legifrance.gouv.fr.

[11]   Case C–352/98 P *Bergaderm* [2000] ECR I–5291.
[12]   See generally Arnull, A, *et al.* (2006), *Wyatt and Dashwood's European Union Law* (5th ed), Sweet & Maxwell at 490.
[13]   See Cases T–96/00 *FIAMM* and T–383/00 *Beamglow* [2005] ECR II–5393 and II–5459, [2006] 2 CMLR 9 and 10.

limits of the economic risks inherent in operating in the sector concerned and, second, *special* when it affects a particular circle of economic operators in a disproportionate manner by comparison with other operators ...

The requirements for this liability are distinct from those for liability for unlawful act; they may be summarised as follows:

1. actual damage;
2. causal link between the damage and the conduct of the defendant
3. this damage must also be both *unusual* and *special*:
    a) unusual damage goes beyond the limits of the normal (entrepreneurial) economic risks inherent in operating in the sector concerned, and
    b) special damage is a disproportionate impact on a particular circle of economic operators in comparison with the other operators.

This chapter is not the place to explore fully how this ruling under Article 288 EC translates in the context of state action. Surely not any state activity, even when wholly unrelated to Community law, would be capable of triggering possible 'beyond *Francovich* liability', i.e. the obligation to make good loss and damage caused to individuals as a result of 'almost breaches' [?] of Community law. Terminologically, the concept of state liability for lawful acts is somewhat problematic; conceptually, it is not, as clear guidance can be derived from the French notion of equality of public burdens (in French: *principe d'égalité devant des charges publiques*; in German: *Sonderopfer*).[14] Only when a claimant can satisfy the above requirements and the state was acting in the sphere of Community law does a compensation claim in the absence of unlawfulness stand a chance.[15]

However, the appeal rulings by the ECJ in *FIAMM* have significantly reduced the scope of the principle of Community liability for lawful acts.[16] For the first time, the Court ruled in detail and in response to far-reaching pleas by various parties about the very existence of liability under Article 288 EC for lawful acts, as well as, if it does exist, its applicability in the context of non-directly effective WTO rules. Previously, in *Dorsch Consult*,[17] and as noted by the Court itself in

---

[14]   Cf. the leading Dutch case *Hoge Raad* (Netherlands Supreme Court), 18 January 1991, *NJ* 1992, 638, case note CJHB (*Leffers v Netherlands State*). See generally Schueler, BJ (2005), *Schadevergoeding en de Awb* (*Compensation and the General Administrative Law Act*), Kluwer at Chapter. 8.

[15]   Tellingly, the claimants in both *FIAMM* and *Beamglow* failed; see also Arnull, *supra* n. 12 at 494.

[16]   Joined Cases C–120/06 P and C–121/06 P *FIAMM and FIAMM Technologies v Council and Others* [2008] ECR nyr (judgment of 9 September 2008).

[17]   Case C–237/98 P *Dorsch Consult* v *Council and Commission* [2000] ECR I–4549.

the *FIAMM* appeal (paragraph 169), the ECJ had only considered liability in the absence of unlawfulness hypothetically. That is to say, its reasoning focused on the specific requirements in the context of liability for lawful acts, unusual and special damage – applicable instead of the normally applicable unlawfulness requirement, and agreed with the CFI that the claimant had failed to prove that he had suffered this kind of damage. As for the very possibility of Community liability in the absence of fault, like the CFI, the ECJ in *Dorsch Consult* merely considered that 'in the event of the principle of Community liability for a lawful act being recognised in Community law'.[18] In *FIAMM*, by contrast, liability for lawful acts was a live issue before the Court as it was raised in a cross-appeal in two ways: in dispute were 'the very existence or very applicability of the liability regime [for lawful acts] which the judgments under appeal applied'.[19] The ECJ reasoned, in essence, that, unlike liability for unlawful acts, there is no firmly established regime for liability in the absence of unlawfulness at Community level; that such a regime could not be deduced from previous case law and that even Community liability for legislative activity more generally should be incurred only exceptionally and in special circumstances (paragraphs 164–74). In addition the Court noted that, as a matter of comparative law, convergence among Member States can be found where public authority liability, including for legislative acts, for unlawful acts/omissions is concerned, but not with respect to lawful conduct causing harm to certain individuals, 'in particular where it is of a legislative nature'.[20] The ECJ then held as follows:

> 176   In the light of all the foregoing considerations, it must be concluded that, as Community law currently stands, no liability regime exists under which the Community can incur liability for conduct falling within the sphere of its legislative competence in a situation where any failure of such conduct to comply with the WTO agreements cannot be relied upon before the Community courts.[21]

It would seem to follow from this passage that the ECJ has not ruled out liability for lawful act altogether and in all circumstances, but limited the scope of such a regime by making it unavailable in the specific context of (WTO) rules which are of such a kind that they cannot be relied upon before the courts (i.e.

---

[18]   At para. 18. Para. 19 confirms the three conditions cited above for such liability for lawful acts: real damage, causal link and the unusual and special nature of that damage. Remarkably, in the context of a ruling which is precisely about the difference between liability for lawful and *un*lawful acts, para. 53 of the English version of the judgment erroneously talks about *un*lawful acts.

[19]   Para. 162. See also para. 161 summarising the pleading by the Council reported in paras. 141–2 of the judgment.

[20]   Para. 175 of *FIAMM*.

[21]   See also para. 188.

they have no direct effect) in reviewing the legality of secondary Community law, either in annulment proceedings or in the context of a damages action.[22] Although the ECJ concluded that the first plea in the cross-appeals was well-founded, it did not spell out in detail which particular part of that plea was decisive: the first part disputing the very existence of liability for lawful acts altogether or the second part 'merely' disputing the way the CFI had applied this principle – 'even assuming that such a principle can be established' – to the particular situation in hand involving a legislative omission allegedly in conflict with non-directly effective WTO rules.[23] Nonetheless, the decisive passage of *FIAMM* is paragraph 176, quoted above, which does not say that liability for lawful conduct cannot exist at all. Future case law must be awaited to provide more clarity about the situations in which the still existing special regime of liability for lawful acts is applicable.

STATE LIABILITY FOR BREACH OF UNION LAW

Absence of Direct Effect

Above, a key extension of the scope of the liability for non-contractual obligations under the EC Treaty has been examined. This is a development which one might call 'beyond *Francovich*'. The main possibility for 'beyond *Francovich*' developments this chapter would like to explore, however, concerns possible state liability for breach of European *Union* law (as opposed to *Community* law), and in particular measures adopted under the third pillar (Treaty on European Union: Title VI Provisions on Police and Judicial Cooperation in Criminal Matters). An example would be Member State liability for failure to transpose a Framework Decision within the meaning of Article 34 TEU, which is the third pillar equivalent of a Directive within the meaning of Article 249 EC. Equivalent but not identical, as the text of the very provision describing a Framework Decision excludes any possibility of direct effect.[24]

Does the absence of any direct effect of Framework Decisions rule out all possible state liability? The answer has to be no, since direct effect of the relevant norm of EC law is no requirement for *Francovich* liability.[25] It follows that the

---

[22]   See paras. 109–20 confirming well-established previous case law. In para. 133 the ECJ held that the CFI was right in deciding that the legality of the activity of the Community institutions could not be reviewed in the light of these WTO rules.

[23]   Paras. 142 and 141.

[24]   Art. 34(2)b TEU, last sentence.

[25]   Prechal, S (2005), *Directives in European Community law* (2nd ed), OUP at 282; Arnull, *supra* n. 2 at 274.

Treaty based absence of any possible direct effect of a Framework Decision poses no obstacle to a potential extension of state liability for breach of *EC* law to state liability for breach of *EU* law.[26]

Also, there is a precedent of such an extension of a fundamental doctrine of EC law to the context of the EU Treaty: the recognition of the existence of the doctrine of consistent interpretation as a matter of EU law in the *Pupino* case.[27] In terms of content of the duty of *interprétation conforme* there is no difference between the doctrine's application between the EC and the EU contexts. For example, *Pupino* itself (paragraph 47) makes a contribution to one of the general aspects of 'consistent interpretation' by recognising explicitly for the first time that national courts are not obliged to construe their national law *contra legem* in order to attain the result prescribed by the Community norm in issue. Clearly, this proposition applies equally in the context of the EC Treaty.[28]

Consistent Interpretation Indirectly Inherent in the EU Treaty

But in one important respect, dealing with its legal basis, the ECJ did not 'export' the EC doctrine wholly to the EU Treaty context. Until 2004, the duty to interpret national law in conformity with Community law – and in particular directives, which is the most frequent scenario – was founded on a twofold basis of written Treaty law: Article 249(3) EC establishing the binding nature of directives in terms of their result and the duty of loyal cooperation of Article 10 EC.[29] These two provisions were always cited in conjunction and in one and the same sentence; they presumably contributed 50% each to the legal foundation of the doctrine as anchors within the EC Treaty. This changed with *Pfeiffer*,[30] where the ECJ added that the obligation of *interprétation conforme* is inherent in the Treaty. The parallel with state liability is striking for 'inherent in the Treaty' is linked to effectiveness:

> 114. The requirement for national law to be interpreted in conformity with Community law is inherent in the system of the Treaty, since it permits the national court,

---

[26]   See also Prinssen, J (2007), 'Domestic Legal Effects of EU Criminal Law: A Transfer of EC Law Doctrines?' in Obradovic and Lavranos, *Interface Between EU Law and National Law*, Europa Law Publishing, *supra* n. * at section 4.5.

[27]   Case C–105/03 *Pupino* [2005] ECR I–5285, [2005] 2 CMLR 63.

[28]   Prechal, *supra* n. 25 at 194 who herself queries any categorical ruling out of all possible interpretations *contra legem*, however. Case C–212/04 *Adeneler* [2006] ECR I–6057, [2006] 3 CMLR 30, para. 110; Case C–268/06 *Impact* [2008] ECR nyr (judgment of 15 April 2008, [2008] 2 CMLR 47, para. 100.

[29]   See the first judgments on consistent interpretation in Case 14/83 *Von Colson and Kamann* [1984] ECR 1891 and Case 79/83 *Harz* [1984] ECR 1921; followed in numerous subsequent cases, see Arnull, *supra* n. 12 at 168–71.

[30]   Joined Cases C–397/01 to C–403/01, [2004] ECR I–8835, [2005] 1 CMLR 44.

for the matters within its jurisdiction, to ensure the full effectiveness of Community law when it determines the dispute before it. ...

But since the ECJ also reiterated its traditional foundation of Articles 10 and 249 EC, a genuine double basis – written as well as unwritten – seems to be the current position. Whatever one might make of this additional, *ex post facto*, justification for consistent interpretation in the context of the EC Treaty (it is difficult to think of any practical consequences for future cases), the notion of 'inherent in the Treaty' is potentially significant when it comes to extending fundamental doctrines of EC law to the EU law context. Unless one can identify crucial differences between the two legal frameworks – which, moreover, must be relevant to the specific legal issue in hand – it has already been seen above that Framework Decisions cannot have direct effect but direct effect is not a requirement for *Francovich* liability anyway – it is not such a big step to conclude that what is inherent in Pillar One is also inherent in Pillar Three. Before examining in more detail what relevant differences between the EC and EU law framework might potentially form an obstacle to the export of EC doctrines to Union law, first a few words about the precedent value of *Pupino* for the possible extension of *Francovich* liability to infringements of EU law.

Pupino is a relevant precedent to the extent that the ECJ recognised that the duty of consistent interpretation applies in the third pillar just as it does in the first. It held that such a duty follows from the binding nature of Framework Decisions under the EU Treaty comparable to Article 249 EC referring to directives. However, and in my view regrettably, the ECJ did not rule that the duty of consistent interpretation is inherent in the EU Treaty as it is now inherent in the EC Treaty. It indirectly anchored this obligation to the duty of loyal cooperation even though there is no explicit recognition of it in the Treaty on European Union. In response to the objection raised by Italy and the UK that there is no equivalent of Article 10 EC in the TEU – on which the Court 'partially relied in order to justify the obligation to interpret national law in conformity with Community law' (paragraph 39) – the ECJ recognised a kind of unwritten version of Article 10 EC.[31] Citing the TEU's declaration that it constitutes a new stage of European integration, it said:

42   It would be difficult for the Union to carry out its task effectively if the principle of loyal cooperation, requiring in particular that Member States take all appropriate

---

[31]   See also para. 27 of A-G Kokott's Opinion in *Pupino*: '[a]gainst that background, Article 10 EC lays down some axiomatic principles, namely, that obligations must be fulfilled and damaging measures refrained from. The same applies in Union law, without needing to be expressly mentioned.'

measures, whether general or particular, to ensure fulfilment of their obligations under European Union law, were not also binding in the area of police and judicial cooperation in criminal matters, which is moreover entirely based on cooperation between the Member States and the institutions, as the Advocate General has rightly pointed out in paragraph 26 of her Opinion.

In terms of 'inherent in the Treaty', this passage might be read as considering the principle of loyal cooperation as inherent in the Treaty on European Union. Accordingly, rather than directly anchoring the duty of consistent interpretation as a matter of Union law 'inherent in the Treaty', the Court indirectly read the duty into the TEU via the intermediary of a likewise non-textual anchor in the form of the principle of loyal cooperation; it, in turn being based on effectiveness.[32]

Damages Claims for Breach of EU Law before National Courts

As noted below, a damages action against the Union in the context of the second (the TEU's Common Foreign and Security Policy) and third pillars (Police and Judicial Cooperation in Criminal matters, Articles 29–42 TEU) is not available before the Community Courts in the absence of a TEU equivalent of Articles 235 and 288(2) EC conferring (exclusive)[33] jurisdiction on the European Court of Justice. In two judgments of 27 February 2007 the ECJ therefore dismissed appeals against rulings by the CFI dismissing claims for damages allegedly incurred by a number of Basque organisations as a result of a Council Common Position, based on Articles 15 and 34 TEU, including them on a list of entities suspected of involvement with terrorism and against whom measures must be taken.[34] The action for damages is to be seen in the wider context of judicial protection against measures such as in issue here, i.e. the placing on a list pursuant to acts adopted under UN Security Council Resolutions with limited scope for judicial review of such decisions, in particular in the light of the confidentiality of the factual basis for such inclusion hampering the listed persons' ability to challenge such decisions.[35] In *Segi*, the CFI came to the conclusion that 'indeed

---

[32]   See also Ross, *supra* n. 8 at 481–2.

[33]   See Case C–275/00 *First and Franex* [2002] ECR I–10943, [2005] 2 CMLR 12.

[34]   See Case C–354/04 P *Gestoras Pro Amnistía and Others v. Council* [2007] ECR I–1579, [2007] 2 CMLR 22 and Case C–355/04 P *Segi and Others* [2007] ECR I–1657. Appeals from Case T–333/02 *Gestoras*, not published in the ECR, and Case T–388/02 *Segi* [2004] ECR II–1647, [2007] 1 CMLR 8.

[35]   But see the ECJ's ground-breaking rulings in Joined Cases C–402/05 P and C–415/05 P *Kadi* [2008] ECR nyr (judgment of 3 September 2008). 'Normal' judicial review and damages actions are available insofar as implementing measures are taken under the first pillar: see Case T–47/03 *Sison* [2007] ECR II nyr, [2007] 3 CMLR 39; case

probably no effective judicial remedy is available to them, whether before the Community Courts or national courts, with regard to the inclusion of Segi on the list of persons, groups or entities involved in terrorist acts'; it is well-established, however, that that fact as such cannot alter the system of judicial remedies as provided for by the Treaties.[36]

Unsurprisingly, on appeal, the ECJ confirmed these key findings of the CFI. On the judicial remedy point, however, a somewhat novel approach was taken by the ECJ. For the first time it ruled that although the act in question is a Council Common Position, which is not a reviewable act for the purposes of judicial review (Article 35(6) TEU) nor can form the subject of a reference for a preliminary ruling under Article 35(1) TEU, it will nonetheless be reviewable if the Common Position in issue is intended to produce legal effects for third parties. The Court reasoned that Article 35(1) TEU should not be construed narrowly and that it implicitly includes in the class of acts capable of being referred for a preliminary ruling 'all measures adopted by the Council and intended to produce legal effects in relation to third parties'; likewise, a Common Position of this type, one producing legal effects *vis-à-vis* third parties, also constitutes a reviewable act in the context of a direct challenge brought by a Member State or the Commission under Article 35(6) TEU.[37] It follows that the ECJ refers to the mechanism of an indirect challenge pending before a national court which can then refer the question of the legality of the Common Position to the ECJ via the preliminary rulings mechanism. About the claim for damages, the ECJ only said the following:

> 56   Finally, it is to be borne in mind that it is for the Member States and, in particular, their courts and tribunals, to interpret and apply national procedural rules governing the exercise of rights of action in a way that enables natural and legal persons to challenge before the courts the lawfulness of any decision or other national measure relating to the drafting or the application to them of an act of the European Union and to seek compensation for the loss suffered, where appropriate.

Without going into detail the ECJ does recognise a role for national courts in damages claims in this context. Implicitly it must mean that it endorses such actions before national courts even where the defendant is the European Union. Only very little guidance has, however, been given about such an action. More

---

and comment by Angus Johnston, 'Freezing terrorist assets again: walking a tightrope over thin ice?' [2008] *Cambridge Law Journal* 31.

[36]   See para. 38 of Case T–388/02, cited *supra* n. 34, with reference to Case C–50/00 P *UPA* (*Unión de Pequeños Agricultores*) [2002] ECR I–6677, [2002] 3 CMLR 1.

[37]   Paras. 53 and 54 of *Gestoras*, *supra* n. 34. Cf. Peers, S (2007), 'Salvation Outside the Church: Judicial Protection in the Third Pillar after the *Pupino* and *Segi* Judgments', 44 *CMLRev*. 883.

detailed considerations about where, against whom and under which legal system to initiate damages claims for breach of Union law are to be found in Advocate General Mengozzi's Opinion in *Gestoras* and *Segi*.[38]

Suffice it at present to highlight just a few key points particularly relevant to private international law issues, as these were not considered by the ECJ at all whereas they will undoubtedly arise if and when damages claims of this type are brought before national courts as envisaged by the ECJ in the quoted paragraph 56. The Advocate General places the availability of a remedy before a national court in the absence of jurisdiction of the Community Courts firmly in the context of fundamental rights and the rule of law as confirmed by Article 6(1) TEU, the EU Charter of Fundamental Rights and the relationship between the EU and the European Convention on Human Rights.[39] It is noted that in the present state of European *Union* law (as pointed out below, the landscape changes significantly after entry into force of the Treaty of Lisbon), judicial protection, as a matter of EU law, is entrusted to the national courts. Without excluding possible liability of each Member State because of its involvement with adoption of Union acts, the A-G briefly touches on the vexed question of the legal personality of the Union.

Insofar as the Union can be sued as such, as an international organisation, jurisdiction of the courts of the Member States will be determined by the usual rules of Community law: the Brussels I Regulation.[40] Importantly, if and when the question of possible immunity from jurisdiction of the EU arose, the A-G took the view that the Council would then be obliged to waive it; alternatively, a Council Declaration about the right to compensation accompanying the Common Position in issue (2001/931) could be read to constitute implicit waiver already.[41] As for choice of law, such an issue may arise analogously to the possible liability of Member States in the context of the Europol Convention dealing with liability for damage caused by unlawful data processing.[42] Given the recent adoption of uniform rules about choice of law for non-contractual liability, it would seem to follow that those rules, the so-called Rome II Regulation, would apply.[43] In any

---

[38]   Opinion of 26 October 2006 in Case C–254/04 P and Case C–355/04 P, [2007] ECR I–1579.

[39]   Ibid. at paras. 73–97.

[40]   Council Regulation (EC) No. 44/2001 of 22 December 2000 on jurisdiction and the recognition and enforcement of judgments in civil and commercial matters, OJ 2001 L 12/1; latest consolidated version after Council Regulation 1791/2006 available at: eur-lex.europa.eu.

[41]   Opinion, *Gestoras and Segi*, paras. 151 and 152.

[42]   Ibid., para. 154.

[43]   Regulation (EC) No 864/2007 of the European Parliament and of the Council of 11 July 2007 on the law applicable to non-contractual obligations (Rome II), OJ 2007 L 199/40.

event, the A-G notes various options in terms of determining the actual liability conditions, notably, of course, the ones developed by the Community Courts under Article 288 EC. Interestingly, Mr Mengozzi draws a parallel with state liability as noted and advocated above. That is, he considers it a 'given [that] the principle of the right to reparation of damage resulting from unlawful acts adopted by the Council under Article 34 EU [is] a principle inherent in the EU Treaty'.[44] Accordingly, certain key features of a possible *EU* liability regime can be transferred from the case law developed in the context of both state and Community liability. The next section of this chapter looks at an example of such a transfer which has already taken place.

Levels of European Integration

The fact that the EU Treaty constitutes a lesser degree of integration than the EC Treaty was no obstacle to the extension of the doctrine of consistent interpretation, as seen above. The Court of Justice also agreed with A-G Kokott on this point.[45] Some of the fundamental differences between EC and EU law may be summed up as in Table 7.1.

Table 7.1   Differences between EC and EU law

	EC	EU
Infringement actions by Commission/Member States	Arts. 226–228/227	Non-existent
Preliminary rulings	Arts. 234/68	MS decide:[46] Art. 35
Direct effect	Any instrument	Excluded for Framework Decisions
Failure to act actions; damages	Arts. 232 and 235/288(2)	Non-existent

Advocate General Kokott in *Pupino* not only compared and contrasted the EC and the EU Treaties from the perspective of European integration, she also

---

44   Ibid.

45   See in particular paras. 30–37 of her Opinion in *Pupino*.

46   See 'Jurisdiction of the Court of Justice to give preliminary rulings on police and judicial cooperation in criminal matters', available at: curia.eu (Research and Documentation Service; March 2008); see also the summary at OJ 2008 L 70/23 and OJ 2008 C 69/ 1.

considered the EEA: the Agreement creating the European Economic Area (EEA) between most of the EFTA states and the EC.[47] This is another Treaty closely linked to the EC Treaty but containing a lesser degree of integration than the TEC. The lower level of integration, however, did not prevent the EFTA Court from recognising an EFTA version of *Francovich*.

State Liability for Breach of EEA Law

This important development took place within the context of various legal and institutional connections between the EC/EU and the EFTA (the European Free Trade Association).[48] To be more precise, the 'EFTA *Francovich*' recognises the principle of state liability for breach of the EEA. The EFTA Court was established instead of an EEA Court because the latter was held to be incompatible with Community law by the ECJ in *Opinion 1/91*.[49] However, the arrangement of the judicial control under the final, amended, version of the EEA Agreement was subsequently declared compatible in *Opinion 1/92*.[50] A crucial feature of the judicial architecture and its *modus operandi* in the EEA is the link with the case law of the ECJ. The EEA Agreement declares applicable a large part of the *acquis communautaire*, mainly internal market and competition law, in the European Economic Area. Such provisions of EEA law are identical to their EC law counterparts. It is an aim of the EEA Agreement that both sets of rules are interpreted and applied as uniformly as achievable (homogeneity of interpretation; Article 6 EEA).[51]

A number of mechanisms have been put in place to achieve this homogeneity, such as a system of exchange of information between the ECJ, the EFTA Court and the highest courts of the EFTA states about their case law relevant to the EEA. In addition to the cited Article 6 EEA, a Joint Committee was established to accommodate the reception of ECJ case law handed down after the signing of the EEA. Also, a Protocol to the EEA empowers EFTA states to confer on their courts the right to request the ECJ to give a preliminary ruling

---

[47]   OJ 1994 L 1/3.
[48]   See its Website at www.efta.int. Member States are Iceland, Liechtenstein, Norway and Switzerland.
[49]   [1991] ECR I–6079, [1992] 1 CMLR 245.
[50]   [1992] ECR I–2821.
[51]   Which reads as follows: '[w]ithout prejudice to future developments of case law, the provisions of this Agreement, in so far as they are identical in substance to corresponding rules of the Treaty establishing the European Economic Community and the Treaty establishing the European Coal and Steel Community and to acts adopted in application of these two Treaties, shall, in their implementation and application, be interpreted in conformity with the relevant rulings of the Court of Justice of the European Communities given prior to the date of signature of this Agreement.' See also Arts. 105–7.

on the interpretation of EEA rules corresponding to EC rules.[52] However, no EFTA state has given this power to its courts.[53] By contrast, they are entitled to request the EFTA Court to give so-called advisory opinions on the interpretation of the EEA Agreement. In addition, the EFTA states participating in the EEA and the EFTA Surveillance Authority have the right to participate in preliminary rulings procedures before the ECJ and have rights of intervention in any other cases insofar as EEA law can be affected.[54]

In *Sveinsbjörnsdóttir*,[55] the EFTA Court ruled on the failure (correctly) to implement Directive 80/987/EEC on the protection of employees against insolvent employers by Iceland and the liability of an EFTA state (it is recalled that *Francovich* itself involved the same Directive). The EFTA Court observed that there is no explicit provision of EEA law laying down state liability for 'incorrect adaptation of national law' (paragraph 46). But is such a principle implicit in the EEA Agreement, in the light of its stated purpose and legal structure? The EFTA Court notes the requirement of a homogeneous interpretation and application of EEA law with EC law and the acknowledgement of judicial protection of individual rights conferred by EEA law. In a passage well worth quoting in full it said:

> 59   The Court concludes from the foregoing considerations that the EEA Agreement is an international treaty *sui generis* which contains a distinct legal order of its own. The EEA Agreement does not establish a customs union but an enhanced free trade area, see the judgment in Case E-2/97 *Maglite* [1997] EFTA Court Report 127[.[56]] The depth of integration of the EEA Agreement is less far-reaching than under the EC Treaty, but the scope and the objective of the EEA Agreement goes beyond what is usual for an agreement under public international law.

The EFTA Court thus gives a ruling analogous to the ECJ's *Van Gend en Loos* case,[57] recognising a new EEA legal order rather than mere intergovernmental cooperation, albeit of a less far reaching kind than the EC legal order.[58] With

---

[52]   See Protocol 34 on the possibility for courts and tribunals of EFTA states to request the ECJ to decide on the interpretation of EEA rules corresponding to EC rules, available at: www.efta.int.

[53]   Forman, J (1999), 'The EEA Agreement Five Years On: Dynamic Homogeneity in Practice and Its Implementation by the Two EEA Courts', 36 *CMLRev*. 751 at n. 124.

[54]   Statute of the Court of Justice, Arts. 23 and 40; Rules of Procedure of the Court of Justice, Arts.123f and g, latest consolidated versions (2008), ECJ website: curia.eu.

[55]   Case E–9/97, [1998] EFTA Court Reports 95 (Advisory Opinion of 10 December 1998), available at: www.eftacourt.lu; [1999] 1 CMLR 884.

[56]   [1998] 1 CMLR 331.

[57]   Case 26/62 [1963] ECR 1.

[58]   See for a similar appraisal by the CFI Case T–115/94 *Opel Austria* [1997] ECR II–39, [1997] 1 CMLR 733 at paras. 107–8.

this approach, in accordance with the homogeneity principle, the EFTA Court follows the rulings of the ECJ in *Francovich*.[59] The EFTA Court also refers to Article 3 EEA (the equivalent of Article 10 EC Treaty (ex Article 5): loyal cooperation) as a further basis for state liability. The conditions for liability as recognised by the EFTA Court under EEA law faithfully reflect the ECJ's case law, in particular its post-*Francovich* developments in *Brasserie*[60] and *Dillenkofer*,[61] including a sufficiently serious breach.

The principle of EFTA State liability itself is laid down in equally broad terms as under Community law. The EFTA Court:

> 62   It follows from all the forgoing that it is a principle of the EEA Agreement that the Contracting Parties are obliged to provide for compensation for loss and damage caused to individuals by breaches of the obligations under the EEA Agreement for which the EFTA States can be held responsible.

But a specific feature of EFTA state liability under EEA law, as opposed to Member State liability under EC law, is the absence of a transfer of legislative powers by the EFTA states to supranational organs. The EFTA Court thus added that although the principle of state liability is an integral part of the EEA Agreement, it cannot be applied by the national EFTA courts as such, but: 'it is natural to interpret national legislation implementing the main part of the Agreement as also comprising the principle of State liability' (paragraph 63). The EFTA Court could not therefore recognise a form of direct effect of the principle inherent in the Agreement (monism), but instead insists on construing the national implementing laws accordingly (dualism). The existence of state liability for breach of EEA law was confirmed more recently in *Karlsson*,[62] underlining that it is indeed an integral part of the EEA Agreement and that its operation is not contingent on the direct effect of the violated norm of EEA law (mirroring the *Francovich* liability as noted above).

It follows from these rulings that the principle of state liability for breach of EC law has been extended to the Contracting States of the EEA Agreement, i.e. Iceland, Liechtenstein and Norway (Switzerland, although a Member State

---

[59]   Perhaps surprisingly, because of the absence of supremacy and direct effect of the EEA Treaty, A-G Cosmas concluded – unlike the EFTA Court – that *Francovich* could not be extended to the EEA context: see his Opinion in Case C–321/97 *Andersson* [1999] ECR I–3551, [2000] 2 CMLR 191, para. 49. The ECJ ruled it had no jurisdiction to answer the questions.

[60]   Joined Cases C–46 and 48/93 *Brasserie du Pêcheur & Factortame III* [1996] ECR I–1029, [1996] 1 CMLR 889.

[61]   Joined Cases C–178, 179 & 188–90/94 *Dillenkoffer v Germany* [1996] ECR I–4845, [1996] 3 CMLR 469.

[62]   Case E–4/01, [2002] EFTA Court Report 240, available at: www.eftacourt.lu; [2002] 2 CMLR 60.

of EFTA does not participate in the EEA). Meanwhile, in *Rechberger*,[63] the ECJ cited the first EFTA case recognising state liability for breach of EEA law. Like in *Andersson*,[64] a question with respect to the EEA Agreement was put before the ECJ. It was argued that Austria might be liable under EEA law as of 1 January 1994, the date of required implementation of the Package Travel Directive under the EEA Agreement (as opposed to 1 January 1995, the date of accession to the EU). Citing *Andersson*, the ECJ held that it is not competent to rule on the application of the EEA Agreement in connection with Austria before its EU membership. The Court does, however, refer to *Sveinsbjörnsdóttir*, citing the EEA's objective of uniform interpretation and application with EC law.

Nothing stands in the way of the Court being inspired by the EFTA Court's ruling and extending *Francovich* liability to Union law. Indeed, in the light of the appraisal carried out by A-G Kokott in *Pupino* (cited above), comparing the three Treaties' levels of integration, it could even rule that now that state liability exists as a matter of EEA law, it *a fortiori* exists as a matter of Union law, given the more intense level of integration of the TEU compared to the EEA Agreement.

The Treaty of Lisbon

Damages actions became fully available for the kind of acts discussed above as the reforms included in the 2007 Reform Treaty entered into force. This Treaty is also known as the Treaty of Lisbon and is the successor to the failed Constitution.[65] There would no longer be a question whether *Francovich* liability applies under Union law as well as EC law as the whole pillar structure is unpicked by the Lisbon Treaty; the restrictions contained in particular in the current versions of Article 35 and 41 TEU disappear as these provisions are repealed. The distinction between EC and EU law would be obsolete insofar as damages claims are concerned just as had previously been agreed and included in the Constitution.[66] However, there is a five-year transition period pursuant

---

[63]   Case C–140/97 *Rechberger and Others v. Austria* [1999] ECR I–3499; [2000] 2 CMLR 1.

[64]   Case C–321/97, [1999] ECR I–3551, [2000] 2 CMLR 191. As said, the ECJ ruled it had no jurisdiction to answer the questions from the national court about whether *Francovich* liability exists under EEA law. A-G Cosmas, in the alternative proposition that the ECJ were to have jurisdiction, did answer those questions in paras. 37–54 of his Opinion; see also *supra* n. 59.

[65]   OJ 2007 C 306; see generally Dougan, M (2008), 'The Treaty of Lisbon 2007: Winning Minds, Not Hearts', 45 *CMLRev*. 617.

[66]   Opinion of A-G Mengozzi in *Gestoras*, *supra* n. 34, para. 100. See on the merger of the 'old' pillar structure more generally Craig, P (2008), 'The Treaty of Lisbon,

to Article 10 of the Protocol on Transitional Provisions,[67] the effect of which is to continue the 'old regime' with all its limitations on the ECJ's competence to give preliminary rulings and regarding actions for annulment and damages actions in the field of police and judicial cooperation in criminal matters. In other words, the restrictions laid down in Articles 35 and 41 of the previous version of the TEU remain in force until five years after the entry into force of 'Lisbon'. With the latter having been ratified by all the Member States in 2009, a case like *Gestoras* would indeed have to be brought before a national court until 2014/2015.[68]

Given this state of affairs for the next six years or so, it might finally be pointed out that post-Lisbon damages for breach of Union law by the Union would be upgraded to a fundamental right as a component of the right to good administration under the Charter of Fundamental Rights of the European Union.[69] However, the Reform Treaty as well as the Constitution does not contain a written reference to state liability for breach of Union law, but as a firmly established element of the *acquis communautaire* it must be deemed to continue to exist. And since *Bergaderm*, as seen above, the regimes have merged. It follows that state liability for breach of Union law would be part of the legal landscape. Until the Lisbon Treaty enters into force, however, the Charter remains non-binding. Nonetheless, legal effects are being produced by it since it was cited by the ECJ as a relevant benchmark in the context of judicial review of legislation.[70] Accordingly, before it becomes legally binding pursuant to

---

Process, Architecture and Substance', 33 *ELRev.* 137 at 142–3 and Lenaerts, K (2007), 'The Rule of Law and the Coherence of the Judicial System of the European Union', 44 *CMLRev.* 1625 at 1630–33.

[67] Adopted at Lisbon, 13 December 2007, part of Category A. Protocols to be annexed to the Treaty on European Union, to the Treaty on the Functioning of the European Union and, where applicable, to the Treaty establishing the European Atomic Energy Community; Dougan, *supra* n. 65 at 682.

[68] It could be earlier where the act in issue was amended during this 'interregnum': Art. 10(2) of that Protocol. There are also, bewilderingly complex, further transitional rules for the UK only: see Art. 10(4) and (5); Dougan, *supra* n. 65 at 683–4.

[69] OJ 2007 C 303/1. See Art. 41(3): 'Every person has the right to have the Community make good any damage caused by its institutions or by its servants in the performance of their duties, in accordance with the general principles common to the laws of the Member States.'

[70] Case C–540/03 *European Parliament v. Council* [2006] ECR I–5769; [2006] 3 CMLR 28 (Re family reunification), para. 38. See now also Case C–432/05 *Unibet* [2007] ECR I–2271, para. 37; Case C–303/05 *Advocaten voor de Wereld* [2007] ECR I–3633, para. 46; Case C–438/05 *Viking Line* [2007] ECR I–10779, paras. 43–44 and Case C–341/05 *Laval* [2007] ECR I–11767, paras. 90–91; Case C–244/06 *Dynamic Medien* [2008] ECR nyr (judgment of 14 February 2008), para. 41; Case C–450/06 *Varec* [2008] ECR nyr (judgment of 14 February 2008), para. 48.

Article 6(1) TEU (Lisbon version),[71] as pointed out by A-G Poiares Maduro, the Charter performs a double role: it creates a presumption of the existence of a fundamental right, requiring confirmation of its existence in another source, such as the constitutional traditions of the Member States or an international convention, in particular the ECHR; secondly, the Charter is a useful reference point for determining the meaning, scope and content of such a right.[72] *Union* liability can be deemed to be a part of the Charter as also under the current version of Article 6 TEU the European Union must respect fundamental rights as general principles.[73] Although the Charter refers to liability of the Community only, the right to damages as a general principle of EU law must be accepted.[74] A building block for the Court to go beyond *Francovich* is therefore in place.

Indeed, it can be inferred from *Unibet* that the right to effective judicial protection would require national courts to construe their law so as to ensure that damages actions for breach of EU law are available.[75] As pointed out by Arnull,[76] the ECJ imposed a wide interpretive duty on national courts in order to ensure effective protection of, in the *Unibet* context, Community law, with a formulation that is very similar to what is now Article 19(1) TEU (Lisbon version): '1. ... Member States shall provide remedies sufficient to ensure effective legal protection in the fields covered by Union law'. Admittedly, one still needs to transpose the *Unibet* rulings from Community to Union law, but since the European Union is just as bound by the general principle of effective judicial protection as the European Community it would seem to follow that the cited provision of the TEU post-Lisbon is already current law.

---

[71]   Which provides as follows: '1. The Union recognises the rights, freedoms and principles set out in the Charter of Fundamental Rights of the European Union of 7 December 2000, as adapted at Strasbourg, on 12 December 2007, which shall have the same legal value as the Treaties. The provisions of the Charter shall not extend in any way the competences of the Union as defined in the Treaties. The rights, freedoms and principles in the Charter shall be interpreted in accordance with the general provisions in Title VII of the Charter governing its interpretation and application and with due regard to the explanations referred to in the Charter, that set out the sources of those provisions.'

[72]   Opinion of 14 December 2006 in Case C–305/05 *Ordre des barreaux francophones and germanophone and Others* [2007] ECR I–5305, [2007] 3 CMLR 28, at para. 48.

[73]   Cf. Lenaerts, K and Corthaut, T (2006), 'Of Birds and hedges: the role of primacy in invoking norms of EU law', 31 *ELRev.* 287 at 314 referring to Art. 47 of the Charter as a possible justification for state liability for breach of EU law; however, they also note that there is currently no liability of the EU itself for a breach of second pillar law making it difficult to justify state liability in that context.

[74]   Opinion of A-G Mengozzi in *Gestoras, supra* n. 34, para. 73–107.

[75]   Case C–432/05 *Unibet* [2007] ECR I–2271, [2007] 2 CMLR 30, para. 44.

[76]   See case note Arnull, A (2007), on *Unibet* in 44 *CMLRev.* 1763 at 1769.

FINAL REMARKS

From a single, not at all specific, reference to non-contractual liability of the Community in the EC Treaty, a much more comprehensive liability regime encompassing both the European Community and its Member States has been judicially developed over the last 15 years or so. All the cases were concerned with either the Community's or the Member States' liability for breach of Community law as opposed to European Union law, with the exception of the *Gestoras* and *Segi* judgments.[77] These rulings, in the current state of the law, confirmed that the Community Courts have no jurisdiction to entertain damages claims based on breach of Union law. But it does not follow that such liability, be it by the EU and/or the Member States, does not exist. On the contrary, all it means is that the competence to deal with such claims resides with the national courts.

This chapter examined various strands of judicial developments in support of the proposition that current law does recognise such claims. It built on a recent extension of the Article 288 EC case law from liability for unlawful to lawful acts, covered a number of differences between the level of legal integration in the EU and EC Treaties, and drew on an analogy with liability of EFTA states for breach of EEA law. Finally it was noted that the Community Courts would be able to entertain such direct damages claims for breach of Union law upon the entry into force of the Lisbon Treaty. However, until at least approximately 2015, jurisdiction for damages claims against the Union, as opposed to the Community, remains unavailable. The first port of call for claimants even when they are suing the Union is therefore a national court. The current case law of the ECJ in the context of the EC Treaty contains a number of building blocks, in particular regarding fundamental rights and the principle of effective judicial protection, for those national courts to adjudicate upon such claims. There are of course many unanswered questions which are likely one day to end up before the ECJ.

---

[77] See also Case T–47/03 *Sison* [2007] ECR II nyr, [2007] 3 CMLR 39.

8. International law on the carriage of goods by sea: UNCITRAL's most recent harmonisation efforts

Miriam Goldby*

INTRODUCTION

In the course of its forty-first Session in New York which took place between 16 June and 3 July 2008, the United Nations Commission on International Trade Law (UNCITRAL) adopted a decision whereby it submitted the final draft of a new Convention on Contracts for the International Carriage of Goods Wholly or Partly by Sea to the United Nations General Assembly for its consideration with a view to adoption.[1] The adoption by the General Assembly took place on 11 December of the same year. A signing ceremony was held in Rotterdam in 2009 and the Convention became known as the 'Rotterdam Rules'.[2] To date, 24 states have signed the Convention, one of which, Spain, has also ratified it.

The Convention was drafted by UNCITRAL's Working Group III on Transport Law in collaboration with the Comité Maritime International (CMI). This is the fourth international convention on this subject which has been produced since 1924, the first three being the International Convention for the Unification of Certain Rules of Law relating to Bills of Lading 1924 (Hague Rules), the Hague Rules as Amended by the Brussels Protocol 1968 (Hague-Visby Rules) and the UN Convention on the Carriage of Goods by Sea 1978 (Hamburg Rules). These Conventions aim to regulate the rights and obligations of parties to contracts for the carriage of goods by sea, contracts whereby party A agrees to carry goods for party B between ports in different jurisdictions.

The purpose of these Conventions is to limit the extent to which carriers can limit or exclude their liability under contracts for the carriage of goods by sea

---

* Visiting Scholar, George Washington University, USA
[1] See *Report of the United Nations Commission on International Trade Law Forty-first Session* (16 June–3 July 2008) (UNCITRAL document A/63/17) para. 298, available at http://www.uncitral.org/uncitral/en.commission/sessions/41st.html (visited 17 May 2011).
[2] See ibid.

which are usually entered into on the carrier's standard terms,[3] and the terms of which are usually found in bills of lading and other transport documents. Charterparties (contracts for the charter of ships where the parties have comparable bargaining power) are excluded from the application of these Conventions. Of the three instruments that preceded UNCITRAL's latest Convention, the first two were widely adopted by major maritime nations. The Hamburg Rules which made several radical departures from the previous instruments[4] were adopted by only 34 states,[5] none of them major maritime nations. Thus their contribution to this area of law has been limited.

The new Convention is much longer and more detailed than any of the previous Conventions on this subject, running to 96 provisions. The Convention seeks to bring the law on carriage of goods up to date by addressing the shortcomings of the previous Conventions that have come to light over the years, introducing provisions that reflect current practice and prepare for future developments. It also seeks to achieve the purpose of any harmonisation exercise, namely, to introduce a greater amount of uniformity in the way that relevant contracts of carriage are regulated in different jurisdictions.

SIGNIFICANCE OF STATE IMPLEMENTATION TO THE AIM OF UNIFORMITY

The aims of the harmonisation exercise would obviously be prejudiced if adoption were not widespread among states, not less because there are already three different regimes which are applicable in different jurisdictions, in certain circumstances mandatorily,[6] and which put varying limits on the carrier's power to exclude and limit his liability. Thus if many states decide not to switch from their current regime to the new Rotterdam Rules, the effect will simply be to introduce further potential conflicts of law problems by adding a fourth regime to the already existing ones.[7]

---

[3]   For a historical account of the genesis of the Conventions see Reynolds, F (1990), 'The Hague Rules, the Hague-Visby Rules, and the Hamburg Rules', 7 *Australian and New Zealand Maritime Law Journal* 16, available at www.austlii.edu.au/au/journals/ANZMLJ/1990/2.pdf.

[4]   For an account of these see Wilson, JF (2010), *Carriage of Goods by Sea* (7th ed), Pearson Longman at 215–9.

[5]   A list of these is available at www.uncitral.org/uncitral/en/uncitral_texts/transport_goods/Hamburg_status.html.

[6]   See Article X Hague-Visby Rules and Article 2 Hamburg Rules.

[7]   For states' comments on the final draft of the Convention see *Draft convention on contracts for the international carriage of goods wholly or partly by sea: Compilation of comments by Governments and intergovernmental organizations*, UNCITRAL

In practice adoption and implementation at state level are likely to be problematic. States may be reluctant to overhaul their applicable regime without first consulting extensively with local practitioners and interest groups. Furthermore reform of the law on carriage of goods by sea is unlikely to be viewed as a pressing matter by legislatures as, even if it is successful, it is unlikely to have any political impact (from the average voter's point of view it is a non-issue). Therefore even if the new Convention is well received, reform is unlikely to occur with great speed, and if uptake by states is too slow, the instrument may become outdated before it has been put to significant use.

The above drawbacks are certainly likely to stall adoption in the UK which participated for the last three years in the drafting negotiations that led up to the Convention through the Department for Transport (DfT). The following reactions were expressed by a representative of the DfT when questioned regarding implementation:[8]

> While we can see positive benefits from adopting the new Rules, no agreed UK Government position exists on UK adoption, or not, of them and further consultation with our stakeholders and legal practitioners will be important before we would be prepared to recommend ratification (and consequential amendments to English law). Ratification will also depend on how other nations respond positively [*sic*] to the Rules i.e will the Rules be adopted by the great majority of UN member states, a level of support which is required if they are to supersede the Hague, the Hague-Visby ... and the Hamburg Rules ..., together with national codes, and thus achieve 'uniformity'. A number of issues caused strong debate/divided opinion throughout the course of negotiations ... on the Rules and it is probably fair to say that adoption might not be a straightforward issue.

More recently, the DfT reiterated this position as follows:

> The UK Government continues to support the principle of consolidating, harmonising and modernising existing rules governing the carriage of goods by sea. However, we consider this can only be successfully achieved by having an internationally agreed and workable regime that is broadly acceptable to all the commercial parties.
>
> In the absence of a consensus of opinion on the Rotterdam Rules by UK business engaged in international trade, the Government remains neutral on them. We are nevertheless continuing to maintain a watching brief on international reaction to the Rules and will review the UK position if other leading maritime and trading nations ratify them.[9]

---

documents A/CN.9/658 plus Addenda 1–14. These comments were presented in the course of UNCITRAL's forty-first session in June–July 2008.

[8]   Email to the author dated 31 July 2008. See also *Draft convention on contracts for the international carriage of goods wholly or partly by sea: Compilation of comments by Governments and intergovernmental organizations*, Addendum 13: United Kingdom, 11 June 2008, UNCITRAL document A/CN.9/658/Add.13, for an overview of the UK's concerns regarding the text of the Convention itself.

[9]   Email to the author dated 18 March 2011.

This position is understandable. The ratification of the new Convention would bring about major changes to current UK law and it is likely that the consultation will raise the same objections as are frequently levelled against proposals to adopt the Vienna Convention on the International Sale of Goods,[10] i.e. that changing the well-established and developed current laws would introduce uncertainties which in turn might decrease the popularity of English law as applicable law and London as a centre for dispute resolution. Thus adoption, while a possibility, is not likely to take place very speedily in the UK, and this is likely to apply also to a number of other major maritime nations, albeit a number of them, including Denmark, France, Greece, the Netherlands, Norway, Spain, Switzerland and USA,[11] have all signed the Convention.

The question that this chapter deals with is whether the value of this harmonisation exercise depends solely on whether or not a large enough number of states decide to show support for these aims by adopting the Convention and implementing it into their national laws. It is worth considering two questions. First of all is there the option of autonomy? That is can the Convention be used independently of whether or not it is adopted by nation states? And secondly, if the answer to the first question is yes, what is the likelihood that it will be so used?

AUTONOMY

We shall deal first with the question whether the Convention may be used to govern contracts for the international carriage of goods by sea in the absence of widespread adoption by states. Theoretically it is possible to apply the Convention to one's contract of carriage with the inclusion of appropriate governing law and dispute resolution clauses. The governing law clause would need to indicate the Convention (a non-state body of law) to be the governing law of the contract. The Convention governs rights, duties and liabilities in a great amount of detail and its provisions could by themselves provide an answer to most disputes in connection with contracts of carriage. In order for this choice of law to be upheld, however, such disputes would have to be decided outside

---

[10] See for example Forte, A (1997), 'The United Nations Convention on Contracts for the International Sale of Goods: Reason or Unreason in the United Kingdom', 26 *University of Baltimore Law Review* 51 at 56–63.

[11] All these countries are listed in UNCTAD's list of the 35 countries and territories with the largest fleets owned by nationals according to deadweight tonnage, as of 1 January 2009. See United Nations Convention on Trade and Development, *Report on Maritime Transport 2009*, New York and Geneva, 2009, 53. Table 12. Available at http://www.unctad.org/en/docs/rmt2009_en.pdf (visited 17-05-2011).

national courts, as the latter would not readily recognise a non-state body of law as the governing law of a contract[12] and would apply conflict rules to lead them to a particular jurisdiction whose law would be the applicable law for the purposes of the dispute. Therefore an arbitration clause would also have to be included in the contract of carriage.[13]

Some excellent centres of maritime arbitration have become established over the years, among them the London Maritime Arbitrators Association (LMAA) and the Society of Maritime Arbitrators of New York (SMA),[14] which give parties to contracts of carriage a very good alternative to courts for the resolution of their disputes. Arbitrators are apt to apply the parties' choice of law even if it is not the law of a state.[15] Article 28(1) of UNCITRAL's Model Law

---

[12]   Where national courts are concerned, they would usually recognise the parties' autonomy in choosing the law applicable to their contract under certain conditions, one of them being 'that the law chosen should be that of a contemporary municipal legal system and that the parties are bound by any subsequent changes therein'. See Nygh, P (1999), *Autonomy in International Contracts*, Clarendon Press at 46. Thus under Article 3(1) of the Rome Convention, which provides that 'a contract shall be governed by the law chosen by the parties', 'law' means 'the law of a State' (ibid. at 60). The same author, ibid. at 61, observes that '[r]eceived wisdom in virtually all countries at present [1999] precludes the choice of a law which is not part of a municipal system. Such a purported choice would be ineffective and the objectively applicable law would prevail'. Note that a provision in the European Commission's *Proposal for a Regulation of the EU Parliament and Council on the law applicable to contractual obligations (Rome I)* (Brussels, 15 December 2005, COM(2005)650 final, 2005/0261 (COD), available at http://europa.eu.int/eur-lex/lex/LexUriServ/site/en/com/2005/com2005_0650en01.pdf) allowing parties to choose a non-state body of law as the applicable law of the contract (Article 3(2)) was deleted from the text of the proposal in the Compromise Package recommended by the Presidency to the European Council in April 2007 (see *Proposal for a Regulation of the European Parliament and of the Council on the law applicable to contractual obligations (Rome I) – Compromise package by the Presidency*, 13 April 2007, Brussels, 8022/07 ADD 1 REV 1, available at http://www.consilium.europa.eu/cms3_applications/applications/openDebates/openDebates-PREVIEW.ASP?id=301&lang=en&cmsID=1105) and does not appear in the adopted text of the Regulation (see Regulation EC 593/2008 of the European Parliament and of the Council of 17 June 2008 on the law applicable to contractual obligations (Rome I) available at http://eur-lex.europa.eu/LexUriServ/LexUriServ.do?uri=OJ:L:2008:177:0006:0016:EN:PDF).

[13]   The arbitration agreement itself is likely to be upheld by national courts as most states have arbitration laws that provide for a stay of court proceedings where there is an arbitration agreement between the parties.

[14]   Though there are numerous maritime arbitration centres throughout the world, these two centres share approximately 90% of the worldwide maritime arbitration market. See Riccomagno, M (2004), 'Maritime Arbitration', 70 *Arbitration* 267 at 271.

[15]   In fact arbitrators will even recognise governing law clauses which refer simply to the Lex Mercatoria. An example of a governing law clause referring to the Lex Mercatoria would read as follows: '[this agreement is subject to] the customs and usages of international trade, to the rules of law which are common to all or most of the States

on International Commercial Arbitration (Model Law)[16] provides that '[t]he arbitral tribunal shall decide the dispute in accordance with such rules of law as are chosen by the parties as applicable to the substance of the dispute'. The use of the words 'rules of law' (or '*règles de droit*')[17] 'should be interpreted as permitting a choice beyond national law'.[18] This is important as the Model Law's provisions are based on worldwide consensus on the principles of international arbitration practice,[19] and were meant to provide a model for updating national laws which had become inadequate,[20] as well as to help do away with disparities among national laws on arbitration.[21]

The only reason why arbitrators might set aside the parties' chosen law would be if they saw the choice as an attempt to circumvent the mandatory application of whichever international convention would have been mandatorily applicable in the absence of such choice (for example, in the case of shipments taking place from the UK, the Hague-Visby Rules).[22] However this reason for setting aside

---

engaged in international trade or to those States which are connected with the dispute. Where such common rules are not ascertainable, the arbitrator applies the rule or chooses the solution which appears to him to be the most appropriate and equitable.' See Lando, O (1985), 'The Lex Mercatoria in International Commercial Arbitration', 34 *International and Comparative Law Quarterly* 747 at 747. The same clause is quoted with disapproval by Flanagan, PM (2004), 'Demythologising the law merchant: the impropriety of the Lex Mercatoria as a choice of law', 15 *International Company and Commercial Law Review* 297 at 297–8.

[16] A number of countries have enacted arbitration laws based on UNCITRAL's Model Law. At present this number stands at over 60. A list of countries that have used the model law in enacting legislation is available at www.uncitral.org/uncitral/en/uncitral_texts/arbitration/1985Model_arbitration_status.html.

[17] Nygh, *supra* n. 12 at193, explains that 'the use of the French words *règles de droit* is significant. Unlike *loi*, the meaning of *droit* is not confined to a law emanating from a sovereign authority but includes rules of moral or social force.'

[18] Ibid.

[19] See Explanatory Note by UNCITRAL Secretariat on the Model Law on International Commercial Arbitration, in *Model Law on International Commercial Arbitration*, United Nations, 1994, paragraph 2.

[20] Ibid., paragraphs 5–6.

[21] Ibid., paragraphs 7–8.

[22] See *The Hollandia* [1983] 1 AC 565, 576: 'What the arbitration clause does is to leave it to the arbitrator to determine what is the "proper law" of the contract in accordance with accepted principles of conflict of laws and then to apply that "proper law" to the interpretation, and the validity of the contract and the mode of performance and the consequences of breaches of contract. One, but by no means the only, matter to be taken into consideration in deciding what is the "proper law" is the particular choice of substantive law by which the contract is to be governed, made by an express clause in the contract itself. But if the particular choice of substantive law made by the express clause is such as to make the clause null and void under to the law of the place where the contract was made, or under what, in the absence of such express clause, would be the

the choice of law is not likely to arise because the level of carrier liability laid down by the new Convention is higher even than the level applicable under the Hamburg Rules[23] which is considerably higher than that applicable under the Hague or Hague-Visby Rules, and therefore the choice of the new Convention as applicable law is hardly likely to be viewed as an attempt by the carrier to avoid the mandatory application of a lower level of liability.[24] Thus it is likely that an arbitrator would uphold such a choice of law.

The Convention itself contains provisions on arbitration. Under Article 75(1) of the Convention 'parties may agree that any dispute that may arise relating to the carriage of goods under this Convention shall be referred to arbitration'. The subsequent paragraphs of Article 75 go on to make detailed provisions regarding the place of arbitration, provisions which apply mandatorily and restrict the carrier's ability to determine the place of arbitration through contractual designation.[25] These provisions are meant to grant additional protection to the party to the contract of carriage whose standard contract terms are not being

---

proper law of the contract, I am very far from accepting that it would be open to the arbitrator to treat the clause as being otherwise than null and void, or to give any effect to it.'

[23]   See Article 59 of the Convention where the limitation is set at 875 units of account per package or other shipping unit, or 3 units of account per kilogram of the gross weight of the goods, whichever amount is the higher. Cf Article 6 of the Hamburg rules where the limitations are set at 835 units of account and 2.5 units of account respectively. In addition the carrier's liability has increased in relation to his liability under the Hague-Visby Rules in the following ways: under Article 62 the period of time for suit against the carrier has been doubled from one to two years as under the Hamburg Rules. In addition, and in contrast to the Hague-Visby Rules, the exception of error in navigation has been excluded (see Article 17(3)), the obligation to exercise due diligence to make the vessel seaworthy must be exercised throughout the voyage rather than merely at its commencement (see Article 14) and the carrier is liable for delay in delivery (see Article 17).

[24]   See Article V of the Hague-Visby Rules whereby 'a carrier shall be at liberty to surrender in whole or in part all or any of his rights and immunities or to increase any of his responsibilities under these Rules, provided such surrender or increase shall be embodied in the bill of lading issued to the shipper.'

[25]   A note by the Secretariat (*Arbitration: Uniform international arbitration practice and the provisions of the draft instrument*, 2 March 2005, UN Document A/CN.9/WG.III/WP.45) issued at the time these provisions were being drafted would suggest that 'place' here means 'seat' rather than 'location' (see paragraph 14). Merkin, R (2005), *Arbitration Act 1996* (3 ed), LLP at 22 explains the distinction as follows: '[t]he seat of the arbitration is not necessarily the same place as that in which some or all of the arbitration is physically conducted: the seat is a juridical concept.' Indeed an arbitration which has its seat in England will be recognised as being within the English legislation even though various parts of the arbitration are conducted abroad (e.g. for the convenience of arbitrators or witness, or to facilitate the inspection of any property forming part of the dispute). See for example *Naviera Amazonica Peruana SA v. Compania Internacional de Seguros del Peru* [1988] 1 Lloyd's Rep. 116; *Union of India v. McDonnell Douglas* [1993] 2 Lloyd's Rep. 48; *Sumitomo Heavy Industries v. Oil and Natural Gas Commission* [1994] 1 Lloyd's Rep. 45.

used (i.e. the party who is not the carrier) and apply specifically to liner carriage. In addition, special provisions apply where the designation of the place of arbitration is contained in a volume contract.[26]

Article 76 expressly excludes bulk trades from the provisions in Article 75,[27] thus allowing more freedom in drafting the arbitration agreement applicable to the contract of carriage in these cases. Article 76(1) provides that nothing in the Convention affects the enforceability of an arbitration agreement in a contract of carriage in non-liner transportation to which this Convention or the provisions of this Convention apply by reason of (a) the application of Article 7 (which refers, among other things to the holder of a charterparty bill of lading who is not an original party to the charterparty[28]) or (b) the parties' voluntary incorporation of the Convention in a contract of carriage that would not otherwise be subject to this Convention (which may include a contract of carriage contained in a transport document or electronic transport record that refers to the Convention as applicable law).

Sub-article (2) goes on to provide as follows:

> Notwithstanding paragraph 1 of this article, an arbitration agreement in a transport document or electronic transport record to which this Convention applies by reason of the application of article 7 is subject to this Chapter [i.e. the restrictions in Article 75] unless such a transport document or electronic transport record:
>   (a)   identifies the parties to and the date of the charterparty ...; and
>   (b)   incorporates by specific reference the clause in the charterparty ... that contains the terms of the arbitration agreement.

Where Article 76 is applicable, it would seem that if an appropriately drafted[29] arbitration clause were included in the contract of carriage, any disputes arising

---

[26]   A volume contract is defined, for the purposes of the new Convention, as 'a contract of carriage that provides for the carriage of a specified quantity of goods in a series of shipments during an agreed period of time. The specification of the quantity may include a minimum, a maximum or a certain range.' See Article 1(2) of the Convention.

[27]   See *International Chamber of Shipping, BIMCO and the International Group of P&I Clubs' Comments on the Draft Convention on the Carriage of Goods [wholly or partly] [by Sea]* (UNCITRAL A/CN/9.WGIII/WP.81) (undated) at 8, available at www.marisec.org/news/Industry%20Submissions/Mar%2007%20ICS%20BIMCO%20IG%20comments%20on%20Draft%20Convention%20on%20the%20Carriage%20of%20Goods%20Final.pdf.

[28]   It is common for charterparty bills of lading to incorporate charterparty arbitration clauses by reference.

[29]   The careful drafting of these clauses is essential to their enforceability. See Debattista, C (2005), 'Drafting Enforceable Arbitration Clauses', 21 *Arbitration International* 233. See also Bond, SR (2005), 'How to Draft and Arbitration Clause (Revisited)' in Drahozal, CR and Naimark, RW (eds), *Towards a science of international arbitration: collected empirical research*, Kluwer Law International at 65.

in connection with that contract would be referred to arbitration in accordance with the provisions of that clause,[30] without the restrictions found in Article 75. Even where Article 75 is applicable, opting for arbitration is still possible, albeit subject to certain protections for the person having a claim against the carrier, who would not usually have been directly involved in the drafting of the arbitration clause.

The use of such choice of law and arbitration clauses would give the Convention autonomy from state law and permit parties to contracts for the international carriage of goods by sea to use it regardless of whether or not it is widely implemented at state level. It is not completely clear what the implications of this approach would be for uniform interpretation and application of the Convention's provisions. There is of course no rule of precedent in maritime arbitration, but neither is there a rule of precedent in many of the jurisdictions that would adopt and apply the Convention. *Jurisconsultorium*,[31] through use of UNCITRAL's Case Law on UNCITRAL Texts (CLOUT) system[32] would be possible if publication of relevant awards took place. Publication of maritime arbitral awards is envisaged under both the SMA Rules (Section 1) and the LMAA Terms (paragraph 26), but in each case the parties to the dispute may object to publication. Under the SMA Rules, the parties must exclude publication at the time they agree to apply the Rules to their arbitration, otherwise publication of the award will take place as a matter of course in the Society's *Award Service*. Under the LMAA terms the parties may object to publication after the award is made, i.e. at the time publication is proposed by the arbitrator.

A questionnaire was sent by the author to all 34 LMAA arbitrators in June 2008 (LMAA Questionnaire), and ten of them responded. To the question 'how often do you propose publication of an award you made?' the responses ranged from 'never' (three responses) to 'in almost all cases where there has been an award' (one response). Respondents were also asked how often the parties objected to publication. Objection by one or both of the parties to publication appears to be very frequent. One respondent stated that in his experience the parties had objected every time he asked so he had ceased to suggest it. More

---

[30] Resolution of disputes in connection with the transfer of ownership of the goods represented by the bill of lading would of course be subject to separate rules.

[31] Baasch Andersen, C (2005), 'The Uniform International Sales Law and the Global Jurisconsultorium', 24 *Journal of Law and Commerce* 159, explains that '[t]his term is offered by Vikki Rogers and Albert Kritzer in their excellent trade law thesaurus on terminology of international sales, and they use it to denote the need for cross-border consultation in deciding issues of uniform law. It is an excellent descriptive term for the phenomenon of the meeting of minds across jurisdictions in the shaping of international law.'

[32] The system is available at www.uncitral.org/uncitral/en/case_law.html.

than one respondent observed that it is usually (but not exclusively) the losing party who objects to publication. The estimation of the number of times that publication had been objected to after it was proposed ranged among the respondents from 50% to 90%. In spite of this, awards are occasionally published in *Lloyd's Maritime Law Newsletter*. It is noted on the LMAA website that '[in] 2009 LMAA Full Members received about 4445 new arbitration appointments and more than 647 awards were published by them'.[33]

In view of these responses, it looks likely that there is potential for some degree of uniformity, though of course some variation would still be likely to occur as not all awards would be published, and even those that are would not be binding on arbitrators deciding subsequent disputes.[34] However it must also be noted that because the number of established maritime arbitration centres (and arbitrators) that are likely to be deciding these disputes is far smaller than the number of jurisdictions whose courts may potentially be interpreting these provisions, one may argue that there may be less scope for variable interpretation if this method of dispute resolution were chosen.

---

[33] See www.lmaa.org.uk/about-us-Introduction.aspx (visited 17 May 2011).

[34] For example, from an overview of published SMA awards it appears that previous awards are frequently cited as precedents before SMA arbitral tribunals. They are also referred to by arbitrators themselves. As may be expected, however, they are not always followed rigorously. See *Arbitration between Maersk Line Ltd, as Claimants and U.S. Ship Management, Inc., as Respondents No. 3862* dated 24 September 2004 where the tribunal observed that '[w]hereas most arbitrators will consider and incorporate legal principles into the arbitral process in order to achieve a result which will acknowledge the commercial equities, the contract language as well as the applicable law, arbitrators are not bound by either legal precedent or prior arbitration decisions. The Award Service of the SMA is replete with cases supporting this proposition. The adherence to precedent, in the form of prior arbitration decisions, is at best a discretionary one, under which arbitrators view not only the substance of the prior award and result, but also consider the panel composition, the reasoning process and, quite importantly, the underlying facts. As brief examples to demonstrate this point, one can look at the arbitration decisions on the ATLANTIC MONARCH n15 and the PEGNY n16. Both cases involved the very narrow issue of whether charterer is entitled to six-hour free time after the tender of a Notice of Readiness when the vessel is already on demurrage. The charterer was the same in both cases, the owners were different. In the first decision, a panel of three lawyers found for the charterer; the second decision was heard before a panel of commercial men, who decided in owner's favor. Is this inconsistent and a disregard of *stare decisis?* On the face of it, it appears so. However, when reading these awards and those which followed on the same issues, one finds order and consistency. True to their background and training, the attorneys took a legal (and somewhat esoteric) approach, whereas the commercial arbitrators drew from their work experience, applying a more practical interpretation.'

VOLUNTARY APPLICATION?

But the essential question is would carriers voluntarily apply this Convention to their contracts of carriage unless they were obliged to by national law? The Convention does present certain advantages over its predecessors for carriers. To begin with, it codifies certain rules and principles developed by the courts, and it brings the law up to date. For example, Article 24 lays to rest any doubts that may remain as to the effects of fundamental breach of contract by deviation.[35] Secondly, the Convention makes clear the duties not only of the carrier but also of the shipper and the consignee.[36] Thirdly, it is very detailed and comprehensive and is largely able to function independently of state law, which can be very advantageous in a situation where, by definition, the regulated contract involves different jurisdictions.[37] This provides parties with clarity as to the applicable regime regardless of the state where loading or delivery takes place, or the law of the forum, and because arbitrators are usually professionals with extensive experience in the field, they are likely to be able to draw on their experience and their knowledge of practice to fill in any gaps. It also provides legal certainty with regard to the functional equivalence of electronic alternatives to transport documents, an area not covered by any of the previous Conventions.[38]

Finally, as far as dispute resolution by arbitration is concerned, any arbitral award that is made would be capable of enforcement through the national courts of most jurisdictions due to the wide adoption of UNCITRAL's Convention

---

[35] For a discussion of the problems that have arisen over the years in relation to fundamental breach by deviation see Wilson, *supra* n. 4, 20–25.

[36] See Articles 27–34 and 43–44.

[37] Possible conflicts and overlaps which can occur are well described by Wilson, *supra* n. 4, at 227, where he takes the example of the possibility of having the simultaneous application of both the Hague/Visby and the Hamburg Rules to the same contract of carriage: '[i]n practice … a carrying voyage may be mandatorily subject to two conflicting conventions. To take, for example, a carrying voyage from a port in the United Kingdom to a port in a Hamburg state, the contract of carriage would be governed by the Hague/Visby Rules at the port of shipment, and by the Hamburg Rules at the port of discharge. Which set of Rules would actually be applied would depend on the forum in which the dispute was litigated.'

[38] Re this see Van der Ziel, G (2003), 'The Legal Underpinning of E-Commerce in Maritime Transport by the UNCITRAL Draft Instrument on the Carriage Of Goods By Sea', *CMI Yearbook 2003*, 260 at 270, available at www.comitemaritime.org/year/2003/pdfiles/YBK03-12.pdf; and Goldby, M (2007), 'The Performance of the Bill of Ladings Functions under UNCITRAL's draft Convention on the Carriage of Goods: Unequivocal Legal Recognition of Electronic Equivalents', 13 *Journal of International Maritime Law* 160; and Goldby, M 'Electronic Alternatives to Transport Documents: a framework for future development?', Chapter 9 in D Rhidian Thomas (ed.) (2010), *A New Convention for the Carriage of Goods by Sea – The Rotterdam Rules*, Law Text Publishing.

on Recognition and Enforcement of Foreign Arbitral Awards (New York Convention).[39] This Convention has proven extremely popular and currently the number of states which are parties to it stands at 145.[40]

However, as can be imagined, these advantages are somewhat overshadowed by a number of factors that carriers would view as disadvantages. First of all, as mentioned above, the new Convention contains provisions on the carrier's liability that are less advantageous than those found in the Hague or Hague-Visby Rules which currently apply in many jurisdictions.[41] Secondly, non-state laws are not currently chosen as the applicable law of carriage contracts contained in a bill of lading or other transport document.[42] Venturing into new territory brings with it risks and potential costs that carriers might not want to take on. Also the choice might confuse arbitrators who may apply conflict rules to find an applicable state law anyway, thus complicating the dispute.[43] Furthermore, the Convention is designed for use as implemented into state law, and this is reflected in some of its provisions which would have to be adapted or interpreted creatively by arbitrators.

---

[39]   National courts have shown themselves willing to uphold even arbitral awards based on non-national legal systems such as the Lex Mercatoria. Railas, L (2004), *The Rise of the Lex Electronica and the International Sale of Goods* Faculty of Law, University of Helsinki, at 468–9 cites as examples the *Norsolar* case (ICC Case 3131/1979) upheld by the Austrian Supreme Court; the *Fougerolles* case upheld by the French Cour de Cassation and *Deutsche Schachtbau und Tiefbohrgesellschaft mbH v. Ras Al Khaimah National Oil Co and Shell International Petroleum Co Ltd* [1987] 2 Lloyd's Rep. 246 where the English Court of Appeal upheld an arbitral award based on the Lex Mercatoria. See also Nygh, *supra* n. 12 at 195–6, who cites *Channel Tunnel Group Ltd v. Balfour Beatty Constructions Ltd* [1993] AC 334, as the prime example of such cases.

[40]   A list of states parties is available at www.uncitral.org/uncitral/en/uncitral_texts/arbitration/NYConvention_status.html.

[41]   See *supra* n. 23.

[42]   The author has not come across any evidence that suggests otherwise and, indeed, in many if not most jurisdictions an international set of Rules will apply mandatorily, precluding this from happening. The same would also seem to be true where arbitration agreements apply. Responses to the LMAA Questionnaire suggest that practically all disputes that come before these arbitrators are governed by English law and the very few exceptions involve the law of another state. One response stated: 'Hamburg Rules can be incorporated by contract but the matter still subject to English Law'.

[43]   One response to the LMAA questionnaire indicated that the arbitrator would 'apply the appropriate conflict of laws rules' in a situation where interpretation and gap-filling were required due to the choice by the parties of a law other than a national law to govern their contract. Other responses indicated that the arbitrator would 'consider all surrounding circumstances' or use 'common sense informed by well-known principles of law that are common to most jurisdictions'. Still others said they would base themselves on the parties' submissions. Most responses (four out of ten) simply replied 'not applicable' or indicated that it was difficult for them to respond as such a situation had never arisen in their experience.

For example, the wording of Article 5(1) provides:

> ... this Convention *applies* to contracts of carriage in which the place of receipt and the place of delivery are in different States, and the port of loading of a sea carriage and the port of discharge of the same sea carriage are in different States, *if*, according to the contract of carriage, any one of the following places is located in a Contracting State: (a) The place of receipt; (b) The port of loading; (c) The place of delivery; or (d) The port of discharge.

The word 'if' would seem to imply that the circumstances indicated are a condition precedent for the Convention to apply – i.e. the provision could be seen as stating that the Convention applies *exclusively* in these circumstances. This would be problematic as we are considering a situation where 'contracting states' are not involved. But one could also read this provision as meaning that the Convention applies *mandatorily* in these circumstances, but its application is not precluded in other instances. Arbitrators would have to perform a similar interpretative activity with other articles, e.g. Article 19(1)(a) which also refers to 'contracting states'.

Thirdly, contracts of carriage contained in transport documents are not usually subject to arbitration, except for standard charterparty bills of lading (e.g. CONGENBILL). Change of practice would be required and as far as liner carriage is concerned, it might well have to occur within the limits allowed by Article 75 discussed above. In addition, the carrier would have to consider the question whether transport documents with such choice of law clauses would be acceptable to shippers/transferees/consignees.[44] There is also the chance that these parties might attempt to challenge the choice of law clause as null and void, and while, as explained above, there is not a high likelihood of a successful *Hollandia*-style challenge, the mere possibility of one is still not a risk that carriers might be willing to take.

Thus one cannot realistically conclude that this option for autonomy would be very attractive to carriers, or is likely to be adopted widely in practice, if at all.

---

[44] There have been some objections to the new Convention, most notably from the European Shippers' Council which has in two documents referred to what it believed was a bias against shippers since, for example, they have strict liability for breach of certain duties as laid down by the Convention (Article 31(2)). See *Comments of the European Shippers' Council regarding the draft convention on the carriage of goods [wholly or partly] [by sea]*, 27 January 2006, UN Document A/CN.9/WG.III/WP.64, paragraphs 41–9; and *Position of the European Shippers' Council submitted to UNCITRAL Working Group III (Transport Law)*, 14 February 2007, UN Document A/CN.9/WG.III/WP.83, paragraph 12.

CONCLUSIONS

The major problem with UNCITRAL's most recent harmonisation efforts in the area of international carriage of goods by sea is the addition of a fourth regime to those that have already been produced on this subject. These regimes apply simultaneously in different jurisdictions and there is much potential for the new Rotterdam Rules to increase diversity and conflicts of law rather than harmonisation, unless they are widely adopted by states to replace currently applicable regimes.

The aim of this chapter was to show one of the ways in which this harmonisation exercise could be of value even in the event that states fail to show any interest in adopting the new Convention. It suggests that the new Convention may be used autonomously of state laws by parties to contracts which it seeks to regulate in order to enjoy certain disadvantages, e.g. the avoidance of conflicts of laws issues. This can be done through the inclusion of appropriate choice of law and arbitration clauses in the contract of carriage. This approach could allow the aims of the harmonisation exercise to be reached regardless of whether the Convention proves popular with states.

Because of the practical drawbacks discussed, the autonomy approach is unlikely to be an attractive option for carriers across the board. However, there are some situations where the advantages offered may outweigh the drawbacks. For example, if the carrier wishes to make available an electronic alternative to the usual transport documents to his clients, the autonomy approach would be ideal as the legal status of these instruments remains largely uncertain in most jurisdictions and they are not covered by any of the previous Conventions.

Were the autonomy approach to be adopted, the publication of arbitration awards and their inclusion in UNCITRAL's CLOUT service could do much to encourage a more uniform interpretation of the new Convention's provisions. Publication of awards is envisaged by the terms of the two major centres of maritime arbitration and, while not compulsory, does happen occasionally in LMAA arbitration and more frequently for awards given by SMA arbitrators. Thus *jurisconsultorium* on the Convention's provisions could still take place if this approach were adopted.

9. Demandeur-centricity in transnational commercial law

Sandeep Gopalan[1]

Theoretical explanations for the structuring of transnational commercial law agreements are limited by their focus on the state. Given the dispositive nature of transnational commercial law, this chapter contends that the key actors are private demandeurs, and that agreements are reflective of their preferences and relative power. I have explained the limitations of the state-centric approach in other works,[2] and do not elaborate on those arguments here. This chapter will limit itself to outlining the central claims of the demandeur-centric approach for the process of creating transnational commercial law. It demonstrates that agreement design is predicated on two variables – bargaining costs and enforcement costs. The operation of these variables spawns agreements ranging from non-convention agreements, which result when demandeurs possess the ability to strike agreements at low cost and are able to enforce them without much reliance on state actors, to conventions, which result when bargaining and enforcement costs are high.

Theories about the design of transnational commercial law agreements have extensively applied the contract lens, assuming that states mimic private contracting parties and seek to enhance the credibility and enforceability of their agreements.[3] The central players are rational states which act to maximize contractual surplus.[4] Putting mutual promises in contract form makes them binding

---

[1]   Professor and Head of Department of Law, National University of Ireland, Maynooth.
[2]   See Gopalan, S (2008), 'A Demandeur-Centric Approach to Regime Design in Transnational Commercial Law', 39 *Georgia Journal of International Law* 327, upon which some of the points of this chapter are based.
[3]   See, e.g., Guzman, AT (2005), 'The Design of International Agreements', 16 *European Journal of International Law* 579, at 581.
[4]   See Abbott, KW (1989), 'Modern International Relations Theory: A Prospectus for International Lawyers', 14 *Yale Journal of International Law* 335; Keohane, RO (1984), *After Hegemony: Cooperation And Discord In The World Political Economy*, Princeton University Press (1984) at 27.

and facilitates compliance by stipulating mechanisms to measure satisfactory performance and breach. Although there are no threats of damages actions to keep states in line, the fear of suffering reputational damage satisfies the coercive function.[5] However, there is a marked difference that cannot be ignored – in private contract law, the damages are a measure of the non-breaching party's loss and are paid to it, whereas, in international law, reputational damages do not compensate for the non-breaching state's loss. Further, the contract analogy has limitations because of the absence of the interpretive role played by courts to limit opportunism. Consider the following example: A and B enter into a contract for the sale of a horse. If A, the seller, delivers a mule at the time of performance and claims that he subjectively understood 'horse' to mean 'mule', B will prevail in court because the court is likely to regard A's self-serving interpretation as no more than horse dung. This is key to A (and other contracting parties) using terms with due consideration to how courts are likely to enforce them. Contrast this with disputes between states over the use of river waters, where each state argues that its use is consistent with the agreement. The two examples are distinguished by the limitation of opportunistic auto-interpretation by *ex ante* judgments about enforceability. In the absence of a neutral player, merely embodying promises in contractual form does little to limit opportunism. The fact that state commitments are largely free from such checks means that the contract analogy can be taken only so far. Despite these limitations, the contract law lens has been favoured with the concomitant obsession with monitoring mechanisms, sanctions, and sanction inflicting bodies.

State-centric theories posit that in structuring international agreements states are most concerned about the *impact* that the agreement will have in changing state conduct. Impact determines whether states choose *hard* or *soft* law. If states desire to have low impact, then they are more likely to choose soft law. Conversely, if they desire a high impact, agreements will be structured as hard law. Empirical examination does not always support a positive correlation between impact and form.[6]

Explanations premised on the state have limited traction in transnational commercial law. To begin with, states are not the dominant actors in transnational commercial law. Even when they are significant actors, compliance and monitoring concerns are manifestly underappreciated based on the drafting history. Indeed, most transnational commercial law conventions have no monitoring mechanisms whatsoever, and do not have unified dispute resolution mechanisms

[5]   Downs, GW and Jones, MA (2002), 'Reputation, Compliance, and International Law', 31 *Journal of Legal Studies (Special Issue) 95*, at 95–6, 98–100.

[6]   See, e.g., Franck, TM (1988), 'Legitimacy in the International System', 82 *American Journal of International Law*, 705 at 705.

or tribunals. These mechanisms do not seem to occupy much attention in drafting discussions and diplomatic conferences, suggesting that they are either unnecessary or unlikely to be feasible. Given that such mechanisms feature in public international law conventions, their absence in transnational commercial agreements is probably more indicative of the former belief. The drafters of the 1980 United Nations Convention on Contracts for the International Sale of Goods (hereinafter referred to as the CISG), for example, could have provided for the constitution of an international tribunal for the disposition of CISG cases without leaving it to domestic courts with the obvious risk of disharmony caused by divergent interpretations.

The absence of compliance monitoring mechanisms might be explained by the qualitative differences between transnational commercial law and public international law agreements. The former are largely aimed at tackling problems stemming from incomplete contracts between private parties. As such, much like domestic commercial law in sophisticated legal systems, their ambition is limited to the efficient interpretation of commercial agreements. One measure of their success is their ability to offer default rules at lower cost than those that could potentially be crafted by the parties. Over time, these rules as interpreted contribute the (intended) additional educational externality which standardizes commercial practices and drafting language as parties internalize lessons from the interpretive process. To be sure, some transnational commercial law agreements seek to achieve the standardization result without the sacrifice of time required for it to be achieved organically by creating new legal concepts in international conventions. The success or failure of these short-cut methods will ultimately depend on the interpretive function being performed uniformly by other states.

The application of rational choice theory to contracting parties, rather than states, explains why conventions succeed or fail. If the convention is precise in its terms on the ambits of cooperative action, contracting parties will find it hard to behave opportunistically and then turn round and claim that the opportunistic conduct did not violate the requirements of a cooperative game.[7] The conclusion is similar in the context of coordination. Contracting parties subject themselves to a convention not because of its *binding* nature, but *inter alia* to assuage another party's fear of being subject to a foreign legal system, because their interests might be better protected by the convention, and to reduce transaction costs. The *binding* nature does not add much value to either party, except insofar as it imposes some obligations on courts if a dispute arises.[8] Routine

---

[7]   Goldsmith, J and Posner, E (2003), 'International Agreements: A Rational Choice Approach', 44 *Virginia Journal of International Law* 113, at 118.

[8]   This may be of limited utility if, as is common, the contract contains an arbitration clause. Even where the dispute is before a court, the binding nature of a convention can be stymied by interpretative devices aimed at applying domestic law.

exclusions of instruments like the CISG are not indicative of its qualitative failure and might be explained by path dependence[9] and network externalities. Thus, although the CISG might be a better solution, a suboptimal uniformity continues to persist because contracting parties are reluctant to change their existing practices.[10]

A. EVALUATION OF FUNCTIONAL THEORIES

Functional theories posit that agreement design is predicated on desired outcomes.[11] Thus, drafters choose soft law because of its greater flexibility, conduciveness to incremental expansion, non-state entity participation, and lack of need for ratification.[12] A key assumption is that hard law impacts on state behaviour more than soft law.[13] States prefer soft law when uncertainty is high, their interests are divergent, informational costs are low, and, consequently, reputational sanctions are low.[14] Soft law also offers flexibility, which is valuable in areas where states are strongly wedded to their preferences. It is an intermediate option when the expected modification in behaviour is burdensome.[15]

In keeping with the contract lens, agreement design is functionally responsive to the need to ensure the credibility of state commitments by limiting 'self-serving auto-interpretation'.[16] Hard law represents maximum credibility, and is chosen when domestic political costs are low. Hard law also offers a better guarantee of binding successive governments, and might be better suited to modifying the behaviour of relevant domestic actors.[17] Given that states are repeat players in the international legal system, there is an expectation that the opportunistic interpretation of a particular convention or treaty will trigger

---

[9]   Kahan, M and Klausner, M (1996), 'Path Dependence in Corporate Contracting: Increasing Returns, Herd Behavior and Cognitive Biases', 74 *Washington University Law Quarterly* 347, at 347.

[10]   *Ibid.* at 349. Kahan and Klausner have suggested 'that corporate contract terms can frequently offer "increasing returns" as more firms employ the same contract term. Value arises from the common use of a contract term ... as the use of a term increases, it becomes significantly more attractive (at least up to a critical point), and its attraction becomes self-perpetuating.'

[11]   Abbott, KW and Snidal, D (2000), 'Hard Law and Soft Law in International Governance', 54 *International Organization* 421.

[12]   *Ibid.*

[13]   E.g., Guzman, *supra* n. 3, at 584.

[14]   Raustiala, K (2005), 'Form and Substance in International Agreements', 99 *American Journal of International Law* 581, at 591–2.

[15]   Abbott and Snidal, *supra* n. 11, at 423.

[16]   *Ibid.* at 427.

[17]   *Ibid.* at 426.

negative consequences for the bad actor in other areas.[18] Agreements with binding dispute resolution mechanisms check auto-interpretation.[19] Abbott and Snidal espouse a narrow role for tribunals, only to apply and interpret hard law. This does not account for the ability of these tribunals to apply soft law. The unexpected success of soft law agreements like the UNIDROIT Principles and the Principles of European Contract Law (PECL) is attributable to their application by tribunals and courts.

Abbott and Snidal predict that hard law results where 'the benefits of cooperation are great but the potential for opportunism and its costs are high, where noncompliance is not easy to detect, where states want to form clubs of very committed states, and where executive agencies within a state want to commit other domestic actors such as the legislature to the international agreement'.[20]

While functionalism has some explanatory power, it leaves several puzzles unanswered. Consider, for example, the CISG: if Abbott and Snidal are correct the drafters chose a convention over soft law because the benefits of cooperation are great but the potential for opportunism is high. A convention that provides a unified system of law for contracts for the sale of goods between parties in different countries could provide cooperative benefits.[21] Arguably, differences in national laws may cause 'legal risk', and stand in the way of cooperative interactions.[22] Legal risk can encourage opportunism by contracting parties who may, for example, race to litigate in a forum that will suit their interests in appropriate cases,[23] creating fear and chilling potentially profitable contracts, or imposing additional costs to cover such risks.[24]

Assuming opportunism could be significant, eliminating or minimizing legal risk would play a salutary role in promoting contracts across national borders.[25] In addition to legal risk, the differences in national laws impose transaction costs on contracting parties, ranging from the cost of obtaining legal opinions, fulfilling formal requirements, and obtaining translations, to the varying court costs of different legal systems. While large businesses may be able to absorb these costs, they can be prohibitive to small enterprises.

---

[18] *Ibid.*

[19] *Ibid.*

[20] *Ibid.* at 429–30.

[21] This point is valid even after the adoption of the CISG. See von Bar, C and Lando, O (2002), 'Communication on European Contract Law: Joint Response of the Commission on European Contract Law and the Study Group on a European Civil Code', 10 *European Revue of Private Law* 185.

[22] See Stephan, PB (1999), 'The Futility of Unification and Harmonization in International Commercial Law', 39 *Virginia Journal of International Law* 743, at 746.

[23] *Ibid.*

[24] *Ibid.*

[25] *Ibid.*

If Abbott and Snidal are correct, the drafters' choice of convention for the CISG should address these problems.[26] The difficulty is that the CISG's convention form does very little for it in terms of limiting opportunism. Contracting parties are just as free to exclude the law in whole or in part regardless of the fact that it is a convention.[27] The only value from choosing a convention is that courts in contracting states are bound to apply it unless the parties have excluded it by contract.[28] The utility of this is dependent on the willingness of domestic courts to avoid contriving reasons for the application of their domestic law. [29] In any event, a significant number of commercial parties exclude the CISG; thus, the binding nature is of limited utility.[30] Even in cases where the CISG has been applied, it has come as a surprise to parties.[31] Lawyers either do not know of the application of the convention or choose to apply domestic law instead.[32] A simple questionnaire study of the Maricopa County Bar association by this author yielded similar results. On the evidence, if the drafters chose convention over soft law, they did so in a way that does almost nothing to stop opportunism.

Functionalists also explain choices of form in terms of contracting costs – soft law is less costly than hard law.[33] This is only partly true – the principal

---

[26] What kind of opportunistic conduct would the delegates worry about? Would it be that parties in some states would not be subject to the agreement? Would it be that courts in some states would not apply the agreement? Would it be that parties could act opportunistically and pick and choose the instrument or its component parts depending on their interests? These do not appear to be prevented by the CISG.

[27] CISG, Art. 6: 'The parties may exclude the application of this Convention or, subject to article 12, derogate from or vary the effect of any of its provisions.'

[28] United States Federal Appellate Court Judgment of 21 June 2002 (*Schmitz-Werke v. Rockland*), available at http://cisgw3.law.pace.edu/cases/020621u1.html: '[w]hen two nations are signatories to the CISG, the treaty governs contracts for the sale of goods between parties whose places of business are in those two nations, unless the contract contains a choice of law clause.'

[29] See United States cases *Zapata Hermanos Sucesores, S.A. v. Hearthside Baking Co.*, 313 F.3d 385 (7th Cir. 2002); *MCC-Marble Ceramic Ctr., Inc. v. Ceramica Nuova D'Agostino, S.P.A.*, 144 F.3d 1384 (11th Cir. 1998); *Delchi Carrier SpA v. Rotorex Corp.*, 71 F.3d 1024 (2d Cir. 1995).

[30] Smits, J (2007), 'Law Making In The European Union: On Globalization And Contract Law In Divergent Legal Cultures', 67 *Louisiana Law Review* 1181, at 1187.

[31] Behr, V (1998), 'The Sales Convention in Europe: From Problems in Drafting to Problems in Practice', 17 *Journal of Law and Commerce* 263, at 265.

[32] A study on the CISG in Florida showed that it was 'largely unknown to crucial legal audiences in Florida.': see Gordon, M (1998), 'Some Thoughts on the Receptiveness of Contract Rules I the CISG and UNIDROIT Principles as Reflected in One State's (Florida) Experience of (1) Law School Faculty, (2) Members of the Bar with an International Practice, and (3) Judges', 46 *American Journal of Comparative Law Supp.* 361.

[33] Abbott and Snidal, *supra* n. 11, at 434: [l]egal specialists must be consulted; bureaucratic reviews are often lengthy. Different legal traditions across states complicate the

difference between hard and soft law costs pertains to the need for ratification in the former. All the other costs are incurred for both. Experts have to be consulted, differences between legal families and systems must be resolved, and negotiation is still contentious as proponents of various interests argue just as vigorously.[34] There is no noticeable improvement in terms of time expended either. The UNIDROIT Principles have been a work in progress for over 20 years.[35] In contrast, the Hague Convention on Certain Rights with respect to Securities held with Intermediaries took about two years from start to finish.[36]

Abbott and Snidal's examples distinguishing hard and soft law can be better explained by focusing on ratification costs. Even so, soft law instruments have to be marketed to the relevant constituencies, and entail some of the same kinds of expenditures as conventions. Notwithstanding these criticisms, it is true that agencies creating transnational commercial law are conscious about ratification costs. A perception exists that the labour expended in creating the instrument is largely wasted if the instrument does not achieve a high number of ratifications.

A low number of ratifications is not necessarily indicative of failure and may be attributed to a number of reasons: the instrument is inadequate in comparison to domestic law,[37] legislatures are not interested in the subject matter, international law is not needed, the state was not actively engaged in the drafting process,[38] the perception that the instrument panders to inimical interest groups,[39] and pressure from conflicting interest groups.[40]

---

exercise. Approval and ratification processes, typically involving legislative authorization, are more complex than for purely political agreements'.

[34]   If it were otherwise, it might suggest that the parties do not intend that the instrument be of much use.

[35]   International Institute for the Unification of Private Law (UNIDROIT) – Home Page, www.unidroit.org.

[36]   See Press Release, Hague Conference on Private Int'l Law (HCCH), *New Hague Convention increases legal security for cross-border securities transactions* (13 Dec. 2002), available at http://www.hcch.net/index_en.php?act=events.details&year=2002&varevent=8. See also HCCH, Conclusions of the Special Commission Held from 1–3 April 2003 on General Affairs and Policy of the Conference, para. 1, available at www.hcch.net/upload/wop/genaff_concl2003.pdf, noting that '[t]he Commission welcomed the flexibility and innovative character of the working methods used for this project and the speed at which the project has been completed without a vote being cast'.

[37]   This explains the lack of ratification of the ULIS and ULIF conventions drafted by UNIDRIOIT.

[38]   This explains the United States' refusal to ratify ULIS and ULIF.

[39]   This explains the reluctance of developing countries to ratify the Hague-Visby Rules.

[40]   This explains the United States' refusal to ratify the United Nations Convention on the Law of the Sea. This last reason is the least powerful in the transnational commercial law context. None of these reasons pertains to cost or seriousness. Unless each

These alternative explanations call into question Abbott and Snidal's claim that 'softer forms of legalization will be more attractive to states as contracting costs increase'.[41] Rather than the increased cost, in many instances what seems to be motivating the choice against hard law is the realization that the cost of ratification is only worthwhile in some instances because of the dispositive nature of conventions. Ratification may not add much by way of bindingness or, more importantly, impact. Thus, it is unclear if the trade-offs between contracting costs and the choice between hard law and soft law occurs, except for the marginal ratification costs.

Professor Raustiala writes that technocratic subjects are more amenable to soft law.[42] He provides examples to support both the functionalist claim that uncertainty influences the form of international agreement and the liberal claim that pledges are 'most common in areas of low domestic salience'.[43] However, one example in the technocratic area directly contradicts this claim – the Hague Convention on the Law Applicable to Certain Rights in Respect of Securities Held with an Intermediary ('Hague Convention'),[44] which is a hard law agreement necessitated by the enormous uncertainty that threatened the very survival of the global financial system.[45] The project took just over two years from start to finish.

Raustiala's work posits that depth and form are negatively correlated: pledges (soft law) are deeper than contracts (conventions) because they do not raise compliance worries. States prefer pledges to make deep commitments rather than shallow ones. Conversely, hard law is chosen when states make shallow commitments. Given the low levels of behaviour modification needed, compliance levels are higher in hard law. This runs counter to the low numbers of ratifications for several transnational commercial law conventions if one assumes that ratification is a proxy for compliance, suggesting that other factors affect ratification. In any event, compliance in terms of ratification has little or no meaning in the transnational commercial law context because of its dispositive nature.

---

instrument is evaluated based upon the reasons for the lack of ratifications, it is impossible to prove that the same instrument could have been more successful had the drafting agency chosen soft law as the vehicle. This is surely a mammoth task and is beyond the purview of this chapter.

[41]　Abbott and Snidal, *supra* n. 11, at 436.

[42]　Raustiala, *supra* n. 14, at 600.

[43]　*Ibid*. at 600–601.

[44]　HCCH, Convention on the Law Applicable to Certain Rights in Respect of Securities Held with an Intermediary, available at http://hcch.e-vision.nl/index_en.php?act=conventions.text&cid=7.

[45]　Raustiala, *supra* n. 14.

Raustiala also argues that legality correlates positively with depth: deep commitments are in hard law form.[46] The positive and negative correlations may serve a signalling function: a negative correlation exists when a state may not want to comply, and a positive correlation exists when a state wants other states to comply.[47] Further, positive correlation between legality and depth signals the support of powerful domestic constituencies whereas negative correlation suggests weakness in domestic constituencies.[48]

Despite their explanatory power in public law, these correlations do not translate to transnational commercial law. The International Chamber of Commerce (ICC) and its constituents possess significant political power but still chose to draft the UCP 600 and the Incoterms as non-convention law. Conversely, the aircraft manufacturing and leasing industries also possess enormous political clout, and, unlike the ICC, chose to structure their agreement as a convention.[49] One could reasonably conclude that political clout can be employed to choose both hard law and soft law, thus diluting its explanatory power. For example, consider a segment of the economy that does not have much political power – small businesses that enter into international contracts on a daily basis. If Professor Raustiala is right, the CISG should have been designed as soft law rather than a convention. The same is the case with the UNIDROIT Conventions on International Financial Leasing, and International Factoring.[50] However, contrary to the correlation thesis, both international commercial agreements took the form of hard law.

B.   THE DEMANDEUR-CENTRIC APPROACH

How, then, does the demandeur-centric approach offer greater explanatory power? In this scheme, agreement design is essentially a game of regulatory competition between demandeurs and states. The central trade-off is not between depth and legality but between state involvement and exclusion. Deep agreements can result if the demandeurs believe that state involvement can be minimal or non-existent, and equally if they decide that state involvement is essential. Depth is thus not tied to determinations as to form, but rather connected to the degree of demandeur

---

[46]   *Ibid.* at 602.

[47]   *Ibid.*

[48]   *Ibid.* This may explain the deep commitments in the WTO agreements.

[49]   See Gopalan, S (2003), 'Securing Mobile Assets: The Convention on International Interests in Mobile Equipment', 29 *North Carolina Journal of International Law and Commercial Regulation* 59, at 80.

[50]   UNIDROIT, Convention on International Financial Leasing (Ottawa, 1988), available at www.unidroit.org/english/conventions/1988leasing/main.htm.

integration. The more diffuse the demandeurs, the shallower the agreement, regardless of whether the agreement is a convention or a non-convention.

If demandeurs are tightly integrated and capable of self-policing, they prefer non-convention law because state enforcement powers are unnecessary. Integration confers on demandeurs state-like police powers and they serve as enforcers outside the state system. In this case, the choice of convention law would be inimical to their interests because of the exposure of the rules to greater scrutiny. Demandeurs' choice of a convention form may signal a low level of integration.

Demandeurs seem less concerned with the formal hard law/soft law distinction than appreciated by other theories. The UNIDROIT Principles and the UCP 600 contradict Professor Raustiala's claim that 'there is a dearth of state practice in support of the idea that formally non-legal agreements are actually quasi-legal'.[51] Courts and arbitral tribunals in several countries have referred to the UNIDROIT Principles in deciding cases, even when the disputed contracts do not refer to them. When compared with the CISG and other hard law conventions, which have provisions allowing parties to exclude them, the Principles are not that 'soft'.[52] The hard law versus soft law distinction means little in the transnational commercial law setting; soft law often includes obligations derived either from membership of the organization that promulgated it, or incorporation into the contract. This makes it functionally equivalent to state law.[53]

1.   Demandeur Preferences Determine Form and Structure

Demandeurs choose form and structure based on relative power. The Cape Town Convention is a classic example.[54] Prior to commencing work on the

---

[51]   Raustiala, *supra* n. 14, at 590.

[52]   CISG, Art. 6: '[t]he parties may exclude the application of this Convention or, subject to article 12, derogate from or vary the effect of any of its provisions'); United Nations Convention on the Assignment of Receivables in International Trade, Art. 6: '[s]ubject to article 19, the assignor, the assignee and the debtor may derogate from or vary by agreement provisions of this Convention relating to their respective rights and obligations. Such an agreement does not affect the rights of any person who is not a party to the agreement.'

[53]   I make no claims about the functionalist claim that soft law, characterized as non-state law in my scheme, is a way station to hard law. It could serve as a way station because integration collapses or because demandeurs realize that state sanctions are needed to recognize private agreements.

[54]   See UNIDROIT, Convention on International Interests In Mobile Equipment (Cape Town, 2001), available at www.unidroit.org/english/conventions/mobile-equip-ment/conference2001/main.htm (note that 68 nations attended the diplomatic conference in Cape Town, South Africa and 53 nations signed the final act); see also UNIDROIT Protocol to the Convention on International Interests in Mobile Equipment on Matters Specific to Aircraft Equipment, (Cape Town, 2001), available at www.unidroit.org/

convention, UNIDROIT sought empirically to demonstrate the need for a new law facilitating the taking of security over movables.[55] About 1,000 copies of the questionnaire and an explanatory report were sent to financial institutions, industry representatives, and airlines. The response rate was very low: only 93 entities replied. The bulk of the respondents were lenders – 52 out of the 93.[56] Despite the low response rate, UNIDROIT was satisfied that there was sufficient support and determined that a convention was appropriate. The aircraft industry was involved from the early drafting stages and slowly came to drive the entire process. Airbus Industry and Boeing formed an aviation working group, and framed the drafting process in terms of a sophisticated asset-based financing regime.[57]

They were the demandeurs of the Aircraft Protocol to the Convention, and with their dominant position in the market and enormous economic clout, it was no surprise that the legal regime for aircraft assets was the first to be adopted. Thereafter, they used their leverage to convince states to ratify the convention and protocol. Demandeur clout also explains the relatively large number of mandatory provisions[58] in contrast to the CISG. The drafting of controversial provisions as opt-in or opt-out clauses also allowed the industry to bargain more strategically. But for the demandeurs' economic clout, the convention likely would not have included many of these provisions. Even if they had been included, they would have been watered down versions. Because Airbus and Boeing, the two dominant aircraft companies, worked together, the agreement reflected their preferences. Airbus and Boeing desired a binding convention that created an 'international interest', provided expeditious recourse to the asset in case of default, established an international registry, and made available self-help remedies. These are deep commitments and necessitated state involvement.

---

english/conventions/c-main.htm. The Convention and its Protocol have been ratified by 20 nations to date. See UNIDROIT, Status of the Convention on International Interests in Mobile Equipment, available at www.unidroit.org/english/implement/i-2001-convention. pdf.

[55] See UNIDROIT, *International Regulation of Aspects of Security Interests in Mobile Equipment: Questionnaire*, Study LXXII-Doc. 2 (1989).

[56] See UNIDROIT, *Analysis of the Replies to the Questionnaire on an International Regulation of Aspects of Security Interests in Mobile Equipment*, Study LXXII-Doc. 3 (1991) (concluding that 'the types of legal problems arising in the context of the international recognition of security interests in mobile equipment could be adequately addressed through an international convention containing a mix of choice of law and substantive rules the implementation of which would not require sweeping changes in the municipal law of most States').

[57] UNIDROIT, *Study Group for the Preparation of Uniform Rules on Int'l Interests in Mobile Equip.: Subcomm. For The Preparation of a First Draft*, Memorandum, at 1, Study LXXII – Doc. 16 (May 1995).

[58] Mandatory provisions cannot be modified or excluded by contract.

Since state approval was virtually guaranteed because of superior economic power, they chose to embody the agreement in convention form.

The Cape Town convention casts doubt on Professor Raustiala's depth–legality correlation.[59] The international demandeurs seem to have defeated any hostile domestic demandeurs. In the Cape Town convention, the largest number of domestic demandeurs should have been from developing countries, a group that consists of borrowers rather than lenders. Rational self-interest might dictate that actors from developing countries ought to prefer less depth: as borrowers, they could default and systemic weaknesses in the domestic legal system might offer strategic advantages. However, their interests yielded to the more powerful international demandeurs. Lenders and aircraft manufacturers protected their interests by ensuring a pro-lender framework in the protocol.

2.   Demandeurs Choose Non-Legal Agreements When They Do Not Need State Involvement

The term 'soft law' is problematic because of the lack of definitional consensus. Some define 'soft laws' as pledges, which are not laws at all.[60] Other scholars define soft law as incorporating legal obligations enshrined in 'hard law' in a weak form. For them, treaties without substantive requirements are 'soft law'.[61] Under this conception, hard law can be soft in whole or in part. It is unclear if these scholars apply the same standards to soft law to determine if the obligations therein are actually of a substantive nature and hence more appropriately labeled hard law.

a.   Legality and soft law
Professor Raustiala argues that states 'carefully choose the legal nature of their agreements dichotomously'.[62] States focus on the binding nature of an agreement as an *ex ante* certainty when deciding whether to enter into an international agreement.[63] Thus, a state, when participating in international agreement design, will ask itself if it wants to be bound by the agreement in question. If the answer

---

[59]   Raustiala, *supra* n. 14, at 603: there will be 'a positive correlation between depth and legality when the domestic demandeurs of cooperation are politically privileged, and a negative correlation when they are not'.

[60]   *Ibid.* at 586–7.

[61]   See Baxter, RR (1980), 'International Law in "Her Infinite Variety"', 29 *International and Comparative Law Quarterly* 549, 554; Chinkin, CM (1989), 'The Challenge of Soft Law: Development and Change in International Law', 38 *International and Comparative Law Quarterly* 850, at 851.

[62]   Raustiala, *supra* n. 14, at 587.

[63]   *Ibid.*

is yes, it will be in favour of structuring the agreement in the form of hard law. If the answer is no, it will be in favour of structuring the agreement in the form of soft law. This argument does not address the intentions of non-state actors – do non-state actors structure agreements in the form of soft law when they do not want to be bound by the agreement?

Another view is that international law lacking enforceability is soft law.[64] This view is too simplistic. In the context of international private law, agreements lacking direct enforcement nevertheless can become binding in some form. One example is the UNIDROIT Principles of International Commercial Contracts which were drafted almost entirely at the instance of academics without any state involvement.[65] They have been applied by courts and arbitral tribunals and have become binding by incorporation, suggesting that non-legal agreements can perform the function of the law without state involvement at the drafting stage. Demandeurs possessing low power and requiring no state involvement would prefer non-legal agreements.

b. Flexibility and soft law

Some scholars focus on the flexibility offered by soft law.[66] It is flexible in terms of substantive provisions, party applicability, the absence of ratification requirements, and ultimately bindingness or *impact*. Flexibility also pertains to the relevant actors. This is particularly important in the transnational commercial law area and seems to have greater explanatory power than the other kinds of flexibility discussed by public international law theorists. Flexibility in terms of implementation, by executive action rather than ratification, is important in the transnational commercial law area because of legislative disinterest and apathy.[67] Given the rather technical nature of transnational commercial law

---

[64] See Baxter, *supra* n. 61.

[65] See Society of Public Teachers of Law in Great Britain and Northern Ireland, *Response to Communication from the European Commission on European Contract Law COM(2001)398 final*, para. 20, available at http://ec.europa.eu/consumers/cons_int/safe_shop/fair_bus_pract/cont_law/comments/5.21.pdf. The response further states that the UNIDROIT Principles could form the basis of a legal 'restatement' of contract principles to which contracting parties could subscribe on a voluntary basis on a European level. Moreover, an English court would give effect to a contractual agreement to apply the UNIDROIT Principles in place of the general rules of English law.

[66] Abbott and Snidal, *supra* n. 11 at 445; Lipson, C (1991), 'Why are Some International Agreements Informal?', 45 *International Organization* 495, at 500: '[I]nformal bargains are more flexible than treaties. They are willows not oaks'. See also Raustiala *supra* n. 14, at 591–2.

[67] Scholars have argued that implementation flexibility is important when speed is of the essence and/or when legislative support is doubtful because of the hostility of legislators to the substantive commitments in the international instrument. While this can be a powerful motivation in controversial areas like nuclear weapons control or anti-terror

instruments, legislators rarely place them at the top of the legislative agenda. Despite their great importance for the economy, they may be trumped on the legislative calendar by politically attractive subjects. Legislators worry more about re-election than passing significant commercial legislation.

Flexibility, one scholar argues, is important because of opposing interest group pressure.[68] Professor Guzman writes that when domestic interest groups are championing international agreements they are likely to favour conventions because they prefer the most binding form possible.[69] Accordingly, when competing interest groups collide, states are likely to adopt soft law. In fact, the evidence in the transnational commercial law area does not support this view. International agreements appear to be concluded almost entirely in the absence of colliding interest group pressure of any significance. Agreements result almost exclusively when dominant interest groups push for them, and in the few instances where opposition has materialized, the proposed agreement has been dropped from the legislative agenda of the law-making agency.[70]

3. Demandeurs Choose Deep Non-legal Agreements When They are Integrated

The most powerful example is the work of the ICC, particularly the drafting of the Uniform Customs and Practice for Documentary Credits and the Incoterms. Other examples are agreements drafted by commodities associations like the Refined Sugar Association (RSA), the Sugar Association of London, the Federation of Oils, Seeds and Fats Associations (FOSFA), the American Cotton Shippers' Association, the American Cotton Exporters' Association (ACEA), and the Grain and Feed Trade Association (GAFTA). These associations dominate their trade sectors and have succeeded in almost entirely preempting state involvement. Standard form agreements adopted by commodities associations invariably contain binding arbitration clauses, and are designed to facilitate expeditious dispute resolution without many of the systemic protections offered by state mechanisms. The level of integration of these demandeurs allows them to opt for deep commitments because of an alignment of interest, and the power to exclude recalcitrant actors from membership benefits. They choose non-legal agreements because they do not need state involvement, and actively desire to avoid state scrutiny.

---

activities, legislative boredom is more plausible in the case of franchising conventions and conventions on international receivable financing.

[68] Guzman, *supra* n. 3, at 591–3.

[69] *Ibid.* See also Raustiala, *supra* n. 14 at 596–7.

[70] The hoteliers' liability convention that was dropped by UNIDROIT is a classic example.

4. The Regulatory Competition Game

The demandeur-centric approach sheds light on agreement design being a competition between state and non-state actors, political institutions intra-state, and among international organizations. Traditional theories have ignored this competition and assume that their objectives are largely complementary. They also presume that states possess the power to subsume and subdue non-state entities. This explains their understanding of how the states are mediating demandeurs and designing agreements considering the preferences of these groups. However, the reality may frequently be the opposite. Non-state actors compete with state actors and dominate them in certain areas of international law – the work of the ICC in occupying the field of documentary credits has particular salience here. Non-state entities dominate these fields because of technical expertise and policing mechanisms. In the demandeur-centric approach, the non-state demandeur mediates state preferences, not vice versa.

Competition can also exist at an intra-state level between various political institutions. Demandeur preferences are also at play in mediating this competition. All other things being equal, a legislature ought to prefer a convention rather than a non-legal agreement as it has the opportunity to participate in the former whereas it would be completely excluded in the latter. In terms of institutional competition, the legislature comes off second-best when non-legal agreements are chosen as both the other institutions – the executive and the judiciary – have a role to play. The executive branch can sign non-legal agreements and courts may be able to leave their stamp on non-legal agreements that have been contractually incorporated and are the subject of disputes before them. Thus the choice of legal versus non-legal is frequently a choice of legislative versus non-legislative participation.

Institutional competition can stymie effectiveness because of concerns about demandeurs playing too powerful a role in the drafting of an agreement. This may be behind concerns expressed by the European Parliament in its analysis of the Hague Securities Convention, '[r]eiterat[ing] the need for democratic checks on the negotiations carried on in the context of the Hague Conference on Private International Law'.[71] The Parliament called for an impact study even though the European Commission had been involved in the drafting of the convention. Regardless of the relative merits of the competing positions, the delay in ratification caused by the stance of the Parliament illustrates the need for demandeurs to be cautious in their co-opting of international organizations, and to pay heed to intra-state and intra-organization competition.

---

[71] Resolution on the Implications of Signing the Hague Securities Convention, Eur. Parl. Doc. P6_TA(2006)0608 (14 Dec. 2006), available at www.europarl.europa.eu/sides/getDoc.do?pubRef=-//EP//TEXT+TA+P6-TA-2006-0608+0+DOC+XML+V0//EN.

C. CONCLUSION

Traditional theories have serious limitations in explaining the design of international commercial agreements. They assume that states are the primary actors, that law is binding and non-excludable, and that soft law is inferior to hard law.[72] These assumptions are problematic when applied to transnational commercial law. The correlation between legality and depth predicted by functionalism is rebutted by the CISG – choice of convention yields little benefit because of its dispositive nature. The prediction that soft law will be more common in arcane areas is rebutted by the adoption of the Hague Convention on the Law Applicable to Certain Rights in Respect of Securities Held with an Intermediary.

The choice of hard law seems to be a function of the extent to which the area is conducive to self regulation. If state assistance is needed for regulation, hard law will result; if not, non-convention law is likely to be adopted. Further, demandeurs are often highly integrated and thus possess sanctioning mechanisms that stem from membership, negating the need for state-preference capture.

The demandeur-centric approach offers significant explanatory advantages over other theories. It demonstrates the relative primacy of demandeurs as the motivating force in transnational commercial law agreement design. Agreement design is thus a function of relative demandeur power. If demandeurs are highly integrated and do not depend on states for enforcement, they are more likely to opt for non-convention vehicles that contain deep commitments. This is exemplified by the UCP 600.[73] To the extent that demandeurs depend on state enforcement, deep commitments in convention form are likely to result if demandeurs are integrated and possess the ability to obtain ratification. This is exemplified by the Cape Town convention. If demandeurs are integrated, but unable to obtain ratification, they are likely to opt for non-convention vehicles containing deep commitments. If demandeurs are not integrated, and lack the ability to obtain ratification, they are likely to opt for non-convention law containing weak commitments, as exemplified by the UNIDROIT Principles.

As the examples show, regime design is a function of demandeur preference, and state preferences are often subordinated. States have to be aware that they are ceding legislative power in significant areas to organizations that are not

---

[72]   The last of these is clearly rebutted by the perceptions of non-state actors. See ICC comments on the 'Communication from the European Commission to the Council and the European Parliament on European Contract Law': COM(2001)398 final, 3, available at http://ec.europa.eu/consumers/cons_int/safe_shop/fair_bus_pract/cont_law/comments/2.5.2.pdf: 'ICC has produced many soft law instruments that have been so widely used in practice that they have become as important as black-letter legislation'.

[73]   Uniform Customs and Practices in Documentary Letters of Credit, ICC Banking Regulation no. 600.

democratically elected, and difficult to access. Consultation in the agreement design process is frequently restricted to the membership, and even copies of the agreements are not available without paying a cost – a feature that sits uncomfortably with modern notions of participatory legislation and accessibility. It is not uncommon for some organizations to act like regulatory monopolies.[74] There are serious consequences for states – legal business is monopolized by those with greater access to the demandeur, dispute resolution is often taken away from the jurisdiction of otherwise appropriate state courts or tribunals, state legislative power is eroded, the legal system may, after a time, possess very little expertise in an area because of a complete absence of relevant work for the local bar, and citizens are deprived of participation. The demandeur-centric approach predicts outcomes in transnational commercial law design and states have to decide if these outcomes are in their best interests.

---

[74] One might contend that these laws only apply in commercial transactions where the parties have the benefit of legal counsel, and that there is no element of coercion. Allowing sophisticated commercial parties to act in ways that maximize joint gains is in conformity with autonomy. To the extent that there are no externalities on third parties, these arguments might have some merit. However, it is disingenuous to believe that there are no externalities to parties subjecting themselves to agreements structured by demandeurs outside the pale of state regulation.

10. International commercial harmonisation and national resistance – the development and reform of transnational commercial law and its application within national legal culture

Maren Heidemann*

1. INTRODUCTION

1.1 General Theory of Harmonisation

A theory of harmonisation has to be based on sound analysis of the underlying concepts in both law and its language. While one difficulty in developing a coherent theory of harmonisation of laws is the fact that the term is used in the context of a specific area of EU legislative activity, an excellent starting point is the word harmony itself. The word appears in only slightly different versions in many languages across the world. The meaning depends on the context, but certainly includes a pleasant accord of circumstances. Going beyond this rather vague and seemingly random meaning of harmony one has to realise that harmony was an important element in all the classic Greek scientific disciplines, and therefore plays a part not only in the seemingly vague concept of musical harmony (which springs to mind first) but also in mathematics, physics, astronomy, philosophy and certainly medicine. The reason is that harmony describes a precise system of proportionality, of proportions as they occur in nature. Harmony is part of the laws of nature. An harmonious chord is built on an exact ratio between individual tones, ie, their amplitudes, for instance, the octave, the third and the fifth. This is a natural phenomenon which has been used in architecture and all arts throughout history. Harmony depicts the natural

---

* University of London, UK.

proportions of nature, such as the human body and even the universe. We can therefore say that harmony is a very precise concept, not at all vague or random, and can therefore also serve as a scientific term in the legal science. Developing a meaningful theory of harmonisation of laws could among other things entail an attempt to analyse which figures and numbers can be observed within the process in order to work out whether it might be possible to achieve an ideal proportion. On a more general level, it is my submission that a theory of harmonisation must include a two-way activity. The one-way legislative process currently carried out by the EU can lead to resistance within the national legal systems and would therefore amount to a uniformisation process. Harmonisation would require a complementary action emanating from the national legal systems with a view to achieving harmony on a transnational level. Examples have been presented throughout the workshop in the context of, e.g., international criminal law, the European Human Rights Convention and its margin of appreciation, and even in the area of EU regulations which unwittingly fail to achieve their goal of uniformity and depend on this active harmonising contribution on the part of the national legal systems.

This complementary role of national law in the harmonisation process is the subject of my contribution.

1.2   Harmonisation as a Two-way System

International contract and commercial law has recently been subject to reform through a process of co-operation in civil and commercial matters within the EU.

A number of EU directives and regulations in the area of private and commercial law have been adopted or are being drafted and in the process of formal adoption. The complementary element to this growing effort of harmonisation and uniformisation in order to advance the internal market cross-border trade is, of course, the application of substantive legal norms forming part of international and transnational law. Without a culture of applying international and transnational legal rules, the process of harmonisation remains a 'top-down' process which may not achieve its ultimate objectives.

In the area of private and commercial law, three elements of applying law to cross-border situations can be identified and illustrated here:

- the skill of applying substantive norms of transnational contract law;
- the willingness to acknowledge foreign legal concepts and draft legislation with a view to developing international instruments; and
- the appropriate consideration of foreign legal positions or even precedence in domestic proceedings in international matters.

2.   THE APPLICATION OF TRANSNATIONAL CONTRACT LAW: SKILFUL LEGISLATION AND APPLICATION IS A PREREQUISITE TO UNFOLD ITS POTENTIAL

The application of transnational contract law requires two stages – the stage of the conflict of laws and that of the application of individual rules.

2.1   Transnational Law in the Conflict of Laws: Legislators and the Courts

The conflict of laws position distinguishes between the areas of state court litigation and of arbitration. Legal doctrine has developed a mode of language whereby 'law' stands for the law of a state and 'rule of law' includes so-called 'soft law' which comprises instruments such as Model Laws, UNIDROIT principles, PECL or CISG.

The reform of the conflict of laws through the proposed 'Rome I' Regulation originally intended to allow in its Article 3(1) for certain non-state laws to govern international contracts (by way of express choice of law) by introducing a previously unused formula: 'recognised internationally or in the Community'.[1]

The idea of allowing 'soft law' to govern international contracts had already been manifested in the UNCITRAL Model Law on International Arbitration. The reformed German code of civil procedure,[2] however, does not reflect the effort of incorporating this Model into the German law of arbitration.[3]

In the UK, the Arbitration Act 1996 does leave room for the open choice corresponding to the Model. The generally skeptical attitude of the courts towards a choice of non-state law does not generally preclude this possibility.[4]

However, a quantitative study[5] shows a marginal use of non-state law in international arbitration. (Between 1 and 2% of reported ICC arbitration cases between 2000 and 2006 show the use of transnational law as the law governing the contract). So, is the current legal framework the reason for the low numbers of awards based on non-national law? Is the low number of published arbitration awards based on non-state law a reason to abandon further research into this matter or is it an indicator of a need to support this type of legal regime?

---

[1]   Draft Council Regulation, COM(2005)650 final. See below, 3.1.2, for further discussion.

[2]   Code of Civil Procedure, *Zivilprozessordnung*, the ZPO, in §§1025–1066 (10th book), revised 22 December 1997 and in force since 1 January 1998.

[3]   See below, 3.1.1, for further discussion.

[4]   See below, 3.1.2, for further discussion.

[5]   Dasser, Felix (2008, forthcoming), 'Mouse or Monster? Some Facts and Figures on the *Lex Mercatoria*', 4 in R Zimmerman et al. (eds) *Globalisierung und Entstaatlichung des Rechts* (Mohr Siebeck, 2008), 129 et seq.

It seems that choice of law clauses to the exclusion of national contract law are a regular occurrence[6] and hence a need in commercial contracts. Given the high financial value of international commercial arbitration this ought to be of concern to legislators. Transnational contract law is the response to the need for a specialised law for international commercial contracts, a form of *lex specialis*.

The concept of transnational contract law is still treated with great caution within national legal systems, and as a result is accompanied by a considerable degree of legal uncertainty. Transnational law is therefore a good example to illustrate differing standards of legislative skill in recent law reform projects in English and German arbitration and conflict law.

The purpose now is not primarily to look at the effect of the legal rules mentioned above but rather the process of their making.[7]

2.1.1   Reform of the German arbitration law

Recent reform projects concerned arbitration law, both in Germany and in England. The new §1051 ZPO had been expressly drafted with a view to incorporating the UNCITRAL Model Law and with reference to other European arbitration laws. The objective was to make Germany a more attractive place for arbitration and, to this end, to approximate the German arbitration law to international standards. This can be seen from the Official Reasons published by the government.[8]

Now, looking at the text of the UNCITRAL Model Law, it can be seen that a choice of non-national law was intended to be permissible by the drafters of this text. This can be deduced from the wording 'rules of law' which by convention hints at the application of state law and soft law, while the wording 'law' would indicate that only state law is encompassed by the term. The German ZPO incorporated this aspect in its paragraph 1 ('according to the rules of law') on express choice of law. However, in the second paragraph, the legislator has stipulated that, in the absence of choice, 'the tribunal applies the law of the state with which the matter is most closely connected'. This differs from the provision in paragraph 2 of Article 28 of the Model Law which gives the arbitration tribunal a discretion to decide which 'conflict of laws rules it considers applicable'. This wording gives the arbitrator a maximum of flexibility in order to deal with

---

[6]   A good example from state court litigation is *Eurotunnel v. Balfour Beatty* [1992] 2 Lloyd's Rep 7 (CA); [1993] 1 Lloyd's Rep 291 (HL), and an illustrative example in arbitration is ICC No 7110, cf Ly, F d (1999) 'Dutch National Report' in Bonell, MJ (ed.) *A New Approach to International Commercial Contracts* (Kluwer Law International) at 203–35.

[7]   Contrary to the advice of our elder statesmen never to investigate the making of sausages or the making of laws.

[8]   *Bundestags-Drucksache (BT-Drucks)* 13/5274.

the individual case on behalf of the parties without overstepping the marks still guarded by traditional legal science.

The German legislator, however, has created a different and, looking at both form and substance, rather peculiar rule. Not only is there no mention of a discretion for the arbitrator and the allusion to non-state law but, on the contrary, the section prescribes a very strict rule: 'the tribunal applies the law of the state with which the matter is most closely connected'. This makes a clear choice in favour of state law exclusively, and at the same time prescribes the criterion to be applied in order to arrive at the proper law of the contract, which the UNCITRAL Model Law does not. Formally, this rules poses a riddle: the legislator has set this brief rule up but has not clarified how it relates to the general rules of the German conflict law which is incorporated in the so-called 'Introductory Code to the Civil Code', the EGBGB.[9] In this codification, the legislator implemented the Rome Convention in 1986, and its Article 28 is nearly identical to the Convention. This means that Article 28 EGBGB gives a list of guidelines relating to specific contract types and in its paragraph 5 offers an exception to these in order to give effect to unusual situations: '[t]he presumptions of paras 2, 3 and 4 are not to be applied if on the whole the contract has a closer connection with a different state'. Now, it seems that the German legislator of the new ZPO assumed that these guidelines and the whole Article 28 EGBGB would automatically apply to §1051 ZPO and therefore the rules did not need repeating. This is not the case, however. Methodically, it is clear that the ZPO is a *lex specialis* and will supersede the general rules of the EGBGB, not to mention the difference in wording between the two rules which suggests that §1051 (2) ZPO is not identical in substance with Article 28 EGBGB.[10] The questions which this poses have not been answered by the legislator. On the contrary, the *Official Reasons* state that it was assumed that Article 28 EGBGB would automatically apply; they also state that this provision was identical with the arbitration laws of many other European jurisdictions, for example, the Swiss. Both suggestions are incorrect.[11] In addition, it has to be mentioned that should the arbitrator ignore §1051 ZPO and, for instance, decide according to the Model Law and arrive at a law or set of rules which is not in accordance with §1051 ZPO, this decision

---

[9] *Einführungsgestz zum Bürgerlichen Gesetzbuch* (EGBGB), 'Introductory Law to the BGB', first enacted on 18 August 1896.

[10] Cf. in more detail Solomon, D (1997), 'Das vom Schiedsgericht in der Sache anzuwendende Recht nach dem Entwurf eines Gesetzes zur Neuregelung des Schiedsverfahrensrechts', 12 *Recht der InternationalenWirtschaft* 981–90 and Heidemann, M (2007), *Methodology of Uniform Law: the UNIDROIT Principles in International Legal Doctrine and Practice* (Springer) Chapter 8.

[11] For reasons of space, this question cannot be analysed any further here, but compare, ibid.

would not be overturned by a German court. Unlike English law, German law does not review arbitration awards on the merits (regarding the application of German law) but would overturn the award only if the arbitrator has exceeded his powers, for example, if he had decided *ex aequo et bono* without being authorised to do so. As long as the arbitrator announces that he or she is applying law or rules of law, however, this will not be assumed to be the case.[12]

Conclusion 1:   The German legislator has enacted a rule which is not only meaningless but obviously very insufficiently thought through. It has to be assumed that it was unknown or irrelevant to the drafters how this new rule would fit in with this area of law. This is unfavourable for the development of international commercial law and does not help the express aim of the legislator of making the German law of arbitration both more attractive and more consistent with international models.

2.1.2   Transnational law in the courts

Despite the critical attitude of both the German and the English legislatures, the courts, both in England and Germany have never overturned an arbitration award based on anational law so far. This is particularly interesting in the case of English courts as the Arbitration Act 1996 upholds the traditional powers to review awards on grounds of wrongly applying English law and the attitude of English judges is traditionally very critical towards arbitration and the application of non-state rules.[13] Two cases in more recent times have come very close to the question of the legitimacy of non-state law or whether 'soft law' could be the proper law of the contract: *Eurotunnel v. Balfour Beatty* [1992] 2 Lloyd's Rep 7 (CA); [1993] 1 Lloyd's Rep 291 (HL) and *Halpern & Ors v. Halpern & Anr* [2007] EWCA Civ 291. In the first case, the House of Lords confirmed that an arbitration clause was to be respected, and did not, as might have been hoped for by the parties, consider that the choice of 'principles common to both English and French law' was an inadmissible choice of law. The case did not, however, require this question to be decided, and a warning remark was included in the judgment questioning the advisability of such choices. In the case of *Halpern*, an inheritance dispute among members of an orthodox Jewish family, the defendants sought Jewish law to be the proper law of the contract.[14] This submission was by no means bluntly rejected by the judge (Waller LJ). The

---

[12]   BGH NJW (1986) 1437, which also expressly states that the wrong application of the correct law is not subject to judicial review. See also Heidemann, *supra* n. 10, at 210.

[13]   Cf. *Charnikow v. Roth Schmidt & Co* [1922] 2 KB 478.

[14]   As this would have allowed a more favourable law of restitution: see case note by Heidemann, M (2008), '*Halpern v Halpern*: Zur Anwendbarkeit nicht-staatlichen Rechts und "Rom I" in England – Entscheidung des englischen Court of Appeal vom 3 April 2007', 3 *ZEuP*, 618.

court considered that there might be circumstances in which such law could be the proper law of the contract, but that it was not to be regarded as an express choice of law under the Rome Convention and consequently under the Contracts (Applicable Law) Act 1990. This is a remarkable way of putting it, as it does not expressly exclude the possibility of choosing a national law but states that in this case, under English law, it did not amount to an express choice and was not applicable otherwise. The new draft Rome I Regulation on choice of law within the European Community was discussed in the course of the proceedings. The first draft of this Regulation suggested the applicability of certain 'soft law' which the defendant's/respondent's counsel mentioned. Again, this argument did not make a difference to the position under English law, and with the new draft all these considerations will be irrelevant, anyway.

Conclusion 2:   Despite the indifferent or outright negative attitude of legislators towards non-state contract law, courts have maintained a more open-minded attitude with a view to allowing the evolution of international commercial and private international contract law as far as a wider use of non-state law would be desired. The use of uniform, tailor-made rules of law can aid and benefit international trade and other private cross-border activities. This development has been jeopardised by the enactment of the Regulation (EC) No. 593/2008, (Rome I).

2.2   Reform of the German Civil Code

A second example from recent German law reform is to be found in the new BGB which was reformed with effect from 2002. Again, the legislator has published the intention to align German law with international instruments (in the *Official Reasons*).[15] In order to disentangle the highly complicated structure of the German law of impossibility, non-performance and frustration in contractual relations, a new notion was devised – the so-called breach of duty. I have deliberately translated this expression as literally as possible from the German word *Pflichtverletzung* in order to illustrate all its implications within the context of international instruments of contract law. For instance, the *Official Reasons* refer to the 1980 Vienna Sales Convention, the CISG, pointing out that German law has incorporated the notion used in this Convention: non-performance. The text states that the difference in wording is only clerical or editorial, a mere verbal difference but with no legal meaning. One does not have to be a specialist in private international law to detect a problem with such an attitude to legal texts. Non-performance and breach of duty are very much two different legal concepts. As with many international instruments, the CISG was drafted in the

---

[15]   *Official Reasons*, BGB, Parliamentary Bulletin No 14/6040, 14 May 2001, at 1992.

form of a blend or a compromise between various legal traditions and concepts so as to find the best solution, and one which would be acceptable to as many jurisdictions as possible. The concept of non-performance is not equal to the common law concept of breach of contract, but is based on this, in so far as it pursues a more holistic understanding of the contract. It is an attempt to simplify contractual performance and reach clear-cut solutions in cases where performance does not go to plan. The so-called civil law or continental systems which work with the law of obligations have a different understanding of contract. A contract is a network of obligations which are reciprocal, and all of these need to be discharged in order for the contract to be fulfilled or the obligations otherwise lifted. This structure was taken to the extreme in the German BGB and in particular the old §323 and the whole network of provisions relating to cases of impossibility and non-performance. Non-performance was not a starting point as such, but rather what was called a disturbed performance. This expression sought to describe the act of discharging the various elements of the contract in a value-neutral way. Contract law, civil law in general, has never been about value judgements or moral attitude, but rather first and foremost about balancing economic interests. The new expression, 'breach of duty', reminds one too much of a moralising attitude towards dutifulness and does not fit the picture from this angle alone. Furthermore, it is a new concept and expression which is not in line at all with either common law systems or international instruments which incorporate a completely different concept of contract. This is not what the German legislator had in mind though. The general system of individually connected obligations has been maintained, rather than replaced with a more simplistic concept of non-performance. It is not the breach of a duty but the non-performance which is the basis of contractual failure in international instruments. If the German legislator had wanted to align the contract law to international instruments, this would have been the best choice. The now existing solution represents a completely novel concept, which needs explaining to both German and international lawyers.

Conclusion 3:   The German legislator has failed to align the German contract law with international instruments despite express intentions to do so. Subtleties of different legal concepts seem to be unnoticed by the drafters, which suggest a lack of interest or skills. This is unfavourable for the development of a culture of transnational law.

2.3   Application of Individual Norms of Transnational Contract Law

In order to complete the picture, some thoughts should be sketched here regarding the application of rules of uniform commercial law such as CISG, the PECL or the UNIDROIT Principles of Commercial Contracts. By way of example it is interesting to look at an instance where Article 7.2.1 of the UNIDROIT

Principles has been analysed by a scholar[16] in a way which shows how problems arise which could be easily avoided. Professor Schwenzer considered the payment rule in Article 7.2.1 UPICC an overly rigid rule which would not be compatible with any European jurisdiction, as none of them grants an unqualified right to performance. She arrived at this conclusion by comparing Article 7.2.1 with Article 7.2.2, which contains a list of exceptions to the general rule of requiring performance (of non-monetary obligations). She did not, however, take a closer look at the UPICC and she did not apply them as a whole in the way of a contract code. Therefore, she did not consider all the limitations and exceptions which the Principles contain as general rules (just as any domestic law does) and which by no means create an overly rigid right to performance which would clash with domestic legal systems. The UPICC are one of several international instruments which allow a comprehensive application of all their rules in the way of a contract code. If this were done in the same way as lawyers apply their own domestic law, comprehensively, they would see fewer 'gaps' in the uniform international law to start with.[17]

A similarly fragmentary method of application can be observed in some case law, often in the context of trying to establish general principles of law.[18] The good faith rule of the UPICC is often quoted as proof of this principle in international law, but often in an isolated manner as if the UPICC were a collection of random rules when they are really a unique set of rules that is extraordinarily suited to be used in the style of a code. The isolated way of using these rules can lead to misconceptions and subsequently to a general sense of unsuitability of such law to solve complex cases.

More conceptual resentments such as the general rejection of the concept of specific performance upon a brief inspection of Article 7.2.1 UPICC are equally based on a very superficial look at one's own legal system. A careful comparison of the extent to which both the German (as a civil law system) and the English (as a common law jurisdiction) legal systems grant payment rights demonstrates that the UPICC, if applied properly, will in substance be compatible with those systems and how an application can be facilitated.[19]

The willingness to apply such uniform law is an indispensable prerequisite for a successful integration into the legal process. And this includes the aspect of conflict of laws which functions as a gateway for uniform commercial law

---

[16]   Schwenzer, I (1998/1999), 'Specific Performance and Damages According to the 1994 UNIDROIT Principles of International Commercial Contracts', 1 *European Journal of Law Reform* 289.

[17]   See for in-depth discussion of this method Heidemann, *supra* n. 10, Chapters 4 and 5.

[18]   Available at www.unilex.info.

[19]   See Heidemann, *supra* n. 10.

into the sphere of domestic law. Legal doctrine has to provide solutions for this if this law is to play a role in cross-border trade. Questions of legitimacy have to be addressed in view of the fact that national law will necessarily always address domestic contracts as the national legislator's competence ends at the borders of a territory while international contracts can span the whole globe. So, rules of international trade law have a quality of *lex specialis* as they deal with international contracts.[20]

Conclusion 4:   In conclusion, it can be said that many of the current problems in international trade law are based on misconceived aspects of private law which can be avoided by referring to the jurisprudential foundations of each jurisdiction's own tradition. Theories of contract law and the general doctrine of construction can help overcome prejudices and seemingly insurmountable obstacles in the application of modern trade law.

3   'RESISTANCE' BY WAY OF EXTRA-LEGAL ARGUMENTS: THE *HORROR ALIENI*

3.1   International Company Law: Adverse Practices

On a more anecdotal level, it must be observed that, even after the decisions of the ECJ on freedom of establishment and free movement of companies, migrating companies are still not exactly welcome in the host European state. The German business community still maintains a campaign-style adversity against specifically English limited companies. Following a wave of formation of 'Ltds' predating the *Überseering*[21] decision by the ECJ, by what is thought to be 46,000[22] German small businesses, both private actors[23] and state authorities[24] started to denigrate this form of incorporation. Banks are known to refuse to open accounts for 'Ltds', business partners are reluctant to enter into contracts and the tax offices are advised that most Ltds are 'letter box' companies (because the practice of having the registered office and the head office in different places is not familiar to them). These assumptions were of course originally based on the doctrine of the real seat[25] which was

---

[20]   See below at 3.2.

[21]   Case C–208/00.

[22]   This is said to be the unofficial count, dramatically called *Dunkelziffer*, while about 7,000 English private limited companies are registered in the German *Handelsregister*.

[23]   Banks refusing to open accounts for 'Ltds'.

[24]   The Federal Tax Office regularly found that 'Ltds' were not to be recognised in terms of a permanent establishment in Germany.

[25]   *Sitztheorie*.

subsequently dismissed by the ECJ in favour of the doctrine of incorporation. The mindset did not change, though, with the case law. Critics wait for a sign in the ECJ decisions allowing the reintroduction of the seat theory. They find hints in the concession that 'abuse' should certainly not be supported in *Cadbury Schweppes*.[26]

The arguments on which the rejection of foreign companies, and in particular the British limited company, is based are the difference in minimum share capital which is said to pose an enormous risk to creditors,[27] a lack of personal liability of the directors and a dubious degree of truthfulness of the register at Companies House.[28] These arguments are, of course, wholly unfounded.[29] However, the extent of this attitude clearly shows that irrational behaviour reigns, rather than the principle of mutual recognition and non-discrimination, and the wrong subject is targeted by these campaigns: as much as it might be unfavourable for sole traders such as hairdressers or plumbers to set up an English Private Limited Company because they incur double filing obligations in both countries in terms of annual reports and tax returns, it is not the Limited Company as such which poses the problem, and ignorance is no excuse for the unhelpful behaviour towards foreign companies.

3.2   Cartesio: *AG Maduro's Opinion*

This problem stems from and illustrates once again the complex relationship between private law and the state. Looking at the latest case brought before the ECJ regarding international company law, *Cartesio*,[30] this comes to the fore once again. Advocate General Maduro gives an interesting description of the issues involved in his Opinion.[31] He states, in paragraph 31:

---

[26]   *Centros Ltd v. Erhverus- og Selskabsstyrelsen*, Case C–196/04.

[27]   In Denmark this problem was apparently solved by effectively transferring the requirement of a minimum share capital into tax law to prevent Centros from registering in Denmark (cf. Case C–21/97).

[28]   The practice of acquiring 'off-the-shelf companies', as well as the practice of having a separate registered and head office, leads to the assumption that every British company is a 'letterbox company' and cannot be trusted. The register at Companies House is feared not to provide up-to-date information about the authorised representatives of companies.

[29]   Not many creditors really turn to the share capital in order to satisfy outstanding debts, but rather to the established and well known procedures of debt collection through different types of security. The German company registers can certainly contain incorrect information in certain instances, as can the records at Companies House. Of course, there is a director's liability in certain cases under English law.

[30]   *Cartesio Oktató és Szolgáltató bt*. Case C–210/06.

[31]   Opinion of Advocate General Poiares Maduro delivered on 22 May 2008 (1) in Case C–210/06, *Cartesio Oktató és Szolgáltató bt*.

In sum, it is impossible, in my view, to argue on the basis of the current state of Community law that Member States enjoy an absolute freedom to determine the 'life and death' of companies constituted under their domestic law, irrespective of the consequences for the freedom of establishment. Otherwise, Member States would have *carte blanche* to impose a 'death sentence' on a company constituted under its laws just because it had decided to exercise the freedom of establishment.

The question really is: what does the state have to do with the establishment of a company which is ultimately a contract between several private individuals to carry on a commercial activity? The company registers are not necessarily a state organ or run by a state organ and do not as such confer legal status on the companies, and so while the company owes its status as a legal person to the law in the state where it is established, does this mean it vanishes when it 'leaves' that state? This touches on the quality of law as such, in particular in private law. The current prevailing doctrine of the unity of law and state will find it hard to give answers which further the development of the Community trade which we currently see evolving. The solution, in my view, has to come from the recognition of a legal pluralism, for instance in the way which Gunther Teubner has suggested by 'reframing' legal sources,[32] and of course by genuinely recognising party autonomy.

Another important argument in this context is mentioned in paragraph 32 of AG Maduro's Opinion:

> Consequently, even though the restriction on the right to freedom of establishment at issue in the present case arises directly from national rules on the incorporation and functioning of companies, the question has to be asked whether they can be justified on grounds of general public interest, such as the prevention of abuse or fraudulent conduct, or the protection of the interests of, for instance, creditors, minority share-holders, employees or the tax authorities.

The argument of abuse is, as I mentioned briefly above, eagerly welcomed by those who prefer to classify companies purely under the doctrine of the real (*de facto*) seat, the place of the operational headquarters, and disagree with the free movement of companies throughout the EU. This argument, however, is in my view totally out of place in the context of the EU. The act of forming a company in any of the European Member States must pre-empt any reproach of abusive behaviour. Moving freely across borders needs to be fully recognised and practised by both individuals and state authorities as it is an important objective of the EU.

Last but not least, it appears questionable whether the tax authorities can claim an independent right to have taxation opportunities arising from their

---

[32] Teubner, G (2002), 'Breaking Frames: Economic Globalisation and the Emergence of the *Lex Mercatoria*', 5 *European Journal of Social Theory* 199.

national laws or even the movement of the companies, protected, as confirmed in *Daily Mail*.[33] After all, even if Cartesio will be allowed to move to Italy without dissolving and re-establishing themselves under Hungarian and Italian company law, the *Daily Mail* principle still holds, and it is clear that at least the German hairdressers and plumbers will find it difficult to tax their business assets (*stille Reserven*) in the country of origin and start again in the new country.

3.3 Professional Envy

In a similar way of veiling alleged economic advantages, the preoccupation with transnational law is deemed to be a purposeful development of young scholars who want to create their own niche subject. Repeatedly, arguments against choices pointing away from Germany include the economic advantage and success of the City of London as a place of arbitration and the seat of wealthy law firms as an ulterior motive of canny lawyers to sway the judgment of naive recipients of advice.[34] This just underlines that there is and should be a competition between the different European jurisdictions, and that the citizens are making choices in order to find the best solutions for themselves.

4   THE ROLE OF THE LEGAL UNDERSTANDING OF THE OTHER SIDE: INTERNATIONAL PRECEDENCE, INTERPRETATION OF TREATIES AND COMITY

The previous discussion has shown that taxation law is an integral part of the free movement of companies and individuals within Europe and it is intrinsically linked to freedom of establishment. As there is only a rudimentary and fragmentary body of EC taxation law most of these issues are still subject to national laws and bilateral treaties between the Member States. It is therefore interesting to look at the standards that apply to promoting cross-border activity in this area.

---

[33]   Case 81/87. This might even be the strongest driving force behind the reluctance to embrace the free movement of companies which the Danish example illustrates.

[34]   Cf Mankowski, P (2003), 'Rechtswahl für Verträge des internationalen Wirtschaftsverkehrs' 1 *Recht der Internationalen Wirtschaft (RIW)* 2 and Heidemann, *supra* n. 10, Chapter 8. In this article, Mankowski recommends the use of CISG for international commercial contracts – however he discourages the use of UNIDROIT Principles even though the very same arguments which he uses obviously speak in favour the UPICC, too. CISG needs this support from scholarly writing in Germany as routinely excluding it from applying to international contracts still is standard practice in the legal profession.

What I am looking for here is the extent to which the attitude within the national legal system supports or acknowledges the fact that cross-border activity is increasing within the EU and also worldwide.

Comparing practices in the UK and Germany, it can be seen that there are differing ways of including foreign legal positions, and in particular judgments, in legal reasoning. While it is fairly common in English judgments to consider case law from other jurisdictions, this is not common in Germany. With regard to Double Taxation Treaties (DTTs), this has been analysed by Moessner, Lang and Waldburger, three tax experts (law professors and senior judges) from Germany, Austria and Switzerland who have analysed the considerations of foreign decisions in German judgments of the Federal Taxation Court, the *Bundesfinanzhof*, BFH, between 1957 and 1994. Professor Moessner found 27 instances of consulting foreign case law in those 37 years. While this is not a high number, it is also striking that those instances mostly concerned the DTTs entered into by Germany with the USA and Switzerland. Due to the fact that a large proportion of the German case law on double taxation has emanated from litigation concerning those two treaties, it is all the more interesting to look at the position regarding the DTT between Germany and the UK.

4.1   Different Views on the Application of a Bilateral Treaty: the Silent Partnership

A peculiar example to observe in German–UK taxation law is the taxation of the silent partnership. We can observe two interestingly diverging legal standpoints as well as, after all, a positive move within German case law towards recognising the view of the other party (if yet again arising from a case about the German–US DTT).[35] The German courts have ignored the British viewpoint on the matter entirely, in contravention of international law, but there is now a move towards recognising the view of the partner of the bilateral treaty.

Between the UK and Germany there are considerable discrepancies as to the understanding of silent partnerships. Some legal systems, such as the German, subdivide silent partnerships into plain ones and so-called atypical silent partnerships. English law does not recognise this distinction. Not surprisingly, the distinction is not expressly mentioned in the DTT. (Only four DTTs concluded by Germany with other states include this distinction, those with Luxembourg, the Netherlands, Austria and Tunisia.) The current German practice classifies income and proceeds from sales of atypical silent partnerships as business profits, attributed to the permanent establishment of this entity (Article 3

---

[35]   See below.

DTT), while the UK sees these earnings merely as dividends[36] or – in the case of the sale of the main share – simple debt collection (Article 6(4) DTT). This discrepancy arises not only from a generally diverging company law, but predominantly due to a flawed technique of applying rules of international law by the German authorities and courts. The DTT contains substantive rules creating sources of income *sui generis* and includes provisions about the distribution of income between the contracting states, as well as about avoidance of double taxation and double non-taxation (tax avoidance). The fact that the atypical silent partnership is not mentioned in the DTT does not justify the application of Article II (3) DTT[37] in a way which amounts to using the rule in the sense of a conflict rule, pointing to the full application of German law.[38] This method is contrary to Article 31 (1) of the Vienna Convention on the Law of Treaties, which states that the wording of a rule is the limit of possible interpretation. The correct development of a treaty-specific autonomous meaning of the relevant terms of the DTT (*enterprise, business profits, silent partnership*) can be found, however, in the English cases of *Memec plc*,[39] where the courts set out the criteria by which the meaning is to be established and point out that understanding of the terminology in DTTs has to be specific to each Article and cannot simply be taken from another DTT Article or from English law. The starting point for the analysis is the understanding of the ordinary businessman. Notably, the judges also take German case law (again, on the Swiss DTT) into account when determining the nature of the German silent partnership. No mention is made of an atypical form of silent partnership, even though Memec plc was in fact an atypical silent partner of its German subsidiary. Instead, the nature of the business venture of the (atypical) silent partner Memec plc was correctly described as:

> The position of Plc was that of a purchaser who, for a consideration consisting of the contribution of a capital sum and an undertaking to contribute to losses of the owner

---

[36] *Memec plc v. Inland Revenue Commissioners (IRC)* [1996] STC 1336 (Ch D); [1998] STC 754 (CA).

[37] The interpretation rule of Art. 2(3) DTT, the so-called *Oeffnungsklausel*.

[38] German law classes the profits of the atypical silent partner as business profits according to §15 EStG, the domestic income tax law going merely by the fact that the silent partner has agreed to take part in the losses of the principal as well as hold certain information rights in respect of the principal's business which itself can be a share in another business. There are inconsistencies between this legal situation and other taxation laws such as the definition of business in the law of corporation tax and value added tax. There are also clashes with the company law aspect of this scenario. Thus the whole viewpoint of the German tax authorities and courts on this matter appears highly remote, even within domestic law.

[39] See previous note.

of a business up to the amount of the contribution, purchased a right to income of a fluctuating amount calculated as a share of the annual profits of the business. Neither in English nor in Scottish law would that have left Plc a partner with GmbH.[40]

The English court arrived at the conclusion that such an activity cannot generate business profits under the German-British DTT – exactly the opposite stance to that which the German courts have been taking in cases which notably did not involve the German–British DTT but mainly Swiss cases.[41] The last relevant decision was made by the BFH in 1999[42] (regarding a German–Swiss case) and this ended a previously lively academic discussion about the correct way of classifying the atypical silent partnership according to an autonomous interpretation of the DTT.[43] On the part of the tax authorities, the underlying argument seems to be that insofar as there is no double taxation resulting from the different views on the qualification of the sources of income, there is no need for a coherent application of the DTT.[44] This is an insufficient argument under international law. The *Memec* decisions and the 1999 BFH decisions were followed by the OECD *Report on the taxation of partnerships*[45] which seemed to induce this line of argument. It does, however, presume that a sufficient interpretation and application of DTTs has been carried out before gaps or unregulated matters can be assumed. This is not the case in the silent partnership cases.

Newer German case law shows a shift towards an awareness of the significance of the legal position in the partner country. The BFH's judgment of 17 October 2007, IR 5/06 concerned the taxation of interest which a US-based shareholder earned under the German–USA DTT. The BFH made it very clear that the mere non-intervention of the US authorities with regard to a practice of the German authorities which contravened the DTT does not amount to an

---

[40]   Henry LJ in *Memec plc v. Inland Revenue Commissioners* (IRC)CA [1998] STC 754, 756. Memec plc was consequently denied the set-off of German local business tax *(Gewerbesteuer)* paid on the profits.

[41]   It should be noted that the outcome of these cases by no means always favours the German *fiscus*. This can therefore not be the motivation for the legal views of the courts on this point of law.

[42]   BFH (German Supreme Tax Court) Urteil vom (judgment of) 21 July 1999, BStBL II 1999, 812 = FR 1999, 1361.

[43]   A comprehensive overview of this discussion is given by Geuenich, M (2005), *Qualifikationskonflikte im OECD-Musterabkommen und deutschen Doppelbesteuerungsabkommen am Beispiel der atypisch stillen Gesellschaft* (Schriften zum Steuerrecht, Duncker & Humblot, 2005) at 46–7.

[44]   Cf BMF *(Bundesministerium für Finanzen)* 'letter' of 28 December 1999, IV D 3-S 1300-*25/99, in Internationales Steuerrecht* (IStR) 2000, at 24.

[45]   OECD, *The Application of the OECD Model Tax Convention to Partnerships* (OECD Publications, 1999).

'understanding'[46] between the contracting parties, and hence to an agreement about this practice. Here, for the first time, the BFH looks at the viewpoint of the partner state.[47] The court applies the Vienna Convention on the Law of Treaties extensively. The BFH also expressly distinguishes between legal solutions applicable under the German–US Treaty and potentially different solutions under the German–Swiss DTT, i.e., the court recognises that the DTTs have to be individually interpreted in the light of the intentions and mutual understanding of the contracting parties.[48]

This has a lot of potential for the future development in this area of law and means that the German authorities and courts may have to recognise the English view expressed in *Memec plc*.

4.2 International Precedent?

The previous considerations have aimed at demonstrating instances of recognising foreign law within the formation of domestic legal opinions and case law.

Taking this idea further, there are considerations within the framework of civil and commercial co-operation as to whether judgments of supreme national courts can affect the interpretation of Community law, for instance in insolvency proceedings. While this could be resolved by way of a preliminary ruling as it is part of the *acquis*, recourse needs to be had to general principles in the case of bilateral treaties.

These general principles are discussed within German-speaking doctrine in the context of *Entscheidungsharmonie*, harmonising decision-making (also discussed within the context of DTTs) and *Vertrauensprinzip*, the principle of mutual trust in international public law.[49]

Three Austrian cases of the supreme court (*Oberster Gerichsthof*)[50] apply Article 15 of the Insolvency Regulation (1346/2000) differently from the way the High Court did in the case of *Mazur Media* (HC 03 C4269, July 2004, paragraph 70). There is a discrepancy between the way the relationship between Article 4 and Article 15 of Regulation 1346/2000[51] is seen and the way the

---

According to Art. 31 (3) of the Vienna Convention on the Law of Treaties (1969) (signed 23 May 1969, entered into force on 27 January 1980).

BFH 17 October 2007 – I R 5/06, II b) dd) bbb).

Ibid., at II b) ee).

Mössner, JM, Waldburger, R and Lang, M, *Die Auslegung von Doppelbesteuerungsabkommen in der Rechtsprechung der Höchstgerichte Deutschlands, der Schweiz und Österreichs* (Linde Verlag, 1998) at 57 et seq.

8 Ob 131/04d; 9 Ob 135/04z and 10 Ob 80/05w; available at www.ris.bka.gv.at.

Art. 15 of Reg. 1346/200: '[e]ffects of insolvency proceedings on lawsuits pending –The effects of insolvency proceedings on a lawsuit pending concerning an asset or a right of which the debtor has been divested [Art 4, *lex loci concursus*] shall be

national law is applied under Article 15. In order to achieve an accord between the decisions, one could argue that the preceding decision should prevail. A preliminary ruling has not been considered by the courts involved in this matter, as the Austrian supreme court considered the question sufficiently clear. So, is the harmony among supreme court decisions about the *acquis* an independent objective within EU law? Or do we accept that, as with many other instruments of international law, discrepancies are unavoidable in the context of procedural autonomy of the Member States or indeed any other parties to international conventions and other uniform legal instruments?

Conclusion 5:   An awareness of legal positions in other jurisdictions is increasingly important for the successful development of an ever closer European Union and free world economy as a whole. In some areas of law some progress can be observed, but a lot of work needs to be put into the foundations of legal theory in order to create a convincing basis for cross-border interaction of the law.

5   CONCLUSION

It is important to raise the level of awareness of foreign law and transnational law in legal science and practice, including legislation. The use of transnational law must be improved by suggesting practical methods of application of such law. Prejudices should be replaced by familiarity with concepts of combining different spheres of legal origin and law-making.

---

governed solely by the law of the Member State in which that lawsuit is pending [*lex loci processus*].'

11. Methodological challenges of codifying or consolidating national and international sales law based on CISG Article 35

Rene Franz Henschel[1]

1. INTRODUCTION

This chapter centres on the impact the CISG Convention has had on the national and international development of law. It focuses on the rules in Article 35 CISG, as the content of the provision has gained wide recognition in a number of jurisdictions. However, this recognition has resulted in changes and alternative expressions of the legal contents of the provision. If the provision is used as a model for preparing national as well as international rules but is changed more or less extensively, the question is whether these rules have to be interpreted and applied in the same way as the Convention rules, or whether legislators intended the new rules to have different and separate contents and objectives. The following analysis will show that it is sometimes impossible to determine whether this was intended or not, and this leads to uncertainty as to the contents of the new rules. The thesis of this chapter is that these uncertainties can be avoided if the focus is shifted to the method used in preparing the new rules. This thesis should be seen against the background that doubts appear to arise because it is uncertain whether legislators intended *consolidation* with the rules in the CISG, or whether they intended proper *codification* based on the rules of the CISG – a difference that can explain the different interpretations of the contents of the new rules.

Consequently, the focus should be on the method used in preparing the new rules based on the CISG. It is obvious that the method must be based

---

[1]   Associate professor, Ph.D., Department of Law, Aarhus School of Business and Social Sciences, University of Aarhus, Denmark. This is a revised version of an article first published in Baasch Andersen, C and Schroeter, UG (eds) (2008), *Sharing International Commercial Law across National Boundaries : Festschrift for Albert Kritzer on the Occasion of his Eightieth Birthday*, Wildy, Simmons and Hill.

on comparative tools. The point of departure is a famous article by Clive M. Schmitthoff from 1968 which is a prominent publication in the history of IALS: 'The Unification or Harmonisation of Law by Means of Standard Contracts and General Conditions'.[2] This article examines the development of international, common or uniform trade law regulations on the basis of what is described as a non-national, analytical-synthetic comparative method. This description of the method appears to be well suited to an analysis of the creation of rules based on the CISG, because there are many parallels between the creation of rules for the development of international uniform or harmonized law and the creation of rules based on international uniform or harmonized law. The following section will therefore focus on what Schmitthoff understands by a non-national, analytical-synthetic method and how this method can be used to illustrate the development of the legal rules inspired by Article 35 CISG.[3]

2.   THE CONSOLIDATING AND THE CODIFYING METHOD

In his article Schmitthoff describes two preferred comparative methods used in developing common or uniform rules of trade law. The first method, called the consolidating method, aims to ascertain a common core of case law or applicable standard terms and express this core in a new rule. This synthetic method is particularly popular in developing international standard terms such as ICC Incoterms and ECE standard contracts.[4] In some cases, Schmitthoff writes, the result of this method can even be described as synthetic law.[5]

The other method, called the codifying method, aims to compare the doctrines of different jurisdictions in order to establish a desirable legal norm and

---

[2]   Schmitthoff, CM (1968), 'The Unification or Harmonisation of Law by Means of Standard Contracts and General Conditions The Unification or Harmonisation of Law', in 17 *International & Comparative Law Quarterly* 551.

[3]   It is obvious that such a methodological approach in no way pretends to be the only or the most complete methodological approach for such an analysis. See also the summary and conclusion below.

[4]   See Schmitthoff, CM, *supra* n. 2 at 565: '[i]n modern applied comparative law, i.e. comparative law employed for a practical purpose and not merely as an academic exercise, two methods are used, which may be called the consolidating and the codifying method. The object of the consolidating method is to ascertain the common content of various legal regulations and thus to define the "common core of law" of them; this method aims at a factual ascertainment but not a doctrinal improvement of law'.

[5]   See ibid., at 565: '[a]s regards the results of the application of the comparative method to standard contracts, it should be realised that this application has in some instances produced an entirely new type of legal regulation which can only be described as synthetic law'.

express this in a new rule *de lege ferenda*,[6] i.e. an analytically based method. This method, Schmitthoff writes, is the one most often preferred by comparative scholars and is used, *inter alia*, in the preparation of international conventions.

At the same time, Schmitthoff observes that the elements from these methods are combined, for instance when protectable interests developed by case law affect and create balanced rules in standard terms such as ECE 188.[7] In the light of subsequent developments it is possible to add that this may also be the case when conventions such as the CISG apply solutions that some times disguise which doctrinal invention is definitely inherent in a rule, because the rule was a result of a compromise between different legal traditions and doctrinal approaches.[8] Similarly, if the rules in the CISG are applied as a basis for new rules without specifying a clear analytical-doctrinal objective or rules are prepared in the practical spirit of compromise.

Schmitthoff ends his article from 1968 by concluding that, in future, we will be accustomed to working with this type of non-national, analytical-synthetic rules of law which will form the core basis of the harmonization or unification of the law of international trade.[9] The last 50 years have shown that Schmitthoff's prophecy has been fulfilled and his ideas are still important for understanding the methodological development of international trade law and how the results of this process – the rules of law – have to be understood and interpreted.[10]

---

[6]   See ibid., at 565: '[t]he codifying method, on the other hand, compares in order to establish a desirable, improved legal norm; it amends the found regulation in a manner desirable *de lege feranda*'.

[7]   See ibid., at 570: '[i]n future it will be necessary to effect a combination between the realistic approach characteristic of international standard contracts and the doctrinal approach of international legislation'.

[8]   However, it is important to point out that the preparation of conventions is often the result of a compromise between different doctrinal approaches, and the doctrinal approach expressed in the convention rule may not be anything like an expression of all the doctrines of the participating states, let alone the doctrinal approach of a particular state, even though the contrary is often claimed to be the case. In this context the large number of reservations made by CISG ratifying states should be mentioned. For a detailed discussion see Baasch Andersen, C (2006), *The Uniformity of the CISG and its Jurisconsultorium. An Analysis of the Terms and a Closer Look at Examination and Notification* (Kluwer, London).

[9]   See Schmitthoff, CM, ibid., at 565: '[i]n the law of international trade of the future, we shall become increasingly accustomed to working with synthetic non-national legal concepts. The production of such concepts which are internationally acceptable is the greatest contribution which comparative law can make to the unification or harmonization of the law of international trade'. More recent discussions of the problems addressed by Schmitthoff can be found in: Fletcher, I, Mistelis, L and Cremona, M (eds) (2001), *Foundations and Perspectives of International Trade Law*.

[10]   See Mistelis, L (2001), 'Is Harmonisation a Necessary Evil? The Future of Harmonisation and New Sources of International Trade Law' in ibid., at 3.

This applies to the development of international standard terms and contracts, which formed the core of Schmitthoff's ideas, but also to the development of conventions such as the CISG, and to the development of national sales laws and the EU Sale of Consumer Goods Directive.

In order to make an operational analysis possible, the following discussion will focus on a single Article of the CISG, namely Article 35 concerning the conformity of the goods and its impact on a selective sample of regional and domestic rules governing the law of sales; accordingly, the results of the analysis should be seen in this light.

This selection may of course be criticized inasmuch as the sample units represent a limited – and Eurocentric – selection of legislative rules, as the application of the comparative method in connection with such a selection of rules is faced with many challenges and difficulties,[11] and as the analysis is mainly based on a non-exhaustive and rough outline of the non-national, analytical-synthetic comparative method. However, the purpose is not to carry out an in-depth, comparative analysis of all the questions that emerge in connection with this issue, but merely to identify the central themes in the light of Schmitthoff's description of certain rules as having a non-national, analytical-synthetic comparative origin and the challenges this poses. The starting point of the analysis is that there is not one – and only one – real and true solution, but that legal rules should chiefly be understood on the basis of the economic, cultural and social contexts of the specific jurisdiction in which the rules are rooted.[12] On the other hand, it may be possible that a rule can be criticized from a functional-legal point of view, i.e. whether the rule fulfils its intended purpose.[13] This will be discussed in more detail in the analytical sections below using the above-mentioned non-national, analytical-synthetic comparative method.

3. INTRODUCING CREATION OF RULES BASED ON ARTICLE 35 CISG IN NATIONAL AND INTERNATIONAL LAW

The United Nations Convention on the International Sale of Goods, CISG, is the fruit of several decades of work in an attempt to harmonize international

---

[11] See e.g. Twining, W (2006), 'Diffusion of Law: A Global Perspective', 1/2 *Journal of Comparative Law* 237 and Legrand, P (2006), 'Comparative Legal Studies and the Matter of Authenticity', 1/2 *Journal of Comparative Law* 365.

[12] See also Legrand, P (2006), 'On the Singularity of Law', 47/2 *Harvard International Law Journal* 517.

[13] See also Twining, W, *supra* n. 11 at 260.

sales law. The seeds were sown as early as in 1926 when UNIDROIT[14] was established, and in this connection the groundbreaking comparative research of Ernst Rabel prepared the ground for future harmonized rules.[15] In 1964 this work resulted in the adoption of ULIS[16] and ULF[17] (the Hague Conventions), which, however, failed to get the necessary international acceptance.[18] For this reason, a working group under the auspices of the newly founded United Nations Commission on International Trade Law, UNCITRAL,[19] was set up, and its task was to prepare a treaty that could get the wide international acceptance that had eluded the Hague Conventions. After more than ten years of dedicated work, the CISG Convention was adopted by a diplomatic conference in Vienna in 1980, and this new fruit appealed to the taste of the discriminating audience. Now 72 countries – representing several of the most important economies in the world – have ratified the CISG.[20]

However, the CISG has been widely criticized – as a compromise between different legal traditions – for not being a real fruit but a peculiarity, a synthetic fruit, which will never have the same taste and texture as naturally grown fruits. This is likely to affect its functionality, i.e. forming a satisfactory framework for solving international sales law conflicts,[21] because the interpretation of the CISG is hampered by its mixed nature. The harmonization of the rules by reducing them to text does not directly lead to the harmonization of results.[22] Even though some commentators believe that the fruit was picked too early and therefore did not have sufficient time to ripen,[23] there is no doubt that the CISG has fairly strong genes that have affected the genes of other fruits, both nationally and internationally.

---

[14]   International Institute for the Unification of Private Law (www.unidroit.org).

[15]   Rabel, E (1968), *Das Recht des Warenkaufs, 2. Band. Unveränderter Neudruck der Ausgabe von 1958* (Berlin).

[16]   Uniform Law on International Sales.

[17]   Uniform Law on the Formation of Contracts in International Sales.

[18]   Only 9 states, 2 of them non-European, ratified the Hague Conventions.

[19]   UN Commission on International Trade Law, established in 1966.

[20]   See www.uncitral.org (last visited 1 September 2008). The ratifying states include the USA, China and Russia plus all EU Member States, except the United Kingdom, Ireland and Portugal.

[21]   See e.g. Bridge, M (2003) 'Uniformity and Diversity in the Law of International Sale', 15 *Pace International Law Review* 15 at 55.

[22]   For a further discussion see Baasch Andersen, C (2006), *The Uniformity of the CISG and its Jurisconsultorium. An Analysis of the Terms and a Closer Look at Examination and Notification* (Kluwer, London).

[23]   See e.g. Bailey, JE (1999), 'Facing the Truth: Seeing the Convention on Contracts for the International Sale of Goods as an Obstacle to a Uniform Law of International Sales', 32 *Cornell International Law Journal* at 273.

The Conventions rule on non-conformity, Article 35, has been a significant source of inspiration for preparing the new Nordic sales laws,[24] for modernizing the contract law of a number of other European[25] and East European[26] countries, for the new Chinese contract law,[27] and for the new common sales laws of the OHADA states,[28] to mention but a few. Recently, the provision has affected EU law as the rules on non-conformity in the Sale of Consumer Goods Directive are widely based on Article 35 CISG. The influence ranges from almost complete copying of the contents and systematic approach of the provision to almost complete rewriting and reorganization of the systematic approach. This challenges the extent of the influence Article 35 has had on the end result.

The following section opens with a preliminary description of Article 35 with reference to leading case law and scholarly writings. Section 5 will analyse the impact of the provision on the Finnish, Norwegian and Swedish sales laws, which were some of the first national Acts to take the definition of non-conformity of the goods in Article 35 as their source of inspiration; the Nordic legislators also extensively copied the contents and structural approach of the provision. Section 6 then addresses the EU Sale of Consumer Goods Directive, which was partly inspired by Article 35 in order to create a common definition of non-conformity that applies to both contracts of a commercial nature and consumer contracts. Section 7 examines the transposition of this Directive in selected European countries in order to clarify the differences and similarities between the ways in which legislators have coped with the relationship with the CISG in terms of systematic and doctrinal approaches – what may be called creation of rules on the third tier. Section 8 sums up the analysis and the thesis

---

[24] See The Nordic Sales Law Report NU 1984:5 (1985), *Nordiska köplager. Förslag av den nordiska arbetsgruppen för köplagsstiftning.*

[25] For example the Dutch Wetboeks: see Schlechtriem, P (2000), *Kommentar zum Einheitlichen UN-Kaufrecht – CISG* (3rd ed) at 35; Schlechtriem, P (2001), '10 Jahre CISG – Der Einfluß des UN-Kaufrechts auf die Entwicklung des deutschen und des internationale Schuldrechts', 1 *Internationales Handelsrecht* (IHR) 12; Hondius, E and Jeloschek, C (2000), 'Die Kaufrichtlinie und das Niederländische Recht: Für den Westen kaum etwas Neues' in Grundmann, S, Medicus, D and Rolland, W (eds), *Europäische Kaufgewährlesitungsrecht. Reform und Internationalisierung des Deutschen Schuldrechts, Hallesche Schriften zum Recht, Band 13* at 197.

[26] For example the Russian Contracts Act: see Schechtriem, P *supra* n. 25 at 35.

[27] See Yingxia, SU (1996), *Die vertragsgemäße Beschaffenheit der Ware im UNCITRAL-Kaufrecht im Vergleich zum deutschen und chinesischen Recht* at 150 and 205; and Heutger, V (2002), 'Worldwide Harmonisation of Private Law and Regional Economic Integration – 75 Jahre UNIDROIT – Rom, 27.–28. September 2002', 6 *European Review of Private Law* 857.

[28] Organisation pour L´Harmonisation du Droit des Affaires en Afrique: see Rösler, H (2006), '70 Jahre Des Warenkaufs Von Ernst Rabel', 70 *Rabels Zeitschrift für ausländisches und internationales Privatrecht* 803.

of the non-national, analytical-synthetic comparative method and how it affects the development of law and puts them into a wider perspective.

4. CONFORMITY OF GOODS IN ARTICLE 35 CISG

Article 35 CISG contains a rather comprehensive and explicit provision on determining lack of conformity, which is a novelty in many jurisdictions. Moreover, Article 35(1) CISG lays down the principle that the contract of the parties forms the principal basis for determining any lack of conformity, which is emphasized by the words conformity of the goods. These words have already influenced the way in which the issue of conformity has been expressed in doctrinal terms in several jurisdictions, irrespective of whether the sales are domestic or international.[29] Except where the parties have agreed otherwise, the subsidiary provisions contained in Article 35(2) apply, setting forth a number of positively worded presumptions concerning the conformity of the goods. These rules may be regarded as aids in interpreting contracts and set out, at the same time, certain burden-of-proof rules. Finally, Article 35(3) contains an exemption to the seller's liability for lack of conformity if the buyer knew or could not have been unaware of the lack of conformity.

A number of concepts and distinctions known from domestic law play no separate part in relation to determining the conformity of the goods under Article 35,[30] which must be interpreted autonomously and uniformly as provided by Article 7(1). This applies, *inter alia*, to the distinction between defective performance and *aliud pro alio* (delivery of goods completely different from those contracted for);[31] containers and packaging regarded as part of the concept of

---

[29] Danish law, for instance, generally uses the term *defects* (*mangler*) to refer to performance that does not conform to the terms of the contract. In the Danish translation of the CISG provided by the Danish Ministry of Justice the heading of the section containing Art. 35 reads: *Conformity of the goods with the contract (defects) and third party claims*. Furthermore, the Danish Act transposing the EU Sale of Consumer Goods Directive uses the phrase: *Conformity with the contract*. As a result the heading of the part containing the consumer protection provisions on defects has been changed and a parenthesis added: *Conformity of the goods with the contract (defects)*. Even though the use of parentheses in statutes may be questioned from an aesthetic point of view, the phenomenon may be taken to reflect a change in terminology in domestic Danish sales law brought about by outside pressure.

[30] However, this does not mean that the distinctions are not important in other relations, for example in relation to remedies for breach (e.g. trivial defects).

[31] See Oberster Gerichthof (Austria), 21 March 2000, available at: http://cisgw3.law. pace.edu/cases /000321a3.html; Oberster Gerichthof (Austria), 29 June 1999, available at: http://cisgw3.law.pace.edu/ cases/990629a3.html; and Bundesgerichtshof (Germany), 3 April 1996, available at: http://cisgw3.law. pace.edu/cases/960403g1.html, on the sale

lack of conformity and not merely as an ancillary obligation;[32] and the delivery of less than agreed quantities (shortage) treated as late delivery and not as lack of conformity.[33]

Article 35(2)(a) provides that the goods only conform with the contract if they: 'are fit for the purposes for which goods of the same description would ordinarily be used.' This rule seems to be generally accepted.[34] The basis for determining whether the goods are fit for ordinary use is the objective norm applied by the trade concerned. According to the predominant view found in case law and scholarly writings, the seller cannot be expected to know special rules relating to the ordinary use of the goods applicable only in the country of destination, e.g. rules on health, safety, etc. Consequently, it seems reasonable generally to base the assessment on the norm applicable in the seller's country when the conformity of the goods has to be determined.[35] However, this principle does not apply to cases where the information about the norm in the country of destination is brought within the seller's sphere of influence, for instance if the seller is aware of the rules, if the parties have previously done business with each other and the seller knows the buyer's expectations, or if the seller has marketed the goods in the buyer's country.[36] A logical conclusion is that, as to ordinary use, the seller must be required to give the buyer any necessary instructions and directions so that the buyer will be able to use the goods for the purpose for which they would ordinarily be used.

Under Article 35(2)(b) the seller must deliver goods that are fit for any particular purpose of the buyer which, based on an objective assessment of the

---

of a consignment of cobalt sulphate, which does not reject, in principle, that it may be possible to treat such serious cases of *aliud pro alio* as non-delivery if the goods are significantly different from those contracted for.

[32] See decision of COMPROMEX (Mexico), 29 April 1996, available at: http://cisgw3.law.pace.edu/ cases/960429m1.html.

[33] In its judgment of 10 February 1994, Oberlandesgericht Düsseldorf (Germany) heard a case concerning the lack of conformity of about a quarter of the goods under Art. 35(2)(b) but nevertheless determined the case under Art. 47(2) on *Nachfrist* (extension of time to fulfil obligations) and the court referred to *aliud pro alio*. The case is available at: www.unilex.info/case.cfm?pid=1&id=68&do=case. The judgment has been criticized for having ignored Art. 35(1), for considering *aliud pro alio* and must therefore be considered wrong; see also Veneziano, A (1997), 'Non Conformity of Goods in International Sales', 1 *International Business Law Journal* 39.

[34] See Henschel, RF (2005), *The Conformity of Goods in International Sales: An Analysis of Art. 35 in the United Nations Convention on the International Sale of Goods (CISG)*, (Forlaget Thomson) at 190.

[35] See generally Henschel, RF, *supra* n. 34 at 4.

[36] These basic principles were established by the Bundesgerichtshof (Germany) in its judgment of 8 March 1995 (*New Zealand Mussels* case), available at http://cisgw3.law.pace.edu/ cases/950308g3.html.

buyer's statements and conduct, was expressly or impliedly made known to the seller at the time of conclusion of the contract. CISG case law has generally regarded this as a standard of negligence, i.e. the seller has a duty to know the buyer's purpose, as the seller has acted negligently. In other words, the buyer's expectations derived from any given conduct of the seller are protected. However, the protection the buyer is afforded by Article 35(2)(b) is limited if the buyer did not rely, or if it was unreasonable for him to rely, on the seller's skill and judgement.

Article 35(2)(c) contains the presumptive rule in contract law that the goods must possess the qualities of goods that the seller has presented to the buyer as a sample or model. Article 35(1) and Article 35(2)(d) provide that the container and packaging of the goods are an integrated part of the conformity of the goods, i.e. part of the seller's obligation to render proper performance.

Finally, the provision in Article 35(3) is a limited *caveat emptor* rule that applies in case of non-conformity. Whether or not the goods conform to the contract determines when the provision applies, which means that the delimitation of this provision as against Article 35(1) is *de facto* difficult. Both case law and scholarly writings show Article 35(3) applied directly in connection with Article 35(1) with reference to doctrines of good faith and fair dealing, *venire contra factum proprium* as well as observance of the principle of good faith in international trade: see Article 7(1) CISG.[37] However, there is no reason to have recourse to such principles before attempting to interpret the requirements as to the quality of the goods: see Article 35(1) CISG. Similarly, the application of a *caveat emptor* rule in international sales is limited, as the buyer is often unable to examine the goods prior to conclusion of the contract. Therefore, Article 35(3) does not impose on the buyer a general duty to examine the goods prior to the conclusion of the contract on his own initiative. If the buyer examines the goods prior to contract or in any other way may be deemed to have become aware of any lack of conformity, both case law and scholarly writings agree that the buyer could not have been unaware of the non-conformity if he had been grossly negligent.[38]

In the following section, the provisions on conformity of goods in the Nordic Sales Acts will be analysed.

---

[37] See e.g. the judgment of Tribunal Cantonal de Vaud (Switzerland), 28 October 1997, available at: www.unilex.info/case.cfm?pid=1&id=311&do=case.

[38] See Henschel, RF, *supra* n. 34 at 199.

5. CONFORMITY OF GOODS IN NORDIC SALES ACTS

The provisions on conformity of the goods in the Nordic Sales Acts[39] are almost identical to the provisions in Article 35 CISG except for a few important details.[40] The Finnish,[41] Norwegian[42] and the Swedish[43] Acts are based on Article 35 CISG.[44] The Danish legislators chose not to implement these changes, but have subsequently changed the definition of lack of conformity so that it corresponds to the Sale of Consumer Goods Directive. As the Sale of Consumer Goods Directive was partly inspired by Article 35 CISG – as shown below – traces from Article 35 have found their way into Danish sales law using EU law as a conduit. Section 17 of the Finnish Sales Act (*köplagen*), section 17 of the Norwegian Sales Act (*lov om kjøp*), and section 17 of the Swedish Sales Act (*köplagen*) substantially correspond to Article 35(1) and Article 35(2) CISG.

The provision of Article 35(3) CISG has found its way into section 20 of the Nordic Sales Law providing, however, that if the buyer has any knowledge of the lack of conformity the prejudicial effects of this are not only limited to the implicit requirements contained in section 17(2) but apply to the entire provision, including the requirements in the contract between the parties. As indicated above, this corresponds with the case law on Article 35 CISG.

In addition, section 18(2) of the Nordic Sales Acts contains a rule on the seller's liability for marketing the goods, as the seller is generally liable for information provided by an earlier sales channel and manufacturers. As to the relationship between section 18 and Article 35 it is important to appreciate that CISG applies only to the contract between the buyer and the seller (see

---

[39]   This does not include the consumer sale provisions nor the Danish Sale of Goods Act, which did not implement the changes proposed by the Nordic fact-finding committee in report 'NU 1984:5'.

[40]   The discussion below is primarily based on Ramberg, J (1997), 'The New Swedish Sales Law', 28 *Saggi, Conferenze e seminari*; Hellner, J (1997), 'Die bedeutung des UN-Kaufrechts in Skandinavien', in Neumeyer, KH (ed), *Emptio-Venditio Inter Nationes. Wiener Übereinkommen über den internationalen Warenkauf* at 151.

[41]   Finnish Sales Act (*köplag*) of 27 March 1987/355.

[42]   Norwegian Sales Act (*lov om kjøp*) (Act 1988-05-13 no. 27). The Norwegian Sales Act was changed on 1 July 2002 and the former section 17(3) was removed and inserted in the Norwegian Sale of Consumer Goods Act (Act 2002-06-21 no. 34) as part of approximating Norwegian law to the Sale of Consumer Goods Directive. For a detailed discussion of the relationship between the Norwegian Sales Act and Art. 35 CISG and the former provision on defects in the BGB see Kjelland, C (2000), *Das Neue Kaufrecht der nordischen Länder im Vergleich mit dem Wiener Kaufrecht (CISG) und dem deutschen Kaufrecht. Eine vergleichende Darstellung unter besonderer Berücksichtigung des norwegischen Rechts der Sachmangelhaftung.*

[43]   Swedish Sales Act (*köplag*) (1990:931).

[44]   See Report 'NU 1984:5' at 155.

Article 4), so importance cannot generally be attached to material not provided by the seller unless the seller knew or could not have been unaware that the buyer regarded this material as part of the terms of the contract: see Article 8. Accordingly, the CISG does not impose on the seller general liability for marketing the goods in contrast to section 18(2) of the Nordic Sales Acts;[45] see also Article 8(3) and the CISG case law developed by the Austrian Supreme Court.[46] The Norwegian Sales Act also applies to international sales and is therefore problematic because it imposes on the seller a duty that does not follow from the Convention rules.[47] It is very doubtful whether foreign courts will apply this provision when Norwegian law governs the international contract of sale. Despite the substantial correspondence between the lack of conformity principle in Article 35 CISG and the Nordic sales acts, some significant differences should not be ignored.

6. CONFORMITY OF GOODS IN THE SALE OF CONSUMER GOODS DIRECTIVE

EU law recognizes that CISG is part of the common European body of law, its *acquis communautaire*, and thereby also part of the development of future European contract law.[48] In framing the principle of non-conformity with the contract in the Sale of Consumer Goods Directive the European Parliament and the European Council – just as the Nordic legislators – were inspired by Article 35 CISG.[49] Like Article 35 CISG the Sale of Consumer Goods Directive is based

---

[45]   See e.g. Hagstrøm,V (1995), 'Kjøpsrettskonvensjon, Norsk Kjøpslov og International Rettsenhet', 4 *Tidskrift for Rettsvetenskap* 561.

[46]   See Oberster Gerichsthof (Austria),11 March 1999, available at: http://cisgw3.law.pace.edu/cases/ 990311a3.html.

[47]   See further Kjelland, C, *supra* n. 42 at 94. See also Lookofsky, J (2003), 'The Scandinavia Experience' in Ferrari, F (ed), *The 1980 Uniform Sales Law: Old Issues Revisited in the Light of Recent Experiences* (Giuffrè/Sellier European Law Publishers) at 120, re. section 18 in the Norwegian Act and the requirement that the seller 'knew or must have been aware' of the buyer's special purpose, which does not reflect Art. 35(2)(b) which hardly requires some active participation on the part of the buyer.

[48]   See Troiano, S (2003), 'The Exclusion of the Seller's Liability for Recognizable Lacks of Conformity under the CISG and the new European Sales Law: The CISG and the New European Sales Law: The Changing Fortunes of a Notion of Variable Content' in Ferrari, F, *supra* n. 47 at 147.

[49]   The following discussion is primarily based on: Staudenmayer, D (2000), 'EG-Richtlinie 1999/44/EG zur Vereinheitlichung des Kaufgewährleistungsrecht' in Grundmann, S, Medicus, D and Rolland, W, *Europäisches Kaufgewährleistungsrecht. Reform und Internationaliserung des Deutschen Schuldrechts* 27 et seq.; Staudenmayer, D (2000), 'The Directive on the Sale of Consumer Goods and Associated Guarantees – a

on the contract between the parties (see Article 35) as this is a common principle in the legal systems of Member States.[50] When something may be deemed agreed, as provided for in Article 2(1), it is left for the Member States to decide according to their own contract law rules.[51] However, some uniform interpretation rules in the sale of consumer goods framework may be important for the interpretation of the contract between the parties – and also for the principle of non-conformity – see the Unfair Contract Terms Directive.[52]

Article 2(2) introduces a number of presumptions concerning the requirements a buyer may have of goods in the same way as provided in Article 35 CISG, as the sale is often not based on a written contract for the sale of consumer goods.[53] This should also affect the burden-of-proof rules, just as is the

Milestone in European Consumer and Private Law', 8 *European Review of Private Law* 547; Lando, O (2000), 'International Trends: Requirements concerning the quality of movable goods and remedies for defects under the Principles of European Contract Law' in Grundmann, S, Medicus, D and Rolland,W, *Europäisches Kaufgewährleistungsrecht* 61; Magnus, U (2000), 'Die Verbrauchergüterkauf-Richtlinie und das UN-Kaufrecht' in ibid., at 79; Krusinga, SA (2001), 'What do consumer and commercial sales have in common? A comparison of the EC Directive on consumer sales law and the UN Convention on contracts for the international sale of goods', 2 & 3 *European Review of Private Law* 177; Lorenz, S (2005), 'Schuldrechtsreform 2002: Problemschwerpunkte drei Jahre Danach', 27 *Neue Juristische Wochenschrift* 1889.

[50] 'The seller must deliver goods to the consumer which are in conformity with the contract of sale.' This is further explained in the preamble to the Directive: '[w]hereas the goods must, above all, conform with the contractual specifications; whereas the principle of conformity with the contract may be considered as common to the different national legal traditions; whereas in certain national legal traditions it may not be possible to rely solely on this principle to ensure a minimum level of protection for the consumer; whereas under such legal traditions, in particular, additional national provisions may be useful to ensure that the consumer is protected in cases where the parties have agreed no specific contractual terms or where the parties have concluded contractual terms or agreements which directly or indirectly waive or restrict the rights of the consumer and which, to the extent that these rights result from this Directive, are not binding on the consumer.'

[51] See Danish Ministry of Justice Report on the Consumer Sales Directive no. 1403/2001, p. 58. For a recent discussion of European contract law see Communication from the Commission to the Council and the European Parliament on European contract law, COM(2003)68 final of 12 February 2003.

[52] Directive 93/13/EEC of 5 April 1993 on unfair contract terms in consumer contracts.

[53] 'Whereas, in order to facilitate the application of the principle of conformity with the contract, it is useful to introduce a rebuttable presumption of conformity with the contract covering the most common situations; whereas that presumption does not restrict the principle of freedom of contract; whereas, furthermore, in the absence of specific contractual terms, as well as where the minimum protection clause is applied, the elements mentioned in this presumption may be used to determine the lack of conformity of the goods with the contract; whereas the quality and performance which consumers can reasonably expect will depend inter alia on whether the goods are new or second-hand;

case with CISG.[54] Firstly, Article 2(2)(a) provides that the goods must comply with the description given by the seller and possess the qualities of the goods that the seller held out to the buyer as a sample or model.[55] This corresponds to the provision of Article 35(2)(c) CISG in its entirety.

Secondly, Article 2(2)(b) provides that the goods must be fit for any particular purpose required by the buyer which he has made known to the seller and which the seller has accepted.[56] *Prima facie* this rule differs from the provision of Article 35(2)(b) CISG, which does not make the same explicit requirements concerning the apparent positive acceptance of the seller.[57] In the case law on Article 35(2)(b) CISG emphasis is put on the seller's blameworthy conduct; in particular grossly negligent conduct on the part of the seller is equated with 'expressly or impliedly made known'. Whether this apparent limitation of the seller's liability for non-conformity contained in the Sale of Consumer Goods Directive compared with Article 35 CISG shall apply is left to the decision of the Member States, as the Directive is a minimum directive;[58] therefore it is possible to maintain an interpretation rule that is restrictive for sellers. A rule of implied acceptance or negligence on the part of the seller as sufficient may be justified by the interests of consumer protection and will at least correspond to the rule in Article 35(2)(b) CISG, and also leading case law and academic writings. The rule in Article 2(2)(b) of the Sale of Consumer Goods Directive therefore illustrates the need for clarification that may arise when rules governing the sale of consumer goods in one jurisdiction have their genealogical roots in other rules relating to contracts of a commercial character. A general need has therefore arisen for an adjusting, purposive interpretation of the Sale of Consumer Goods Directive in this respect;[59] see also the discussion of the transposition of the Directive into Danish law below.

Article 2(2)(c) – and partly also Article 2(2)(d) – of the Sale of Consumer Goods Directive contains the rule found in Article 35(2)(a) CISG providing

---

whereas the elements mentioned in the presumption are cumulative; whereas, if the circumstances of the case render any particular element manifestly inappropriate, the remaining elements of the presumption nevertheless still apply; ...'

[54] See paragraph 8 of the preamble to Directive 93/13/EEC, *supra* n. 52.

[55] '[C]omply with the description given by the seller and possess the qualities of the goods which the seller has held out to the consumer as a sample or model'.

[56] Art. 2(2)(b) provides: 'are fit for any particular purpose for which the consumer requires them and which he made known to the seller at the time of conclusion of the contract and which the seller has accepted'.

[57] Art. 35(2)(b) provides: 'are fit for any particular purpose expressly or impliedly made known to the seller at the time of the conclusion of the contract, except where the circumstances show that the buyer did not rely, or that it was unreasonable for him to rely, on the seller's skill and judgement'

[58] See Art. 8 of the Directive, *supra* n. 52.

[59] See e.g. Troiano, S, *supra* n. 48 at 147.

that the goods must be fit for the purposes for which goods of the same type are normally used. On the basis of the reason for the rule and its wording, the rule must be deemed to be substantively identical to the provision of Article 35(2)(a) CISG. However, Article 2(2)(d) introduces a further rule on the seller's liability for marketing the goods – which is similar to the rules found in the Nordic Sales Acts. This applies to the sale of consumer goods where a large part of the principal information about the goods is often contained in the marketing material, but this does not apply to contracts of a commercial character to the same extent. However, the seller is not unconditionally liable in all cases for such marketing material, and this limits the scope of the rule somewhat.

Article 2(3) of the Directive provides that there is no lack of conformity with the contract if the buyer was aware or could not reasonably have been unaware of the lack of conformity. This rule modifies Article 35(3) somewhat.[60] The additional rule in Article 2(3) of the Sale of Consumer Goods Directive providing that there shall not be deemed to be a lack of conformity if the non-conformity has its origin in materials supplied by the buyer also applies to the application of Article 35(3) CISG. Finally, CISG case law indicates that the lack of instructions may result in the goods being deemed not to conform with the contract (see Article 35(2)(a)),[61] which corresponds to the provision in Article 2(5) of the Sale of Consumer Goods Directive (the so-called 'IKEA clause').

The conclusion must be that the Sale of Consumer Goods Directive substantially corresponds with Article 35 CISG in relation to the definition of lack of conformity even though it differs in some respects on the grounds of special consumer protection interests. The Member States should take this into account when transposing the Directive in so far as the rules of the Sale of Consumer Goods Directive apply as a model for contracts of a commercial character. At the same time, the development of consumer law reflects a return to the general law of contract. Accordingly, Article 35 as well as case law and scholarly writings on the provision are applicable to the interpretation of closely related rules. Therefore, the European Court of Justice will have to interpret the Sale of Consumer Goods Directive on the basis of Article 35 CISG.[62]

---

[60]   See e.g. ibid., at 147.

[61]   This is confirmed by the decision of Arbitration Institute of the Stockholm Chamber of Commerce, 5 June 1998, available at http://cisgw3.law.pace.edu/cases/980605s5. html, where an American seller had sold a press to a Chinese buyer. It was held that the improper installation of a lockplate could have been avoided if the seller had provided the buyer with correct instructions. See also Magnus, U, *supra* n. 49 at 79.

[62]   Further see Grundmann, S (2000), 'Generalreferat: Internationalisierung und Reform des deutschen Kaufrechts' in Grundmann, S, Medicus, D and Rolland,W, *supra* n. 49 at 290.

7.   TRANSPOSITION OF THE SALE OF CONSUMER GOODS DIRECTIVE INTO NATIONAL LAW

As mentioned above, the Sale of Consumer Goods Directive is a minimum directive and has to be transposed into national law. The road is thus paved for divergent transposal measures as well as major or minor divergences in relation to Article 35 CISG. Furthermore, combined transposition of the Directive so that it will apply to both contracts for the sale of consumer goods and contracts of a commercial character may entail the application of a common yardstick even though consumer contracts and contracts of a commercial character should not always be subject to the same assessment in relation to the conformity of the goods, as shown above.

It is beyond the scope of this chapter to examine the transposition of the Directive by all Member States. Suffice it to say that a few examples of transposal measures warrant attention as they illustrate the problems involved. The following discussion primarily focuses on the transposal measures in Danish and German law, but also transposition of the Directive into Austrian and French law will be addressed.

The *travaux préparatoires* concerning the transposition of the Sale of Consumer Goods Directive into Danish law are contained in Report No. 1403/2001 on the transposition of the Sale of Consumer Goods Directive into Danish law. The report concludes that there was no general need to introduce a new definition of conformity of the goods into Danish law, but such a new definition was nevertheless adopted for sales of consumer goods on the ground that, firstly, it would improve the informative value of the Act and, secondly, the Danish Sale of Goods Act would be approximated to the Sale of Consumer Goods Directive, the Nordic Sales Acts and the CISG. However, the report emphasized that no substantive change was intended in respect of the Danish non-conformity concept applicable to the sale of consumer goods.[63] It should be noted that this non-conformity concept in consumer sales is widely deemed to correspond

---

[63]   'Even though it cannot be deemed necessary for the proper transposition of the Sale of Consumer Goods Directive, the working group suggests that – in line with Finnish, Norwegian and Swedish law – the concept of lack of conformity in the Danish Sale of Goods Act is supplemented by a positive statement of the criteria the goods must have to conform with the contract; see section 1(v) of the Bill (the proposed section 75A). No substantive changes were intended with this provision as it is merely a detailed description of the elements forming part of the general non-conformity concept applicable under section 76(1)(iv) of the Danish Sale of Goods Act. However, the provision may be appropriate for several reasons. Firstly, the informative value of the provision of the Sale of Goods Act is increased, because the criteria are not clearly expressed in the currently applicable provision on the non-conformity concept and secondly, the change facilitates an approximation of the Danish rules to the non-conformity concepts in the Sale of Consumer Goods Directive, the CISG and the other Nordic countries.'

to the definition of non-conformity applicable to contracts of a commercial character which are not subject to an explicit definition of non-conformity. The non-conformity rules in the part of the Act governing consumer sale are applied by analogy, and the references to the CISG and contracts of a commercial character in the *travaux préparatoires* should be read in this light.

Legislators introduced a provision into the Danish Sale of Goods Act, section 75A, which appears to be a compromise between the systematic approach and the contents of Article 35 CISG and the contents of the Sale of Consumer Goods Directive in general. Section 75A appears to be an amalgamation of Article 35(1) CISG and Article 2(2), 2(2)(a) and 2(5) of the Sale of Consumer Goods Directive. Section 75A(2) is practically identical to Article 35(2) CISG and its presumptions and it generally follows the wording of Article 35(2) CISG more closely than the wording of the Sale of Consumer Goods Directive. Section 75A(2)(ii) of the Danish Sale of Goods Act corresponds to Article 35(2)(a) CISG, and section 75A(2) (iv) of the Act corresponds to Article 35(2)(c) CISG, whereas the rule on particular purposes is contained in section 75A(2)(ii). However, this section provides that the goods must be fit for the particular purpose if the seller has 'confirmed the buyer's expectations in that respect'. It seems as if the Danish legislators have opted for a compromise between a direct agreement and acceptance, on the one hand, and Article 35 CISG and its words 'expressly or impliedly made known' on the other hand. It should also be noted that the Danish Sale of Goods Act does not contain a rule corresponding to Article 35(2)(b) CISG, which provides that the seller shall not be liable if the buyer did not rely, or that it was unreasonable for him to rely, on the seller's skill and judgement, on the grounds that a consumer should generally be able to rely on the seller's skill and judgement. There are undoubtedly consumer sales in which this situation will occur.

Even though the Sale of Consumer Goods Directive does not mention discrepancies in quantity and nature (shortage and *aliud*), section 75A of the Danish Sale of Goods Act governs these situations, thereby clearly revealing its affinity with Article 35 CISG. This also coincides with the position in German law (see the discussion of the changes to the BGB below) because, as 'parent' of the Sale of Consumer Goods Directive, Article 35 CISG has specifically been singled out as the reason for such interpretation of the Directive.[64] Similarly, it has been argued that the Directive may be applied to factual non-conformity as well as legal non-conformity, though this argument has been countered by, for instance, French legal scholars.[65]

---

[64]   See Grundmann, S (2001), 'European sales law – reform and adoption of international models in German sales law, 2 & 3 *European Review of Private Law* 250.

[65]   See Rohlfing-Dijoux, S (2000), 'Umsetzungsüberlegungen zur Kaufgewährleistungs Richtlinie in Frankreich' in Grundmann, S, Medicus, D and Rolland, W *supra* n. 49 at 149, referring to Art. 1626 of the French Civil Code.

Article 2(3) of the Sale of Consumer Goods Directive corresponds to Article 35(3) CISG. Consequently, what the buyer ought to know cannot be relied on, but only circumstances the buyer knew or could not have been unaware of may be relied on. Previously, the provision of section 47 of the Danish Sale of Goods Act – which still applies to contracts of a commercial character and of a civil character – applied to consumer contracts, and the decisive factor was what the buyer ought to know. This has now been changed so that an assessment that is more favourable to the consumer and contained in the Sale of Consumer Goods Directive applies: see section 77B of the Danish Sale of Goods Act.[66]

German legislators have also transposed the Sale of Consumer Goods Directive into German law but used an approach that was different from that used by Danish legislators, as the transposition of the Directive was part of a major overhaul of the German law of obligations.[67] The most far-reaching change was the modernization of the BGB as only few changes were made to the HGB.[68] The main reasons for the changes were the serious problems of delimitation caused by the differentiations in the BGB and the HGB and the consequential need for clarification in case law. Moreover, the changes were also the result of an intention to effect an approximation to the clearer and more stringent structure of the CISG, and the transposition of the Sale of Consumer Goods Directive into German law required certain adjustments, in particular concerning the principle of lack of conformity.[69] However, the German legislature did not adopt the changes until its arm was twisted, and therefore had to transpose the Sale of Consumer Goods Directive and hence the effects of the CISG.[70]

Legislators adopted an integrated approach when transposing the provisions of the Sale of Consumer Goods Directive into German law. Instead of a separate Sales Act – as in French law[71] – or a modernization of consumer sale provisions in the general Sales Act – as in Danish law – the legislators integrated the provi-

---

[66] See further the Danish Justice Ministry report 1403/2001 on the Sale of Consumer Goods Directive, at p. 65.

[67] The folowing discussion is primarily based on: Schimmel, R and Buhlmann, D (2002), *Frankfurter Handbuch zum neuen Schuldrecht Luchterhand: Hermann*; Dauner-Lieb, B, Heidel, T, Lepa, M and Ring, G (2001), *Das Neue Schuldrecht in der anwaltlichen Praxis*; and generally Grundmann, S, Medicus, D & Rolland, W, *supra* n. 47.

[68] This concerns the repeal of section 378 of the HGB, which treated certain cases of *aliud* and material defects equally (see the following discussion in the main text). The provision was repealed as a result of section 434(3) of the BGB, which is also discussed in the following main text.

[69] See Dauner-Lieb in Dauner-Lieb, B, Heidel, T, Lepa, M & Ring, G, *supra* n. 67 at 15.

[70] See Herber, R (2003), 'The German Experience' in Ferrari, F, *supra* n. 47 at 66.

[71] The French rules were incorporated in the *Code de la consommation* by decree of 17 February 2005.

sions into the BGB so that they generally apply to all types of sale. The reason for adopting this approach was that legislators wanted to ensure a certain degree of transparency and clarity in German law. At the same time the legislators are forced to provide reasons for those provisions that should be worded differently because of special stakeholder interests.[72]

It is interesting to note that the new non-conformity concept in the BGB retains the word defects and not conformity of the goods, which is the phrase used in the CISG and the Sale of Consumer Goods Directive. This solution has been criticized because it is natural to question whether the German legislators intended to create a new non-conformity concept that is different from that in the CISG and the Directive, or whether they had no such intention despite their choice of words.

Section 433 of the BGB provides that the seller must deliver goods that are free from material defects and legal defects, which means that the provisions rank these two types of defects equally.[73] At the same time, the BGB introduces a general definition of defects which extends but also simplifies the concept of defects compared to the former section 459 of the BGB. The new definition of defects is partly based on the Sale of Consumer Goods Directive and partly on Article 35 CISG.[74] The first sentence of section 433 corresponds to Article 35(1) CISG though it only contains the general provision that goods are free from material defects if they have the agreed quality. The third sentence of section 434(1) contains provisions that *prima facie* correspond to Article 35(2)(a) and 35(2)(b) but are phrased differently, and they also introduced the liability for marketing goods inspired by the provision in Article 2(2)(d) of the Sale of Consumer Goods Directive. Section 434(2) contains the same 'IKEA clause' as that found in the Directive but which is unknown to the CISG. Finally, section 434(3) puts an end to the distinction between material defects and the supply of goods different from those contracted for (*aliud*) and also introduces a rule governing the supply of a lesser amount of goods than contracted for (shortage), so that the BGB is now in line with Article 35 CISG.[75]

In contrast to this the Austrian transposition of the Sale of Consumer Goods Directive does not take this into account, as legislators intended to give consumers the possibility of using the favourable rules on giving notice of lack of conformity caused by *aliud* classified as late delivery.[76] The French transposal

---

[72] See Dauner-Lieb, B, *supra* n. 67 at 15.

[73] The definition of legal defects is now contained in section 435 of the BGB.

[74] The provisions described below cannot be derogated from in consumer sales: see section 475 of the BGB.

[75] See Rösler, H (2006), '70 Jahre Des Warenkaufs Von Ernst Rabel', 70 *Rabels Zeitschrift für ausländisches und internationales Privatrecht* 804.

[76] See Welser, R (2002), 'Die Verbrauchergüterkauf-Richtlinie und ihre Umsetzung in Österreich und Deutschland', in Schlechtriem, P (ed.), *Wandlungen des Schuldrechts* 87.

measures appear to leave this problem unsolved.[77] Finally, section 442 of the BGB contains the same provisions as those found in Article 35(3) CISG but it also introduces liability based on a negligence criterion.[78] This criterion closely resembles the case law developed – primarily in German law – on Article 35 CISG. The definition of lack of conformity contained in Article 35 CISG, which was also adopted in the Sale of Consumer Goods Directive, is therefore one of the CISG provisions that has had the strongest influence on German law.[79]

8. CONCLUSION

Article 35 CISG, the origin of which can be traced back to the comparative work of Ernst Rabel, has had a surprising effect far beyond what was originally intended, i.e. harmonization of international trade law.[80] The provision has affected a whole range of legal rules, from national sales law regulations to EU directives. This brings methodological implications into focus.

As Schmitthoff described, the development of uniform or harmonized rules of law is partly based on a non-national, analytical codifying and partly on a non-national synthetic consolidating comparative method. At the same time the two methods interact. This description seems to fit the characteristics of the legal rules based on Article 35 CISG. Indeed the development of rules based on Article 35 CISG in some cases appears to be motivated by an intention to achieve a clearly dogmatic-analytical approximation – e.g. the Nordic sales laws – whereas in other cases the intention to achieve an 'approximation' to the systematic approach and structure of Article 35 CISG is found, without intending any real substantive change to the existing legal rules – e.g. as clearly expressed by the Danish legislators. In other instances it is impossible clearly to ascertain whether an analytical or a synthetic method has been adopted, or

---

[77] See Witz, C and Schneider, W (2005), 'Die Umsetzung der europäishen Richtlinien über den Verbrauchsgüterkauf in Frankreich', 12 *Recht der Internationalen Wirtschaft* 921 at 926.

[78] 'Knowledge of the buyer. The rights of the buyer due to a defect are excluded if he has knowledge of the defect at the time when the contract is entered into. If the buyer has no knowledge of a defect due to gross negligence, the buyer may assert rights in relation to this defect only if the seller fraudulently concealed the defect or gave a guarantee of the quality of the goods'.

[79] See Herber, R, *supra* n. 70 at 64.

[80] See Rösler, H, *supra* n. ?: '[z]usammenfassend hat das Vorstehende die faszinerende Kontinuität im kühn und breit angelegten Gesamtschaften von Rabel aufgezeigt. Sein Einfluß erstreckt sich – mit dem Recht des Warenkaufs als wissenschaftlichen Kristallisationspunkt – über das Einheits- und Gemeinschaftskaufrecht bis in das rechtsvergleichend reformierte BGB, und geht in Raum und Zeit doch weit darüber hinaus.'

whether – intentionally or unintentionally – an analytical-synthetic compara-tive method has been adopted. Consequently, the contents and functionality of the rule may be questioned – for example whether the new rule is actually best suited to regulating commercial matters, or whether it is best suited to regulating consumer matters. Schmitthoff's prophecy that, in future, we need to grow accustomed to working with rules based on a non-national, combined analytical-synthetic comparative method therefore seems to have been fulfilled. However, it is debatable whether we have become accustomed to understanding the implications of working with rules that occasionally arise on the third tier, for instance the CISG – the Sale of Consumer Goods Directive – the BGB, which refers to provisions based on specific principles.

Firstly, it is worth noting that Schmitthoff characterizes some of these rules as synthetic, but also recognizes that the analytical and the synthetic methods are combined. This refers to the comparative process under which the rules arise as well as the result of the process.[81] However, this statement must have some consequences for the application of these rules – e.g. which *travaux pré-paratoires* or which interests should guide the interpretation of a rule. This can often be determined by applying general rules of interpretation – e.g. whether most weight should be given to the interests of consumers.

Secondly, it is worth considering whether there is still – now 50 years on – anything special in working with rules that have a non-national, combined analytical-synthetic comparative origin, including whether the distinctive features should be reserved for the rules of international trade law discussed by Schmitthoff, or whether we have generally become accustomed to working with rules that have a different and more complex background. If that is the case, a very large part of the modern development of law is characterized as being based on a non-national comparative analytical-synthetic method, which turns Schmitthoff's description into a general characterization of many parts of contemporary legal scholarship.[82] Accordingly, there is less reason to classify certain rules as synthetic, because the synthetic nature – if this is your preferred term – is rather a fundamental ground for many rules. Several factors seem to point to the latter solution. Globally, the increasing prevalence of convention or treaty law such as the CISG is one example of this; regionally, the harmonization of rules, e.g. EU law, is found, and, nationally, the transposition of harmonized law and the modernization of domestic legal rules and principles are cases in point. The carrying out of these processes often involves the use of a combined

---

[81]   See Schmitthoff, CM, *supra* n. 2 at 565.

[82]   See e.g. Jørgensen, S (1968), 'Rudolph v. Jhering and Nordic legal scholarship', *Ugeskrift for Retsvæsen* 245 and the discussion of *inter alia* Thibaut's and Savigny's application of an analytical-synthetic method inspired by e.g. the philosophy of Kant.

comparative analytical-synthetic method that does not seek a special national solution, but rather an ideal solution.

In general, the comparative method therefore appears destined to play an important role as an integrated part of legal method and not only as an academic research discipline,[83] whether it concerns a synthetic, analytical, functional or other comparative method. It may also be difficult to differentiate between these methods, as discussed above, and in continuation of this analysis and Schmitthoff's characterization, legislators often fail to indicate whether they intended a doctrinal innovation, or whether they merely intended to modernize legislation with a view to harmonizing the terminology and language without introducing any dogmatic changes to the existing state of the law.[84] It seems that this realization may actually be the strong point in using Schmitthoff's characterization.

Moreover, it should be pointed out that some jurisdictions have structures and sets of rules that are in effect based on the reception of elements from other jurisdictions with the intention, *inter alia*, to introduce certain new analytical features, which is the case with large parts of the Turkish legal system and the so-called mixed jurisdictions whereby the existence of a combined analytical-synthetic nature follows *a priori*.[85] Experience from these jurisdictions is therefore significant in further clarifying the issues addressed in this chapter.

The existing comparative methods may well be insufficient, and it cannot be ruled out that legal scholars should learn from other social science disciplines in order to find the proper methods to meet these challenges.[86] Nevertheless, Schmitthoff's ideas also seem of interest to contemporary scholars and legislators, at least as a characterization that shifts the focus to the combined, including international, genealogical origin with the implications for the application of law that follows from this.

On the face of it, it appears that the introduction of Article 35 has planted a seed, a potential genetic mother code for a future, universal understanding of

[83]   See e.g. Berger, KP (2001), 'Harmonisation of European Contract Law. The influence of Comparative Law', 50 *International and Comparative Law Quarterly* 877.

[84]   See section 4 above discussing the Danish transposition of the Sale of Consumer Goods Directive because legislators intended to change the Danish Sale of Goods Act having regard to the Sale of Consumer Goods Directive and the CISG but did not intend any *substantive change* of the Danish principle of non-conformity with the contract.

[85]   See Örücü, E (2006), 'A Synthetic and Hyphenated Legal System: The Turkish Experience', 2 *Journal of Comparative Law* 261. See also Zimmerman, R, Visser, D and Reid, K (2004), *Mixed Legal Systems in Comparative Perspective*.

[86]   See e.g. McCrudden, C (2006), 'Legal Research and the Social Sciences', 122 *Law Quarterly Review* 632, who refers to the criticism of legal scholarship as a closed (internal) science in contrast to an open (external) science and calls for greater focus on the method used in legal research. Further to this see Samuels, G (2007), 'Taking Methods Seriously (Part One)', 2 *Journal of Comparative Law* 94.

the principle of non-conformity with the contract.[87] Nonetheless, a different and perhaps more realistic approach seems to be restricted to the determination of whether or not jurisdictions display an increased willingness and openness concerning reception from other jurisdictions without this necessarily resulting in a future, global uniform set of rules, because the development takes the form of a symbiosis between – including but not limited to – a synthetic and an analytical method that is difficult to control and which therefore opens up for divergences between rules and jurisdictions.

The merits of the non-national, analytical-synthetic comparative method are not necessarily – as perhaps assumed by Schmitthoff – that it provides or must provide uniform or harmonized rules of law. On the contrary, its greatest achievement may be that it opens up for a dialogue across jurisdictions and cultures – a dialogue that will continue for decades to come.

---

[87]   For a Global Commercial Code for the future see e.g. Herrmann, G, 'The Future of Trade Law Unification', 1 *Internationales Handelsrecht* 6; and for future global principles see Lando, O (2005), 'CISG and its followers: A Proposal to Adopt Some International Principles of Contract Law', LIII - 2 *The American Journal of Comparative law* 379.

12. How far are national broadcasting orders converging as a consequence of European media law and policy?

Irini Katsirea*

INTRODUCTION

The European Union policy in the audiovisual sector is guided by the alleged existence of a 'European audiovisual model'. At the heart of this model lies the recognition that the production and distribution of audiovisual media services are not only economic, but also cultural activities calling for the protection of a range of objectives of general interest: cultural diversity, protection of minors, consumer protection, particularly in the field of advertising, media pluralism, and the fight against racial and religious hatred. It is considered essential, in the interests of the maintenance of these values, that the 'European audiovisual model' be founded on 'a balance between a strong and independent public service sector and a dynamic commercial sector'.

This chapter will address the question whether the presumed 'European audiovisual model' really exists, whether cultural values still matter in national broadcasting policy despite the fact that technological progress and a general ideological shift across Europe have put regulation for the public interest under strain. If so, the next question to be asked is whether these values are converging and whether they have been furthered or jeopardized by the involvement of the European Union in this area, mainly the Television without Frontiers (TwF) – now Audiovisual Media Services (AVMS) – Directive. This chapter will draw examples from the broadcasting orders of four Member States: France, Germany, the Netherlands and the United Kingdom.[1] By focusing on public broadcasters' cultural obligations, the principle of separation of advertising from

---

* Middlesex University, UK.

[1] For a more comprehensive account of public broadcasting regulation in these Member States as well as in Greece and Italy see Katsirea, I. (2008), *Public Broadcasting and European Law. A Comparative Examination of Public Service Obligations in Six Member States* (Kluwer).

editorial content, the protection of minors and the right of reply, this chapter will demonstrate that in some respects national legislation exceeds the standards set by the TwF (now AVMS) Directive, while in others it still lags behind.

SELECT ASPECTS OF THE TWF DIRECTIVE AND THEIR IMPLEMENTATION

The European Quota

The European broadcasting quota, originally laid down in Article 4 of the TwF (now Art. 16 AVMS) Directive, obliges Member States to ensure, where practicable and by appropriate means, that broadcasters reserve for European works a majority proportion of their transmission time, excluding the time appointed to news, sports events, games, advertising, teletext services, and teleshopping. European works are defined in a rather complex way in Article 6 of the same Directive.

Quotas were a favoured instrument for protecting cultural identity and for stimulating programme-making in France. Programming quotas go beyond the requirements of the TwF Directive. Broadcasters are required to reserve at least 60 per cent of their yearly audiovisual and cinematographic productions for European creations and at least 40 per cent for French language productions.[2] Interestingly, the French language quota was lowered from an initial 50 per cent as a result of an agreement reached with the Commission in the beginning of the 1990s, so as to allow a wider 'corridor' for European works.

In Germany, there are no precise cultural quotas as they would go against the grain of the highly valued programming autonomy of broadcasters. The quota rules of the TwF Directive have been rather loosely transposed into German law. The *Rundfunkstaatsvertrag* (RStV) (Interstate Treaty on Broadcasting) only requires broadcasters to reserve the main part of their broadcasting time for European works.

In the Netherlands, public broadcasters are obliged to devote at least 50 per cent of their television broadcasting time to programmes originally produced in either of the two national languages: Dutch or Frisian.[3] In addition, they are obliged to devote at least 50 per cent of their broadcasting time to European works.[4]

---

[2]   Law 86-1067 of 30 September 1986, Art. 27 and Decree 90-66 of 17 January 1990, Arts 7, 13, 14. For the distinction between audiovisual and cinematographic productions, a number of criteria are laid down in Arts 2, 3, 4 of Decree 90-66. French language productions are defined in Art. 5 of Decree 90-66, European productions in Art. 6 of the same Decree that implements Art. 6 of the TwF Directive.

[3]   Dutch Media Act, Art. 54 (a) (1).

[4]   Ibid., Art. 54 (1).

The United Kingdom has not adopted any quota as regards the broadcasting of programmes of European origin. The Broadcasting Act 1990 only refers to a 'proper proportion' of programmes of European origin.[5] However, the BBC agrees targets with the Office of Communications (Ofcom) regarding the programming of European output each calendar year.

The Principle of Separation of Advertising from Editorial Content

The principle of separation marks the dividing line not only between advertising and editorial content but also between the conception of television as a cultural experience and its conception as an economic good like any other. It ensures audiences are not misled about the nature of content – programming or advertising – they are consuming. It also ensures that broadcasters retain full responsibility and control for their programmes without further interference from advertisers, thus safeguarding the independence and credibility of the mass media.[6]

The TwF Directive endorsed the principle of separation of advertising from editorial content in Article 10(1), which stipulated that 'television advertising and teleshopping shall be readily recognisable as such and kept quite separate from other parts of the programme service by optical and/or acoustic means'. Also, Article 10(4) of the Directive prohibited surreptitious advertising, which was defined in Article 1(d) as 'the representation in words or pictures of goods, services, the name, the trade mark or the activities of a producer of goods or a provider of services in programmes when such representation is intended by the broadcaster to serve advertising and might mislead the public as to its nature. Such representation is considered to be intentional in particular if it is done in return for payment or for similar consideration.'

Surreptitious advertising (*publicité clandestine*) is one of the main reasons for intervention by the *Conseil Superieur de l'Audiovisuel* (CSA), the French broadcasting authority, and for the imposition of numerous sanctions.[7] Its definition in French law was, however, stricter than the one laid down in the Directive.[8] The CSA did not consider it necessary to prove the existence of remuneration in order to establish its surreptitious nature. Even if a television station has

---

[5]   For instance, Broadcasting Act 1990, s. 25 (2) (e) for Channel 4.

[6]   Ofcom, 'Product placement. A consultation on issues related to product placement', available at: www.ofcom.org.uk/consult/condocs/product_placement/product.pdf, 4 September 2007.

[7]   CSA, 'Chaînes hertziennes nationales: une observation systématique', available at: www.csa.fr/infos/controle/controle_chaines.php, 18 July 2007; Debbasch, C., Agostinelli, X. *et al.* (2002), *Droit des médias* (Dalloz) para. 1454.

[8]   Decree 92-280, Art. 9.

only been incautious, but had not drawn any financial or other advantage, the surreptitious character of advertising could not be excluded.[9]

On the contrary, Germany had incorporated the tight definition of the Directive and a proof of intentional acting by the broadcaster. As well as the existence of payment the following were deemed to be strong indications of such intentional acting: contractual arrangements for the representation of goods, services, etc.; the production of a programme with a view to including such promotional references; the discounting of programme rights in return for product placement.[10] It goes without saying that all these factors were very hard to prove. The interpretation given to the definition of surreptitious advertising in § 2 (6) RStV by the German authorities even falls behind the Directive's standard in some respects. The existence of a similar consideration is disputed where goods are provided free of charge.

The Dutch Media Act did not explicitly mention surreptitious advertising. Nonetheless, the Dutch approach to it was especially severe as far as programmes were concerned that had been produced by the public broadcasting company itself. Such programmes should not contain any avoidable advertising, unless it was explicitly permitted.[11] Under the Dutch rules, advertising could be avoidable when the broadcasting company had mentioned or shown products or company names with the intention to serve advertising. It was immaterial whether the representation of these products might mislead the public.[12] However, Article 28(1) of the Media Decree allowed avoidable advertising that involved displays of or references to a product or service provided that: such display or reference was in keeping with the context of the programme service; did not affect the editorial integrity of the programme service; was not exaggerated or excessive; and the product or service was not specifically recommended. However, this exception was not applicable if the broadcaster had received remuneration of some kind.[13]

---

[9] Debbasch *et al.*, *supra* n. 7, para. 1454.

[10] Hartstein., R., Ring, W.-D., Kreile, J., Dörr, D. and Stettner, R. (2003), *Rundfunkstaatsvertrag Kommentar* (Jehle-Rehm) vol. I, sect. 7 RStV para. 48.

[11] Dutch Media Act, *supra* n. 3, Art. 52.

[12] In the course of the consultations for the modernization of the Directive, the Netherlands suggested that the requirement of 'misleading the public' ought to be removed from the definition of surreptitious advertising. In its view, the present definition is impracticable, as advertising is not surreptitious once the viewer realizes that a programme is commercially biased. It considers that the broadcaster's intention to serve advertising is sufficient. See Dutch Government, 'Response to the Television without Frontiers Directive', available at: http://ec.europa.eu/comm/avpolicy/docs/reg/modernisation/2003_review/contributions/wc_nederland_en.pdf, 16 April 2007.

[13] Schaar, O. (2001), *Programmintegrierte Fernsehwerbung in Europa: Zum Stand der kommunikationsrechtlichen Regulierung in Europa* (Nomos) at 228.

In the UK, the principle of separation between the advertising and programme elements of a service was contained in section 10 of the Ofcom Broadcasting Code.[14] This section only applied to the commercial public service broadcasters, not to the BBC which is not allowed to carry advertising on its public television programmes. Rule 10.4 of the Broadcasting Code prohibited the giving of any undue prominence to a product or service in a programme. Undue prominence may result from the lack of editorial justification for a commercial reference or from the manner in which the reference is made. Under Rule 10.5 of the Broadcasting Code, product placement was also prohibited.

It is clear that all of the examined Member States endorsed the principle of separation of advertising from editorial content. It is also worth noting that all of them had more lenient rules in place for the inclusion of products or services in films made for the cinema. In other respects, however, their rules differed considerably and some interpreted the Directive's prohibition of surreptitious advertising more narrowly than others.

Protection of Minors

As far as the protection of minors from offensive content is concerned, the relevant norm is Article 22 of the TwF (now Art. 27 AVMS) Directive. This provision absolutely bans programmes which might *seriously* impair the physical, mental or moral development of minors, in particular those that involve pornography or gratuitous violence. This prohibition extends to programmes which are likely to impair the physical, mental or moral development of minors, except where it is ensured, by selecting the time of the broadcast or by any technical measure, that minors will not normally hear or see such broadcasts.

France has only partially transposed the TwF Directive's requirements since it allows pornographic and extremely violent programmes on authorized channels subject to a specific dual access lock between 12 midnight and 5 am.[15] Such programmes fall under the highest category of the French youth certificate rating system, which is based on a classification according to age. Each channel has a viewing committee that is responsible for the classification of programmes. The CSA monitors the coherence of the classifications. As a result of the Directive's imperfect transposition, Canal Plus and certain cable channels are allowed to transmit pornographic programmes in the small hours.[16] CSA proposals to

---

[14]   See also the BCAP Television Advertising Standards Code, s. 2.1.1.

[15]   Such channels need to enter into a contract with the CSA, which specifies the maximum number of broadcasts allowed per year, and obliges the channels to invest in film production. Vedel, T. (2005), 'France' in *Television across Europe: Regulation, Policy and Independence*, Open Society Institute at 698.

[16]   Franceschini, L. (2003), *Télévision et Droit de la Communication* (Ellipses) at 136.

modify Article 15 of the Broadcasting Law of 30 September 1986 so as explicitly to ban pornographic and extremely violent programmes were dropped as a result of allegations that the CSA President at the time, Dominique Baudis, was involved in sadomasochistic orgies.[17]

In Germany, the *Jugendmedienschutz-Staatsvertrag* (Interstate Treaty on Protection of Minors) and the broadcasting laws of the *Länder* are fully in accordance with Article 22 of the TwF Directive. Classifications of programmes into three categories is carried out by the *Freiwillige Selbstkontrolle der Filmwirtschaft* (FSK). Compliance with this system relies on the social responsibility of public broadcasters which, together with all other national broadcasters, are obliged to appoint Commissioners for Youth Protection.

In the Netherlands, regulation concerning classification is provided by the Netherlands Institute for the Classification of Audiovisual Media (NICAM). Only broadcasters that are members of this Institute are allowed to air programmes suitable for viewers older than 12 years of age. Programmes containing hardcore pornography or gratuitous violence are absolutely prohibited in line with Article 22(1) of the TwF Directive. Since 2001, programmes have been classified into four categories according to the 'Kijkwijzer' rating system. Complaints of violations of these rules are dealt with by NICAM in the first instance. The Dutch Media Authority supervises this self-regulatory system.

In Great Britain, the law is unique in that it seeks to protect not only minors but also adults from violent or sexually explicit programmes. The Ofcom Code distinguishes more clearly than its predecessor, the ITC Code, between provisions protecting those under the age of 18 and provisions for the protection of adults. Material that might seriously impair the physical, mental or moral development of people under 18 is prohibited. Other material that is unsuitable for minors has to observe the watershed and to be scheduled appropriately. There is no classification system.

Right of Reply

Finally, the right of reply was originally laid down in Article 23 of the TwF (now AVMS) Directive. Article 23(1) stipulates that '[w]ithout prejudice to other provisions adopted by the Member States under civil, administrative or criminal law, any natural or legal person, regardless of nationality, whose legitimate interests, in particular reputation and good name, have been damaged by an assertion of incorrect facts in a television programme must have a right of reply or equivalent remedies...The reply shall be transmitted within a reasonable

---

[17]   Harcourt, A. (2005), *The European Union and the Regulation of Media Markets* (Manchester University Press) at 191.

time subsequent to the request being substantiated and at a time and in a manner appropriate to the broadcast to which the request refers.'

The right of reply is triggered in France by allegations in a television programme that are likely to affect a person's name or reputation. These allegations do not need to be factual ones, nor do they need to be incorrect. The conditions for the exercise of the right of reply in France are therefore less stringent than under Article 23 of the TwF Directive. An even wider right of reply has recently been adopted for the online media.

In Germany, the right of reply is granted to every person who has been affected by a factual allegation in a television programme. Again, there is no express requirement that the allegation has to be incorrect.

The Netherlands have failed to implement Article 23 so far. Dutch law does not provide a formal right of reply for fear of excessively restricting broadcasting freedom. Besides the civil remedies available, an injured party can only file a complaint with the Netherlands Press Council. However, not all broadcasters are members of the Council. Moreover, the Council cannot impose binding sanctions, but will only give its opinion on the complaint which will then be published on the Council's website.

In the United Kingdom, there is no right of reply either. The right of complaint to Ofcom does not constitute an equivalent remedy to the right of reply, given that it is subsidiary to the avenue of judicial review. Also, the only redress offered is the publication on Ofcom's website or the transmission by the broadcaster of a summary of Ofcom's decision.

AVMS DIRECTIVE: A ROADMAP FOR CONVERGENCE?

The TwF Directive was adopted in 1989 and was amended for the first time in 1997. A second revision has been completed. The TwF Directive only covered the simultaneous transmission of a predetermined schedule of programmes to more than one recipient, but not on-demand services such as video-on-demand. After a lengthy consultation process that began in 2003 and was concluded in 2005 and a legislative process of 18 months, a new Audiovisual Media Services without Frontiers (AVMS) Directive has been agreed upon. The new Directive covers all audiovisual media services, both scheduled and on-demand ones, the principal purpose of which is the provision of programmes. It also includes more flexible rules on television advertising. We will now look at the changes introduced by the new Directive in the areas under discussion and try to assess their future impact on national broadcasting orders.

Despite widespread criticisms of the European broadcasting quota, this provision has been incorporated *in toto* in the AVMS Directive as far as linear services are concerned. As regards non-linear services, the Commission decided to strike a middle path. It did not impose a quota on on-demand services but asked Member States to ensure that such services provided by media service providers under their jurisdiction promote, where practicable and by appropriate means, production of and access to European works. It clarified further that '[s]uch promotion could relate, *inter alia*, to the financial contribution made by such services to the production and rights acquisition of European works or to the share and/or prominence of European works in the catalogue of programmes offered by the on-demand audiovisual media service'.[18] However, the implementation of this provision is left to the individual Member States, which is problematic from the point of view of legal certainty.

As far as the principle of separation is concerned, the AVMS Directive maintains the prohibition of surreptitious advertising. It distinguishes it, however, from product placement, which is exceptionally allowed for certain types/genres of programmes: cinematographic works, films and series made for audiovisual media services, light entertainment and sports programmes, or in cases where no payment is made but certain goods or services are merely provided free of charge. Children's programmes are specifically excluded from this derogation. Moreover, programmes that contain product placement must meet a number of requirements, which seek to protect, on the one hand, viewers from being misled about the advertising intention behind the product placement and, on the other hand, the editorial independence of broadcasters. However, it is questionable whether these requirements suffice to ward off the dangers lurking for the editorial integrity of programmes.

The explanation given in recital 91 of the AVMS Directive for the liberalization of product placement is that it is 'a reality in cinematographic works and in audiovisual works made for television, but Member States regulate this practice differently. To ensure a level playing field, and thus enhance the competitiveness of the European media industry, it is necessary to adopt rules for product placement.' Indeed, as we have seen, its treatment in the Member States varied considerably. By taking this regulatory mosaic as its starting point for the liberalization of product placement, the Commission might have paved the way for increased convergence, albeit at the expense of the trustworthiness and editorial integrity of programmes. Also, despite this harmonisation drive, considerable variation remains in the way in which Member States have implemented the AVMS Directive rules, in some respects exceeding the Directive's standard, while in others deviating from it or even falling behind. The UK, for instance, prohibits placement of a greater range of products than prescribed under the AVMS Directive, but has failed to clearly outlaw thematic placement. Germany

---

[18]　AVMS Directive, Art. 13(1).

has adopted tighter identification requirements for acquired programmes, and has adopted a narrower definition of 'product placement'.

Turning now to the protection of minors, the AVMS Directive does not attempt to define notions of pornography and gratuitous violence nor the kind of programmes which are likely to impair the development of minors. Likewise, the definition of the time that is suitable for adult programmes to be transmitted is still left to the discretion of the Member States. This is a wise choice of the European Union legislator, since the above mentioned differences between national laws reveal a diversity of opinion on the upbringing and education of young people and, ultimately, of moral standards.[19] These cultural differences also explain why recent suggestions for a common European rating system did not meet with acceptance.

As far as on-demand audiovisual media services are concerned, the AVMS Directive does set a new common standard, albeit at the lowest possible level. Article 12 states that 'Member States shall take appropriate measures to ensure that on-demand audiovisual media services provided by media service providers under their jurisdiction which might seriously impair the physical, mental or moral development of minors are only made available in such a way that ensures that minors will not normally hear or see such on-demand audiovisual media services'. In other words, programmes involving pornography and gratuitous violence can be shown in on-demand services as long as measures are taken to minimize the chances that minors will have access to them.[20] This limited protection offered to minors from harmful content in a non-linear environment is hardly compatible with the proclamation in recital 104 that this Directive aims at ensuring 'a high level of protection of objectives of general interest, in particular the protection of minors and human dignity'. It also ignores the Commission Study on Parental Control of Television Broadcasting which suggested that it might well be too early to rely exclusively on technical measures as regards seriously harmful material on non-linear services.[21]

---

[19]   2nd Report from the Commission to the Council, the European Parliament and the Economic and Social Committee on the application of Dir. 89/552/EEC 'Television Without Frontiers', 24 October 1997, COM(97)523 final, para. 4.2; Council Recommendation 98/560/EC of 24 September 1998 on the protection of minors and human dignity in audiovisual and information services, OJ L270/48, 1998, recital 18; contra Woods, L. and Scholes, J. (1997), 'Broadcasting: The Creation of a European Culture or the Limits of the Internal Market?', 17 *Yearbook of European Law* 47 at 80.

[20]   Only child pornography is explicitly banned according to the provisions of Council Framework Decision 2004/68/JHA of 22 December 2003 on combating the sexual exploitation of children and child pornography, OJ L13/44, 2004. See AVMS Directive, *supra* n. 18, recital 46.

[21]   Levy, D. A. L. (1999), *Europe's Digital Revolution. Broadcasting Regulation, the EU and the Nation State* (Routledge) at 148 n. 8 notes characteristically that 'the weakest

Finally, as far as the right of reply is concerned, the European Parliament and the Council, together with the public broadcasters, have been in favour of extending it to the online media.[22] This right would have a more extended scope than the right of reply for traditional broadcasting services. It would be granted to every natural or legal person whose legitimate interests have been affected by an assertion of facts in a transmission regardless of whether these facts were incorrect or not. This proposal has been vigorously opposed by the United Kingdom, the commercial broadcasters, the written press and most telecom operators and internet service providers (ISPs) with the argument that it would stifle the development of the European internet and other digital platform industries and restrict their ability to compete with non-European operators.[23] Therefore, the European Parliament's proposal did not find its way in the final text of the AVMS Directive in the end. It is therefore up to each Member State whether it wishes to introduce a right of reply for the online domain or not.

CONCLUSION

Having examined the broadcasting systems of France, Germany, the Netherlands and the United Kingdom, it is possible to discern considerable commonalities among them, which arguably amount to a 'European audiovisual model'. They all subscribe to the principle of separation of advertising from editorial content, to the need to protect minors and to granting a right of reply against offending broadcasts. Some of these commonalities can be attributed to the TwF Directive's harmonization impetus, leading to a certain convergence in national broadcasting regulation across Europe.[24] However, these commonalities cannot mask the diversity of the broadcasting systems of these countries, which also accounts for the different forms and methods they have chosen in order to implement European Union rules.

In some respects the four Member States examined in this chapter exceed the minimum standard set by the Directive, while in others they fall behind it.

---

link in most parental control systems is frequently the parents themselves, particularly when it is their children who are the most technically adept users in the household.'

[22] See Recommendation of the European Parliament and of the Council of 20 December 2006 on the protection of minors and human dignity and on the right of reply in relation to the competitiveness of the European audiovisual and on-line information services industry OJ L378/72, 2006, recital 15.

[23] See DCMS, 'Protection of Minors and Human Dignity: Right of Reply', available at: www.culture.gov.uk/what_we_do/Broadcasting/international_broadcasting/, 15 May 2007; Liverpool final report of the Working Group 6, 'Protection of Minors and Human Dignity: Right of Reply', 20–22 September 2005.

[24] Harcourt, *supra* n. 17 at 158 *et seq.*, 194.

France imposes cultural obligations that are more far-reaching than the quotas set by the TwF Directive, and defined surreptitious advertising more widely than prescribed by the Directive. On the other hand, it has not adequately implemented the Directive's requirements on the protection of minors. The Netherlands have high standards as regards the protection of minors, and NICAM is considered a role model for non-state regulation in this field.[25] However, a formal right of reply has yet to be introduced in this country. Germany has correctly transposed the Directive's provisions on the protection of minors. However, it has implemented the European quota rule in narrow terms while initially defining surreptitious advertising in an unduly restrictive manner.

The fact that Member States impose standards on their own broadcasters that are in some respects higher than required by the TwF Directive is not surprising. The method of minimum harmonization has been expressly chosen in an area that is so close to Member States' cultural sensibilities as to accommodate national diversity above the minimum standards set in the Directive. What is perhaps more surprising is the fact that national laws to some extent still lag behind the Directive's requirements. Obviously, even the minimum standards adopted at EU level are sometimes hard to reconcile with basic tenets of the national broadcasting orders.

Broadcasting standards are at the interface between conflicting constitutional rights and freedoms.[26] Setting them involves a fine balancing exercise between interests of equal value. Member States hold on to their power to resolve these tensions in accordance with their own constitutional traditions, even in defiance of the imperatives of European Union law. Germany values its constitutional principle of freedom from state control over the quota requirements of the TwF Directive. The Netherlands resist the introduction of a right of reply so as not to jeopardize broadcasting freedom. The uneasy relationship between EU law and national constitutional orders, ostensibly settled by the principle of supremacy, may well resurface in the field of broadcasting law in the future.

The AVMS Directive takes the TwF Directive's harmonization programme further by setting new rules for the promotion of European works and the protection of minors in the online domain and by liberalizing product placement. It still leaves great scope for differentiation in the way in which Member States choose to implement it. Convergence is used as a welcome excuse for harmonization at all cost, even if it means sacrificing the vulnerable values that are the *raison d'être* of broadcast regulation.

---

[25] Hans-Bredow-Institut, 'Final Report: Study on Co-Regulation Measures in the Media Sector', June 2006, available at: www.ec.europa.eu/avpolicy/docs/library/studies/coregul/coregul-final-report_en.pdf, 12 July 2007 at 188.

[26] See Leidinger, A. (1989), 'Programmverantwortung im Spannungsfeld von Programmgrundsätzen und Rundfunkfreiheit', *Deutsches Verwaltungsblatt* 230.

13. The fallacy of the common core: polycontextualism in surety protection – a 'hard case' in harmonisation discourse

Mel Kenny* and James Devenney**

'Take but degree away, untune that string,
And hark what discord follows. Each thing meets
In mere oppugnancy.'
– W. Shakespeare, *Troilus and Cressida*, Act 1, Scene iii, 109–110

I. INTRODUCTION

This chapter is located in the context of EU initiatives aimed at creating a single market in financial services[1] and the increasingly acrimonious debate on the future of European Private Law.[2] More specifically, this chapter focuses on the protection

---

* Reader in Commercial Law, School of Law, University of Leicester, UK.

** Chair in Commercial Law, School of Law, University of Exeter, UK. We are grateful to the participants and organisers of the 2008 WG Hart Workshop (Institute of Advanced Legal Studies, London).

[1] See Kenny, M (2007), 'Standing Surety in Europe: Common Core or Tower of Babel', 70 *Modern Law Review* 175 at 177–9.

[2] See, for example, Markesinis, B (1997), 'Why a Code is Not the Best Way to Advance the Cause of European Legal Unity', 5 *European Review Private Law* 519; Legrand, P (1997), 'European Legal Systems are Not Converging', 45 *International and Comparative Law Quarterly* 52; Legrand, P (1997), 'Against a European Civil Code', 60 *Modern Law Review* 44; Legrand, P (2003), 'The Impossibility of Legal Transplants', 4 *Maastricht Journal of European and Comparative Law* 111; Legrand, P (2006), 'Antivonbar', 1 *Journal of Contract Law* 1; von Bar, C (2002), 'From Principles to Codification: Prospects for European Private Law', 8 *Columbia Journal of European Law* 379; Lando, O (2003), 'Does the European Union need a Civil Code?', *Recht der Internationalen Wirtschaft* 49; and von Bar, C, Lando, O and Swann, S (2002), 'Communication on European Contract Law: Joint Response of the Commission on European Contract Law and the Study Group on a European Civil Code', 10 *European Review of private law* 183.

afforded to non-professional sureties across the EU.[3] It is argued that this area of law demonstrates some of the challenges which a harmonisation agenda may face. Indeed we would argue that by focusing on problematic areas, such as the protection afforded to non-professional sureties, it is possible to further illuminate the current debate on the future of European private law. In particular it is argued that non-professional surety protection in individual Member States often involves different complex, context-specific orchestrations of various legal fields, concepts and mechanisms (the 'uncommon core'). Moreover it will be argued that it would be unwise for any harmonisation strategy in this area to lose sight of overall, context-specific, non-professional surety protection orchestrations in particular Member States; to focus too heavily on a particular aspect of that orchestration is dangerous for – in the words of Shakespeare – 'untune that string [...a]nd hark what discord follows.' For this reason we will argue that a dual-track harmonisation strategy – involving measures of legislative and non-legislative harmonisation – recommends itself in relation to non-professional suretyship protection.

II.   THE NATURE AND KEY CHARACTERISTICS OF NON-PROFESSIONAL SURETY AGREEMENTS

There is broad accord across the EU on the general characteristics of suretyship agreements.[4] These agreements are, in some ways, an atypical form of agreement. Essentially the surety guarantees the performance of a principal debtor and the liability which the surety assumes is of a secondary and accessory nature.[5] Thus if the liability of the principal debtor is reduced, the liability of the surety is reduced *pro tanto*. Where the suretyship agreement involves a non-professional surety, the surety often does not directly benefit from the transaction.[6] In such cases the surety and principal debtor are often closely associated through, for example, familial relations.[7]

There has also been a broad consciousness across Europe of the potential vulnerability of non-professional sureties.[8] In particular, a non-professional

---

[3]   For a review of harmonisation initiatives in this area see Kenny, M (2007), 'Standing Surety in Europe: Common Core or Tower of Babel?', 70 *Modern Law Review* 175.

[4]   See ibid.

[5]   Ibid.

[6]   Ibid.

[7]   Devenney, J; Fox-O'Mahony, L and Kenny, M (2008), 'Standing Surety in England and Wales: the Sphinx of Procedural Protection', *Lloyds Maritime and Commercial Law Quarterly* 527 at 528.

[8]   Parry, R (2005), 'The Position of Family Sureties within the Framework of Protection for Consumer Debtors in European Union Member States', 13 *European Review of Private Law* 357.

surety is typically in a weak bargaining position with the creditor.[9] Moreover, a non-professional surety may also be in a weak position as regards the principal debtor; for example, there may be a danger that a close association between the surety and principal debtor has engendered inappropriate relational pressures.[10] This may result in a situation where the potential liability involved is out of all proportion to the surety's resources, and this may result in the surety being subject to an indefinite obligation.[11]

Yet, whilst most Member States have attempted to increase surety protection, there is, as we shall see, marked diversity in the nature and extent of the protection provided by individual Member States.[12] Indeed the diversity is such that it underlines the polycontextual nature of suretyship agreements. Suretyship agreements transcend traditional legal boundaries, and it is, perhaps, therefore unsurprising that non-professional surety protection in individual Member States often involves different complex, context-specific orchestrations of various legal fields, concepts and mechanisms including (aspects of):

* specific suretyship law;
* contract law;
* consumer law;
* insolvency law;
* family law;
* constitutional law; and
* property law.

Moreover, as we shall see below, the level of surety protection is also affected by the behavioural patterns of financial institutions in each Member State.

The atypical, polycontextual nature of suretyship agreements has already contributed to difficulties in relation to a number of EU harmonisation initiatives. First, one can point to the debate over whether or not Council Directive 85/577/EEC on contracts negotiated away from business premises[13] covers suretyship transactions, and the subsequent controversial, and somewhat ambiguous,

---

[9]   Devenney, J; Fox-O'Mahony, L and Kenny, M, *supra* n. 7 at 528.
[10]   Ibid.
[11]   Ibid.
[12]   See Colombi Ciacchi, A (2005), 'Non-legislative Harmonisation of Private Law under the European Constitution: the Case of Unfair Suretyships', 13 *European Review of Private Law* 297; Kenny, M, Devenney, J and Fox O'Mahony, L (2010), 'Conceptualising unconscionability in Europe: in the kaleidoscope of public and private law', in Unconscionability in European Private Financial Transaction: Protecting the Vulnerable (CUP), 377–99.
[13]   OJ 1985 L 372/31.

decision of the European Court of Justice in *Bayerische Hypothekenbank v. Edgar Dietzinger*[14] that *some* suretyship transactions were covered by that Directive. Secondly, there was the potential gap in consumer protection in relation to suretyship agreements and Council Directive 87/102/EEC for the approximation of the laws, regulations and administrative provisions of the Member States concerning consumer credit,[15] which was exposed by *Berliner Kindl Brauerei AG v. Andreas Siepert*.[16] Thirdly, there is the continuing debate on the applicability of Council Directive 93/13/EEC on unfair terms in consumer contracts[17] and the subsequent, somewhat unsatisfying,[18] judgment of the High Court of England and Wales in *The Governor and Co of the Bank of England v. Singh*[19] that it does not apply to contracts of guarantee. Finally, one can refer back to the debates on the new Consumer Credit Directive in relation to suretyship transactions.[20]

Yet, as we have already noted, it is important not to lose sight of *overall*, context-specific, non-professional surety protection orchestrations in particular Member States, and it is our contention that the atypical, polycontextual nature of suretyship agreements also presents challenges for EU harmonisation initiatives at a more macroscopic level. Before developing this theme, we will review the different non-professional surety protection orchestrations across the EU; identifying the five central orchestrations and their divergent treatment of surety protection.

---

[14] [1998] ECR 1–1199, Case C–45/96. See also Rott, P (2005), 'Consumer Guarantees in the Future Consumer Credit Directive: Mandatory Ban on Consumer Protection?', 13 *European Review of Private Law* 383, at 384.

[15] OJ 1987 L372/31.

[16] [2000] ECR 1–174, Case C–208/98.

[17] OJ 1993 l95/21.

[18] See Beale, HG (ed.) *Chitty on Contracts*, (2004) Vol. II (Sweet & Maxwell), para.44–133. For full discussion: Devenney, J and Kenny, M (2009), 'Unfair terms, surety transactions and European harmonisation: a crucible of European led private law', *The Conveyancer and Property Lawyer* (73) 295–308.

[19] (QBD, unreported, 17 June 2005). In *Barclays Bank plc v. Kufner* [2008] EWHC 2319 at [29] Field J, relying on *Bayerische Hypothekenbank v. Edgar Dietzinger*, declined to follow *Singh*.

[20] See Kenny, M (2007), *supra* n. 1 at 180.

III. NON-PROFESSIONAL SURETY PROTECTION ORCHESTRATIONS ACROSS THE EU

Great Britain and Ireland

England and Wales

As we shall see, social welfare provisions and bankruptcy regimes may make a significant contribution to non-professional surety protection.[21] However, in England and Wales the protection afforded by bankruptcy laws to sureties is extremely limited[22] and the relevant social welfare provisions have been severely curtailed in recent times.[23] Instead, in England and Wales non-professional suretyship agreements are policed by a medley of legal doctrines and principles. For example, under the Statute of Frauds 1677, a suretyship agreement is unenforceable 'unless the agreement upon which such action shall be brought or some memorandum or note thereof shall be in writing and signed by the party to be charged therewith'.[24] This provision has been said to:

> protect people from being held liable on informal communications because they may be made without sufficient consideration or expressed ambiguously or because such communication might be fraudulently alleged against the party to be charged.[25]

There are also situations where a creditor will be under a duty to disclose certain information to the surety.[26] Furthermore there are a number of principles which afford as surety some measure of protection in England and Wales during the currency of the suretyship transaction. For example, a surety's liability may be reduced, or even extinguished, where the creditor negligently realises the relevant securities.[27]

Yet, notwithstanding the foregoing, it is clear that general contractual vitiating factors are the mainstay of the protection afforded to non-professional sureties in England and Wales.[28] More specifically, much of the protection afforded to

---

[21]   Parry, R, *supra* n. 8 at 358.

[22]   Fox, L (2006), *Conceptualising Home: Theories, Laws and Policies* (Hart Publishing) at 220–28.

[23]   Devenney, J, Fox-O'Mahony, L and Kenny, *supra* n. 7.

[24]   S.4.

[25]   *J. Pereira Fernandes SA v. Mehta* [2006] EWHC 813 (Ch) at [16] *per* Judge Pelling QC.

[26]   See, for example, *Levett v. Barclays Bank plc* [1995] 1 WLR 1260, *Crédit Lyonnais Bank Nederland v. Export Credit Guarantee Department* [1996] 1 Lloyd's Rep 200, and *Royal Bank of Scotland v. Etridge (no. 2)* [2001] UKHL 44.

[27]   *Mutual Loan Association v. Sudlow* (1858) 5 C.B.(N.S.) 449.

[28]   Devenney, J, Fox-O'Mahony, L & Kenny, M, *supra* n. 7 at 529.

non-professional sureties in England and Wales stems from the concept of undue influence.[29] This raises two issues. First, what are the parameters of the protection afforded by the doctrine of undue influence? Secondly, what is the position where, as is more usual, the suretyship agreement has been procured not by the undue influence of the creditor but by the undue influence of the principal debtor?

The first issue is connected to the jurisprudential basis of undue influence, a subject upon which there has been intense debate.[30] In particular there has been a tension between restrictive, capacity-driven approaches to undue influence and more expansive unconscionability-based approaches to undue influence.[31] One

---

[29]   See, generally, Fehlberg, B (1997), *Sexually Transmitted Debt* (Clarendon).

[30]   See, for example, Birks, P and Chin, Y (1995), 'On the Nature of Undue Influence', in Beatson, J and Friedmann, D (eds), *Good Faith and Fault in Contract Law* (Clarendon); Bigwood, R (1996), 'Undue Influence: "Impaired Consent" or "Wicked Exploitation"', 16 *Oxford Journal of Legal Studies* 503; O'Sullivan, J (1998), 'Undue Influence and Misrepresentation after O'Brien: Making Security Secure', in Rose, J (ed.), *Restitution and Banking Law* (Mansfield Press) at 42–69; Fehlberg, B (1997), *Sexually Transmitted Debt* (Clarendon) at 24–5; Smith, S (2002), *Atiyah's Introduction to the Law of Contract* (6th ed, Clarendon) at 288–91; Pawlowski, M and Brown, J (2002), *Undue Influence and the Family Home* (Cavendish) at 7–17, 27–30 and 205–12; Oldham, M (1995), '"Neither borrower nor lender be" – the life of O'Brien', *Child and Family Law Quarterly* 104, at 108–9; Chen-Wishart, M (1997), 'The O'Brien Principle and Substantive Unfairness', *Cambridge Law Journal* 60; Capper, D (1998), 'Undue Influence and Unconscionability: A Rationalisation', 114 *Law Quarterly Review* 479; Price, S (1999), 'Undue Influence: finis litium', 115 *Law Quarterly Review* 8; McMurtry, L (2000), 'Unconscionability and Undue Influence: An Interaction?', 64 *Conveyancer and Property Lawyer* 573, Chen-Wishart, M (2006), 'Undue Influence: Beyond Impaired Consent and Wrongdoing towards a Relational Analysis', in Burrows, A and Rodger, A (eds), *Mapping the Law: Essays in Memory of Peter Birks*, OUP, Chapter 11, p. 201; and Devenney, J and Chandler, A (2007), 'Unconscionability and the Taxonomy of Undue Influence', *Journal of Business Law* 541. Furthermore in *Niersmans v. Pesticcio* [2004] EWCA Civ 372 at [2] Mummery LJ lamented that:

'The striking feature of this appeal is that fundamental misconceptions [about the doctrine of undue influence] persist, even though the doctrine is over 200 years old and its basis and scope were examined by the House of Lords in depth … less than 3 years ago in the well known case of Royal Bank of Scotland Plc v. Etridge (No.2) [2002] 2 AC 773. The continuing confusions matter. Aspects of the instant case demonstrate the need for a wider understanding, both in and outside the legal profession, of the circumstances in which the court will intervene to protect the dependant and the vulnerable in dealings with their property.'

[31]   See, generally, Elvin, J (2007), 'The Purpose of the Doctrine of Presumed Undue Influence', in Giliker, P (ed), *Re-examining Contract and Unjust Enrichment: Anglo-Canadian Perspectives* (Martinus Nijhoff Publishers) 231 In *Portman Building Society v. Dusangh* [2000] 2 All ER (Comm) 221 at 233 Ward LJ stated:

'Professors Birks and Chin…see undue influence as being "plaintiff-sided" and concerned with the weakness of the plaintiff's consent owing to an excessive dependence

of the current authors has argued strongly that undue influence is founded upon a particular concept on unconscionability.[32] We shall say no more on this issue, except to note the versatility of the doctrine of undue influence; for example in *Royal Bank of Scotland v. Etridge*[33] Lord Nicholls stated that:

> there is no single touchstone for determining whether the principle is applicable. Several expressions have been used in an endeavour to encapsulate the essence: trust and confidence, reliance, dependence or vulnerability on the one hand and ascendancy, domination or control on the other. None of these descriptions is perfect. None is all embracing. Each has its proper place.[34]

Where a suretyship agreement has been procured not by the undue influence of the creditor but by the undue influence of the principal debtor, the courts have to balance the interests of the surety with the interests of the creditor in the light of any public interest.[35] Following *Barclays Bank plc v. O'Brien*[36] in such cases a surety would be able to have the suretyship agreement set aside only if the creditor had actual or constructive notice of the debtor's undue influence. Constructive notice, of course, refers to situations where a creditor is *deemed* to have notice of the debtor's undue influence by virtue of a failure to take certain steps once they have been 'put on notice', and, importantly in the present context, a creditor is now[37] always 'put on notice' when the creditor knows that the surety is not a commercial party. Essentially, once 'put on notice' the creditor must:

> take reasonable steps to satisfy itself that the…[non-commercial surety…] has had brought home to her, in a meaningful way, the practical implications of the proposed transaction.[38]

One way in which this may be satisfied is by requiring the surety to obtain legal advice on the nature and risks involved in the transaction.[39] At first glance these steps do not appear onerous. However, as we have argued elsewhere,[40] it

---

upon the defendant, and unconscionability as being "defendant-sided" and concerned with the defendant's exploitation of the plaintiff's vulnerability. I do not find it necessary to resolve this debate.'

[32]   Devenney, J and Chandler, A, *supra* n. 30.
[33]   [2001] UKHL 44.
[34]   Ibid. at [11].
[35]   *Royal Bank of Scotland v. Etridge (no. 2)* [2001] UKHL 44 at [34]–[37].
[36]   [1994] 1 AC 180.
[37]   Following *Royal Bank of Scotland v. Etridge (no. 2)* [2001] UKHL 44.
[38]   Ibid., at [54].
[39]   Ibid., at [79].
[40]   Devenney, J; Fox-O'Mahony, L and Kenny, M, *supra* n. 7 at 548–9.

is possible to underestimate the utility of this approach. In particular – and in contrast to, for example, the German approach which institutes a much higher threshold for intervention – creditors are now, to a certain extent, incentivised to be pro-active in *all* cases of non-commercial sureties.

Scotland

In Scotland the case law has adopted a more restrictive approach to non-professional surety protection.[41] This *may* be attributed to the fact that equitable remedies are unknown in Scotland and that constructive notice does not exist. This approach was confirmed in *Smith v. Bank of Scotland*[42] where it was held that undue influence could not be presumed in close family relationships. On the other hand *Smith v. Bank of Scotland* extended – on the basis of good faith – the 'reasonable steps' owed by the creditor to ensure that the surety is alerted to the risks of the transaction.[43] Yet the 'reasonable steps' are incumbent on the creditor only when he/she is put on notice that the transaction was entered into as a result of undue influence, and this will be a matter of fact. Meanwhile, in *Forsyth v. Royal Bank of Scotland*[44] it was held that banks were entitled to place a normal degree of reliance on solicitors' due diligence;[45] good faith required no more than that the creditor should not take securities where there was reason to think that consent had been vitiated by misrepresentation, undue influence or some other wrongful act. Subsequently, while *Clydesdale Bank plc v. Black*[46] and *Thomson v. The Royal Bank of Scotland plc*[47] confirmed *Smith v. Bank of Scotland*, they made it clear that the English 'core minimum requirements' of *Etridge (No.2)* do not apply in Scotland.

Nevertheless, there has always been a practical interest in ensuring consistency between England and Scotland. The major British banks and building societies have all taken on board the *Etridge* 'core minimum requirements', and the Conveyancing Committee of the Law Society of Scotland has issued guidelines similar to those issued by the Law Society of England and Wales.

---

[41]   Smith, LJ (2007), 'Deferential Spouses and Cautionary Wrecks: Personal or *Cautionary* Obligations in Scots Law', in Colombi Ciacchi, A (ed.), *Protection of Non-Professional Sureties in Europe: Formal and Substantive Disparity* (Nomos) at 185–200.
[42]   1997 SC (HL) 111.
[43]   Ibid., at 122 *per* Lord Clyde: '[a]ll that is required of him (the creditor) is that he should take reasonable steps to secure that… he acts throughout in good faith. So far as the substance of those steps are concerned it seems to me that it would be sufficient for the creditor to warn the… cautioner of the consequences of entering into the obligation and advising him or her to take independent advice.'
[44]   2000 SLT 1295.
[45]   See also *Royal Bank of Scotland v. Wilson and another* [2003] SCLR 716.
[46]   2002 SLT 764.
[47]   [2003] SCLR 964.

These guidelines are flanked by provisions on conflicts of interests and the rules relevant to professional misconduct.[48] Thus in practice banks and professionals have ensured that much the same result obtains in Scotland as across the border.

Ireland

Despite the, as yet unexplored, basis for protective standards contained in the Constitution (protection of family interests and Directive Principles of Social Policy), Equity plays the lead role in Irish suretyships law.[49] Yet important distinctions from England emerge. On undue influence, the Irish Supreme Court in *Bank of Nova Scotia v. Hogan*[50] followed *O'Brien* but underscored that the husband/wife relationship did not automatically raise a presumption of undue influence. Meanwhile, the court in *Ulster Bank v. Fitzgerald* held that constructive notice was too easily triggered in England:[51] banks were on notice only if aware of special circumstances substantiating the principal's wrongdoing. A potentially lower protective standard than in England and Wales emerged. However, in May 2003, the Central Bank and Financial Services Authority of Ireland Act (2003) came into effect with the aim of ensuring a more consumer friendly focus in financial services. The Irish Financial Services Authority subsequently issued a Consumer Protection Code which came into force on 1 August 2006. Chapter 4(3) of the Code requires all financial services providers to issue a warning on all guarantee contracts.[52] Thus emphasis was placed on an 'information paradigm' model, rather than the 'proceduralised' lead given in England and Wales in *Etridge.*

---

[48]   Contained in the Solicitors (Scotland) Practice Rules, 1986 and the Solicitors (Scotland) Act, 1980 respectively. See generally: 'Inter-spouse guarantees: an update' thejournalonline (*Journal of the Law Society of Scotland*). October 2003, at 34 available at: www.journalonline.co.uk/article/1000542.aspx

[49]   O'Callaghan, P (2007), 'Protection from Unfair Suretyships in Ireland' in Colombi Ciacchi, A, *supra* n. 41 at 201–14. Art. 41, Irish Constitution on Fundamental Rights and the protection to be afforded the Family, and Art. 45, Irish Constitution on Directive Principles of Social Policy. See: Martin, F (1998), 'The Family in the Constitution – Principle and Practice'; and Murphy, T (1998), 'Economic Inequality and the Constitution', both in Murphy, T and Twomey, P (eds), *Ireland's Evolving Constitution* (Hart), at 79–95 and 163–81.

[50]   *Bank of Nova Scotia v. Hogan* [1996] 3 IR 239.

[51]   *Ulster Bank v. Fitzgerald* [2001] IEHC 159: 'the relationship of husband and wife does not give rise to a presumption of undue influence... the burden of proving undue influence is on the party alleging it'.

[52]   Chapter 4(3) Irish Consumer Protection Code reads as follows: 'Warning: As a guarantor of this loan you will have to pay off the loan, the interest and all associated charges if the borrower does not. Before you sign this guarantee you should get independent legal advice'.

Established Civil Law Tradition

Germany

The Constitutional Court *(Bundesverfassungsgericht)* has laid down the need for a substantive control of suretyships;[53] freedom of contract exists only where parties have similar bargaining power and the courts must intervene to protect in cases of inequality. Where an *excessive burden* between the sum guaranteed and the surety's assets and income exists, the courts must apply the doctrines of immorality and good faith.[54] Yet the reality of protection is that Supreme Court *(Bundesgerichtshof)* decisions have simply caught the most extreme cases, and, as all property assets must be liquidated before an *excessive burden* can be found, the surety can lose his home without this being seen as excessive. Moreover, a finding that the agreement was immoral can be avoided procedurally.[55] The approach has been criticised: too little emphasis is placed on party autonomy; there is a lack of transparency and flexibility.[56]

Austria

Despite case law approving the German approach,[57] Austrian courts pursue a traditional approach. There are three sources of protection: the Civil Code (immorality, mistake or fraud and surprising terms),[58] the Consumer Protection Act (paragraph 25d CPA, allowing judges to reduce obligations on the basis of an unfair disparity) and the Bankruptcy Regulation; which allows for the discharge of residual debts in cases of personal insolvency.

---

[53]   BverfG *(Bundesverfassungsgericht)* 19 October 1993, BverfGE 89, 214 *(Bürgschaft)*.

[54]   Doctrines of immorality *(Sittenwidrigkeit)* 138 BGB and good faith *(Treu und Glauben)* 242 BGB applied.

[55]   Para. 688 German Code of Civil Procedure *(Zivilprozessordnung)*. Such an order can be avoided only if the guarantor can prove the bank chose the order with the sole purpose of avoiding the immorality assessment; this is almost impossible to establish.

[56]   Hesse, HA and Kaufmann, P (1995), 'Die Schutzpflicht und die Privatrecht-sprechung' *Juristenzeitung* 219; Teubner, G (2000), 'Die Familienbürgschaft in der Kollision unverträglicher Handlungslogiken' *Kritische Vierteljahresschrift fuer Gesetzgebung und Rechtswissenschaft* 288, 296; Diederichsen, U (1998), 'Das Bundesverfassungsgericht als oberstes Zivilgericht', *Archiv fuer die civilistische Praxis* 179 at 247; Rott, P (2007), 'German Law on Family Suretyships: An Overrated System' in Colombi Ciacchi, A, *supra* n. 41 at 51–70.

[57]   Austrian Supreme Court, judgment of 27 March 1995, OGH SZ 68/64. *Discussion:* Faber, W (2007), 'Protection of Non-Professional Sureties in Austria Austrian Reactions to German Developments and Original Ways of Consumer Protection' in ibid., at 71–102.

[58]   Ibid., citing provisions on: Immorality *(Sittenwidrigkeit)*, para. 879 ABGB (Austrian Civil Code) on good faith and fair dealing; special rules on usury (para. 879(2)4 ABGB); mistake *(Irrtum*, para. 871 ABGB); fraud *(Arglist*, para. 870 ABGB) and surprising terms *(Geltungskontrolle*, para. 864a ABGB).

Belgium
Consumer protection was extended to sureties under the 1991 Consumer Credit Act (CCA). The Act restricts the surety's obligations: sums guaranteed must be specified (Article 34, CCA) while 'all sums' guarantees are void. Family law also intervenes; contracts endangering family interests can be declared void. Insolvency law plays an important role in allowing for the discharge of non-professional sureties where the obligation is not *proportionate* to the surety's income and assets. But many problematic distinctions continue: why should the bankrupt debtor's surety be better placed than a non-bankrupt debtor's surety, and why the differences between cases of bankruptcy and those of collective debt?[59]

The Netherlands
Here a layered structure of protection emerges with provisions drawn from different parts of the Civil Code: Book 3, on patrimonial law; Book 6, on contract; Book 7, on special contracts including suretyships; Book 1, on family protection. A hybrid strategy between English proceduralisation and German constitutionalisation has thus been adopted; maintaining a general duty on banks to protect customers, yet obliging sureties to inform themselves on their potential liability. Stringent due diligence requirements apply.[60] Similarly, the assessment of mistake (paragraph 6.228, Civil Code) hinges upon the veracity of the creditor's information.[61]

France
Consumer protection was extended to all guarantors of non-professional *and* professional debts in 2003, as a move to increase protection for family property. Consumer protection considerations now predominate in the treatment of professional and non-professional sureties; contract and surety law playing a residual role. The balance struck favours consumer protection, yet the 'inflation of protection' has caused anomalies in the protection achieved: why should the ex-spouse be better placed than the surety-widow or the principal's dependants? Why should consumer protection be extended to businessmen?[62]

---

[59]   Sagaert, V (2007), 'The protection of non-professional sureties in Belgian law' in Colombi Ciacchi, A, *supra* n. 41 at 121–40.

[60]   Van Erp, JHM (2007), 'Protection of non-professional sureties under Dutch law: a fragmented approach' in ibid., at 141–52. On the treatment of due diligence see *Mees Pierson v. Ten Bos*, Hoge Raad, 3 January 1998, Nederlandse Jurisprudentie 1999, 285.

[61]   *Van Lanschot Bankiers v. Mrs Bink*, Hoge Raad, 1 June 1990, Nederlandse Jurisprudentie 1991, 759.

[62]   Vigneron, S (2007), 'Protection of Non-professional Sureties in France: A trop embrassé, mal étreint', in Colombi Ciacchi, A, *supra* n. 41, referring to s.L. 341–1 to 341–6, Consumer Code.

Spain

The complex demarcation of commercial, civil and consumer law means that the accessority principle precludes the protective principles of consumer law being applied to commercial agreements in Spain. Unfair suretyships are thus dealt with by a cocktail of general principles of contract law, consumer protection and unfair contract terms. A lack of choice in entering such agreements due to emotional dependency is analysed in terms of consent. Similarly, courts look to the standard contract terms to review the validity of such agreements. Family and insolvency law also influence the validity and extent of surety agreements. This diversity of protection is held responsible for the overall under-protection of sureties.[63]

Nordic Countries

Finland

Finnish experience with surety protection is stark: following a credit boom in the 1980s a housing slump ensued and, as debts were called in, sureties began to realise the extent of their obligations.[64] Developments culminated with the 1999 Guaranties and Third-party Pledges Act (GPA) which aimed at giving guarantors a better insight into what suretyships involve. The GPA distinguishes private and commercial agreements: where the agreement is private the provisions of the Act are mandatory, and the maximum liability and the duration of the obligation must be specified. Meanwhile, creditors are placed under compulsory and continuing disclosure duties and sureties have rights to revocation or to have their liability adjusted where they have not received information. Disclosure is comprehensive, embracing information that must be given before and after the agreement, and as regards the surety's information rights. Yet the provisions do not ensure that sureties have *understood* the information. Meanwhile, section 39 GPA, requires the Consumer Ombudsman to supervise the general terms of the agreement, while the Market Court supervises unfair terms. The formation and content of agreements may also be determined by contract law (fraud, duress, undue influence, and misrepresentation). Insolvency law provides some protection, while provisions of Consumer and Family law also intervene. As there has been no case law on the GPA, the level of protection remains to be determined.

---

[63]   Rodriguez de las Heras Ballell, T (2010), 'Spanish report', in Colombi Ciacchi, A and Weatherill, S (eds) *Regulating Unfair Banking Practices in Europe: The Case of Personal Sueretyships* (OUP), 519–45.

[64]   Mikkola, T (2010), 'Finnish Report', in Colombi Ciacchi, A and Weatherill, S (eds), 207–27

Sweden

There is no suretyship law in Sweden. Instead, a general framework is supplied by provisions of the Civil Code, the Contract Act and the Consumer Credit Act. The important role of coordinating this framework falls to judges.[65] Whilst suretyships are widely used, they are not related to over-indebtedness, a state of affairs which has been attributed to bank practice and debt-restructuring; social provision is seen as defusing the issue of over-indebtedness.

The Baltic States

Estonia

European model laws (PECL and PICC) and conventions (CISG) have been influential on Estonian law.[66] Yet the social and economic context in which these rules operate is quite different: first, creditors do not find taking personal securities attractive and prefer to take securities in property or waive security altogether; second, there is evidence that traditional suretyship gender assumptions have been reversed. While the Law of Obligations (2002) provides a framework, protection is supplied in practice by a diverse body of case law. Non-professionals are protected by a number of mechanisms: Article 143 Law of Obligations specifies that the duration and extent of the obligation must be set. The surety is also protected by accessority and subsidiarity, as well as by the creditor's obligations to provide information. The surety may also be protected by the good faith, unconscionability, mistake and fraud provisions in the General Part of the Civil Code. The dearth of case law suggests that the standard of protection is likely to be low.

Lithuania

Non-professional suretyships are uncommon in Lithuania, creditors preferring to rely on *in rem* security. In addition, the law does not draw a distinction between commercial and non-professional suretyships; and does not classify the surety agreement as a consumer contract.[67] UNIDROIT and PECL rules have been transplanted into a different social reality and the few cases that have arisen have concerned commercial agreements. Surety protection is supplied through

[65] Perrson, AH (2010) 'Swedish Reports', in Colombi Ciacchi, A and Weatherill, S (eds), 547–70.

[66] Kull, I (2010, 'Estonian Report' in Colombi Ciacchi, A and Weatherill, S (eds), 179–206.

[67] Smaliukas, A and G Šulija (2010), 'Lithuanian Report', in Colombi Ciacchi, A and Weatherill, S (eds), 401–14. On reform see Smaliukas, A (2004), 'Reform of Security over Movable Property in Lithuania: Evaluation *de lege lata* and proposals *de lege ferenda'*, *European Business Law Review* 879.

the general law of obligations, contract law on good faith and gross disparity (Article 3.10, UNIDROIT Principles (1994)). To a limited extent, family law is relevant.

Latvia

The Latvian Civil Code, based on the Swiss Civil Code, aims to ensure protection for the vulnerable surety. Surety agreements are important and the majority are attached to real property. Given intense competition financial institutions have been lowering their security requirements and regulation is regarded as lax.[68] Non-professional sureties are not clearly demarcated from commercial sureties, and there are no rules relating to consumers and on the circumstances in which a non-professional agreement will be considered unfair. Section 1415 of the Latvian Civil Code on 'impermissible or indecent actions' may be applicable to sureties where there is a gross disproportion between the amount of the debt and the surety's assets and income. However, there is no case law amplifying this point; court practice suggests that courts would adopt a *laissez-faire* approach to protection.

Central and Eastern Europe

Poland

There is a strong link between non-professional suretyships and indebtedness in Poland.[69] Polish law regulates such agreements in the Civil Code in Articles 876–887. The provisions supply protection to all types of surety. Whilst there is no Consumer Code there is a Family and Guardianship Code, providing additional protection. The Civil Code stipulates that the suretyship must take written form. According to Article 880, the creditor must notify the surety immediately on the principal's default. The surety's defences against his/her obligations comprise defences arising out of the primary debt and the surety's personal defences (intent, misrepresentation, mistake). Additionally, Article 357 allows parties to argue an extraordinary, unforeseeable change in circumstances rendering performance impossible or difficult. Articles 58 and 353, allowing the courts to rule on the validity of contracts contravening principles of community life and the lawfulness of the contract, provide additional protection.

---

[68]   Klauberg, T (2010), 'Latvian Report', in Colombi Ciacchi, A and Weatherill, S. (eds) 389–99.
[69]   Lobocka, I (2010), 'Polish Report', in Colombi Ciacchi, A and Weatherill, S. (eds), 435–52.

Hungary

The Hungarian legislator reacted to the issue of surety protection with a secured transactions law in 1996.[70] To protect themselves, creditors responded by accumulating as many security instruments as they could. More recently, bank competition has led to the introduction of more 'consumer friendly' financing aimed at 'riskier' social groups. The perception that suretyships could be unfair has not yet arisen.

Slovenia

Personal security is frequently the only means by which loans can be secured in Slovenia.[71] The Code of Obligations confirms the accessory and subsidiary nature of the agreement. However, the subsidiary nature of the obligation is frequently undermined by bank practice whereby the surety is transformed into a joint debtor. Consumer protection is supplied by the Consumer Protection Act and by the Consumer Credit Act. Both Acts apply to the relationship between the non-professional consumer and the professional lender. There is no duty incumbent on credit institutions to inform sureties on the risks they are assuming. Potentially unfair agreements have to be assessed in the light of the general rules on unfair contracts: usury (Article 119 Code of Obligations) and immorality (Article 86 Code of Obligations). Given legislative inaction, sureties rely on judicial activism.

IV.   HARMONISATION PROPOSALS: UNTUNING THE STRINGS?

Study Group Proposals

Notwithstanding the divergence of national approaches identified in this chapter, the Study Group on a European Civil Code (SGECC), in work led by Professor Ulrich Drobnig, [72] assigned protection of the vulnerable surety to the general law of contract as fleshed out in the *Principles of European Contract Law* (PECL)[73] and the provisions elaborated by the SGECC.[74] These instruments appeared to

---

[70]   Tajti, T (2010), 'Hungarian Report', in Colombi Ciacchi, A and Weatherill, S. (eds), 303–38.

[71]   Mežnar, S (2010), 'Slovenian Report', in Colombi Ciacchi, A and Weatherill, S. (eds), 505–18.

[72]   Working Team on Credit Securities: www.mpipriv-hh.mpg.de/deutsch/Forschung/ Kredit sicherheiten.html.

[73]   PECL: http://frontpage.cbs.dk/law/commission_on_european_contract_law.

[74]   Provisions available at: www.sgecc.net. Particular rules available at: www.sgecc. net/pages/en/texts/index.draft_articles.htm.

adopt a more traditional private law (Austrian) rather than a constitutionalised (German) approach: unfair suretyships were to be challenged where their provisions contravened substantive legal norms on good faith and fair dealing (Article 1:201 (ex 1.106) PECL), the provisions on excessive benefit and unfair advantage (Article 4:109 (ex 6.109) PECL) and, finally, the provisions on unfair contract terms which have not been individually negotiated (Article 4:110 (ex 6.110) PECL). Controversially, in the light of the problems identified of relying on the information paradigm in the context of surety agreements, the framework for protection relied heavily on *duties to inform* (Personal Security Contracts, Chapter 4, Articles 4:101–4:108 SGECC) which, apart from rules on pre-contractual information (Article 4:103 SGECC), also includes the creditor's duty to inform the surety of the precise extent of his/her liability annually (Article 4:107 SGECC).

Draft Common Frame of Reference

The latest stage of the Commission's 'greater coherence' initiative[75] is the production of the Draft Common Frame of Reference (DCFR), produced jointly by the SGECC and the Acquis Group.[76] This instrument is planned as preparatory for the Common Frame of Reference (CFR) which, according to the Commission's 2004 Communication, was to provide 'fundamental principles, definitions and model rules' to assist in improving the existing *acquis* and act as a basis for any subsequent *optional instrument* were one found to be necessary.[77] Model rules were to be the central elements of the CFR, its purpose being to act as a 'tool box' for legislators. In parallel, the Acquis Group was charged with the review of the eight consumer directives central to the emergent body of European private law.[78] Though based on the PECL principles, the DCFR goes

---

[75] Action Plan on A More Coherent European Contract law, COM(2003)68 final, OJ 2003 C63/1.

[76] Study Group on a European Civil Code/Research Group on EC Private Law (eds, 2008) *Draft Common Frame of Reference (DCFR): Principles, Definitions and Model Rules of European Private Law* Sellier: www.law-net.eu. Subsequently, since paper delivered, see C von Bar and E Clive, *Principles Definitions and Model Rules of European Private Law: Draft Common Frame of Reference (DCFR)*, (OUP, Oxford, 2010); Commission Decision 2010/233.EU; 2010 OJ L 105/109.

[77] 2004 Commission Communication, European Contract Law and the revision of the acquis: the way forward, COM(2004)651 final.

[78] Directive 85/577 on Doorstep Sales, OJ 1985 L372/31; Directive 90/314 on Package Travel, OJ 1990 L158/59; Directive 93/13 on unfair terms in Consumer Contracts, OJ 1993 L95/29; Directive 94/47 Timeshare Directive, OJ 1994 L280/83; Directive 97/7 on Distance Contracts, OJ 1997 L144/19; Directive 98/6 Indication of Prices of Products offered to Consumers, OJ 1998 L80/27; Directive 98/27 Injunctions for the Protection

beyond, varies and re-numbers the PECL provisions. The DCFR also admits that its purpose is still unclear and that the values underlying the wider 'coherence' project are contested.[79] Helpfully, the DCFR includes a table of DCFR derivations from the original PECL; thus, for example, on good faith: III 1:103 (ex Article 1:201 PECL) DCFR; on unfair advantage: II 7.207 (ex Article 4:109 PECL) DCFR and on terms which have not been individually negotiated: II 9.404–409 (ex Article 4:110 PECL) DCFR.

As previously alluded to, the DCFR extends into a series of model rules on broader areas of Private Law: to 'specific contracts' and the rights and obligations arising from them (Book IV); non-contractual obligations (Book VI); rights and obligations arising from unjust enrichment (Book VII); and damage caused to another and benevolent intervention in another's affairs (Book V). While the breadth of the DCFR suggests a CFR functioning as more than a 'tool box' intended for legislators; it also implies an *optional instrument* – if not cast in the form of a European Civil Code – of more substance than a simple measure of harmonisation. In one of the chapters in this collection, Professor Hugh Beale, one of the Editorial Team, has emphasised the interim character of the DCFR. Clearly, the interim nature of these provisions – given their links to what some regard as an embryonic European Civil Code – makes assessment doubly difficult.

For our purposes the most intriguing section of the DCFR is the provisions in Part G of Book IV on Personal Security. Part G applies to suretyships, indemnities and co-debtorship.[80] The protection of sureties is expanded upon in Book IV, Chapter 2, and while the subsidiary and accessory nature of the agreement is straightforward,[81] the DCFR appears not to relate the principal's insolvency protection comprehensively to any protection due to the surety (G – 2:102 (2) (a)). Similarly the DCFR lays down that while the amount of the obligation need not be fixed, it cannot exceed the amount of the secured obligations at the time the security became effective (G – 2:102 (3)). Again the subsidiary and accessory nature of the obligation is underscored in G – 2:103 in terms of the debtor's defences and subsequently in the coverage of security and the subsidiary nature of the security provider's liability (G – 2:106). The creditor

of Consumers' Interests, OJ 1998 L166/51; Directive 99/44 Sale of Consumer Goods and Associated Guarantees, OJ 1999 L171/12, available at: http://eur-lex.europa.eu.

[79] DCFR, *supra* note 76, Introduction, at paras. 61 and 15–25. Since this paper was delivered the purpose of the DCFR has generated much academic discussion, e.g. Vogenauer, S (2010), 'Common frame of reference and UNIDROIT Principles of International Commercial Contracts, coexistence, competition or overkill of soft law', 6 *ERCC*, 148 at 149.

[80] Ibid., Book IV. Part G – 1:102: Scope at 281.

[81] Ibid., Book IV. Part G – 2:102.

is required to notify the failure of the principal debt (G – 2:107 (1)) but would also be allowed to notify of any increase in a global security (G – 2:107 (2)). The creditor's pre-contractual duties are, meanwhile, specified in G – 4:103 and the creditor must, where suspecting undue influence, ensure *independent advice*. While the common law rather than civil law approaches seems the model here, it is unclear whether 4:103 equates to constructive notice as it is understood in England or whether it is more in line with the information paradigm operable in Irish law. Similarly, what is the nature of the undue influence at the heart of G. – 4:103? The provision appears effectively to recast undue influence as a relatively narrow concept relating to a lack of information. Meanwhile, though the amount of the obligation would appear not to require specification, it is held to depend on the extent of the principal obligation (G – 4:105); a problem here is whether a high maximum amount can simply be specified by creditor and principal debtor at the outset of the agreement. Additionally, the creditor under the DCFR is under an obligation to supply annual information (G – 4:106), while the surety may limit liability either through a time limit or, on notice, variation to a time limit (G – 4:107).

V. CONCLUSIONS: THE UNCOMMON CORE

This chapter has sought to map the uncommon core of non-professional surety protection across the EU. In particular, we have sought to demonstrate that the protection afforded to non-professional sureties in individual Member States often involves different complex, context-specific orchestrations of various legal fields, concepts and mechanisms. This diversity underlines the polycontextual, aptypical nature of such agreements and can, in part, be explained by the fragmentation of the context in which such agreements operate. In each legal order sureties take a unique place in a subtle web of legal, social and behavioural standards. Thus, when comparing national levels of protection one needs to consider a number of norms and doctrines, social and economic factors, and differences in banking practice. For example, social welfare may influence the likelihood of the principal's default (Sweden); whilst banking practice may influence the real level of protection (Scotland).

Accordingly, it would be dangerous for any harmonisation strategy in this area to lose sight of overall, context-specific, non-professional surety protection orchestrations in particular Member States. Indeed such a strategy would risk further fragmentation.[82] Moreover, a harmonisation strategy in this area with

---

[82] Heß, B (2001), 'Die Integrationsfunktion des Europäischen Zivilverfahrensrechts', *Praxis des Internationalen Privat- und Verfahrensrechts* 389. Polycentricity dominates

a narrow focus may result in unintended consequences. For example, if additional obligations are placed on creditors it may be that suretyship transactions will tend to lose their appeal and resort will be made, instead, to other types of guarantees. Thus the perverse result of *raising* protection for sureties may be that the poorest are either offered worse terms on guarantees or refused access to prime credit altogether. The paradox of protection is that less can be more; promoting standards of weak 'constitutional' protection, as in Germany, may ensure broader and less costly access to credit. In effect there may be a double paradox: the 'lower' the effective level of protection, the more equitable the access to credit; the 'higher' the level of protection, the greater the problem of social exclusion. But we can go further: the treble paradox is that our concern with the social justice implications of the treatment of sureties works to obscure the reality of sub-prime lending in Europe; a paradox in which we can see the danger of charging private law with too many objectives. Furthermore, the problem of over-indebtedness does not disappear in those countries with 'higher' standards of protection; they are simply transformed by the market into charges on mortgages and resort to demand guarantees. Inevitably there are associated implications for banking practice; 'low' protection levels can represent a moral hazard for creditors.

On the other hand it can be argued that some commonality is present in surety law, but at a different level; that uniformity emerges from the tension in the uncommon core. If we can understand surety law as the law of overlapping legal systems, then, whilst some elements may require uniform treatment, we can otherwise rely on competition and spontaneous harmonisation. The idea here is that law depends on contradiction; that systems can also work as a unitary network: '(o)nly the combination of both sides of the difference... brings out the special nature of the hybrid: neither mediation nor syntheses, but extremely ambivalent unity'.[83] Can we use Teubner's juxtaposition of hybridisation (integrating networks) and differentiation (closed systems) to illuminate the blindspots in suretyships law: to see the spectrum of protection, and the variable access to credit in terms of a unitary network?[84] Can an ambivalent unity be seen in the simultaneous promotion of surety protection and private

the law relating to cross-border trade: EC law, new *lex mercatoria*, UN Vienna Convention, Unidroit Principles and 1980 EC Rome Convention.

[83] Teubner, G (2001), 'In the Blindsopot: The Hybridisation of Contracting', at 11 available at www.jura.uni-frankfurt.de/ifawz1/teubner/dokumente/VERTRAG_eng_TheoreticalInquiries.pdf. Teubner, G (2001), 'Das Recht hybrider Netzwerke', *Zeitschrift fuer das gesamte Handels- und Wirtschaftsrecht* 550.

[84] Ibid., Teubner asks at 11: '[c]an we, using two mutually contradictory, equally entitled theories neither reducible to the other see the contract as a multiplicity of systems and simultaneously as a unitary network'.

autonomy? Here freedom of contract can be seen as a much broader concept, engaging constitutional law in a mediating role.[85]

Yet, alternatively to this language of discursivity and hybridisation, the common law can be seen as providing a more pragmatic and rigorous standard of protection. Coupled with a competition of legal orders, case law allows for the adoption of more efficient 'due diligence' solutions and experimentation.[86] Furthermore, even in Teubner's terms, constitutionalism can be unsatisfactory and compromise the real level of protection. Whilst application of a constitutionalised approach could work to strike down the most egregious types of guarantees, caution counsels against relying on such a strategy.[87]

Overall a dual-track strategy involving measures of legislative and non-legislative harmonisation recommends itself for European suretyship law. While the case for codification, given the heterogeneity identified in this chapter, will be rare, European legislation could play a role, for example, in ensuring broader access to credit, or establishing criteria for responsible lending or community reinvestment.[88] More common will be non-legislative harmonisation through judicial convergence; a more effective and legitimate way of harmonising private law.[89] What matters, after all, is that the courts achieve the same results regardless of which norms, doctrines or procedures they apply.

Finally, a number of propositions emerge from this work, the most important of which relate to the caveats to our understanding of European private law as a law possessing a clearly identifiable common core, susceptible to a broad exercise in codification. Given the serious fragmentation which may ensue from the application of either the PECL or the DCFR proposals in the complex field

---

[85]   Teubner, G, ibid., at 18. '[c]ontract as interdiscursivity raises ... the issue of constitutional rights ... these rights can no longer be seen as protecting only the individual actor against the repressive power of the state, but... need to be reconstructed as "discourse rights"'. See Weatherill, S (2002), 'The Commission's Options for Developing EC Consumer Protection and Contract Law: Assessing the Constitutional Basis', *European Business Law Review* 497. Gerstenberg, O (2004), 'Private Law and the New European Constitutional Settlement', 10 *European Law Journal* 766. Schepel, H (2004), 'The Enforcement of EC Law in Contractual Relations: Case Studies in How Not to "Constitutionalise" Private Law', *European Review of Private Law* 661.

[86]   Kähler, L (2005), 'Decision-Making about Suretyships under Empirical Uncertainty – How Consequences of Decisions about Suretyships Might Influence the Law', *European Review of Private Law* 333.

[87]   McCormack, G (2007), 'Protection of surety guarantors in England – prophylactics and procedure' in Colombi Ciacchi, A, *supra* n. 41, cites judicial circumspection towards developing broad doctrine; a lack of a tradition in constitutional adjudication and a reluctance to tying the hands of future legislatures as grounds against constitutionalising private law.

[88]   Cf. US Community Reinvestment Coalition: www.ncrc.org.

[89]   Colombi Ciacchi, A, *supra* n. 12 at 296.

of surety protection, the dangers of harmonisation cannot be ignored. Recalling de Sousa Santos, and looking at the law in action, we find divergence rather than convergence; a picture of fragmentation and tension.[90] The superficial attraction of harmonisation cannot hide the disastrous de-orchestration of a whole web of norms, doctrines and protective instruments.

---

[90] 'We live in a time of porous legality ... of multiple networks of legal orders forcing us to constant tranitions and trespassings': de Sousa Santos, B (1997), 'Law a Map of Misreading: Towards a Post-modern Conception of Law', *Journal of Law and Society* 279 at 298.

14. Harmonisation of business law: the experience of Africa

Jimmy Kodo*

INTRODUCTION

In order to create a better environment for business in their countries, 16 African Heads of State[1] signed in Port Louis (Mauritius) on 17 October 1993 the Treaty relating to the Organisation for the Harmonisation of Business Law in Africa (referred to as OHADA). The aim of this treaty is the promotion of regional integration and economic growth; securing legal environment through the harmonisation of business law. Its specific objectives are a single, modern, flexible, and reliable business law, adapted to each country's economy; arbitration as an appropriate and trustworthy way to settle disputes; an opportunity for training judges and judiciary staff and ensuring their specialisation. The treaty is open to any other country, whether member of the African Union or not. Some institutions have been created to help the new organisation run smoothly. The main institutions are the Permanent Secretary in Cameroon, the Regional School or training of lawyers and judges in Porto-Novo (Benin), and the Common Court of Justice and Arbitration (CCJA) which is the key institution. The CCJA is established in Abidjan, Ivory Coast.

Business law has a wide scope in the context of the OHADA. It covers commercial law, corporate companies, secured transactions, debt recovery and enforcement, bankruptcy, arbitration, accounting, contract for the carriage of goods by road; but also labour law, 'and any other matter the Council

---

*   University of Hertfordshire, UK.

[1]   The Treaty was signed originally by 14 states. On 31 December 2000, it was ratified by these 16 states, in the order of ratification: Guinea Bissau (15 January 1994), Senegal (14 June 1994), Central Republic of Africa (13 January 1995), Mali (7 February 1995), Comoros (20 February 1995), Burkina-Faso (6 March 1995), Benin (8 March 1995), Niger (5 June 1995), Ivory Coast (29 September 1995), Cameroon (20 October 1995), Togo (27 October 1995), Chad (13 April 1996), Democratic Republic of Congo (28 May 1997), Gabon (2 February 1998), Equatorial Guinea (16 April 1999), Guinea (5 May 2000). This list is available at: www.ohada.com/chrono.php.

of Ministers would decide to include in the meaning of business law'.[2] The derivative legislation of the OHADA is formed of two entities: the regulations and specific rules governing proceeding[3] and the Uniform Acts.[4] So far eight Uniform Acts have been enacted and are enforceable:

1. Uniform Act relating to general commercial law
2. Uniform Act relating to commercial companies and economic interest groups
3. Uniform Act organising securities
4. Uniform Act organising simplified recovery procedures and measures of execution
5. Uniform Act relating to arbitration
6. Uniform Act organising collective proceedings for wiping off debts
7. Accounting law Uniform Act relating to accountancy of corporate companies
8. Uniform Act relating to contracts for the carriage of goods by road.

Three Uniform Acts are currently being drafted.[5] According to Article 10 of the treaty, 'Uniform Acts are directly applicable and overriding in the Contracting States notwithstanding any conflict they may give rise to in respect of previous or subsequent enactment of municipal laws'. The Uniform Acts become part of the national law of Member States and are binding without further administrative measures in the Member States. As a matter of course Uniform Acts are mandatory in the entire Member States after their entry into force; they repeal existing legislation but they do not have direct effect as in the European Union system.

Litigation regarding the implementation of Uniform Acts is settled in the first instance and on appeal by the courts and tribunals of the Contracting States.[6] The Common Court of Justice and Arbitration will rule on the interpretation and enforcement of the OHADA Treaty, on Regulations laid down for their application, and on the Uniform Acts. As final court of appeal, the CCJA has jurisdiction over the decisions of the appellate courts of Contracting States in all business issues raising questions pertaining to the application of Uniform Acts, but decisions regarding penal sanctions are pronounced by the appellate courts. While sitting as a court of final appeal, the Court can hear and decide points of fact.[7]

---

[2] Article 2 of the OHADA Treaty.
[3] There are two main regulations addressing proceedings before the CCJA and arbitration proceedings.
[4] Article 5 of the OHADA Treaty.
[5] They are about contract law, consumer law and labour law.
[6] Article 13 of the OHADA Treaty.
[7] Ibid., article 14.

Unification of case law by the CCJA within the Member States is the king-pin of the OHADA since there would not be any harmonisation otherwise. The aim of this chapter is to present findings from our doctoral research on the reception and application of OHADA Uniform Acts in national courts. In most cases, the Uniform Acts are properly implemented. As the treaty allows, national judges contribute widely to the building of the sources of the new harmonised law where a legal vacuum exists. Nevertheless, the legitimacy of legislation giving more power to the Common Court of Justice and Arbitration (CCJA) is questioned, as many judges are reluctant to cede their power of decision-making to the CCJA. Supreme Courts of some Member States have challenged the authority of the CCJA, deciding cases that are outside their competence since the entry into force of the treaty. We will focus on the resistance of national judges to business law harmonisation in Africa. The main features of this resistance are the violation of the authority of the Uniform Acts (section 1) and the challenge of the CCJA's jurisdiction by national judges (section 2).

1.   CHALLENGE OF THE AUTHORITY OF THE UNIFORM ACTS

On one hand the authority of the Uniform Acts is challenged by violation of some of their mandatory provisions (see section A). On the other hand we noticed a prevalence of the will of parties over Uniform Acts and refusal to implement them (see section B).

A.   Violation of Mandatory Provisions

The Uniform Act Organising Simplified Recovery Procedures and Measures of Execution (UAOSRPME) established a specific regime for the nullity of some procedural deeds without required information. On one hand, specific procedural deeds lacking required information are automatically void. On the other hand, a party alleging missing information in a procedural deed will have to provide evidence of the grievance or harm the missing formality has caused him before annulment. In other words, there is a regime of automatic nullity and a regime of nullity subject to evidence of grievance or harm. The violation of these provisions needs careful attention as almost all of them are mandatory. In many cases some national judges make a confusion of these mandatory rules. As a result, some of them require evidence of grievance or harm where this is not required (see below 1), and declare automatically null and void some deeds where evidence of grievance is required (see 2 below).

1. The wrongful requirement of grievance

The UAOSRPME says in its Article 297:

> The time limits provided for in Articles 259, 266, 268, 269, 270, 276, 281, 287, 288(7) and (8) and 289 above shall be prescribed, under penalty of forfeiture. The formalities provided for by these instruments and by Articles 254, 267 and 277 above shall only be penalized by nullity where the irregularity had the effect of causing a prejudice to the interest of the party invoking it.
>
> Nullity pronounced because of lack of adequate description of one or more of the estates included in the seizure shall not necessarily entail nullity of the proceedings as concerns the other estates.

The general principle in this Uniform Act regarding proceedings lacking essential information is nullity. In a case about lack of essential information in a sequestration report, a creditor carries out a sequestration of his debtor properties and asks for their conversion into seizure for sale, after issue of a writ of execution. The debtor invokes the nullity of the action for many reasons among which is violation of Article 64 of the UAOSRPME. This Article sets ten essential requirements, the failure of which has specific implications. Normally the lack of any of the ten requirements in Article 64 above should result in nullity, and this was the demand of the debtor. But the judges dismissed the case. In their decision, they held that the requirements of Article 64 are not mandatory and therefore their violation is not to be sanctioned by nullity.[8] They based this decision on an old piece of French legislation[9] and case law[10] which were in force in Niger before the enactment of the Uniform Acts of OHADA. At that time there was a need to provide evidence of harm or grief resulting from lack of such essential information before nullity was granted. But the Uniform Acts changed the regime of nullity of many proceedings as noted above. The reference to national legislation prior to the UAOSRPME misled the judges and they rendered a wrong decision. And to some extent this can be assimilated to refusal to implement the new legislation.

In a case of omission of the registered office of a corporate body in a writ of garnishment, a party alleged the violation of the mandatory provisions of Articles 157 and 160 of the UAOSRPME. The court ruled that if the failure to fulfil some formalities required by the Uniform Act deserves nullification, in some cases this nullification can be awarded only if the omission of the formality

---

[8]   See Tribunal Régional de Niamey (Niger), n° 435, 3 October 2001: *Hamani Yaye v. Boukary Maïga Adamou*, available at: www.ohada.com/jurisprudence/ohadata/J-02-70.

[9]   See the Decree of 30 November 1931 reorganising the bailiff's proceedings.

[10] CAOF 19 February 1937, Dalloz périodique 1930, Ière partie, p. 223; 30 December 1949; CAOF 19 February 1932, Dalloz périodique 1933, Ière partie, p. 65; Gazette du Palais 1977, IIème partie, Doctrine, p. 552; Cour de Cassation, 2ème chambre civile, 9 February 1983, Gazette du Palais, 1983.

was detrimental to the demanding party. So the lack of the registered office of a company does not have importance as the information results from a bailiff's official report, which is an authentic document. Therefore with no evidence of financial loss there is no need to take into account the omission of the required information.[11] This decision is open to criticism, as one cannot imagine how the bailiff's report would mention the registered office if the writ of garnishment itself has no mention of it. Moreover, the regime of nullity provided by Articles 157 and 160 of the Uniform Act does not require evidence of any harm or financial loss, unlike what the court held. Some other inferior national courts have had similar rulings.[12]

The Uniform Act relating to simplified debt recovery has established the injunction to pay[13] which is a very simple procedure for recovering debts. It is simple because a party whose debt is 'unquestionable and due for immediate payment'[14] can ask for the issue of an injunction to pay. The judge assesses the claim and issues the injunction to pay if the requirements are met. But the simplicity of the procedure allows the debtor to lodge an objection to the injunction to pay by the procedure of opposition.[15] This procedure has specific requirement as laid by the Uniform Act Organising Simplified Recovery Procedures and Measures of Execution:

> The opposing party shall, under penalty of forfeiture and in the same act as that of the opposition:
> – notify his opposition to all the parties and to the registrar of the court which pronounced the injunction to pay;
> – serve a summons to appear before the competent court on a fixed date not exceeding a period of thirty days from the opposition.[16]

We note that notification of the opposition must be made in the same act to all parties involved, i.e. to the creditor, to the bailiff and to the registrar of court. Failure to do so should result in forfeiture of the petition. But a court held that the failure of the debtor to notify his opposition to the registrar and the bailiff in the same act as that of the opposition could not result in forfeiture, since the

---

[11]   Tribunal de Première Instance de Yaoundé (Cameroon), Ordonnance n° 762/C, 1 July 2004: *Crédit Lyonnais Cameroun, Me NDENGUE KAMENI et Me NGONGO OTTOU v. Sté BIOTECH Srl, Me NGONGANG SIME Alain, BEAC*, available at: www.ohada.com/jurisprudence/ohadata/J-04-421.

[12]   Tibunal Régional Hors Classe de Dakar (Senegal), Ordonnance de référé n° 924, 19 May 2004: *SODIMA v. Ndiogou SECK*, available at: www.ohada.com/jurisprudence/ohadata/J-05-104.

[13]   See UAOSRPME, Articles 1–18.

[14]   Ibid., article 1.

[15]   Ibid., Article 9.

[16]   Ibid., Article 11.

creditor had not provided evidence of any harm or financial loss resulting from it and because the provisions of Article 11 quoted above are not mandatory.[17] Instead of deciding that way, the judge should have taken notice of the conspicuous defect and forfeited the opposition. By the way another jurisdiction ruled that the provisions of Article 11 of the UAOSRPME are mandatory.[18]

2. Automatic nullification of deeds where evidence of harm is required

An example will be given to illustrate this tendency. It relates to seizure of real estate.[19] A court held that the declarations and observations relating to a seizure of real estate must be presented before the possible hearing under penalty of forfeiture. But the court can move *sua sponte* to nullify the proceedings because of latent defects such as non-respect for the set date of the auction sale.[20] The proceedings prior to this decision are confusing and the reading of the decision itself is not easy, because of some mistakes in the indication of the Articles of the Uniform Act upon which it was based. However the laconic justification of this judgment and its conclusion are of interest. It is true that the provisions referred to in the decision have specific requirements which would result in nullity if they were missing. But in this specific case it was not an automatic nullity. See page 255 above.[21] In its decision the court added a condition not required by the applicable law. The judges were not entitled to nullify the proceedings *sua sponte* as they did, since no party had provided evidence of harm, which was an essential requirement in this case. There have been some similar cases in various matters.[22] But the Common Court of Justice and Arbitration (CCJA) has resolved this issue. Henceforth 'in the matter of real estate and in the context of Article 297 of the UAOSRPME there is no nullity without harm or tort'.[23]

---

[17] Tribunal de Première Instance de Gagnoa (Ivory Coast), n°8, 20 January 2000: *époux K. v. BICICI*, available at: www.ohada.com/jurisprudence/ohadata/J-02-102, note Joseph Issa-Sayegh.

[18] Tribunal de Première Instance de Douala Ndokoti (Cameroon), n° 23/com., 16 September 2004: *Sté KASA v. Ets Distribution Stores*, available at: www.ohada.com/jurisprudence/ohadata/J-05-144.

[19] Some use the expression 'attachment of real property'.

[20] Tribunal de Grande Instance du Mfoundi (Cameroon), n° 677, 25 September 2002: *YOUMBI Richard v. BICEC*, available at: www.ohada.com/jurisprudence/ohadata/J-04-211.

[21] Article 297 of the UAOSRPME.

[22] Tribunal Régional Hors Classe de Dakar (Senegal), 28 October 1998: *Abdoulaye Niang et Cheick Tidiane Niang v. Banque Islamique du Sénégal*, available at: www.ohada.com/jurisprudence/ohadata/J-03-351.

[23] Cour Commune de Justice et d'Arbitrage (CCJA), n° 25, 15 July 2004: *Dame M. v. SCB-CL*, available at: www.ohada.com/jurisprudence/ohadata/J-05-168.

B.   Other Challenges to the Uniform Acts

They relate to prevalence of the will of parties upon mandatory provisions and refusal to implement the Uniform Acts.

1.   Prevalence of the will of parties over mandatory provisions

The first example is about acceptance of a shorter term of notice for a commercial lease. The parties to a commercial lease can terminate it by giving notice. This requirement has been defined by the court of appeal of Niamey (in Niger) as 'a unilateral deed ending a lease without need to validate it; no formal procedure is needed as far as the deed clearly expresses the will to end the lease'.[24] The notice term for a commercial lease as laid down by the Uniform Act relating to general commercial law is six months.[25] Surprisingly the court of appeal of Niamey ruled in the same decision that 'a month term notice is valid even if it is shorter than the six-month legally required, as far as the parties made a mutual agreement which has not been terminated so far'.[26] That decision seems to infringe a mandatory rule by lowering the protection provided by Article 93 for the lessee.

There is an example of undue extension of the length of a preventive composition agreement. According to the Uniform Act organising collective proceedings for wiping off debts,

> the competent court shall ratify the preventive composition agreement where … the *deadlines given do not exceed three years* for all the creditors and one year for creditors due wages.[27]

But a court went beyond the allotted time, saying that Article 15 above mentioned is not mandatory; therefore the creditors could extend the deadline by mutual agreement and this preventive composition agreement which met the requirements could be ratified.[28] It is difficult to agree with this decision when it says that Article 15 above is not mandatory. In fact this Article highlights the need to protect creditor(s) particularly since it forbids creditors to discharge the

---

[24]   Cour d'Appel de Niamey (Niger), n° 57 réf., 4 June 2003: *S. B. v. E. H. M.*, available at: www.ohada.com/jurisprudence/ohadata/J-05-181, note Brou Kouakou Mathurin.

[25]   See the Uniform Act relating to general commercial law, Article 93.

[26]   Cour d'Appel de Niamey (Niger), n° 57 réf, 4 June 2003: *S. B. v. E. H. M.*, available at: www.ohada.com/jurisprudence/ohadata/J-05-181, note Brou Kouakou Mathurin.

[27]   Article 15 of the Uniform Act organising collective proceedings for wiping off debts. Our emphasis.

[28]   Tribunal Régional Hors Classe de Dakar (Senegal), n° 1466, 30 July 2001: *règlement préventif de la SNCDS*, available at: www.ohada.com/jurisprudence/ohadata/J-04-339.

debts.[29] Therefore this provision does not allow creditors to discharge debts at their disposal; and it is a confirmation of its mandatory nature.

2. Refusal to implement the uniform acts

There is another type of resistance of national courts to the OHADA: refusal to implement the Uniform Acts. There have been several cases where judges continued to settle disputes according to national laws instead of the Uniform Acts, at the very time that these should have been being used in specific cases relating to business. This situation is very important as it has been reported by several authors.[30] Some cases can illustrate this. More than five years after entry into force of the Uniform Act Organising Simplified Recovery Procedures and Measures of Execution, some courts continue to order a *saisie-arrêt des rémunerations* (attachment of earnings in civil law systems) instead of a *saisie-attribution* (garnishment) introduced by the Uniform Act.[31] There are other examples, such as founding a guarantee on Article 1626 of the Civil Code of Bukina Faso instead of Articles 202 to 288 of the Uniform Act relating to general commercial law;[32] use of *liquidation judiciaire* (official receivership) instead of *liquidation des biens* (liquidation of assets) as established by the Uniform Act organising collective proceedings for wiping off debts.[33] Paradoxically, as some judges refuse to implement the Uniform Acts, some other judges implement them beyond their time limit of application.[34]

---

[29] Ibid.

[30] See for example Mamadou, D, 'Les procédures simplifiées et les voies d'exécutions: la difficile gestation d'une législation communautaire', available at: www.ohada.com/doctrine/ohadata/D-05-10; Pascal, N K, 'Le domaine d'application du nouveau droit des sociétés commerciales de l'OHADA', available at: www.ohada.com/doctrine/ohadata/D-04-41.

[31] Tribunal de Première Instance de Bouaflé (Ivory Coast), n°14, 17 September 2003: *V. v. Sté DALI*, available at: www.ohada.com/jurisprudence/ohadata/J-04-394. Tribunal de Première Instance de Port-Gentil (Gabon), ordonnance de référé n°40/98–99, 10 October 1999: *Sté Gras-Savoye et Sté Foraid v. Izakino Augustin*, available at: www.ohada.com/jurisprudence/ohadata/J-02-150

[32] Tribunal de Grande Instance de Ouagadougou (Burkina Faso), 26 March 2003: *NJM v. RJF*, *Revue burkinabé de droit*, n° 43–44, 1 et 2ème semestres 2003, p. 149, note Pierre Meyer; available at: www.ohada.com/jurisprudence/ohadata/J-05-42.

[33] Tribunal de Grande Instance de Ouagadougou (Burkina Faso), n° 20, 29 January 2003: *Requête de IFEX aux fins d'être admise au bénéfice du règlement préventif*, available at: www.ohada.com/jurisprudence/ohadata/J-04-188. See also Cour d'Appel de Ouagadougou, n° 40, 14 September 1999: *SONAPHARM v. SOPAL*, available at: www.ohada.com/jurisprudence/ohadata/J-02-48; Cour d'Appel de Ouagadougou (Burkina Faso), Chambre civile et commerciale, n° 39, 5 April 2002: *SONABHY v. Liquidation judiciaire TAGUI*, available at: www.ohada.com/jurisprudence/ohadata/J-04-14.

[34] See Tribunal de Première Instance d'Abidjan, 1ere chambre civile, n°246, 13 December 2001: *Sté de Transport Burkina Faso – Côte d'Ivoire v. CFAO et CICA*

2. THE CHALLENGE OF THE CCJA'S AUTHORITY BY NATIONAL JUDGES

The authority of the Common Court of Justice and Arbitration is challenged by violation of its jurisdiction (section A below) and refusal to follow its rulings (section B below).

A.   Challenge of the CCJA's Jurisdiction

Normally all disputes arising in the matters covered by the Uniform Acts are settled by national jurisdictions only at first instance and by courts of appeal.[35] When it comes to decisions against which no appeal is possible or decisions of courts of appeal, only the CCJA has jurisdiction.[36] However some national supreme courts continue to settle many cases involving the Uniform Acts. Although most of the decisions we will present hereafter make a correct application of the Uniform Acts, they have not been made by the right court, which is the CCJA. Before presenting the future prospect of improvement (section 2 below), we will present some cases illustrating this tendency (section 1 below).

1.   The extent of the situation
Decisions presented hereafter are wrong, not necessarily because of their rulings, but because they have been made out of jurisdiction. Below are few examples.

Consequences of non-payment of an item sold: a national Supreme Court held that a commercial sale is governed not only by the Uniform Act relating to general commercial law, but by some other ordinary rules. Therefore the seizure under a prior claim by a seller of a movable the price of which has not been paid by the buyer must be carried out within eight days of delivery of the sold item if it is still in the same state as it was at the time of delivery. Seizure under a prior claim carried out after eight days is void and must be withdrawn.[37]

Auto, available at: www.ohada.com/jurisprudence/ohadata/J-02-116. In this decision, the judges applied the Uniform Act relating to General Commercial Law to a case started in 1995, although that Uniform Act entered into force (or was enforceable) only from 1998.

[35]   This is the regime set by the OHADA Treaty in its Article 13.

[36]   Ibid., Article 14-3 and 14-4 and Article 15.

[37]   Cour Suprême Abidjan (Ivory Coast), chambre judiciaire, n°57, 6 February 2003: *El Achkar Hadife Jean-Claude v. Abdallah Nawfla*, available at: www.ohada.com/jurisprudence/ohadata/J-03-233, note Joseph Issa Sayegh.

The effects of a termination clause in a commercial lease: it has been held that parties are bound by their agreements; therefore in presence of a termination clause for non-payment of rents giving jurisdiction to the emergency judge to terminate the lease and evict the lessee, such clause must be applied.[38]

The jurisdiction entitled to cancel a commercial lease: according to Article 101 of the Uniform Act relating to general commercial law, which is mandatory, the cancellation of a commercial lease must result from a judgment. And the emergency judge who issues interim orders does not have jurisdiction to terminate such lease.[39]

The Supreme Court of Ivory Coast had ruled on 4 July 2002 that it is not possible to appeal against a decision for sale by auction. In case of seizure of real estate, an appeal is possible only against decisions settling contested debts, incapacity of parties, property, and exemption from seizure or inalienability of real estate.[40] There have been some decisions in the field of commercial companies.[41] There are some prospects of improvement to this situation. First of all we may try to understand the causes of this situation. The explanation can be traced to the litigants themselves, and particularly to their counsel. Generally it is Counsel who act on behalf of litigants and represent them before courts. They are the main characters in litigation since, owing to their training and competences, they start actions and organise proceedings. Counsel know better than their clients which arguments to use and they choose to bring cases to a national Supreme Court instead of the CCJA. Therefore the first question to answer could be why in cases which come under the exclusive jurisdiction of the CCJA some litigants continue to take their final appeals before national High Courts. We have identified four possible hypotheses.

Would it be for practical reasons: the closeness of the national supreme judge in contrast with the CCJA which is quite far from some litigants? But this argument is not strong enough as the CCJA is in Abidjan (Ivory Coast) and most of the decisions violating the CCJA's jurisdiction have been made by the Supreme

---

[38] Cour Suprême, Abidjan, chambre judiciaire, n° 136, 15 March 2001: *Ali GAD-DAR v. Dame BOURICHIA Eliane Juliette*, available at: www.ohada.com/jurisprudence/ohadata/J-02-86. (Second decision).

[39] Cour Suprême, Abidjan, n° 209, 6 April 2000: Spromaci u. Able Frederic available at: www.ohada.com/jurisprudence/ohadata/J-02-86 (first case).

[40] Cour Suprême, Abidjan, chambre judiciaire, n° 116, 6 March 2003: *époux Diaby Niteh Mohamed v. CFAO-CI*, available at: www.ohada.com/jurisprudence/ohadata/J-03-232, note. Joseph Issa-Sayegh.

[41] Cour Suprême, Abidjan, chambre judiciaire, n° 570/02, 4 July 2002: *Wan Kul Lee v. Jeon Kuk Hyun*, available at: www.ohada.com/jurisprudence/ohadata/J-04-64. Cour Suprême, Abidjan, chambre judiciaire, n° 152/04, 11March 2004: *Adama Koita; Odie Mathieu v. Assane Thiam; SODEFOR*, available at: www.ohada.com/jurisprudence/ohadata/J-05-125, note Kassia Bi-Oula.

Court of Ivory Coast which is in the same town.[42] Would it be for economic reasons? Some authors deplored the high cost of the OHADA's justice for businesses not located in Abidjan;[43] but this assumption must also be set aside since bringing a case to the CCJA would be less expensive to a litigant based in Ivory Coast than to one in Congo for example. Would it be for sociological reasons (attachment of litigants to their own national legal system)?[44] Finally this phenomenon might be explained by a lack of diligence of some lawyers inattentive to the provisions of the OHADA treaty, as mentioned earlier.

The second possible question would be why national Supreme Courts do not decline their jurisdiction *sua sponte* in favour of the CCJA, since Article 15 of the treaty expressly allows cases relating to the Uniform Acts to be transferred to the CCJA by national Supreme Courts themselves. It might be appropriate to rewrite that Article of the treaty to make it an obligation for national Supreme Courts to decline their competence in favour of the CCJA when the conditions for this are met. Then there would not be any ambiguity regarding the CCJA's jurisdiction. In the meantime there is no need to overemphasise this situation as it is not dramatic and a solution is emerging from precedent.

2.   The emergence of a solution from precedent

There is a tendency among some national courts to disagree with or overrule decisions rendered made in violation of the CCJA's jurisdiction. For example the Court of Appeal of Abidjan held that only the CCJA has jurisdiction over matters governed by Uniform Acts according to Articles 2, 10 and 14 of the OHADA treaty. Therefore any attachment carried out on the basis of a decision made in violation of these Articles is void and can have no effect, even if the decision has been made by a national Supreme Court.[45] We note that this interesting decision has been made by an Ivorian court. The Supreme Court of Cameroon also ruled that appeals relating to the application of the Uniform Acts must be transferred to the CCJA. A national Supreme Court must decline its

---

[42]   Six of the seven decisions that we found to be violating the jurisdication of the CCJA were rendered by the Supreme Court of Ivory Coast. But we acknowledge that these data are based only on the decisions published on our main source of information (the OHADA website: www.ohada.com) on 31 December 2006; so there is a need to check the situation again in the near future.

[43]   René, F and Vicaire, O B (2006), 'Le droit de l'Ohada: un capital vital pour le redressement de l'économie africaine', in Gatsi, J (ed.), *L'effectivité du droit de l'Ohada*, Yaoundé, Presses Universitaires d'Afrique, at 59.

[44]   A sociological study could have been interesting on this subject but was not possible during our research.

[45]   Cour d'Appel d'Abidjan (Ivory Coast), Chambre civile et commerciale, n° 617, 8 June 2004: *CFAO v. Ouedraogo Broureima et autres*, available at: www.ohada.com/jurisprudence/ohadata/J-05-263.

jurisdiction in favour of the CCJA in such a case as provided by Article 15 of the treaty.[46] We can assume from this decision that the highest court of Cameroon has completely recognised the exclusive jurisdiction of the Common Court of Justice and Arbitration in the different areas of OHADA law.[47]

The position of the Supreme Court of Niger has been slightly different. The Court ruled about Article 18 of the treaty that the CCJA does not always have exclusive jurisdiction over national Supreme Courts, especially when the cases involved are subject to the application of both Uniform Acts and national laws. Moreover a national Supreme Court does not have to transfer to the CCJA cases which are mainly about national laws and to which Uniform Acts have little relevance.[48] But the position of the Supreme Court of Niger has changed; it seems to have accepted the exclusive jurisdiction of the CCJA too. Since 2006, it has transferred at least three cases to the CCJA, clearly declining its jurisdiction.[49]

There are some other cases of violation of jurisdiction which are not specific to the jurisdiction of the CCJA. For example a court ruled in an appropriation case instead of its president who alone had jurisdiction in that matter;[50] a *juge des référés* (judge with power to hear urgent applications) ruled in a case instead of the full court.[51]

---

[46] Cour Suprême du Cameroun, n° 189/CC, 15 May 2003: *Ansary Trading Company s/c Abba Lamine v. SCB-CL*, available at: www.ohada.com/jurisprudence/ohadata/J-05-23.

[47] No decision has been found proving the contrary of this; but it is possible that all decisions are not published.

[48] Cour Suprême du Niger, chambre judiciaire, n° 1-158/C, 16 August 2001: *SNAR-LEYMA v. Groupe Hima Souley*, available at: www.ohada.com/jurisprudence/ohadata/J-02-28. About this decision see Alassane, K, 'La détermination de la juridiction compétente pour statuer sur un pourvoi formé contre une décision rendue en dernier ressort en application des Actes Uniformes (observations sur l'arrêt de la Cour Suprême du Niger du 16 août 2001)', available at: www.ohada.com/doctrine/ohadata/D-02-29.

[49] Cour Suprême du Niger, n°06-159/C, 1-6-2006: *M.A. v. I.S.*, available at: http://juriniger.lexum.umontreal.ca/juriniger/publication.do?publicationId=25; Cour Suprême du Niger, n° 06-235/C, 5-10-2006: *S. I. v. CFAO-NIGER*, available at: http://juriniger.lexum.umontreal.ca/juriniger/publication.do?publicationId=30. Cour Suprême du Niger, n° 07-085/S, 5-04-2007: *ICRISAT v. M. M. & 21 autres*, available at: http://juriniger.lexum.umontreal.ca/juriniger/publication.do?publicationId=238.

[50] Cour d'Appel de Dakar (Senegal), 2ème chambre civile et commerciale, 4 January 2001: *Sté AFRICARS v. GIE AL ZAR et Mourtada CISSE*, available at: www.ohada.com/jurisprudence/ohadata/J-03-58, obs. Ndiaw Diouf.

[51] Cour d'Appel d'Abidjan (Ivory Coast), 1ère chambre civile et commerciale, arrêt de référé n° 452, 27 April 2001: *AXA-IARD v. Alain Guillemain et Jean-Luc Henri Ruelle*, available at: www.ohada.com/jurisprudence/ohadata/J-02-79.

B. Violation of the CCJA's Rulings by National Courts

In their implementation of the Uniform Acts some national lower courts tend to have dissenting opinions. But this situation is more serious than a simple dissent as in the common law system. In the civil law system on which the OHADA is mainly based, there is almost no place for dissenting opinions. Moreover the harmonisation expected with the creation of the OHADA would not make any sense if there was no unification of the rulings of courts of appeals by the CCJA. Although the dissenting decisions are not too many, it is worth analysing them to see whether they could present a hindrance to the harmonisation process set in motion. There are some decisions violating the CCJA's rulings in the field of garnishment and some in some other fields such as appeals.

1. Decisions in the field of garnishment
Three examples will be provided.

Omission of essential information in the petition: we said above that the lack of some essential information in a writ of garnishment should result in avoidance of the writ, according to Article 157 of the Uniform Act Organising Simplified Recovery Procedures and Measures of Execution. The CCJA upheld this position in an important decision made on 9 October 2003.[52] However an inferior court of Yaoundé (Cameroon) ruled in a decision on 1 July 2004 that the lack of the registered office in a writ of seizure-award could only result in nullity if evidence of harm has been provided by the demanding party.[53] The real question the judge should have asked is whether an error in the indication of the registered office (Douala instead of Yaoundé) could be assimilated to not indicating the registered office at all and result in the nullity of the writ as required by Article 157. The answer seems to be no, according to the CCJA.[54] But the court implies in its decision that it would have nullified the writ only if there had been harm, contrary to the ruling of the CCJA.

---

[52]   Cour Commune de Justice et d'Arbitrage, n° 17/2003, 9 October 2003: *SIB v. CIENA*, available at: www.ohada.com/jurisprudence/ohadata/J-04-120.

[53]   Tribunal de Première Instance de Yaoundé, Ordonnance n° 762/C, 1 July 2004: *Crédit Lyonnais Cameroun, Me Ndengue Kameni et Me Ngongo Ottou v. Sté BIOTECH srl, Me Ngongang Sime Alain, BEAC*, available at: www.ohada.com/jurisprudence/ohadata/J-04-421.

[54]   The CCJA ruled that an error in the writing of the name of a party caused him no harm justifying nullity of a writ of appeal; see Cour Commune de Justice et d'Arbitrage (CCJA), n° 8/2002, 21 March 2002: *Sté Palmafrique v. Etienne Konan Bally Kouakou*, Le Juris Ohada, n°4/2002, October – December 2002, p. 19 By analogy if indication of another town can be assimilated to a simple error of writing we assume it could not result in the nullity of the writ.

The term of notification of a garnishment: the CCJA ruled on 26 February 2004 that mention of the date on which the allotted term of one month expires and the court having jurisdiction are mandatory according to Article 160 of the Uniform Act Organising Simplified Recovery Procedures and Measures of Execution. Their omission must result in the nullity of the writ without need to provide evidence of harm. The court of appeal that stated otherwise without verification of their presence in the writ violated Article 160 and its decision must be overruled.[55] Despite the clear position of the CCJA, the *Tribunal de Grande Instance* (court of first instance in civil and criminal matters) of Bangangte (Cameroon) refused to penalize omission of the essential information without harm.[56] Similarly a court of appeal[57] refused to follow the ruling of the CCJA[58] in a similar matter.

The court of appeal of Libreville (Gabon) ruled that failure to summon a garnishee to the hearing of a dispute raised by a distrainee debtor invalidates the contesting of the garnishment. Therefore the first judges were right to cancel of the proceedings.[59] Less than one month before that decision the CCJA made it clear that Article 170 of the UAOSRPME allows nullification of the proceedings only in case of non-respect of the time allotted to bring the action before a court, not for failure to summon the garnishee.[60] Once again we are in the presence of a dissenting decision. But such decisions originate also from other areas.

The time limit for contesting attachment of earnings: in one of its decisions, the court of appeal of Abidjan ruled that there is no time limit set by the UA-OSRPME for contesting attachment of earnings; therefore one should refer to the national Civil Procedure Code of Ivory Coast to determine that time limit.[61]

---

[55]   CCJA, n° 08, 26 February 2004: *BCN v. Hamadi Ben Damma*, available at: www.ohada.com/jurisprudence/ohadata/J-04-293.

[56]   Tribunal de Première Instance de Bangangté (Cameroon), Ordonnance de référé n° 09/ORD, 8 April 2004: *Satellite Insurance Company SA v. Tchakoutio Jeannette, ayant droit de Feu Beteba Albert*, available at: www.ohada.com/jurisprudence/ohadata/J-05-165.

[57]   Cour d'Appel d'Abidjan, n° 374, 2 March 2004: *GANAMET Gabriel v. Emilio Christoyannis*, available at: www.ohada.com/jurisprudence/ohadata/J-04-498.

[58]   CCJA, n° 08, 26 February 2004: *BCN v. Hamadi Ben Damma*, available at: www.ohada.com/jurisprudence/ohadata/J-04-293.

[59]   Cour d'Appel de Libreville (Gabon), chambre civile et commerciale, arrêt de référé n°7/2001/2002, 6 February 2002: *Kamdje Elise v. Tchana Kweze*, available at: www.ohada.com/jurisprudence/ohadata/J-02-125.

[60]   Cour Commune de Justice et d'Arbitrage (CCJA), n° 3/2002, 10 January 2002: *SIEM v. Sté Atou et Bicici*, available at: www.ohada.com/jurisprudence/ohadata/J-02-25, note Joseph Issa-Sayegh.

[61]   Cour d'Appel d'Abidjan, n°731, 7 June 2002: *SOGEFIBAIL v. Demard Michel Georges Elie*, available at: www.ohada.com/jurisprudence/ohadata/J-03-13.

But there is a previous case in which the CCJA settled this question[62] and many other national courts have followed the same path.[63]

2.   Other decisions violating mandatory rules

In some specific cases some national courts apply general principles of law instead of mandatory provisions of Uniform Acts. On 18 March 2004, the CCJA held that the essential information required by Article 100 of the UAOSRPME must be fully written in any writ of seizure, otherwise the writ will be void with no necessity to prove financial loss. The judge must cancel all the proceedings when any of the required information is missing.[64] Notwithstanding this decision, the regional tribunal of Dakar (Senegal) considered that Article 297 of the UAOSRPME does not exclude application of the general principle of law according to which evidence of harm must be provided before lack of the missing information can be sanctioned by nullity.[65]

Future prospects seem interesting. In fact our research has shown that there are fewer courts of appeal violating the CCJA's rulings.[66] In the meantime a possible solution could be the institution of an electronic transmission system, or a simple telephone conference call just after the reading of each decision by the CCJA, followed by a fax transmission of the decision to all the courts of appeal and bar associations of the OHADA member states. A slight adjustment

---

[62]   Cour Commune de Justice et d'Arbitrage, n° 4/2002, 10 January 2002: *BOA v. BHCI*, available at: www.ohada.com/jurisprudence/ohadata/J-02-26, note Joseph Issa-Sayegh. CCJA, n° 12/2002, 18-4-2002, available at: www.ohada.com/jurisprudence/ohadata/J-02-65; the proceedings of seizure-award are governed by Article 49 of the UAOSRPME. See also CCJA, n° 4/2002, 10-1-2002, www.ohada.com, Ohadata J-02-26; CCJA, n° 13/2002, 18 April 2002, available at: www.ohada.com/jurisprudence/ohadata/J-02-66.

[63]   Cour d'Appel d'Abidjan (Ivory Coast), n° 89, 26 March 2002, available at: www.ohada.com/jurisprudence/ohadata/J-02-200; Cour d'Appel de Bouaké (Ivory Coast), n° 89, 13 June 2001, available at: www.ohada.com/jurisprudence/ohadata/J-02-2-139; Cour d'Appel de Libreville (Gabon), arrêt n° 7/2002 , 6 February 2002, available at: www.ohada.com/jurisprudence/ohadata/J-02-125; Tribunal Régional Hors Classe de Dakar (Senegal), judgment n° 333, 26 March 2002, available at: www.ohada.com/jurisprudence/ohadata/J-02-200; Tribunal Régional de Niamey (Niger), ordonnance de référé n° 67/2001, 10 April 2001, available at: www.ohada.com/jurisprudence/ohadata/J-02-124; Tribunal de Première Instance de Port-Gentil (Gabon), ordonnance de référé n° 15/2001, 28 December 2001, available at: www.ohada.com/jurisprudence/ohadata/J-02-124.

[64]   CCJA, n° 12, 18-3-2004: *BCN v. Hamadi Ben Damma*, note Brou Kouakou Mathurin; available at: www.ohada.com/jurisprudence/ohadata/J-04-297.

[65]   Tribunal Régional Hors Classe de Dakar (Senegal), Ordonnance de référé n° 924, 19 May 2004: *Sodima v. Ndiogou Seck*, available at: www.ohada.com/jurisprudence/ohadata/J-05-104.

[66]   See Kodo, J (2010) *L'application des Actes uniformes de l'OHADA*, Academia-Bruylant.

of the tasks of the registrar of the CCJA could be useful for this purpose. We could wish the suggestions above to be taken into account for the soon-to-be amendment of the OHADA treaty.

CONCLUSION

The resistance noted above can be explained by the novelty of OHADA, which is very young legislation and needs to be asserted from time to time in the near future. So far the CCJA has already done much to affirm its authority and unify case law. There is an ongoing revision of the treaty and the new draft takes into account the four languages spoken within the Member States of OHADA (French, English, Spanish and Portuguese); but some conceptual conflicts may rise in the future and require further consideration.

15. Achieving optimal use of harmonisation techniques in an increasingly interrelated twenty-first century world–consumer sales: moving the EU harmonisation process to a global plane

Louis F. Del Duca, Albert H. Kritzer and Daniel Nagel*

INTRODUCTION

There has been, and continues to be, robust and interesting scholarship generated in the last decade on the need, feasibility and content of a harmonised European Civil Code, the Common Frame of Reference 'tool box' approach, the harmonisation of European Contract law or the European Law of Obligations, and the decision of the Commission of the European Community to focus on harmonising the existing Acquis Communitaire of the already promulgated consumer protection directives has been well documented.[1]

---

* Louis F. Del Duca is Edward N. Polisher Distinguished Faculty Scholar, The Pennsylvania State University Dickinson School of Law. Albert H Kritzer (Deceased) was formerly Executive Secretary of the Institute of International Commercial Law of the Pace University School of Law, USA. Ph.D. candidate Daniel Nagel studied law at the University of Heidelberg and Leeds University. This chapter is based on a paper given at the 14th conference of the International Academy of Commercial and Consumer Law in Bamberg, 31 July to 2 August 2008, also published in the UCC Law Journal. Copyright 2008 Louis Del Duca, Albert Kritzer and Dan Nagel. Reprinted with permission.

[1] Michael Joachim Bonell, The CISG, European Contract Law and the Development of a World Contract Law, 56 Am. J. Comp. L. 1, 9–15 (2008), available at <http://cisgw3.law.pace.edu/cisg/biblio/bonell4.html>; Principles, Definitions and Model Rules of European Private Law, 1–40 (Study Group on European Civil Code and the Research Group on EC Private Law edited by Christian von Bar, Eric Clive and Hans Schulte-Nölke, Hugh Beale, Johnny Herre, Jérôme Huet, Peter Schlechtriem, Matthias Storme, Stephen

The paper entitled 'Developing Global Transnational Harmonization Procedures for the Twenty First Century – The Accelerating Pace of Common Law and Civil Law Convergence' presented at the 13th Biennial Conference of the International Academy of Commercial and Consumer Law, reviewed procedural options for addressing the new harmonisation challenges and opportunities which the twenty-first century presents.[2]

Noting the wide variation in consumer law in the domestic law of states around the world and the anticipated difficulties and probable inability to achieve broad based acceptance and enactment of any proposed harmonisation of consumer law, organizations like UNCITRAL and UNIDROIT explicitly exclude consumer transactions from the International Sale of Goods Convention and the Principles of International Commercial Contracts. Utilization of hard law harmonisation techniques (i.e., conventions, model laws, regulations or directives by the European Community) would therefore not be broadly accepted for enactment or implementation. Exploration of procedures and methods for utilizing soft law techniques to be voluntarily incorporated by the parties to business to consumer (B2C) contracts is an alternative method for offering a harmonised approach to interested parties. The comments which follow provide initial observations regarding use of this approach to achieve benefits for both consumer and business parties to consumer agreements.

I. THE STATUS OF E-COMMERCE AND CONSUMER SALES AT THE OUTSET OF THE TWENTY-FIRST CENTURY

- Just as the UNIDROIT Principles of International Commercial Contracts are a valued aid to the global harmonisation of commercial contract law, a comparable aid to the global harmonisation of consumer contract law can be beneficial.
- The elevation of the EU harmonisation process to the global arena:

  - takes advantage of the enriched frame of reference offered by the EU harmonisation process and related work underway elsewhere; and

---

Swann, Paul Varul, Anna Veneziano and Fryderyk Zoll ed., 2008); Jan M Smits, The Draft-Common Frame of Reference (CFR) for a European Private Law: Fit for Its Purpose? 15 Masst. J. Eur. & Comp. L. 145 (2008); see also Norbert Reich, 'Transnational Consumer Law – Reality or Fiction?, Draft of a paper presented at the 14th conference of the International Academy of Commercial and Consumer Law in Bamberg, 31.7–2.8.

[2] See http://tilj.org/journal/entry/42_625_del_duca/; 42 *Tex. Int'l L.J.* 625.

  – affords consumers and business groups in the world trade community the opportunity to interact in developing a fair, rational set of principles which parties are free to incorporate into their consumer agreements.
  – The emergence of the Internet provides a special incentive for such work; however, although the emphasis in this chapter is on the Internet and on international sales, it should be understood that the Global Principles of Consumer Contracts to be developed under this initiative are not to be limited to either Internet sales or international sales of consumer goods or services.

● It should also be understood that the principles under this initiative are to be fair and balanced and not one-sided in either direction: they are to be balanced principles, reflecting the needs of both business and consumers.

Five hundred years ago, Erasmus wrote *'Immortal God! What a century do I see beginning!'*[3] We who live at the dawn of the Information Age can also say *'What a century do we see beginning!'*.

The twenty-first century is the 'Age of the Internet'. The Internet has evolved from a medium only for scientists and scattered experts to a resource for all of us. In recent years, globalization and the growth of electronic networking have advanced at an incredibly fast pace. New companies are continually emerging and are already gaining prominence throughout the world. And e-commerce has now arrived in the homes of families all over the world.

As laptop users with Internet connections, we can replace tiresome shopping trips with enhanced experiences. A few clicks on a screen enable us to see more items than we have ever dreamed of, from clothing and iPods to tropical fruit and exceptional design. The Internet has brought these items only a mouse-click away from our cosy armchair. It is no wonder that this 'burgeoning area of commerce ... promises to be the most rapidly growing type of retail distribution for years to come'.[4]

Although e-commerce has had a wide-ranging influence on our lives, it has also been accompanied by drawbacks. Several stems are still lacking petals when it comes to cross-border consumer sales. Several factors explain this phenomenon:

---

[3]   Erasmus to Guillaume Budé (1517), cited in Barzun, J (2000), *From Dawn to Decadence: 1500 to the Present; 500 Years of Western Cultural Life* (Harper Collins Publishers), at 8.
[4]   Mann RJ and Siebeneicher, T (2008), 'Just One Click: The Reality of Internet Retail Contracting', 108 *Colum. L. Rev.* 984, at 1010–11.

1. Many consumers still consider the Internet a lawless frontier. Haunted by doubts, they can never be absolutely sure of the actual consequences of agreeing to online 'terms and conditions'.

    The price sounds good, but what happens if:

    – The arrangement of wine bottles I ordered arrives in pieces; or
    – The trousers do not match the colour that I saw on the screen; or
    – The label on the goods is a counterfeit; or
    – No goods were sent at all even though I paid for them?

    Where do I go for relief?

    – Which court will provide justice?
    – What law applies?
    – Would I be subject to any limitations of service, although I did not explicitly agree to them?
    – Would I have to spend more money on attorneys' fees than the actual value of my transaction to receive what had I hoped to buy?

2. It is also questionable whether there is a sufficient level of protection for the legitimate interests of businesses. Arguably, different legal systems have made great achievements in consumer and business protection. However, the benefits of these achievements are only guaranteed so long as the jurisdictional sphere covers the contract. The Internet does not stop at national borders. Legislation, unfortunately, does. For this reason, an international consumer legal regime is desirable.

3. Some truly great harmonisation steps have been taken in the field of international contracting, such as the CISG and the UNIDROIT Principles. Nevertheless, these regulations either do not apply to consumer contracts or apply only to a certain region or to certain transactions.[5]

There is a clear need for a regulatory scheme which can overcome these difficulties, help shield consumers from e-commerce predators,[6] and simultaneously help businesses boost e-commerce by enhancing consumer trust.[7]

---

[5] See, e.g.,The Principles of European Contract Law, Commission on European Contract Law, available at http://frontpage.cbs.dk/law/commission_on_european_contract_law/index.html (which have been drafted for consideration by the European Community. Although these principles have not been designed to apply globally, they have a broader scope than the CISG or UNIDROIT Principles. Like the US UCC, they apply to consumer sales as well as commercial sales).

[6] See Craigslist.com (2006), *Avoiding Scams and Fraud*, available at www.craigslist.org/about/scams.html (example of guidance offered on avoiding scams and frauds).

[7] See Brussels European Council (20 June 2008), 'Gap Between Domestic and Cross-Border E-Commerce Grows Wider, Says EU Report', Press Release IP/08/980, available at http://ec.europa.eu/consumers/strategy/docs/i08_980_en.pdf:

II. A SOFT LAW PROPOSAL FOR OPTIONAL GLOBAL USE

For commercial sales, two global aids serve the international community:

- The United Nations Convention on Contracts for the International Sale of Goods (CISG); and
- The UNIDROIT Principles of International Commercial Contracts.

The CISG is a treaty (*hard law*) that has been adopted by countries accounting for more than three-quarters of all world trade. The UNIDROIT work product is a set of principles (*soft law*), a 'Restatement' or model law that has proven to be of immense benefit.[8]

Neither global aid to consumer sales now exists.

- Although it would of course be helpful if an acceptable global Convention on Contracts for the International Sale of Goods to Consumers could be devised, that is not realistic at the present time.[9]

'EU Consumer Commissioner Meglena Kuneva today announced the results of a new EU wide survey on e-commerce and cross border trade. The figures show that even though e-commerce is taking off at national level, cross-border e-commerce is failing to keep pace. From 2006 to 2008, the share of all EU consumers that have bought at least one item over the internet has increased significantly (from 27% to 33%) whilst cross border e-commerce is stable (6% to 7%). The pattern is similar for those with internet access at home – 56% of consumers with internet at home have made a purchase (in any country including their own) by e-commerce compared to 50% in 2006, while only 13% (of those with internet access at home) made a cross-border e-commerce purchase compared to 12% in 2006. ['Data gathering was carried out in February–March 2008 amongst more than 26,000 consumers and 7,200 businesses in the 27 EU-countries and Norway.'] See 'Gap between domestic and cross-border E-commerce grows wider, says EU report', Press release IP/08/980, Brussels European Council (20 June 2008), available at http://ec.europa.eu/consumers/strategy/docs/i08_980_en.pdf.

This announcement further notes that these figures underline how much work is needed to boost confidence in the online internet market. It observes that consumers and retailers are beginning to embrace e-commerce at a national level but internal market barriers still persist online. The potential of the online internal market to deliver greater choice and lower price to consumers and new markets for retailers is considerable.

[8]   See sections on 'The UNIDROIT Principles as a Model for National and International Legislators', 'The Choice of the UNIDROIT Principles as the Law Governing the Contract', and 'The UNIDROIT Principles Applied in Dispute Resolution' in Bonell, J, *supra* n. 1.

[9]   See Schulte-Nölke (ed.) in cooperation with Twigg-Flesner and Ebers (2008), *The EC Consumer Law Compendium: Comparative Analysis*, available at http://ec.europa. eu/consumers/cons_int/safe_shop/acquis/comp_analysis_en.pdf (an 845 page report on

– However, a global soft law or set of principles *is* realistic and we should aim to set one in place. It would be a consumer counterpart to the UNIDROIT Principles of International Commercial Contracts.

Comparable to the case today with the UNIDROIT Principles, an appropriate set of Consumer Principles could serve the world trade community as follows:

– The Global Consumer Principles as a model for national and international legislators;
– The Choice of the Global Consumer Principles as the law governing the contract; and
– The Global Consumer Principles applied in dispute resolution.[10]

A shield can be a symbol of these Principles; consumershield.org is a website domain name that has been registered on the Internet for this purpose. The set of Principles, with its website, could be presented as a voluntary code[11] for consumer contracts for cross-border Internet sales. Such a set of soft law principles will contain provisions that are relevant to concluding contracts for the sale of goods and services from e-merchants to consumers. It will be a global tool to avoid and resolve disputes between the contracting parties.

The applicability of these soft law principles will depend solely on the intent of the parties. Participation would be completely voluntary and will be effected via an explicit opt-in. E-merchants interested in participating can apply for a registration, which could be awarded subject to requirements, such as posting a bond or providing a letter of credit from a reputable bank or a statement from a national registering authority. The register would be compiled, maintained and updated by consumershield.org. Upon successful registration, the programme will award a seal to e-merchants, which they can present on their homepages with a link to consumershield.org, thereby documenting their adherence to the relevant soft law principles.

Consumers who wish to buy goods from a registered e-merchant and participate will be able to choose the application of the soft-law code by opting in during their purchase.

---

challenges associated with efforts to devise a single, simple set of consumer contract laws for the European Community). See also Schulte-Nölke, Twigg-Flesner and Ebers (eds) (2008), *EC Consumer Law Compendium: The Consumer Acquis and its transposition in the Member States* (Sellier European Law Publishers).

[10] See *supra* n. 8 (reference to these applications of the UNIDROIT Principles of International Commercial Contracts).

[11] An example of the positive influence that voluntarism can exert can be found in the Sullivan Principles, the firms that have subscribed to them, and the impact they have had. See www.thesullivanfoundation.org/gsp/about/governance/default.asp.

There can be a grievance procedure to enable consumers to comment on e-merchants and transactions.[12] This feedback would be reviewed by consumershield.org, translated into statistics and made readily accessible on the Internet to any consumer interested in doing business with a registered e-merchant.[13]

III.   BENEFITS

The general benefits of such a programme are obvious:

1. The global soft-law code would be easily accessible; it would be available to e-merchants and consumers on a public site.
2. The legal provisions would be available in different languages so that users of many countries can access them. The intent is to draft them carefully so they will be easily understood.
3. Consumer participation would be free of charge and thus affordable for consumers around the world.
4. The approach is simple and quick because no lengthy discussions or ratification processes will be necessary.
5. The programme would encourage mediation, which represents a potential way to resolve disputes that is usually cheaper than court proceedings.
6. The approach mirrors the idea of contractual freedom because the parties voluntarily agree to have it govern their contractual relationship.

Furthermore, there are several specific advantages to both the consumer and the e-merchant.

Advantages for the E-Merchant

The added demonstration of credibility should help e-merchants attract consumers from all over the world.[14] The e-merchant will also benefit from protective features applicable to his goods, services and transactions.

---

[12]   See the information presented at www.rocketlawyer.com/documents/legal-form-Complaint+Letter+to+a+BBB+or+attorney+General.aspx?partner=111&HelpTopic=BBB+Info for a report on an effective complaint mechanism involving the Better Business Bureau, that has been set in place in the United States and Canada. For other approaches recommended see the EBay report on 'What steps can I take to protect when purchasing items on EBay' and the PayPal recommendation recited at http://pages.ebay.com/help/tp/questions/avoid-fraud.html and http://pages.ebay.com/help/tp/isgw-buyer-protection-steps.html.

[13]   See the procedure along these lines offered by EBay, *supra* n. 12.

[14]   To be noted is the fact that the programme may not be as important to the large firm with an established world-world reputation. However, for other firms – businesses

Advantages for Consumers

1. Consumers, on the other hand, would not face legal insecurity with respect to hidden terms that contradict the principles recited in the programme because they would be shielded from such terms.
2. The shield would provide a powerful additional resource for consumers, namely, the complaint mechanism.[15]
3. Consumers would have more confidence in purchasing goods that meet their special needs but are not regularly sold without having to pay for intermediaries.[16]
4. Finally, transactions would be conducted on a more level playing field because purchases would be subject to more evenly balanced contract terms rather than pre-drafted, one-sided terms.

IV.   ANTICIPATING DIFFICULTIES

1. The Consumershield approach will, of course, face some criticism. Its first deficiency is that it is *only* soft law. The main point here is that it is simply impossible to regulate every matter with hard law.[17] A prominent example

---

that can offer much value to consumers – a suitable programme can be of considerable interest. Moreover, larger firms would also benefit from added protections offered against counterfeits of their products.

[15]   See *supra* n. 12 for description of such a complaint mechanism.

[16]   An added step to bolster consumer confidence in the integrity of businesses displaying the Consumershield that might be considered could be to require a satisfactory independent evaluation report prior to granting the business the authorization to display the shield. For examples of such evaluations see the reports provided pursuant to the International Company Profile service of the US Department of Commerce. The US Commerce Department profile reports provide considerable data on the business and include an assessment of the business' reputation. For a fee, the Consumershield Programme could obtain profile reports of this nature from independent evaluation firms retained for this purpose. A global contract would reduce the costs of the reports. Businesses that wish to include the Consumershield logo in their advertisements would pay a fee for this privilege. The fees would defray the costs of the evaluation reports.

[17]   Soft law offers the following advantages over hard law. Comparing a soft law such as Incoterms or the UNIDROIT Principles with a hard law such as the CISG:

- After a hard law has been enacted, if one sees a cavity, how can it be filled? How do you rectify other errors that you may detect? Or implement improvements that you want to make? – improvements that you did not previously consider, perhaps could not have previously considered.
- As of July 2008, the CISG has been enacted by 71 separate national legislatures. Needs such as the above can be satisfied for this hard law either by national

is the Internet: no state or legal entity has succeeded so far in effectively regulating Internet activities. In addition, the approach is applicable internationally, whereas the political borders of a particular state that passes hard law also restrict it.

2.   People may also question the authority of the programme because it lacks the official approval of state authorities. Nevertheless, a uniform global law of consumer sales is not realistic at the present time. The Principles approach is much more flexible and universal so long as the interests of the parties, rather than national interests, give it life.[18]

3.   Furthermore, doubt may be cast upon the necessity of such an approach because international choice-of-law rules or conflict-of-law rules already exist. Such rules, however, do not guarantee a result that is foreseeable, as a court might have to interpret an unfamiliar foreign provision, or, as Cardozo said, these rules are 'more remorseless, more blind to the final cause than in other fields'.

4.   Finally, the approach's opponents might see it as a blunt tool because enforcing one's legal remedies might result in difficulties. Arguably, an approach that is based on the voluntary opt-in of parties depends to a large extent on their integrity and honesty. Trusting someone across the ocean from you is less promising. Cross-border enforcement always presents difficulties irrespective of the legal background on which it is based. In addition, a soft-law scheme has the characteristic feature of firing rifle shots and not shotgun blasts, simply because in the latter case nobody would opt in.

---

re-enactments or by accommodating interpretations (or re-interpretations) of its terms, neither of which provides a simple solution. It is, however, much easier to devise soft law solutions. Take, for example, the realization some years ago of the growing importance of containerization. It was much easier for the ICC to implement an appropriate soft law accommodation. The ICC simply issued a new set of Incoterms that took proper cognizance of this development.

For related comments see Abbot, KW and Snidal, D (2000), 'Hard Law and Soft Law in International Governance', 54 *Int'l Org.* 421 and Gopalan, S (2008), 'A demandeur-centric approach to regime design in transnational commercial law', 39 *Georgia J. Int'l L.* 327. Devising the proper Consumer Sales Code for global use presents many challenges. Commencing on a soft law basis is the primary recommendation of this presentation. This permits us to take advantage of current wisdom in the field (wisdom coming out of Europe and elsewhere) and gives us the opportunity readily to adjust the principles we set forth to take advantage of future wisdom as it emerges.

[18]   Moreover, where contracting parties adopt the Principles, state-backed enforcement mechanisms are available – to the extent that the principle of freedom of contract is an integral part of the applicable governing law.

In conclusion, even though the Consumershield approach would not offer perfect solutions, in many cases it can surely provide better ones.[19] As we saw with the UNIDROIT Principles, the global soft law for international commercial sales transactions, the future of which some doubted at the outset, has become a universally acclaimed success.[20]

V. A CAVEAT

Subject to one exception, none of the Consumershield proposals presented in this chapter should be regarded as final-final.

– The exception is recognition of the desirability of a global set of Principles for Consumer Sales Contracts, a counterpart to the UNIDROIT Principles of International Commercial Contracts.

---

[19]   See, e.g., Carvajal DC (2008), 'EBay Ordered to Pay 61 Million Euro in Sale of Counterfeit Goods', *NY Times*, 1 July 2008, available at www.nytimes.com/2008/07/01/technology/01ebay.html?_r=1&sq=ebay&st=nyt&oref=slogin (a report that highlights a scam that led to a huge judgment against EBay. The scam was the sale of counterfeit Luis Vuitton bags and Dior perfumes by businesses utilizing EBay.) The Consumershield programme could not prevent scams such as this; however, it can shorten their duration. As currently visualized, e-commerce purchasers who click the Consumershield emblem presented on the homepage of participating businesses would obtain the following types of information:

– The consumershield.org Consumer contract provisions to which each participating business has agreed to abide;
– Information on how long the business has been a consumershield.org participant; and
– A report on unresolved complaints. See *supra* n. 12 for data on a manner in which complaint mechanisms have been applied. Use of the Internet would help assure timely and current information on this subject.

Where there is a procedure such as this and a scam of the type reported in the *New York Times*, consumers aware of the misrepresentation would have an opportunity to report it immediately to the programme administrator. The business would be requested to respond. If the consumer's report is determined to be valid; notice to that effect could be posted; the business could be de-registered from the programme, and, if a bond had been required to participate in the programme, the bond could be forfeited.
The amount that owners of brands lose due to counterfeit goods is enormous. It may be that, because a properly devised Consumershield programme can be a helpful response to such scams, owners of vulnerable brand names could be looked to for donations of funds to cover expenses associated with the meetings of the Working Groups referred to in Phase Three of the Action Plan described below. To achieve balance business representatives as well as consumer representatives will participate on the Working Groups formulating the specifics of the Consumershield programme.
[20]   See *supra* n. 8 for comments on the benefits being derived from these Principles.

- Development of such a set of Principles should be resolved as a move-
forward objective. All other observations and proposals presented in this
chapter should be regarded as tentative and subject to further refinement.[21]

---

[21] A possible Action Plan follows. It is patterned after the development of the CISG.
The Working Groups that helped develop that Convention commenced with texts that
were primarily European accomplishments: the 1964 Hague Formation and Sales Conventions. After much deliberation over the course of many meetings, they devised the
refinements that, in their judgement, were best suited to the global audience they served.
The Consumershield Working Groups will have an opportunity to proceed in a similar
manner. The Consumershield Working Groups can build upon the harmonisation work
underway in the European Community.
    There are many aspects to the harmonisation work underway in the European Commu-
nity. In addition to the Principles of European Contract Law (PECL), Chapter 2 of which
on Obligations of the Seller is very relevant, Viola Heutger classifies some of the related
European aproaches to harmonising private law into three channels: the Accademia dei
Giusprivatisti Europei, the Acquis Group, and the Study Group on a European Civil
Code. She introduces her helpful elaboration on these activities with the statement that:

> [The Accademia] concentrates on an already existing codification and aims to create a
> whole civil code. [The Acquis Group] deduces some principles for European use from
> the already existing acquis communautaire. [The Study Group] is drafting principles
> on various fields of law on the basis of national legislation, the acquis communautaire
> and international instruments and will later combine these principles in a Civil Code.
> All three groups consist of international scholars and are all busy drafting principles
> on European Sales Law, as well as other parts of contract and patrimonial law.
>
> All of these academic groups have specific ideas on how their own results will
> later be used on a European level. The principles seek to serve different purposes. On
> the one hand, they will be an academic answer to the ongoing process relating to the
> EU-wide harmonization of contract law and will therefore offer their own dogmatic
> system. On the other hand, they could also be a model law for further comparative and
> legislative activities within European contract law. The principles may offer a solid
> basis for a common frame of reference as requested in the Commission's Action Plan
> on a more coherent European Contract Law. The Principles may serve as an optional
> instrument in cross-border transactions, allowing the parties simply to refer to this
> instrument as the applicable law. In addition, the principles may provide a solution
> when it proves impossible to establish the relevant rules of the applicable law. Like
> the PECL and the UNIDROIT Principles, the principles may be used to interpret or
> supplement international or European uniform law instruments and customs.

Heutger, V (2004), 'Do We Need a European Sales Law?', 4 *Global Jurist Topics* 2,
Article 1 (citations omitted), available at www.bepress.com/gj/topics/vol4/iss2/art1.
    All of this is relevant to and should be considered by those who wish to look at the
subject on a broader global plane. The subjects Europe is focusing on merit consideration not only for that region, but also for markets of Asia, the Americas, Africa, the
Middle East and Oceana. That is the primary thesis of this chapter: these subjects merit
examination on a global plane.

VI. AN ACTION PLAN

Speaking in the context of the European Union, EU Consumer Commissioner Meglena Kuneva has said:

> In the world we live in, we are not obliged to shop in the supermarkets and stores of our postal codes. We are not constrained to buy in our municipalities. We should also not be forced to shop within our national borders. ... [T]here is no place ... for artificial geographical restrictions which hold consumers back within national borders.[22]

While these comments are on target, they have a broader application than the European Union. We need a *global* set of Principles that takes cognizance of the fine work underway in Europe and also underway elsewhere.[23] The global set of Principles would be designed to benefit consumers and businesses of all countries.

We submit a four-phase action plan for the development and oversight of the requisite Principles and aid to consumers and businesses.

Phase One: A Preliminary Articulation of Goals and Objectives

This chapter has been prepared as a Phase One response.

Phase Two: The Refinement of these Goals and Objectives

- A Dialogue Planning Group has been set in place to refine the goals and objectives of this endeavour and review the Business Plan requisite to accomplishing them. The dialogues will be online and in print. The current participants in the Dialogue Planning Group are the following members of the International Academy of Commercial and Consumer Law: Yesimar Atamer, Immaculada Barral Viñals, Michael Joachim Bonell, Neil Cohen, Ross Cranston, Louis F. Del Duca, Mary Hiscock, Eva-Maria Kieninger, Donald B. King, Albert H. Kritzer, Hans Micklitz, Norbert

---

[22]   See 'Consumers: Commission sets out 5 priorities for consumer policy in a digital age', Press Release IP08/979, Brussels European Council (20 June 2008), available at http://europa.eu/rapid/pressReleasesAction.do?reference=IP/08/979&format=HTML& aged=0&language=EN.

[23]   See, e.g., the Principles of the Law of Software Contracts submitted for discussion at the Eighty-Fifth Annual Meeting of the American Law Institute on 19, 20, and 21 May 2008. See also the activities of the International Consumer Protection and Enforcement Network. Information on this network is available at www.icpen.org. See their list of other organizations concerned with consumer issues or e-commerce, available at www. icpen.org/related.htm.

Reich, Alex Schuster, Takis Tridimas, Kazuaki Sono, and Jay Westbrook They are being joined by Margaret F. Moses, Dean for Faculty Research and Development at Loyola University, Chicago. The Secretary *pro tem* of the Dialogue Planning Group is Daniel Nagel of Heidelberg University, Daniel.N@gmx.ch.

A Consumershield blog will be set in place to facilitate the further sharing of insights – on a global basis. In addition, the Internet website on uniform and harmonised international law of the Pace University School of Law, http:// cisgw3.law.pace.edu, and the popular *Lex mercatoria* site http://lexmercatoria. net[24] can serve as platforms for sharing information on the programme. A promotion of this initiative on the Pace site and on the *Lex mercatoria* site can bring the Consumershield programme to the attention of an enormous global audience.[25]

---

[24]   A 13 July 2008 entry of 'International Commercial Law' on a Yahoo search form lists the Pace site First, the *Lex mercatoria* site second and the Pace site third out of 444 million sites listed under this subject heading, A similar entry on a Google search form lists the Pace site first and second and the *Lex mercatoria* site fourth out of 17.8 million sites listed under this subject heading. The third most prominent source for Internet searches, Microsoft's MSN, lists the Pace site second, third and sixth and the *Lex mercatoria* site seventh and eighth out of 77.5 million sites listed there under this heading.

[25]   During the first six months of 2008, the Pace site received 10 million Internet 'hits', an average of over 50,000 per day. The 'hits' have come from the following jurisdictions: Albania, Algeria, Andorra, Angola, Anguilla, Antigua & Barbuda, Argentina, Armenia, Aruba, Australia, Austria, Azerbaidjan, Bahamas, Bahrain, Bangladesh, Barbados, Belarus, Belgium, Bermuda, Bhutan, Bolivia, Bosnia-Herzgovina, Brazil, Brunei, Bulgaria, Burkina Faso, Cambodia, Cameroon, Canada, Chile, China, Colombia, Cook Islands, Costa Rica, Croatia, Cuba, Cyprus, Czech Republic, Denmark, Dominica, Dominican Republic, Ecuador, Egypt, El Salvador, Estonia, Ethiopia, Faroe Islands, Finland, France, Fiji, Gabon, Gambia, Georgia, Germany, Ghana, Gibraltar, Greece, Greenland, Guatemala, Guinea, Guinea Bissau, Honduras, Hong Kong, Hungary, Iceland, India, Indonesia, Iran, Ireland, Israel, Italy, Jamaica, Japan, Jordan, Kazakhstan, Kenya, Republic of Korea, Kuwait, Kyrgyzstan, Laos, Latvia, Lebanon, Lesotho, Libya, Liechtenstein, Lithuania, Luxembourg, Macau, Macedonia, Maldives, Malaysia, Mali, Malta, Mauritius, Mexico, Micronesia, Moldova, Monaco, Mongolia, Morocco, Mozambique, Myanmar, Namibia, Nepal, Netherlands, Netherlands Antilles, New Caledonia, New Zealand, Nicaragua, Niger, Nigeria, Norway, Palestine Territories, Panama, Papua New Guinea, Paraguay, Peru, Philippines, Poland, Polynesia, Portugal, Qatar, Romania, Russian Federation, St Kitts-Nevis, Saint Lucia, San Tome and Principe, Saudi Arabia, Senegal, Singapore, Slovak Republic, Slovenia, Solomon Islands, South Africa, Spain, Sri Lanka, Sudan, Sweden, Switzerland, Syria, Taiwan, Tanzania, Thailand, Togo, Trinidad and Tobago, Tunisia, Turkmenistan, Turkey, Turks and Caicos Islands, Uganda, Ukraine, United Arab Emirates, United Kingdom, United States, Uruguay, Uzbekistan, Vanuatu, Venezuela, Viet Nam, Yugoslavia, Zambia and Zimbabwe.

An extremely high rate of usage can also be reported for the *Lex mercatoria* site.

Phase Three can begin when the goals and objectives of the endeavour have been sufficiently developed.

Phase Three: Formation of Working Groups to Promulgate the Principles and Methodology to be Followed in the Design of Related Aids to Consumers and Business

We seek to develop global principles. Representation on the Working Groups should therefore be global. We also seek balanced principles. The Working Groups should therefore represent business interests as well as consumer interests.

The activities of the Working Groups could be sponsored by an academy, an institution accustomed to managing such work, or a consortium of universities dedicated to the advancement of world trade on a fair and equitable basis.

Phase Four: Formation of an Oversight Committee

Following approval of the Working Groups' recommendations, an Oversight Committee should be created. Incoterms work well – extremely well – and remain current, among other reasons because they are revisited on a decennial basis. Once adopted, the Consumershield Principles should also be revisited on an appropriate cycle.

VII. CONCLUSION

Moving the EU Consumer Law harmonisation process to a global plane makes sense:

- A suitable Consumershield programme can safeguard consumers' and merchants' interests;
- The dialogues associated with the process can enhance domestic and global relations.

The time to begin working on the process is now.

16. The meaning of harmonisation in the context of European Union law – a process in need of definition

Eva J. Lohse*

Harmonisation of laws is a multifaceted development. We are yet to comprehend the many processes and implications involved in harmonising law. Any account of harmonising processes depends on what is understood by 'harmonisation' or by 'approximation', a term which is often used synonymously to refer to the abolition of different legal rules within a given entity[1] (section A). This chapter will not tackle the issues why or how to harmonise. It will focus on defining the process of harmonisation by elaborating cornerstones of a definition of harmonisation in the context of European former Community law.[2]

The term 'harmonisation' is, however, restricted neither to the context of the European Union (EU),[3] nor to legal contexts, but is commonly used in order

---

* University of Erlangen-Nürnberg, Germany.
[1] This synonymous use will be elaborated further in section A below. See also Eiden, C (1984), *Die Rechtsangleichung gemäß Art. 100 des EWG-Vertrages* (Duncker & Humblot) at 15; Hallstein, W (1964), 'Angleichung des Privat- und Prozessrechts in der Europäischen Wirtschaftsgemeinschaft', 28 *RabelsZ* 211 at 217 and Ihns, A (2005), *Entwicklung und Grundlagen der europäischen Rechtsangleichung* (Heymans) at 15.
[2] This chapter refers mainly to the situation under the former 'First Pillar', i.e. the core of the European Union (EU). It is still a moot point whether there is harmonisation in the areas covered by the Treaty on the European Union (EU), particularly by framework decisions, although some of the recent case law of the European Court of Justice (ECJ) hints at that. See Case C–176/03 *Commission v. Council* [2005] ECR I–7879; Case C–440/05 *Commission v. Council* [2007] ECR I–9097. Generally see Craig, P and de Búrca, G (2008), *EU Law* (4th edn, OUP) at 238–9; Curtin, D and Dekker, I (2002), 'The Constitutional Structure of the European Union: Some Reflections on Vertical Unity-in-Diversity' in Beaumont, P, Lyons, C and Walker, N (eds), *Convergence and Divergence in European Public Law* (Hart Publishing) 59 at 72–4; Calliess, C (2008), 'Auf dem Weg zu einem einheitlichen europäischen Strafrecht? – Kompetenzgrundlagen und Kompetenzgrenzen einer dynamischen Entwicklung', *Zeitschrift für Europäisches Strafrecht* 3.
[3] David, R (1982), 'L'avenir des droits européens: unification ou harmonisation' in David, R (ed.), *Le Droit Comparé* (Economica) 295, at 298–9 names e.g. the United

to refer to a process of 'combination or adaptation of parts, elements or related things, so as to form a consistent and orderly whole', presupposing 'the diversity of the objects harmonized'.[4] It is not a very precise concept, entailing an array of terms and definitions,[5] and it remains to be seen whether the above definition suits the specific setting of the EU.

Harmonisation within the European Communities (EC) has been subject to alternating policies and approaches over the last 50 years (section B). Nonetheless, there is no clear idea of what harmonisation means. A lack of methodology has been noted.[6] Many actors participate in the development of EU law. They use the term 'harmonisation' in regard to this process and their contribution, but do not offer a concise definition. This is problematic because there are other processes that are comparable in some aspects, but significantly different in others. If harmonisation is not clearly differentiated from those processes, there is an acute danger of talking at cross purposes. Terms used include 'unification', referring to the creation of identical legal rules, and 'convergence', 'Europeanisation', 'cross-fertilisation' or 'spill-over', referring to the mutual influence between legal systems within Europe.[7] A classification and differentiation of those terms can contribute to a better understanding and a definition of harmonisation. It will also become clear that some of them, in the context of EU law, merely refer to aspects of harmonisation, whereas others have a different quality. This is why we will scrutinise each of the terms individually.

Imprecise terminology is interlinked with vague ideas about the substance of the process. Due to this lack of definition, the description of legal and

States of America or the Commonwealth; for the context of conflicts of law see Aubin, BCH (1955), 'Europäisches Einheitsrecht oder intereuropäische Rechtsharmonie? Grundfragen einer europäischen Zusammenarbeit im Privatrecht' in Zweigert, K (ed.), *Europäische Zusammenarbeit im Rechtswesen* (Mohr) 45 at 48–55.

4   Boodman, M (1991), 'The Myth of Harmonization of Laws', 39 *American Journal of Comparative Law* 699 at 700–701.

5   Ibid., at 705–7. See also Jeammaud, A (1998) ,'Unification, uniformisation, harmonisation: de quoi s'agit-il?' in Osman, F (ed.), *Vers un code européen de la consommation/ Towards a European consumer code* (Bruylant) 35 at 43: 'la réalisation, dans le respect de la pluralité des droits étatiques, d'une équivalence des règles nationales' ('the realisation of an equivalences of national norms while respecting the plurality of domestic law').

6   Fischer, N (2003), '"Rechts-Harmonisierung" – Schlagwort oder Rechtsprinzip? – Kritische Anmerkungen zum Prozess der "Rechts-Angleichung"', 10 *Verbraucher und Recht* 374.

7   For the latter terms see also Birkinshaw, P (2003), *European Public Law* (Butterworths) at 7–8; Bell, J (1998), 'Mechanisms for Cross-fertilisation of Administrative Law in Europe' in Beatson, J and Tridimas, T (eds), *New Directions in European Public Law* (Hart Publishing) 147 at 147; and Wahl, R (1999), 'Die zweite Phase des öffentlichen Rechts in Deutschland – Die Europäisierung des Öffentlichen Rechts', 38 *Der Staat* 495 at 495–6.

judicial instruments of harmonisation and their effects can easily be mistaken for attempts to define the overarching process. Equally, critical accounts of the objectives of harmonisation and alternative ways to reach them are used as a definition. It will be shown that instruments, effects and objectives should be seen as inductive (instruments and effects) or deductive (objectives) means contributing to a definition (section C).

A definition cannot be drawn out of nothing but must be based on characteristics that can be distilled from various sources in order to approach what might be a working definition of harmonisation in the EU context (section D).

A. WORDS, WORDS, WORDS – A BABYLONIAN CONFUSION OF TERMS

Searching for a definition, the wording of the official legal documents of the EU springs to mind. One is soon let down, however, by the confusing use of terms in these legal documents. In the English version of the Treaty on the Functioning of the European Union (TFEU), for example, different terms such as 'approximation' (Articles 114, 115 TFEU), 'coordination' (Articles 50(2) (g), 52(2), 53(2) TFEU), or 'harmonisation' (Articles 113 and 191(2) EU), are applied without clear distinction or definition,[8] each of them to refer to what can roughly be described as the process of creating similar legal rules in fields considered crucial for the functioning of the internal market.[9] A comparison of the 23 language versions does not add to a more precise idea, as the terms are used inconsistently in each version and are also translated inconsistently in the official versions of the TFEU.[10] The interpretative problems created thereby have not improved since 1959.[11] Whereas in the early days of the European Economic Community (EEC) there was a constant effort to find ways of differentiating between the aforementioned terms by comparing the then only four language

---

[8] For a (non-exhaustive) list of terms used see Merryman, J (1978), 'On the Convergence (and Divergence) of the Civil Law and the Common Law' in Cappelletti, M (ed.), *New Perspectives for a Common Law of Europe/ Nouvelles Perspectives d'un Droit Commun de l'Europe* (Badia Fiesola) at 197; Lochner, N (1962), 'Was bedeuten die Begriffe Harmonisierung, Koordinierung und gemeinsame Politik in den Europäischen Verträgen?', 118 *Zeitschrift für die gesamte Staatswissenschaft* 35.

[9] See for example Craig, P and de Búrca, G (2008), *EU Law* (4th edn, OUP) at 1170.

[10] This means that approximation is not always translated by '*Rechtsangleichung*', but may also be translated by '*Harmonisierung*'.

[11] Polach, JG (1966), 'Harmonization of Laws in Western Europe' in Yntema, HE (ed.), *The American Journal of Comparative Law Reader* (Oceana Publications) 433 at 436–8.

versions,[12] it was soon realised that this endeavour would not be successful. As neither the use in positive law[13] nor that in the practice of the EU organs[14] is consistent, a literal interpretation does not lead anywhere. In practice, not even gradual differences can be clearly attributed to the different wordings, although this seems theoretically possible based on the very meaning of the words.[15]

As a result, it is common understanding today that the terms are mutually replaceable synonyms.[16] What should be kept in mind from this obsolete debate is that a definition of 'harmonisation' in the EU context is deemed to fail if the definition is based on literal meanings in one language. Therefore, criteria for a definition must be drawn elsewhere the most conceivable and promising categories being function, process and result.

B. THE DEVELOPMENT OF EUROPEAN HARMONISATION – HARMONISING FOR A COMMON MARKET?

In order to set the basis to elaborate on those categories an overview of some specific structural characteristics and developments of harmonisation in the EU context will be provided.

---

[12]   Dutch, French, German, and Italian. Cf Lochner, N (1962), 'Was bedeuten die Begriffe Harmonisierung, Koordinierung und gemeinsame Politik in den Europäischen Verträgen?', 118 *Zeitschrift für die gesamte Staatswissenschaft* 35.

[13]   Cf ibid., at 39 et seq.; Seidl-Hohenveldern, I (1971), 'Rechtsakte der Organe der EWG als Mittel der Angleichung', 11 *Kölner Schriften zum Europarecht* 170 at 170 giving further references; Schmeder, W (1978), *Die Rechtsangleichung als Integrationsmittel der Europäischen Gemeinschaft* (Heymann) at 5; Osman, F (1998), 'Codification, unification, harmonisation du droit en Europe: un rêve en passe de devenir réalité?' in Osman, F (ed.), *Vers un code européen de la consommation/ Towards a European consumer code* (Bruylant) at 15.

[14]   Cf Opinion of AG Stix-Hackl in Case C–436/03 *European Parliament v. Council* [2006], ECR I–03733, paras 41 and 71: 'Harmonisierung in Sinne von Rechtsangleichung' '[e.g. harmonisation in the sense of reducing disparities; l'harmonisation au sens de rapprochement des législations; la armonización en el sentido de aproximación; harmonisatie in de zin van onderlinge aanpassing; en åtskillnad i harmoniseringen mellan ett tillnärmande; harmonizáciou v zmysle aproximácie právnych ...]'. Likewise Case C–217/04 *ENISA* [2006], ECR I–03771, paras 11, 15: 'Harmonisierungsmaßnahme im Sinne von Art. 95 EG' ['harmonising measures in the sense of Art 95 EC']. Likewise Commission of the European Communities, *White Paper on the Completion of the Internal Market*, COM(85)310 final at 17.

[15]   Attempts to do so can be found at Lochner, N (1962), 'Was bedeuten die Begriffe Harmonisierung, Koordinierung und gemeinsame Politik in den Europäischen Verträgen?', 118 *Zeitschrift für die gesamte Staatswissenschaft* 35 at 48 et seq.

[16]   Bock, Y (2005), *Rechtsangleichung und Regulierung im Binnenmarkt – Zum Umfang der allgemeinen Binnenmarktkompetenz* (Nomos) at 53.

Particular Setting of the EU Legal Order

There have been attempts to harmonise law by international instruments before.[17] However, harmonisation in the context of the EU is different. It is a distinguishing feature about the EU legal order that harmonisation happens within a unique institutional framework, where institutions, entitled by the 'signatories' to enact unifying law, issue harmonising measures independently from the 'signatories'. This means that primary and secondary Union law does not have to rely on the transposition and agreement of signatory states but is binding for the Member States without further action. It can even directly transfer rights to the citizens, be it due to directly applicable Treaty provisions, to regulations (Article 288(2) TFEU) or to directly effective directives.[18] Therefore, the Member States are 'forced' to adopt all harmonising measures regardless of whether they like the particular objective or deem it suitable for their own national policies.[19] Due to the specific setting, 'harmonisation' within the EU context has obtained a specific meaning and entails specific characteristics that are not readily deducible from general discussions on harmonisation of law. Rather, 'harmonisation' in the EU context has to be seen against the particularities of the European legal order.

From Full Harmonisation to Minimum Harmonisation and Back – the Interplay of Positive and Negative Harmonisation

The perception of harmonisation has changed over the years. There are at least three developments concerning harmonisation to be kept in mind. In the beginning, the ideal of a uniform law for Europe was still lingering in people's

---

[17]   See e.g. the United Nations Convention on the Sale of Goods or treaties within the WTO. On the latter see Reich, A (2004), 'The WTO as a law-harmonizing institution', 25 *University of Pennsylvania Journal of International Economic Law* 321. Further examples are given by Dölle, H (1963), 'Gezielte und gewachsene Rechtsvereinheitlichung', *Zeitschrift für Rechtsvergleichung* 133 at 135.

[18]   For the particular institutional and legal framework see e.g. Schwarze, J, Becker, U and Pollak, C (1994), *The Implementation of Community Law* (Nomos) at 30–35; Weatherill, S (1995), *Law and Integration in the European Union* (Clarendon Press) at 58–9 and 81–4; de Witte, B (1999), 'Direct Effect, Supremacy and the Nature of the Legal Order' in Craig, P and De Búrca, G (eds), *The Evolution of EU Law* (OUP) 177 at 208–10.

[19]   Stein, E (1994), 'International Law in Internal Law: Toward Internationalization of Central-Eastern Constitutions?', 88 *American Journal of International Law* 472 at 472 and Everling, U (1986), 'Rechtsvereinheitlichung durch Richterrecht in der Europäischen Gemeinschaft', 50 *RabelsZ* 193 at 194. This has become even more true since the introduction of what is now Art. 114 TFEU.

minds and was reflected in the prevailing use of total harmonisation measures.[20] Mainly after the Single European Act 1987, the EC came to realise that an encouragement of differentiated legal environments and a competition between legal systems was also needed.[21] Thus 'minimum harmonisation' rose to importance, where Community legislation sets a floor, and the Treaty provisions set the ceiling.[22] Member States remain free to pursue more stringent policies within this framework.

Nowadays, approximation of law by positively set secondary legislation and approximation by negatively prohibitive provisions of free movement in Articles 18, 21 and 34 *et seq.* TFEU are interdependent. They are combined in order to abolish differences between the legal orders that might hinder free movement.[23] It misses the mark to view the approximation of law by secondary legislation being in conflict with negative integration, or to restrict the examination of harmonising processes to secondary measures under Article 113 et seq. TFEU.[24] The four freedoms[25] prohibit national legislation that creates obstacles to the internal market. As they are not restricted to discriminating measures,[26] there

---

[20]   Everling, U (1987), 'Zur Funktion der Rechtsangleichung in der Europäischen Gemeinschaft – Vom Abbau der Verzerrungen zur Schaffung des Binnenmarktes' in Capotorti, F and others (eds), *Du droit international au droit de l'intégration – Liber Amicorum Pierre Pescatore* (Nomos) 227 at 233–5; Schmitt von Sydow, H (1988), 'The Basic Strategies of the Commission's White Paper' in Bieber, R and others (eds), *1992: One European Market?* (Nomos) 79 at 79–85; Streinz, R (1997), 'Mindestharmonisierung im Binnenmarkt' in Everling, U and Roth, W-H (eds), *Mindestharmonisierung im Europäischen Binnenmarkt* (Nomos) 9 at 10–17.

[21]   Dougan, M (2000), 'Minimum Harmonization and the Internal Market', 37 *Common Market Law Review* 853 at 857. Also Kurcz, B (2001), 'Harmonisation by means of Directives – never-ending story?', *European Business Law Review* 287 at 287.

[22]   Dougan, M (2000), 'Minimum Harmonization and the Internal Market', 37 *Common Market Law Review* 853 at 855.

[23]   Everling, U (1987), 'Zur Funktion der Rechtsangleichung in der Europäischen Gemeinschaft – Vom Abbau der Verzerrungen zur Schaffung des Binnenmarktes' in Capotorti, F and others (eds), *Du droit international au droit de l'intégration – Liber Amicorum Pierre Pescatore* (Nomos) 227.

[24]   E.g. Amato, G (1995) 'Convergence, Harmonization, Standardization of Legislation in Europe' in Karpen, U and Wenz, EM (eds), *National Legislation in the European Framework* (Nomos) 17 at 17; Burrows, N and Hiram, H (1995), 'The Legal Articulation of Policy in the EC' in Daintith, T (ed.), *Implementing EC Law in the United Kingdom: Structures for indirect Rule* (Wiley and Sons) 29 at 40; Ihns, A (2005), *Entwicklung und Grundlagen der europäischen Rechtsangleichung* (Heymans) at 196–7.

[25]   The four freedoms are, as stated in Art. 26(2) TFEU, free movement of goods, of persons, of services and of capital, complemented by the right of establishment. They are considered essential for the establishment and functioning of the single market. For a comprehensive overview see Barnard, C (2004), *The Substantive Law of the European Union – The Four Freedoms* (OUP).

[26]   Case 8/74 *Procureur du Roi v. Dassonville* [1974] ECR 837, para. 5.

is a great amount of domestic law to be measured against the market freedoms. Due to the *Cassis* case,[27] which allows the Member States to bring up various kinds of non-economic justifications for their derogation from the prohibitive provisions, harmonisation through positive legal instruments is still necessary, however. Once a regulation or directive is enacted, justification of national measures is no longer possible.[28]

This is also where the requirement of mutual recognition comes to play a part. As it is too costly to create detailed harmonising legislation, especially as regards product standards, the idea that different national regulations will lose their limiting effect if each Member State accepts 'foreign' solutions as being equal to its own is appealing. As a result harmonisation (above a minimum standard, if required for health or security reasons, as opposed to market reasons) will not be necessary.[29]

Nevertheless, the outlined interdependence also means that approximation of law within the EU needs both positive and negative harmonisation.[30] The main reason is that the principle of minimum standards and mutual recognition works well with technical (product) standards. It poses a problem, though, with non-technical barriers to trade stemming mainly from the fact that there are different legal regimes within the Member States, which might discourage cross-border transactions.[31] Here, the only possibility of creating an encouraging environment for movements throughout the EU is to introduce similar or even uniform law.

Approximation of Laws for the Common Market

Before the Treaty of Lisbon the approximation of the laws of Member States was one of the activities of the EC according to Article 3(1)(h) EC Treaty. Despite the abolition of Article 3(1)(h) EC Treaty, this has not changed as can be deduced from Articles 114 and 115 TFEU. Approximation can be characterised as

---

[27] Case 120/78 *Rewe-Zentrale AG v. Bundesmonopolverwaltung für Branntwein (Cassis de Dijon)* [1979] ECR 649, para. 8.

[28] See Slot, PJ (1996), 'Harmonisation', 21 *European Law Review* 378 at 379–80; likewise Craig, P and de Búrca, G (2008), *EU Law* (4th edn, OUP) at 717.

[29] For an overview of mutual recognition see Bock, Y (2005), *Rechtsangleichung und Regulierung im Binnenmarkt – Zum Umfang der allgemeinen Binnenmarktkompetenz* (Nomos) at 60–61; Craig, P and de Búrca, G (2008) *EU Law* (4th edn, OUP) at 620–626.

[30] For the use of this term see Kurcz, B (2001), 'Harmonisation by means of Directives – never-ending story?', *European Business Law Review* 287 at 287–8.

[31] In a way, private international law has always had this function as it tries to define the applicable law and often only requires equivalence. See e.g. Case C–302/05 *Commission v. Italy* [2006] ECR I–10597, para. 28. European Commission, *Green Paper on the Review of the Consumer Acquis*, COM(2006)744 final, 2007/C 256/05 at 4.

'driving change in legal and administrative rules and structures'[32] by conscious and intended Union action. Articles 114, 115 TFEU also provide a first indication of what the function of harmonisation is. Approximation is meant to take place to the extent required for the functioning of the common market. It cannot be concluded that everything that serves the common market is harmonisation. Still, approximation of laws and the establishment of a common market are inextricably linked, since harmonised law is perceived as one of the main instruments to build a common market and differences in the legal orders are seen as obstacles to the free movement of production factors, the core element of the internal market (Article 26(2) TFEU).[33]

Approximation of Laws for Further Purposes

Initially the EC merely pursued the economic goal of a common market, harmonisation thus concerning the few areas of law directly related to competition and free movement of goods and persons.[34] However, the competences have since stretched to loosely related areas like environmental protection (Article 192 TFEU) and the realisation of common values like fundamental rights.[35] Despite the core provisions of Articles 114 and 115 TFEU, harmonisation today does not only cover measures that are intended to create a single market, but also those aimed at creating equal conditions and to find common solutions within the EU. So after more than 20 years of the New Approach,[36] secondary legislation and a reliance on Article 21 TFEU, which is not directly market-related, will rise to new importance.

In addition, although harmonisation is a pivotal part of the establishment of the common market, a definition cannot rely solely on this function by taking

---

[32]   Burrows, N and Hiram, H (1995), 'The Legal Articulation of Policy in the EC' in Daintith, T (ed.), *Implementing EC Law in the United Kingdom: Structures for indirect Rule* (Wiley and Sons) 29 at 41.

[33]   For the question whether internal market and common market are interchangeable, synonymous, concepts see Ludwigs, M (2004), *Rechtsangleichung nach Art. 94, 95 EG-Vertrag – Eine kompetenzrechtliche Untersuchung unter besonderer Berücksichtigung des Europäischen Privatrechts* (Nomos) at 158–83.

[34]   This is reflected by the older literature concerning harmonisation: see e.g. Everling, U (1986), 'Rechtsvereinheitlichung durch Richterrecht in der Europäischen Gemeinschaft', 50 *RabelsZ* 193 at 194 who claims that the closer a field is related to economy and the functioning of the internal market the more likely it is it will be affected by harmonisation and the more likely is the success of harmonising measures.

[35]   See e.g., Großfeld, B and Bilda, K (1992), 'Europäische Rechtsangleichung', *Zeitschrift für Rechtsvergleichung* 421 at 422; Slot, PJ (1996), 'Harmonisation', 21 *European Law Review* 378 at 378, 384–5.

[36]   Commission of the European Communities, *White Paper on the Completion of the Internal Market*, COM(85)310 final.

harmonisation to be 'the finishing touch for the completion of the internal market'[37] or 'the method or policy through which internal barriers within the Community to Community trade were dismantled'.[38] Even if this might have been true in the early days of the EEC, today integration goes much further.[39] For a functional approach to a definition (with all its short-comings as regards process and outcome), it has to be extended to all measures that are instruments in pursuance of common policies and are intended to achieve the objectives of the EU by setting common standards.

C.   CRITERIA OF HARMONISATION

In this section, six defining parameters of EU harmonisation will be scrutinised, looking at the factors both from the European and the Member States' perspective, as harmonisation happens through dialogue and cooperation between the two levels. The parameters are (1) conscious setting of a standard, (2) contribution by the Member States, (3) actors involved, (4) objectives, (5) object and standard, and (6) result.

Why these six parameters? (1) Harmonisation is a process that begins at the first stage by creating a concept at the European level. (2) It does not, however, stop there, but involves at the second stage insertion of the European concept into the domestic legal orders and at the third stage formation and development by the Member States. (3) Harmonisation at all three stages is furthered by different actors, both at the European and at the national level. Therefore, it is important to consider those actors involved in the harmonising process. (4) Harmonisation in the EU serves a function and this function determines harmonisation: (5) Harmonisation understood as a process requires an object that undergoes harmonisation and a direction the law is approximated to. (6) Finally, there should be an intended result, as otherwise neither can the success of a project be determined nor can it be discerned if the aim has been achieved.

---

[37]   Slot, PJ (1996), 'Harmonisation', 21 *European Law Review* 378 at 378.
[38]   Birkinshaw, P (2003), *European Public Law* (Butterworths) at 13.
[39]   Everling, U (1986), 'Rechtsvereinheitlichung durch Richterrecht in der Europäischen Gemeinschaft', 50 *RabelsZ* 193 at 193: '*[d]as Recht ist einerseits Gegenstand der Integration als Teil der geistigen, kulturellen und sozialen Wirklichkeit der zu integrierenden europäischen Staaten und Völker, andererseits aber auch Mittel der Integration*' ('law is on the one hand object of the integration as part of the spiritual, cultural and social reality in the European countries and peoples to be integrated, but on the other hand also a tool of integration').

1. European Standard-setting: Instruments and Process

Harmonisation is an active, steered process originating from an independent entity[40] and must therefore be differentiated from other processes occurring within Europe. On the one hand, (1) not every process that leads to approximated legal orders is harmonisation. On the other hand, (2) harmonisation is not limited to certain legal instruments and (3) comprehends nearly any kind of legislative activity by the EU.

Harmonisation versus convergence

The approximation of laws requires something, i.e. a point of reference, which the law is approximated to. This could be another pre-existing legal concept or legal order[41] or a standard of approximation created specifically for the purpose of harmonisation. Within the European legal order, there are examples of both: of slow, 'bottom-up' convergence or Europeanisation of legal orders, and of to-the-point, 'top-down' harmonisation. The difference between harmonisation and convergence is as follows.

Harmonisation seen through the lens of the founding Treaties is conscious, intended, and requires the volitional setting of a European standard by a European institution to which the Member States adapt their legal orders. Convergence functions without a predefined standard. Instead, private actors use concepts from other European legal orders whilst derogating from their own. Legislators draw their inspiration for legal reform from the European or domestic legal orders.[42] Member States borrow principles from judgments of the European Court of Justice (ECJ) on an ostensibly voluntary base or autonomously extend the scope of directives.[43] Sometimes courts even use

---

[40] See above section B.

[41] As can be observed with cross-fertilisation and convergence between legal orders: cf Harlow, C (2002), 'Voices of Difference in a Plural Community' in Beaumont, P, Lyons, C and Walker, N (eds), *Convergence and Divergence in European Public Law* (Hart Publishing) 199 at 202; Lyons, C (2002), 'Perspectives of Convergence Within the Theatre of European Integration' in Beaumont, P, Lyons, C and Walker, N (eds), *Convergence and Divergence in European Public Law* (Hart Publishing) 79 at 81; Bell, J (1998), 'Mechanisms for Cross-fertilisation of Administrative Law in Europe' in Beatson, J and Tridimas, T (eds), *New Directions in European Public Law* (Hart Publishing) 147 at 147; Örücü, E (2002) 'Law as transposition', 51 *International and Comparative Law Quarterly* 205 at 205; Birkinshaw, P (2003), *European Public Law* (Butterworths) at 7–8.

[42] Cf van Hoecke, M (2000), 'The Harmonisation of Private Law in Europe: Some Misunderstandings' in van Hoecke, M and Ost, F (eds), *The Harmonisation of European Private Law* (Hart Publishing) 1 at 2–3.

[43] Anthony, G (2002), *UK Public Law and European Law* (Hart Publishing) at 1; Schnorbus, Y (2001), 'Autonome Harmonisierung in den Mitgliedsstaaten durch die Inkorporation von Gemeinschaftsrecht – Eine Untersuchung zur einheitlichen

European or foreign legal concepts for the interpretation of national law.[44] Especially in the context of a European Contract law a slow convergence is promoted.[45]

Harmonisation implies setting a standard. First of all, this is the content of measures taken on the basis of Article 113 et seq. TFEU. But it is also part of measures based on provisions which are not directly market-related, like Article 192 TFEU. At least as a secondary objective they aim at creating a common European standard, as otherwise their main aim, e.g. the protection of the environment, could not be reached. The same is true when we look at negative harmonisation through fundamental freedoms and even at the development of legal principles through the interpretation of the Treaties by the ECJ. The principles developed by interpretation are also geared towards the abolition of legal barriers to free trade or at the creation of a European legal order, and thus constitute European standard-setting.

This sets harmonisation apart from mere convergence. When legal orders converge, the EU does not and cannot actively influence the process and outcome of this convergence, even if the existence of the EU undeniably creates a framework of common interests and the basis for exchange. This framework might in particular be created through the principle of mutual recognition or partial harmonisation. Foreign rules having to be recognised as equivalent to internal rules it is very costly to uphold different legal regimes within one legal order – one for internal and third-country relations and one for European cross-border trade. Hence, there is factual pressure on legal orders to converge, but there is no means of channelling or directing this *rapprochement* the EU can use.

Anwendung und Auslegung europäischen und autonomen nationalen Rechts und zur entsprechenden Zuständigkeit des EuGH im Vorabentscheidungsverfahren', 65 *RabelsZ* 654 at 656.

[44] A well-known example is the use of the German interpretation of human dignity, which was borrowed by the Hungarian Constitutional Court: cf Dupré, C (2003), *Importing the Law in Post-Communist Transitions – The Hungarian Constitutional Court and the Right to Human Dignity* (OUP). Other examples from UK law can be found at Anthony, G (2002), *UK Public Law and European Law* (Hart Publishing) at 4.

[45] Cf Eidenmüller, H and others (2008), 'Der Gemeinsame Referenzrahmen für das Europäische Privatrecht', *Juristische Zeitschrift* 1 at 2; Harlow, C (2002), 'Voices of Difference in a Plural Community' in Beaumont, P, Lyons, C and Walker, N (eds), *Convergence and Divergence in European Public Law* (Hart Publishing) 199 at 200; Gebauer, M (1998), *Grundfragen der Europäisierung des Privatrechts* (Universitätsverlag C. Winter) at 105–6; van Hoecke, M (2000), 'The Harmonisation of Private Law in Europe: Some Misunderstandings' in van Hoecke, M and Ost, F (eds), *The Harmonisation of European Private Law* (Hart Publishing) 1 at 3.

Instruments for standard-setting

Harmonisation happens through manifold mechanisms. In the context of the establishment of a single market, 'positive' and 'negative' integration are distinguished.[46] Positive integration relates to the active introduction of a 'common' legal standard by Union legislation on the basis of Articles 114 and 115 TFEU[47] as well as e.g. Articles 153, 192 and even 352 TFEU.[48] This includes any form of secondary legislation mentioned in Article 288 TFEU. Before the Treaty of Lisbon, Article 3(1)(h) EC Treaty did not restrict harmonisation to directives nor even to secondary legislation. The limitation to directives in what is now Article 115 TFEU reflects the fear of a loss of competences,[49] but it does not imply that directives are the sole instrument of approximation of laws. Excluding regulations from the tool box of harmonisation just because they create law that remains at the European level[50] contravenes Articles 113 and 115 TFEU. Moreover, it disregards the fact that regulations, owing to their direct applicability, become part of the national legal orders. This leads to the existence of identical norms within the legal orders and to the stimulation of processes that result in a common European principle. Finally, it is worth bearing in mind that even recommendations, opinions and non-binding guidelines can have a factual harmonising effect comparable to that of 'open coordination'.[51]

The term 'negative integration' is used to describe the abolition of differing national standards by means of the four freedoms in the TFEU in their interpretation by the ECJ.[52] It leads to an approximation of legal orders, since it

---

[46]   For the differentiation between those forms of integration see Craig, P and de Búrca, G (2008) *EU Law* (4th edn, OUP) at 97.

[47]   This is the most restrictive meaning of harmonisation and also its original one: cf ibid., at 1190 referring to Case 120/78 *Rewe-Zentrale AG v Bundesmonopolverwaltung für Branntwein (Cassis de Dijon)* [1979] ECR 649.

[48]   See Barnard, C (2004), *The Substantive Law of the European Union – The Four Freedoms* (OUP) at 12; Oppermann, T (2005), *Europarecht* (3rd edn, C.H.Beck) at 385.

[49]   Cf Vignes, D (1991), 'Le rapprochement des législations mérite-t-il encore son nom?' in Debbasch, C and Venezia, J-C (eds), *L'Europe et le droit Mélanges en hommage à Jean Boulouis* (Dalloz) 533 at 542–3.

[50]   VerLoren van Themaat, P (1965), 'Die Rechtsangleichung als Integrationsinstrument' in Hallstein, W and Schlochauer, H-J (eds), *Zur Integration Europas – Festschrift für Carl Friedrich Ophüls aus Anlass seines siebzigsten Geburtstags* (C.F.Müller) 243 at 244.

[51]   Bock, Y (2005), *Rechtsangleichung und Regulierung im Binnenmarkt – Zum Umfang der allgemeinen Binnenmarktkompetenz* (Nomos) at 56; Harlow, C (1999), 'European Administrative Law and the Global Challenge' in Craig, P and de Búrca, G (eds), *The Evolution of EU Law* (OUP) 261 at 276–7.

[52]   See Kurcz, B (2001), 'Harmonisation by means of Directives – never-ending story?', *European Business Law Review* 287 at 287. Likewise McGee, A and Weatherill,

introduces a 'permissible' canon of internal law in compliance with the Treaties. It indirectly requires Member States to adapt their laws to the 'Euro-standard' pronounced by the ECJ, as otherwise they may be liable for a breach of Union law. Thus, harmonisation happens through primary law, not through judicial law-making. The instruments of negative harmonisation are the provisions on free movement.[53]

More recently, this harmonising effect of primary law was stretched from Article 26(2) TFEU to Article 18 in combination with Article 21 TFEU. This has far-reaching consequences as it is interpreted as a general provision ruling out any internal provisions that might deter citizens from exercising free movement – market-related or not.[54] Even Union fundamental rights can lead to negative harmonisation, not so much because Member States adapt their constitutions to Union fundamental rights,[55] but rather because internal measures are scrutinised against the standard of Union fundamental rights and deemed inapplicable if they contravene them.[56] This is mainly the case because the ECJ applies Union fundamental rights to any situation where Member States handle

---

S (1990), 'The Evolution of the Single Market – Harmonisation or Liberalisation', 53 *Modern Law Review* 578 at 580. Barnard, C (2004), *The Substantive Law of the European Union – The Four Freedoms* (OUP) at 14–15 shows how positive and negative integration interact in the creation of the single market and argues that there is 'a spill-over from one type of integration to another'. Other authors use harmonisation only in relation to 'positive integration' and harmonising legislation and oppose it to the prohibitions in the free movement provisions: see e.g. Slot, PJ (1996), 'Harmonisation', 21 *European Law Review* 378 at 379–80. Craig, P and de Búrca, G (2008) *EU Law* (4th edn, OUP) at 1171, similarly refer to integration through the free movement provisions as 'judicial contribution to market integration' as opposed to the legislative contribution through harmonisation of laws.

[53]   Cf Kurcz, B (2001), 'Harmonisation by means of Directives – never-ending story?', *European Business Law Review* 287 at 288 who considers negative harmonisation chronologically to be the first. On the contrary see Everling, U (1986), 'Rechtsvereinheitlichung durch Richterrecht in der Europäischen Gemeinschaft', 50 *RabelsZ* 193 at 215 et seq.; Schießl, H (2005), 'Europäisierung der deutschen Unternehmensbesteuerung durch den EuGH', *Neue Juristische Wochenschrift* 849 at 849: 'ECJ as surrogate legislator'.

[54]   Case C–209/03 *Bidar v. London Borough of Ealing* [2005] ECR I–2119 and Joined Cases C–11/06 and C–12/06 *Rhiannon Morgan v. Bezirksregierung Köln and Iris Bucher v. Landrat des Kreises Düren* [2007] ECR I–9161.

[55]   The most commonly known example in Germany is Case C–285/98 *Kreil v. Bundesrepublik Deutschland* [2000] ECR I–68, which led to the change of Art. 12a(2) of the German Constitution by allowing female soldiers to join the armed forces; cf Schwarze, J (2005), 'Der Schutz der Grundrechte durch den EuGH', 48 *Neue Juristische Wochenschrift* 3459 at 3462 and Craig, P and de Búrca, G (2008) *EU Law* (4th edn, OUP) at 911.

[56]   Joined Cases C–465/00, 138 and 139/01 *Rechnungshof v. Österreichischer Rundfunk* [2003] ECR I–12489, where the conformity of national law that might touch the scope of a directive was at stake.

EU law.[57] Thereby a Union-wide consent on legal measures in conformity with fundamental rights is created.

European legislation as harmonisation

Harmonisation is an act of European legislation, i.e. the regulation of political, social, economic, or environmental issues transferred to the European level by the Member States.[58] It should be contemplated, however, whether each European legislative action constitutes harmonisation.[59] There may be a domain of genuine European law-making: first, when new legal concepts are created that have not existed in any domestic legal order before; second, if after the approximation of law the 'Euro-standard' is modified; and finally, if concepts are instituted that are not meant to replace national law but to leave it untouched and co-exist.

The creation of a concept that has not existed in any of the Member States before is also referred to as 'preventive harmonisation' as it suppresses differences between the legal orders before they even spring up. This, too, is harmonisation, as it is intended to create common legal rules in the Member States.[60]

---

[57]   Case C–260/89 *Elleniki Radiophonia Tileorass AE (ERT) v. Dimotiki Etairia Pliroforissis and Sotirios Kouvelas* [1991] ECR I–2925, paras 42 et seq.

[58]   Commission of the European Communities, *White Paper on the Completion of the Internal Market*, COM(85)310 final, paras 67 et seq. Cf Slot, PJ (1996), 'Harmonisation', 21 *European Law Review* 378 at 380–81 and Streinz, R (1997), 'Mindestharmonisierung im Binnenmarkt' in Everling, U and Roth, W-H (eds), *Mindestharmonisierung im Europäischen Binnenmarkt* (Nomos) 9 at 10 et seq. Further Weatherill, S (2004), 'Why Harmonise?' in Tridimas, T and Nebbia, P (eds), *European Union Law for the Twenty-First Century – Rethinking the New Legal Order* (Hart Publishing) 11 at 20.

[59]   In this direction see Verloren van Themaat, P (1965), 'Die Rechtsangleichung als Integrationsinstrument' in Hallstein, W and Schlochauer, H-J (eds), *Zur Integration Europas – Festschrift für Carl Friedrich Ophüls aus Anlass seines siebzigsten Geburtstags* (C.F.Müller) 243 at 244; in favour of two different categories see Schwartz, IE (1987), '30 Jahre EG-Rechtsangleichung' in Mestmäcker, E-J, Möller, H and Schwarz, H-P (eds), *Eine Ordnungspolitik für Europa – Festschrift für Hans von der Groeben* (Nomos) 333 at 333; von der Groeben, H and Schwarze, J (2003), *Kommentar zum Vertrag über die Europäische Union und zur Gründung der Europäischen Gemeinschaft* (Nomos) Art. 94 para. 12.

[60]   Case C–377/98 *Netherlands v. Parliament and Council* [2001] ECR I–7079, para. 15; Eiden, C (1984), *Die Rechtsangleichung gemäß Art. 100 des EWG-Vertrages* (Duncker & Humblot) at 18–19; Ihns, A (2005), *Entwicklung und Grundlagen der europäischen Rechtsangleichung* (Heymans) at 86; Calliess, C and Ruffert, M (2007), *EUV/EGV – Das Verfassungsrecht der Europäischen Union mit Europäischer Grundrechtecharta – Kommentar* (3rd edn, C.H.Beck) Art. 94 para. 9; Bell, J (1998), 'Mechanisms for Cross-fertilisation of Administrative Law in Europe' in Beatson, J and Tridimas, T (eds), *New Directions in European Public Law* (Hart Publishing) 147 at 149 et seq.

The problem of the modification of the Euro-standard is one of competences[61] rather than of whether it constitutes harmonisation. If understood literally, a modification of the European standard is not admissible under Article 114 TFEU once the approximation of law has been attained by the original measure, since differences between the legal orders have been eliminated. However, whether or not a (necessary) modification or renewal of the Euro-standard is based on Article 114 or rather on Article 352 TFEU, it is still harmonisation, as it sets a new standard and thus results in a process of approximation to this new standard.

Only the third category is problematic from the point of view of harmonisation. When European legal concepts are not intended to replace or even to modify national concepts (e.g. the European cooperative society[62]), the fundamental difference is that the law of the Member States continues to exist in its full diversity.[63] As was claimed by the Council in the *Cooperative Society* case 'a harmonisation measure must necessarily lead to a result which ... would have been possible to achieve by simultaneously adopting identical legislation in each Member State'.[64] This is not the case when over-arching European concepts are created. Neither do they result in a process of adaptation within the Member States. This is the only incident of genuine European legislation, which can naturally only be based on Article 352 TFEU. However, this does not mean *a contrario* that no measure based on Article 352 TFEU constitutes harmonisation. A measure under Article 352 TFEU can still harmonise as long as it sets a standard that substitutes or modifies norms in the Member States.

In summary, from the European perspective harmonisation requires the setting of a common standard by any existing legislative or judicial means that is intended (at least as a secondary objective) to replace or modify law in the Member States towards a Euro-standard.

2.   Extent of Member States' Contribution

The process of harmonisation requires some kind of Member State involvement. There is no harmonisation if a principle is bluntly forced onto legal orders or if it is created at the European level, but co-exists with pre-existing Member States'

---

[61]   See Bock, Y (2005), *Rechtsangleichung und Regulierung im Binnenmarkt – Zum Umfang der allgemeinen Binnenmarktkompetenz* (Nomos) at 159.

[62]   Further examples are provided by Ludwigs, M (2004), *Rechtsangleichung nach Art. 94, 95 EG-Vertrag – Eine kompetenzrechtliche Untersuchung unter besonderer Berücksichtigung des Europäischen Privatrechts* (Nomos) at 228–9.

[63]   Case C–436/03 *European Parliament v. Council* [2006] ECR I–3733, paras 43–4.

[64]   Ibid., para. 32.

concepts. Harmonisation entails not only standard-setting at the European level, but also legislative and judicial implementation and adoption at the national level. The Member States are involved at all three stages of the harmonisation process, namely standard-setting, insertion and moulding of a European concept.

At the first stage, Member States participate in the procedure of setting the European standard, although, depending on the circumstances, this may be the smallest and less decisive contribution.[65]

The more determining contribution happens at the second stage, when the European concept is actively inserted into the national legal order, commonly by a domestic legislative act,[66] exceptionally by judicial interaction. Harmonisation is mostly (but not necessarily) two-tiered legislation, i.e. undertaken by directives.[67] Some kind of activity in order to trigger the harmonising process at the national level is always required, although there are gradual differences. The least contribution is obviously required for regulations to be effective. As they are directly applicable law according to Article 288(2) TFEU,[68] which replaces domestic law within its scope, they only rarely require to be fitted into the domestic law.[69] It is claimed that approximation entails modification, but not substitution of domestic law, requiring that the area is regulated by Member States' law before and after the insertion of the principle.[70] This would not be the case in regard to regulations. However, this is only a formal difference but not a substantial one, attached to the intervening act of a national legislator. A (partial) substitution effectuates a change in the legal order, and implementation of directives constitutes a modification and a partial substitution of the previ-

---

[65] See section below C 3.

[66] Case C–361/88 *Commission v. Germany* [1991] ECR I–2567 declaring administrative directives insufficient for implementation due to their non-binding character towards third parties.

[67] Taupitz, J (1993), *Europäische Privatrechtsvereinheitlichung heute und morgen* (Mohr) at 18–20.

[68] On its meaning see Case 34/73 *Variola v. Amministrazione delle Finanze* [1973] ECR 981, paras 10–11.

[69] Joined Cases 146, 192 and 193/81 *BayWa AG and others v. Bundesanstalt für landwirtschaftliche Marktordnung* [1982] ECR 1503. Cf Wagner, M (2000), *Das Konzept der Mindestharmonisierung* (Duncker & Humblot) at 36–7; Ihns, A (2005), *Entwicklung und Grundlagen der europäischen Rechtsangleichung* (Heymans) at 19–20; Bock, Y (2005), *Rechtsangleichung und Regulierung im Binnenmarkt – Zum Umfang der allgemeinen Binnenmarktkompetenz* (Nomos) at 54–5; Craig, P and de Búrca, G (2008) *EU Law* (4th edn, OUP) at 84.

[70] von der Groeben, H and Schwarze, J (2003), *Kommentar zum Vertrag über die Europäische Union und zur Gründung der Europäischen Gemeinschaft* (Nomos) Art. 94 para. 12; Usher, J (1981), 'Harmonisation of Legislation' in Lasok, D and Soldatos, P (eds), *Les Communautés Européennes en Fonctionnement – The European Communities in Action* 171 at 174.

ously existing national law as well.[71] Moreover, the classical two-tier legislation through directives, where the involvement of the Member States' legislature is paramount as it has to transpose the directive, does not always entail as much contribution by the Member States as one could gather from the wording of Article 288(3) TFEU. Due to considerably detailed directives and the intervention by the ECJ,[72] the scope of discretion for the Member States is often minimal. Then the only contribution consists in enacting the implementing legislation that complies with the European blueprint.[73]

Harmonisation also occurs through the effects of primary legislation, most importantly through the four freedoms. As they are directly applicable law, their harmonising effect is mainly realised by domestic courts when interpreting, or deciding not to apply law that would otherwise contravene the fundamental freedoms. Additionally, if the ECJ has declared a national solution inapplicable in Union contexts, it is up to the Member States to adapt the domestic law to the newly realised European standard. They must react in accordance with the ECJ's decision by harmonious interpretation[74] or modification of the existing law.[75] This applies not only to the Member State which has been party to the proceedings, but also to other Member States where similar legislation is in force, as it constitutes a breach of Union law if clear interpretations of Union provisions are not respected by the Member States.[76] Even if harmonisation takes place via general principles of law developed by the interpretation of the ECJ, e.g. fundamental rights, the Member States are essential to trigger the harmonising process. It is the domestic courts that apply and respect those principles, thus making them part of the national legal order, and indirectly also the legislature, which may change the law in order to accommodate those principles.[77]

---

[71]   See Opinion of AG Stix-Hackl in Case C–436/03 *European Parliament v. Council* [2006] ECR I–03733, para. 60.

[72]   Cf Fischer, N (2003), '"Rechts-Harmonisierung" – Schlagwort oder Rechtsprinzip? – Kritische Anmerkungen zum Prozess der "Rechts-Angleichung"', 10 *Verbraucher und Recht* 374 at 376 concerning European consumer law; Tonner, K and Lindner, B (2002), 'Immaterieller Schadensersatz und der EuGH', *Neue Juristische Wochenschrift* 1475 at 1476.

[73]   Taupitz, J (1993), *Europäische Privatrechtsvereinheitlichung heute und morgen* (Mohr) at 24.

[74]   On the concept of harmonious interpretation in Community law see Craig, P and de Búrca, G (2008) *EU Law* (4th edn, OUP) at 287–96.

[75]   See e.g. the modification of German statutes on state grants for German students going abroad in the wake of Joined Cases C–11/06 and C–12/06 *Rhiannon Morgan v. Bezirksregierung Köln and Iris Bucher v. Landrat des Kreises Düren* [2007] ECR I–9161.

[76]   Cases C–46 and 48/93 *Brasserie du Pêcheur SA v. Germany* [1996] ECR I–1029; Case C–244/01 *Köbler v. Republik Österreich* [2003] ECR I–10239.

[77]   Case C–285/98 *Kreil v. Bundesrepublik Deutschland* [2000] ECR I–68.

The third stage of harmonisation, the creation of a common though not necessarily uniform European concept, is reached as soon as the European principle has been inserted. Approximation means that law gets closer to the European standard. The insertion of similar sounding norms is the trigger for harmonisation, but does not result in the elimination of differences between the national legal orders, as application and interpretation of law may differ vastly. Thus, an important part of the Member States' involvement in harmonisation is to create a common interpretation and application in dialogue with the European level by referring questions for preliminary rulings to the ECJ (Article 267 TFEU), using harmonious interpretation,[78] respecting court and administrative decisions in other Member States and trying not to stick to a national interpretation of norms of Union origin.[79].

To sum up, harmonisation is characterised by Member States' contribution at three levels. This leads to the insertion of the concept to be harmonised into the national legal orders and to a process of adaptation, in which 'one' European concept is formed.

3. Actors

The aforementioned criteria have already shown that harmonisation is not limited to the legislator–legislator relationship. Already at the first stage of the process, the creation of the concept requires actors from the European and the Member State level alike, although to a different degree depending on the instrument of harmonisation. As far as secondary legislation is concerned, Member States and the Commission are involved in the legislative procedures (Articles 16, 17 TFEU in combination with Article 294 TFEU) although due to majority voting (Article 114 TFEU) the influence of a single state may be rather small. National legal orders also provide ideas to be moulded into a European concept.[80] Politically undesirable decisions are transferred to the European level and Europe is 'blamed' for them. Even outside the scope of secondary law, Member

---

[78]   See the impact of Case C–168/00 *Leitner v. TUI Deutschland* [2002] ECR I–2631; Case C–144/04 *Mangold v. Helm* [2005] ECR I–9981; Cases C–397–403/01 *Pfeiffer et al. v. Deutsches Rotes Kreuz, Kreisverband Waldshut eV* [2004] ECR I–8835 on the respective domestic laws; also Tonner, K and Lindner, B (2002), 'Immaterieller Schadensersatz und der EuGH', *Neue Juristische Wochenschrift* 1475 at 1476.

[79]   Case C–237/02 *Freiburger Kommunalbauten GmbH Baugesellschaft & Co. KG v. Ludger Hofstetter und Ulrike Hofstetter* [2004] ECR I–3403, paras 19–20 and 25.

[80]   E.g. the idea of good faith, which forms part of Art. 3 of Council Directive 93/13/EEC of 5 April 1993 on unfair terms in consumer contracts, OJ 1993 L 095 29–34, is supposed to be derived from §242 of the German BGB. See Beale, H (2004), *Chitty on Contracts* (29th edn, Sweet & Maxwell) at 1–019–1–023; Tenreiro, M and Karsten, J (1999), 'Unfair Terms in Consumer Contracts: Uncertainties, contradictions and novelties

States have a slight influence, because it is they who bring cases before the ECJ and plead their case in favour of a certain development. The ECJ often refers to the domestic legal orders when developing new principles.[81] So it may be said that, at first, national law influences Union law, and then, in a second phase, those newly created European principles influence national law.[82]

The setting of standards at the European level is primarily undertaken by the European legislature, i.e. the Commission and the Council. The question remains whether the ECJ can be considered an autonomous creator of European legal concepts at the first, the standard-setting level. If negative harmonisation takes place, it functions through primary law, set by the signatories mainly in order to remove barriers to a common market. The ECJ's task is to realise the vague provisions rendering them enforceable, but it does so only because the legislature has left the power of realising them to the ECJ. It is an important role, for even though it is not an autonomous contribution to the standard-setting procedure, it shapes the standard to which Member States' legal orders are to adhere. This means that although judge-made law is not an instrument of harmonisation,[83] the ECJ is an actor in the standard-setting process because the 'masters of the Treaties' left it with the task of realisation.

At the second stage, harmonisation happens mainly through Member States' contributions – insertion of secondary legislation by the national legislators, compliance with standards derived from primary legislation mainly by the national courts and only occasionally and in the long run by the national legislators.

Influence at the third stage, the carving and moulding of the common European concept, is mainly exercised by the national courts in cooperation with the ECJ. 'Legal interpretation is another important, if not an indispensable, link in a successful unification process.'[84] National courts are to apply the concepts of

---

of a Directive' in Schulte-Nölke, H and Schulze, R (eds), *Europäische Rechtsangleichung und nationale Privatrechte* (Nomos) 223 at 224.

[81] A quite exhaustive list of what has been 'borrowed' can be found in Schwarze, J (1996), *Das Verwaltungsrecht unter europäischem Einfluß – zur Konvergenz der mitgliedstaatlichen Verwaltungsrechtsordnungen in der Europäischen Union* (Nomos) at 15–16. It was mainly general principles, but also some institutions, like the ombudsman, which were inspired by national legal orders. See also Tridimas, T (2006), *The General Principles of EU Law* (OUP) at 5–7.

[82] See Schwarze, J (1996), *Das Verwaltungsrecht unter europäischem Einfluß – zur Konvergenz der mitgliedstaatlichen Verwaltungsrechtsordnungen in der Europäischen Union* (Nomos) at 12–13 and 15–17 and Birkinshaw, P (2003), *European Public Law* (Butterworths) at 12.

[83] The term 'judicial harmonisation' constitutes a confusion of terms, a good example of this confusion is Ihns, A (2005), *Entwicklung und Grundlagen der europäischen Rechtsangleichung* (Heymans) at 25 et seq.

[84] Polach, JG (1966), 'Harmonization of Laws in Western Europe' in Yntema, HE (ed.), *The American Journal of Comparative Law Reader* (Oceana Publications) at 443.

European origin in a Europe-friendly way and to refer interpretative questions to the ECJ. Although the ECJ only announces its understanding of the (secondary) Union law[85] and therefore the national courts are left to decide how to apply this interpretation within their legal orders, this is a promising way of controlling and also of creating a common application of law as part of the harmonising process.[86]

4. Reasons and Objectives – Why Harmonise?

The question 'Why harmonise?' has been asked many times, mostly because it is felt that there are more promising ways of reaching the intended result than active approximation of law, such as regulatory competition.[87] I will not go into details, as it does not contribute to a definition. As mentioned above, approximation of law is meant to serve a function, and what is not intended to serve this function cannot be harmonisation in the context of EU law. Harmonisation is not done '*l'art pour l'art*' or simply in order to obtain a European *ius commune*.[88]

Conceivable reasons are: (1) the establishment of a functioning common market, (2) the use of law as a means of integration ('integration through law'), (3) the pursuit of European legal policy in order to provide common European solutions for common European societal questions, and (4) 'pressure' of the legal system due to fundamental principles inherent in the Union legal system.

Establishment of a functioning common market
This first objective is pronounced within the Treaties as one of the core tasks of the EU. The common market can function only if competition is not distorted

---

[85]   See eg Case C–168/00 *Leitner v. TUI Deutschland* [2002] ECR I–2631, paras 23–4.

[86]   '*Rechtsanwendungsgleichheit*' (equal application of law): cf Taupitz, J (1993), *Europäische Privatrechtsvereinheitlichung heute und morgen* (Mohr) at 14 and 37.

[87]   See some more recent publications: Weatherill, S (2004), 'Why Harmonise?' in Tridimas, T and Nebbia, P (eds), *European Union Law for the Twenty-First Century – Rethinking the New Legal Order* (Hart Publishing) 11 at 11; Birkmose, HS (2006), 'Regulatory Competition and the European Harmonisation Process', 4 *European Business Law* 1075; Franck, J-U (2006), 'Rechtssetzung für den Binnenmarkt: Zwischen Rechtsharmonisierung und Wettbewerb der Rechtsordnungen' in Riesenhuber, K and Takayama, K (eds), *Rechtsangleichung: Grundlagen, Methoden, Inhalte – Deutsch-Japanische Perspektiven* (De Gruyter Recht) at 47 at 47.

[88]   See von der Groeben, H (1970), 'Die Politik der Europäischen Kommmission auf dem Gebiet der Rechtsangleichung', *Neue Juristische Wochenschrift* 359 at 359. However, the Opinion of AG Stix-Hackl in Case C–436/03 *European Parliament v. Council* [2006] ECR I–3733, para. 59 could be read in that way: '[t]he aim of approximation of laws within the meaning of Article 95 EC is to reduce disparities between legal systems' (emphasis added).

and free movement of production factors is not prevented by existing disparities between national legal orders.[89] It is long-standing practice to create common rules in order to further inter-state trade and economic integration.[90] The content of these rules does not matter as long as they do not obstruct free movement. The functioning of the common market is the regulatory aim pursued. Some authors see this as the sole purpose of harmonisation within the EU that sets European harmonisation apart from other processes of harmonisation, which are undertaken to facilitate legal relations between states.[91] Until the Treaty of Lisbon, Article 2 EC Treaty showed that the Community is committed to tasks other than the establishment of a common market. This is now reflected by Articles 2 and 3(1), (3), (5) and (6) TFEU in an even stronger way. Although approximation of laws is not explicitly mentioned as a means to pursue those tasks, it is hard to see how the Union could reach a certain level e.g. of environmental protection within Europe other than by approximation of the Member States' environmental legislation – even though, undeniably, those policies might also indirectly support the establishment of the common market.[92]

Integration through law

Law is seen not only as the object, but also as the main tool of integration, as long as it is law that is capable of being uniformly implemented.[93] Integration means 'a coming together'.[94] This coming together can be economic. In that case, the

---

[89] Cf Commission of the European Communities, *White Paper on the Completion of the Internal Market*, COM(85)310 final at 4; Eiden, C (1984), *Die Rechtsangleichung gemäß Art. 100 des EWG-Vertrages* (Duncker & Humblot) at 21; Kurcz, B (2001), 'Harmonisation by means of Directives – never-ending story?' *European Business Law Review* 287 at 288; Collins, H (1994), 'Good Faith in European Contract Law', 14 *Oxford Journal of Legal Studies* 229 at 237.

[90] Barnard, C (2004), *The Substantive Law of the European Union – The Four Freedoms* (OUP) at 14–15; for the 19th century inter-state trade cf Behrens, P (1981), 'Integrationstheorie – Internationale wirtschaftliche Integration als Gegenstand politologischer, ökonomischer und juristischer Forschung', 45 *RabelsZ* 8 at 10–11.

[91] Taupitz, J (1993), *Europäische Privatrechtsvereinheitlichung heute und morgen* (Mohr) at 35.

[92] Streinz, R (1997), 'Mindestharmonisierung im Binnenmarkt' in Everling, U and Roth, W-H (eds), *Mindestharmonisierung im Europäischen Binnenmarkt* (Nomos) 9 at 22.

[93] Everling, U (1986), 'Rechtsvereinheitlichung durch Richterrecht in der Europäischen Gemeinschaft', 50 *RabelsZ* 193 at 193; Himsworth, C (2002), 'Convergence and Divergence in Administrative Law' in Beaumont, P, Lyons, C and Walker, N (eds), *Convergence and Divergence in European Public Law* (Hart Publishing) 99 at 99.

[94] Ward, I (2003), *A Critical Introduction to European Law* (2nd edn, LexisNexis UK) at 103. See also Meyer-Cording, U (1987), 'Fortschritte der Europapolitik nur mit wirklich integrierenden Maßnahmen möglich!' in Mestmäcker, E-J, Möller, H and

second objective of harmonisation equals the first. But integration can also be political or cultural.[95] In that respect the second objective is different. If Member States cannot pursue their political objectives on their own – either because they have transferred competences to the EU or out of factual constraints – it may not be sufficient to create common markets through common rules. It further necessitates pursuing a common policy at the European level and therefore creating a common core of values. That is why the aim of integration stretches further than economic integration, namely to other policies and law.[96] The instrument for creating a *'Rechtsgemeinschaft'*[97] that may become a *'Wertegemeinschaft'*[98] is law. By law, common values are transferred and promulgated throughout Europe, giving the people of Europe a common legal identity and thereby creating an integrated European society – first at the level of law but gradually also at the levels of social, cultural or political values transferred by the legal rules.

Pursuit of a common European policy

For the markets it is in most cases not sufficient to create a level playing field where private actors can interact, but states have to pursue their respective policies.[99] When competences are transferred to the Union, the objective of Union legislation is to create common European solutions. Regulatory aims are transferred to the Union level, so most 'modern' directives pursue not only the aim of liberalising trade, but also further policies, like consumer protection.[100] Thus, approximation of law is intended to serve all tasks of the Union.[101] This

---

Schwarz, H-P (eds), *Eine Ordnungspolitik für Europa – Festschrift für Hans von der Groeben zu seinem 80 Geburtstag* (Nomos) 221 at 221–2.

[95] Ward, I (2003), *A Critical Introduction to European Law* (2nd edn, LexisNexis UK) at 102; Behrens, P (1981), 'Integrationstheorie – Internationale wirtschaftliche Integration als Gegenstand politologischer, ökonomischer und juristischer Forschung', 45 *RabelsZ* 8 at 35.

[96] Cf Ward, I (2003), *A Critical Introduction to European Law* (2 edn, LexisNexis UK) at 102–3.

[97] 'Community of law'.

[98] 'Community of values'.

[99] Behrens, P (1981), 'Integrationstheorie – Internationale wirtschaftliche Integration als Gegenstand politologischer, ökonomischer und juristischer Forschung', 45 *RabelsZ* 8 at 13.

[100] Examples are the Food Labelling Directive 79/112, OJ 1999 L 69 22–3 or considerations (3) and (4) of the first Tobacco Products Advertising Directive 98/43/EC; OJ 1998 L 213 9–12. For further examples see Daintith, T (1995), 'Showing your Strength: Alcohol Content Labelling and the Beer Industry' in Daintith, T (ed.), *Implementing EC Law in the United Kingdom: Structures for indirect Rule* (Wiley and Sons) 113 at 120.

[101] Lochner, N (1962), 'Was bedeuten die Begriffe Harmonisierung, Koordinierung und gemeinsame Politik in den Europäischen Verträgen?', 118 *Zeitschrift für die gesamte Staatswissenschaft* 35 at 52.

is also caused by the interplay of positive and negative harmonisation described above. If Member States are not able to protect interests of public policy as 'mandatory requirements' because the EU enacts harmonising legislation in order to counter the diversity of law,[102] this protection has to be ensured by the EU. Here, the third reason for harmonisation comes in. Law is used not only as an instrument for creating a community,[103] but as a regulatory instrument in order to pursue certain policies. This may not have been the original intention of the EEC (European Economic Community), but the transferral of non-market related competences shows the development towards a political union.

Principles inherent in Union law

When developing general principles of Union law, a European standard may be set, not primarily to create a common law, but because the principle arrived at by the judges is inherent in the legal order. It would be against the systematic or the underlying reasoning of Union law if this principle were not applied. This applies to some of the administrative principles (proportionality, due process, access to documents), to state liability, and to fundamental rights. They were the logical consequences of the legal development within Europe and were needed in order to limit state power and to confer rights on the individual.[104] Their very idea is inherent in any democratic legal order. As they are realised very differently in the Member States, however, it was important to declare a common European standard of those ideas to be applied by the Member States when acting as Community agents. Harmonisation furthered by the ECJ was needed in order to fill in lacunas in Community law.[105] Unless those general principles of Union law are organising principles for the common market or the functioning of the EU, not deemed to be harmonising standards but ordinary

---

[102]   This has been established in a series of cases by the ECJ and can be seen as re-cognized principle now: see e.g. Weatherill, S (2004), 'Why Harmonise?' in Tridimas, T and Nebbia, P (eds), *European Union Law for the Twenty-First Century – Rethinking the New Legal Order* (Hart Publishing) 11 at 13 and Kurcz, B (2001), 'Harmonisation by means of Directives – never-ending story?', *European Business Law Review* 287 at 292.

[103]   As has been done before, e.g. in the process of German unification in the 19th century.

[104]   Tridimas, T (2006), *The General Principles of EU Law* (OUP) at 7; Möllers, C (2002), 'Verfassungsgebende Gewalt – Verfassung – Konstitutionalisierung' in von Bogdandy, A (ed.), *Europäisches Verfassungsrecht – Theoretische und dogmatische Grundzüge* (Springer) 1 at 49; Emiliou, N (1996), *The Principle of Proportionality in European Law – A Comparative Study* (Kluwer International) at 119.

[105]   Joined Cases 201 and 202/85 *Klensch v. Secrétaire d'Etat à l'Agriculture et à la Viticulture* [1986] ECR 3477. Cf Groussot, X (2006), *General Principles of Community Law* (European Law Pub.) at 11; Tridimas, T (2006), *The General Principles of EU Law* (OUP) at 8.

constitutional principles,[106] they are not associated with the establishment of the common market.

We can thus conclude that harmonising measures are effectuated in order to prepare, yet not to complete, the unification of law.[107] At the same time they are used to promote economic, social and political changes in the Member States in order to create a single market and a union of values.[108] Law is at the same time the object and the tool of integration.[109]

5. Objects and Directions

Another defining element of harmonisation is the object to be harmonised. On a macro-level it seems to be the legal orders that converge as a whole due to the process of harmonisation, even though it is quite clear that the result will not be a uniform law within Europe. Yet, the actual object of harmonisation is much smaller and subject to many debates. It is the 'law'. What is law? This is a moot question, and the understanding of law diverges in the Member States and the various schools of thought, but for our purpose it suffices to state that law is more than rules; it is also the application and use of these rules by courts, administrative bodies and even sometimes private actors, i.e. the legal practice.[110] Article 114 TFEU speaks of 'laws, regulations or administrative provisions' referring primarily to approximation by the means of positive (statutory) law.

---

[106]   Koopmans, T (1991), 'The Birth of European Law at the Crossroads of Legal Traditions', 39 *American Journal of Comparative Law* 493 at 497–8.

[107]   See Teubner, G (1998), 'Legal Irritants: Good Faith in British Law or How Unifying Law Ends Up in New Divergences', 61 *Modern Law Review* 11 at 13.

[108]   For those two (of three possible) general incentives for legal transplantation see Kahn-Freund, O (1974), 'On Uses and Misuses of Comparative Law', 37 *Modern Law Review* 1 at 2. The third one, 'giving adequate legal effect to a social change shared by the foreign country', thus looking for similar solutions, cannot be said to be part of the idea of harmonisation.

[109]   Everling, U (1986), 'Rechtsvereinheitlichung durch Richterrecht in der Europäischen Gemeinschaft', 50 *RabelsZ* 193 at 193.

[110]   See especially Sacco, R (1991), *La Comparaison juridique au Service de la Connaissance du Droit* (Economica, Collection Etudes Juridiques Comparatives) at 33, who claims that one has to talk about '*règles légales, doctrinales et prétoriennes ainsi que des constantes tirées des décisions des cours et des exemples des manuels*' ('legal rules, rules of the doctrine and pretorian rules as well as constants of law drawn from court decisions and examples in textbooks') instead of '*la règle de droit de tel pays*' ('the statutory rule of this country') and at 35: '*[l]a première constatation est qu'en chaque système nous trouvons chacun de ces divers ensembles, que nous pouvons appeler "formants" du système: nous parlerons ainsi d'un "formant légal", d'un "formant doctrinal", etc.*' ('First we have to state that in each system we will find each of those diverse aspects that we could call "formants" of a system: thus, we talk of "legal formants", "doctrinal formants" etc.').

This must, however, also include approximation at the level of application and interpretation.[111] Negative harmonisation, on the contrary, affects any national measure at a broader scale, hence also administrative and judicial practice, and case law. Indirectly, the approximation of laws means also an approximation of policies, as Member States are barred from enacting their own legislation once an area has been harmonised.[112] Legislation is meant to govern the behaviour of individuals in order to attain the purpose of the norm. After harmonisation has taken place this is guaranteed at the European level, thus creating a common European policy.[113]

If law is to be approximated, the question is whether this requires pre-existing, diverging regulations of the matter within the Member States and, consequently, whether the standard is derived from within this framework spanned by the Member States' solutions. Are the legal provisions of the Member States adapted to each other, to an abstract 'third' standard not necessarily derived from the pool of the Member States' solutions, or to a minimum level required for the functioning of the common market?

While outside the context of EU law approximation of law is mostly used in the sense of approximation to existing standards within the legal orders (not exclusively, as the parties to a treaty might also agree on a 'third' standard),[114] the standard in EU law is strongly influenced by the function of approximation as mentioned in Articles 113–115 TFEU and the former 3(1)(h) EC Treaty. As harmonisation is mainly aimed at establishing a common market, approximation of the Member States' law to each other is not sufficient as soon as all existent laws owing to their very content obstruct the market. Approximation requires a European standard which is autonomously set. As the EU pursues tasks transferred to it by the Member States, it can enact an autonomous standard within its margin of discretion.[115] This is valid even when harmonisation is extended

---

[111]   Case C–361/88 *Commission v. Germany* [1991] ECR I–2567. This means also rule-making by precedents in the Common Law countries: see Bock, Y (2005), *Rechtsangleichung und Regulierung im Binnenmarkt – Zum Umfang der allgemeinen Binnenmarktkompetenz* (Nomos) at 67.

[112]   Schwartz, IE (1987), '30 Jahre EG-Rechtsangleichung' in Mestmäcker, E-J, Möller, H and Schwarz, H-P (eds), *Eine Ordnungspolitik für Europa – Festschrift für Hans von der Groeben* (Nomos) 333 at 337.

[113]   Slot, PJ (1996), 'Harmonisation', 21 *European Law Review* 378 at 381; not solely for the EC context see Taupitz, J (1993), *Europäische Privatrechtsvereinheitlichung heute und morgen* (Mohr) at 14–15.

[114]   Cf Großfeld, B and Bilda, K (1992), 'Europäische Rechtsangleichung', *Zeitschrift für Rechtsvergleichung* 421 at 426–7 and Örücü, E (2002), 'Law as Transposition', 51 *International and Comparative Law Quarterly* 205.

[115]   Cf Lochner, N (1962), 'Was bedeuten die Begriffe Harmonisierung, Koordinierung und gemeinsame Politik in den Europäischen Verträgen?', 118 *Zeitschrift für*

to areas not directly connected with the internal market (e.g. Article 153 or 192 TFEU or general principles of Union law). Approximation to an autonomous standard results in the convergence of the legal orders.[116]

The concept does not need to have been part of Member States' legal orders before harmonisation, as differences between the legal orders exist even if there are no laws for a certain issue in some Member States. The ECJ deems an approximation to be admissible even if the concept is created at the European level for the first time, without the pre-existence of similar regulations in at least one Member State.[117] This is criticised as a creeping gain of competence,[118] but it is the consequence of an understanding of harmonisation that is not based on the approximation of legal orders to each other (and hence automatically only within the available array of national solutions), but on the approximation to a set Euro-standard.[119] Harmonisation requires compliance with this standard. So even if there were no pertinent regulative acts in the Member States it would still be approximation, as the differences to be eliminated are not determined by differences between the Member States' legal orders, but by a divergence from the European standard determined by the requirements of Article 3 TFEU.

The same applies when all existing laws are identical, as long as they are not identical with the European standard. Harmonisation does not require discrepancy between the Member States' legal orders. There is only one exception. If

die gesamte Staatswissenschaft 35 at 56: '[a]nnäherung an ein neu festzustellendes gemeinsames Ideal' ('approximation to common ideal to be defined'). Likewise von der Groeben, H and Schwarze, J (2003), *Kommentar zum Vertrag über die Europäische Union und zur Gründung der Europäischen Gemeinschaft* (Nomos) Art. 94 para. 22. On the question of discretion see Bock, Y (2005), *Rechtsangleichung und Regulierung im Binnenmarkt – Zum Umfang der allgemeinen Binnenmarktkompetenz* (Nomos) at 164.

[116] Neri, S (1971), 'Les actes des organes de la C.E.E. en tant que moyen du rapprochement', 11 *Kölner Schriften zum Europarecht* 199 at 201.

[117] Case C–376/98 *Germany v. Parliament and Council* [2000] ECR I–8419, para. 86; Case C–377/98 *Netherlands v. Parliament and Council* [2001] ECR I–7079, para. 15 and Case C–491/01 *R v. Secretary of State for Health, ex parte British American Tobacco (Investments) Ltd and Imperial Tobacco Ltd* [2002] ECR I–11453, para. 6.

[118] Eiden, C (1984), *Die Rechtsangleichung gemäß Art. 100 des EWG-Vertrages* (Duncker & Humblot) at 18–19; Ihns, A (2005), *Entwicklung und Grundlagen der europäischen Rechtsangleichung* (Heymans) at 86; Calliess, C and Ruffert, M (2007), *EUV/EGV – Das Verfassungsrecht der Europäischen Union mit Europäischer Grundrechtecharta – Kommentar* (3rd edn, C.H.Beck) Art. 94 para. 9; Seidl-Hohenveldern, I (1971), 'Rechtsakte der Organe der EWG als Mittel der Angleichung', 11 *Kölner Schriften zum Europarecht* 170 at 177; Ludwigs, M (2004), *Rechtsangleichung nach Art. 94, 95 EG-Vertrag – Eine kompetenzrechtliche Untersuchung unter besonderer Berücksichtigung des Europäischen Privatrechts* (Nomos) at 98.

[119] Cf Bell, J (1998), 'Mechanisms for Cross-fertilisation of Administrative Law in Europe' in Beatson, J and Tridimas, T (eds), *New Directions in European Public Law* (Hart Publishing) 147 at 149 et seq.

approximation under Article 114 TFEU is motivated by the existence of differing regulations that hinder the functioning of the internal market, real differences are needed.[120] However, this is only a question of competences. Existing differences can still be eliminated or mitigated by raising all regulations to a new, common level.[121]

6. Intended and Real Results – Unity in Diversity?[122]

Harmonisation aims at a legal result. This result is not to be confused with the objective of harmonisation. The legal result serves to achieve the objective and is at the same time determined by the objective. One must differentiate between objective and result, as otherwise causal relationships are confounded. An

---

[120] See Case C–376/98 *Germany v. European Parliament and Council* [2001] ECR I–8419, paras 83–5; Case C–491/01 *R v. Secretary of State for Health, ex parte British American Tobacco (Investments) Ltd and Imperial Tobacco Ltd* [2002] ECR I–11454, paras 69, 75.

[121] Case C–436/03 *European Parliament v. Council* [2006] ECR I–0373,3 para. 44; Opinion of AG Kokott in Case C–217/04 *United Kingdom and Northern Ireland v. European Parliament and Council (ENISA)* [2006] ECR I–03771, paras 23–4.

[122] This 'motto' of the EU was meant to be integrated in the failed European Constitutional Treaty, where the preamble contained the passage: '[c]onvinced that, while remaining proud of their own national identities and history, the peoples of Europe are determined to transcend their ancient divisions and, united even more closely, to forge a common destiny, convinced that, thus "united in its diversity", Europe offers them the best opportunity'. The motto, created in 2000, is still part of the Declaration 52 to the consolidated EU Treaties, signed by 16 Member States. It is an old idea which has its roots in Indian philosophy and has often been used in relation to culture, language or ethnic groups. As many national rules reflect cultural or societal values and differ exactly for this reason from rules in other Member States, it can also be applied to the laws in Europe, meaning that harmonisation of law is only admissible as long it is needed for common policies and safeguards national idiosyncrasies. See e.g. Curtin, D and Dekker, I (2002), 'The Constitutional Structure of the European Union: Some Reflections on Vertical Unity-in-Diversity' in Beaumont, P, Lyons, C and Walker, N (eds), *Convergence and Divergence in European Public Law* (Hart Publishing) 59 at 60; von Bogdandy, A (2003), 'Europäische Prinzipienlehre' in von Bogdandy, A (ed.), *Europäisches Verfassungsrecht – Theoretische und dogmatische Grundzüge* (Springer) 149 at 166–9 and 184 et seq.; Jeammaud, A (1998), 'Unification, uniformisation, harmonisation: de quoi s'agitil?' in Osman, F (ed.), *Vers un code européen de la consommation/Towards a European consumer code* (Bruylant) 35 at 43; Toggeburg, G (2004), 'Unification via Diversification – what does it mean to be "united in diversity"?, *Eumap Online Journal*, available at: www.eumap.org/journal/features/2004/bigday/diversity; David, R (1955), 'Die Zukunft der europäischen Rechtsordnungen: Vereinheitlichung oder Harmonisierung?' in Zweigert, K (ed.), *Europäische Zusammenarbeit im Rechtswesen* (Verlag J.C.B. Mohr) 1 at 1–3; Calliess, C and Ruffert, M (2007), *EUV/EGV – Das Verfassungsrecht der Europäischen Union mit Europäischer Grundrechtecharta – Kommentar* (3rd edn, C.H.Beck) at 1252.

example of the importance of this aspect can be found in the German perception of harmonisation. In the German version, Articles 114 and 115 TFEU confer competences for *Rechtsangleichung* ('assimilation'), whereas in most other versions mere 'approximation', thus a getting closer, seems to suffice.[123] I have earlier pointed out that we ought not to draw legal conclusions from the use of terms in Europe, as it is not uniform and not used with a specific intent.[124] The use of words, however, coins academic writing in the respective language families. Consequently, in Germany a higher amount of identity of European norms as a result of approximation is subconsciously presupposed than in most other countries.[125] The term 'harmonisation', which is used in all versions, i.e. the creation of harmony, order or concordance, does not indicate that at the European level the aim could go any further than mere approximation or creation of similar law. Harmonisation is mostly understood as avoiding complete uniformity.[126] The reality within the EU seems to teach us a different lesson, as often detailed requirements and a unifying interpretation by the ECJ create more than merely approximated law.[127] But what is the intended result?

Approximation or unification of norms and of applied law
It has often been claimed that unification is not the intended result of European harmonisation.[128] However, leaving aside literal interpretation, there are more indicators for gradual than for qualitative differences between harmonisation and unification within the EU legal order. Some claim that since Article 288 TFEU distinguishes between directives (which allegedly equal approximation) and regulations (which allegedly equal unification) there must be a substantial

---

[123]   ES: *la aproximación*; FR: *rapprochement*; IT: *ravvicinamento*; NL: *aanpassing*; PT: *aproximação*.

[124]   See above section A.

[125]   See however Everling, U (1987), 'Zur Funktion der Rechtsangleichung in der Europäischen Gemeinschaft – Vom Abbau der Verzerrungen zur Schaffung des Binnenmarktes' in Capotorti, F and others (eds), *Du droit international au droit de l'intégration – Liber Amicorum Pierre Pescatore* (Nomos) 227 at 229 who remarks that this is due to last minute changes.

[126]   See Boodman, M (1991), 'The Myth of Harmonization of Laws', 39 *American Journal of Comparative Law* 699 at 701; Jeammaud, A (1998), 'Unification, uniformisation, harmonisation: de quoi s'agit-il?' in Osman, F (ed.), *Vers un code européen de la consommation/Towards a European consumer code* (Bruylant) 35 at 41–2.

[127]   Cf Neri, S (1971), 'Les actes des organes de la C.E.E. en tant que moyen du rapprochement', 11 *Kölner Schriften zum Europarecht* 199 at 201.

[128]   Slot, PJ (1996), 'Harmonisation', 21 *European Law Review* 378 at 379; Kurcz, B (2001), 'Harmonisation by means of Directives – never-ending story?', *European Business Law Review* 287 at 288; Jeammaud, A (1998) 'Unification, uniformisation, harmonisation: de quoi s'agit-il?' in Osman, F (ed.), *Vers un code européen de la consommation/Towards a European consumer code* (Bruylant) 35 at 39–43.

difference.[129] This is, however, not as obvious as it seems at first sight. Since the introduction of what was then Article 100a TEC (now Article 114 TFEU) it has become clear that regulations may also be used in order to achieve approximation. Even before that there have been regulations entitled 'for the approximation of law'.[130] In practice, many directives, due to the way they are formulated or the type of concepts they try to introduce, do not leave much leeway for the Member States when enacting implementing legislation.[131] Moreover, the doctrine of direct applicability of directives[132] approximates their effects to that of regulations, because the Euro-standard can be directly applicable in the Member State, if there is no implementing legislation.

The difference between approximation and unification seems therefore predominantly a formal one. As directives require implementation by the Member States and are thus two-tiered legislation, the difference can be defined as follows: 'Rechts*vereinheitlichung* durch ein *einheitliches Gesetz*, Rechts*angleichung* durch eine *Vielzahl inhaltlich gleicher oder jedenfalls materiell gleichwertiger Gesetze*'.[133] It is certainly true that if a single, directly applicable law is the source for regulation, there is an identical, positive legal basis in all Member States. Directives, on the contrary, theoretically combine an abstract standard at the European level and the discretion to realise this standard on the part of the Member States. This does not, however, constitute a substantial difference. It cannot be concluded that implementation of directives will only result in an adjustment of legal orders while safeguarding their identity and idiosyncratic characteristics and prohibiting unification.[134] Harmonisation brings with it the loss of certain legal options, also meaning a certain loss of legal

[129] See Schnorbus, Y (2001), 'Autonome Harmonisierung in den Mitgliedsstaaten durch die Inkorporation von Gemeinschaftsrecht – Eine Untersuchung zur einheitlichen Anwendung und Auslegung europäischen und autonomen nationalen Rechts und zur entsprechenden Zuständigkeit des EuGH im Vorabentscheidungsverfahren', 65 *RabelsZ* 654 at 657 and 662.

[130] Cf Lagrange, M (1969), 'Contribution to the Discussion' in 11 *Kölner Schriften zum Europarecht* 223 at 223; Usher, J (1981), 'Harmonisation of Legislation' in Lasok, D and Soldatos, P (eds), *Les Communautés Européennes en Fonctionnement – The European Communities in Action* (Bruylant) 171 at 174 et seq.

[131] See e.g. Art. 3 of Council Directive 93/13/EEC of 5 April 1993 on unfair terms in consumer contracts, OJ 1993 L 095 29–34.

[132] For an overview on direct applicability see Craig, P and de Búrca, G (2008), *EU Law* (4th edn, OUP) at 279–84.

[133] 'Unification by one uniform law, approximation by a multitude of laws that are identical or at least equivalent in content': Taupitz, J (1993), *Europäische Privatrechtsvereinheitlichung heute und morgen* (Mohr) at 20 (emphasis as in the original text).

[134] Contrary Schnorbus, Y (2001), 'Autonome Harmonisierung in den Mitgliedsstaaten durch die Inkorporation von Gemeinschaftsrecht – Eine Untersuchung zur einheitlichen Anwendung und Auslegung europäischen und autonomen nationalen Rechts

identity. Even by the introduction of identical rules or by reference to the same source a common European principle can only evolve if there is uniform, or at least similar, Union-wide application. So it is the case neither that approximation safeguards national principles nor that unification enforces common principles *per se*.

Both share the grade of harmonisation as common criteria for their respective effects. As a result, unification is only the most intensive form of harmonisation. Approximation can be sufficient if that way obstacles to free movement are removed or, respectively, the aim of the European legislative act can be reached. This is when non-identical law suffices to govern the behaviour of the European citizens. The permissible variety depends solely on the aim of the harmonising measure. As long as the principle of mutual recognition is applicable, a great variety is possible. If laws are harmonised in order to encourage cross-border trade, there must be less variety (although higher protection through national laws may be permissible).[135] If uniform Union-wide behaviour is needed (e.g. in order to protect the environment), then harmonisation must result in uniform law and application.

Thus, no matter whether the Euro-standard is inserted by means of approximation or unification, the process of formation of a European principle triggered by the insertion of a new concept is the same and its outcome not predictable – a common European principle that substitutes for all pre-existing national law may evolve or it may only result in a minimum standard and divergence in national application.

Uniformity of the legal order or uniformity of concepts
The determination of the intended result of harmonisation also depends on perspective. Regarding the whole European legal order, a uniform European law is clearly not intended and would neither be useful nor required for the aims of the EU. It would mean that in all areas of law, or at least in single, definable areas, the same rules had to be applied. In respect to the whole legal order, Union law is meant to coexist with national solutions, as the approaches of minimum harmonisation, mutual recognition and equal treatment show – thus, diversity in unity. However, looking at a specific harmonising measure or even more closely at one of the legal concepts within a non-technical directive, e.g. 'product' or 'defect' in the Directive on Product Liability,[136] the difference

---

und zur entsprechenden Zuständigkeit des EuGH im Vorabentscheidungsverfahren', 65 *RabelsZ* 654 at 663.

[135] Cf Case C–52/00 *Commission v. French Republic* [2002] ECR I–3827, para. 17.

[136] Council Directive of 25 July 1985 on the approximation of the laws, regulations an administrative provisions of the Member States concerning liability for defective products 85/374/EEC, OJ 1985 L 210 29–33.

between an approximated concept and a unified one is hard to determine. The elimination of differences in product liability law makes sense only if the same regime applies all over Europe.[137] The same is true regarding minimum product safety standards – as far as minimum standards are concerned they must be exactly the same and not only similar throughout Europe.

'Spill-over'[138] effects

The pointillist[139] approximation or unification, however, induces changes in the whole legal order. Principles, policies and ideas developed at the Union level are the (binding) blueprint for developments in the domestic legal orders. Theoretically, the scope of harmonisation only entails legislation for situations with a Union dimension. In practice, this results in a large 'penetration' of national law by Union standards, which transcends those areas actually subject to harmonisation and within the direct competence of the Union.[140] It further leads to a Union-directed development and interpretation of the harmonised areas detracted from the competence of the Member States.[141] Thus, 'passive' harmonisation goes much further than intended by 'active' harmonisation of relatively small fields. AG Stix-Hackl noted, 'The aim of approximation of laws within the meaning of Article 95 EC Treaty is to reduce disparities between legal systems'.[142] This is not as circular as it may seem; it rather points to the fact that

---

[137]   Ibid., recital 1.

[138]   This term is mainly used in order to refer to the spread of European ideas to purely domestic contexts: see e.g. Birkinshaw, P (2003), *European Public Law* (Butterworths) at 7; Anthony, G (2002), *UK Public Law and European Law* (Hart Publishing) at 13; Craig, PP (1997), 'Once more unto the breach: the Community, the State and damages liability', *Law Quarterly Review* 67 at 89.

[139]   The picture of 'pointillist' directives has been coined by Roth, W.-H. (2002), 'Transposing "Pointillist" EC Guidelines into Systematic National Codes – Problems and Consequences', 6 *European Review of Private Law* 761 at 761.

[140]   Großfeld, B and Bilda, K (1992), 'Europäische Rechtsangleichung', *Zeitschrift für Rechtsvergleichung* 421 at 422; Weatherill, S (2004), 'Why Harmonise?' in Tridimas, T and Nebbia, P (eds), *European Union Law for the Twenty-First Century – Rethinking the New Legal Order* (Hart Publishing) 11 at 26–7.

[141]   See also Everling, U (1986), 'Rechtsvereinheitlichung durch Richterrecht in der Europäischen Gemeinschaft', 50 *RabelsZ* 193 at 195.

[142]   Opinion of AG Stix-Hackl in Case C–436/03 *European Parliament v. Council* [2006] ECR I–3733, para. 59. In other language versions this reads for example: D: 'Das Ziel der Rechtsangleichung im Sinne von Artikel 95 EG besteht in einer Annäherung der Rechtssysteme'; F: 'L'objectif du rapprochement des législations au sens de l'article 95 CE consiste à rapprocher les systèmes juridiques'; ES: 'El objetivo de la aproximación de las legislaciones en el sentido del artículo 95 CE consiste en una armonización de los sistemas jurídicos'; SV: 'Syftet med harmoniseringen i den mening som avses i artikel 95 EG är en tillnärmning av rättssystemen'; SK: 'Cíl sbližování práva ve smyslu článku 95 ES spočívá ve sblížení právních systémů.'

the over-arching aim of particular harmonising measures is to bring the legal systems as a whole closer together. Furthermore, even if unity is not intended, it may still be the factual result, as Member States stick closely to the European standard and the common application is controlled by the ECJ.[143] Therefore, harmonisation tries to 'smooth' the national legal orders. At the same time, it transports common values, which should prevail throughout the single market.

D.   A UNIFORM DEFINITION OF HARMONISATION

Having considered all this, what definition can be derived?

First, harmonisation is a process. It begins with the conscious creation of a concept at the European level by various actors and included in various normative instruments, which has the intent and the potential to develop towards a common European law. This is the standard for harmonisation to which the domestic law is to be approximated. Instruments are not only secondary legislation, but also primary legislation in its interpretation by the ECJ and general principles of Union law. Harmonisation requires the insertion and adaptation of the concept into the domestic legal orders by different means, as only thereby is the important part of the process triggered. After the insertion the actual moulding of a common European concept, which may or may not resemble the original standard, but which is common to all Member States, begins. This task is mainly undertaken by cooperation between domestic and European courts and influenced by specific mechanisms in the EU legal order such as preliminary ruling, harmonious interpretation, infringement procedures and state liability.

Second, harmonisation has an intended result. This is to create a law as uniform as is needed for the goals to be achieved. Most importantly, similarity in norms, i.e. texts and rules, is not enough. Rather, the intent is to create a harmonised application of the concept throughout Europe. That is why a harmonising process is needed.

Finally, harmonisation serves a function, namely effectively to pursue the tasks of the European Union. This can be the establishment of the common market, but also the pursuance of common policy goals.

Harmonisation can thus be defined as a conscious process that has the aim of leading to the insertion of a concept into the national legal orders, which triggers a process of adaptation to form a European concept as uniform as required to serve the objectives of the European Union.

---

[143]   See Eiden, C (1984), *Die Rechtsangleichung gemäß Art. 100 des EWG-Vertrages* (Duncker & Humblot) at 14.

17. Theory and practice of harmonisation in the European internal market

Isidora Maletić*

This chapter[1] purports to explore the theory and practice of harmonisation by using as a test case a pivotal legislative provision of the European Treaty. Article 95 EC,[2] which enables the Community institutions to adopt measures for the approximation of Member States' norms relating to the establishment and functioning of the internal market, constitutes one of the most powerful instruments for the advancement of European harmonisation. However, there seems to be a fundamental divergence between the theory and practice of harmonisation under this provision. Under the Treaty, it is envisaged that, *in theory*, the process of harmonisation will be complemented by the possibility for Member States, in accordance with the procedure contained within paragraphs (4) to (9) of Article 95 EC, to maintain or introduce national measures even following harmonisation. Nevertheless, *in practice*, this derogation procedure 'has proved to be relatively infrequently invoked and its use even less frequently authorised'.[3] It is the object of this chapter to analyse to what extent this discrepancy between the theory and practice of harmonisation under Article 95 EC has resulted in a loss of regulatory differentiation, and to investigate more generally how harmonisation under this provision, which characterises much of the European legislative agenda, may be reconciled with regulatory variation at national level.

As illustrated by the seminal *Tobacco Advertising*[4] case, harmonisation under Article 95 EC is inextricably linked to the creation of the internal market. It will be remembered that the Court annulled a directive which had allegedly been adopted to promote the formation of the internal market, on the suspicion

---

* King's College, London, UK.
[1] The present chapter is based on my doctoral studies.
[2] Article 95 EC has, following the completion of this chapter, become Article 114 TFEU as a result of the Lisbon Treaty amendments (OJ 2007, C306).
[3] Weatherill, S (2006), 'Supply of and Demand for Internal Market Regulation: Strategies, Preferences and Interpretation', in Shuibhne, NN (ed.), *Regulating the Internal Market* (Edward Elgar Publishing) 29 at 41.
[4] Case C–376/98 *Germany v. Parliament and Council* [2000] ECR I–8419.

that the measure was intended, in reality, to harmonise rules governing public health, a matter lying beyond the Community's competence. So, in line with the principle of attributed powers, harmonisation under Article 95 does not give the Community institutions a general regulatory power, but rather enables them to adopt measures specifically designed to facilitate the establishment and functioning of the internal market. It may therefore be wondered whether, in the aftermath of harmonisation, the reallocation of powers between Community legislation and Member State residual autonomy caters satisfactorily for the often diverging interests of, on the one hand, the internal market and, on the other, non-market values safeguarded at national level, such as consumer protection, environmental policies, and public health.

It is clear, however, that despite an indubitable emphasis on economic legislative advancement, harmonisation under Article 95 EC also presupposes the furtherance of related welfare policies. Indeed, paragraph 3 of Article 95 requires the Commission, in its proposals on the establishment and functioning of the internal market concerning health, safety, environmental protection, and consumer protection, to take as a base a high level of protection, taking account in particular of any new development based on scientific facts.

The concern for the regulatory quality of legislative norms is reinforced by the 'horizontal' provisions, such as Articles 6, 153(2) and 152(1) EC (post-Lisbon, Articles 11, 12, and 168 TFEU respectively), directing that environmental, consumer and health protection be considered in the implementation of Community policies.[5] This concern would also seem to be reflected in the jurisprudence of the Court: indeed it has long been clear, especially from the *Tobacco Advertising* saga,[6] that despite the Court's insistence in the first *Tobacco Advertising* case[7] that harmonisation norms adopted under Article 95 must be genuinely intended to promote the internal market, a Community measure will not be annulled because it also takes into account correlated welfare concerns. Thus, for example, in the second *Tobacco Advertising* case,[8] a directive purporting to harmonise national rules on tobacco advertising and adopted on the basis of Article 95 EC with the presumed objective of promoting the establishment and functioning of the internal market was not annulled despite the fact that public

---

[5]   See for a discussion of these issues Weatherill, S (2005), 'Harmonisation: How Much, How Little?', 16 *European Business Law Review* 533 at 535.

[6]   See the established line of jurisprudence, including cases like Case C–491/01 *British American Tobacco (Investments) and Imperial Tobacco* [2002] ECR I–11453; Case C–434/02 *Arnold André* [2004] ECR I–11825; Case C–210/03 *Swedish Match* [2004] ECR I–11893, and most recently Case C–380/03 *Germany v. European Parliament* [2006] ECR I–11573.

[7]   Case C–376/98 *Germany v. Parliament and Council* [2000] ECR I–8419.

[8]   Case C–380/03 *Germany v. European Parliament* [2006] ECR I–11573.

health had been a decisive factor informing the Community legislature's choice to introduce the relevant norm. Clearly, therefore, both the Treaty text and the jurisprudence of the Court would seem to endorse a harmonisation trend away from strict economic integration and open to the legislative pursuit of related welfare policies.

Yet, it is notable that even though the EC Treaty seeks a high level of regulatory protection, it does not oblige the EC legislature to adopt the highest level of protection that can be found in any particular Member State.[9] Thus, although not insensitive to regulatory advancement, harmonisation at Community level may still differ from or fail to attain the standards selected by individual Member States. This issue would however appear to be addressed by the Treaty: indeed, it is important to remember that Article 95 does contain a derogation mechanism enabling Member States, under carefully delineated circumstances, to derogate from harmonisation norms in order to safeguard specific values, even at the irrefutable expense of Community legislation and economic integration. In view of the importance of this procedure, the most relevant sections deserve to be mentioned briefly in full. Thus, it may be recalled that paragraph (4) of Article 95, allows a Member State, following the adoption of a harmonisation norm, to *maintain existing* national provisions on grounds of major needs referred to in Article 30 (post-Lisbon, Article 36 TFEU),[10] or relating to the protection of the environment or the working environment, by way of notification to the Commission. Paragraph (5) of Article 95 provides for the further possibility, following the adoption of a harmonisation measure, of *introducing* national provisions based on new scientific evidence relating to the protection of the environment or the working environment on grounds of a problem specific to that Member State arising after the adoption of the harmonisation measure. The Commission is then under an obligation within six months of the notifications made under either paragraph (4) or (5), to approve or reject the relevant national provisions, after having verified whether or not they are a means of arbitrary discrimination or a disguised restriction on trade between Member States and whether or not they constitute an obstacle to the functioning of the internal market. In the absence of a decision by the Commission within this period the notified national provisions are deemed to have been approved. However, when justified by the complexity of the matter and in the absence of danger for human health, the

---

[9]   See Rott, P (2003), 'Minimum Harmonization for the Completion of the Internal Market? The Example of Consumer Sales Law', 40 *Common Market Law Review* 1107 at 1108.

[10]   These are 'public morality, public policy or public security; the protection of health and life of humans, animals or plants; the protection of national treasures possessing artistic, historic or archaeological value; or the protection of industrial and commercial property', which notably excludes consumer and environmental protection.

Commission may notify the Member State that the six month deadline is to be extended for a further period of up to six months. In the case of a Member State being permitted to maintain or introduce national provisions derogating from a harmonisation measure, the Commission has a duty to consider whether it is necessary to propose an adaptation to that measure.

Enabling Member States to apply higher regulatory standards even after harmonisation, the significance of Article 95(4) *et seq.* cannot be overemphasised. This derogation mechanism has been seen as presenting 'real opportunities for protectionist abuse'[11] and is one of the key reasons why, when initially introduced in 1987 by the Single European Act, this legislation was regarded 'as an instrument of destruction'[12] for what had already been achieved by the Community. Yet, inherent in this notification procedure is the constitutionally imperative compromise between the Community's legislative competence and national autonomy. At least in theory, harmonisation under Article 95 EC, which is representative of the European legislative process, would appear to envisage a possible balance between the two. Exploring the derogation mechanism under Article 95 with reference to a recent ruling in this field concerning national provisions banning genetic engineering[13] could help determine the extent to which European harmonisation can co-exist with national regulatory differentiation in practice as well as in theory.

The case arose following the adoption of a 2001 directive[14] on the deliberate release into the environment of genetically modified organisms (GMOs). The objective of the directive was stated as being to approximate the laws of the Member States and to protect human health and the environment, first, when the deliberate release into the environment of GMOs for any purposes other than placing on the market within the European Community is carried out and, second, when GMOs are placed on the market in products within the Community. The Directive was adopted on the basis of Article 95 EC. In 2003, Austria notified the Commission under Article 95(5) EC of a draft law of 2002 banning genetic engineering in the hope of securing a derogation from the Community norm. The Austrian law was intended to prohibit the cultivation of seed and planting material containing GMOs and the breeding and release, for the purposes of hunting and fishing, of transgenic animals. In response to a request by the Commission for an analysis of the probative value of the

---

[11]   Bermann, G (1989), 'The Single European Act: a New Constitution for the Community?', 27 *Columbia Journal of Transnational Law* 529 at 543.

[12]   Pescatore, P (1987), 'Some Critical Remarks on the "Single European Act"', 24 *Common Market Law Review* 9 at 18.

[13]   Case C–439/05 *Land Oberösterreich v. Commission* [2007] ECR I–7141.

[14]   Directive 2001/18/EC of the European Parliament and of the Council of 12 March 2001 on the deliberate release into the environment of genetically modified organisms and repealing Council Directive 90/220/EEC (OJ 2001 L 106 at 1).

scientific information relied on by Austria, EFSA, the European Food Safety Authority, issued an opinion in which it essentially concluded that the data supplied did not contain any new scientific evidence which could justify banning GMOs. Against this background, the Commission rejected Austria's request for derogation,[15] concluding that the conditions in Article 95(5) EC had not been satisfied as Austria had failed to provide new scientific evidence or demonstrate that a specific problem in the Province of Upper Austria had arisen following the adoption of the relevant directive which made it necessary to introduce the notified national measure. Following the dismissal of the action brought by Austria before the CFI[16] seeking the annulment of the Commission decision, Austria and the Province of Upper Austria initiated proceedings before the ECJ. In support of their appeal, they raised two pleas for annulment, alleging, first, infringement of the right to be heard and, second, infringement of Article 95(5) EC. The ECJ rejected both pleas and the action was dismissed.

The ruling, insofar as the application for derogation of the Member State was refused, appears to be in line with other judgments relating to the notification procedure under Article 95. The cases before the Courts and decisions of the Commission would seem to indicate a fairly narrow reading of this derogation mechanism. In view of the positioning of this procedure within the Treaty, namely Article 95, the oxygen for the establishment and functioning of the internal market, the cautious attitude of the Community institutions would seem understandable. It may also be that that procedure has been invoked in a somewhat uncertain manner by the Member States, with the cases often revolving round procedural aspects of the derogation mechanism rather than lending themselves to a more extensive substantive analysis of this device.[17]

On the other hand, an almost systematic rejection of Member States' applications to maintain or introduce more stringent national measures following harmonisation would seem to be in contravention of the concern for regulatory differentiation enshrined in the Treaty. Indeed, while it is clear that *in theory* at least the process of harmonisation does not preclude the possibility for continued national regulatory variation, it may be wondered whether excessively tight control over the conditions that must be fulfilled for a derogation to be granted makes the procedure a truly viable option *in practice*. Looking at Article 95(5)

---

[15]   Commission Decision 2003/653/EC of 2 September 2003 relating to national provisions on banning the use of genetically modified organisms in the region of Upper Austria notified by the Republic of Austria pursuant to Article 95(5) of the EC Treaty (OJ 2003 L 230 at 34).

[16]   Joined Cases T–366/03 and T–235/04 *Land Oberösterreich and Austria v. Commission* [2005] ECR II–4005.

[17]   See, for example, Case C–512/99 *Germany v. Commission* [2003] ECR I–845; Case T–234/04 *Kingdom of the Netherlands v. Commission* [2007] ECR II–4589.

EC, it is evident that a number of conditions need to be satisfied and that these are cumulative, so that all must be met for the derogating national measures to be allowed by the Commission. In particular, as aforementioned, under Article 95(5) EC it is apparent that the introduction of novel national provisions derogating from a harmonisation measure must be based on new scientific evidence relating to the protection of the environment or the working environment made necessary by reason of a problem specific to that Member State arising after the adoption of the harmonisation measure. The case examined above on genetic engineering illustrates in particular the difficulty of proving the existence of a problem specific to the notifying Member State justifying a purported derogation. It is noteworthy that the ECJ emphasised that the lawfulness of national measures notified under Article 95(5) EC is closely linked to the assessment of the scientific evidence put forward by the notifying Member State. The EFSA opinion found that there was no scientific evidence demonstrating the existence of a specific problem, on the basis that no scientific evidence proving the existence of unusual or unique ecosystems requiring separate risk assessments from those conducted for Austria as a whole or in other similar areas of Europe had been submitted. Thus, it is clear that there was a contrast between the scientific opinion of the notifying Member State and EFSA, which found that Austria had not provided any new information capable of calling into question the 2001 directive. In this respect, the dismissal of the application for derogation raises the fundamental issue regarding the extent to which it is really accepted that Member States may legitimately differ in their risk assessments from harmonisation norms. Again, the outcome of the ruling ultimately casts doubt on the notion that the derogation mechanism contained in Article 95 may be a truly viable option in *practice* as much as in *theory*.

It is difficult to draw a definitive conclusion on the significance of the case for the notification procedure under Article 95, and more broadly for harmonisation within the internal market. It is noteworthy however, that from the opening paragraphs of her Opinion, Advocate General Sharpston emphasised that the case concerned an attempt by one of the Austrian *Länder* to introduce, with a view to creating a farming area free of GMOs, a law imposing a *general* ban, whereas under the relevant directive the placing on the market of a GMO is subject to an authorisation regime which requires a health and environmental risk assessment on a *case-by-case* basis. Rather than being necessarily reflective of a narrow reading of the procedure contained within Article 95, the case could merely be in line with the Court's general application of the principle of proportionality. On this reading, it would appear that the Austrian notification was rejected primarily because the national provisions concerned sought to introduce a *general ban* rather than a more qualified monitoring of the cultivation of GMOs.

At the same time, however, the case could also have more profound implications for the concept of harmonisation within the European legislative process, and in particular the form harmonising instruments should take. As aforementioned, the 2001 directive at issue in the ruling established a notification and authorisation regime preceded by an assessment on a case-by-case basis of potential adverse effects on human health and the environment. The outcome of the ruling would seem to imply that the regime set out by the Directive was viewed as being self-sufficient, not to be undermined by additional and *ad hoc* Member State derogations. In this respect, it would be plausible to interpret the rejection of the notified provision in the Austrian case on genetic engineering as being indicative of the increasingly comprehensive nature and all-inclusive role attributed to directives. In practice, therefore, harmonisation under Article 95 would seem to assume a definitive character, sealing the possibility for Member States to add further conditions except for in circumstances provided by the relevant directive itself. The presumption would appear to be that Member States should raise any legitimate concerns they may have at the stage of the negotiation of directives. This implication is not without difficulties, however, for arguably an excessively narrow reading of the notification procedure under Article 95 could result in harmonisation being perceived as an almost static process, in the sense that once it has occurred, save for the exceptions provided in the relevant directives themselves, it would be difficult to use the derogation mechanism in paragraphs (4) to (9) of Article 95 EC to improve attained legislation in line with scientific progress. It may indeed be wondered whether an almost systematic rejection of applications under this notification procedure would be compatible with the initial insertion of this device within the Treaty and the concern for regulatory differentiation which it encapsulates.

In reality therefore, the notification procedure under Article 95 EC raises more profound constitutional dilemmas on the form harmonisation should take. While it is clear that the need for harmonisation within the internal market is considerably reduced by a rigorous process of negative integration, legislative harmonisation obviously remains a key instrument for the approximation of the laws of the Member States.[18] As recognised by the Commission, '[m]utual recognition is not always a miracle solution for ensuring the free movement of goods in the single market. Harmonisation or further harmonisation remains without doubt one of the most effective instruments, both for economic operators and for the national administrations.' Yet, nothing in Article 95 EC seems to suggest in a conclusive way a predilection for either minimum or maximum harmonisation as the preferred method of harmonisation for the purposes of the internal market. Nevertheless, recent practice would seem reflective of an

---

[18]   Commission Second Biennial Report on the Application of the Principle of Mutual Recognition in the Single Market, COM(2002)419.

increasing trend towards exhaustive harmonisation.[19] Examining in greater detail the notification procedure under Article 95 EC may be particularly useful for determining whether a potential inclination towards exhaustive harmonisation and away from minimum approximation norms might represent an automatic elimination of national regulatory autonomy. Furthermore, if it was concluded that the current trend gravitates indeed towards exhaustive harmonisation under Article 95 EC, the need to examine the derogation mechanism contained therein in greater detail would appear to be even more pressing.

In particular, it may be desirable to consider the possibility of reform of the notification procedure, especially with reference to the accepted grounds on which Member States may rely to deviate from a harmonisation norm and the current time limits allowed for the Commission to reach a decision in response to an application for derogation. Indeed, it is clear from the jurisprudence of the ECJ that a Member State is not authorised to apply the national provisions notified by it under Article 95 EC until after it has obtained a decision from the Commission.[20] As aforementioned, under paragraph (6) of Article 95, the Commission is under an obligation to reject or approve the national measures within six months. It may be wondered, however, whether the time allowed is compatible with a situation of real urgency arising at national level. Furthermore according to paragraph (6), when justified by the complexity of the matter and in the absence of danger for human health, the time allowed may be extended for a further period of up to six months. It is surprising to note that whilst the six month deadline cannot be extended where there is a danger for human health, there is no similar safeguard in the case of damage to the environment. Assessing any shortcomings of the derogation procedure and the extent to which these may be rectified could help to understand whether the current model of harmonisation under Article 95 caters satisfactorily both for promoting the establishment and functioning of the internal market and preserving a degree of national regulatory differentiation as prescribed by the Treaty, or whether alternative methods of harmonisation for the purposes of the internal market should be explored.

---

[19] See Case C–376/98 *Germany v. Parliament and Council* [2000] ECR I–8419; Case C–380/03 *Germany v. European Parliament* [2006] ECR I–11573. For a discussion see Weatherill, S (2006) 'Supply of and Demand for Internal Market Regulation: Strategies, Preferences and Interpretation', in Shuibhne, NN (ed), *Regulating the Internal Market* (Edward Elgar Publishing) 29; Rott, P (2003), 'Minimum Harmonization for the Completion of the Internal Market? The Example of Consumer Sales Law', 40 *Common Market Law Review* 1107.

[20] See Case C–41/93 *France v. Commission* [1994] ECR I–1829; Case C–319/97 *Kortas* [1999] ECR I–3143.

CONCLUDING REMARKS

As it has been tried to illustrate, the notification procedure under Article 95 is at the crossroads between theory and practice of harmonisation. In theory, the derogation mechanism is arguably intended to create a balance between Community harmonisation and the residual autonomy of national legal systems, as well as to reconcile economic integration with related welfare policies. However a narrow application of the notification procedure in practice, either through improper or a negligible use of the Member States or through a strict interpretation of the Commission and Courts, seems to give rise to an appreciable discrepancy between theory and practice of harmonisation for the purposes of the internal market. In the light of the defining character of Article 95 for the European legislative agenda, it would be useful to reassess the overall functioning of the derogation mechanism contained therein. In particular, as seen above, the possibility of reforming the procedure could be explored in greater detail. Assessing the advantages and shortcomings of the notification procedure contained within this important provision would in turn help one to make a more informed decision as to what form harmonisation for the purposes of the European legislative process should take. Indeed, as has been seen above, the current discrepancy between theory and practice with respect to the Article 95 notification procedure casts doubt on the extent to which the current model of harmonisation is truly compatible with national regulatory variation and whether it is ultimately suitable for the successful continuation of the European integration project.

18. International competition law harmonisation and the WTO: past, present and future

Jurgita Malinauskaite*

INTRODUCTION

The globalisation process together with technological advancements, dilution of trade barriers and liberalisation as well as privatisation programmes, has shaped the global landscape, which has resulted in the augmentation of cross-border businesses. The expansion of businesses beyond national borders has raised the issues of international anti-competitive practices. On the one hand, businesses are becoming international, whereas competition laws are national with their curbs and limits. Due to these boundaries, national competition authorities are unable to address international anti-competitive behaviour effectively, especially if the authority lacks experience, knowledge or resources and does not have vision when the anti-competitive issues transcend their domestic boundaries. As a result, some international anti-competitive transactions can escape effective regulatory mechanism, which is known as under-regulation. On the other hand, globalisation and therefore international anti-competitive practices have driven competition authorities to apply their laws beyond national boundaries. Many countries have introduced the extra-territoriality principle, where national competition authorities apply their domestic law to extra-territorial conduct that has effects in their nations. Hence, extra-territorial effects of competition bring various countries' competition laws into contact and quite often into confrontation. Apart from the harm that may be caused to the relationships between the different countries, conflicting results may be damaging to the firms concerned, as their transactions are subjected to investigation by various competition authorities worldwide. This phenomenon is known as over-regulation. For instance, if a cross-border merger was approved by one side of the Atlantic, but blocked

* Lecturer in Law, Brunel University, UK.

by the other, this conflicting result would place an unnecessary burden on the undertakings involved. Firms are concerned about the compliance cost of their international transactions due to these conflicting or duplicative policies by different national competition authorities.

Problems in dealing with these cross-border challenges have brought scholars and practitioners as well as various international organisations together to discuss harmonisation of international competition law and its importance in today's global world. Hence, this chapter will discuss the prospect of harmonisation of international competition law in light of the World Trade Organisation (WTO), its past, present and future. It will also evaluate the benefits and the pitfalls of international competition law, as to whether the notion of 'one size fits all' could be the best solution for competition law in an international context, especially from the position of small and developing countries. The question will be raised what are the strengths and limitations of the WTO in harmonising and enforcing international competition law.

THEORETICAL FRAMEWORK OF HARMONISATION

The harmonisation of law generally has been an aspiration of the international legal community since the fall of the Roman Empire, mainly to serve practical needs.[1] The globalisation process in today's world has brought businesses closer and instigated once again the necessity of harmonising laws. In general terms, harmonisation is about elimination of differences among legal regimes. However, the notion of harmonisation of laws is far from clear. René David, for instance, declared that the harmonisation of laws entails 'effectuating an understanding about the significance of certain concepts, on certain modes of rule formulation, and on the recognition of authoritative sources'.[2] Meanwhile, Goldring indicated that under the process of harmonisation 'the effects of a type of transaction in one legal system are brought as close as possible to the effect of similar transactions under the laws of other countries'.[3] Professor Boodman has further searched for a definition of harmonisation and defined it as 'a process in which diverse elements are combined or adapted to each other so as to form a coherent whole while retaining their individuality. In its relative sense, harmonisation is the creation of a relationship between diverse things. Its absolute

---

[1]   Hessel E. Yntema (1942), 'Comparative Research and Unification of Law', 41 *Michigan Law Review* 261–8.

[2]   David, R (1968), 'The Methods of Unification', 16 *The American Journal of Comparative Law* 13 at 15.

[3]   Goldring, J (1978), 'Unification and Harmonization of the Rules of Law', 9 *Federal Law Review* 284 at 289.

and most common meaning, however, implies the creation of a relationship of accord or consonance'.[4] Such a variety in concepts suggests that harmonisation of law *per se* has no general meaning. It is a pragmatic concept that cannot be separated from its particular context or applied use.[5]

This chapter will discuss attempts by the WTO to harmonise competition law, as a response to globalisation, which led to global markets and therefore to international anti-competitive behaviour. There is a variety of terms used in the literature on competition law to describe the process of 'harmonisation', such as the terms 'harmonisation', 'unification', 'convergence', and 'internationalisation'. However, quite often these terms are not defined or explained by scholars. Two main reasons may explain this. The first reason relies on the assumption that these terms are self-defining and broadly accepted and no further explanation is necessary. The second reason could be that these terms are so confusing and unclear that any attempt to define them will further muddle already 'murky water'. Either way, the result is not satisfactory. Nonetheless, it seems that scholars use different terms to define similar or even the same processes. Dabbah,[6] for instance, refers to 'internationalisation' as a means to move closer to a position of similarity (in the case of antitrust policy).[7] He further provides four examples of internationalisation,[8] one of them being convergence towards some common standards in order to harmonise the different antitrust laws of different countries. Neither 'convergence' nor 'harmonisation' is further explained.[9] First refers to strong-form harmonisation, which means having an international agency with enforcement power; meanwhile weaker-form harmonisation would consist of enforcement assistance agreements between national

---

[4]   Boodman, M (1991), 'The Myth of Harmonization of Laws', 39 *The American Journal of Comparative Law* 699 at 705.

[5]   For further discussion see ibid., at 707.

[6]   Dabbah, M (2003), *The Internationalisation of Antitrust Policy* (Cambridge University Press) at 4.

[7]   Although some scholars refer to antitrust law, which is an accepted term by the US, this chapter will define it as competition law (as referred to in the EU).

[8]   First, bilateral co-operation between different antitrust authorities around the world; secondly, convergence of domestic antitrust laws towards some common standards; thirdly, creation of a detailed international antitrust code; and finally, establishment of an international system of antitrust within a framework of autonomous international institutions: Dabbah, *supra* n. 6, at 9.

[9]   Yet the term 'internationalisation of antitrust policy' is distinguished from 'system of antitrust' and 'international system of antitrust' and serves as a 'double-edge sword', combining both the need to accept various national interests and decision processes into international institutions design and also reference to the actual penetration of international pressures into the functioning of domestic institutions. For further reading see Dabbah, *supra* n. 6, at 10–12.

competition authorities.[10] Moreover, Taylor[11] provides a more detailed explanation – distinguishing 'full harmonisation' and 'partial harmonisation' from 'convergence'. According to Taylor's convergence–harmonisation continuum, 'full harmonisation' is where two or more countries exhibit near uniformity of their substantive competition obligations and procedures for more than 80% of their competition laws;[12] therefore 'partial harmonisation' is accordingly between 60% and 80%. 'Convergence', on the other hand, refers to a state where two or more countries achieve a reasonable degree of similarity in their domestic competition laws but continue to retain different standards and approaches.[13] Although the given percentage points out the difference between the terms, it is not very clear whether substantive competition obligations are binding. In the context of this chapter, harmonisation refers to a process of negotiation and agreement on common substantive standards that have a binding nature and are accepted by various countries with divergent competition cultures, that are at different economic development stages and have different sized economies. This means that each country would require to amend its domestic laws to adopt an internationally-agreed 'ideal' standard. Meanwhile, the notion of 'convergence' will refer to a process of competition law of different countries getting closer but not quite reaching the level of harmonisation. The EU has achieved a successful harmonisation at the regional level in competition law. This chapter will examine whether it can be achieved at a global level. However, in contrast to the EU, where both voluntary and mandatory harmonisation was used,[14] this chapter will discuss 'voluntary' harmonisation: to what extent countries around the world having divergent competition cultures and different development levels of their economies are willing to accept an internationally-agreed 'ideal' standard of competition rules. It is important to distinguish between core (referring to developed countries) and peripheral (meaning developing or less developed) countries. On the one hand, the core countries may be keen 'to sell' their competition law model. On the other hand,

---

[10] First, H (1998), 'Theories of Harmonization: a cautionary tale' in Ullrich H (ed), *Comparative Competition Law: Approaching an International System of Antitrust Law* (Nomos Verlagsgesellschaft) 17 at 33.

[11] Taylor, M (2006), *International Competition Law. A new dimension for the WTO?* (Cambridge University Press) at 337–9.

[12] Note: this 80% figure, according to Taylor, is arbitrary, but necessary to demonstrate the contrast between full and partial harmonisation.

[13] For further reading see Taylor, *supra* n. 11, at 337–9.

[14] Voluntary harmonisation in this context refers to the founding Member States of the EU, which were initiators of competition law in the EU. Meanwhile, mandatory harmonisation alludes to the Member States of later accession waves, especially of 2004 and 2007, where the introduction of competition law (framed on the EU model) was a pre-condition for membership.

peripheral countries may feel political pressure from core countries to accept it, which can jeopardise 'voluntary' harmonisation.

THE SCHOOLS OF THOUGHT

The analysis of the school of thought can be of assistance in this chapter in order to explain the rationale for the WTO to integrate competition law. Two main schools will be discussed – the theories of neo-functionalism and of neo-realism. In general terms, neo-functionalism is a political theory of integration which endeavours to understand the variables leading to regional integration.[15] One of the main mechanisms of integration by the neo-functionalist theory is positive spill-over. It suggests that integration between states in one economic sector would create strong incentives for integration in further sectors in order fully to obtain the benefits of integration in the original sector. Overall, neo-functionalism brought notions of social pluralism to the centre arena and spill-over effect as a leading dynamic in furthering the integrative process.[16] McGowan argues that the EU competition law and policy mechanism epitomises one of the best successes in the history of regional integration processes, which can be used to rebut criticisms of neo-functionalism's value. He has also suggested that a competition regime may arise as 'the first example of genuine supranational, international and global regulation'.[17] Along these positive lines, Dabbah relied on neo-functionalism in order to explain how spill-over from trade to competition policy can help advancing competition policy[18] in the international arena, which could be carried out in two stages. First, there could be a spill-over from trade policy with an effective market access principle to competition policy. This will lead to adoption of a general market access principle in private anti-competitive behaviour. Secondly, after the first stage, the principle could be adapted to specific types of restraints, such as cartels and mergers, and then to vertical agreements and abuses of dominance. Although the theory of neo-functionalism can be useful in this context, i.e. to explain how the WTO's policy can be extended to

---

[15] This theory has been largely used by scholars examining European integration. See Haas, EB (1958), *The Uniting of Europe: Political, Social and Economic Forces 1950–1957* (2nd edn, Stanford University Press); Moravcsik, A (2005), 'The European Constitutional Compromise and the Neofunctionalist Legacy', 12/2 *Journal of European Public Policy* 349; O'Neill, M (1996), *The Politics of European Integration: a Reader* (Routledge); McGowan, L. (2007), 'Theorising European Integration: revisiting neo-functionalism and testing its suitability for explaining the development of EC competition policy?', *European Integration online Papers*, 25 May 2007.

[16] McGowan, *supra* n. 15.

[17] Ibid., at 14.

[18] Dabbah, *supra* n. 6, at 232–3.

embrace competition law, it is doubtful whether it would present a successful model. On the one hand, the WTO's achievement in trade liberalisation policy is undeniable. Having 152 members,[19] the WTO is one of the largest international organisations which deals with the rules of trade between nations at a global or near-global level. Yet, the WTO's efforts in removing the various internal barriers for international trade would be curtailed if these governmental restraints were replaced by private anti-competitive restraints, otherwise known as the next 'generation' of barriers to trade in the world. Accordingly neo-functionalism in this context would explain the necessity of spill-over from trade to competition policy in order to achieve the full benefits from the former. However, the expansion of the market access principle by the WTO to cover both public and private restrictions is not an easy task. Scholars argue that it is difficult to ascertain the precise split of all restraints producing an effect on international trade, especially having an effect equivalent to governmental barriers to trade and restraints that do not have such effect.[20] Moreover, limiting competition harmonisation to specific trade-related restrictive business practices may cause more problems than produce benefits. If international competition rules were subject to a trade linked criterion, the results could be worse due to nations' different interpretations based on their national notion of free trade and the mutual benefits associated with them.[21] This is because even identical words in statutes could be interpreted and applied differently due to differences in legal systems, legal cultures or mentality. Overall, competition law objectives would be undermined if justified solely on market access grounds.

The rapid advance of global economic integration means that there is a need for new perspectives of the international economy. Neo-functionalists suggest that while the process of integration proceeds, pure national orientation should be re-valued and superseded by 'a new and geographically larger set of beliefs'.[22] In this context, it would mean that national states should think globally and consider protecting global markets and global consumers. However, competition law is national in nature and, therefore, it is not clear whether (and if yes, to what extent) national competition authorities would be prepared to prioritise protecting global markets or global consumers over national markets and national consumers, and therefore how this can be effectively achieved?

---

[19] For the date of 16 May 2008, available at: www.wto.org/english/thewto_e/whatis_e/tif_e/org6_e.htm.

[20] See for instance, Ullrich, H (1998), 'International Harmonisation of Competition Law: Making Diversity a Workable Concept' in Ullrich H (ed.), *Comparative Competition Law: Approaching an International System of Antitrust Law* (Nomos Verlagsgesellschaft) 43 at 56.

[21] For further discussion see ibid., at 56–8.

[22] Haas, *supra* n. 15, at 13.

In contrast, neo-realism suggests looking behind the formal texts of rules and employs a sceptical approach towards harmonisation of substantive bodies of law such as competition law.[23] Successful harmonisation has the attributes of values, norms and actual behaviour rather than rules and text.[24] The neo-realist model suggests harmonising values, not rules. This is because competition law and policy do not exist in a vacuum and may not sit tightly with other social values. Waller points out that countries need to understand how competition policy of their own and of other states reflects unexpressed governance norms before considering common international competition rules, as to where the promotion of competition ranks on the hierarchy of social values. To what extent does the promotion of competition threaten the general social, political or economic stability of the country, and finally should competition rules incorporate only nationalistic concerns, or should the interests of foreign entities and the international system be considered in the decision making process? This means that a multinational agreement without a consensus as to the values and norms underlying the rules is meaningless – 'each society should implement its unique vision with a set of carefully considered indigenous laws, not a set of rules that represents the vision and voice of another'.[25]

This chapter will rely on both theories. First of all, it will argue that if international competition rules were introduced, then relying on the theory of neo-functionalism spill-over effect would be a logical option: the WTO's success in trade policy could be expanded to introduce international competition rules as well fully to achieve the benefits of international trade regulation. However, the chapter will conclude that this daunting task is hardly achievable based on the theory of neo-realism – no consensus on international competition rules has been reached between developed and developing countries and between large and small countries due to their differences in 'values'. Unless the agreement on common values is met, the 'ideal' international competition law model will not materialise in reality.

---

[23]   Weber Waller, S. (1994), 'Neo-Realism and the International Harmonization of Law: Lessons from Antitrust', 42 *Kansas Law Review* 557 at 591.

[24]   Prof. Joel Trachtman suggested areas that are appropriate for international discipline and those that should be left to competition: Trachtman, JP (1993), 'International Regulatory Competition, Externalization, and Jurisdiction', 34 *Harvard International Law Journal* 47 at 51. Weber Waller, *supra* n. 23, at 591.

[25]   Ibid., at 604.

GLOBALISATION AND COMPETITION POLICY

The globalisation process, together with technological advancements, domestic government policies with the opening up of borders for foreign traders and signing up to the international and/or regional organisations, dilution of trade barriers and customs distortions, liberalisation of capital movement and investment, and privatisation programmes, has changed the global landscape over time, where global transactions whirl over national borders, bringing businesses together. Apart from a liberalised environment that enables businesses to carry on their activities at a global level, they also have the technological means and resources to do so. With markets and competition becoming increasingly international, anti-competitive practices have also become trans-national. Hence, anti-competitive behaviour in the global market is not uncommon. The difference between national and international anti-competitive practices lies in the cross-border dimension of anti-competitive behaviour, which is harder to challenge. Examples of anti-competitive practices that can cause global economic damage are international anti-competitive agreements or concerted practices, anti-competitive merger transactions with spill-over effects and abuse of a dominant position by global firms. For instance, the consolidation of industries through mergers or other means may lead to global oligopolies where pricing and output decisions are made by each global firm depending on the conduct of its few remaining competitors. Practices of this nature can lead to the transfer of wealth from consumers in one country to producers in another. Consequently, consumers in one or more countries will directly or indirectly bear the cost of these unlawful activities, which may result in higher prices and reduced choice. Similarly, consumers in different nations could be worse off due to the hard-core cartels arrangements which are difficult to deter, especially if international ones, because they operate in secret and relevant evidence may be located in different countries.

Competition law together with competition enforcement institutions was introduced to many jurisdictions in the world. However, the governments from different jurisdictions have soon realised that national competition law could not give a final solution, as trade has been increasing globally whereas competition law is essentially national in scope. In a global world where multinational firms become dominant, national competition authorities cannot guarantee full protection from cross-border anti-competitive practices. Although national competition authorities attempt to deal with these practices effectively through increased levels of co-operation and consultation, their application of national regulatory tools to international anti-competitive practices is inevitably a complicated matter. While domestic markets are regulated by national authorities through their competition law or other measures, there is hardly any mechanism for regulating the international market with regard to competition law issues.

Globalisation has a significant impact for competition policy and law in the global economy; it has almost made it inevitable to change competition law. As a response to these international competition issues, the harmonisation of international competition law has evolved into a topic of significant contemporary importance. Scholars and practitioners around the world have questioned whether there is a necessity to set up a global competition agency in order to enforce international competition law and, if yes, which international body is the most suitable and what role should it play in order to enforce the principles of international competition. Many organisations, such as the International Competition Network (ICN),[26] the Organisation for Economic Cooperation and Development (OECD),[27] the United Nations Conference on Trade and Development (UNCTAD)[28] and others, have considered or even introduced soft law to deal with international competition issues. The WTO is no exception. Before exploring the WTO's response to globalisation and its attempts to harmonise competition law, it is important to discuss the principle of extra-territoriality employed by national competition authorities to deal with international anti-competitive behaviour.

---

[26] The ICN is devoted exclusively to competition law enforcement. Although it does not exercise any rule-making function, the ICN can issue recommendations or 'best practices', and then individual competition authorities decide whether and how to implement the recommendations, through unilateral, bilateral or multilateral arrangements, as appropriate. For further information on the ICN, see www.internationalcompetition-network.org.

[27] The OECD has been active in encouraging soft convergence amongst member countries by adopting a number of non-binding recommendations on competition law and policy. For instance, *OECD Guiding Principles for Regulatory Quality and Performance* (2005), *Best Practices for the Formal Exchange of Information Between Competition Authorities in Hard Core Cartel Investigations* (2005), *Recommendation of the Council concerning merger review* (2005), *Recommendation of the Council concerning structural separation in regulated industries* (2001), *Recommendation of the Council concerning effective action against hard core cartels* (1998), and *Recommendation of the Council concerning co-operation between member countries on anticompetitive practices affecting international trade* (1995), also available at: www.oecd.org/document/59/0,3343,en_2649_34535_4599739_1_1_1_1,00.html.

[28] The UNCTAD provides national competition authorities from developing countries and economies in transition with an intergovernmental forum for addressing practical competition law and policy issues. It is also a depository of international competition legislations, the Model Law on Competition (TD/RBP/Conf.5/7/Rev.2) and the United Nations Set of Principles on Competition ((td/rbp/conf/10/rev.2) 01/01/01).

THE PRINCIPLE OF EXTRA-TERRITORIALITY AND ITS LIMITATIONS

The issue of extra-territoriality has become increasingly important as the globalisation of the world economy advances. Many national competition authorities around the world have introduced the principle of extra-territoriality as a response to the globalisation process, which led to the increase in international anticompetitive practices. The public international law principle of territoriality establishes one of the fundamental attributes of sovereignty, where each country is able to enact and enforce law within its territory. If one country seeks jurisdiction outside its boundaries, it may infringe the sovereignty of other countries and therefore violate the principles of public international law. Yet, as international competition law has developed the exceptions were inevitable. One of the exceptions is harmful economic effects, where a country can claim jurisdiction over conduct that occurred outside its boundaries, but has effects within its territory. National competition authorities rely on a 'doctrine of effects', which serves as a basis to the doctrine of extra-territoriality in competition policy.[29]

The 'effect doctrine' was first propounded in the US courts. However, the application of extra-territoriality in US antitrust law has been controversial. Initially, in the *American Banana* case,[30] Justice Holmes stated that 'the general and almost universal rule is that the character of an act as lawful or unlawful must be determined wholly by the law of the country where the act is done'. However, the US courts soon changed this approach and began to apply the US antitrust rules to extra-territorial conduct. In the famous *Alcoa* case[31] it was decided that the US can assert jurisdiction over a cartel agreed outside its territory without the US firm being party to the agreement. Judge Hand explained that an agreement (although having a completely foreign nature) could still be declared unlawful and a country may punish an economically harmful act which has consequences within its borders that the state reprehends. However, other countries did not appreciate extra-territorial reach into their domestic competition systems and extra-territorial application was met with hostility from other states. As a response to this, in the *Timberlane* case[32] Judge Choy placed limits on the *Alcoa* effects doctrine, suggesting that its application had to be balanced against the interests of international

---

[29]   Dabbah, *supra* n. 6, at 162.

[30]   213 US 347, 1909 (*American Banana Co v. United Fruit Co.*).

[31]   US Court of Appeals, 148 F 2d 416 (2nd Circuit) 1945, (*United States v. Aluminum Co. of America*) at 443–4.

[32]   US Court of Appeals (9th Circuit), 549 F 2d 597, 1976 (*Timberlane Lumber Co. v. Bank of America*)

comity.[33] Thus, the US courts have attempted to limit the scope of the extra-territoriality principle, placing certain conditions, such as the existence of a direct and substantial effect within the US and most importantly a balance of the respective interests of the US in asserting jurisdiction and other country or countries affected by such assertion.[34] In 1982, the US amended its antitrust laws to include extra-territorial jurisdiction in non-import cases, where there is a 'direct, substantial, and reasonably foreseeable' effect.[35] However, the US authorities have not been consistent in the application of the principle of extra-territoriality or comity.[36] Earlier the Department of Justice stated that the main task of the principle of extra-territoriality was to protect US exports and investment opportunities, and then later the additional condition was put in place to include adverse effects on competition that would harm US consumers. In the early 1990s this condition was repealed, suggesting that US antitrust law was not limited to direct harm to consumers and both imports and exports are equally important to the US economy.[37] In the 1995 Antitrust Enforcement Guidelines for International Operations, issued jointly by the Department of Justice and the Federal Trade Commission, it was stated that both agencies may take action against anti-competitive conduct, wherever occurring, that restrains US exports, if (a) the conduct has a direct, substantial, and reasonably foreseeable effect on exports of goods (or services) from the US, and (b) the US courts can obtain jurisdiction over persons (or entities) engaged in such conduct.[38] The Guidelines also state that both agencies are committed to the

---

[33]   The term 'comity' means that a country in its enforcement should take into consideration important interests of other countries, in return expecting the same from these countries.

[34]   Fox, E (1986), 'Extraterritoriality and Antitrust – Is Reasonableness the Answer?', 49 *Fordham Corporate Law Institute* 54.

[35]   Foreign Trade Antitrust Improvement Act of 1982 § 7, 15 USC § 6(a) (1) (1994).

[36]   Although the *Timberlane* case developed a comity balancing test placing limits on extra-territoriality, the US Supreme Court in the *Hartford Fire* case ruled that the principle of international comity should be used only in circumstances where there is a true conflict between US and foreign law: 509 US 764, 1993 (*Hartford Fire Ins. v. California*). For further comments on this case see Ferencz, BB (1995), 'Extraterritorial Application of American Law After the Insurance Antitrust Case: A Reply to Professors Lowenfeld and Trimble', 89 *American Journal of International Law* 750; Lowenfeld, AF (1995), 'Conflict, Balancing of Interests, and the Exercise of Jurisdiction to Prescribe: Reflections on the Insurance Antirust Case', 89) *American Journal of International Law* 42; Trimble, PR (1995), 'The Supreme Court and International Law: The Demise of Restatement Section 403', 89 *American Journal of International Law* 53.

[37]   Dabbah, *supra* n. 6, at 170.

[38]   The 1995 Antitrust Enforcement Guidelines for International Operations, US Department of Justice and the Federal Trade Commission (April 1995) at 3.122, available at http://www.justice.gov/atr/public/guidelines/internat.htm.

principles of international comity, relating to their own enforcement actions, and to the possibility of cooperating with foreign competition authorities.

The principle of extra-territoriality has also been adopted on the other side of the Atlantic. Although Articles 81 and 82 EC (now Articles 101 and 102 TFEU, the Treaty on the Functioning of the European Union) are silent on the principle,[39] it has been introduced through the case law. The effects doctrine for the very first time was raised in the *Dyestuffs* case,[40] where the Commission established that Article 81(1) EC (now Article 101(1) TFEU)[41] catches all agreements that have the effect of preventing, restricting or distorting competition within the Common Market regardless of whether the undertakings involved have their seat within or outside the Community. The CJEU (Court of Justice of the European Union) refrained from comments on this issue and approved the Commission's decision based on a less controversial ground known in the EU as the single economic entity doctrine.[42] In the *Wood Pulp* case, the ECJ established that Article 81 (now Article 101 TFEU) could be applied extra-territorially, but based its extra-territorial jurisdiction decision on implementation rather than the effects doctrine developed in the US. In the *Gencor* merger case,[43] the General

---

[39]   The EC Merger Regulation, although not expressly addressing the extra-territoriality principle, contains a jurisdictional threshold where merger transactions between undertakings established outside the EU could be caught if they meet the turnover thresholds set out in the Regulation: EC Council Regulation 139/2004, OJ [2004] L 24/1, Article 1.

[40]   Case 48/69 *ICI v. Commission* [1972] ECR 619, [1972] CMLR 557.

[41]   Article 101(1) TFEU provides:

'The following shall be prohibited as incompatible with the common market: all agreements between undertakings, decisions by associations of undertakings and concerted practices which may affect trade between Member States and which have as their object or effect the prevention, restriction or distortion of competition within the common market, and in particular those which:
   (a)   directly or indirectly fix purchase or selling prices or any other trading conditions;
   (b)   limit or control production, markets, technical development, or investment;
   (c)   share markets or sources of supply;
   (d)   apply dissimilar conditions to equivalent transactions with other trading parties, thereby placing them at a competitive disadvantage.'
   (e)   make the conclusion of contracts subject to acceptance by the other parties of supplementary obligations which, by their nature or according to commercial usage, have no connection with the subject of such contracts.'

[42]   The single economic entity doctrine means that parents and subsidiaries are considered to be one undertaking for the purposes of the application of the EU competition rules. For further reading see Jones, A and Sufrin, B (2008), *EC Competition Law* (3rd ed. Oxford University Press) at Chapter 3.

[43]   Case T–102/96 *Gencor Ltd. v. Commission* [1999] ECR II–753, [1999] 4 CMLR 971.

Court stated that the application of the EC Merger Regulation is justified under public international law 'when it is foreseeable that a proposed concentration will have an immediate and substantial effect in the Community'.[44] This and other EU cases[45] suggest that the EU applies the principle of extra-territoriality, which is close to that of the US.

Throughout the world, the effects doctrine has found acceptance by countries as a tool to combat the impact of globalised business activity on their own economies. However, national competition authorities encounter practical problems in applying their laws to extra-territorial conduct. Usually an activity that affects the international commerce of one country also has influence on the others too. Quite often it is difficult to say which country's economic interests have been affected more: that in which activity takes place or that which applies the effects doctrine. Also, some nations lack the experience or resources adequately to enforce their laws extra-territorially. National competition authorities of a single country are unable on their own satisfactorily to deal with giant global transactions, because the enforcers of competition law are territorially fragmented while those giant undertakings are trans-nationally integrated and territorially flexible in their operations.[46] This is why many nations have entered into bilateral agreements to tackle these international anti-competitive concerns. The EU, for instance, has dedicated cooperation agreements on competition policy with the United States, Canada, Japan and other countries.[47] Under these agreements, competition authorities on both sides exchange information and coordinate their enforcement activities. The EU entered into two agreements with the US: the 1991 EU/US Competition Cooperation Agreement,[48] and the 1998 EU/US Positive Comity Agreement[49] which further clarifies that the competition authorities of a requesting party will normally defer or suspend their own enforcement actions: (i) if the anti-competitive activities do not have a direct, substantial and reasonably foreseeable impact on consumers in the requesting party's territory; or (ii) where the anti-competitive activities do have such an impact on the requesting party's consumers, and they occur principally in and

---

[44] Ibid., at para 90.

[45] For example, extra-territoriality was applied in the following cases: *GE/ Honeywell Case No COMP/M.2220 OJ L048, 18/02/2004, p. 00001–0085*; *WorldCom/MCI Case No IV/M.1069 OJ L116, 04/05/1999 p. 0001–0035*; *MCI/ World Com/Sprint Case No COMP.M.1741, OJ L300, 18/11/2003, p. 0001–0053*; *AOL/Time Warner Case No COMP/M.1845 OJ L268, 09/10/2001, p. 0028000048*; *Oracle/People Soft Case No COMP/M.3216, OJ L218, 23/08/2005, p. 0006–0012*; *Microsoft Case COMP/C-3/37.792 [2005] 4 CMLR 965.*

[46] Joelson, MR (2006), *An International Antitrust Primer* (Kluwer) at Chapter 15.

[47] Available at: http://ec.europa.eu/comm/competition/international/bilateral/.

[48] 1991 EU/US Competition Cooperation Agreement, OJ [1995] L95, 47–52.

[49] 1998 EU/US Positive Comity Agreement, OJ [1998] L 173, 28–31.

are directed principally towards the other party's territory.[50] However, these agreements do not apply to mergers, which have caused tension between the authorities on both sides of the Atlantic.

Although the bilateral agreements have eased some problems between countries in relation to access to information or evidentiary matters which usually surface in competition cases, yet they have not eliminated the conflicts between them. For instance, the contrasting positions taken by the US and EU competition authorities in cases such as *Boeing McDonnell Douglas*,[51] *G.E./Honeywell*[52] and *Microsoft*[53] suggest that there exist significant limits to regulatory approaches regardless of close co-operation between the authorities. As Schaub, a former EU Director-General of Competition at DGIV, has explained, there are the 'natural limits' of the EU/US co-operation: 'procedures of notification and consultation and the principles of traditional and positive comity allow us to bring out respective approaches closer in cases of common interest but there exist no mechanism for resolving conflicts in cases of substantial divergence of the analysis'.[54] Apart from the differences in competition rules worldwide, some countries do not have any competition law enforcement mechanisms and there is no binding requirement under international rules for them to introduce them and there is no binding requirement for them to entry into bilateral agreements with other competition authorities even if they have a competition law regime. This means that there is no legal international mechanism to ensure that a national competition authority will take adequate action to stop or prevent anti-competitive activities that have significant extra-territorial harm.[55] Hence, the rapid advance of global economic integration means that while bilateral co-operations remain important, they are not sufficient to address successfully the new perspectives of the international economy. The following sections will examine the first attempts to form international competition rules at the WTO and its predecessors.

---

[50]   1998 EU/US Positive Comity Agreement, OJ [1998] L 173, Article IV, 28–31.

[51]   Case M.877, OJ [1997] L 336/16. For comments on this case see Bavasso, A (1998), 'Boeing/McDonnell Douglas: Did the Commission Fly too high?', 19 *European Competition Law Review* 243.

[52]   Case COMP/M.2220, OJ [2001] L 162, 0001–0085.

[53]   Case COMP/C–3/37.792, [2005] 4 CMLR 965.

[54]   Schaub, A (1998), 'International co-operation in antitrust matters: making the point in the wake of the Boeing-MDD proceedings', 4 *EC Competition Policy Newsletter*, No. 1.

[55]   Hansen, P (1999), 'Antitrust in the Global Market: Rethinking "Reasonable Expectations"', 72 *Southern California Law Review* 1601 at 1614.

COMPETITION ISSUES AND THE PREDECESSORS OF THE WTO

Despite the absence of binding competition rules within the WTO, competition issues have been an important question within the international trading system for some time. As early as in 1948 the draft of the 1948 Havana Charter, which was aimed at establishing the International Trade Organisation (ITO), addressed issues on restrictive business practices. Article 46 of the Charter imposed an obligation on member countries to prevent firms from engaging in activities that 'restrain competition, limit access to markets or foster monopolistic control whenever such practices have harmful effects on the expansion of production or trade'.[56] However, the ITO never materialised and the Charter was deemed to fail after the US Senate objected, partly because of the US's concern over involvement of possible compromises and balancing of many divergent views and therefore an inability to enforce its own anti-trust law, which they believed to be the best.[57] All that survived after the ITO was the General Agreement on Tariffs and Trade (GATT[58]), which in 1995 was superseded by the WTO.[59] The GATT was designed to provide a general framework that encouraged free trade between contracting nations by regulating and reducing tariffs on traded goods and by providing a common mechanism for resolving trade disputes. The explicit aim of GATT is to eliminate all trade restrictions. Article III (paragraph 4) of the GATT provides that 'the products of the territory of any contracting party imported into the territory of any other contracting party shall be accorded treatment no less favourable than that accorded to like products of national origin'. Although the GATT prohibits trade restrictions on international trade, it does not directly address anti-competitive issues.[60] Nonetheless, there are some provisions that to some extent address competition rules. For instance,

---

[56]   Havana Charter for an International Trade Organization, UN Doc. E/Conf.2?78 1948, available at www.worldtradelaw.net/misc/havana.pdf.

[57]   Klein, JI (1996), 'A Note of Caution with Respect to a WTO Agenda on Competition Policy', Address before the Royal Institute of International Affairs, 18th November 1996, at 14.

[58]   General Agreement on Tariffs and Trade, 1947, 61 Stat. A-11, TIAS 1700, 55 UNTS 194.

[59]   'Havana Charter for an International Trade Organization', in UN Conference on Trade and Employment: Final Act and Re Documents in UN Doc.E/Conf.2/78, 1048; Wilcox, C (1949) *A Charter for World Trade* (Macmillan); Brown Jr, WA (1950) 'The United States and the Restoration of World Trade. An Analysis and Appraisal of the ITO Charter and the General Agreement on Tariffs and Trade' (Brookings Institution).

[60]   Though several Articles to some extent address anti-competitive issues, for instance, Article III on National Treatment; Article XI on prohibition of quantitative restrictions; Article VIII of GATS on monopoly service supplier providers etc.

Article VIII of the GATS (the General Agreement on Trade in Services) states that where a Member's monopoly supplier competes, in the supply of a service outside the scope of its monopoly rights which is subject to that Member's specific commitments, the Member shall ensure that such a supplier does not abuse its monopoly position in its territory in a manner that would prevent Members' specific commitments to keep their markets open to foreign services suppliers.[61] Article IX also recognises that certain business practices of service suppliers may restrain competition and thereby restrict trade in services.[62] Moreover, the contracting parties adopted a decision that the members should consult with each other concerning allegedly restrictive business practices.[63] According to Marsden, the GATS, while providing for consultations only, was the first binding international agreement to address the practices of private business in such a manner.[64] The WTO's other agreements, likewise the TRIPS (the Agreement on Trade-related aspects of Intellectual Property Rights), also have some reference to competition issues, preventing anti-competitive practices by the use of intellectual property rights that may affect trade.[65]

The GATT helped to establish a strong and prosperous multilateral trading system that became more liberal through rounds of trade negotiations; however, by the 1980s the system needed to be reformed. This led to the Uruguay Round and subsequently to the WTO.

COMPETITION ISSUES AND THE WTO

In 1995 the GATT was superseded by the WTO. The WTO is an organisation that deals with the rules of trade between nations at a global or near-global level. It has a multi-functional task, being an organisation for liberalising trade, a forum for governments to negotiate trade agreements, and a place to settle trade disputes.[66] Despite these roles, the WTO is not Superman and cannot solve all the world's problems. This can be seen from the limited power of the WTO dispute settlement to deal with competition issues. The globalisation process has brought trade law and competition law into contact; anti-competitive

---

[61]   GATS, Annex 1B to the WTO, Article VIII.

[62]   GATS, Annex 1B to the WTO, Article IX (para 1).

[63]   GATS, Annex 1B to the WTO, Article IX (para 2). Decision on Restrictive Business Practices: Arrangements for Consultations, 18 November 1960, GATT, BISD (9th Supp.) at 28.

[64]   In contrast to a decision or recommendation. For further discussion see Marsden, P (2003), *A Competition Policy for the WTO* (Cameron May) at 53.

[65]   TRIPS, Annex 1C to the WTO Agreement, Article 40.

[66]   Available at www.wto.org/english/thewto_e/whatis_e/tif_e/fact1_e.htm.

practices have been recognised by some scholars[67] as the next 'generation' of barriers to trade in the world. Anti-competitive behaviour by private firms that can affect the flows of trade and investment between countries has increased in recent years. Although the efforts of the international community have been on removing barriers to the flow of trade, anti-competitive practices of firms that hinder the expansion of world trade have not been left unnoticed. Following a proposal from the European Commission that suggested the possibility of reaching international agreement in some key competition law areas, such as the response to international cartels,[68] the first WTO Ministerial Conference in Singapore in 1996 under the chairmanship of the French Vice President of the *Conseil de la Concurrence* (Competition Council) formed the Working Group on the Interaction between Trade and Competition Policy 'to study issues raised by Members relating to the interaction between trade and competition policy, including anti-competitive practices, in order to identify any areas that may merit further consideration in the WTO framework'.[69] This Group was given a mandate to explore these issues with the possibility of negotiating an agreement. It meant to cover a wide range of issues, including the impact of competition on trade and, vice versa, the impact of trade policy on competition, gathering information from member countries and evaluating alternatives of international co-operation.[70] This promising start can be further seen in the Doha Ministerial Declaration, where Ministers 'recognized the case for a multilateral framework to enhance the contribution of competition policy to international trade and development, and the need for enhanced technical assistance and capacity-building in this area'.[71] They instructed the Working Group to focus on the clarification of the following: core principles, including transparency, non-discrimination and procedural fairness; hardcore cartels; modalities for voluntary cooperation; and support for reinforcement of competition authorities in developing countries through capacity building. Unfortunately, during the subsequent meetings, members failed to reach a consensus on the content of possible competition rules, with much of the opposition coming from small and developing countries that

---

[67] See, for instance, Lee, K (2005), 'The WTO dispute settlement and anti-competitive practices: lessons learnt from trade disputes', University of Oxford press, Working paper, 10/05.

[68] Commission Press Release (1995) IP/95/752, 12 July.

[69] WTO, Singapore Ministerial Declaration, Conference Doc WT/MIN(96)/DEC/W, 13 December 1996, 96-5315, at para 20. For further discussion see www.wto.org/english/thewto_e/minist_e/min96_e/min96_e.htm.

[70] Yun, M (2001), 'Trade and Competition Policy in WTO', Chapter 7 in UNESCAP, *Regional Perspectives on the WTO Agenda: Concerns and Common Interests*, at 122, available at www.unescap.org/tid/publication/chap7_2161.pdf.

[71] WTO, Doha Ministerial Declaration, WT/MIN(01)/DEC/W/1, 14 November 2001, at paras 23–5, available at www.wto.org/english/tratop_e/comp_e/history_e.htm.

feared intrusive competition law enforcement designed by developed countries. Thus, negotiations on competition policy ended in deadlock at the Cancun Ministerial Conference in 2003. From a promising start, the last step adopted by the WTO is rather disappointing. In the so-called 'July 2004 package' the WTO General Council remarked that the issue of competition policy 'will not form part of the Work Programme set out in that Declaration and therefore no work towards negotiations on any of these issues will take place within the WTO during the Doha Round'.[72] Hence, the Working Group is currently inactive and the Doha Round of multilateral trade negotiations, launched in November 2001 under the aegis of the WTO, remains stalled. According to Jackson, the WTO's reluctance explicitly to address competition policy could be explained by various constitutional and procedural constraints.[73] For example, it is difficult to harmonise existing national regimes into a single standard, especially since national competition policies not only employ different standards but also require complex factual determinations of changed performance in specific markets as a result of designated actions, for instance, for tying agreements, parallel import restrictions, and merger transaction deals. Despite this deadlock at the WTO, the following section will further explore to what extent competition policy and trade policy intersect and why without competition policy the objectives of trade policy cannot be fully achieved.

COMPETITION POLICY AND TRADE POLICY

This section considers the complex relationship between competition and trade policy. It examines how trade policy interacts with competition policy in a liberalised global economy and to what extent those two disciplines could reconcile. In order to establish this, it is necessary to discuss the objectives of each discipline. Anti-competitive behaviour is controlled by competition law and policy. In general terms, the objective of competition law and policy is to enhance efficiency and consumer welfare,[74] which allows wider choices for

---

[72]   WTO, The General Council's post-Cancun decision, the 'July 2004 package', WT/L/579, 2 August 2004, at para (g), available at: www.wto.org/english/tratop_e/dda_e/draft_text_gc_dg_31july04_e.htm.

[73]   Jackson, J (2006), *Sovereignty, the WTO, and Changing Fundamentals of International Law* (Cambridge University Press).

[74]   Usually accepted by most competition authorities, though some authorities might still consider total welfare instead. Total surplus is the sum of producers' surplus and consumers' surplus. Producer surplus is the difference between the price in the market that producers collectively receive for their products and the sum of those producers' respective marginal costs at each level of output. Meanwhile, consumer surplus is the

consumers between domestic and foreign goods and services, wider economic opportunities for firms by allowing them to enter any activity they want and by giving them an incentive to innovate. Trade law and policy, on the other hand, deal with the rules to handle trade between countries; primarily they concentrate on removing obstacles to the flows of trade and investment between countries. Removing barriers to trade is necessary in order to enhance a state's ability to engage in international trade and achieve efficiency gains from specialisation and exchange. Hence, international trade policy is aimed at achieving liberalised trade (otherwise known as 'free trade') where there is no denial to foreign firms of access to a country's domestic market. Meanwhile, competition policy and law deal with market structures and practices and promote competitive markets rather than the interest of specific competitors, which is trade policy's concern. In general terms, trade policy is concerned with protecting the interest of competitors, whereas competition law deals with the interest of consumers.[75]

International trade law, including the WTO rules, does not cover anticompetitive behaviour of private firms and apply to barriers to trade that are governmental in nature, in contrast to competition law which principally deals with anti-competitive practice of private firms. Anti-competitive behaviour by firms that affects the flows of trade between countries is the main area where trade policy and competition policy intersect. This means that the benefits from international trade policy allowing foreign firms to enter national market can be reduced or eliminated if they are replaced by anti-competitive practices that exclude a foreign firm from national markets as effectively as a high tariff.[76] Competition policy regards a barrier to trade as a form of barrier to market entry. If trade barriers are significant, then foreign firms are unable to enter domestic markets and therefore competition is reduced, as foreign firms cannot provide additional competition to domestic firms. In contrast, if such trade barriers are reduced, enabling foreign firms to enter domestic markets, competition will increase. In this context, international trade policy that reduces trade barriers is complementary to competition law objectives, as it facilitates competition by promoting greater market entry.[77] Furthermore, in the EU Report to the WTO Working Group it was expressed that '[a] practice which has a foreclosure effect would negatively affect consumer welfare in the country where the practice is

---

difference between what a consumer is willing to pay for goods and what the consumer actually pays when buying them.

[75] Many competition authorities around the world (i.e. the European Commission, the US Department of Justice, the US Federal Trade Commission) emphasise consumer welfare rather than total welfare in their assessments.

[76] Tarullo, D (2000), 'Norms and Institutions in Global Competition', 94 *American Journal of International Law* 478 at 483.

[77] Taylor, *supra* n. 11, at 177.

being implemented and, at the same time, affect the legitimate interests of the country whose producers are being denied equality of competitive opportunities. This is both a market access and a competition law problem'.[78] Hence, international trade law and international competition law intersect or even, as Taylor expresses it 'exhibit synergies' in their approaches by first of all having the effect of increasing domestic competition.[79] International trade law opens market access by removing trade obstacles, enabling foreign firms to enter the domestic market and therefore increase competition. Secondly, both disciplines have the effect of increasing international trade. International trade law promotes market access by reducing governmental barriers to trade, whereas international competition law does so by means of reducing the scope for anti-competitive behaviour, otherwise private trade barriers. Neo-functionalism's spill-over effects could be applied here with the adoption of a general market access principle in private anti-competitive practice; more specifically, if adopted, international competition law could provide a key mechanism regulating a particular form of trade barrier, namely private trade barriers generated from anti-competitive behaviour and allow greater market access for foreign firms. This means that international competition law would prevent private anti-competitive practices from impeding the magnitude of trade liberalisation achieved by trade negotiations.[80]

Although both international trade and international competition law share some complementary concerns and competition policy seems to complement trade policy's goal of market access, in-depth analysis proves that these two disciplines do not sit neatly together. Certain trade measures that may be permitted by international trade law could be prohibited under international competition law and vice versa. For instance, prohibiting exclusionary activity that has the effect of blocking markets would be likely to be given a green light by trade representatives. Yet, these exclusionary practices that have an impact on foreign competitors and therefore restrict trade do not suffice to prove harm to competition. Competition lawyers may have a 'more tolerant' approach towards exclusionary practices depending on whether such restraints enhance efficiency.[81] Trade policy places its attention in many cases on the denial to a foreign competitor of access to a country's market. Meanwhile, competition policy employs a broader approach and tests this denial of access to market from a different perspective by questioning whether this denial also generates

---

[78]   EU Communication 62, at 12–13.

[79]   Taylor, *supra* n. 11, at 176.

[80]   Ibid., at 178.

[81]   For in-depth analysis of exclusive arrangements see Marsden, *supra* n. 64, at Chapter III.

efficiencies.[82] As Tarullo suggests, trade policy is mainly concerned with a government's efforts to promote exports by its state's industries regardless of whether foreign markets are workably competitive or not in an economic sense.[83] Competition policy, on the other hand, deals with industry structures and practices and promotes competitive markets. Trade representatives stress the result of effective access rather than 'the relative competitiveness of the market in an economic or antitrust sense'.[84] In this context it is not clear what decision would be made if measures were allowed by one discipline but prohibited by another; otherwise, will priority be given to trade policy over competition policy, to governmental measures over private restrictions, protection of specific competitors over consumers or vice versa? If competition law harmonisation is justified on market access grounds in order to complement trade policy's objectives, it may quite easily jettison competition law principles. Along similar lines, Tarullo said, 'forcing the square peg of competition policy into the round hole of trade policy will change the shape of the peg'.[85] Thus, neo-functionalism's model does not fit smoothly in this case scenario. Nonetheless, Marsden proposed a test balancing both trade and competition policies.[86] According to Marsden, the necessary consensus needs to be built in recognising that trade policy and competition policy have much more in common than once thought. Furthermore, he suggested a test where the WTO members 'would undertake to prohibit those business arrangements that substantially impede access to their market and which are thereby likely to lessen competition substantially in the relevant market for the products at issue'.[87] Although this 'guideline' is a valuable step, the author argues that it is too early to discuss it at this point, considering that members cannot determine the rationale for international competition law, define the regulatory objectives and agree on the meaning of competition policy terms. Further research and analysis need to be done before the particular mechanisms can be discussed. Nonetheless, with support from trade policy or without it, the benefits of international competition law rules cannot be undermined. The next section will further explore the gains that international competition law may produce.

---

[82] ABA, *Report of the ABA Task Force on International Trade and Antitrust concerning Private Anticompetitive Practices as Market Access Barriers* (January 2000), available at www.abanet.org/antitrust/reports at 26–7.

[83] Tarullo, *supra* n. 76, at 483.

[84] For further discussion see ibid., at 483.

[85] Ibid., at 479.

[86] Marsden, *supra* n. 64, at Chapter VII.

[87] Ibid., at 284.

BENEFITS OF INTERNATIONAL COMPETITION LAW HARMONISATION AND THE WTO

Due to the globalisation process, there has been a significant rise in the number of large cross-border transactions, potentially requiring clearance from a multitude of national competition authorities. Also, the detection of anti-competitive practices, for instance, in hard-core cartel cases or merger transactions with spill-over effects, affecting multiple jurisdictions, has surged. Such anti-competitive practices have harmful consequences for society at large, and therefore can create private obstacles to market access, nullifying the advances made by governments in trade liberalisation and regulatory reform. These issues could potentially be solved through international competition law mechanisms. Harmonisation is arguably desirable for its efficiency effects which, for instance, can reduce the burdensome costs of legal uncertainty imposed by divergent local standards. The EU has argued in favour of the harmonisation of competition law, most notably under the auspices of the WTO. This is because the WTO has a near universal membership; it can provide a balanced response sensitive to the varying interests and concerns of both developed and developing countries; the WTO is the recognised institution for trade-related international economic rules, which are closely related to competition issues (some of its agreements already have a number of specific provisions to address anti-competitive practices, i.e. in the area of anti-dumping); the institutional infrastructure of the WTO includes a system of transparency and surveillance through notification requirements and monitoring provisions; it contains the general rules relating to non-discrimination and transparency; the WTO also provides a forum for continuous negotiation and consultation, where its members could take their trade-related competition concerns; and most importantly the WTO has a well established, reinforced and legalised dispute settlement mechanism between governments.[88]

Presuming that the WTO is the best body for the job, it can provide the following benefits with regard to international competition issues. First of all, Brittan and Van Miert stated that international competition rules may help tackle market access issues.[89] For instance, anti-competitive practices keep European firms out of third country markets, and they cannot, in the absence of proper enforcement measures in those third country markets, be effectively dealt with without international rules. European firms also face a competitive disadvantage if they

---

[88]   Communication submitted by Sir Leon Brittan and Karel Van Miert towards an international framework of competition rules; Communication to the Council, COM(96)284, available http://ec.europa.eu/comm/competition/international/com284.html. Also see Dabbah, *supra* n. 6, at 224.

[89]   Brittan and Van Miert, *supra* n. 88.

have to compete on world markets with foreign producers operating from home markets that are subject to lax competition policies. Firms in other countries may also encounter similar problems. In this context multilateral rules would promote more equal conditions of competition world-wide.

Secondly, international competition rules can help to avoid conflicts of law and jurisdiction between countries and to promote a gradual convergence of competition laws.[90] As aforementioned, some competition authorities, including those of the EU and US, apply the 'effect doctrine' to deal with international anti-competitive practices, assuming jurisdiction even if all the conduct complained of takes place in other countries. However, jurisdiction is a central and vital attribute of state sovereignty; a country is able to enact and enforce laws within its boundaries and must not intervene in the domestic affairs of other nations. This means that some countries may not appreciate extra-territorial reach into their domestic competition law systems, especially if they do not have a similar belief as to what constitutes anti-competitive harm. Sovereignty concerns may limit the potential benefits of extra-territoriality.[91] It means that national competition authorities may fall short of providing a remedy when more than one jurisdiction is involved, especially when it comes to collecting information and evidence from foreign countries. This is why there is a real need to minimise jurisdictional conflicts, arising not only from the extra-territorial application of certain competition laws, but also from the application of competition law to anti-competitive practices conceived abroad but implemented within one's jurisdiction.

Thirdly, apart from sovereignty concerns, other problems can also occur in the application of the 'effect doctrine' by various competition authorities. The same international transaction can be subjected to different competition authorities, which imposes conflicting obligations on firms. One might say that firms in question need simply to confirm their conduct to whichever competition law regime is more restrictive. However, this can lead to global over-regulation.[92] Furthermore, conflict in policy objectives may also occur, for instance, in the cases where one country allows certain conduct generally agreed on the conclusion that its pro-competitive effects are likely to outweigh any anti-competitive concerns. For another country to restrict that conduct is thus to deny those pro-competitive effects to the first nation, which is contrary to its policy preferences. This can instigate policy conflicts where countries differ on what count as pro-competitive effects and to what extent they should be taken into consideration.[93]

---

[90]   Ibid.

[91]   Sokol, D (2007), 'Monopolists without borders: the Institutional Challenge of International Antitrust in a Global Gilded Age', 4.1 *Berkeley Business Law Journal* 46.

[92]   Suggested by Elhauge, E and Geradin, D (2007), *Global Competition Law and Economics* (Hart) at 1011–12.

[93]   For further discussion see ibid., at 1011–12.

Harmonisation of competition laws could reduce these problems and help to achieve 'transactional smoothness', as to obtaining transaction cost efficiencies arising from standardisation of procedures (i.e. filing requirements) and 'functional smoothness' – the ability of business transactions to carry on businesses across borders without being subject to inconsistent regulation.[94] Indeed, harmonisation could reduce contradictory decisions (or duplicative proceedings) and therefore reduce firms' costs and time of compliance with competition laws or any conflicts in their competition policies, and most importantly increase legal certainty for firms operating in different jurisdictions.

Finally, there is the necessity for an international instrument with a binding nature to respond to globalisation and trans-national transactions. This is because the non-binding nature of current agreements may not always provide satisfactory results. Many countries which have implemented comprehensive competition policies, nonetheless, lack the necessary knowledge, experience or even resources to apply domestic competition rules to anti-competitive practices with an international dimension. For instance, if a cartel affects many small and/ or developing countries and each of them hopes to free ride off the enforcement efforts of others and is unwilling to investigate the matter on its own, it will be under-regulation which will be harmful to all of them collectively.[95] Lack of any competition laws in a number of jurisdictions worldwide adds to further international problems. All these issues suggest the importance and necessity for international competition law rules. However, these benefits do not come without costs. Thus, the following section will examine what are the pitfalls of international competition law harmonisation and to what extent they should be addressed.

'ONE SIZE FITS ALL' – THE PITFALLS OF INTERNATIONAL COMPETITION LAW HARMONISATION AND THE WTO

The WTO provides a framework of binding rules together with an effective dispute resolution mechanism, however, with the *raison d'être* being solely that of global trade policy. Competition policy intersects with trade policy when anti-competitive practice eliminates a foreign firm from a national market as effectively as a high tariff would, and when the national competition authority fails to provide a remedy for such conduct. Although international trade and competition policy are inter-related (as discussed in the previous sections), this

---

[94]   The concepts suggested by First, *supra* n. 10, at 34.
[95]   Elhauge and Geradin, *supra* n. 92, at 1014.

does not necessarily mean that the WTO is well equipped to take on anti-competitive issues. In contrast, the past proves that the WTO in its present capacity is incapable of dealing with competition issues satisfactorily. For instance, the *Kodak-Fuji*[96] and *Telmex*[97] cases show that the WTO was unable properly to address the problems of anti-competitive practices which foreclose market access. The WTO panel had a difficult dilemma to deal with: the complex issue of private agreements and hybrid government–private restrictions (as the new barriers to a liberalised marketplace) in the absence of international competition rules and out of reach of international trade law as well as national competition laws. These cases suggest that in the situations where an interaction between private anti-competitive practices and government measures is involved, the WTO panel may exhibit a more cautious engagement of trade tools to address anti-competitive issues.[98] This is because access to the WTO dispute resolution process is limited to governments and the WTO rules apply to governments only, and therefore it is not open to governments to challenge private measures in this way. These examples also highlight the main differences between trade and competition policies; trade rules address governmental practices as opposed to anti-competitive conduct by private firms covered under competition law. The WTO is centrally focused on governmental restraints that affect trade flow, whereas competition policy is much wider. Hence, the WTO's mandate of rules negotiation together with dispute resolution mechanism is not suitable for competition issues, which require 'to be discussed broadly and in a consultative manner'.[99]

Along similar lines, the differences in objectives may even increase the problem. The WTO's main task is to deal with trade policy, which is mainly concerned with market access, as discussed in the previous sections. If the scope of the WTO were extended to include competition rules (as suggested by some scholars[100]), then it may appear that competition policy at the WTO would be overwhelmed by the market access norms of trade policy at the expense of distorting the consumer welfare norm of competition law and policy; especially if there was a conflict between them, the WTO would most likely decide in favour of trade norms. No matter how these two sets of norms reconcile in theory,

---

[96] WTO, *Japan – Measures affecting consumer photographic film and paper*, 31 March 1998, WT/DS44/R.

[97] WTO, *Mexico – Measures affecting Telecommunications Services*, 2 April 2004, WT/DS204/R.

[98] For further discussion see Lee, *supra* n. 67.

[99] ICPAC (International Competition Policy Advisory Committee) (2000), *Final Report* at 282–3.

[100] See, for instance, Hansen, *supra* n. 55; Dabbah, *supra* n. 6, at 224–5 and at Chapter 9.

they cannot work happily in practice.[101] For instance, when there is an overlap in competition and trade policy issues, different conclusions may be reached regarding the effect of a particular restraint.

The nature of competition issues is too complex to be cast in a binding international regime established and enforced by a dispute settlement body, such as the WTO, which lacks the legitimacy and expertise to manoeuvre the difficult analytical tools of competition law. Lee argues that to allow WTO tribunals to exercise a judicially created or gap-filling role would stagger the legitimacy of not only the dispute settlement mechanism but also the WTO system as a whole.[102] Along similar lines, Professor Jackson claims that the use of WTO tribunals to resolve competition policy disputes to 'plug gaps' in the WTO agreement 'places too much of the problem-solving burden on the dispute settlement process'.[103] However, other scholars like Hansen have faith in the WTO and argue that the WTO can and should step into the legal gap concerning competition policy in order to safeguard the international trading system.[104] Furthermore, Hansen suggests that a rule requiring governments to negotiate an adjustment for their policies that have a disproportionate impact on imports is consistent with the text and purpose of the WTO. It is possible that governmental tolerance towards restrictive business practices could render meaningless existing commitments reached at the WTO, and encourage behaviour that the WTO rules were designed to prevent. The absence of specific rules for competition places a difficult task on the WTO tribunal to resolve disputes over these policies. However, the author disagrees that the WTO should stretch its powers in order to cover competition issues without having a consensus from its members on what competition rules should be, in what forms, and to what extent they should be addressed in international trade disputes.

Competition law has national roots and is usually designed to be a function of a nation's economic, cultural, social and institutional structure. Countries tend to make competition-law related decisions based on the effects on their national markets rather than considering any international effects. International anti-competitive practices bring nations of different economic development into contact with one another. Countries do not share common competition policy traditions; some of them do not even have any competition laws in place. Considering the complex nature of competition, reaching an agreement among many countries with too diverging competition cultures becomes a formidable task. Presumption of the 'ideal' international competition law model

---

[101]   For further discussion see Tarullo, *supra* n. 76, at 478–504.
[102]   Lee, *supra*, n. 67.
[103]   Jackson, J (1998), 'Expert Warns of Burden to WTO Dispute Settlement', 15 *International Trade Representative* (BNA) No. 18, 6 May 1998 at 778.
[104]   Hansen, *supra* n. 55, at 1601.

as 'one size fits all' may be misleading. For instance, the model of competition law from developed countries (otherwise core countries) is not necessarily ideal for small, emerging market economies or developing countries (peripheral countries). It has been suggested that developed countries first developed an industrial policy and then modified it in the light of international commitments. During times of rapid structural change, developed countries could modify their competition policy to facilitate necessary changes; however, the same is not possible for economies in transition due to their international obligations and imposed models from the developed countries.[105] Parachuting competition laws from developed countries to developing countries would mean that they would not be able to develop competition rules to suit their own legal, economic and political conditions. Similarly, small market economies require different competition rules, as laxer competition rules. This is because there are a limited number of market players in small markets that the market can serve and in order for these countries to achieve economies of scale they would require to have more concentrated markets.[106] The concerns, such as the admission of sales below costs, refusals to sell, geographic market divisions in intellectual property licences and others, may have a different impact on competition in large and in small countries, especially if the latter do not have the scope of what may be called a domestic market since, with regard to small markets, compensation by remaining competition may be less likely.[107] Those differences in competition law between countries worldwide suggest that the likelihood of them making concessions during multilateral negotiations in order to accommodate the ideals of other countries is relatively low. For instance, the US was reluctant to make any compromises in accepting an international competition model, which would be second best to its anti-trust law.[108] Similarly, in the past, peripheral countries also declined the international competition law model, fearing intrusive competition enforcement designed to be optimal for core countries.[109] Accordingly, the peripheral countries' concerns are not without reason. Scholars suggest that multilateral negotiations are usually influenced by nations with greater economic and

---

[105]   Vissi, F (1995), 'Challenges and Questions around Competition Policy: the Hungarian Experience', 18 *Fordham International Law Journal* 1230. Also see Dabbah, *supra* n. 6, at 126–9.

[106]   Gal, M (2003), *Competition policy for small market economies* (Harvard University Press).

[107]   First, *supra* n. 10, at 51.

[108]   Referring to the example during the ITO debates.

[109]   Referring to the Doha negotiations at the WTO, August 2004, where the negotiations on international anti-trust rules collapsed due to the opposition from small and developing countries.

political power.[110] This would mean that stronger (otherwise core) countries can influence negotiations in a manner favourable to them at the expense of peripheral countries. Although the WTO to some extent addresses specific features of developing and less developed countries with regard to trade issues, it is not clear to what extent the specific attributes of developing or small countries would be taken into consideration *vis-à-vis* competition issues. Thus, harmonisation based on the 'ideal' competition law model would fail to recognise the differences in the nations' economies, markets, policies and their convergent distributional objectives or otherwise their values, as suggested by neo-realists.

Finally, benefits and costs analysis should also be mentioned. It may be the case that an international competition law agreement is not worth having if the gains in achieving it are outweighed by the implementation costs. Although there is a demand for international competition law, in relation to the costs of an international regime the benefits could be just too small. It has to be taken into account that each nation would have to deviate from its competition policy (presumably tailored to serve its needs) to compromise on a common international regime, which will take time and costs to introduce.[111]

To summarise, an 'ideal' model which assumes that 'one size fits all' is unlikely to be created in the near future. The differences in competition law and policies and economic development between nations make harmonisation an ambitious task that requires outstanding efforts from all members to reach consensus on multilateral agreement. As the neo-realist model suggests, there is a need to harmonise values, not rules. However, international competition law may not sit tightly with other social national values, which may differ from one country to another. Unless all nations agreed on the superiority of international values or global values over national ones, hardly any consensus could be achieved.

CONCLUSION

The globalisation process has shaped the global landscape leading to the increase in cross-border businesses. With markets and competition becoming increasingly international, anti-competitive practices also cut across national and regional boundaries. Many countries in the world have introduced

---

[110]   See, for instance, Schoppa, LJ (1999), 'The Social Context in Coercive International Bargaining', 53 *International Organization* 307. Bagwell, K and Staiger, RW (2000), 'Multilateral Trade Negotiations, Bilateral Opportunism and the Rules of GATT', Internet Working Paper, March 2000. Also see Taylor, *supra* n. 11, at 342–3.

[111]   For further discussion see Elhauge and Geradin, *supra* n. 92, at 1011–12.

competition laws together with competition enforcement institutions to control anti-competitive behaviour. However, governments from different jurisdictions have soon realised that national competition law could not offer a final solution as trade has been increasing globally whereas competition law has national roots. This chapter addressed the complex issues of international competition law. On the one hand, the globalisation process, therefore international anti-competitive practices, has initiated the negotiation of international competition rules and their importance. An international competition law mechanism could cover global anti-competitive transactions unreachable by domestic competition authorities. It could eliminate contradictory decisions from different jurisdictions, and save time and costs for firms involved in international transactions, as well as providing legal certainty and transparency. It would eliminate the limits of the 'effect doctrine'. However, on the other hand, reaching an agreement among many countries with very diverging competition cultures, acting at different development scales and varying in the size of their economies becomes a formidable task. Countries do not share common competition policy traditions; the model that suits developed countries is not necessarily ideal for developing countries. Although the WTO with its well established dispute resolution mechanism has its benefits, the lack of consensus among the nations on international competition policy and law suggests that an 'ideal' model of international competition law is unlikely to appear on the horizon in the near future. The time is not yet ripe for the creation of a global competition regime with a competition enforcement mechanism, and it probably will never be ripe until all nations consider and agree upon some common values and adopt the concept of global welfare rather than national welfare.

19. Convergence, path-dependency and credit securities: the case against Europe-wide harmonisation*

Gerard McCormack**

Within Europe in recent years there have been two pressure points for reform of the law governing secured transactions.[1] The first pressure point arises out of the desire by some to create a European Civil Code, a common law for Europe as you will, and this Civil Code (or Common Frame of Reference, as it is now less contentiously termed) is envisaged as extending to security rights over property. The second pressure point stems from lobbying to promote the merits of Article 9 of the American Uniform Commercial Code as the basis for European (and indeed international) harmonisation of the law of secured transactions. Behind the second point is the view that Article 9 is normatively superior to other systems and that, irrespective of national frontiers, the law should converge towards the best model. This chapter suggests that these theories fail to take adequate account of the 'path-dependent' nature of legal development. They also fail to pay sufficient regard to the role of national lawyers and other interest groups in the reform process. To illustrate my thesis, the English experience with an attempted transplant of Article 9 is singled out for discussion.

* The author would like to thank the British Academy Leverhulme Trust for funding some of the research on which this chapter was based. An earlier version of this paper was presented at the WG Hart Workshop at the Institute of Advanced Legal Studies, London, in June 2008.
Editor's note: This contribution has been affected by rapid developments in the field, see the Preface on p. xi for details.
** University of Leeds, UK
¹ See generally U Drobnig, H J Snijders, E-J Zipporo (eds), *Divergences in Property Law – an Obstacle to the Internal Market* (Munich, Sellier, 2006); H C Sigman and E-M Kieninger (eds), *Cross-Border Security over Tangibles* (Munich, Sellier, 2007); W Faber and B Lurger (eds), *Rules for the Transfer of Movables: A Candidate for European Harmonisation or National Reforms?* (Munich, Sellier, 2008); EM Kieninger, 'Securities in Movable Property withing the Common Market' [1996] *European Review of Private Law* 40.

The chapter begins by examining the case that is being made for a European Civil Code and its extension to security rights over property. I suggest that the argument for such a code can only be understood in the context of a desire to promote an ever closer European Union. It is essentially a political, rather than an economic or a social project. The economic case, at best, is unproven. Insofar as the lack of uniformity of secured transaction laws across European frontiers is seen as presenting an obstacle to intra-community trade, there is no particular evidence of such a hindrance that needs removing by a European Civil Code. Moreover, such a code would substantially limit the scope for national autonomy and potentially fruitful experimentation at the local level.

The chapter then looks at theories of convergence and path dependency in the corporate and commercial law sphere. The English example provides an illustration of how a jurisdiction may successfully resist a transplant from a supposedly normatively superior system. The English example is also highlighted as illustrating the importance of lawyers and legal doctrine in shaping and muting the reform agenda.

The chapter concludes by suggesting that convergence, to the extent that it is achieved in this area, is much more likely to be formal rather than functional. The results achieved in a particular respect may be substantially the same, but the language of the law and the way in which these results may be expressed will be different.

A EUROPEAN CIVIL CODE AND ITS APPLICATION TO SECURITY RIGHTS OVER PROPERTY

At the institutional political level the genesis of the proposal for a European Civil Code comes from the 2001 European Commission communication on contract law.[2] The communication suggested four possible courses of action. The

---

[2]   For background see the three primary European Commission documents – Communication from the Commission to the Council and the European Parliament on European Contract Law, COM(2001)398; 'A More Coherent European Contract Law, An Action Plan', COM(2003)68; 'European contract law and the revision of the acquis: the way forward', COM(2004)651. For more detail see the 'European Contract Law' website of the Directorate General for Health and Consumer Protection accessible via the Europa website at www.ec.europa.eu/. See also the von Bar Study Group on the European Civil Code – www.sgecc.net/ – and the Acquis Group on European Private Law – www.acquis-group. org/ and – see also the Joint Network on European Private Law – www.copecl.org. There is a vast academic literature, and for a taster see A Hartkamp *et al*. (eds) *Towards a European Civil Code* (Nijmegen, Kluwer Law International, 3rd ed 2004); M Van Hoecke and F Ost (eds), *The Harmonisation of European Private Law* (Oxford, Hart Publishing, 2000). See also M Kenny, 'The 2004 Communication on European Contract Law: Those Magnificent

first was no action at all. The second was to encourage the drafting of relevant principles by scholars. Another possibility involved thinking about a European Civil Code or a Common Frame of Reference (CFR), as it was called. A final possibility involved the revision and reorganisation of existing European law in the field – the so-called *acquis*. Existing European instruments pertained principally to consumer contracting and consisted primarily of a series of vertical provisions applying to particular areas of business operations such as Distance Selling, Timeshares, Electronic Commerce, etc., though there was also a more 'horizontal' measure regulating unfair terms in consumer contracts. This body of law was somewhat unwieldy and inconsistent however, applying, for example, different levels of protection and different cooling-off periods in different sectors. Moreover, the European measures had been implemented differently in the various countries, leading to further national divergence. Revision of the *acquis* would entail rationalisation and systematisation of this body of law.

The 2003 Action Plan suggested three avenues of development. Firstly, it encouraged the creation and refinement by European businesses of Europe-wide standard terms and the dissemination of best practice. Secondly, it suggested the revision of the *acquis* and, thirdly, it encouraged further thought about a Common Frame of Reference. The Common Frame of Reference was envisaged as having various functions. One function would be to provide a set of model terms for contracting parties. Another function would be to serve as a toolbox or source of inspiration for European institutions (or even national legislatures) contemplating further legislative initiatives. Another possibility saw the CFR standing as an optional instrument applying to cross-border contractual relationships and expressly or impliedly selected by the parties, whether on an 'opt-in' or 'opt-out' basis. It should be noted that in the whole process the European Commission took great care to avoid use of the Code or 'C' word. Instead it adopted the strategy of small steps at a time and spoke of a non-sector-specific legislative device and of a Common Frame of Reference (CFR). At the same time however, one might argue that the Commission gave the game away by entrusting the task of drafting the CFR to a network led by a group called the Study Group on a European Civil Code.

The Study Group has now produced a draft academic CFR, including a part dealing with secured transactions or 'credit securities' as they are called in the

---

Men in Their Unifying Machines' (2005) 30 *European Law Review* 724; 'Constructing a European Civil Code: Quis Custodiet Ipsos Custodes?' (2006) 12 *Columbia Journal of European Law* 775. See Green Paper from the Commission on policy options for progress towards a European Contract law for consumers and businesses (Brussels, European Commission, July 2010) Com(2010)348 final; and see generally R Zimmerman and N Jansen 'A European Civil Code in All but Name: Discussing the Nature and Purposes of the Draft Common Frame of Reference (2010) 69 *Cambridge Law Journal*, 98.

language of the CFR.[3] The standard reason given for the inclusion of credit securities in the CFR seems to be that they are part of private law, being generally the product of contract, and have often been included in Civil Codes, though usually not in an exhaustive way.[4] Moreover, it might be easier to find agreement on the content of such provisions than on, say, provisions of family law where moral and ideological differences run deeper. It is up to the European political institutions to refine and develop the 'academic' CFR into a political CFR. It may be that in this process some of the wider contractual and extra-contractual material such as credit securities will be excised from the eventual product.

In general terms, the case for the CFR is presented in terms of removing barriers to intra-European trade. In *Netherlands v. Parliament and Council*[5] it was held that the institutions had legislative competence 'if the aim is to prevent the emergence of future obstacles to trade resulting from multifarious development of national laws provided that the emergence of such obstacles is likely, and the measure in question is designed to prevent them.' On the other hand, in the *Tobacco Advertising Case*[6] the European Court of Justice held that a 'mere finding of disparities between national rules and of the abstract risk of obstacles to the exercise of fundamental (economic) freedoms or of distortions of competition liable to result therefrom' was not sufficient to justify the vesting of legislative competences in the European Community institutions. It may be however that there is no particular hindrance to cross-border European trade resulting from divergent national legal regimes.[7] While cross-border transactions may be more expensive than purely domestic transactions in terms of transaction costs, these legal uncertainties can always be factored into the price and reflected in the terms of the agreement. A common European Civil Code may not actually achieve greater trade flows. Barriers to cross-border contracting are often

---

[3]   A team headed by Professor Ulrich Drobnig (Hamburg) produced the draft dealing with credit securities: see www.sgecc.net.

[4]   See generally J Basedow, 'The Case for a European Contract Act' [2001] *Journal of Business Law* 569. See also U Drobnig, 'A Subsidiary Plea: A European Contract Law for Intra-European Border-Crossing Contracts' in S Grundmann and J Stuyck (eds), *An Academic Green Paper on European Contract Law* (The Hague, Kluwer, 2002) 343.

[5]   Case C–377/98 [2001] ECR 1–7.

[6]   Case C–376/98 *Germany v. Parliament and Council* [2000] ECR 1–8419.

[7]   But see O Lando, 'Why Does Europe Need a Civil Code' in S Grundmann and J Stuyck (eds), *An Academic Green Paper on European Contract Law* (The Hague, Kluwer, 2002) 207: '[i]n Europe the existing variety of contract laws is a non-tariff barrier to the inter-Union trade. It is the aim of the Union to do away with restrictions of trade within the Communities, and therefore the differences of law that restrict this trade should be abolished.' See generally S Vogenauer and S Weatherill, 'The European Community's competence for a comprehensive harmonisation of contract law – an empirical analysis' (2005) 30 *European Law Review* 821.

psychological or social rather than merely legal. Non-legal considerations such as language barriers, lack of a common basis of trust and understanding, lack of local knowledge and lack of familiarity with local business practices are likely to loom in terms of impeding cross-border trade.[8]

A second justification for the CFR focuses more on the goal of promoting European political integration, or at least sees political integration sitting side by side with economic integration. But one's opinion on this justification is likely to turn on the relative weighting that one attaches to the potentially competing principles of national sovereignty and European integration. Or, to put it in a less conflictual way, '[t]he fundamental issue is whether some form of harmonisation of contract law can contribute to a form of better economic integration that nevertheless respects an appropriate degree of political sovereignty for nation states.'[9]

If the CFR is presented merely as an optional instrument[10] that supplements national law rather than tying to supersede it, then some of the potential opposition to its creation may be defused. The change in terminology from Civil Code to CFR may also help in this respect, though it may be unwise to assume that the desire of Euro enthusiasts for a binding instrument has been dimmed by this linguistic sleight of hand.

An additional argument for an optional instrument may be raised in terms of enlarging contracting choice. In other words, contracting parties should be at liberty to choose the optional instrument to govern their transaction if they wish. But objections may still be raised on the basis of the additional costs and complexities caused by its introduction. [11] Parties may have to expend

---

[8]   See generally S Macaulay, 'Non-contractual Relations in Business' (1963) 28 *American Sociological Review* 55; 'The Real and the Paper Deal: Empirical Pictures of Relationships, Complexity and the Urge for Transparent Principles' (2003) 66 *Modern Law Review* 44. See also J Michie and S Deakin, *Contracts, Co-operation and Competition: Studies in Economics, Management and Law* (Oxford, Oxford University Press, 1997).
[9]   See H Collins, 'Transaction Costs and Subsidiarity in European Contract Law' in S Grundmann and J Stuyck (eds), *An Academic Green Paper on European Contract Law* (The Hague, Kluwer Law International, 2002) 269.
[10]   See generally S Grundmann and J Stuyck (eds), *An Academic Green Paper on European Contract Law* (The Hague, Kluwer Law International, 2002), and in particular Part IV, 'An optional European Code supplementing, not substituting national laws'; S Vogenauer and S Weatherill (eds), *The Harmonisation of European Contract Law: Implications for European Private Laws, Business and Legal Practice* (Oxford, Hart Publishing, 2006).
[11]   See H Collins, 'Transaction Costs and Subsidiarity in European Contract Law' in S Grundmann and J Stuyck (eds), *An Academic Green Paper on European Contract Law* (The Hague, Kluwer Law International, 2002) 269 at 281: '[t]ransnational regulation can reduce transactions in commercial transactions only by becoming a compulsory

time and energy in coming to grips with the CFR as well as understanding and appreciating its effects. The CFR will not be rooted in a national legal system. It will be a wholly new instrument and its proper interpretation may take some time, thus generating uncertainties. In the words of Professor Hugh Collins:[12]

> With respect to the creation of an optional set of rules that could be chosen by the parties, the transaction cost approach cannot point to any advantages. The creation of [another] system of law, which the parties may select as their choice of law, neither reduces uncertainty nor ignorance. It has no benefits from a transaction cost point of view. Indeed, as is the case with any transnational and novel law, it is likely in fact to increase uncertainty, at least in the medium term, so that it would provoke increased transaction costs.

There may be spillover effects of the CFR on non-contracting parties who have not bargained for the application of the CFR – so-called negative externalities. In addition, the laws of many countries contain mandatory provisions that contracting parties are not free to depart from. The CFR cannot be expected to replicate the mandatory principles of each and every European state, not least because such principles may be contradictory from one state to another. Making use of the CFR would seem to provide an avenue for escaping from the effect of such mandatory principles. This argument has particular resonance in the sphere of secured transactions or credit securities, where an intimate connection with property law should be noted. In the CFR context, credit securities can be defined as rights against property to ensure the payment of money or the performance of some other obligation. A security right is a right over property and property law is often considered to be within the exclusive domain of national governments. Many countries have a closed list of property rights – a *numerus clausus* – and it is not permissible for parties by contract to add to the list of property rights. The CFR may enlarge the permissible scope of property rights under national law, and if parties are empowered to adopt the CFR as the basis for their security arrangement, effectively they are pushing out the boundaries of the so-called closed list.

More general arguments that are part and parcel of the objections to a European Civil Code may also be deployed. These objections involve an intricate

---

uniform law, but the real benefits only emerge if the transnational regulation becomes reasonably certain or predictable'.

[12]   See 'Transaction Costs and Subsidiarity in European Contract law' in S Grundmann and J Stuyck (eds), *An Academic Green Paper on European Contract Law* (The Hague, Kluwer Law International, 2002) 269 at 277. See also the views of a former English Law Lord, John Hobhouse, on international instruments (and presumably a Common Frame of Reference), 'International Conventions and Commercial Law: In Pursuit of Uniformity' (1990) 106 *Law Quarterly Review* 530.

interlinking of constitutional, economic and cultural considerations.[13] Firstly, the European Civil Code trenches upon national sovereignty and entails the arrogation by the European Union of powers which it does not possess and ought not to possess.[14] While cooperation between nation states is seen as acceptable, creeping encroachments on the sovereignty of nation states are viewed as completely unacceptable. The European Civil Code is seen as involving a frontal assault on the sovereignty of states which is perceived of as more invidious still. It also smacks of a nineteenth century exercise in nation-building, adding to the symbols of the European Union and strengthening and deepening the bonds of its citizens.[15] This nineteenth century approach may not be apposite in a new [16] millennium of new fangled and multi-centric modes of governance.

Focusing on more economic concerns, the European Civil Code suppresses national differences for the sake of uniformity with no opportunity for national autonomy and divergence. [17] The end of jurisdictional diversity eliminates opportunities for competition between national legal orders.[18] There is no scope for innovation at the local level and the creation of uniformity

---

[13]   See generally S Weatherill, 'Why Object to Harmonization of Private Law by the EC?' [2004] 12 *European Review of Private Law* 633.

[14]   On the legal basis for a European Civil Code see generally W van Gerven, 'Coherence and National Laws: Is there a Legal Basis for a European Civil Code?' [1997] 22 *European Review of Private Law* 465; 'Codifying European Private Law? Yes, If' [2002] 27 *European Law Review* EL Rev 156.

[15]   See generally T Wilhelmsson, 'The Legal, the Cultural and the Political – Conclusions from Different Perspectives on Harmonisation of European Contract law' [2002] 13 *European Business Law Review* 541.

[16]   On nation-building and the idea of civil codes see generally W van Gerven, 'Codifying European Private Law: Top Down and Bottom Up' in S Grundmann and J Stuyck (eds), *An Academic Green Paper on European Contract Law* (The Hague, Kluwer, 2002) 405.

[17]   See, for example, P Legrand, 'European Legal Systems are Not Converging' (1997) 45 *International of Comparative Law Quarterly* 52; 'Against a European Civil Code' (1997) 60 *Modern Law Review* 44; 'On the Unbearable Localness of the Law: Academic Fallacies and Unseasonable Observations' [2002] 10 *European Review of Private Law* 61; 'The Impossibility of Legal Transplants' (2003) 4 *Maastricht Journal* 111; 'Antivonbar' (2006) 1 *JCL* 1. And for a slightly different perspective that such a Code may be an impossibility see G Teubner, 'Legal Irritants: Good Faith in British Law or How Unifying Law Ends Up in New Divergences' (1998) 61 Modern Law Review 11. See also B Markesinis, 'Why a Code is Not the Best Way to Advance the Cause of European Unity' [1997] 5 *European Review of Private Law* 519.

[18]   See R. Van den Bergh, 'Forced Harmonisation of Contract Law in Europe: Not to be Continued' in S Grundmann and J Stuyck (eds), *An Academic Green Paper on European Contract Law* (The Hague, Kluwer Law International, 2002) 249 at 267: '[t] he advantages of competition between legal rules must not be underestimated: if rules differ, more preferences can be satisfied and learning processes remain possible'.

can lead to economic sterility.[19] As a result there is less chance for initially unpromising, but ultimately beneficial, ideas to win through and gain general acceptance. The absence of an all-pervasive European norm means that seeds of ingenuity can be sown, tested and put into play at the local national level and then reproduced across national frontiers if they turn out to be generally beneficial. The creation of a pan-European legal order would submerge these potentially enriching seedbeds of dynamism and innovation in a sea of sterile uniformity. This proposition builds upon the celebrated article by Charles Tiebout suggesting that decentralised governance, with horizontally arrayed jurisdictions competing to attract residents on the basis of differing tax and benefit structures, generates increased social welfare and produces a Pareto-superior outcome.[20] Applying this analysis, Professor Easterbrook has made the point that[21] '[w]hen governments become sufficiently plentiful, and when the scope of laws matches the domain of their costs and benefits (that is, when costs and benefits are all felt within the jurisdiction enacting the laws), competitive forces should be as effective with governments as they are with private markets.'

On the cultural front, it can be argued that a Civil Code is closely connected with a country's history and development,[22] and that the replacement of national Codes by a supra-European one would involve casting aside a lot of a country's historical legacy.[23] While not all aspects of a country's cultural and historical

---

[19]   See generally A Ogus, 'Competition Between National Legal Systems: A Contribution of Economic Analysis to Comparative Law' (1999) 48 *International of Comparative Law Quarterly* 405 and see also U Mattei, 'A Transaction Costs Approach to the European Civil Code' [1997] 5 *European Review of Private Law* 537.

[20]   See generally C Tiebout, 'A Pure Theory of Local Expenditures' (1956) 64 *Journal of Political Economy* 416, and see generally D C Esty and D Geradin, *Regulatory Competition and Economic Integration Comparative Perspectives* (New York, OUP, 2001).

[21]   See F Easterbrook, 'Federalism and European Business Law' (1994) 14 *International Review of Law and Economics* 125 at 127–8.

[22]   See generally H Collins 'European Private Law and Cultural Identity of States' [1995] *European Review of Private Law* 353.

[23]   See S Weatherill, 'Why Object to the Harmonization of Private Law by the EC?' [2004] *European Review of Private Law* 633 at 647: '[t]his objection to harmonization is driven by the perception that legal culture, represented in part by the shape of private law, has undergone a long-term, frequently unplanned evolution in the Member States, reflecting a range of influences. To confine such richness within the straightjacket of harmonization is to rob Europe of its past. It is to sacrifice a multi-textured private law tradition to the narrow demands of economic integration built on regulatory homogeneity. A harmonized private law will not display the susceptibility to local preference that is the preserve of a more decentralized system. More broadly still, stretching far beyond the domain of private law, this dissenting vein is nurtured by the profound belief that Europe is strengthened by its diversity.'

baggage are necessarily worth keeping, national champions may consider deeply troubling the large-scale submergence of national legal institutions in a pan-European order. Differences between national legal orders are perhaps at the most stark in relation to the common law/civil law divide, with lawyers trained in the common law and civilian traditions approaching legal issues in different ways. They have different legal mindsets, in that civilians tend to start off with statements of general principles while the common lawyer works more from the specific to the general. For the common lawyer, the facts of a specific situation come first, and this leads through a process of analogy and induction to a statement of general principle. The civilian lawyer deduces the approach to be adopted in a particular case from an initial statement of general principle, thus working the other way round. The differences can be exaggerated, in that most areas of private law in the common law world are largely governed or, at the very least, deeply encrusted by statute. But it remains the case that an appreciation of the effects of statute often requires an understanding of the common law backdrop since common law norms continue to apply in areas not regulated by the statute.

A European Civil Code might involve marginalising the common law canon of experience in favour of the civilian tradition, with lawyers trained in the common law tradition becoming second class citizens compared with their civilian counterparts. As an overall proposition, the English common law does not make use of general codes, while such Codes are a foundation stone of the civilian tradition. It has been suggested that the very existence of a European Civil Code means bowing to the Civil Law in preference to the common law. This argument has been advanced forcefully by Professor Pierre Legrand who speaks of 'political correctness a l'européenne' or the desire to eliminate difference across laws or to pretend that it is not there. He also says:[24]

> Nowadays, there is only way in which one can be a 'good European' and it is to support the suppression of local particularlism. Any expression of doubt in favour of cultural diversity, any critique of centralising legal integration processes is rapidly construed as inimical to the grand European project, its author being branded as a reactionary, someone who is on the wrong side of History. An extreme illustration of this discourse of 'closure' is, of course, the speech which then Chancellor Helmut Kohl delivered in Louvain in February 1996 where he said that European integration was a 'question of war and peace in the twenty-first century.' Another German political leader opined that after Auschwitz it was no longer permissible to be 'against Europe'.

---

[24] See P Legrand, 'On the Unbearable Localness of the Law: Academic Fallacies and Unseasonable Observations' [2002] *European Review of Private Law* 61 at 66. For a more measured but occasionally critical voice see MW Hesslink, *The New European Legal Culture* (Deventer, Kluwer, 2001).

One may fairly suggest that both the rhetoric and the sentiments appear over-blown.[25] Certainly, the description of European legal systems appears to be grounded on stereotypes and, moreover, it may ignore the receptivity of particular legal systems to change. A stereotyped presentation depicting the common law as based on case law and civil law as founded on a legislative basis does not necessarily tell us about the reality of the living law. This snapshot does not reproduce the oscillation and fragmentation of sources in national legal systems. Cultures, traditions and legal practices are not rooted to a particular historical epoch but transform themselves with time.

Moreover, the common law equals case law/civil law equals legislation dichotomy does not hold good when it comes to secured transactions/credit securities. In the European mainland, this area of law, by and large, is not codified law and legal recognition and expansion of security rights has occurred, in the main, through statutory supplements to the Civil Code and case law developments. It has been remarked that 'the development of secured transactions law ... largely took place (and continues to take place) outside the national Civil Codes. The legal regime is either entirely based on case law, as for example in Germany, or contained in special, fragmented legislation as, for example, in France, Italy and Spain.'[26] The position is not fundamentally different in the UK where, unlike the position in the US under Article 9 of the Uniform Commercial Code, there is no comprehensive statutory code on secured transactions.[27]

Conclusions on a Code/CFR

Objections to the proposal for a European Civil Code/CFR may be made on constitutional, economic and cultural grounds and, while some of the criticisms may be exaggerated, it is submitted that in the main they are well-founded. Moreover, the case for a CFR is ultimately a political case based on advancing the goal of European legal integration. It is submitted that, in the wake of the rejection of the

---

[25] See A Chamboredon, 'The Debate on a European Civil Code: For an "Open Texture"' in M Van Hoecke and F Ost (eds), *The Harmonisation of European Private Law* (Oxford, Hart Publishing, 2000) 63 at 66.

[26] See E-M Kieninger (eds), *Security Rights in Movable Property in European Private Law* (Cambridge, Cambridge University Press, 2004) at 647.

[27] See generally on the presentational difficulties caused by this M Bridge, 'The Law Commission's Proposals for the Reform of Corporate Security Interests' in J Getzler and J Payne (eds), *Company Charges: Spectrum and Beyond* (Oxford, OUP, 2006) at 267 who concludes at 289: '[t]hose who have participated in international gatherings will be acutely aware that the absence of a presentable package of English commercial law is a major hindrance to its international influence.' See also R Goode, 'Insularity or Leadership? The Role of the United Kingdom in the Harmonisation of Commercial Law' (2001) 50 *International of Comparative Law Quarterly* 751.

Lisbon Treaty by Irish voters and the earlier rejection of the European Constitution by French and Dutch voters, the prospects of this case being accepted by citizens of Europe is a remote one. Nevertheless the European Commission has pressed on, and published a Green Paper on 'progress towards a European Contract Law for consumers and businesses'.[28] The Green Paper canvasses various policy options on the final form of the CFR and whether it should serve as (a) An official 'toolbox' for the legislator; (b) the basis of Commission Recommendation on European Contract Law; (c) a Regulation setting up an optional Instrument of European Contract Law; (d) a Directive on European Contract Law; (e) a Regulation establishing a European Contract; (f) Regulation establishing a European Civil Code. Among these various options the Optional instrument approach seems to find most favour with the Commission though it does see possible complications with its introduction. The Commission has established an Expert Group comprising mainly academics and those previously associated with the CFR project and this Expert Group has been primarily charged with the task of converting the academic CFR into an optional instrument. The expert Group has a number of decisions to make on the structure and form of the Optional instrument; whether it should cover business-to-business contracts, business-to-consumer contracts, and on-line transactions; whether it should cover both cross-border and domestic contracts and whether it should be available on an 'opt-in' or 'opt-out' basis. There is also the possibility that the Optional Instrument may cover 'credit securities' or proprietary interests in movable assets, as well as the law of unjustified enrichment. Political, popular and academic opposition has not gone away however and it may that the entire Commission endeavour turns out to be stillborn.

CONVERGENCE OF NATIONAL LAWS ALONG THE LINES OF ARTICLE 9 OF THE UCC

While the European Civil Code/CFR is best seen as a possible political or integrationist imposition, a move of national laws in the direction of Article 9 of the Uniform Commercial Code is seen as more the product of spontaneous convergence. There is a widespread view that an efficient secured credit system should improve the availability and reduce the cost of credit. For example, studies in emerging and transitional economies suggest that weaknesses in functioning collateral-based credit provision hinder financial and economic development.[29]

---

[28]   (Brussels, European Commission, July 2010) COM(2010)348 final.
[29]   See generally H Fleisig, 'Economic Functions of Security in a Market Economy' in J Norton and M Andenas (eds), *Emerging Financial Markets and Secured Transactions* (London, Kluwer, 1998) at 15. Fleisig examines legal deficiencies in the framework governing secured transactions over movable property in Argentina. Theoretical and

Simply stated, banks and other financial institutions will not engage in large-scale lending activities if their position as secured creditors in the liquidation of their borrowers is not sufficiently certain or sufficient means for the enforcement of security are not available. More controversially, it has also been suggested that businesses in less developed financial systems and civil law countries substitute less efficient forms of external finance, trade credit and other sources of funds for bank loans and equity.[30] This assertion ties in with the proposition that Article 9 is the 'most modernised, rational and comprehensive system of security interests in the present world',[31] and that legal systems should converge towards the best model. The proposition however is questionable on a number of levels. For instance, one may query whether Article 9 in its entirety is necessarily the best system. Others may argue that the proposition conflates the 'is' and the 'ought' in various respects.

Convergence theorists may take some heart from the fact the most recent, and arguably the most representative, international instrument in the field is close to Article 9 in tone. This is the United Nations Commission on International Trade Law (UNCITRAL) Legislative Guide on Secured Transactions, which has been heavily shaped by American law and American lawyers.[32] The intellectual case for convergence has also been extensively aired in the closely-aligned sphere of corporate governance where Professors Hansmann and Kraakman have predicted the end of history for corporate law.[33] They speak of a widespread normative consensus that corporate managers should act exclusively in the interests of shareholders, including minority shareholders. In their view, while differences may persist as a result of institutional and historical contingencies, the bulk of legal development worldwide will be towards a standard model of the corporation. Others such as Professor Klaus Hopt have acknowledged

---

empirical perspectives are presented and the author concludes that 'three-quarters of the problem of high interest rates facing borrowers who do not use real estate as collateral is a problem that arises from the laws and legal procedures that govern lending against immovable property'. See also World Bank, *Building Effective Insolvency Systems* (World Bank, 1999), A report from the Working Group on Debtor-Creditor Regimes at 3 and see generally D W Arner, *Financial Stability, Economic Growth and the Role of Law* (New York, CUP, 2007).

[30] See generally ibid.
[31] Professor Ulrich Drobnig: see (1977) 8 *UNCITRAL Yearbook* at 171.
[32] Up-to-date information on the secured transactions guide may be found on the UNCITRAL website, *www.uncitral.org/*, and see generally S Bazinas, 'UNCITRAL's Work in the Field of Secured Transactions' in J Norton and M Andenas (eds), *Emerging Financial Markets and Secured Transactions* (London, Kluwer, 1998).
[33] See generally on what interests corporate law should serve H Hansmann and R Kraakman, 'The end of history for corporate law' (2001) 89 *Georgetown Law Journal* 439.

a greater role for path-dependent differences between corporate governance regimes that are deeply embedded in a country's tradition, history and culture but, at the same time, suggest that market forces can be expected to be stronger in the long run.[34] In general, all proponents of convergence are committed to the idea that global competition is a strong enough force to bring about change in the laws. They assume that it is possible for a country to amend its existing legal norms to any degree that is desired or, in other words, that legal systems are free to choose from an open-ended menu of legal rules.[35]

Professor Mark Roe has broken somewhat from this consensus, arguing that political forces cause legal systems to develop path-dependently.[36] I would submit that Roe's work, while going some way to explain the persistence of divergence, fails to pay sufficient regard to the role of existing legal norms in shaping subsequent legal developments.[37] A distinction may be made between the factors that bring about changes in the law and the form in which the law absorbs the need for change. In short, politics, economics and culture as well as changing social and commercial norms can generate the need to alter legal rules, but once such a need has emerged, the reform process has historically been shaped by legal doctrine. The result of legal doctrine is to cause the law to develop in a path-dependent fashion. While the law will change and adapt to new demands and circumstances, the change is effected by adapting existing legal concepts rather than by introducing new ones. Legal systems are equipped with a certain limited set of doctrinal tools, and this has a self-perpetuating effect. Legal problems are invariably solved by making use of existing concepts that are most developed and therefore safest to use. The law and lawyers tend to absorb change by digging deeper into existing soil, rather than branching out into new fields. Political and other influences may trigger legal development and cause the law to produce certain outcomes, but the form that represents these outcomes is determined by the legal doctrine prevailing in the jurisdiction

[34] See K J Hopt, 'Common Principles of Corporate Governance in Europe?' in J McCahery *et al.*, *Corporate Governance Regimes, Convergence and Diversity* (Oxford, OUP, 2002) 175.
[35] See generally E Micheler, *Property in Securities: A Comparative Study* (Cambridge, CUP, 2007).
[36] See M Roe, *Political Determinants of Corporate Governance* (Oxford, OUP, 2003); M Roe, 'Chaos and Evolution in Law and Economics' (1996) 109 *Harvard Law Review* 641; L Bebchuk and M Roe, 'A Theory of Path Dependence in Corporate Ownership and Governance' (1999) 52 *Stanford Law Review* 127, and see generally P Gourevitch, 'The Politics of Corporate Governance Regulation' (2003) 112 *Yale Law Journal* 1864.
[37] See generally E Micheler, *Property in Securities: A Comparative Study* (Cambridge, CUP, 2007) chapter 15: 'Legal development as a path-dependent process', and see the statement at 228: '[l]egal doctrine causes the law to develop path-dependently'.

concerned. Legal doctrine is an independent factor that determines the form of future development.

The institutions that prevail in a particular jurisdiction influence future developments, and lawyers, by virtue of their role in shaping legal doctrine, are in a prime position to play an important role as a pressure group.[38] Their preference for certainty and predictability causes them to favour the use of familiar doctrinal tools rather than a process of experimentation with more straightforward, but unfamiliar and untested, legal techniques. The preference is for reform that requires little modification of existing rules over reform that requires significant change. Moreover, once a solution has been found to overcome what has been perceived to be a problem or an obstacle by the commercial market place, legal practice likes to stick to this solution even though a more straightforward solution may now appear on the horizon. These points are well illustrated by the English experience of proposals for reform of secured credit law put forward by the Law Commission. The Law Commission advocated an Article 9 type scheme for England, but this endeavour has been resisted successfully thus far. At the forefront of resistance has been an influential lawyers' group that has essentially argued that any reform should occur within the existing legal landscape rather than by seeking a transformation exercise. The English experience will now be looked at in detail

ENGLAND AS A CASE STUDY OF SECURED CREDIT LAW REFORM

For over 30 years successive official bodies and government reports have endorsed the idea of reforming the English law of personal property security along the lines of Article 9 of the United States Uniform Commercial Code. The latter was first adopted in the 1950s and its influence has since spread to the common law provinces of Canada and to New Zealand,[39] with Australia currently contemplating Article 9 type change. Legal practitioners in England, however, have generally been, at best, indifferent, and at worst, outrightly hostile to the idea. Their general stance is best encapsulated in the maxim that the present law, while it may do with the occasional incremental adjustment, works well,

---

[38] This may be referred to as 'structure-driven path dependence': see L Bebchuk and M Roe, 'A Theory of Path Dependence in Corporate Ownership and Governance' (1999) 52 *Stanford Law Review* 127.

[39] See generally: P Ali, *The Law of Secured Finance* (Oxford, OUP, 2002); G McCormack, *Secured Credit under English and American Law* (Cambridge, CUP, 2004). It should be noted that Australia is also actively considering similar reforms. For up-to-date information on the reform process in Australia see www.ag.gov.au/pps.

and if it is not broke, there is no need to fix it. The Law Commission started on the project of comprehensive personal property security law reform in 2001 following a reference from the Company Law Review Steering Group.[40] The way forward then seemed clear. There was a strong steer from the Company Law Review Group suggesting that legislation based on Article 9 of the Uniform Commercial Code was the appropriate path to follow. The Law Commission endorsed this approach in the Consultation Paper *Registration of Security Interests*[41] and the basic approach is confirmed and extended in the Consultative Report, *Company Security Interests*.[42]

In its Final Report, the Law Commission, in response largely to pressure from lawyers' groups, watered down its original approach.[43] The US Article 9 influence is still apparent, though the comprehensive cutting edge of Article 9 has been blunted in a big way. The Law Commission also shied away from amendments to insolvency legislation. The appetites of users of the system were not sufficiently robust to stomach the changes originally contemplated. More generally, the change of heart by the Law Commission demonstrates the persuasive power of existing legal doctrine as well as lobbying by lawyers' groups. Particularly influential in this regard has been the pressure applied by the Financial Law Committee of the City of London Law Society.[44] As the

---

[40]   See *Modern Company Law for a Competitive Economy* (London, TSO, 2001).

[41]   See Consultation Paper No 164, *Registration of Security Interests: Company Charges and Property other than Land* (London, TSO, 2002), hereafter 'Consultation Paper'. See generally on the Consultation Paper Gullifer, L 'Will the Law Commission sink the floating charge?' [2003] LMCLQ 125; McCormack, 'Quasi-securities and the Law Commission Consultation Paper on security interests – a brave new world' [2003] *Lloyds Maritime and Commercial Law Quarterly (LMCLQ)* 80; note also Davies, I, 'The Reform of English personal property security law: functionalism and Article 9 of the Uniform Commercial Code' (2004) 24 *Legal Studies* 295.

[42]   See *Company Security Interests: A Consultative Report* (London, TSO, 2004); hereafter 'Consultative Report'; on which see G McCormack, 'The Law Commission Consultative Report on Company Security Interests: An Irreverent Riposte' (2005) 68 *Modern Law Review* 286.

[43]   Law Com No 296 with accompanying draft Company Security Regulations 2006. See Ziegel, 'The travails of English chattel security law reform – a transatlantic view' [2006] *LMCLQ* 110 at 119: '[i]n my view, …the Law Commission's revised proposals, as reflected in the draft Regulations, do not by any reasonable yardstick amount to a mini-Art 9 style Code and, it is safe to assume, were not meant to do so. They contain important building blocks in the realization of such a goal but in their present form too many critical blocks are missing to justify such an ambitious claim.' For a different perspective see the paper by Law Commissioner H Beale, 'The Exportability of North American Chattel Security Regimes: the Fate of the English Law Commission's Proposals' [2006] 43 *Canadian Business Law Journal*, 177.

[44]   Its comments on the Law Commission proposals can be found on the website, www.citysolicitors.org/. The chair of the working group which produced this response

Law Commission noted, this committee 'examined our proposals in particular depth, and their response was adopted by a further 11 respondents, some of whom added comments and clarifications of their own.'[45] The Law Commission proposals were not acceptable to the City of London Law Society even in their watered down form, and in response to this practitioner opposition the Companies Act 2006 simply re-enacted the existing legislative provisions in what was designed to be a more user-friendly and accessible form.

Existing Legal Doctrine in England

There are four types of security right currently known to English law – mortgages, charges (fixed and floating), pledges and liens.[46] Mortgages and charges are both non-possessory consensual rights. They are created by agreement between security giver and security taker and the security giver retains possession of the property that serves as security. In *NatWest Bank plc v. Spectrum Plus Ltd*[47] Lord Scott suggested that the essential characteristic of a floating charge, and the characteristic that distinguishes it from a fixed charge, is that the 'asset subject to the charge is not finally appropriated as a security for the payment of the debt until the occurrence of some future event. In the meantime, the charge giver was left free to use the charged asset and to remove it from the security.'

Sometimes, the expressions 'mortgage' and 'charge' (meaning a fixed charge) are used interchangeably.[48] On other occasions, however, the expression 'charge' may be used as a general umbrella concept that also embraces mortgages,[49]

---

was Richard Calnan of Norton Rose and he has synopsised the report in an article, 'The Reform of Company Security Interests' in [2005] *Butterworths Journal of International Banking and Financial Law* 28. This article will be referred to as Calnan [2005] *BJIBFL* 28.

[45] See Final Report, Law Com No 296 at para. 1.19. There were a total of 70 responses to the Consultative Report, including 21 from practitioners and practitioners' organisations, 10 from banks and banking organisations and 12 from academics – '[i] nevitably, we received more responses from lawyers and lenders than from companies' The City Solicitors' Group has produced a follow-up document, 'The Registration of Companies' Security Interests', the appearance of which coincided with the appearance of the Law Commission's Final Report. This document will be referred to in the chapter and appears on the City of London Law Society website, www.citysolicitors.org/. The group continues to be critical of the Law Commission proposals.

[46] See generally *Re Paramount Airways Ltd* [1990] BCC 130 at 149 *per* Browne-Wilkinson VC.

[47] [2005] 2 AC 680 at para. 111.

[48] The Law of Property Act 1925 s. 205(1)(xvi) states that 'mortgage' includes any charge or lien on any property for securing money or money's worth, and see also Insolvency Act 1986 s. 248.

[49] The Companies Act 1985 s. 396(4) provides that 'charge' includes 'mortgage'; see now to the same effect Companies Act 2006, s. 861(5).

but it has been suggested that there is a narrow technical difference between a mortgage and a charge. A mortgage involves the transfer of ownership to the security taker, with a re-transfer once the obligation secured has been discharged, whereas the charge involves no transfer of ownership but merely a right of recourse against the property to ensure the discharge of the relevant obligation.[50]

The pledge is also created by agreement between security giver and security taker, but it differs from the mortgage or charge in that actual or constructive possession of the property serving as security, or documents representing the same,[51] is handed over to the security taker.[52] A lien can take at least two forms.[53] The common law lien gives the lien holder the right to retain possession of items originally delivered for some other purpose until some outstanding indebtedness is discharged.[54] The lien holder has a passive power to retain possession but no power of sale over the assets, though statute sometimes brings into existence a power of sale.[55] The equitable lien, on the other hand, is essentially an equitable charge over property, arising by operation of law rather than by agreement between the parties.[56]

Whereas property law serves to determine what security rights may be created, contract law sets out the formalities for the creation of consensual security rights. These requirements are not onerous. In the generality of cases, a simple oral contract is all that is required, though, in practice, there will be writing in considerable and expensive detail. For security interests relating to land the writing requirement is mandatory under the Law of Property (Miscellaneous Provisions) Act 1989 and, before that, the Statute of Frauds.

Once a security right has been created then it is good, not only as between the security giver and the security taker, but also with respect to third parties. Chapter 25 of the Companies Act 2006 lays down, however, that particulars of certain types of charge created by a company, along with the original instrument

---

[50]   See the comments of Slade J in *Re Bond Worth Ltd* [1980] Ch 228 at 250, but compare however Lord Hoffmann in *Re BCCI (No 8)* [1998] AC 214 at 226.

[51]   See *Harrold v. Plenty* [1901] 2 Ch 314.

[52]   The Privy Council explained the nature of a pledge in *Official Assignee of Madras v. Mercantile Bank of India Ltd* [1935] AC 53 at 58–9.

[53]   In *Re Cosslett (Contractors) Ltd* [1998] Ch 495 at 508 Millett LJ referred to a contractual lien and distinguished it from a pledge, stating that in the case of pledge the owner delivers possession to the creditor as security, whereas, in the case of a lien, the creditor retains possession of goods previously delivered to him for some other purpose. Under the draft Company Security Regulations 2006, published as an appendix to the Law Commission's Final Report, a contractual lien is considered to be a pledge.

[54]   See *Tappenden v. Artus* [1964] 2 QB 185.

[55]   See *Bristol Airport plc v. Powdrill* [1990] Ch 744.

[56]   For descriptions of equitable liens see *Re Bond Worth Ltd* [1980] Ch 228 at 251 and *Re Bernstein* [1925] Ch 12 at 17–18.

of charge, must be delivered to a public register – namely Companies House – within 21 days from the creation of the charge. If this is not done, then the charge is invalid in the event of the corporate charge giver going into liquidation or administration. Registration requirements apply to the most common types of charge, including floating charges and fixed charges over land, goods, debts, ships, aircraft and intellectual property rights. The list of registrable charges is set out in section 860(7) Companies Act 2006 and only charges on this list are registrable. To use Article 9 jargon, the requirement of registration is a 'perfection' requirement.

The purpose behind Part 25 of the Companies Act is the provision of information[57] about a company's secured lending, and this information may be of use to such persons as later lenders, rating or credit reference agencies, potential investors or financial analysts. Essentially Part 25 prevents the implication of false wealth. It also has an incidental effect in determining priorities, in that an unregistered, but registrable, charge is void in a company's liquidation or administration. According to Lord Hoffmann in *Smith v. Bridgend County Borough Council*, 'The plain intention of the legislature was that property subject to a registrable but unregistered charge should be available to the general body of creditors (or a secured creditor ranking after the unregistered charge) as if no such charge existed'.[58]

Part 25, however, plays no comprehensive role in determining priorities. Priority between competing security interests in the same property turns on a number of factors as well as the fact of registration. These factors include the order of creation of the respective security interests; whether the security interest in question is a fixed or floating charge; and whether one security interest holder had notice of another earlier security interest before taking its later security interest. Where the security interests are charges, the order of priority is roughly as follows: assuming that all the charges have been duly registered, fixed charges run ahead of floating charges irrespective of the order of creation unless the floating charge contains a restrictive or negative pledge that forbids

---

[57] According to the DTI, *Regulatory Impact Assessment on Proposals for the Registration of Companies' Security Interests* (London, DTI, July 2005) at para. 2.7 'The system for registration of company charges is needed to address the following risks:

- the concealment of secured credit with markets being misled by the apparent unencumbered ownership by companies of assets which in fact are encumbered in favour of prior creditors,
- uncertainty over the rights of secured parties in the event of the borrower's insolvency,
- uncertainty over the rights of those who buy assets that are subject to security interests.'

[58] [2002] 1 AC 336 at para. 68.

the creation of subsequent fixed charges having priority and the fixed chargeor has actual notice, not just constructive notice, of the restrictive clause.[59]

The basic priority position is complicated further by the freedom of contract principles that underlie English law. Security interest holders are free to alter the order of priority amongst each other by contractual provision.[60] Moreover, while there is a finite list of security interests, parties can often achieve the functional equivalent of security through other legal strategies. The retention of title by the seller of goods pending payment of the purchase price serves the same legal effect as a loan of money on the security of goods. In the same way, the assignment of debts by a company to a finance house will provide the company with immediate funds to the same extent as a loan of money on the security of the debts. Both these kinds of transaction are referred to as 'quasi-security', i.e. functionally equivalent legal devices to security rights strictly so-called. Moreover, quasi-security rights are generally stronger than security rights since the holder of the quasi-security right has ownership of the asset in question.

Criticisms of the English Law and Comparisons with the Article 9 Approach

The Law Commission voiced certain criticisms of the current English law, pointing out, for example, that the registration provisions were far from being comprehensive. These provisions applied to an important, but comparatively limited, range of security interests and registration did not serve as an over-riding reference point for determining priorities. Quasi-security interests were also outwith the registration system. Moreover, the system was one of transaction filing rather than notice filing. The original instrument of charge had to be submitted, along with the requisite particulars to Companies House. The latter compared the two and, if satisfied that the filed particulars were accurate, issued a certificate of due registration which was stated to be con-clusive evidence that all the requirements of the legislation as to registration

---

[59]   See generally *G & T Earle Ltd v. Hemsworth Rural District Council* (1928) 44 TLR 605; *Re Standard Machine Co Ltd* (1906) 95 LT 829, *Wilson v. Kelland* [1910] 2 Ch 306; and for possible circularity problems see *Re Portbase Clothing Ltd* [1993] Ch 388 and *Re Woodroffes (Musical Instruments) Ltd* [1986] Ch 366.

[60]   See *Cheah v. Equiticorp Finance Group Ltd* [1992] BCC; *Re SSSL Realisations Ltd* [2004] EWHC 1760; *Re Maxwell Communications Corp (No 2)* [1993] 1 WLR 1402; *Re British & Commonwealth Holdings plc (No 3)* [1992] 1 AC 472. Note also E Ferran, 'Subordination of Secured and Unsecured Debt' in *Company Law and Corporate Finance* (Oxford, OUP, 1999) at chapter 16; R Nolan, 'Less Equal than Others' [1995] *Journal of Business Law* 485.

had been observed.[61] There was a considerable administrative burden imposed on Companies House against a backdrop of potential liability to prejudicially affected parties if it transpired that the certificate of due registration was issued in error. Transaction filing related necessarily to a single transaction rather than to a chain of potential transactions. Additionally, the filing was, by definition, after the event. It was not possible to file in advance of the conclusion of a security agreement.

The Law Commission's consideration of the issue arose from a reference by the Company Law Review Steering Group and must be understood against that backdrop. As part of a thorough review of company law, the Steering Group considered the company charge provisions. It seems that there was some determined and sustained arm-twisting behind the scenes by highly-placed advocates of the Article 9 philosophy such as Professor Sir Roy Goode, who has criticised the present English position in strident terms[62] adding:[63]

> this state of affairs continues to be tolerated in the 21st century, when the United States and Canada have for many years had highly developed, market-responsive legislation which has worked and when successive government reports have recommended the adoption of similar legislation in this country, is a shocking indictment of the indifference of successive governments to the modernisation of our commercial law.

Article 9 is based on notice filing.[64] 'The most characteristic difference between notice filing and traditional systems of registration is that notice filing is parties-specific rather than transaction-specific. What is filed are not the details of a particular security but notice that certain parties have entered into, or may in future enter into, a secured transaction in relation to specified property. This approach has certain implications. ... the information given on the register is necessarily rather general in character, being an invitation to further inquiry rather than a full account of the right in security.' The notice may be filed before any security interest is concluded and a single filing may relate to a series of security interests between the parties.

---

[61] S. 869(6)(b) Companies Act 2006. For cases on the conclusiveness of the registrar's certificate see *Re CL Nye Ltd* [1971] 1 Ch 442; *Re Central Bank of India Ltd* [1986] QB 1114.

[62] See generally R Goode, 'Insularity or Leadership? The Role of the United Kingdom in the Harmonisation of Commercial Law' (2001) 50 *International of Comparative Law Quarterly* 751 at 759–60. Professor Goode acted as a consultant to the Law Commission during the project.

[63] *Legal Problems of Credit and Security* (3rd ed, London, Sweet & Maxwell, 2003) at 156.

[64] Scottish Law Commission discussion paper, *Registration of Rights in Security by Companies* (Edinburgh, TSO, October 2002) at 8.

Filing is the generally accepted method of perfecting a security interest or making it effective against third parties though, in certain circumstances, handing possession over to the secured party may serve as an alternative to filing. Moreover, certain security interests are automatically perfected, i.e. no filing is necessary, and for certain types of intangible property investing the secured party with control over the property is a superior method of perfection. If there is more than one security interest over the same item of property, then priority is normally determined by the application of a first to file (more accurately first to perfect) priority principle, though there are exceptions for purchase money security interests ('PMSI'). A PMSI is a loan of money, or more generally the extension of credit, that is conditioned on the acquisition of particular property and where the credit provider takes a security interest in the property that is thereby acquired. The PMSI will outrank an earlier general creditor whose security interest extends to the later property by virtue of an after-acquired property clause in the security agreement.[65] The Article 9 filing and priority rules also extend, in the main, to the assignment of receivables and to title retention devices, though finance leases have posed particular problems for the conceptual and practical design of an Article 9 scheme. Article 9 therefore has more of a comprehensive scope than the English company charge registration system.

The Original Law Commission Proposals

The Law Commission was convinced of the merits of Article 9 as a suitable guide for English law to follow. It suggested that a new English system would be modelled along the lines of Article 9 and the Personal Property Security Acts in the common law provinces of Canada and in New Zealand. Overseas legislation was used as a guide, the Law Commission explained, partly because of the constraints of time but also because the Law Commission saw 'no need to re-invent the wheel'.[66] It was said that there was not necessarily an assumption that what has worked well in North America will work well in England, but 'the fact that Article 9 and the PPSAs have been so successful means that they deserve very

---

[65]   For a theoretical justification of PMSI super-priority see the discussion at para. 17.7 of the Diamond Report, *A Review of Security Interests in Property* (London, HMSO, 1989) (Chairman Professor AL Diamond) and for a law and economics perspective see H Kanda and S Levmore 'Explaining Creditor Priorites' (1994) 80 *Virginia Law Review* 2103 at 2138–41. See also A Schwartz, 'The Continuing Puzzle of Secured Debt' (1984) 37 *Vanderbilt Law Review* 1051 who argues that whereas a general financier takes account of average risk, the PMSI lender may have particular skills and is able to lend on particularly advantageous terms because of its special knowledge of the collateral.

[66]   See Consultative Report at para. 1.20.

careful consideration'.[67] The Law Commission thought that notice filing could be applied to a broader range of transactions, and not just the current list of registrable charges set out in what is now section 860(7) of the Companies Act 2006. In particular, it singled out factoring, i.e. the assignment of receivables, and retention of title clauses in sale of goods transactions. The first tranche of reform would involve the introduction of notice filing for an amended list of company charges and, in its view, preferably also for 'quasi-security' interests, with the vehicle of reform being regulations made under a new Companies Act. Later on, the reform might be extended to non-corporate legal actors and a further stage of reform would entail a comprehensive restatement of the law of security interests.

A major selling point used by the Law Commission was registration of security interests over the internet. Registration could be carried out on-line, without the active intervention of Companies House, other than the provision of the necessary facilities. This would produce a saving of staff time and less administrative hassle. The Law Commission stated that notice filing would be advantageous primarily for the following reasons:[68]

1. Electronic filing would be fast, simple and cheap in the long run.
2. In a companies-only scheme, the risk of an error that might invalidate a filing would be very small since companies have a unique registration number.
3. A simple description of the secured property – the 'collateral' – would suffice. This would reduce the risk of inaccurate descriptions and also protect third parties because a security interest would not be effective as regards property that fell outside the description in the financing statement.
4. Filing would become permissible in advance of a security agreement being concluded, and this would enable a lender to protect its priority position while negotiations over security were continuing.
5. Dual registration would become generally a thing of the past. Security interests over land, ships, aircraft and intellectual property rights would remain registrable in the specialist asset registers but would no longer be registrable at Companies House, though, to ensure that there was no loss of valuable information, there would be an automatic forwarding of information from the Land Registry to Companies House.
6. Time of filing would become the crucial reference point for determining priorities subject to the recognised Article 9 exception for PMSIs.[69]
7. The Law Commission suggested that the fixed/floating charge distinction could disappear under the new system. No longer would complicated

---

[67] See Consultative Report at para. 1.5.
[68] See Consultative Report at para. 2.43.
[69] See Consultative Report at para. 2.43.

boundary demarcation exercises of the kind necessarily engaged in by the Privy Council in *Re Brumark Ltd*[70] and the House of Lords in *Re Spectrum Plus Ltd*[71] be the order of the day. The floating charge would be superseded by a single type of security interest that would have all the advantages of the floating charge but fewer disadvantages to the lender.

It is the case however that some of the advantages claimed by the Law Commission bear no necessary connection with the introduction of a notice filing system. Indeed the Government has recently brought forward proposals for the electronic registration of charges under a revised version of the present system.[72] This would be done in conjunction within the existing company charge registration framework. Moreover, in practice under the existing system, given the fact that companies have a unique registration number and given the certificate of due registration issued by Companies House, there is no appreciable risk of an error in the registration process that would invalidate a complete filing. Simple descriptions of the secured property, while making it easy to file for a secured party, also provide less information to a potential searcher of the register. Divorcing registration from the actual conclusion of a security agreement also opens up the possibility that the state of the register may become remote from the factual realities concerning the state of a debtor's secured borrowings. A notice on the register may relate not to an actual transaction but to one of a multitude of possible transactions that never in the event materialised.

The presence or absence of dual registration has nothing to do with notice filing. One could have a transaction filing system with registration not being required in respect of security interests that are the subject of separate registration in an asset-based register. Equally one could introduce a notice filing system that also includes security interests that are the subject of separate registration in an asset-based register. Dual registration, or the absence thereof, and notice filing are logically separate and distinct concepts. There is no necessary connection between the two.

Moreover, notice filing and 'first to file has priority' are logically separate and distinct concepts. One could devise a system which makes notice filing, whether before or after the formalisation of a security agreement, a condition of the validity of certain security interests in certain circumstances, but which

---

[70]   *Re Brumark Ltd: Agnew v. CIR* [2001] 2 AC 710.

[71]   [2005] 2 AC 680.

[72]   BIS (Department of Business, Innovation and Skills) 'Government Response on Registration of Charges created by Companies and Limited Liability Partnerships'), December 2010. According to the DTI, *Regulatory Impact Assessment on Proposals for the Registration of Companies' Security Interests* (London, DTI, July 2005) the idea of computerised registration of company security interests has pretty near universal support.

leaves priority between two or more security interests in respect of the same property turn on factors other than filing. Equally, one could have a transaction filing system where the time of registration determines priority questions. Indeed, the current asset-based registers for ships, aircraft, etc. involve a variant of this approach. Notice filing and the statutory or judicial recognition of PMSIs are also independent from one another. The PMSI is not inherently part and parcel of a notice filing system. One could have notice filing without any PMSI component. Alternatively, one could have special priority status for the PMSI even under a transaction filing system, and, arguably, this is the case in England. In *United Malayan Banking Corp v. Aluminex*[73] courts in Malaysia recognised the PMSI on the basis of old English authorities like *Re Connolly Bros Ltd (No 2)*[74] and *Wilson v. Kelland.*[75] In England, more recently the Court of Appeal in *Whale v. Viasystems Ltd*[76] gave further judicial blessing to the PMSI and reinforced the comments of Professor Sir Roy Goode about 'the inequity that would result in allowing the prior chargee a windfall increase in his security brought about not with the debtor's money or new funds injected by the prior chargee but with financing provided by a later incumbrancer'.[77] Finally, while the floating charge is a time-honoured feature of English law, fixed and floating charges could be assimilated without doing undue violence to the current transaction filing system. Indeed, a noted critic of notice filing has also endorsed assimilation of fixed and floating charges, or at least similar treatment of the two for most salient purposes.[78]

Practitioner Objections to the Original Law Commission Proposals

There were some practitioner objections to the original Law Commission proposals, but these were muted, in the main. As time went on, the objections began to harden. The Law Commission noted in its consultative report, *Company Security Interests*, that 'at least one respondent representing legal practitioners may now have moved to a position where it considers only minor reform of the law relating to registration of company charges is desirable'.[79] It is believed that

---

[73] (1993) 3 MLJ 587. For discussion of the case see H Tjio, 'Personal Property Security Interests in Singapore and Malaysia' (1995) 16 *Company Law* 28.

[74] [1912] 2 Ch 25.

[75] [1910] 2 Ch 306.

[76] [2002] EWCA Civ 480, notably the comments of Jonathan Parker LJ at para. 72.

[77] *Legal Problems of Credit and Security* (2nd ed., London, Sweet & Maxwell, 1988) at 99–100, and see now the third edition at 192–3.

[78] See R Calnan 'Floating Charges: a proposal for reform' [2005] *Butterworths Journal of International Banking and Financial Law* 341.

[79] See Consultative Report at para. 2.7 n 21.

this is a reference to the Financial Law Committee of the City of London Law Society, and one of the leading lights in this group, Richard Calnan, has warned graphically about the dangers of throwing out the baby with the bathwater. He suggested that there was nothing fundamentally wrong with the present system that a bit of incremental amendment could not mend,[80] whereas the Law Commission's[81] 'imperative seems to be to introduce a US-style functional system as a wholesale replacement for our current system. On a cost-benefit analysis, this seems difficult to justify. The implementation costs will be very large, and it is difficult to see what material benefits will result from it.' He added that one of the advantages of English law for domestic and international investors is the ease of creation of security and quasi-security, and it would be most unfortunate if the effect of the proposals were to make it more complicated and expensive.

In a sense, resistance from practitioners to the Law Commission proposals should hardly occasion surprise. Similar proposals by the Crowther Committee Report on Consumer Credit in 1971[82] and in the Diamond Report in 1989[83] met with stubborn practitioner resistance, and ultimately floundered. In 1991 it was announced that the Government would not be proceeding with the Diamond recommendations. It was suggested that Article 9 style reforms would be costly and, in view of proposed registration requirements, difficult to implement as well as cutting across potential EC initiatives.[84] Moreover, there was no major demand for such reforms.

The City of London Solicitors' Group has made the same point in relation to the Law Commission recommendations while, at the same time, emphasising its own objectivity:

> [W]e believe that there is no desire amongst those who use the English law of security for a wholesale change, and we have a real concern that the proposed changes will

---

[80]	See R Calnan, 'The Reform of the Law of Security' [2004] *Butterworths Journal of International Banking and Financial Law* 88.

[81]	See Calnan, n. 51 above, at 92. For a response by the Law Commissioner responsible for the Commercial and Common Law team, Professor H Beale, see 'Reform of the Law of Security – Another View' [2004] *Butterworths Journal of International Banking and Financial Law* 117.

[82]	*Report of the Committee on Consumer Credit* (London, HMSO, 1971) (Chairman Lord Crowther), Cmnd 4596 at Parts IV and V.

[83]	*A Review of Security Interests in Property* (London, DTI, 1989); on which see generally Prentice, 'The Registration of Company Charges: Ripe for Reform' (1985) 101 *Law Quarterly Review* 330; Davies 'the Reform of English Personal Property Security Law' (1990) 30 *Malaya Law Review* 88; Lawson, 'The Reform of the Law Relating to Security Interests in Property' [1989] *Journal of Business Law* 287; Diamond, 'The Reform of the Law of Security Interests' (1989) 42 *Current Legal Problems* 231.

[84]	See (1991) HC debates Vol 189, col 482, 24 April 1991 per Peter Lilley MP, the then Secretary of State for Trade and Industry.

reduce the efficiency, effectiveness and competitiveness of London as an international financial centre. We are concerned that the only beneficiaries of the changed law will be lawyers, whose services will be in demand to advise clients on the implications of the proposals and to litigate areas of uncertainty. We believe it right to make this observation: looking to the long-term health of the UK economy and against our firms' immediate financial interest.

There are some, perhaps cynical, observers who might take these professions of impartiality and disinterestedness at less than face value. It is worth noting however that the introduction of such reforms in New Zealand did not meet with similar levels of opposition from the practising legal profession, and there are some suggestions that the legal profession in New Zealand saw reform in the personal property security sphere as potentially a valuable source of new business.[85]

The City of London solicitors voiced some general criticism of the reform proposals in terms of fragmentation of the law, lack of flexibility, additional complication, constraints on contractual freedom and the introduction of increased uncertainty. Land was excluded from the scheme, so that one was left with one set of rules in the case of land and a different set for personal property. Also major capital assets such as ships and aircraft were excluded. The overall effect would be a fragmented enforcement system, whereas much security consisted of fixed and floating charge debentures over all corporate assets. Also, they believed that the imposition of mandatory duties, and the requirement to treat transactions which did not create security as if they did, resulted in artificial distinctions, making it more difficult for the parties to be able to document the transaction. It was also felt that the introduction by the Law Commission of American concepts produced complexity. Many of the Law Commission proposals, it was suggested, would make the law less flexible.[86] 'We do not believe that there is any desire for a wholesale change of the law of security by those who use it in practice, whether they are lenders, borrowers, lawyers or other professionals. They recognise the great benefits of the way in which the English law of security works at the moment, and do not wish to jeopardise it.'

---

[85] See generally on the New Zealand system the official website, www.ppsr.govt.nz; note also M Gedye, R Cuming and R Wood, *New Zealand Personal Property Securities Act* (Wellington, Thomson, 2002); L Widdup and L Mayne, *Personal Property Securities Act: a conceptual approach* (Wellington, Butterworths, 2002); B Allan, *Guidebook to New Zealand Personal Property Securities Law* (Auckland, CCH, 2002).

[86] See at 3 of the City Solicitors' Group's 2004 submission.

Revised Law Commission Proposals

Under revised Law Commission proposals the reform agenda was watered down considerably.[87] They proposed a new system of electronic notice filing for companies that would apply to traditional security interests (essentially mortgages and charges) and also to sales of receivables. The new scheme would not extend to title retention techniques such as finance leases and reservation of title under sale of goods agreements. While priority was linked to the date of registration, the fixed/floating charge distinction was preserved, particularly in the context of insolvency.[88]

In the revised proposals, the Law Commission suggested that ships, aircraft and intellectual property rights should still be registrable for validity purposes at Companies House and, for priority purposes, under the specialist asset registers. In the original scheme, registration at the specialist asset registers was all that was required. Consultees were of the view that double registration in both the specialist register and at Companies House was worthwhile because of the advantages in finding information at one source. As far as land was concerned, Companies House would simple serve as a reception point for information transmitted from the Land Registry with the validity and priority of charges over land being dependent solely on rules of land law.[89] The scheme included specific proposals on financial collateral[90] but there was no provision for PMSI super-priority. Also excluded from the legislative agenda was a statutory statement of the rights and remedies of the parties and the imposition of obligations on secured parties to disclose information about the security.

---

[87]   For a synopsis of the revised proposals see 'Company Security Interests: Developing a Final Scheme' (May 2005) available on the Law Commission's website, www.lawcom.gov.uk/. The Final Report was published at the end of August 2005 – Law Com No 296.

[88]   See 'Company Security Interests: Developing a Final Scheme' at para. 1.3. *See also Regulatory Impact Assessment on Proposals for the Registration of Companies' Security Interests* (London, DTI, July 2005) at 66.

[89]   But see *Regulatory Impact Assessment on Proposals for the Registration of Companies' Security Interests* at 12: '[t]his may depend on the introduction of e-conveyancing in England and Wales'.

[90]   See regulations 36–41 of the draft Company Security Regulations 2006 which are found as an appendix to the Law Commission's Final Report. Basically, as an alternative to registration, the regulations allow a charge holder to take 'control' of financial collateral. Taking 'control' renders the charge effective in the debtor company's liquidation and also confers priority advantages over a charge rendered effective through registration.

Analysing the Revised Proposals – Floating Charges

The Law Commission advocate a 'first to file has priority' principle, but the preservation of the fixed/floating charge distinction renders this less important in practice. To use an inexact metaphor, the Law Commission deliberations on the fixed/floating charge issue may remind one of the old dance – 'she steps out, she steps in and she steps out again'. Originally, the Law Commission proposed the retention of the floating charge. It suggested that 'a charge that permits the debtor to dispose of the assets in the ordinary course of business free of the charge may still be described accurately as a floating charge'.[91] Therefore, it was still subject to the provisions of the Insolvency Act 1986 giving priority to preferential creditors and to section 245, which invalidates floating charges granted to secure past indebtedness in the immediate run up to liquidation or administration. There was criticism of this approach, for practitioners would not only have to get used to a new notice filing system, they would also have to bear in mind the fixed/floating charge distinction and its continued importance.[92] Moreover, while pre-Article 9 United States law did not have any functional equivalent of the floating charge[93] as such, floating charges were an important part of the commercial landscape in Canada and New Zealand before the Article 9 style reforms.[94] The original reform statute in Ontario in 1967 tried to retain the floating charge, but this approach was widely considered to be unsatisfactory and later legislation went for an assimilation approach. In *Royal Bank of Canada v. Sparrow Electric Corp.*[95] the Supreme Court of Canada declared that the legislative effect was to abolish the old fixed and floating charge distinction together with that between legal and equitable security interests. As one commentator remarks, 'In a PPSA statutory regime, all security interest attach on the debtor's acquisition of rights in the collateral, regardless of whether the collateral is specific or circulating, and regardless of the scope of the debtor's licence to deal. In thus establishing

---

[91] See Consultation Paper at para. 4.133.

[92] See, for example, L Gullifer, 'Will the Law Commission sink the floating charge?' [2003] LMCLQ 125, 144.

[93] See: *Zartman v. First National Bank of Waterloo* (1907) 189 NY 267; *Benedict v. Ratner* (1925) 268 US 253. The progenitor of Article 9, Professor Grant Gilmore, has argued that if floating charges had been accepted in the US, then some of the pressure for change which brought about Article 9 would have been absent: see *Security Interests in Personal Property* (Boston, Little Brown, 1965) at 359–61. Note also the comments of Lord Walker in *NatWest Bank plc v. Spectrum Plus Ltd* [2005] 2 AC 680 at para. 133.

[94] See generally G McCormack, 'The Floating Charge in England and Canada' in J de Lacy (Ed), *The Reform of United Kingdom Company Law* (London, Cavendish, 2002) at 389.

[95] (1997) 143 DLR (4th) 385; on which see generally K Davis, 'Priority of Crown claims in insolvency' (1997) 29 *Canadian Business Law Journal* 145.

a unitary attachment regime independent of the concept of crystallisation, the PPSA legislators had effectively signalled to the courts that all security interests were henceforth to be characterised as fixed ... in their proprietary effect.'[96]

In the Consultative Report, *Company Security Interests*, the Law Commission changed tack and, though somewhat coy about the matter, seemed to accept that its proposals would see the disappearance of the floating charge, to be replaced by a super security interest that had the advantages of the floating charge in terms of ease of creation and management autonomy yet none of the disadvantages, such as inferior priority status to the fixed charge.[97] Legal commentators have written elegies to the floating charge,[98] and in *Re Brumark Ltd*[99] Lord Millett remarked:

> The floating charge is capable of affording the creditor, by a single instrument, an effective and comprehensive security upon the entire undertaking of the debtor company and its assets from time to time, while at the same time leaving the company free to deal with its assets and pay its trade creditors in the ordinary course of business without reference to the holder. Such a form of security is particularly attractive to banks, and it rapidly acquired an importance in English commercial life which ... should not be underestimated.

The Crowther Committee on Consumer Credit back in 1971 went so far to observe that the floating charge was so fundamentally a part of commercial lending practice that its abolition could not seriously be contemplated.[100]

In its Final Report, the Law Commission has done a turnaround and reverted to its original thinking – retention of the fixed/floating distinction though priority

---

[96] See C Walsh, 'The Floating Charge is Dead: Long Live the Floating Charge' in A Mugasha (Ed), *Perspectives on Commercial Law* (St Leonards, NSW, Prospect, 1999) 129 at 146.

[97] Professor Sir Roy Goode has long propounded this view, arguing that 'a unified concept of security interests in which rules of attachment, perfection and priority are clearly laid out and are designed to produce results that are fair in the typical case is greatly preferable to the uncodified and unsystematised collocation of rules we have painfully developed in this country over the past century'; see 'The Exodus of the Floating Charge' in D Feldman and F Meisel (eds), *Corporate and Commercial Law: Modern Developments* (London, Lloyds of London Press, 1996) chapter 10 at 202–3.

[98] See R Mokal, 'An Elegy to the Floating Charge' in S Worthington (ed.), *Commercial Law and Commercial Practice* (Oxford, Hart Publishing, 2003) at 479.

[99] [2001] 2 AC 710. In *NatWest Bank plc v. Spectrum Ltd.* [2005] 2 AC 680, Lord Scott at paras. 95–7 explained the history and development of the floating charge. He pointed out that by the last decade of the 19th century the 'floating security' had become firmly established and in regurlar use. This new form of security was not the creature of statue but had been bred by equity lawyers and judges out of the needs of the commercial and industrial entrepeneurs of the time.

[100] See Crowther Report at para. 5.7.77.

between competing charges, whether fixed or floating, will be by date of filing, unless otherwise agreed between the parties involved.[101] As the Law Commission explained:

> Under current law, chargees use negative pledge clauses to attempt to alter the 'default' priority position for a floating charge that enables a charger to grant subsequent fixed charges that will rank ahead of the floating charge. However, such clauses are not always effective against subsequent chargees. Dating priority from time of registration will make it unnecessary for a chargee to rely on a negative pledge clause in order to prevent subsequent charges gaining priority.[102]

But why the *volte face*? This was explained on the basis that the complete assimilation of fixed and floating charges would mean major implications for insolvency law and matters such as the unsecured creditors' lifeboat.[103] Under section 176A of the Insolvency Act 1986 (introduced by virtue of the Enterprise Act 2002) a proportion of floating charge recoveries, calculated on a sliding scale, but not fixed charge recoveries, is required to be set aside for the benefit of unsecured creditors. Also under sections 40 and 175 of the Insolvency Act 1986, if unsecured assets are insufficient to discharge preferential debts, the latter can be recouped out of floating charge assets but not fixed charge assets.[104] The Law Commission suggested that for these provisions there was an appropriate replacement – preferential creditors and the unsecured creditors' fund should have first claim on:

1. Any inventory or receivables belonging to the company;
2. Any other assets of the company that, under the charge agreement, the company had the right to dispose of free from the charge.

In its view, the effects of adopting this test would be broadly 'insolvency neutral' and, furthermore, the test would be easier to apply than the current one.[105]

There are other possible solutions. One could, for instance, earmark a proportion of all charge recoveries, irrespective of how the charge is categorised, for

---

[101]   See Law Com No 296 (2005) at para. 3.158: '[i]n the light of responses to the CR we have decided that, for the time being at least, the distinction between fixed and floating charges should be retained'.

[102]   'Company Security Interests: Developing a Final Scheme' at para 1.16. See also regulation 24 of the draft Company Security Regulations 2006.

[103]   See Law Com No 296 at para. 3.166.

[104]   The Enterprise Act 2002 continues to enshrine the fixed/floating charge distinction in various other respects including making the floating charge more vulnerable to challenge in a liquidation in certain circumstances.

[105]   See 'Company Security Interests: Developing a Final Scheme' at para. 1.31; Law Com No 296 at para. 3.170.

preferential creditors and for unsecured creditors, thereby building upon section 176A of the Insolvency 1986 and the Enterprise Act reforms. The 'solution' envisaged by the Law Commission is not free from difficulty.[106] What about 'receivables' factored by the company? Would they be caught by the provision? A similar provision in New Zealand has generated substantial difficulties, not least in terms of drafting.

The Law Commission however stepped back from the brink, recognising 'that insolvency law has undergone significant change in recent years, and that there is great unwillingness to see further changes in the immediate future.' As a result, the Law Commission was not minded to recommend the steps that would result in fixed/floating charge distinction being rendered obsolete.[107]

The end result of the Law Commission's proposals is a somewhat messy and anomalous priority picture. A floating charge may have priority over the fixed charge under the first to file principle, yet a fixed charge outranks all other creditors whereas a floating charge is subject to the claims of preferential creditors[108] and to the unsecured creditors' lifeboat, etc. Regulation 45 of the draft Company Security Regulations 2006 attempts to square this particular circle by adopting a 'statutory subrogation' solution – the floating charge will step into the shoes of the fixed charge so that, as against the preferential creditors and the unsecured creditors' fund, the floating charge should have priority to the extent of any fixed charges over which it has priority.[109]

Analysing the Revised Proposals – Title Retention and Purchase Money Security Interests

In its earlier consultative exercises, the Law Commission was adamant that title retention devices should be included in the new legislative scheme.[110] The Law Commission suggested that filing on-line would be cheap and easy. Moreover, for high volume users such as suppliers who normally used retention of title clauses in their conditions of sale, special arrangements were envisaged under which information entered into a secured party's own system could be forwarded to the registry without further data input.[111]

---

[106]   See the response of the Insolvency Law Committee of the City of London Law Society to the Law Commission at 6–7, available at wwww.citysolicitors.org/.

[107]   In the Consultatative Report the Law Commission recognised that insolvency matters were a political hot potato: see para. 2.60.

[108]   Insolvency Act 1986, ss. 40 and 175.

[109]   'Regulatory Impact Assessment', above n. 60, at 84, and for analagous examples under current law see *Re Portbase Clothing Ltd* [1993] Ch 388; *Re Woodroffes (Musical Instruments) Ltd* [1986] Ch 366.

[110]   Consultative Report, above n. 4, at para. 2.87.

[111]   See Consultative Report at para. 2.103.

The Law Commission recognised that its proposals meant a major expansion of the filing system, in that the penalty for failure to register a deemed security interest would be loss of the security interest in the debtor's insolvency.[112]

In effect, two types of contractor, the finance lessor and the simple retention of title supplier, who never considered that they were bringing into existence a security interest at all, are magically transformed by legislation into doing what they never wanted to do.[113] This 'recharacterisation' has troubled even arch exponents of an Article 9 regime:[114]

> There are two features of the UCC, Article 9 approach that appear to be troublesome even to those who are attracted to it. The first is the total reconceptualisation that it requires in the context of types of transactions that traditionally are not viewed as secured financing devices. ... The second feature ... is the extent to which it requires a bifurcated approach to the characterisation of certain types of transactions. Since a title retention sales contract or a lease falls within a secured financing regime because it functions as a security device, it follows that the seller or lessor is not the owner of the goods sold or leased .... What is troublesome is that outside this regime, the recharacterisation might not be acceptable with the result that same transaction is viewed differently depending on the legal issues being addressed.

Critics have also focused on the complexity of the resultant legislative scheme. Statutory recognition of the PMSI is meant to accommodate title retention devices, but with a new scheme there are difficult questions about how PMSI super-priority should extend into proceeds and products. Another issue is the conditions that must be satisfied before PMSI status can be obtained and whether a distinction should be drawn, as in some schemes, between inventory and capital equipment, with PMSI status in the latter being more difficult to establish. Under current English law, if a creditor can claim ownership of property in a debtor's insolvency, the creditor's ownership interest will prevail against charge holders who are also laying claim to the property through the debtor. A retention of title claim is valid

---

[112]   The New Zealand Personal Property Securities Act prvovides protection in this situation by allowing an unregistered security interest to remain valid in liquidation. Failure to file only means loss of priority to competing parties claiming an 'ownership' or security interest in the goods: see e.g. New Zealand Personal Property Securities Act 1999, s 52, and see generally the New Zealand Law Commission Report No 8, *A Personal Property Securities Act for New Zealand* (Wellington, 1989) at 115.

[113]   See the comment by I Davies, 'The reform of English personal property security law' [2004] LS 295 at 321: '[t]he difficulty with the functionalism as applied in Article 9-type regimes is that it can be both over-inclusive and also under-inclusive at the same time. A more appropriate approach in any reform of English personal property security law is to operate within the existing legal landscape rather than to seek to transform it.'

[114]   Professor R Cuming, 'The Internationalisation of Secured Financing Law' in R Cranston (ed.), *Making Commercial Law: Essays in Honour of Roy Goode* (Oxford, OUP, 1997) at 522–3.

with respect to goods in their original condition, but claims by the supplier to proceeds or products of the goods are likely to fall by the wayside. It would seem extraordinary if all new legislation was doing was reproducing this general pattern, but doing so in a very complicated way, by introducing a new registration apparatus and complicating this with a new conceptual structure.

The City of London Solicitors' Group argued strongly that there was no material benefit to be obtained from requiring quasi-security to be registered, 'both because of the very material uncertainty which will result and because the requirement to recharacterise quasi-security will unnecessarily interfere with the ability of the parties to structure their business transactions as they wish'. It was suggested that parties in international financial transactions, including sale and repurchase agreements (repos), choose English law precisely because of their confidence that the English courts will not generally engage in a recharacterisation exercise.[115]

In its view, there was a fundamental distinction between a company granting an interest over its own asset and a company obtaining limited rights in someone else's assets. This was not an arcane legal concept which served to obscure the reality of the transaction but, instead, was the reality of the transaction. In the second scenario, the company never owned the asset and so could not grant security over it. The inclusion of quasi-security in the legislative scheme would alter these fundamental legal conceptions.[116]

The Law Commission withdrew its original proposals in the light of this criticism and decided not to recommend the registration of title-retention mechanisms.[117] The Law Commission also noted that the priority rules on PMSIs were included on the assumption that title-retention devices were to be covered and, given the fact that the initial stages of reform would not include such devices, PMSI rules would also be excluded.[118]

There has been a lot of opposition to the PMSI provisions from legal professionals. For example, the City of London Solicitors' Group observed:[119]

> It is by no means self-evident that a creditor which can identify funds lent by it to acquire a particular asset should be in a better position than a creditor which has

---

[115] See Calnan [2005] *BJIBFL* 25 at 28.

[116] See R Calnan, above n 91, at 29. For a different perspective see J Ziegel, 'The travails of English chattel security law reform – a transatlantic view' [2006] *LMCLQ* 110 at 116: 'a conditional sale agreement is only a short form of chattel mortgage and that in each case the seller or mortgagee merely retains or obtains title as security for performance of the buyer's obligation'.

[117] 'Company Security Interests: Developing a Final Scheme', above n. 58, at para. 1.26, and see Law Com No 296, above n. 5, at para. 1.66.

[118] Ibid., at para. 3.146.

[119] See Calnan [2005] *BJIBFL* 25 at 30.

taken general security over all the company's assets and which has provided it with the benefit of working capital. Who is to say that one is more valuable than the other? The effect of these arrangements will be to prefer vendor credit to lender credit. The implications of such a change in a market which has traditionally relied on lender credit are difficult to establish. We do not believe that such a major change should be contemplated without proper economic investigation of its effects.

Analysing the Revised Proposals – Assignment of Receivables

The Law Commission stuck to the view that absolute assignments of receivables should be subject to notice filing requirements and to the 'first to file has priority' principle. There are essentially two reasons for this. The first is that the present rules for determining priorities between competing assignments of the same debt are widely considered to be unsatisfactory. Under the rule in *Dearle v. Hall*[120] priority goes to the first assignee to give notice to the debtor, unless that assignee has actual or constructive notice of an earlier assignment at the time that the later assignment was taken. The Law Commission points out that it is not practicable to check 'with each account debtor to find out whether a notice of assignment of the debt has been given, nor will the assignee always wish to give notice simply in order to preserve its priority as against a competing assignment'.[121] The second reason is the very narrow defining line between absolute assignments of receivables and security assignments.[122] The latter, where executed by a company, are registrable under current English law as charges over book debts, but absolute assignments are not. In the Law Commission's view, it was hard to distinguish between assignments that resemble a secured transaction and those that do not. Nevertheless, in any reforming legislation some fine distinctions may have to be drawn to avoid undue disturbance in the financial markets. In the US, financial intangibles, i.e. where the account debtor's principal obligation is a monetary one, are excluded from filing requirements. This was done to safeguard the loan participation market where parts of loans may be in sold in an intense, fast-moving market.[123]

---

[120]   (1828) 3 Russ 1, and for criticism of the rule see F Oditah, 'Priorities: Equitable versus Legal Assignments of Book Debts' (1989) 9 *Oxford Journal of Legal Studies* 521. Note also J de Lacy, 'Reflections on the Ambit of the Rule in *Dearle v. Hall* and the Priority of Personal Property Assignments – 11' (1999) 28 *Anglo-American Law Review* 197 at 214.

[121]   See Consultative Report, above n. 4, at para. 2.87.

[122]   See generally *Re George Inglefield Ltd* [1933] Ch 1; *Lloyds & Scottish Finance v. Cyril Lord (Carpet Sales) Ltd* [1992] BCLC 609; *Crown Finance Ltd v. Orion* [1996] BCC 621.

[123]   For an explanation see generally C Bjerre, 'Secured Transactions Inside Out: negative pledge covenants, property and perfection' (1999) 84 *Cornell Law Review* 305

The City of London Solicitors' Group has also expressed opposition to the inclusion of outright sales of receivables in the legislative scheme on the basis that difficulties in defining quasi-security should not result in extending the concept of security to quasi-security and to outright transfers. Instead, it suggested that the attempt to include quasi-security should be abandoned.

Analysing the Revised Proposals – Notice Filing as Opposed to Transaction Filing

Stripped down to its bare bones, the revised Law Commission scheme suggested the application of notice filing to security interests, narrowly so-called, though the current list of registrable charges would be replaced by a provision that any charge was registrable unless specifically exempted.[124] The Law Commission considered that this was more in line with practitioner thinking – when in doubt, register. In this sense, the Law Commission proposals do not change anything much in practice, but they may have the effect of altering the language in which the debate is framed. At the moment, one can focus on the wording of what is now section 860(7) of the Companies Act 2006 and ask whether a particular transaction is a registrable charge within that list.[125] Under the new regime, the debate will focus, not on any list, but on whether the transaction amounts to a 'charge' – a question which may not be susceptible of easy answer.[126]

What is the magic about notice filing that so attracted the Law Commission?[127] It said that[128] 'it will be necessary only to provide brief particulars of the charge

---

at 392; S Harris and C Mooney, 'How Successful was the Revision of UCC Article 9?: Reflections of the Reporters' (1999) 74 *Chicago-Kent Law Review* 1357 at 1369–73.

[124] 'Company Security Interests: Developing a Final Scheme', above n. 58, at para. 1.13; Law Com No 296 at paras. 3.14–3.16

[125] To be registrable a security interest must constitute a 'charge'; be created by a company and also come within the list set out in the section: see generally H Bennett, 'Registration of Company Charges' in J Armour and H Bennett (eds), *Vulnerable Transactions in Corporate Insolvency* (Oxford, Hart Publishing, 2003) 217 at 243.

[126] 'Charge' is defined by s. 396(4) Companies Act 1985 to include a mortgage (also s. 861(5) Companies Act 2006) but there is no other amplification of the term in the statute.

[127] It should be noted that the Scottish Law Commission refused to recommend a notice filing system for Scotland: see *Report on Registration of Rights in Security by Companies* Scottish Law Commission Report No 197 (Edinburgh, TSO, September 2004) at para. 1.5. In its view, a notice filing system could not readily be modified to accommodate the very different structures and concepts of Scots property law. See generally D Cabrelli, 'Joined up thinking? An analysis of the Scottish and English Law Commissions' proposals for the reform of rights in security and charges granted by companies' [2004] *Journal of Corporate Law Studies* 385.

[128] See 'Company Security Interests: Developing a Final Scheme' at para. 1.8, and see also Law Com No 296 at paras 3.107–3.109.

in a simple, electronic format. It will no longer be necessary to send the original charge document. Charges will appear on the register and be searchable on-line as soon as the registration procedure has been complied with: thus there will be no period of 'invisibility' between submission of the particulars and their appearance on the register.'

Responsibility for filing would be transferred from the corporate charge giver to the secured party. In practice, it is the latter that attends to registration at the moment, although the charge giver is subject to the theoretical possibility of a criminal penalty if there is no registration. Currently, failure to file renders the charge invalid in an administration or liquidation. This would continue, though the 21-day time limit from the date of creation for registering a charge would disappear. So too would the checking function performed by Companies House. The instrument of charge would not have to be delivered to Companies House and, consequently, no longer would there be any scope for Companies House to compare the submitted particulars against the instrument of charge. As a result, Companies House would no longer issue a conclusive certificate of registration, though registration could be proved by the electronic record, a copy of which is to be sent to the secured party. It is part of the scheme that a secured party may not rely on rights that are in excess of those referred to in the particulars delivered for registration.[129]

Some of this is very worthwhile. Removing the invisibility gap and cutting down on staff time at Companies House are worthwhile endeavours. On the other hand, removing the time limit for registration opens up the possibility that the register may become seriously out of date and not provide a complete picture of a company's secured borrowings. It also creates the risk of last minute filings by connected parties.

The Law Commission stressed that, with notice filing, it would be possible to file in advance of the transaction and that a single filing may cover a series of similar transactions between the same parties.[130] But with security interests in the strict sense, these supposed advantages are very small beer. First of all, how likely is it that a prospective borrower would be in contact with a number of potential lenders and that each lender wishes to file to protect its position lest some other secured party sneak into the breach in the meantime?[131] A lender

---

[129]   Law Com No 296 at paras. 3.74–3.76 and 3.124–3.131, and see also 'Regulatory Impact Assessment' at 71: 'the charge will not be effectively registered in respect of collateral that was omitted from the description of the collateral'.

[130]   Law Com No 296 at para. 1.32: '[t]his will be particularly important for sales of receivables ...'.

[131]   See the comment by the City Solicitors' Group at 9 of 'The Registration of Companies' Security Interests' (31 August 2005): '[w]e do not believe that this is a material issue in practice. It is not something which, in our experience concerns lenders'. To deal

can always make it a condition of the loan that there are no other charges on the property[132] or insist on an interval of at least 21 days between the execution of a charge and the release of funds. Moreover, a single charge can cover an ongoing credit facility with the borrower having general, or limited, drawdown facilities.

On 'advance filing', one critic has suggested that the notice filing system may lead to the underproduction of valuable information, in that a searcher of the register does not know whether a particular registration relates to an actual transaction or to an intended transaction that never in fact materialised. Furthermore, fewer details of the transaction are available than under transaction-filing,[133] though the Law Commission has now addressed the latter concern by allowing a full description of the property subject to the charge.[134]

More generally, the Law Commission responded by saying that the risk of clutter was small for two reasons:[135]

> First, filing will only be effective if done with the debtor's consent and it can be expected that debtors will be circumspect in giving their consent to a filing. Secondly, if further finance is sought from another secured party, it will insist before anything else that any filings that are not concerned with existing security agreements are removed.

In response, one might say the expense in getting unnecessary registrations removed may cause delay in financing transactions and also add to transaction costs.

It may be that the supposed advantages of notice-filing could equally be achieved in a reformed transaction filing system. For example, there is no reason why the current paper-based English company charge registration regime could not be switched on-line. Indeed, Companies House is currently exploring the possibility. Moreover, some jurisdictions require the filing of transactions, but there is no checking of documents performed by the equivalent of Companies House. The applicant simply gets a statement – perhaps computer generated – that the particulars of the transaction have been filed on such and such a date.[136] Also the

---

with the issue the group suggests a priority notice system of the kind used by the Land Registry in relation to registered land for many years.

[132]   Breach of the condition would render the loan immediately repayable.

[133]   R Calnan, 'The Reform of the Law of Security' [2004] *Butterworths Journal of International Banking and Financial Law* 88 at 89–90: 'the effect of the proposals would be to make the system less informative and reliable'.

[134]   See 'Regulatory Impact Assessment', above n. 60, at para 3.2: '[a] brief general description will suffice, but there will be a facility to enable the party filing to copy a full description from the charge document into the financing statement'. See also Law Com No 296 at paras 1.32(7) and 3.107–3.109.

[135]   See Consultative Report at para. 2.54.

[136]   For details of the Irish position see Irish Companies Act 1963, s. 99, and for reforms envisaged by the Irish Company Law Review Group see the website, www.clrg.

criminal sanction for failure to register is not a necessary part of a transaction filing system. The sanction is rarely applied at the moment and could usefully be scrapped.[137] Likewise, the time limit for failure to register under a transaction based registration system could be removed, with registration being permissible at any stage up to the commencement of liquidation or administration, coupled with presumably some sanction to prevent last minute filing by corporate insiders or other connected persons. Whether or not this is a wise step is another question entirely. If disclosure of charges becomes in this sense 'voluntary', then the register will lose its utility in providing information about the state of a company's secured borrowings to potential lenders and investors, and other secured parties. The City of London solicitors'group argued that[138] if the security was not registered within a comparatively short period, the security but not the secured indebtedness should become void. The group's strong preference was for a registration system for all charges with appropriate penalties for failure to comply.

AN OVERVIEW AND ASSESSMENT

This chapter has suggested that there are two, possibly intersecting, pressure points for Europe-wide harmonisation of the law of credit securities. The first stems from the desire of some Euro enthusiasts, at least partially sanctioned by the EC institutions, to create a European Civil Code/Common Frame of Reference (CFR) that would extend to credit securities. The second comes from the argument that Article 9 of the US Uniform Commercial Code ought to form the basis of a European or indeed international harmonisation in this field. This ties in with convergence theory, i.e. the theory that legal systems in the commercial sphere will converge towards the best system and that, normatively speaking, Article 9 is the best.

The chapter argues that while the CFR might be useful as a toolbox or source of ideas for reform-minded national legislatures it ought not to have any mandatory or binding effect. The objections are founded on constitutional, economic and cultural concerns that link up with each other. On the constitutional level, the enactment of the CFR as a legally effective instrument can be seen as involving a further erosion of national sovereignty and another milestone in the

---

org/. The Singapore system under s. 131 of its Companies Act involves the electronic submission of particulars without the instrument of charge being produced as a matter of course. The registrar of companies is still required to issue a notice or certificate of due registration.

[137] See 'Company Security Interests: Developing a Final Scheme' at para. 1.9; Law Com No 296 at paras 1.32(4) and 3.77.

[138] See Calnan [2005] *BJIBFL* 25 at 30.

creation of a European superstate. Economically speaking, the CFR may lead to sterile uniformity across Europe. The case against uniformity and for states as laboratories for experimentation can equally be made from a neo-liberal as well as a social market perspective.[139] The continued recognition of national legislative autonomy means that states can legislate for security rights differently and assess the impact of such provisions on the cost and availability of credit. [140] Different states may wish to experiment with different degrees of freedom when it comes to sanctioning the creation and enforcement of security. Different states, for example, may have different views on the extent to which secured creditors should prevail over unsecured creditors and whether particular types of creditor, e.g. trade creditors, should prevail over other creditors, e.g. finance creditors.[141]

Concerns about consumers, or about protecting the weaker party to credit relationships, may have motivated many of the limitations on the taking of security that are found in European jurisdictions. If national governments are recognised as having continued autonomy in this area, one state is free to favour an extensive regime of consumer protection whereas another state may be content with more limited measures.

One can plausibly make the argument that the law of credit securities in many European jurisdictions is in need of reform and that economic activity is impeded by archaic rules that owe more to the hang-ups of legal history than the needs of commerce. One comparative study argues that[142] 'none of the ju-

---

[139]   For a reference to separate jurisdictions as legal laboratories see Brandeis J in *New State Ice Corp v. Liebmann* (1932) 285 US 262 at 311.

[140]   See R Goode, 'Security in Cross Border Transactions' (1998) 33 *Texas International Law Journal* 47 at 48: '[c]ommon law jurisdictions, which are generally sympathetic to the concepts of party autonomy and self-help, have a liberal attitude towards security. This attitude allows security interests to be taken with a minimum of formality over both present and future assets to secure existing and future indebtedness....[T]hey allow universal security rather than require specific security. By contrast, civil law jurisdictions have been more cautious in their approach to non-possessory security and have been anxious about the false wealth which such practices are perceived as permitting.... [Therefore, one can find in civil law jurisdictions] requirements of specificity or individualisation of collateral, the requirements of notice to the debtor as a condition of the validity (not merely priority) of an assignment of debts, and restrictions on self help remedies such as possession and sale of the collateral.'

[141]   See H Beale, 'Finding the Remaining Traps' in S Grundmann and J Stuyck (eds), *An Academic Green Paper on European Contract Law* (The Hague, Kluwer Law International, 2002) 67 at 70: 'diversity encourages experimentation and experimentation encourages legal development...[W]e should encourage pluralism. Diversity is one of the things that makes our society interesting to live in ...'.

[142]   See E-M Kieninger (eds), *Security Rights in Movable Property in European Private Law* (Cambridge, Cambridge University Press, 2004) at 648. See also U Drobnig,

risdictions of the EU Member States has developed a comprehensive, functional approach to security rights in movables. Instead, there exists in each jurisdiction a wide range of security devices, which differ from each other with respect to the character of the secured debt, the collateral that may be used, and the legal concept on which the security rights are based: title-based security rights such as retention of title, security transfer of ownership or leasing exist side by side with the possessory pledge and various devices that are based on the idea of the pledge such as non-possessory registered charges in individualised property or entities of assets.'

Given this diversity, does not Article 9 serve as a beacon for reform efforts with divergent national provisions converging towards the supposedly superior US Article 9 model? [143] The English experience however suggests that reform efforts are more likely to go down a functional path-dependent route. Market integration, technological innovation and economic imperatives may inspire reform initiatives in particular states, but the strength of legal doctrine and the influence of legal practice specific to the jurisdiction will shape what emerges at the end of the reform dialogue. For example, the Law Commission started out with a big plan to make the English law of security interests very much like the American – notice filing, extension of the scheme to cover quasi-securities, new rules on priorities and a comprehensive restatement of the law of security interests. The Law Commission stuck to its guns for a couple of years but all the huffing and puffing failed to convince influential practitioner groups whose basic message was – stick to the basics of what we have got at the moment and do not go down the American path. [144]

The Law Commission's message to the practitioner and to business lobby groups was that notice filing etc. would provide all the advantages in terms of flexibility and comprehensive coverage etc. that the present system offers, but also it would add something much more. The additional benefits would include

'Present and Future of Real and Personal Security' [2003] *European Review of Private Law* 623; C Bourbon-Seclet, 'Cross-border security interests in moveable property', [2005] *Journal of International Banking Law and Regulation (JIBLR)* 419.

[143]   See A Ogus, 'Competition Between National Legal Systems: A Contribution of Economic Analysis to Comparative Law' (1999) 48 *International of Comparative Law Quarterly* 405 at 418: 'competition between jurisdictions will generate a tendency for national legal principles to converge in those areas of law designed primarily to facilitate trade'.

[144]   See R Calnan, 'The Reform of the Law of Security' [2004] *Butterworths Journal of International Banking and Financial Law* 88 at 92: '[t]he Law Commission's imperative seems to be to introduce a US-style functional system as a wholesale replacement for our current system. On a cost-benefit analysis, this seems difficult to justify. The implementation costs will be very large, and it is difficult to see what material benefits will result from it.'

ease of registration, greater simplicity and convenience in structuring transactions, plus simpler and more coherent priority principles. But it is a bit difficult to persuade financial lawyers that somebody else knows best for them, and it is not surprising that, ultimately, the Law Commission failed in its task. It is very difficult to persuade banks and their legal advisers that they are not the best judges of their own best interests.

After being repulsed with its 'big plan', the Law Commission then came back with a little plan – notice filing and a few add-ons. While the American antecedents of the little plan are still fairly obvious, the reform agenda has been substantially diluted to the extent that potential advantages could readily be achieved by technological adjustments to the present system.[145] But even this watered down plan failed to convince critics, and the Companies Act 2006 simply re-enacted the existing legislative regime in more accessible and user-friendly language.

---

[145] See statement by City of London Solicitors' Group in 'The Registration of Companies Security Interests' (31 August 2005), that a few, fairly small changes would make the present system work better. In December 2010 the Department for Business, Innovation and Skills brought forward proposals to revise the scheme for registration of charges created by UK incorporated companies. It is proposed that instead of setting out a list of charges requiring registration, the requirement to register should apply to every charge unless expressly excluded either by the Companies Act or Regulations or some other statute. Under the revised regime it would be possible to register a charge electronically and to send a copy of an extract from the charge instrument covering inter alia, the identities of the chargor or charge, the date of the charge and the property covered. The extract may be redacted to conceal information that is not required and provided that it does not exceed a specified limit, the entire instrument may be filed instead. The effect of the certificate of Registration issued by the Registrar of Companies will be reduced somewhat in that the certificate will merely serve as conclusive evidence as to the identity of the chargor and that the charge was registered within 21 days of its date of creation.

20. Lex Mercatoria as transnational commercial law: is the *Lex Mercatoria* preferentially for the *'mercatocracy'*?[1]

Adaora Okwor[*]

INTRODUCTION

As traditional boundaries collapse and the globe shrinks, countries are no longer as discrete as they once were. During the last century, all manner of universal co-operation among private institutions, governments and businesses have been necessitated both by technological advancement and other effects of globalisation. However, increasingly, the traditional conflicts of laws rules and public international law demonstrate their inadequacies in effectively dealing with the different kinds of challenges which globalization presents. Consequently, the *lex mercatoria* has been controversially publicized as a viable option to these other traditional legal systems: 'the most successful example of global law without a state'?[2]

The mercatocracy, described as an elite association engaged in the unification and globalisation of transnational merchant law, exercises a predominant influence 'as the organic intellectuals of the transnational capitalist class'.[3] This assertion appears to expose a crisis of representation and legitimacy. The crisis is in the presumption that if the *lex mercatoria* truly is global law and therefore applies transnationally, should it be preferentially elite in its creation and origin? Surely, this *lex mercatoria* would be unlike the medieval *lex mercatoria* which originated from merchants generally and regulated their commerce irrespective

---

[*]   Formerly of University of Liverpool, UK.
[1]   Cutler, CA, *Private Power and Global Authority, Cambridge Studies in International Relations*, (Cambridge, Cambridge University Press, 2003), 5.
[2]   Teubner, G, 'Global Bukowina: Legal Pluralism in the World- Society' in Teubner, G (ed.), *Global Law Without a State* (Dartmouth, 1996), 1.
[3]   Cutler, supra n. 1 at 181.

of the commercial class to which they belonged? Thus, the discussion focuses on the UNIDROIT Principles of International Commercial Contracts[4] as a transnational legal instrument which allegedly epitomizes the *lex mercatoria* and is quite widely used in transnational commercial practice.

This chapter evaluates the legitimacy of the claim to transnationality that the *lex mercatoria* makes by assessing this instrument of harmonisation based on its origin and use in practice. The first part contains a concise outline of the development of the *lex mercatoria* and its claim as transnational law. The second part reviews the UNIDROIT Principles of International Commercial Contracts and explores whether it is preferential in its creation and use in practice in favour of the commercial elite.

THE DEVELOPMENT OF THE *LEX MERCATORIA* AS TRANSNATIONAL COMMERCIAL LAW: ANCIENT AND MODERN

Transnational law in the broadest sense includes 'all law which regulates actions or events that transcend national frontiers'[5] and transnational commercial law would include all laws which transcend national frontiers and which relate to commercial transactions. The need for such a law is underscored by globalisation and the shifting of borders in the interest of commerce. Proponents of the *lex mercatoria* claim that it is transnational commercial law. In discussing the attributes and development of the *lex mercatoria*, we hope to affirm this claim.

Lex mercatoria is Latin for law merchant. This appears to be the only consensus with respect to the exact meaning of the *lex mercatoria*. Opinions, on what the *lex mercatoria* precisely is range from loosely describing the *lex mercatoria* as 'practices and norms developed and applied predominantly by businesspeople to manage their cross border contractual relationships'[6] to denying its existence and describing the *lex mercatoria* as 'a sort of legal Loch Ness monster – occasionally in the headlines as a result of a purported sighting but ultimately non-existent'.[7] The dismissal of the *lex mercatoria* as non-existent

---

[4] UNIDROIT, UNIDROIT Principles of International Commercial Contracts (Rome, 2004) (The Principles), also available electronically at www.unidroit.org/.

[5] Jessup, P, *Transnational Law* (New Haven, Yale University Press, 1956), 2.

[6] Nottage, L, 'The Procedural Lex Mercatoria: The Past, Present and Future of International Commercial Arbitration', CDAMS Symposium, Kobe University Law Faculty, 29 September 2003.

[7] Molineaux, Book Review of Berger, KP, 'The Creeping Codification of the Lex Mercatoria' 1, (2000) *Journal of International Arbitration* 147.

may stem from the fact that the *lex mercatoria* is intangible and does not have a geographical domain of application.[8] Or that it is not possible to point to any one document and refer to it as the *lex mercatoria*. Proponents of the *lex mercatoria* assert that this fluidity of the *lex mercatoria* is its uniqueness and advantage over the other existing legal systems. Moreover, the fact that the historical roots of the *lex mercatoria* can clearly be found in the law merchant of the Middle Ages is one sure pointer to its existence.[9] Therefore, whatever its exact meaning, it appears that the *lex mercatoria* as law merchant has subsisted for as long as mercantile practice has existed.[10]

The *lex mercatoria* was not established by any sovereign,[11] but is said to have resulted from the effort of the medieval trade community to overcome complex rules of feudal law which could not respond to the needs of the then-new interlocal commerce.[12]

In recent times, as states increasingly participated in international trade, each one invariably propounded its own rules to govern its dealings with other countries. Consequently, cross-border disputes came to be resolved by reference to various national conflict of laws rules or general principles of public international law. These rules have increasingly grown complicated, especially in the face of amazing technological strides and globalisation. As a consequence, harmonisation, or at least some sort of universal co-operation in transnational commerce, became necessary. As in the Middle Ages, where complex feudal laws pressed merchants to seek an alternative in the *lex mercatoria*, so in this age the complexity of the current rules of conflicts of laws and the inadequacies of public international law in dealing with transnational commerce have opened the door to the transnational commercial law which the *lex mercatoria* claims to be.

In the Middle Ages, the *lex mercatoria* was initially administered for the most part in special quasi-judicial courts including regularly constituted courts of '*piepoudre*' or 'dusty feet', which decided cases quickly and according to

---

[8]   Selden, 'Lex Mercatoria in European and US Trade Practice: Time To Take A Closer Look', 2 *Annual Survey of International and Comparative Law*, 111 at 113 and 119 as cited in Berger, KP, The New Law Merchant and the Global Market place: A 21st Century View of Transnational Commercial Law (2000) *International Arbitration Law Review*, 3(4), 92.

[9]   Cf Goode, R, *Commercial Law in the next Millennium* (London, Sweet & Maxwell, 1989), 4, 5 and 81.

[10]   Malynes, G, *Consuetudo Vel Lex Mercatoria*, (Or the Ancient Law-Merchant), 1622, Vol. 1, 3.

[11]   *Ibid*.

[12]   Goode, R, *supra* n 9, at 4; Berger [2000] The New Law Merchant and the Global Market place: A 21st Century View of Transnational Commercial Law *International Arbitration Law Review*, 3(4), 92.

the customs and practices of merchants.[13] In recent times, the *lex mercatoria* finds application chiefly in arbitral tribunals.[14] The constitution and procedure of the courts of 'dusty feet' appear similar to arbitration tribunals which aim to decide cases speedily and according to the law and practice of arbitral parties.

In its application during the Middle Ages, the *lex mercatoria* was at least trans-local because it had 'a peculiar prerogative above all other customs'; they were observed in all places, as opposed to the custom of one place which did not extend in other places.[15] In its application in this age, the *lex mercatoria* supposedly transcends and reaches across national borders to apply to contractual commercial transactions. Rudimentarily, this assertion embodies the essence of the claim which the *lex mercatoria* presently makes as transnational commercial law: that the medieval merchants created a law which was uniform in its application among merchants[16] and that the *lex mercatoria* in modern times can equally apply uniformly to merchants across national frontiers.

The medieval *lex mercatoria* went into a moratorium due to the heightened sense of sovereignty of states coupled with the wave of codification of domestic laws which trailed the last two centuries. The *lex mercatoria* was absorbed into the fabric of domestic laws of individual countries and thus temporarily lost its universality.[17] In the 1960s, attempts were resumed to capture the uniformity of the *lex mercatoria*. These efforts turned to the distillation of the principles of the *lex mercatoria* into a coherent legal system. This systematic arrangement has been pursued through harmonisation of national and international laws on transnational trade and restatements[18] of universal principles of transnational commerce. By making one such restatement, the International Institute for the Unification of Private Law (UNIDROIT) has been described as possessing 'creative powers to harmonise the concept and contents of international law',[19] but not to create transnational law. In this

---

[13]   Cf Bradgate, R, *Commercial Law* (Oxford, Oxford University Press, 2000), 9.

[14]   Some national courts have referred to the *lex mercatoria*. See the Centre For Transnational Law Website: www.tldb.net.

[15]   Malynes, G, *Consuetudo Vel Lex Mercatoria*, (Or the Ancient Law-Merchant) (1622), Vol. 1, 3.

[16]   Goode, R, *supra* n. 9, 1.

[17]   Dalhuisen, J, *Dalhuisen on Transnational and Comparative Commercial, Financial and Trade Law* (3rd edn., Oxford, Hart Publishing, 2007), 217.

[18]   Or prestatements as posited by Berger, KP, 'The New Law Merchant and the Global Market place: A 21st Century View of Transnational Commercial Law', (2000) *International Arbitration Law Review*, 3(4), 91 at 97.

[19]   Rosett, A, *UNIDROIT Principles and Harmonization of International Commercial Law: Focus on Chapter Seven* (1997), at: www.unidroit.org/english/publications/review/articles/1997-3.htm retrieved 22 August 2008.

regard, the UNIDROIT Principles of International Commercial Contracts (UNIDROIT Principles)[20] are seen as evidence of 'an authentical expression of what is usually called "*lex mercatoria*"'[21] and as 'a kind of *ratio scripta* of an emerging supranational legal order – a modern *lex mercatoria*'.[22] It is the source of the Principles and its use in practice which form the crux of the following discussion.

UNIDROIT[23] PRINCIPLES OF INTERNATIONAL COMMERCIAL CONTRACTS

The UNIDROIT was formed in 1926 and has been operating since 1940 as an independent intergovernmental organisation.[24] The UNIDROIT, made up of 61 member states, describes itself as 'intergovernmental' and describes its purpose with particular regard to commercial law as 'between states and groups of states'.[25] This appears to directly contravene the nature of the *lex mercatoria*. Fundamentally, the *lex mercatoria* claims that it side-steps the meddling of states in transnational commerce and that it is a law which emanates from merchants in the course of their dealings with one another. How then could an organisation which is self-professedly intergovernmental produce a document which is considered an authentical evidence of the *lex mercatoria*?

The answer may lie in the fact that the UNIDROIT Governing Council which produced the Principles is comprised of experts in the relevant fields of law. These experts were elected to the Governing Council and are minded to provide implementable general principles addressed directly to commercial people rather than to their governments.[26] Further, the UNIDROIT Principles merely

---

[20]   1994, updated in 2004.

[21]   Bonell, MJ, 'Das UNIDROIT-Projekt für die Ausarbeitung von Regeln für Internationale Handesverträge', 56 *Rabel Journal of Comparative and International Private Law (RabelsZ)* 274 at 287, as cited in Berger, KP, 'The New Law Merchant and the Global Market place: A 21st Century View of Transnational Commercial Law' (2000) *International Arbitration Law Review*, 3(4), 91.

[22]   Bonell, MJ, 'A "Restatement" of Principles for International Commercial Contracts: An Academic Exercise or a Practical Need?' [1988] RDAI 873 at 874 as cited in Berger, KP, 'The New Law Merchant and the Global Market place: A 21st Century View of Transnational Commercial Law' (2000) *International Arbitration Law Review*, 3(4), 91; Dalhuisen, J, in *Dalhuisen on International Commercial, Financial and Trade Law* (2nd edn., Portland, Oregon, Hart Publishing, 2004), 191.

[23]   International Institute for the Unification of Private Law (UNIDROIT), Rome.

[24]   UNIDROIT, An Overview, (electronic version) at: www.unidroit.org/dynasite. cfm?dsmid=84219, retrieved 22 August 2008.

[25]   Ibid.

[26]   Ibid.

claim to be an assembly or distillery of the already existing principles of the *lex mercatoria*.[27] More significantly, the UNIDROIT Principles do not involve the endorsement of governments and it appears that it is this non-involvement with governments that qualifies the UNIDROIT Principles as private rules aimed at transnational commerce.

Work on the UNIDROIT Principles began in 1970 and the Principles generally reflect concepts which are common in most legal systems. They also offer 'best solutions' in the expectation that they will be generally adopted.[28] It is perceived that it is this distillery of the common principles on commercial contracts which qualifies the UNIDROIT Principles as *lex mercatoria*. The Principles' objective is 'to establish a balanced set of rules designed for use throughout the world'[29] and this is reflected in the language employed in the Principles. It is concluded therefore that the contents of the UNIDROIT Principles to the extent that they are a distillery of the principles of transnational commercial contracts which are already in use among merchants are *lex mercatoria*.

Additionally, the Principles 'may be applied when the parties have agreed that their contract be governed by general principles of law, the lex mercatoria or the like'.[30] In practice it has been disclosed that courts and arbitral tribunals are wary of controversial terms like '*lex mercatoria*' and prefer less controversial terms such as 'general principles of law'.[31] Ultimately, the success of the UNIDROIT Principles is evident from their wide acclamation and adoption of their Principles in transnational commerce.[32] A clear empirical indication of this

---

[27]   Cf CENTRAL which states clearly that it is not creating *lex mercatoria* but organising or assembling it. See Transnational Law Digest and Bibliography (electronic version) at: www.tldb.net/ retrieved 22 June 2008.

[28]   UNIDROIT, Introduction to the 1994 Edition, UNIDROIT Principles of International Commercial Contracts, Rome, 1994.

[29]   Ibid.

[30]   UNIDROIT, Preamble, *UNIDROIT Principles of International Commercial Contracts* (Rome, 2004).

[31]   CENTRAL Enquiry, electronic version at: www.tldb.net/, retrieved 22 June 2008; cf. Bonell, MJ, 'The Unidroit Principles in Practice – The Experience of The first Two Years', electronic version at: www.cisg.law.pace.edu/cisg/biblio/pr-exper.html, retrieved 22 June 2008; Bonell, 'Unidroit Principles and Transnational Law', electronic version at www.unidroit.org/english/publications/review/articles/2000-2.htm, retrieved on 22 June 2008.

[32]   Berger, KP, 'International Arbitral Practice and UNIDROIT Principles of International Commercial Contracts', (1998) 46 *American Journal of Comparative Law*, 129 at 132; Bonell, MJ, 'The UNIDROIT Principles and Transnational Law' (2000) at www.unidroit.org/english/publications/review/articles/2000-2.htm, retrieved on 22 June 2008; Bonell, MJ, 'Das UNIDROIT-Projekt für die Ausarbeitung von Regeln für Internationale Handelsverträge', (1992) 56 *RabelsZ* 274 at 287 as cited in Berger, KP, The New Law Merchant and the Global Market place: A 21st Century View of Transnational

success can be found in the enquiry conducted by the Centre for Transnational Law (CENTRAL) of transnational commercial lawyers in 1999 which disclosed that about 11% of the respondents had used the UNIDROIT Principles in contract negotiations and about 13% in arbitration.[33]

IS THE *LEX MERCATORIA* PREFERENTIALLY FOR THE MERCATOCRACY?

The mercatocracy, described as an elite association engaged in the unification and globalisation of transnational merchant law, exercises a predominant influence 'as the organic intellectuals of the transnational capitalist class'.[34] This class of merchant elites is able to exert considerable influence on transnational law in response to challenges it encounters in the course of business. In apparent support, Dezalay describes a case study of the *lex mercatoria*'s use in arbitral practice where the parties encountered 'the grand old men and their *lex mercatoria* – which ended up serving well the interests of the large Western construction companies'.[35] The question which springs to mind then is whether the *lex mercatoria* is guilty of being preferential in serving the interests of the merchant elite. A number of legal theorists[36] believe that the *lex mercatoria* does precisely this. One way to verify the veracity of this claim will be to evaluate the source of the *lex mercatoria*. As already outlined above, the law merchant evolved out of the trade usages and practices of medieval merchants; can the same be said of the modern *lex mercatoria*? If it can, how do the activities of the formulating agencies affect this? Are documents produced by a formulating agency such as the UNIDROIT, mere restatements of these principles or do they create them? If they create them, can these principles be *lex mercatoria*?

Overall, the modern *lex mercatoria* could be said to exist in an environment similar to that which propelled the medieval merchants to escape state-bound laws; the rigidity, complexity, lack of speed and localisation of existing legal structures. The *lex mercatoria* is flexible and unique because its principles originate from and move with current commercial practices. It also does not need promulgation or formal amendment procedure. It is speedy in dispute resolution,

---

Commercial Law (2000) 3(4) *International Arbitration Law Review*, 91; see also Dalhuisen, J, *Dalhuisen on International Commercial, Financial and Trade Law* (2nd edn., Portland, Oregon, Hart Publishing, 2004), 191–2.

[33]   CENTRAL Enquiry, electronic version at: www.tldb.net/, retrieved 22 June 2008.

[34]   Cutler, *supra* n. 1, 181.

[35]   Dezalay, Y, and Garth, B, *Dealing in Virtue* (Chicago, The University of Chicago Press, 1996), 100.

[36]   Including Dezalay and Garth and Cutler.

which is usually achieved through arbitration, and is pragmatic since it uses the facts as they are and decides them on case-by-case basis. Most importantly, *lex mercatoria* does not belong to any one country or sovereign. So the important query at this point is whether the harmonisation instruments produced by such private agencies as the UNIDROIT qualify as *lex mercatoria*. Put conversely, do these instruments owe their creation and source to these formulating bodies or not?

On the face of it, it would appear that these harmonisation instruments owe their existence to the private agencies that produce them. However, this initial assumption is overturned upon a closer examination of these harmonisation instruments as the expression of the emergence of a new world order based on a search for common principles and rooted in the practices and expectations of the commercial community.[37] In the sense that organisations like UNIDROIT are merely systematically organising the principles and rules which comprise the *lex mercatoria*, they are codifying the *lex mercatoria*. This is confirmed by the fact that the principles contained in the UNIDROIT Principles are the principles which comprise the *lex mercatoria*. This brings up the further question whether the *lex mercatoria* owes its essence to mercantile practice or to codification and privately formulated legal instruments. As is uncommon in discussions on *lex mercatoria*, views are largely congruent on this question.

Lex mercatoria is not intentionally fashioned as an instrument of harmonisation.[38] It evolves out of usage, contractual practice and case law of international arbitration, since 'instruments drafted and adopted by private institutions do not automatically assume the quality of law within the *lex mercatoria* context...the rules and principles which are contained in the text of such instruments have to stand the test of transnational commercial practice and international arbitration in order to become acknowledged as part of the *lex mercatoria*'.[39] A codification may in due course establish new usages, but only when it becomes generally known and widely adopted.[40]

This means that instruments of unification and harmonisation merely serve as 'indication for the possible content of the *lex mercatoria* but may not be equated with it'[41] and are at best evidence of previously existing unorganised

---

[37]   Bradgate, R, *Commercial Law* (Oxford, Oxford University Press, 2000), 20.
[38]   Mustill LJ, cited in Goode, R, 'Rule, Practice and Pragmatism in Transnational Commercial Law' (2005), 54 *International Commercial Law Quarterly*, 546; Goode agrees 'because as law the *lex mercatoria* consists of binding usage': ibid.
[39]   Berger, KP, *The Creeping Codification of Lex Mercatoria* (The Hague, Kluwer Law International, 1999), 68; Goode, R, 'Rule, Practice and Pragmatism in Transnational Commercial Law' (2005), 54 *International Commercial Law Quarterly*, 548.
[40]   Ibid.
[41]   Berger, KP, *supra* n. 38, 39 and 179.

rules. By assembling its Principles, the UNIDROIT has been appropriately described as possessing 'creative powers to harmonise the concept and contents of international law',[42] but not to create it. These instruments, although assembled by private agencies, do not therefore create the *lex mercatoria*, but are mere restatements of the principles which comprise the modern *lex mercatoria*.

Since codification may establish new usage if it becomes generally known and widely adopted, and acquiring legitimacy implies that 'there is some form of normative, uncoerced consent or recognition of authority on the part of the regulated or governed',[43] then wide adoption ultimately confers legitimacy on the new usage so that it becomes *lex mercatoria*. Query: does the modern *lex mercatoria* adequately represent a broad spectrum of merchants? In other words, has it acquired legitimacy through this representation? According to CENTRAL, 'the new *lex mercatoria* is born out of practical needs of the business community and not out of the theoretical discussions of some learned law professors'.[44] If this is true, then the *lex mercatoria* should be representative of the business community, since participation in the creation and use of *lex mercatoria* would be born out of the needs of that community. It remains to determine how best to ensure this representation in order to ensure that the assembly of the *lex mercatoria* principles acquires even more legitimacy in accordance with the expressed nature of the *lex mercatoria*. According to those *lex mercatoria* tenets, *lex mercatoria* emanates from mercantile practice and usage. In the event that some merchants and their practice and usage are not represented in the distillation or organising of the *lex mercatoria*, it is likely that their usages of trade will be overlooked. They are thus forced to abide by the *lex mercatoria* of other mercantile communities which have been represented in the organising of the system that is the *lex mercatoria*. This essentially contravenes the fundamental attribute of the *lex mercatoria*, i.e. that it is law which does not emanate from a sovereign but from merchants for merchants.

Empirical research conducted in Nigeria between December 2007 and January 2008 (as part of PhD research) indicates that some developing countries, while being aware of (and possibly using) the *lex mercatoria*, may not have been involved in its assembly. The probable reason for this may be that there has not been a perceived need to participate in the assembly of *lex mercatoria*.

---

[42]   Rosett, A, *supra* n. 19.

[43]   Hall, R, and Biersteker, T. 'The Emergence of Private Authority in the Global International System' in Hall, R. and Biersteker, T. (eds), *The Emergence of Private Authority in Global Governance* (Cambridge, Cambridge University Press, 2002), 5.

[44]   The CENTRAL Enquiry on the Use of Transnational Law in International Contract Law and Arbitration Background, Procedure and Selected Results, Center for Transnational Law (CENTRAL), University of Cologne, Germany, 1999 (electronic version), at: www.tldb.net/ retrieved on 22 June 2008.

This possible explanation is proffered not because transnational commerce does not take place in the country but because the multinational companies maintain a strong monopoly of almost all the transnational business. This business community therefore finds itself legitimising new usage through using the *lex mercatoria* principles already created for it by other business communities. In this sense, the accusation that the *lex mercatoria* serves the interest of the merchant elite becomes true.

Thus, it may be true that the medieval law merchant was inter-local and that the new *lex mercatoria* applies across national boundaries. It may also be true that the *lex mercatoria* is ambitious about being a viable option to the other existing legal orders. However, it seems to be equally true that the *lex mercatoria* as currently emanating from current merchant practice is preferential in serving the interests of the merchant elite. But this does not appear to be intentionally or maliciously so. It appears that the job of assembling these principles has to be done. It is a beginning; a step towards ensuring that the principles of the *lex mercatoria* are organised into a coherent system. However, in order truly to legitimise such restatements, greater representation has to be made of merchants in developing societies and their *lex mercatoria*.

21. The legal basis for harmonisation of environmental criminal law in the EU: past and future challenges

Ricardo Pereira*

I INTRODUCTION

The debate over the appropriate legal basis of a legislative measure harmonising environmental criminal law in the European Union is regarded as being of the highest political importance, since the competence to define criminal offences and penalties has traditionally been regarded as belonging to the sphere of sovereignty of the nation State. However the need to combat crimes effectively, in particular transnational crimes, has been recognised by the governments of the EU Member States as a political priority following the abolition of internal border checks within the EU Member States. The importance of co-operation in criminal matters (including, when necessary, harmonisation of criminal law) was hence stressed during the Tampere European Council in 1999 and the 2004 Hague Programme and Action Plan.[1]

Before the ratification of the Lisbon Treaty in December 2009, the Member States appeared to regard co-operation in criminal matters (including legislative harmonisation) as belonging to the third pillar of the EU (created by the 1993 Treaty on the European Union), being intergovernmental and hence lacking supranational controls. However this view has been open to challenge and the outcome of two legal actions brought by the European Commission against the Council is that legislative measures harmonising environmental criminal law in

* Lecturer in Environmental and Energy Law, Centre for Environmental Policy, Imperial College, London, UK.

[1] For an overview see Elsen (2007), 'From Maastricht to the Hague: the Politics of Judicial and Police Cooperation', *ERA Forum* 13. The Tampere Programme, unlike the Hague programme, expressly referred to need for a certain degree of harmonisation/ approximation of laws (definitions of main elements of crimes and minimum sanctions) in the case of sectors of particular relevance such as (…) *environmental crime* (para. 48).

the EU will be subject (at least partially) to the typical supranational political and judicial control of the so-called called 'first pillar' (Community law).

This dispute led to the ECJ decisions in the *Environmental Crimes* (2005) and *Ship-Source Pollution* (2007) cases which have set important limits of the EC competence in criminal matters and recognized for the first time the competence of the EC under the first pillar to harmonise environmental criminal law. The decision led to the adoption of the directives on environmental crimes in October 2008 and ship-source pollution in September 2009, which require Member States to criminalise serious violations of (EU) environmental law. Subsequently, the ratification of the Lisbon Treaty in December 2009 abolished the third pillar (the original intergovernmental forum established for Member States to cooperate in criminal matters), allowing Member States to pursue further integration in the (environmental) criminal law field at the supranational level.

The chapter discusses the recent dispute over the legal basis for the harmonisation of environmental criminal law between the Community institutions and the Member States and the impact that this had on the format and scope of the adopted legislative measures on environmental crime. In this context, it also addresses some of rationales given for the harmonisation of measures to foster criminal law cooperation between the Member States. The chapter then looks into the reforms introduced by the Lisbon to the Areas of Freedom, Security and Justice (AFSJ) and the extent to which they may impact on any future harmonisation of national legislation aimed at combatting environmental crime.

II OVERVIEW OF EU DEVELOPMENTS

The European Union has attempted to find an instrument of harmonisation of environmental criminal law that would respect the distribution of competences between the EC (now TFEU) and EU (TEU, now amended by the Lisbon Treaty) Treaties and between the EC/EU and its Member States, and which would equally provide an effective response to environmental criminality within the EU. The Kingdom of Denmark launched an initiative for a Framework Decision on environmental crimes in 2000, founded on the EU's third pillar.[2] The Commission subsequently launched a parallel proposal in

---

[2] Initiative of the Kingdom of Denmark with the view of Adopting a Framework Decision on Combating Serious Environmental Crime (05 (2000)/C39/05). Member States shared with the European Commission the power of initiative to write legislative measures under the third pillar, under former Article 34(2) TEU (repealed by Lisbon).

March 2001 for a directive on environmental crimes[3] based on Article 175 EC (since Lisbon, Article 192 TFEU) as amended by the Parliament in 2002[4] to rival the proposal for a Framework Decision based on the Treaty on the European Union (TEU). The presentation of the 2001 directive proposal has successfully delayed the adoption of the Framework Decision by the Council, but it was not sufficient to convince the Member States that the Community had competence in the area of (environmental) criminal law, culminating in the adoption by the Council of a Framework Decision on environmental crimes in January 2003.[5] Given this impasse, the Commission, supported by the European Parliament, brought an annulment action against the Council's Framework Decision on environmental crimes in April 2003 before the European Court of Justice challenging the legal basis of the adopted third pillar instrument. In their view, the third pillar instrument encroached upon the Community's competence under the first pillar.

Finally, in a landmark ruling in the summer of 2005, the ECJ provided some clarification to the question of distribution of competences between the (then) EC and EU Treaties in the area of criminal law and policy. The European Court of Justice decision of 13 September 2005 in *Commission v. Council*[6] (*'Environmental Crimes'*) has established that while the Community (EC) did not have competence in criminal matters *per se*, the Community institutions might require Member States to introduce criminal sanctions in the case of serious violations of environmental law.[7] The ECJ has therefore annulled the Framework Decision of the Council which aimed at harmonising the criminal sanctions for protection of the environment of Member States under the third pillar of the EU (which is intergovernmental), rather than the first pillar (i.e. under the 'environmental title' of the Treaty), which would have allowed the Commission and ECJ to exercise stronger enforcement powers and the European Parliament to have greater participation in decision-making.

---

[3]   Proposal for a Directive of the European Parliament and of the Council on the Protection of the Environment through Criminal Law, COM(2001)139 final, 13 March 2001.

[4]   Amended Proposal for a Directive of the European Parliament and of the Council on the Protection of the Environment through Criminal Law, COM(2002)544 final, 30 September 2002.

[5]   Council Framework Decision 2003/80/JHA on the Protection of the Environment through Criminal Law, 27 January 2003.

[6]   Case C–176/03 *Commission v. Council* [2005] ECR I–7879; [2005] 3 CMLR 20.

[7]   See particular paras 48, 49 and 53 of the judgment. It is still unclear whether the Community competence in criminal matters under the former first pillar extended to other Community policy areas outside the environmental field. See also the ECJ decision in Case C–440/05 *Commission v. Council*, discussed below.

Following the ECJ ruling in 2005, the Commission proposed another directive in February 2007 on environmental crimes[8] based on Article 175 EC (post-Lisbon, Article 192 TFEU), superseding the 2001 proposal. Unlike the 2001 directive proposal, which contained a general provision on the types of criminal sanctions to be introduced by Member States,[9] the 2007 proposal specified not only the types but also minimum levels of criminal penalties to be introduced by Member States.[10] The Commission thereby hoped that harmonisation of environmental criminal law would help improve the implementation deficit of EC environmental legislation and provide a strong deterrent against transboundary environmental crimes within the EU.[11]

Yet even though the ECJ recognised in the *Environmental Crimes* ruling that the European Community had a limited competence in criminal matters (that is, to require Member States to introduce criminal sanctions against serious violations of environmental law), it has fallen short of finding that the Community had competence to define specific offences and penalties. The answer to this question only happened on 23 October 2007 in the follow-up Case C–440/05 *Commission v. Council* (*'Ship-Source Pollution Case'*), in which the Commission challenged the legal basis of a Framework Decision of the Council of July 2005 2005/667/JHA to strengthen the criminal law for the enforcement of the law against ship-source pollution (adopted by the Council under the third pillar). This case concerned the legal basis of a measure adopted by the Council and European Parliament in the aftermath of the *Prestige* oil-spill disaster, which caused severe loss of wildlife on the coasts of Portugal, Spain and France, to strengthen the implementation and enforcement of maritime anti-pollution rules by means of criminal sanctions.[12] Thus on the basis of two 2003 proposals from the European Commission, a Ship-Source

---

[8]   Proposal for a Directive of the European Parliament and of the Council on the Protection of the Environment through Criminal Law, COM(2007)51 final, 9 February 2007.

[9]   See Art. 4 (a) of the 2001 Directive Proposal which states that '[a]s concerns natural persons, Member States shall provide for criminal penalties, involving in serious cases deprivation of liberty'.

[10]   See Arts 5 and 7 of the 2007 'Environmental Crime' Directive proposal. For an analysis of this proposal see Pereira, (2007), 'Environmental Criminal Law in the First Pillar: A Positive Development for Environmental Protection in the European Union?', (2007) 16 *European Environmental Law Review* 254.

[11]   See 4th Recital to the Explanatory Memorandum to the 2007 'Environmental Crime' directive proposal, (*supra* n. 8).

[12]   For a more detailed background to the adoption of the EU Ship-Source pollution instruments, see R Pereira, 'On the Legality of the Ship-Source Pollution Directive – the *Intertanko* Case and Selected Others', (2008) 17 European Energy and Environmental Law Review, 6, 372.

Pollution Directive[13] (which sets out 'infringements' but not criminal sanctions) and a parallel Framework Decision[14] (containing the underlining criminal sanctions) have been adopted on 7 September 2005 and 12 July 2005 respectively[15] to criminalise vessel-source pollution in the seas and to implement the Marpol 73/78[16] standards in the EU.[17] The Commission, supported by the European Parliament, thus aimed in the *Ship-Source Pollution* case to challenge the legal basis of the criminal law provisions adopted under the third pillar, fuelled by the Court's findings in the *Environmental Crimes* ruling.

Finally, the ECJ confirmed in this case its position in the *Environmental Crimes* ruling and annulled the Framework Decision on Ship-Source pollution as, being indivisible, it encroached on the Community's competence.[18] Yet it also stated in clear terms that 'the determination of the type and level of the criminal penalties to be applied does not fall within the Community's sphere of competence'.[19]

Hence the provisions on the type (imprisonment, fines etc) and levels ('minimum maximum' custodial sentences and fines, in line with the Justice and Home

---

[13]   Directive 2005/35/EC of the European Parliament and of the Council on Ship-Source Pollution and on the Introduction of Penalties for Infringements, 7 September 2005, *Official Journal* 1, 255/11, 30.9.2005.

[14]   Council Framework Decision 2005/667/JHA to Strengthen the Criminal-Law Framework for the Enforcement of the Law against Ship-Source Pollution, 12 July 2005, *Official Journal* 1, 255/164, 30.9.2005

[15]   The difference between the dates of adoption of those measures reflects the legislative procedure which applies for their adoption. The adoption of the Directive based on former Article 80(2) EC (post-Lisbon Article 100(2)) requires qualified majority voting and co-decision between the Council and the European Parliament, whereas measures adopted under Title VI TEU required unanimity in the Council and the Parliament is merely consulted.

[16]   International Convention for Prevention of Shipping Pollution from Ships (MARPOL, 1973) as amended in 1978.

[17]   This legislative method was known as the 'double-text' mechanism.

[18]   Case 440/05, Ship-Source Pollution. The Court rules in para. 66: '[a]lthough it is true that, as a general rule, neither criminal law nor the rules of criminal procedure fall within the Community's competence ... the fact remains that when the application of effective, proportionate and dissuasive criminal penalties by the competent national authorities is an essential measure for combating serious environmental offences, the Community legislature may require the Member States to introduce such penalties in order to ensure that the rules which it lays down in that field are fully effective.' Moreover, in para. 69 the Court ruled: 'since Articles 2, 3 and 5 of Framework Decision 2005/667 are designed to ensure the efficacy of the rules adopted in the field of maritime safety, non-compliance with which may have serious environmental consequences, by requiring Member States to apply criminal penalties to certain forms of conduct, those articles must be regarded as being essentially aimed at improving maritime safety, as well as environmental protection, and could have been validly adopted on the basis of Article 80(2) EC'.

[19]   *Ship-Source Pollution*, para. 70.

Affairs Council conclusions on penalties in April 2002,[20] had been properly adopted under the third pillar.

Following this decision, the Council has taken the 2007 Environmental Crimes Directive proposal for discussion. In line with the ECJ decisions in the *Environmental Crimes* and *Ship-Source Pollution* cases, the Council of Ministers[21] and European Parliament,[22] following the co-decision procedure which applies to the adoption of legislative measures based on Article 192 TFEU (former Article 175 EC), have detached the provisions establishing the types and levels of penalties from the proposal, and introduced amendments to it so that only violations of EC environmental law, not national environmental law, needed to be criminalised by Member States.[23] Subsequently, the Draft Report of Harmut Nassauer[24] was approved by the members of the European Parliament Legal Affairs Committee in a close vote[25] on 8 April 2008. The Council and the European Parliament (following the first-reading Plenary session) reached an agreement on the final compromise text of the Directive on 21 May 2008[26] and the Directive was finally adopted with minor amendments by the unanimous vote of the Member States represented in the Council on 24 October 2008.[27]

---

[20]   Justice and Home Affairs Council 2423rd meeting, Luxembourg, April 2002, 25/26.IV.2002.

[21]   See for example Working Party on Substantive Criminal Law, Proposal for a Directive of the European Parliament and of the Council on the Protection of the Environment through Criminal Law 5152/08 DROIPEN 1ENV 12 CODEC 17 11 January 2008, available at http://register.consilium.eu.int/.

[22]   Draft Report on the Directive on the Protection of the Environment through Criminal Law, European Parliament, Committee on Legal Affairs, Rapporteur: Hartmut Nassauer, 26 February 2008.

[23]   Council of the European Union, 6749/1/08 REV 1, DROIPEN 16 ENV 112 CODEC 246, 4 March 2008. See also the Draft Report on the Proposal for a directive of the European Parliament and of the Council on the protection of the environment through criminal law COM(207)0051 C6-0063/2007 – 2007/0022(COD) European Parliament Rapporteur: Hartmut Nassauer, 26 February 2008.

[24]   See Report on proposal for a directive of the European Parliament and of the Council on the protection of the environment through criminal law, A6-0154/2008 of 15 April 2008 [COM(2007)0051 – C6-0063/2007 – 2007/0022(COD)] European Parliament, Committee on Legal Affairs, Rapporteur: Hartmut Nassauer.

[25]   15 Committee members voted in favour while 11 voted against the proposal. There were two abstentions. See http://www.euractiv.com/en/environment/meps-vote-outlaw-green-crimes/article-171498 (accessed on 13 June 2011).

[26]   See Position of the European Parliament Adopted at First Reading on 21 May 2008 with a View to the Adoption of the Directive 2008/.../EC of the European Parliament and of the Council on the Protection of the Environment through Criminal Law, available at www.europarl.europa.eu (accessed on 13 June 2011).

[27]   Directive 2008/99/EC of the European Parliament and of the Council of 19 November 2008 on the protection of the environment through criminal law, *Official Journal*

In turn, the Commission proposed a directive on 11 March 2008 to amend the directive on ship-source pollution,[28] *inter alia* in order to require that sanctions for certain forms of ship-source pollution committed intentionally, recklessly or with serious negligence are of a criminal nature. Following the European Parliament's Transport Committee vote in favour of the Ship-Source Pollution Amending Directive (as proposed in the report drafted by Luis de Grandes Pascual[29] on 17 February 2009), the directive was finally adopted in September 2009.[30] In line with the *Ship-Source Pollution* ruling, this directive does not contain provisions on specific penalties.

Following the ratification of the Treaty of Lisbon in December 2009, the third pillar is abolished and a clear power for the European Union to power to adopt, at the supranantional level, criminal law legislative measures, including criminal penalties and other measures on police and judicial cooperation in criminal matters.[31]

III THE NEED FOR EU ENVIRONMENTAL CRIMINAL LAW[32]

The US government estimates that organisations worldwide earn around US$22–31 billion annually from hazardous waste dumping, smuggling proscribed hazardous materials, and exploiting and trafficking protected natural

L 328, 6 December 2008, at 28–37. See also Directive of the European Parliament and of the Council on the Protection of the Environment through Criminal Law DROIPEN 51 ENV 323 CODEC 652, PE-CONS 3639/08 12 August 2008.

[28] Proposal for a Directive of the European Parliament and of the Council amending Directive 2005/35/EC on ship source pollution and on the introduction of penalties for infringements, COM(2008)0134 final COD 2008/0055.

[29] There were 37 votes in favour of the proposal and 1 against. 'Pollution at Sea: MEPS Vote for Compulsory Criminal Law Penalties' http://www.europarl.europa.eu/news.

[30] Directive 2009/123/EC of the European Parliament and of the Council of 21 October 2009 amending Directive 2005/35/EC on ship-source pollution and on the introduction of penalties for infringements, *Official Journal*, L 280/52 27 December 2009.

[31] See Art. 83 of the Treaty on the Functioning of the European Union (formerly EC Treaty), as amended by the Treaty of Lisbon. This Article is the successor to Art. III-271 of the Draft Constitutional Treaty.

[32] On whether the harmonisation of environmental criminal law could improve the enforcement and implementation of environmental criminal law in the European Union see: Pereira 'Environmental Criminal Law in the First Pillar: A Positive Development for Environmental Protection in the European Union?' (2007) *European Environmental Law Review* 254; and Pereira, 'The Harmonisation of Environmental Criminal Law – International and European Perspectives' Martinus Nijhoff Publishers (forthcoming).

resources.[33] To put this into the EU context, one interesting case is the Commission's recent decision to institute proceedings against Italy before the ECJ for the dumping of waste in illegal sites in Naples on 7 May 2008. Criminal groups control most of Italy's waste disposal contracts (the so-called eco-mafia). According to the Italian authorities 11 million metric tons of toxic and industrial waste are deposited annually in some 2,000 illegal domestic dump sites in local waterways or in the Mediterranean.[34] Not only in Italy but in the EU generally several studies have shown the infiltration of criminal organisations into the waste disposal sector.

International crime does not recognise national borders. Globalisation and the consequent loosening of border controls have meant that nation states are not able to serve as the sole guardians of values protected by criminal law as the principal means to control social deviance. The individual failure of nation states to combat crime (in particular transnational crime) calls for forms of police and judicial cooperation in criminal matters between states, as recognised in several international and regional agreements (e.g. on extradition and mutual assistance on criminal matters[35]).

When the European Union decided to abolish border controls back in 1986 under the Single European Act (SEA) in an ambitious programme to complete the single market by 1992 (where goods, persons, services and capital would move freely), it recognised that flanking policies would need to be introduced in order to combat cross-border crime. Even though the abolition of border controls was initially developed outside the context of European Union law (the so-called

---

[33] See Comte 'Environmental Crime and the Police in Europe: A Panorama and Possible Paths for Future Action' (2006) *European Environmental Law Review* 190.

[34] In Case 297/08 *Commission v. Italy* [2010] the Italian government argued in defence to its failure to prevent illegal waste disposal in the region of Catania that the infiltration of criminal organizations made it impossible for the Italian government to stop the illegal activity. Yet the ECJ found in its judgment handed down on 4 March 2010 that 'as regards the presence of criminal activity, or of persons described as operating "on the fringes of the law" active in the waste management sector it is sufficient to point out that that fact – even if it were assumed to be established – cannot justify the failure by that Member State to fulfil its obligations under Directive 2006/12 (Case C–263/05 *Commission v. Italy*, paragraph 51)'. Moreover, the Court found that by failing to adopt, for the region of Campania, all the measures necessary to ensure that waste is recovered and disposed of without endangering human health and without harming the environment and, in particular, by failing to establish an integrated and adequate network of disposal installations, the Italian Republic has failed to fulfil its obligations under Articles 4 and 5 of Directive 2006/12 on waste management.

[35] See e.g. the 1957 The European Convention on Extradition, ETS 24. 359 UNTS 273; 1959 European Convention on Mutual Assistance in Criminal Matters, ETS 30; and the 1972 European Convention on the Transfer of Proceedings in Criminal Matters, ETS 73, 72 UNTS 185.

'Schengen Acquis'),[36] it was later incorporated into EU law by the Treaty of Amsterdam. Thus, measures to deal with crimes are often regarded as a counter-weight to reduced border controls. Significantly, the fact that criminals are able to exploit the differences in legislation and legal enforcement techniques in different states to their benefit has led to calls for the harmonisation of both substantive and procedural criminal law. Harmonisation of criminal legislation could then be re-garded as a means to facilitate police and judicial cooperation in criminal matters. For example, classic extradition agreements require double criminality in both executing and issuing states, so harmonisation of criminal law would facilitate the operation of those agreements because both states would have criminalised and introduced similar sanctions for similar offences.[37] Yet harmonisation of criminal legislation could also be regarded as an objective in itself. For example it could be argued that some environmental crimes have global or transboundary effects (the deleterious effects of global warming, trade in endangered species and in ozone-depleting substances), and thus eco-criminals would need to be punished with a similar degree of severity everywhere.

The Principle of Mutual Recognition

In order to avert fears from the part of the member states that harmonisation would undermine their sovereignty in criminal matters and ultimately lead to legislative stagnation,[38] the principle of mutual recognition has been chosen as the cornerstone of police and judicial cooperation in criminal matters in the EU.[39] The principle of mutual recognition progressively replaces traditional judicial cooperation by one based on the near automatic acceptance and en-forcement of all judicial decisions made during criminal proceedings taken in

---

[36]   See Schengen Agreement of 1985 and Schengen Implementation Convention (1990): Agreement between the Governments of the States of the Benelux Economic Union, the Federal Republic of Germany and the French Republic on the gradual aboli-tion of checks at their common borders. *Official Journal* L 239, 22/09/2000 P. 0013.

[37]   Though as will be discussed later in the chapter, the European Arrest Warrant and other EU instruments based on the principle of mutual recognition do not require double-criminality for certain crimes, including environmental crimes, when punishable by a maximum custodial sentence or detention order of at least 3 years.

[38]   V. Mitsilegas, 'Trust-Building Measures in the European Judicial Area in Crimi-nal Matters: Issues of Competence, Legitimacy and Inter-Institutional Balance', in T. Balzacq and S. Carrera (eds) *Security Versus Freedom? A Challenge for Europe's Future* (2006), 279.

[39]   This was stressed both at the Tampere 1999 meeting (see paras. 33–7) and at the 2004 Hague Programme. See I. Jegouzo, 'Le development Progressif du Principe de Reconnaissance Mutuelle des Décisions Judiciares Pénal Dans L'Union Europeenne' (2006) 77 *Revue Internationale de Droit Penal* 97.

one member state by the appropriate authorities in all others. The principle of mutual recognition in EU criminal law has been criticized *inter alia* for adapting a judicial framework developed for market regulation to the very different needs of internal security.[40]

Although the principle of mutual recognition is regarded as the cornerstone of police and judicial cooperation in criminal matters in the European Union and underpins a number of initiatives adopted under the third pillar (e.g. the European Arrest Warrant 2002[41] and the European Evidence Warrant 2008[42]), the successful operation of the principle requires the building of mutual trust in each other's legal systems, which in turn may require a degree of harmonisation. For example, one judge may be hesitant to surrender a state's own national under an arrest warrant issued by another Member State if the legal system of that state does not provide minimum guarantees to the defendant in criminal proceedings. Hence in order to build mutual trust in the legal systems of European Union Member States, a degree of harmonisation of criminal law is required. So mutual recognition is not an *alternative* to harmonisation; it is complemented by it.[43]

IV   THE LEGAL BASIS FOR THE HARMONISATION OF ENVIRONMENTAL CRIMINAL LAW: PRE-LISBON DEVELOPMENTS

Following the creation of the three pillars by the TEU in 1993, and particularly after the Treaty of Amsterdam in 1999, the Member States of the EU have found a legal basis (the third pillar) for cooperating in criminal matters and,

---

[40]   V. Mitsilegas, EU Criminal Law, (Hart Publishing, 2009). The principle of mutual recognition was developed by the case law of the Court of Justice in the context of market integration. Once a product is lawfully marketed in one member state another member state cannot not refuse that product unless if based on one of the grounds for derogations under the Treaty or the mandatory requirements. See Case 120/78, *Rewe-Zentral AG v. Bundesmonopolverwaltung für Branntwein* (*'Cassis de Dijon'*) [1979] ECR.

[41]   Council Framework Decision of 13 June 2002 on the European arrest warrant and the surrender procedures between Member States (2002/584/JHA) *Official Journal* L 190/1 18.7.2002.

[42]   Council Framework Decision 2008/978/JHA of 18 December 2008 on the European evidence warrant for the purpose of obtaining objects, documents and data for use in proceedings in criminal matters, *Official Journal* L 350.72 30.12.2008.

[43]   On whether the harmonisation of environmental criminal law could improve the enforcement and implementation of environmental criminal law in the European Union see: Pereira (2007), 'Environmental Criminal Law in the First Pillar: A Positive Development for Environmental Protection in the European Union?', *European Environmental Law Review* 254.

where necessary, harmonising criminal legislation. Yet the intergovernmental method applied under the third pillar was criticised for being undemocratic[44] and for the very limited political[45] and judicial[46] control over policies adopted. As a result, the harmonisation of criminal law left citizens (and indeed third country nationals) particularly vulnerable to the measures adopted at the EU level, in light of the fact that executive action in this field is particularly apt to strike at their most fundamental interests.[47] Hence both the European Commission and European Parliament have called for the harmonisation of criminal law to take place instead under the first pillar.[48] They argued that harmonisation of criminal law under the first pillar would allow enhanced supranational and democratic control of policies, including full ECJ jurisdiction (then known as the 'Community method'). However, this view was not shared by the Council of Ministers and the Member States themselves, who feared losing their sovereignty over criminal matters, often regarded as intrinsic to state sovereignty. Yet even though from the perspective of Member States the intergovernmental model appeared preferable as it would not involve giving away their competence in this sensitive area (criminal law), the ECJ had already started blurring the line between the pillars in a decision in May 2005 in the *Maria Pupino* case,[49] in which the ECJ held that third pillar measures have indirect effect, i.e. it was held that the Member States must interpret national criminal law in line with third pillar measures (even if they have not been implemented in that Member State).

As discussed earlier in the chapter, the Commission had proposed the adoption of a directive on environmental crimes in March 2001 (a first pillar measure) but the Council decided to go ahead and adopt instead a Framework Decision on environmental crimes (a third pillar measure) in January 2003 based on a proposal from the Kingdom of Denmark (2000), a major

---

[44]   Third pillar measures required unanimity in the Council and the European Parliament was merely consulted.

[45]   The Commission could through a scoreboard programme oversee the implementation of those third pillar instruments, but it might not institute proceedings under Art. 258TFEU (ex. Art. 226 EC) before the ECJ for the failure of a Member State to implement a third pillar measure.

[46]   The Member States had the option to declare that they accepted the ECJ jurisdiction to oversee the legality of third pillar instruments in a reference for a preliminary ruling from a national Court (there were restrictions also on which national courts were able to refer questions for a preliminary ruling).

[47]   N. Walker, 'In Search of the Area of Freedom, Security and Justice: A Constitutional Odyssey', in N. Walker (ed.), *Europe's Area of Freedom, Security and Justice* (2004), 10.

[48]   Commission of the European Communities, 'Implementing the Hague Programme: The Way Forward', COM(2006)331 final, at 14.

[49]   Case 105/03 *Criminal Proceedings against Maria Pupino* [2005] ECR 1–5285.

institutional conflict emerged. This institutional conflict was only partially settled following the ECJ decision in Case *Commission v. Council* on 13 September 2005.[50] In this case the Court held that the Community has the power under the first pillar to require Member States to introduce criminal sanctions in the case of serious violations of environmental law. Therefore, the Court has effectively bypassed the negative Dutch and French referenda on the Constitutional Treaty (CT) in the summer of 2005 which, had it been ratified, would have provided a clearer Treaty basis for the Community to harmonise criminal law. However, the decision is not inconsistent with the Court's own case law, in which the Court has consistently held, interpreting the loyal-cooperation principle enshrined in ex-Article 10 of the EC Treaty,[51] that sanctions for the non-implementation of EC law must be 'effective, proportionate and dissuasive' (see e.g. *Greek Maize*[52]) and even that a state's failure to prosecute could amount to a violation of ex-Article 10 EC (*Greek Maize,*[53] *Spanish Strawberries*[54]) – despite the fact that the prosecutorial activities in some countries are ruled by the opportunity principle, and hence there is no duty for the relevant authorites to bring a prosecution in individual cases under the law of those countries. Moreover, despite the fact that there is no explicit reference to the Community competence in criminal matters in the EC Treaty[55] and the third pillar appeared to offer the framework for Member States' co-operation in criminal matters, the Court re-stated in *Environmental Crimes* the rule under ex-Article 47 of the TEU[56] which stated that nothing

---

[50]   Case 176/03 *Commission v. Council* [2005] ECR I–7879: [2005] 3 CMLR 20.

[51]   Post-Lisbon repealed and replaced, in substance, by Article 4, paragraph 3, TEU, which states that: '[p]ursuant to the principle of sincere cooperation, the Union and the Member States shall, in full mutual respect, assist each other in carrying out tasks which flow from the Treaties. The Member States shall take any appropriate measure, general or particular, to ensure fulfilment of the obligations arising out of the Treaties or result-ing from the acts of the institutions of the Union. The Member States shall facilitate the achievement of the Union's tasks and refrain from any measure which could jeopardise the attainment of the Union's objectives.'

[52]   Case C–68/88 *Commission v. Hellenic Republic* [1989] ECR, 2965.

[53]   Ibid.

[54]   Case 265/95 *Commission v. France* [1997] ECR 6959.

[55]   In fact the Council and the Member States argued in *Environmental Crimes* that the effect of ex-Art. 280 (4) EC (replaced by Art. 325 TFEU), which *excluded* the Com-munity competence to lay down rules concerning the application of national criminal law or the national administration of justice in the case of fraud to the financial interests of the Community, would be to rule out the criminal law competence of the Community in relation to other policy areas as well.

[56]   Since Lisbon replaced by Art. 40 TEU. Given that the Lisbon Treaty abolished the third pillar, this article no longer deals with the distribution of competences between the first and third pillars.

in the Treaty on European Union shall affect the Community competence under the EC Treaty.[57] Moreover, the Court found that the main objective of the Framework Decision was the protection of the environment, and hence the measure could have properly been adopted under former Article 175 EC (post-Lisbon, Article 192 TFEU).[58] Hence the Court ruled that 'the entire framework decision, *being indivisible*, infringed [ex-]Article 47 EU as it encroached on the powers in environmental matters which [ex-]Article 175 EC confers on the Community'[59] and thus annulled the 2003 Environmental Crimes Framework Decision.

The Court has however left many questions unanswered in the *Environmental Crimes* case, in particular whether the power of the Community in criminal matters extended beyond the environmental field or not, and whether the Community had the power to approximate the definition of offences and the types and levels of criminal penalties (for example to establish minimum levels of fines or terms of imprisonment, as was already the practice in the third pillar). Indeed, the Court's ruling allows the Community legislature to take '*measures* which relate to the criminal law of the Member States which it considers necessary in order to ensure that the rules which it lays down on environmental protection are fully effective'[60] (emphasis added). The judgment hence fell short of defining what type of criminal law measures can be defined by the Community and must be introduced by Member States in order to achieve the objective of environmental protection. So even though the decision indicated that the nature of the sanction to implement EC law could be established at EC level (i.e. criminal), it was not clear whether this power extended to the definition of specific offences and penalties.[61]

---

[57] Ex-Art. 47 TEU (replaced by Art. 40 TEU) literally stated that 'nothing in [the TEU Treaty] shall affect the Treaties establishing the European Communities or the subsequent Treaties and Acts modifying or supplementing them.'

[58] The Court ruled that 'as general rule, neither criminal law nor the rules of criminal procedure fall within the Community's competence' (para. 47), 'the last-mentioned finding does not prevent the Community legislature, when the application of effective, proportionate and dissuasive criminal penalties by the competent national authorities *is an essential measure* for combating *serious environmental offences*, from *taking measures which relate to the criminal law* of the Member States which *it considers necessary* in order to ensure that the rules which it lays down *on environmental protection are fully effective.*' (emphasis added) (para. 48).

[59] *Environmental Crimes* case, para. 53.

[60] *Environmental Crimes* case, para. 48.

[61] See 42nd Report of Session 2005–2006, House of Lords, European Union Committee, 'The Criminal Law Competence of the European Community. Report with Evidence', 28 July 2006, 21–3. However, as regards the Community competence to harmonise criminal offences, Professor Peers considered that the Community 'must at least have the power to define what criminal offences must be prosecuted by Member

The Commission itself took the view that the Community had the power to harmonise penalties, as seen in its Communication of November 2005 outlining its interpretation of the September 2005 ruling[62] as well as from its second proposal for a directive on environmental crimes of February 2007. Yet many Member States feared that the power of the Community to define criminal offences and the types and levels of criminal penalties would undermine the coherence of their own national legal systems (undermining their powers properly to label offences and grade corresponding sanctions according to their severity), and this view was shared (at least as far as the creation of penalties is concerned) by Advocate General Mazák in his Opinion in the follow-up *Ship-Source Pollution* Case.[63] This view had also been supported by Advocate General Colomer in his Opinion in *Environmental Crimes*, though the question of harmonisation of criminal penalties is not directly addressed by the ECJ in that case.[64] However the argument regarding the coherence of each national legal system is perhaps not so strong if one takes into account that the harmonisation of criminal penalties was already taking place under the third pillar, and it must be remembered that those third pillar legislative measures are legally binding and even – after the *Pupino* decision in June 2005 – have indirect effect.[65] Moreover, the subsidiarity principle does not appear to be a strong enough justification to restrict the Community competence to adopt *minimum* levels of *maximum* criminal penalties, in line with the Justice and Home Affairs Council conclusions on penalties.[66]

The ECJ had the opportunity to rule on this point on 23 of October 2007 in the *Ship-Source Pollution* case, which involved a similar dispute over the legal

States' as 'paragraph 48 [of the judgement] … does not rule out the Community being relatively specific and being very, very prescriptive as to what precisely Member States should ban' (21–2).

[62]   Communication from the European Commission to the European Parliament and the Council on the Implications of the Court's Judgment of 13 September 2005 (Case C–176/03 *Commission v. Council*), COM(2005)583 final/2, 24 November 2005.

[63]   Case 440/05, Opinion of Advocate General, Points 103 to 113. In point 108 he also cites the subsidiarity principle in support of this argument.

[64]   Case 176/03, Opinion of Advocate General Ruiz-Jarabo Colomer, Points 83 to 87.

[65]   For comments on this case see e.g. Peers (2007), 'Salvation Outside the Church: Judicial Protection in Third Pillar after the Pupino and Segi Judgements', *Common Market Law Review*; Herlin-Karnell (2007), 'Recent Developments in the Area of European Criminal Law', 14 *Maastricht Journal of European and Comparative Law* 1 and Betlem (2007), 'Beyond *Francovich*: Completing the Unified Member State and EU Liability Regime. A Comment on the Jan Jans Contribution' in Obradovic and Lavranos (eds), *Interface between EU Law and National Law* (Europa Law Publishing).

[66]   Justice and Home Affairs Council conclusions April 2002. See further Peers (2008) 'The European Community's Criminal Law Competence: the Plot Thickens', *European Law Review* 399 at 407.

basis for a directive and Framework Decision to combat pollution from ships through criminal law (following the *Prestige* oil-tanker disaster). The Court ruled, but without any elaboration, that the Community does not have the power to establish the types and levels of criminal sanctions.[67] Hence eco-criminals would still be able to exploit the differences in the environmental criminal legislation of the Member States (as one Member State may apply a small criminal fine and another a long prison sentence for the same offence) unless it could be established that any criminal sactions set at a low level are not 'effective, proportionate and dissuasive' enough[68] which is difficult to establish in individual cases. Moreover, at the level of police and judicial co-operation in criminal matters a certain level playing field for criminal penalties would be desirable, given that some EU criminal law measures which apply to environmental crimes, such as the European Arrest Warrant (EAW) and the European Evidence Warrant (EEW), require a cetain minimum penalty threshold for their operation without the requirement for double criminality. That is, the issuing of an EAW is only possible (unless the sentence has already been passed) for acts punishable in the issuing state by a custodial sentence or a detention order of at least 12 months. In the case of environmental crime, issuing the EAW without the condition of dual criminality requires that the offence is punishable in the issuing Member State by a maximum of at least three years' imprisonment. Hence the European Commission argues that a minimum level playing field in the area of criminal penalties could facilitate police and judicial cooperation between the Member States.

It was not clear from the 2007 judgment whether the Community power to require Member States to introduce criminal sanctions was only limited to environment-related policies (for example the common transport policy, in the case of ship-source pollution) or whether it extends to other policies without an environmental objective.[69] It was also not clear why the Court does not elaborate on the question of the lack of Community competence to adopt criminal penalties – it has been suggested that this may have been due to political reasons in light of the negotiation process of the EU Reform Treaty[70] which, as will be

---

[67]   See para. 70 of the judgment.

[68]   There is a general requirement under EU law that penalties for failure to comply with EU legislation must be 'effective, proportionate and dissuasive' and the same requirement is inserted in a number of pieces of EU legislation, including the EU directives on environmental crime and ship-source pollution.

[69]   See 10th Report of Session 2007–2008, House of Lords, European Union Committee, 'The Treaty of Lisbon: an Impact Assessment', Volume I: Report, 13 March 2008, Chapter 6 and Peers (2008), 'The European Community's Criminal Law Competence: the Plot Thickens', *European Law Review* 399 at 407.

[70]   Peers, S (2008) 'The European Community's Criminal Law Competence: the Plot Thickens' *European Law Review* 399 at 407.

seen in the next section, has brought about fundamental changes to the area of freedom, security and justice (AFSJ).

V   THE LISBON TREATY AND THE FUTURE OF EU ENVIRONMENTAL CRIMINAL LAW

A)   Overview of Changes to AFSJ

Despite the above discussed litigation in which the Member States sided with the Council against criminal-law powers being transferred to the EC, the Member States themselves recognized the deficiencies under the third pillar by aiming to ratify a treaty that would bring police and judicial cooperation in criminal matters to the 'first pillar'. Following the failed attempt to ratify the Constitutional Treaty in 2005, the Lisbon Treaty was signed on 13 December 2007 by the heads of government and state of the member states and was ratified in November 2009, following the Irish second referendum[71] and the Czech and Polish ratifications. It came into force in December 2009.

Under Lisbon, the intergovernmental third pillar is abolished and two separate bodies of law are generated: an amended version of the Treaty on the European Union (TEU) and the Treaty on the Functioning of the Union (TFEU), which is the new denomination of the Treaty establishing the European Community (TEC).[72] Hence the dispute over the legal basis for the harmonisation of criminal law, highlighted in the ECJ cases discussed above, will no longer be as relevant following the ratification of the Treaty of Lisbon.

The Treaty of Lisbon completes the absorption of the remaining third pillar aspects of Justice and Home Affairs Law – i.e. police and judicial cooperation in criminal matters – into the 'first pillar'. This means that measures under all aspects of the Area of Freedom, Security and Justice will be determined by the ordinary legislative procedure of qualified majority voting and co-decision between the Council and European Parliament, unless otherwise specified. Moreover, subject to transitional, and in the case of the UK, Ireland and Denmark, opt-in arrangements, pre-existing third pillar acts will fall after a five-year transitional period within the jurisdiction of the ECJ.[73]

---

[71]   The Irish 'no vote' on the Treaty on 12 June 2008 had shed doubt on whether the Treaty of Lisbon will indeed be ratified by all Member States.

[72]   S. Carrera and F. Geyer, 'The Reform Treaty and Justice and Home Affairs: Implication for the Common Area of Freedom, Security and Justice', in E. Guild and F. Geyer (eds.) *Security versus Justice: Police and Judicial Cooperation in the European Union* (2008), at 291.

[73]   See 10th Report of Session 2007–2008, *supra* n. 83.

Another innovation introduced by the Lisbon Treaty in the context of criminal law is that it allows a member state to pull the 'emergency brake' when a legislative proposal would bring about fundamental changes to its national criminal justice system. The matter is then referred to the European Council and the ordinary legislative procedure is suspended. If the European Council arrives at a consensus within four months, the matter is then referred back to the Council of Ministers for continuation of the legislative procedure.[74] If no agreement is reached, this would then allow a number of member states (at least nine of them) to initiate enhanced cooperation in order to implement a criminal law proposal to be applicable among themselves. They need to notify the European Parliament, the Commission and the Council and authorization for enhanced cooperation is deemed to have been granted. However, although perhaps a necessary compromise which has arisen in the negotiations of the Lisbon Treaty, this process of enhanced cooperation could be criticized for creating a 'two-speed' Europe. It has been argued that the 'emergency brake' is unlikely to be frequently used in practice, but that it is likely to impact on negotiations in the Council through the possibility of its use.[75]

B)   The Scope of Article 83(1) and (2) TFEU

Under the TFEU, the European Union gains competence at the supranational level to define minimum rules (approximation) regarding the definition of criminal offences *as well as penalties.*

Paragraph 1 of Article 83 of the Treaty on the Functioning on the European Union (which replaces the EC Treaty) states that:

> The European Parliament and the Council may, by means of directives adopted in accordance with the ordinary legislative procedure, establish minimum rules concerning the definition of criminal offences and sanctions in the areas of particularly serious crime with a cross-border dimension resulting from the nature or impact of such offences or from a special need to combat them on a common basis.

> These areas of crime are the following: terrorism, trafficking in human beings and sexual exploitation of women and children, illicit drug trafficking, illicit arms trafficking, money laundering, corruption, counterfeiting of means of payment, computer crime and organised crime.

---

[74]   Ibid., at 118.

[75]   See ibid. On the relevance of the British and Irish opt outs in light of the new 'emergency brake' rules, see Peers (2008), 'EU Criminal Law and the Treaty of Lisbon', 33 *European Law Review* 507. It must be noted that the emergency brake does not apply to mutual recognition measures or Eurojust – only to substantive criminal law and domestic criminal procedure.

> On the basis of developments in crime, the Council may adopt a decision identify-
> ing other areas of crime that meet the criteria specified in this paragraph. It shall act
> unanimously after obtaining the consent of the European Parliament.

The list of offences under paragraph 1 of Article 83 is exhaustive, and does not
include environmental crime. This is perhaps surprising considering the above
discussed ECJ case law emphasising the seriousness of some environmental
offences. However an unanimous decision of the Council might bring environmental crime into the scope of that provision, so ultimately it is not impossible
that Article 82 (1) TFEU will be used in future to amend the Environmental
Crimes Directive to order to e.g. introduce specific criminal penalties.

The approximation of criminal law is also possible under paragraph 2 of Article
83 TFEU:

> If the approximation of criminal laws and regulations of the Member States proves
> essential to ensure the effective implementation of a Union policy in an area which
> has been subject to harmonisation measures, directives may establish minimum rules
> with regard to the definition of criminal offences and sanctions in the area concerned.
> Such directives shall be adopted by the same ordinary or special legislative procedure
> as was followed for the adoption of the harmonisation measures in question, without
> prejudice to Article 76.

Some commentators consider that paragraphs (1) and (2) of Article 83 TFEU
may be *lex specialis* in relation to one another, which would then allow the
adoption of a proposal on environmental crimes, for example, under paragraph
2 only.[76] That is, since the harmonisation of criminal law would be sought as
a means to ensure the effective implementation of a Union policy, it is suggested that any future harmonisation of environmental criminal legislation
would have to be based on Article 83 (2). So it would not be possible for the
Commission to seek harmonisation of environmental criminal law under *either*
one *or* the other paragraph of Article 83, as paragraph 2 is to be regarded as
lex specialis.[77]

Hence it is possible that the EU criminal law measures adopted under the first
pillar in the aftermath of the *Environmental Crimes* and *Ship-Source Pollution*
rulings (i.e. the Environmental Crimes Directive adopted in October 2008 and
the Ship-Source Pollution [Amending] Directive adopted in October 2009)
will be amended for harmonisation of specific penalties (e.g. minimum levels
of maximum prison sentences and fines), and perhaps also other measures on

---

[76] See Peers 'EU Criminal Law and the Treaty of Lisbon' (2008) *European Law
Review* 4, 516–17.

[77] Ibid.

police and judicial cooperation in criminal matters (although the legal basis for this under the TFEU is less clear).[78] The Commission has already indicated that it will propose such amendments when launching the Action Plan to implement the Stockholm Programme in April 2010, which sets out the priorities of EU criminal law for the next five years.[79]

Moreover, it must be noted that any future EC environmental legislation may itself prescribe criminal offences and sanctions by a reference to the Environmental Crimes Directive. Alternatively, the Commission may propose in future an amendment to the Environmental Crimes Directive to amplify the list of offences or (possibly) the list of EC secondary legislation listed in an Annex to the Directive, serious violations of which will need to be sanctioned by means of criminal law.[80]

C) Does Article 83 (2) TFEU Prevail Over the Other TFEU Legal Provisions?

It has been suggested that there is still scope for the EU to harmonise environmental criminal law under Article 192 TFEU i.e. under the environmental title of the TFEU, rather than para. (2) of Article 83 TFEU. Although Article 83 (2) TFEU allows the adoption of minimum criminal rules in order to ensure the effective *implementation of a Union policy* (which clearly includes environmental policies), the *Environmental Crimes* and *Ship-Source Pollution* rulings clarified that there is scope to harmonisation of criminal sanctions under a Treaty article belonging to other policy areas (e.g. Article 192 TFEU on environmental protection). This has potentially important consequences as the UK, Ireland and Denmark have secured in a Protocol to the Lisbon Treaty the option to opt out from the EU initiatives in criminal law *only*.[81] Therefore the British, Irish and

---

[78]   If an amendment to the Directive(s) is proposed along the lines described above, the Directive would have to be based on a dual legal basis, since the amending act would be based on a criminal law provision (quite possibly Article 83 (2) TFEU) while the Directive is based on a environmental protection or the common transport policy legal basis i.e. Article 192TFEU or Article 100 (2) TFEU.

[79]   See European Commission. Communication From the Commission to the European Parliament, the Council, the European Economic and Social Committee and the Committee of Regions. Delivering an Area of Freedom, Security and Justice for Europe's Citizens: Action Plan Implementing the Stockholm Programme, COM(2010)171 final.

[80]   Recital 15 of the preamble to the Environmental Crimes Directive states that '[w]henever subsequent legislation on environmental matters is adopted, it should specify where appropriate that this Directive will apply. Where necessary, Article 3 [which defines the criminal offences] should be amended'.

[81]   See Peers, S (2007) *Statewatch Analysis*, EU Reform Treaty Analysis no. 4: British and Irish Opt-Outs from EU Justice and Home Affairs Law, 26 October 2007, available

Danish opt outs will be irrelevant if the criminal policy finds its legal basis as a means to enforce other policy areas of the EC Treaty (e.g. environmental or consumer protection). Moreover, as discussed above any Member State may pull the 'emergency brake' to prevent a criminal law measure from being adopted by the Council, but this only applies to measures based Article 83 (1) or (2), not to measures adopted under other TFEU provisions.

On the other hand it has been argued that Article 83 TFEU is *lex specialis* in relation to other Treaty provisions, and hence the correct legal basis for the future harmonisation of (environmental) criminal law.[82] This appears to have been the intention of the Member States when negotiating the provisions on police and judicial cooperation under the Lisbon Treaty, in particular when negotiating the provisions on the 'emergency brake'.

D)   A Common 'European Environmental Criminal Law'?

One of the differences between the original 2007 proposal for a directive on environmental crime, and the final compromise text of the directive adopted in 2008 is that under the latter only violations of EU environmental law, not national environmental law, can be criminalised at the EC level, in line with the *Ship-Source Pollution* case.[83] Hence the directive contains an Annex listing over 60 pieces of EC environmental legislation which relate to the environmental offences defined in the directive. Thus no 'autonomous environmental offences' (i.e. criminalising national environmental law, regardless of whether or not they violate EU environmental legislation) is present in the directive.

It is also possible, though perhaps unlikely, that the Commission may wish to amend the Environmental Crime (and ship-source pollution) Directive to create a common 'European environmental criminal law', so that violations of national environmental law can also be criminalised, a possibility which was ruled out under the first pillar by the ECJ *Ship-Source Pollution* ruling.[84] There would be difficulties in securing such an amendment, though. Firstly, it is not clear whether the criminal law provisions of the Lisbon Treaty permit the harmonisation of purely domestic environmental law, as the two possible legal bases for such harmonisation, Article 82(1) and (2) of the TFEU, would

---

online at http://www.statewatch.org [accessed on 13 June 2011]. Obviously those countries also have opt outs in other areas of the EC Treaty, e.g. Title IV on immigration and asylum, and they would retain the right to opt out in those areas post-Lisbon.

[82]   Peers, *supra* n. 90.

[83]   Case 440/05 para. 66: '[…] the Community legislature may require the Member States to introduce such penalties in order to ensure that *the rules which it lays down in that field* are fully effective' (emphasis added).

[84]   Ibid.

appear to rule out the harmonisation of purely domestic environmental law, unless a transnational link with the offence could be made. Paragraph 1 requires a *transnational* element in order for harmonisation of criminal law to be possible, while paragraph 2 allows the harmonisation of criminal law only in order to ensure the effective *implementation of a Union policy* in an area which has been subject to harmonisation measures.

E)   The British, Danish and Irish Opt-outs

If there is an amendment to a EU criminal measure in future, the UK and Ireland (though Denmark's arrangements differ to some extent) secured in Protocol 21 and 22 to the Lisbon Treaty the possibility to opt out from that measure. As for the other Member States, a transitional period of five years would be applicable until a pre-existing criminal-law legislative measure is subject to full ECJ jurisdiction.[85] Yet that does not apply to the Environmental Crimes (or Ship-Source Pollution) Directive, as the Protocol applies to third-pillar measures which preceded the Lisbon Treaty only, not to a directive adopted under the first pillar. So the UK and Ireland may not be able to opt out from those directives (which preceded Lisbon) after (and if) it is eventually amended to harmonise criminal penalties based on a post-Lisbon criminal law legal basis.

CONCLUSION

Although a convenient choice for the Member States, the pillar structure which underpinned integration in criminal matters in the EU between 1993–2009 can hardly be considered a model for interstate cooperation and integration in criminal matters. This is not only because of the general criticism that criminal law measures adopted under the third pillar lacked democratic legitimacy and were deficient from the perspectives of accountability and legal enforcement, but because the exact borderline between the pillars was ill-defined and hence constantly subject to legal dispute.

Before the ratification of the Lisbon Treaty, it appeared that the only way for the Commission to seek harmonisation of environmental criminal law would be to combine supranational and intergovernmental componenets, the principle of criminalisation and the main prohibitions contained in a directive on environmental crime, while the criminal penalties and measures to foster cooperation

---

[85]   See Peers, S (2007) *Statewatch Analysis*, EU Reform Treaty Analysis no. 4: British and Irish Opt-Outs from EU Justice and Home Affairs Law, 26 October 2007, available online at http://www.statewatch.org [accessed on 15 13 June 2011].

between the police and judicial authorities would be harmonised at the third pillar level.

Since the ECJ had already settled in 2005 the most controversial question regarding the competence of the Community (EC) to criminalise environmental offences, the Council and Member States must welcome the reforms introduce by the Lisbon Treaty which will allow them adopt further, more effective measures to combat environmental crime in the EU.

22. Comparative law and European harmonisation – a match made in heaven or uneasy bedfellows?

Dagmar Schiek*

INTRODUCTION

The title of this chapter maintains a contradictory relationship between comparative law and European harmonisation theories. On the one hand, conventional approaches to comparative law are said to have been revived by common core studies, based on their tendency for universalism (Örücü 2007: 51). Traditional comparative law and European harmonisation thus seem a match made in heaven. On the other hand, approaches to comparative law which stress diversity of socio-legal and cultural contexts of legal institutions may well be sceptical of any mission to use comparative law for finding a best (and possibly uniform) European way to any issue (Nelken 2007:1, 31). Such critical branches of comparative law and European harmonisation may thus appear as uneasy bedfellows.

The question behind this is what, if anything, critical comparative law may be able to contribute to a theory of European legal harmonisation. Working towards such a theory, it is worthwhile to consider theoretical approaches to law, among which critical comparative law may have a claim to belong.

In relation to comparative law, this chapter does not make any suggestion that this approach to law is sufficient to form a theory of harmonisation. Under Articles 114–115 TFEU, harmonisation (referred to as 'approximation of laws') is pursued in order to achieve specific goals, mainly to ensure the functioning of the internal market as defined in Article 26 TFEU. Harmonisation is thus inextricably linked to substantive aims of an economic nature, which are again embedded in wider social, environmental and global development aims under articles 2 EU and 8–10 TFEU. Accordingly, a theory of EU harmonisation would have to offer methods of assessing how individual harmonisation projects

*   University of Leeds, UK.

relate to these aims and the tensions between them. It is questionable whether any comparative law exercise could engage with the normative dimensions behind this. It seems that other theoretical contributions would be necessary in addition.

Thus, this chapter aims to show that comparative law is capable of providing critique and analysis of law-making and judicial activity. Such critique seems invaluable in reconciling EU harmonisation with the traditions of Member States, which again may well be a precondition for achieving the policy aims mentioned earlier. It will first establish a notion of critical comparative law, by showing how comparative law may be capable of providing critique and analysis of law-making through judicial and legislative activity at a European level. This will be followed by discussing a few examples of how comparative law is actually used in relation to EU harmonisation through case law, legislation and 'soft law'. It will then consider whether and how these uses would change under a critical approach to comparative law, as well as expanded, before we reach a tentative conclusion.

NOTION OF CRITICAL COMPARATIVE LAW IN RELATION TO EUROPEAN HARMONISATION

Conventional vs Critical Comparative Law

Still a useful dualism?

The distinction between conventional and critical comparative law (and legal studies[1]) runs through many publications on the subject.[2] Although this may seem a rather rough categorisation, maintaining it appears useful, if only for heuristic purposes and for developing future directions of comparative law (Örücü 2004: 203).

The distinction between conventional and critical comparative law starts from dualisms that are so familiar in legal reasoning.[3] One of these – possibly the most important one[4] – is the perceived antagonism between similarity and

---

[1] The double notion of 'comparative law and legal studies' is used by Nelken (2007). Notions used in lieu of 'Conventional comparative law' approaches include traditional approaches.

[2] Notions used in lieu of 'Conventional Comparative Law' include 'Traditional Comparative Law' and 'Mainstream Comparative Law' (see Örücü 2004, 203).

[3] An unusual but useful overview can be found in Leskiewicz (2007).

[4] At least it is one with a long history, as van Gerven reminds us: 'should we pay heed to Montesquieu's warning who, after having analysed the laws of various countries, concluded that, although all laws referred to the same principles of justice, it was better

difference. Viewed from this perspective, conventional approaches to comparative law seem to pursue an agenda of similarity, which can take different forms. The proposition that only similar systems can be fruitfully compared is one of these. It has been the basis for 'families of law', and has often led to restricting comparison to within a family (Dannemann 2006: 387). Conventional approaches are also characterised as interested in evaluating different solutions to perceived similar demands (Michaels 2006: 307). This again leads many of them to pursue an agenda of unifying the law (Zimmerman 2006), which may lead to stressing similarity between legal orders at the expense of acknowledging diversity. Critical comparative law, on the other hand, would acknowledge multiplicity as an inevitable and actually positive characteristic of an increasingly global world (at least in the absence of imperialism and colonialism). Critical comparative law is then characterised by looking for diversity, rather than similarity, and by not shying away from comparing law from different backgrounds (Örücü 1999).

Another duality is that of law in the books and law in action. If that duality were used, conventional comparative law would be comparing legal texts, whereas critical comparative law would compare contexts. It is questionable whether a pure 'black letter approach' to comparative law is upheld nowadays. Even conventional approaches to comparative law do not restrict themselves to analysing statutory or constitutional texts exclusively. For one, comparative lawyers have always considered legal concepts in their historical context (Jansen 2006: 308). Also, functionalist approaches to comparative law refer to socio-legal methodology (Riles 2006: 780–83). However, it may still be possible to distinguish between conventional comparison restricted to texts and traditional legal contexts, such as adjudication, and critical comparativists taking into account more contexts, expanding their research towards socio-legal and linguistic methodologies. It includes interdisciplinary approaches, such as socio-legal approaches (Riles 2006) and cultural-legal discourses (Cotterell 2006). This places functionalist comparative law with its many facets between the camps or in different ones, though.[5]

Much of the discussion summarised rather crudely above has been voiced as a criticism of functionalism as one of the leading methods of comparative law

---

to preserve diversity in laws and forms of government and religion, given the large diversity of historical experience, cultural tradition and geographical location? Or should we rather follow Condorcet who, thirty years later, in his commentary on Montesquieu's *Esprit des Lois*, wrote that "a good law must be good for all men, as a true proposition is true for all"'. (van Gerven 2005: 4, references omitted).

[5] For example, Zweigert and Kötz demand to consider law in action (Zweigert and Kötz 1996: 5, 11), which can be traced back to Durkheimian or classical functionalism (Michaels 2006: 349–50).

(Frankenberg 1985). This again has led to reviews of the functional method (Michaels 2006: 352–5). Similarly, the structuralist approach to comparative law may even form a basis for 'new' critical comparative law (Mattei 2006: 825–7). A theory of 'transplants' as the base of comparative law can be used in different directions. Some use the notion of transplants to maintain that convergence of legal orders is impossible, or at least difficult (Legrand 1999), while others refer to the phenomenon of transplantation as contributing to approximating legal cultures (Graziadei 2006). This critique reveals some merit of the contention that the different directions of comparative law may actually be converging (Dannemann 2006: 391–6); and the future of comparative law may well lie in a less controversial approach (Husa 2003; Örücü 2004, 203–22).

Conventional comparative law and European integration

There is also truth in the contention that conventional approaches to comparative law have been dominant in contributing to European legal integration and harmonisation of laws (Örücü 2007: 51).

The classical treatise on functionalist comparative law clearly saw one of the main functions of the discipline in contributing to unification of law, *inter alia* in the framework of the European Union (Zweigert and Kötz 1996: 27). They also stressed that in modern times such uses should not be confined to advising the legislator, but that a more realistic way to unification of law will be to create a common legal culture between Europe's lawyers, which would induce courts to base their reasoning on legal ideas from other jurisdictions within this sphere (Zweigert and Kötz 1996: 28).[6]

This approach would suggest a number of practical uses of comparative law within the EU law harmonisation project. One, comparison is used in order to determine whether Member States' legal rules and rules demanded by European legislation are sufficiently similar for the Member States to discharge their obligations. Two, the European Court of Justice would use comparative law in order to establish rules that are not defined in the founding Treaties or secondary legislation. Three, comparative law could be used to advise the EU legislator.

The use of comparative law by the European Court of Justice seems to have captured more theoretical attention than its use for assessing Member States' compliance or preparing EU legislation (Kiikeri 2001: 100–62, Lennaerts 2003). Unsurprisingly, the Court makes use of comparative law in its reasoning for the purpose of interpreting EU law and establishing its content in the numerous

---

[6] Depending on the definition, the latter would encompass harmonisation and not only unification in a strict sense. The difference between the two has been characterised as follows: unification aims to substitute several legal systems by one single system, whereas harmonisation only seeks to approximate legal systems or sets of norms by eliminating major differences and creating minimum requirements (de Cruz 2007: 24).

cases when there is no clear determination of this by Treaties or secondary law (Lennaerts 2003: 873). In order for EU law to remain autonomous from national legal orders, the use of comparative law by the EU judge is not without risks (Kiikeri 2001: 100). Explicit recourse to national law might also reveal overreliance on some national legal cultures, which would require a convincing reason (Kiikeri 2001: 119; on influences of French, German and English law: de Cruz 2007: 160–64). This may be the reason for its uses in the judgments often being hidden, while the Advocates General make more extensive use of comparative law (Lennaerts 2003: 875). Above all, it also implies that the CJEU will always use comparative law as a tool to find a uniform meaning, or as inspiration for finding 'the' EU law. This again implies that striving for uniformity will be the natural tendency of the Court when using comparative law. The Court has even rejected the use of comparative law if it did not find sufficient convergence of legal orders (Kiikeri 2001: 115–18 with examples).

Uses of comparative law in legislation are often initiated by the European Commission. In fields such as employment law and discrimination law, but also in company law and tort law, extensive studies of a comparative nature are sometimes conducted in preparation for EU legislation. Naturally, these tend to be geared towards finding best solutions or a common core. Sometimes, a legislative instrument may be rejected because there is not sufficient convergence. On the other hand, this may be the reason to devise a legal instrument based on the assumption that harmonisation is necessary to overcome barriers to establishing transnational markets. One of the most recent projects in this regard is harmonisation of private law beyond specific fields such as consumer law. The Commission has encouraged a large network of academics to draft a 'European civil code', while the Commission itself only wished to generate legislation rounding off the 'consumer aquis'.

We can see that motives for using comparative law in European harmonisation projects are more conducive to supporting an agenda of uniformity, a striving towards unity, and a disregard of differences. Although, as we have seen, projects in this tradition will occasionally point out divergences, their main concern is with harmonisation and convergence. This again can be seen as a continuation of the functionalist project in a conventional sense (Cotterell 2007: 145–7).

Critique of the conventional approach in relation to EU law
The danger of enhancing convergence (or even assimilation) between legal norms in Europe through excessive conventionalism in the use of comparative law by European harmonisation has not remained without criticism.[7]

---

[7] One strand of critique is based on law and economics arguments, and promotes diversity of legal solutions under the notion of a competition of legal orders, labelled

One of the most eloquent critics of the European harmonisation project has been Pierre Legrand, in whose view legal orders in Europe are not converging and should not converge. The ensuing critique of any assimiliationist[8] harmonisation project starts from a 'comparative law and culture' perspective (Legrand 1999) and proceeds to a line of argument that posits market-driven harmonisation against culturally conscientious legal diversity (Legrand 2006). Legrand's principled opposition to any harmonisation of law within Europe has been subject to criticism (Cotterell 2007: 138–45), while the proposal not to disregard differences in legal cultures in which legal norms are embedded is supported (Cotterell 2007: 145–6; Smits 2007: 228). Criticism of conventionalist comparative law as used within the EU harmonisation project has rightly pointed to overly assimilatory tendencies, but has been accused of being unable to offer a comprehensive comparative law method as an alternative (Cotterell 2007: 151–2). One possible contribution is a critical approach to possibilities of 'transplants' (Graziadei 2006: 470–74). Critiques of increasing conventionalism in comparative law inspired by EU harmonisation projects would seem to be able to offer a more intellectually challenging, and more rewarding approach to comparative law within the European harmonisation project. However, there are as yet few practical examples of such studies.

Aim of this chapter
It is hardly necessary to repeat the many reports on the factual uses of comparative law in EU law. The story of the success of a (revised) functional method has been well told (Örücü 2007; Cotterell 2007, each with further references). The aim of this chapter is different. It considers whether it is possible to establish a critique of European harmonisation using comparative law. In other words, it discusses whether critical comparative law can contribute anything to harmonisation theory. Using the notion of critical comparative law, this chapter does thus not aspire to classify comparative law at large. Its aim is rather to provide a critical approach to the questions whether and how far harmonisation is desirable or useful in order to achieve the wider aims of European integration. In this

---

'regulatory competition'. This strand will not be pursued here (for an overview which doubts whether 'Comparative Law and Economics' is a truly distinctive approach to comparative law see Faust 2006). The attempt to found such a distinctive approach was made by Mattei 1997. On some critical evaluation see Schiek 2003. It should be noted that regulatory competition of legal orders has also been viewed as a method of converging different laws, as competition is assumed to reveal the best solution for a certain problem (Smits 2007: 235).

[8]   The analogy between the convergence/difference debate in comparative law and the assimilation/multiculturalism debate in discourses on dealing with (ethnic) diversity is used by Cotterell (2007: 136–9).

regard, critical comparative law is still a useful notion, albeit with some clarifications.

Applied Comparative Law as a Critical Method of Legal Research

Being applied to European harmonisation, comparative law is transformed 'from a purely persuasive and cognitive area of law to one which was to perform a regulatory task of strategic importance' (Barbera and Caruso 2007: 10). At first sight, it may seem questionable whether applied comparative law can be critical at the same time. However, any critique that is not applied to real-world phenomena risks becoming conservative in the literal sense (Mattei and Robilant 2002). If critical comparative law strives to contribute to the European harmonisation theory, its tasks would then be to provide a critique of European harmonisation which is in touch with practical consequences of its application.

Leading questions behind any critique of European harmonisation would include whether harmonisation will contribute to the wider aims of the EU (see Article 3 TEU), or whether it increases the degree to which the EU contributes to a peaceful world-wide legal order. Comparative law, be it critical or not, can only contribute to this in a meta-sphere. To achieve any of the aims internally to the EU, harmonisation needs truly to harmonise legal concepts instead of imposing non-transferable ones, and remain modest in its aims. There is some argument that this would be aided by a considerate approach to national legal cultures. The notion of reflexivity has been used in this regard by several authors (Nelken 2007; Kiikeri). Reflexivity between the European legal order (which increasingly develops its own style) and national legal orders requires (Örücü 2004) harmonisation projects to be tuned with the national legal orders. This might help to avoid unwanted side-effects and to enhance acceptance of harmonisation throughout the Community.

When critical comparative law emerged in the 1980s and 1990s, its proponents were understandably preoccupied with criticising existing methodology. They have in turn been criticised for not providing an alternative one (Mattei 2006; Peters and Schwenke 2000). The critique of conventional comparative law is valuable even without a methodology, as it proposes a different mindset for comparative research, which will be outlined in the next paragraph. In order to be an applied science, critical comparative law is in need of some methodological instruments that enable it to contribute to its aims, which will be outlined after that.

As regards the mindset of comparativists, critical comparative law demands that they should not be positioned on one side of any of the issues posed by the harmonisation project from the outset. For example, comparative law should not take camp with either similarity or diversity as aims of its research. In other words, critical comparative law should start neither from a general assumption that national laws in Europe need to assimilate, nor from a general assumption that they should not be converging or that convergence is indeed impossible. While there are, without any doubt, differences between European national laws in their social and cultural embeddings, it has been argued that European legal systems are rather similar, if compared to legal cultures in other parts of the world (Cotterell 2007: 144). It has even been argued that for European law truly to become a major legal tradition it needs to be complex, and thus accept diversity within its realm (Glenn 2007: 354[9]). Thus, it seems futile to insist on national laws being either fundamentally divergent or convergent. It also seems unlikely that the need for convergence and divergence is the same in all fields of law, or economy, or society. Above all, the aim to approximate the laws of Member States does not necessarily mean that all differences must be squashed by policies of assimilation. Indeed, any policy of assimilation may be at odds with the initial aims of European integration, which was ultimately inspired by maintaining peace in Europe. Thus, in each single field balanced proposals as to in which aspects to maintain difference and in which regards to achieve unification should be made. This means that applied critical comparative law needs to establish a balanced approach to the sameness and difference debate.

In terms of methodology, critical comparative law needs to take into account the ideological framework and style of legal systems – or even legal cultures – as well as socio-legal factors. The latter would seem to include taking a perspective as wide as possible on socio-economic functions of certain pieces of legislation. Although functionalism is often conventional, it may well be capable of being developed into a critical approach by using adequate socio-legal methodology (Scheiwe 2000). This may be of particular use for comparative law to provide an applicable critique of European harmonisation. If providing guidance on a harmonisation project, methodological scrutiny is thus very important. The typical form of guidance (whether taken in the realm of judicial or statutory lawmaking) would start from a question whether a certain field of law is regulated in the same or different ways in different Member States. Formulating this question, the comparative lawyer should be wary of remaining within fields of law as doctrinally defined. This would risk missing the social and/or cultural embedding of the field. Thus, even if in one Member State a certain type of legal rule does not exist or is less elaborated than in other Member States, there may be a different institution or mechanism to achieve the aims pursued by this particular type of legal rule in other Member States.

While this may seem rather straightforward, comparative law studies are not always conducted in this way. For example, a recent study on a common

---

[9]   It should be noted that Patrick Glenn does not categorise Europe as one legal tradition, but distinguishes between civil and common law traditions.

framework of reference for compensation of victims of road accidents (Kadner Graziano and Oerthe 2008) considers the Spanish system difficult fully to integrate, as its legislation establishes specific sums for certain heads of damages in these cases ('*barema*'). The authors rather uncritically consider that the *barema* would automatically produce under-compensation. Their deliberations are devoid of considering the socio-legal context of the rule. Possibly, Spanish victims of road accidents might be covered by different systems from just damages under the law of torts to cover their losses. The comprehensive system of Spanish health care as well as obligatory insurance for the professions against loss of earnings comes to mind. Looking at the problem from this wider perspective may well lead to different conclusions. Kadner Graziano and Oertel advocate that compensation for road accidents in tort law needs to be harmonised in order fully to compensate victims for any loss. A wider perspective that takes into account different sources of means to cope with the consequences of road accidents may still lead to the conclusion that there should be some European harmonisation. After all, road accidents will often involve people from different Member States, and thus have a transnational dimension. However, if harmonisation is needed at all, harmonisation of welfare rules may well be considered in addition to tort law harmonisation. Also, co-ordination of the different national systems for compensating victims may be more adequate than harmonisation.

This section closes with a short and possibly incomplete working definition of applied critical comparative law in relation to European harmonisation. Applied critical comparative law is characterised by a mindset as well as by methodological principles. The mindset required to be a true critic includes impartiality towards the harmonisation project in so far as approximation and unification of laws is not a value in itself – maintaining diversity is just as valuable. Methodological principles would include considering law in context rather than exclusively in the books. These contexts are still national in large parts, but will become increasingly transnational or even EU-wide. Contexts to be considered go beyond socio-economic factors and should include different styles of legal cultures in Europe, including the style of EU law in its interaction with national legal styles. Used in this way, critical comparative law may be able to contribute to reflexivity of European harmonisation. Such reflexivity would ensure that harmonised law reflects socio-legal contexts and cultures in Member States, and is thus more easily accepted as well as equipped to achieve its goals.

CRITICAL USES OF COMPARATIVE LAW IN EU HARMONISATION – WHAT CHANGE?

This chapter cannot offer a fully-fledged analysis of all uses of comparative law in European lawmaking through case law and legislation. The purpose of this section is merely meant to give a taste of what, if anything, would change if critical comparative law were applied. The modest aspiration of these paragraphs is to highlight a few instances. The themes of these are not chosen with any claim to representativity. They are rather meant highlighting the issues against the background of rather recent developments in fields where the author can claim to have the contextual knowledge to give at least an inkling of what applied critical comparative law may be able to contribute to European harmonisation.

Current Uses of Comparative Law in EU Harmonisation – Some Examples

Case law of the CJEU

The Court of Justice of the European Union (CJEU) case law is an important part of the harmonisation project when the CJEU fulfils its task to give an authoritative interpretation of EU law, as well when it establishes general principles of EC law. In both instances, the case law amounts to instances of lawmaking.

It is well known that the Court in developing general principles of EU law first applied its specific comparative method of EU law (Lennaerts 2003). Using this method, the CJEU not only refers to national legal orders as an inspiration for general principles of EU law. It also reserves the right to evaluate the different national conceptions it finds by choosing 'from each of the Member States those solutions which, having regard to the objects of the Treaty, appear to be the best' (GA Lagrange opinion in Case 14/61 *Hoogovens* [1962] ECR 253). It is well known that the CJEU relies mainly on the arguments of its Advocates General in its case law. While the CJEU decisions themselves often do not reveal the extent to which the Court has actually relied on comparative arguments, the opinions of the AG are often much more elaborate.

The chosen fields for highlighting uses of comparative law for European harmonisation are (collective) labour law and discrimination (or equality) law. In both fields, there is younger case law in which comparative reasoning was actually used. As ever, this is more present in the opinions of the AGs than in the reasoning of the Court.

Comparative arguments and collective labour rights   The field of collective labour rights is particularly interesting as an example for several reasons. There is a general assumption throughout comparative labour law that collective labour law is difficult, if not impossible, to harmonise, given its cultural embedding in national law (Kahn-Freund 1974, 24–6). Also, the EU competences regarding collective labour rights are constructed confusingly. While Article 153 (1) TFEU provides for an EU competence for 'representation and collective defence of the interests of workers and employers, including co-determination', Article 137(5) EC excludes the right of association, and the right to collective action from Community competences. Accordingly, any perceived conflict between collective labour rights (which indeed include the right to strike and freedom of association under international obligations of most Member States) and directly binding Community legislation (such as competition rules and fundamental freedoms) will have to be resolved by the ECJ. Use of comparative law may be quite difficult here, as traditions in Member States are far from converging.

Albany Drijvende Bokken (C–67/96 [1999] ECR I–5757)
The *Albany* case posed a nearly classical example for these conflicts, a perceived clash between collective labour agreements and the prohibition of cartels in Article 101 TFEU. The case also concerned a number of other issues which will be disregarded in the following. The argument that any or some collective labour agreements will amount to illegal cartels has been raised in a number of, but not in all, Member States of the EC. Those defending such a view would consider that the consent to the collective agreement is also an agreement between the undertakings or their association bound by it, and as such an agreement between businesses or a decision by an association of undertakings. Those defending the opposite view would usually point to the fundamental importance of collective bargaining, and the human rights guarantees behind it, in order to defend a full or partial exemption of collective labour agreements from competition law.

Advocate General Jacobs provided extensive comparative reasoning in his opinion on this, which is sometimes praised as exemplary (Reich 2005: 29). He used comparative arguments for his analysis of the question whether collective labour agreements should be subject to review by cartel authorities. He compared the legal order of five out of (then) 15 Member States (France, Finland, Germany, Denmark and the UK) and the United States of America, omitting the legal order in which the case had developed (the Netherlands), and Sweden, although both these Member States had submitted statements to the Court. His analysis included case law and statute, as considered appropriate in each of the legal orders examined. He did not, however, consider academic writing and the socio-economic embedding of the court cases he analysed. His conclusion was that the legal orders of the Member States were diverse, although in all of them 'collective agreements ... are to some extent sheltered from the prohibition of anticompetitive cartels' (No 109 of the opinion). There is only scant reference to this result in the final reasoning of the AG. He rejects the existence of a fundamental right to bargain collectively, as there was no 'sufficient convergence'

(No 160). He also takes his comparative overview as proof that there is always a tension between collective bargaining and competition law (No 178). His conclusion that 'Article [81] EC [now Article 101 TFEU] cannot be applied to collective agreements ... on core subjects such as wages and other working conditions' (No 179), 'which do not directly affect third markets and third parties' (No 194) replicates in fact some older case law from Germany and also from the US, but there is no reference to this in the reasoning.

AG Jacobs' reasoning has been characterised as traditional (Kiikeri 2001: 225), in that it does not explicitly consider the socio-economic and legal-cultural background of the court cases discussed, and not even reflect on the rooting of AG Jacobs himself in a certain legal-cultural background that lends itself to reasoning by analogy (again, Kiikeri 2001: 225, 227). This opinion provoked a counter study, commissioned by a Swedish research institute (COLCOM 2001), as the Swedish system of industrial relations would obviously be fundamentally threatened by a Community law system of content control of collective agreements at national level. The COLCOM study not only provided an overview of more legal orders (11 out of 15, including the Netherlands, Sweden, Belgium, Austria, Italy and Spain in addition to those chosen by AG Jacobs). Although based on a questionnaire in the common core tradition, it also considered the socio-legal background in describing the collective bargaining system and the system of enforcing a prohibition of cartels. The study thus went a few steps towards critical approaches to comparative law.

As is well known, the restrictive approach of Jacobs has not been followed by the Court. The Court held that collective agreements may 'by virtue of their nature and purpose' be regarded as falling outside the scope of Article 101 TFEU. This formula was obviously rather vague, and quickly became subject to divergent interpretations in literature. The CJEU did also did not offer any explicit comparative reasoning for its result. It referred to the objectives pursued by the EU and the Member States within the framework of social policy (improved living and working conditions, social protection, dialogue and development of human resources with a view to high employment and the combating of exclusion, No 57). The reasoning of the Court also relied on the fact that competition policy and social policy are on an equal footing in the EU Treaties, as are the aims of promoting a balanced development of economic activities and social protection (No 54). Although the Court's reasoning is regrettably short, these few references could be read as taking into account wider policy contexts of both competition law and legal rules regarding collective agreements. Thus, while less comparative, the Court could be considered to have been more critical.

Laval (C–341/05); ITWF and FSU v Viking (C–438/05)

The relation of directly applicable Community economic law to collective labour rights also arose in the much discussed *Laval* and *Viking* cases. In both cases, an undertaking relied on its rights derived from the four freedoms under Community law in order to have a national court find collective action by trade unions illegal. In the *Laval* case other issues were also at stake, which will be disregarded here. Again, in both cases the main issue at stake was the relation of EU economic law and collective labour agreement, this time relating to the fundamental economic freedoms guaranteed by the EU Treaties. In the *Laval* case, an Estonian undertaking relied on its right to provide services across the border to Sweden against the Swedish construction workers' union and its allies. These unions had launched collective action in the form of a boycott in order to convince the Estonian undertaking to pay its Estonian workers wages as agreed in Swedish collective agreements. The case was fought before a Swedish court. In the *Viking* case, a Finnish shipping company, VIKING, sought an order by an English court to declare void a boycott by the International Transport Workers' Federation and the Finnish Seafarers' Union. This boycott was directed against the company's plan to move its corporate domicile from Finland to Estonia and to pay its crews wages at Estonian rates in the future. The boycott only aimed at the continued application of Finnish collective agreements, not at hindering the company in moving its corporate domicile. These cases would have offered themselves for comparative reasoning for two reasons. On the one hand, the Scandinavian countries, Denmark and Sweden, had insisted that the constitutionally protected rights to collective action should not have been restricted through EU law, as the EU had no competence in this very field. The ensuing comparative question could have been whether the Member States' legal orders would imply such reasoning. Second, the question whether a fundamental right to collective action deserves protection at EU level is once again a question for a general principle of EU law. To derive such principles, the EU Treaty refers to common traditions of the Member States (see also Article 6 (3) TEU).

Despite all this, comparative reasoning is not very developed in the CJEU decisions and the Opinions of the Advocates General. Both Advocates General conclude that a right to strike must be acknowledged as a fundamental right under Community law. Both base this conclusion on fundamental rights instruments. Maduro refers solely to the Charter of Fundamental Rights of the European Union as 'reaffirming' this right (No 60 of his Opinion), thus avoiding the question of its exact base. Mengozzi refers to international law instruments, mainly the ESC, which he considers as having attained a new relevance with the new wording of Article 136 EC (now Article 151 TFEU) after the Treaty of Amsterdam (No 66 and 74 of his Opinion). He only makes a cursory reference to the texts of a number of constitutions of Member States, stating that given the strength of the basis for the right to strike this is not really necessary (No 77 of his Opinion). It could be said that the reasoning of AG Jacobs in *Albany*, which seemed to use comparative law as a mere background or decorative argument, is taken to its logical conclusion in the Opinions in these cases, by leaving out reference to comparative reasoning altogether.

Both AGs came to the conclusion that it is the task of the national courts, in Finland, the UK and Sweden respectively, imposed by Community law, to consider the proportionality of collective action by trade unions and to decide on its legality. None of the Advocates General thought it necessary to employ comparative considerations as regards the juridification (*Verrechtlichung*) of collective labour disputes in the Member States, which may ultimately allow the restriction of the right to strike.[10] Arguably, he thus did not appreciate how much lawyers and citizens from England and also from Ireland would be alienated by his conclusion, that the legality of a strike should be assessed by courts, more specifically by the CJEU in relation to its partitioning effects on markets, and by the national courts in relation to the applicable domestic rules.

A right to equal treatment as a fundamental principle of Community law   There is a wide range of CJEU case law relying on equal treatment of persons as a fundamental principle of Community law, mostly in relation to gender equality. Following legislation on other discriminations in 2000, the first cases on other grounds are emerging. Three have already concerned equal treatment irrespective of age, two in relation to disability, and one in relation to race. One would expect comparative reasoning in such cases.

Mangold (C–144/04 [2005] ECR I–9981)

The decision in *Mangold* was the first to establish a right not to be discriminated against on grounds of age. There has been some argument whether this statement was a mere obiter dictum or really relevant for the decision, which shall not be discussed here (Schiek 2006). Here, AG Tizziano had proposed to decide the case using a general equality clause as a principle of Community law which was derived from former case law, but without using comparative arguments (No 83 of his Opinion).

In this decision, the ECJ did not follow the conclusions of AG Tizziano. However, the Court still concluded that there is a general principle of discrimination on grounds of age, *inter alia* referring to the common constitutional traditions of the Member States, without any comparative reasoning to support this claim.

Palacio de la Villa (C–411/05 [2007] ECR I–8531)

Unsurprisingly, the decision was criticised *inter alia* based on this shortcoming. AG Mazak, in his Opinion in the *Palacios* case, based this critique on comparative arguments. He *inter alia* contended that only a few constitutions of Member

---

10   For a critique see Novitz (2006).

States, among them the Finnish constitution, actually contained an explicit prohibition of discrimination on grounds of age. He then went on that there is a clear convergence between the Member States' constitutions and international agreements in guaranteeing a general principle of equal treatment. Further, he argued (without having recourse to specific national traditions or readings of this principle) that it does not necessarily extend to a principle of non-discrimination on grounds of age. He added that for the purpose of practicability any conclusion towards specific principles of non-discrimination should not be made (No 88–99). As AG Mazak had invited the Court to decide the case on the basis of Directive 2000/78/EC exclusively, there was no need for the Court to engage with his reasoning in relation to the general principle.

Again, this use of comparative law seems rather conventional. AG Mazak compares mainly constitutional texts, not even the actual application of the constitution by courts. The latter might have resulted in finding some applications of a principle of non-discrimination in relation to age. Any further socio-economic arguments might have supported the conclusion that with ageing societies the issue of age discrimination is becoming more and more relevant.

Bartsch (C–427/06 [2008] ECR I–7245)

In her Opinion in Bartsch, AG Sharpstone contradicts Mazak, and argues for upholding the *Mangold* principle. She starts with some comparative reasoning as a basis for her initial thesis that a principle of equal treatment is a common constitutional tradition of Member States, and is for this reason acknowledged as a general principle of Community law. This comparative analysis is again rather conventional, in that it is based on constitutional texts alone. This is followed by a jurisprudential analysis of that principle, based *inter alia* on historical reflections as well as jurisprudential writing from the US and on international law, concluding that a principle of equal treatment is meaningless if it does not specify in relation to which traits equal treatment must be guaranteed. The opportunity to dig deeper into the legal orders of Member States which maintain more emanations of a prohibition of age discrimination on the field of employment and social security law than the Finnish constitution is missed. In this regard, Sharpstone could have compared constitutional case law from a number of Member States, or even legislation or employment case law from others as well. The conclusion may well have been that there is an evolving consensus that a general principle of equal treatment contradicts unreasonable discrimination on grounds of age. The Court did not decide the case on the substance, because the conflict emerged long before Directive 2000/78/EC was due for implementation, and there was no other connection to EU law. Thus, Sharpstone's opinion became less influential than could have been expected.

Summary

These few examples have illuminated uses of comparative reasoning by the CJEU and its Advocates General. These reasonings were mostly rather conventional, in that they relied on texts generated by legislators and courts. Even if this is fleshed out by reference to jurisprudential arguments, as in the opinion of AG Sharpstone in *Bartsch*, a contextual analysis of the concepts analysed within national law is not provided. As the example of *Viking* shows, this may lead to the CJEU case law ultimately losing its moral authority in Member States.

Harmonisation Through Legislation and 'Soft Law'

Legislation through directives

As regards legislative harmonisation, comparative law is used quite frequently. The field of non-discrimination law can be cited as one example. Two comparative studies, from 1992 and 2000 respectively, were commissioned to explore the legacy of prohibiting racial harmonisation in the Member States (European Commission 1992 and 2000), prior to establishing a prohibition of racial discrimination by directive in employment law, social law, and also provision of goods and services.[11] Both studies were based on a purely textual approach to comparison, limited to establishing which Member States prohibited racial discrimination in which fields of law. No assessment was made of different legal traditions or different ideologies behind the different approaches to combating racism, and no discussion of these approaches in the social contexts of the Member States. Unsurprisingly, discrimination law is a field of law where, as Bob Hepple puts it, the technique of uncritical transplantation of a legal concept, taken out of its social context, and not considering its further developments, has occurred (Hepple 2004; see also Schiek et al. 2007; Schiek 2007). Of course, especially in the field of non-discrimination law, a binding obligation on Member States to establish a prohibition of discrimination in the market place is of tantamount importance. However, modelling the relevant directives in the smallest detail upon traditions in only a few Member States is bound to produce unwanted side-effects, which will lower the level of protection available in some Member States.

For example, the definition of direct discrimination repeats the comparator concept which has been developed in English law with its traditional 'concentration on matters of procedure at the expense of matters of substance' (Ibbetson 1998: 235). Although the comparator concept also taints much case law and

---

[11]   Commission of the European Communities, *Report on the Member States' legal provisions to combat discrimination* (2000), available at http://ec.europa.eu/ employment_social/labour_law/docs/reportmsdiscrimination_en.pdf.

legal reasoning on equality even in continental jurisdictions, most of these also acknowledge other methods of establishing a causal relationship between detriment and a trait on the grounds of which one should not be discriminated against. Aping the English concept, EU equality law reduces the rights granted in these continental legal orders.

As another example of legislative harmonisation, we can cite European consumer law. In this field, harmonisation was more often than not policy driven, based on the 'information paradigm' or reference to consumer confidence, which harmonisation purported to strengthen. This argument was also used for justifying maximum harmonisation, which attracted the critique of Thomas Wilhelmsson in relation to insufficiently taking into account socio-legal contexts in several Member States:

> In more general terms, a functioning consumer protection needs to have a close understanding of the expectations of consumers and the prevailing consumer culture. These are not uniform throughout the Union. As has been shown by many, the consumer expectations concerning protects are quite different in Northern and Southern Europe … and the variations will become still greater with the accession of the new Member States in 2004 … . It is easy to see that total harmonisation measures in such an environment most certainly would bring consumer law of the internal market further away from the expectations and culture prevailing in at least some of the national markets. This again would rather decrease than increase the confidence of consumers in their local market place and perhaps as a consequence also in the internal market as a whole [Wilhelmsson 2004: 328].

Again, we can see a limited use of critical comparative law. In one instance, comparative law is restricted to black letter approaches; in the other instance, while there is a conceptual background, there is insufficient analysis of real life background in all Member States.

The open method of coordination (and similar instruments)

Before considering the usage of comparative law arguments within the Open Method of Coordination (OMC), some explanation is needed. Considering the OMC in relation to European harmonisation could provoke criticism. After all, the method is usually based on soft law, and not on legal obligations to harmonise. It focuses on defining common goals for Member States and setting into motion a bench-marking process. During these processes best practices can be developed in accordance with national traditions, as long as the benchmarks are achieved. Although the OMC usually is based on what traditionally is considered as soft law, it is surprisingly effective in promoting convergence. In relation to employment protection, Biagi noted that the common ideology of raising employment figures by deregulation had been rather effective in lowering employment protection standards throughout the Community, without binding measures being taken (Biagi 2000).

The method originated in the field of coordinating economic policies, but is today most developed in employment policies. Indeed, since the Treaty of Nice, Article 137 EC provides that coordination of policies between Member States (where using OMC is implicit) is to be preferred over harmonisation by legislation (Barnard 2006: 71).

The OMC lends itself as an instrument to balance unity and diversity of national systems (Sciarra 2004: 15; Barbera and Caruso 2007: 18), and has been characterised as one of the ways to implement 'machinery for learning from diversity thereby transforming an obstacle to closer integration into an asset for achieving it', thus establishing the third way in European governance (Sabel and Zeitlin 2008: 281). The method is based on a comparison of policies, and such comparison is said to be rather functional than institutional or textual (Sabel and Zeitlin 2008: 285). This would suggest that comparative law is used in a critical, contextual way in applying this method. But is this really the case? Let us consider two examples.

As the OMC has its home in employment law, one would suspect that the uses of comparative law are most developed in this realm. Indeed, given the diversity of labour law across Member States, spontaneous convergence may well be a precondition for successful harmonisation (Bercusson 2008). Such harmonisation may well be aided by OMC procedures. Again, comparative law skills may aid a successful OMC in this respect.

As the OMC is mainly driven by the European Commission, any comparative law activities are also driven by this body. In the field of employment law, interesting cross-communications between the more policy-oriented field of employment policy and the field of employment law are developing. These are also a field for comparative research. One of the much-debated programmatic outputs of the European Commission in the field of employment law, its 2007 Green Paper for the Future of Labour Law (COM 2007), was actually based on a few comparative studies. Following the 'Supiot Report' of 1998 on the 'Future of Labour Law in Europe', the Sciarra Report on 'The evolution of Labour Law' (1992–2002) established a detailed description of developments in Member States, duly informed by socio-legal background studies (Sciarra 2004b; Supiot 1998). These endeavours are not neccessarily mirrored in ensuing Commission documents, in this case the Green Paper on the Future of Labour law. While it recommended to the Member States to consider certain policy models for adoption in their own countries, due regard to socio-legal and legal-cultural embeddings was not always given. For example, the Green Paper recommends adopting the 'Danish model' of labour law, which it characterises as giving up individual rights to employment protection in favour of a high level of social security in cases of dismissal, combined with an active labour market policy. The Green Paper fails to acknowledge that a pre-condition for the functioning of the 'Danish model' is the control of unemployment insurance by the trade unions, as well as a strong role of these unions in general, accompanied by strong rights for collective action.

In the field of contract law harmonisation, van Gerven has characterised the current policy towards a Common Framework of Reference as a first step towards developing an OMC methodology in this field (van Gerven 2005). There are some shortcomings. First of all, the institutional elements of the OMC are certainly not formally applied in the process. Also, while the studies for a common framework of reference are based on academic work of a comparative character, much of these seem to be based on a preference for unification. The underlying thesis thus seems to be that convergence without upholding diversity should be preferred. On the other hand, the regulatory approach to the Common Framework of Reference for European Private Law is one which would uphold diversity. Difference should prevail in hard core legislation, while the CFR only serves as a backdrop for those who wish to use something other than a common frame.

Summary

Our deliberations have demonstrated that in supporting Community legislation comparative law arguments are not always used in the elaborated way that would be required by the critical approach to comparative law sketched above. Having said this, we must acknowledge that the Open Method of Coordination seems to offer opportunities for reflexive uses of comparative law, as have been advocated by Nelken in reflecting on comparative law and culture (Nelken 2007). Such comparative law needs to be reflective of social contexts and legal styles. These are ingredients that only a critical approach to comparative law can achieve.

What Change? And Further Perspectives

We have seen that approaches to comparative law in CJEU case law, legislation and soft law harmonisation are very different. What would change if the role of critical comparative law were expanded in this? The following only attempts to flesh this out in a bare outline.

Comparative Law and Harmonisation Through Case Law

The exemplary cases: Fundamental freedoms and fundamental rights, fundamental principles of law In relation to CJEU case law, a more critical use of comparative law arguments might well enhance acceptance of the case law, or – if used in AGs' Opinions – better enable the Court to appreciate the acceptance of its judgments or potential disruptions caused by these. In the examples discussed above, a more critical approach would have prompted the Advocates General (and possibly also the Court) to consider the embedding of the national legislation and case law they compared in their socio-economic background. They would also have considered the style of the legal orders (to avoid using the notion of formants). Thus, in relation to collective labour rights, the analysis of Member States' legal orders should have included not only legal texts, but also questions such as the real potential of collective actors to safeguard balancing social and economic rights. This could have induced the Court to appreciate the relative strengths of unions and employers with and without the means of collective action in different socio-economic realities. In addition to the insight that in transnational cases employees need to be able to use transnational collective action (Maduro in his Opinion in *ITWF, SFU & Viking*[12], No 70), this would have led to some insights into the effects of obliging national courts to subject trade unions' actions to a test of proportionality.

In the cases relating to equality law and a principle of non-discrimination on grounds of age, the comparative arguments are partly only implicit (*Mangold*), partly fully confined to conventional, textual comparison, partly enhanced by jurisprudential arguments. Applying a more critical comparative approach, the comparativist would have examined the socio-economic background more thoroughly. Such socio-economic arguments might have supported the conclusion that with ageing societies the issue of age discrimination becomes more and more relevant. Relating this back to case law analysis, aided by a discussion of styles of legal cultures, one might question why some legal cultures prefer to respond to ageing through discrimination law, and whether others adequately protect the ageing population. This may well lead to different, or at least diversified, solutions – although the author personally is convinced that discrimination reasoning would be able to address some problems that other reasoning would miss out on.

Potential other cases   Of course, comparative law can also be used in other cases before the CJEU. The CJEU also interprets EU legislation that aims at harmonising national laws. In this regard, considering comparative arguments may be helpful, in that they may enhance effectiveness and acceptance of EU law. Much EU legislation amounts to transplanting legal concepts of one legal order to another. Such endeavour is not necessarily doomed to failure. However, attention must be paid to the different institutions and mechanisms that may in different Member States lead to similar results. This may require a careful analysis of any 'source' legal order and in relation to the question how EU law notions must best be read in order to achieve maximum harmonisation with regard to the differences of this legal order from other legal orders. To enable successful legal transplanting against a background of diversity, it seems that

---

[12]   ECJ 18 December 2007, C–438/05.

careful judicial reasoning, including critical comparative deliberations, would be a precondition.

Before national courts, there is the issue of interpreting national legislation that has been issued in relation to Community law. Interpreting and applying national law is not the task of the CJEU, but rather of national courts. Just as the CJEU would be best advised to take into account the specific structures and the specific culture of that legal order from which the Community law concept has been derived, the national judge should also pursue a comparative assessment of its own. Such assessment would include isolating the specific cultural backgrounds from 'source legal orders', distilling such aims and concepts from the directives that are the kernel of their objectives, and adapting them to the national court's legal system as necessary.

Comparative law, community legislation and the OMC

Adding more critical arguments to the legislative process in EU law would require a more contextual analysis of national legal orders. Thus, before the EU legislator decides to use a certain national model for EU-wide regulation, the embedding of the legal texts in a specific socio-economic environment should be analysed carefully, and different approaches should be evaluated equally carefully. In this regard, the OMC clearly offers some advantages. These advantages derive from the reflexive of comparative law, which is typical for the OMC. While not aiming at hard legal obligations to harmonise, the OMC initiates processes of mutual learning, which again will induce a more considerate approach to foreign legal concepts.

It is questionable whether the reflexive use of comparative law, which may develop in OMC procedures, should not also be possible in relation to harmonisation by directives. When comparing the result of harmonisation activities of the EU legislator, a wide variety of institutional arrangements to enforce employment rights leads to vastly different impacts of actual harmonisation (Malmberg *et al.* 2004). This has led to demands of new methods for comparative law within the context of European harmonisation, *inter alia* stressing the need to view law in context and regard the socio-legal system in which a specific legislative aim is embedded (Malmberg *et al.*, 293–4; Riles, 2006, 790–92). Also, Article 249 EC does not, in any way, envisage the detailed method of regulation by directive as has become the practice in many fields of Community law. On the contrary, the provision envisages that the Community legislator only fixes an aim to be achieved, and leaves the means to such achievement to the Member States. Varga demands only to unify 'the components of legal cultures ... which are of a sine qua non instrumental character in respect to the fundamental target the realisation of which has, by all means to be guaranteed' (Varga 1992: 408). It seems that the original conception of a directive would be ideally suited to achieve this aim.

CONCLUSION

Traditional approaches to comparative law, when applied in specific harmonisation projects, will almost inevitably tend to recommend overly intense unification, based on the false hope that legal transplants do not meet obstacles if harmonisation is focused on such elements where a common core or best regulation exists.

Critical approaches to comparative law, contextualising legal rules both in their social function and the specific style of a legal culture, have a greater potential of contributing to strengthening necessary convergence between European legal orders while reinforcing such diversity that will ultimately further the acceptance of European legal integration. The term 'reflexive convergence' may be a suitable catchword to characterise such a process, which is based on a contextualised reception of diverse national (or even regional) laws.

Certainly, harmonisation processes aided in such a way by critical comparative law would lead to maintaining diversity in more cases than the more conventional style of comparison which is frequently used for real harmonisation projects. After all, universalism colouring traditional comparative law is at odds with the original aims of the European Economic Community and the ongoing aspirations of the EU to build and maintain peace. Also, with multiple enlargements, the EU now not only combines civil law and common law, but also the former socialist legal families, which are of course developing into new diversity (Kühn 2006). It is questionable, whether these can be unified by anything other than a new imperialism (Mattei 2003).

To a certain degree, European harmonisation can also be promoted on the basis of critical comparative law. For example, from Glenn's new edition (2007) of *Legal Traditions of the World* one could take the notion that complex legal traditions are a precondition for reconciling traditions, and that a complex legal tradition needs to reconcile different contradicting trends within it. While risking overestimating the relevance of law to society, the thought of reconciling legal traditions as a contribution towards reconciling people is intriguing. Glenn's complex tradition would seem to imply the development of new forms of harmonisation which enable reconcilability. This may well mean that differences should remain. On a similar line, Nelken argues that Europe as a project of harmonisation is designed to produce more tolerance of difference, advocating an alternative vision of harmonisation as opposed to unification (Nelken 2007).

The story of a happy reunion between European harmonisation and critical comparative law still waits to be written. It seems a worthwhile endeavour to do so, both with regard to European harmonisation without alienating large parts of the population, as well as with regard to European harmonisation as a model for non-imperialist harmonisation in other regions of the world.

REFERENCES

Barbera, M. & Caruso, B. (2007), 'In Search of a New Language: Italian Labour Law Scholarship in the Face of European Integration', Jean Monnet Working Paper 11/07 NYU School of Law & Universita degli Studi di Trento.

Barnard, C. (2006), *EC Employment Law* (3rd ed. Oxford: OUP).

Bercusson, B. (2008), 'Lessons for Transnational Labour Regulation From a Case Study of Temporary Agency Work in the EU', in Ahlberg, K., Bercusson, B., Bruun, N., Kountouros, H., Vigneau, C. and Zappalà, L. (eds.), *Transnational Labour Regulation. A Study of Temporary Agency Work* (Brussels et al: Lang).

Biagi, M. (2000), 'L'impatto della European Employment Stategy sul rualo del diritto del lavoro e delle relazioni industriali', *Rivista italiana di diritto di lavoro*, 414.

COLCOM (2001), 'Collective Bargaining and Competition in the EU', the Report of the COLCOM-project (Brawn, N. and Hellsten, J. (eds) Uppsala: Justus).

Commission of the European Communities (1992), *Legal Instruments to Combat Racism and Xenophobia* (Luxembourg: Office for the Official Publications of the European Communities).

Commission of the European Communities (2000), *Report on the Member States' legal provisions to combat discrimination*, available at: http://ec.europa.eu/employment_social/labour_law/docs/reportmsdiscrimination_en.pdf.

Commission of the European Communities (2007), 'Modernising Labour Law to Meet the Challenges of the 21st Century' (COM(2007)627 fin).

Cotterell, R. (2006), 'Comparative Law and Legal Culture', in Reimann, M. and Zimmermann, R. (eds), *The Oxford Handbook of Comparative Law* (Oxford: OUP), 709–38.

Cotterell, R. (2007), 'Is it so bad to be different? Comparative Law and the Appreciation of Diversity', in: Nelken and Örücü (eds), *Comparative Law. A Handbook* (Oxford: Hart), 133–54.

Dannemann, G. (2006), 'Comparative Law: Study of Similarities or Differences?' in: Reimann, M. and Zimmermann, R. (eds), *The Oxford Handbook of Comparative Law* (Oxford: OUP), 384–419.

De Cruz, P. (2007), *Comparative Law in a Changing World* (3rd edn, London & New York, Routledge Cavendish.

Faust, F. (2006), 'Economic Analysis of Law', in Reimann, M. and Zimmermann, R. (eds), *The Oxford Handbook of Comparative Law* (Oxford: OUP), 837–65.

Frankenberg, G. (1985), 'Critical Comparison: Re-thinking Comparative Law', 26 *Harvard International Law Journal*, 411–45.

Gerven, W. van (2005), 'Bringing (Private) Laws Closer to Each Other at the European Level', available at www.law.kuleuven.ac.be/ccle/pdf/2005-01-18_WvG_.Impact_courts_on_private_law.pdf.

Glenn, P. (2007), *Legal Traditions of The World* (3rd edn, Oxford: OUP).

Graziadei, M. (2006), 'Comparative Law as the Study of Transplants and Receptions', in Reimann, M. and Zimmerman, R. (eds), *The Oxford Handbook on Comparative Law* (Oxford: OUP), 441–75.

Hepple, B. (2004), 'Race and Law in Fortress Europe', 67 *Modern Law Review*, 1–15.

Husa, J. (2003), 'Farewell to Functionalism or Methodological Tolerance?', 67 *RabelsZ*, 419–7.

Ibbetson, D.J. (1998), 'A Reply to Professor Zimmermann' in Watkin, T.G. (ed.), *The Europeanisation of Law*, United Kingdom Comparative Law Series Vol: 18 (London, BIICL 1998), 224–9.

Jansen, N. (2006), 'Comparative Law and Comparative Knowledge', in Reimann, M. and Zimmermann, R. (eds), *Oxford Handbook of Comparative Law* (Oxford: OUP), 305–37.

Kadner Graziano, Th. and Oertel, C. (2008), 'Ein Europäisches Haftungs- und Schadensrecht für Unfälle im Straßenverkehr? Eckpunkte de lege lata und Überlegungen de lege ferenda', 107 *Zeitschrift für vergleichende Rechtswissenschaft* 113–62.

Kahn-Freund, O. (1974), 'On Uses and Misuses of Comparative Law', 47(1) *Modern Law Review* 1–27.

Kiikeri, M. (2001), *Comparative Legal Reasoning and European Law* (Dordrecht: Kluwer).

Kühn, (2006), 'Development of Comparative Law in Central and Eastern Europe', in Reimann, M. and Zimmermann, R. (eds), *Oxford Handbook of Comparative Law* (Oxford: OUP), 215–35.

Legrand, P. (1999), *Fragments of Law and Culture* (Deventer: WEJ Tjeenk Wilink).

Legrand, P. (2006), 'Antivonbar' 1 *Journal of Comparative Law* 13.

Lennaerts, K. (2003), 'Interlocking Legal Orders in the European Union and Comparative Law', 52 *International and Comparative Law Quarterly* (2003), 873–906.

Leskiewicz, M. (2007), 'Comparative Law Methodology, Legal Culture, and Epistemology of Law', *ALSPA net* (www.alpsa.net/documents/comparativeLeskiewicz.pdf).

Malmberg, J. (ed) (2003), *Effective Enforcement of EC Labour Law* (The Hague *et al.*, Kluwer International).

Mattei, U. (1997), *Comparative Law and Economics* (Michigan: University of Michigan Press).

Mattei, U. (2003), 'A Theory of Imperial Law: A Study on U.S. Hegemony and the Latin Resistance',10 *Indiana Journal of Global Legal Studies* 383–448.

Mattei, U. (2006), 'Comparative Law and Critical Legal Studies', in Reimann, M. and Zimmermann, R. (eds), *The Oxford Handbook of Comparative Law* (Oxford: OUP), 816–36.

Mattei, U. & Robilant, A. di (2002), 'The Art and Science of Critical Scholarship. Postmodernism and International Style in the Legal Architecure of Europe', 1 *European Review of Private Law* 29–59.

Michaels, R. (2006) 'The Functional Method of Comparative Law', in Reimann, M. and Zimmerman, R. (eds), *The Oxford Handbook of Comparative Law* (Oxford: OUP) 339–82.

Nelken, D. (2007), 'Comparative Law and Legal Studies', in Nelken and Örücü (eds), *Comparative Law. A Handbook* (Oxford: Hart), 3–42.

Novitz, T. (2006), 'The right to strike and reflagging in the European Union: free movement provisions and human rights', *Lloyd's Maritime and Commercial Law Quarterly*, 243–56.

Örücü, E. (2000), 'Critical Comparative Law: Considering Paradoxes for Legal Systems in Transition', 4.1 *Critical Electronic Journal of Comparative Law 4*, http://www.ejcl.org/41/abs41-1.html.

Örücü, E. (2004), (2004), *The Enigma of Comparative Law* (Leiden: Martinus Nijhoff).

Örücü, E. (2007), 'Developing Comparative Law', in Nelken and Örücü (eds), *Comparative Law. A Handbook* (Oxford, Hart), 43–65.

Peters, A. & Schwenke, H. (2000), 'Comparative Law Beyond Post-Modernism', 49 *International and Comparative Law Quarterly*, 803–34.

Reich, N. (2005), *Understanding EU Law* (2nd edn, Antwerp: Intersentia).

Riles, A. (2006), 'Comparative Law and Socio-Legal Studies', in Reimann, M. and

Zimmermann, R (eds), *The Oxford Handbook of Comparative Law* (Oxford: OUP), 775–813.

Sabel, C. and Zeitlin, J. (2008), 'Learning from Difference: The New Architecture of Experimentalist Governance in the EU', 14 *ELJ* 271–327.

Scheiwe, K. (2000), 'Was ist ein funktionales Äquivalent in der Rechtsvergleichung?' 83 *Kritische Vierteljahresschrift für Gesetzgebung und Rechtswissenschaft* 30–51.

Schiek, D. (2003), 'Comparative Law and Economics. On the Dangers of Interdisciplinary Transplants', in Lichtenberg, H., Scharrelmann, B. Lubach, D., van der Woude I., Scheik D. and Benöhr-Lacquer, S. (eds), *Hanse Law School Cahiers* 3 (Groningen) 49–69.

Schiek, D. (2006), 'The ECJ Decision in *Mangoldt* – a further twist on effects of directives and constitutional relevance of Community equality legislation', 35 (3) *Industrial Law Journal*, 329–41.

Schiek, D., (2007), 'Implementing EU Non-Discrimination Directives. Typologies of legal transplanting' in C. v Schoubroeck & H. Cousy (eds), *Discriminatie in verzekering* (Anwerpen Apeldoorn), 47–83.

Schiek, D., Waddington, L. and Bell, M. (eds) (2007), *Materials, Cases and Text on National, Supranational and International Non-discrimination Law* (Oxford: Hart Publishing).

Sciarra, S. (2004), 'New Discourses in labour law: part-time work and the paradigm of flexibility', in Sciarra, S., Davies, P. and Fredland, M. (eds), *Employment Policy and the Regulation of Part-time Work in the European Union* (Cambridge: Cambridge University Press), 3–33.

Sciarra, S. (2004b), 'The Evolution of Labour Law (1992–2003) General Report' (Brussels: European Commission).

Smits, J. (2007), 'Convergence of Private Law in Europe' in Örücü, E. and Nelken, D. (eds), *Comparative Law. A Handbook* (Oxford et al., Hart), 218–40.

Supiot, A. (1998), 'Transformation of Labour and Future of Labour Law in Europe' (Brussels: European Commission), available at http://metiseurope.eu/content/pdf/n8/15_supiotreport.pdf.

Varga, C. (1992), 'European Integration and the Uniqueness of National Legal Cultures', in de Witte, B. and Forderer, C. (eds), *The Common Law of Europe and the Future of Legal Education* (Deventer: Kluwer), reprinted in ibid. (1994), *Law and Philosophy, Selected Papers in Legal Theory* (Budapest: Larón and Eätuös University) 399–411.

Wilhelmsson, T. (2004), 'The Abuse of the Confident Consumer as a Justification for EU Consumer Law', 27 *Journal of Consumer Policy* 317–37.

Zimmermann, R. (2006), 'Comparative Law and the Europeanization of Private Law', in Reimann, M. & Zimmermann, R. (eds), *The Oxford Handbook of Comparative Law* (Oxford: OUP), 539–77.

Zweigert, K. and Kötz, H. (1996), *Einführung in die Rechtsvergleichung* (3rd edn Tübingen: Mohr).

23. Should the EU be attempting to harmonise national systems of labour law?*

Phil Syrpis**

INTRODUCTION

Throughout the history of European integration, harmonisation has occurred in a piecemeal fashion. Combinations of political factors determine whether particular policy areas become candidates for harmonisation. Likewise, political contingencies dictate not only whether harmonisation initiatives come to fruition, but also the form which any such measures take.

Many of the chapters in this collection address arguments for and against harmonisation of particular aspects of law and practice within the EU. My contention is that it is important to distinguish between the range of principled arguments which may be made both in favour of, and against, various harmonisation initiatives; and on the basis of these distinctions, to attempt to identify criteria which may be used in order to locate those policy areas which may, or may not, be candidates for harmonisation.

The focus of this contribution is labour law. The role of the EU in labour law has always been contentious. There are a number of plausible rationales for EU intervention in domestic labour law. A crucial question is the extent to which these various rationales call for harmonisation or approximation;[1] for the purposes of this chapter, this is taken to involve the elimination (or at least the reduction) of differences between the labour law regimes of the Member States.

---

* A version of this chapter appears in *European Business Law Review* 143 (2010).
** University of Bristol, UK.
[1] It seems that the terms approximation and harmonisation 'are entirely interchangeable'. Dashwood, A (1996), 'The Limits of EC Powers', 21 *European Law Review* 113 at 120. See also Slot, PJ (1996), 'Harmonisation', 21 *European Law Review* 378 at 378; Vignes, D (1990), 'The Harmonisation of National Legislation and the EEC', 15 *European Law Review* 358 at 361; and Pernice, I (1996), 'Constitutional, Federal and Subsidiarity Aspects' in Pernice, I (ed.), *Harmonisation of Legislation in Federal Systems* (Nomos Verlagsgesellschaft) at 10–11.

The structure of this chapter is as follows. The first section discusses the extent to which the Treaties afford the institutions the competence to harmonise in the labour law arena. The second section shifts its focus to the case law of the Court of Justice (including the recent *Viking*, *Laval*, *Rüffert* and *Luxembourg* cases) and explains that, for the Court at least, differences between the labour law regimes of the Member States, exacerbated as they have been by the Eastern enlargement of the EU, are seen as problematic. Some attention is devoted to critiques of the Court's approach. The third, somewhat tentative, section goes on to suggest that, in so far as the case law of the Court is taken as a given, the harmonisation of the labour law regimes of the Member States may provide an attractive option for the legislative institutions; but it also points out the problems which are likely to beset such an approach in the current political climate, in which the views and interests of the Member States diverge significantly.

HARMONISATION IN THE LABOUR LAW FIELD – THE TREATY FRAMEWORK

As we will see in this section, the competence of the EU to act in the labour law field – for example via harmonisation – is contested. There are a number of legal bases which appear to afford European-level institutions the competence to act in the labour law field; but under these legal bases the scope of EU action is restricted, as is the range of objectives which may legitimately be pursued. Moreover, as we shall see, although the wording of the relevant provisions is not perhaps as clear as one might hope for or expect, many of the legal bases under which the EU institutions have acted in the social sphere appear to rule out, or at least caution against, harmonisation. In this section, I examine the boundaries of EU competence, before moving on to consider the rationales for intervention in the labour law arena.[2] The relevant legal bases are also considered in some detail.

My contention is that it is important that the EU, especially in the current climate of popular unease exemplified by the tortuous attempts to find a constitutional settlement which resonates with the citizens of Europe,[3] takes care not to overstep the boundaries of its competence and that it is sensitive to principles, such as subsidiarity and proportionality, respect for which is an important component of good federal governance. The EU is a multi-centred democracy.

---

[2]   The argument in this section is largely based on Syrpis, P (2007), *EU Intervention in Domestic Labour Law* (OUP), Chapters 2 and 3.

[3]   See Dougan, M (2008), 'The Treaty of Lisbon 2007: Winning Minds, not Hearts', 45 *Common Market Law Review* 617, and Syrpis, P (2008), 'The Treaty of Lisbon: Much Ado… But About What?', 37 *Industrial Law Journal* 219.

International units of governance such as the EU, which are still trying to carve out a role for themselves on the world stage, are especially sensitive to legitimacy challenges. It is important that they are able to demonstrate that they are able to 'add value' to policy making processes, and to demonstrate that EU action enables or facilitates the achievement of given goals. Social norms are deeply embedded in the various Member States of the EU. The EU institutions must be able to formulate strong arguments before intervening in any way which might unsettle or destabilise these social norms.

The Boundaries of EU Competence

The EU only has the competence to act in so far as it is granted this power in the Treaties by its constituent Member States. The Treaty of Lisbon reinforces what has been explicit in the Treaties since Maastricht. Article 4 TEU confirms that 'competences not conferred upon the Union in the Treaties remain with the Member States'. Article 5 TEU states that 'the Union shall act only within the limits of the competences conferred upon it by the Member States in the Treaties to attain the objectives set out therein. According to Articles 4 and 5 TEU, Union action must find a legal basis within the Treaty, and must be in conformity with the principles of subsidiarity and proportionality. These twin principles invite the institutions to stop and think before exercising the competence which has been allocated to them in the Treaties.

The subsidiarity principle in Article 5(3) TEU insists that the Union 'shall take action, only if and insofar as the objectives of the proposed action cannot be sufficiently achieved by the Member States either at Central level or at regional and local level, but can rather, by reason of the scale or effects of the proposed action, be better achieved at Union level'. Subsidiarity directs 'a genuine legislative inquiry into the consequences of the Community's refraining from taking a measure that it may legitimately take, in deference to the Member States' capacity to accomplish the same objectives'.[4] Unless there are clear benefits associated with European level intervention, subsidiarity asks that the EU refrain from taking action. The principle, appropriately in my view given the difficulties in establishing the legitimacy of Community level intervention, 'systematically places the burden of proof on the proponents of Community action'.[5] Nevertheless, the principle may be criticised. It takes as its starting point the objectives of the proposed action. It does not acknowledge that the

---

[4]   Bermann, G (1994), 'Taking Subsidiarity Seriously: Federalism in the European Community and the United States', 94 *Columbia Law Review* 331 at 335.

[5]   Ibid. at 453. See also De Búrca, G (1999), 'Reappraising Subsidiarity's Significance After Amsterdam', Harvard Jean Monnet Working Paper 7/99 at 8.

EU and the Member States may have different objectives.[6] The result of this is that although the principle is able to operate well where there is a coincidence between the objectives of the EU and those of the Member States, it does not operate well where there may be a clash. The effect of this is to reduce the value of the principle in certain situations; for example those in which there is a clash between the dictates of the internal market and particular national labour law rules.

According to Article 5(4) TEU, 'under the principle of proportionality the content and form of Union action shall not exceed what is necessary to achieve the objectives of the Treaties'. In order for the principle to be satisfied, it must be shown that action at the European level is suitable for the purpose of attaining the objective pursued, and that it does not go beyond what is necessary to achieve it. Proportionality defines the permissible extent of European level action. 'Every proposed measure must be scrutinised to see whether it could do its job in a way that would be less obtrusive or burdensome for the Member States.'[7] It may be argued that this principle militates against harmonisation – where the EU can achieve its objectives in a way which leaves greater scope for national autonomy, proportionality suggests that such a course of action should be preferred.

Three Rationales for Intervention in the Labour Law Arena

Having examined the principles which create the boundaries of permissible EU action, the rationales upon which European intervention in the labour law field may plausibly be said to be based are explored. In my taxonomy, there are three – these are termed 'integrationist', 'economic' and 'social'. The three rationales are reflected in the Preamble to the Treaty on European Union, in which, at Lisbon, the Heads of State and Government stated that they were 'determined to promote economic and social progress for their peoples … within the context of the accomplishment of the internal market'. This statement is typical of the approach of the institutions, which too often claim that tensions between rationales for, and conceptions of, EU labour law do not exist. In contrast, I argue that the three rationales are, in important respects, distinct. A strong commitment to, for example, the social rationale is likely to lead to a very different set of

---

[6]   Davies, G (2006), 'Subsidiarity: The Wrong Idea, in the Wrong Place, at the Wrong Time', 43 *Common Market Law Review* 63. At 67–8, he argues as follows: '[s]ubsidiarity misses the point. Its central flaw is that instead of providing a method to balance between Member States and Community interests, which is what is needed, it assumes the Community goals, privileges their achievement absolutely, and simply asks who should be the one to do the implementing work'.

[7]   Dashwood, A, *supra* n. 1 at 115.

interventions at EU level in the labour law field from those which would flow from a commitment to the integrationist rationale. Of particular relevance here is that the arguments for and against harmonisation are very different under each of the three plausible rationales for EU intervention. Nevertheless it must be conceded that each of the three rationales is internally contested and that, unsurprisingly, institutional understandings of the three rationales, including of the extent to which the rationales are able to sustain arguments for harmonisation in the labour law field, have altered over time.

The Integrationist Rationale

The rationale which seems to provide the strongest call for harmonisation is the integrationist rationale. Where the EU acts for integrationist reasons, it acts with the aim of establishing, or improving the functioning of, the European market. But, there is little or no agreement over what action is required in order to establish the market in Europe, or to improve its functioning. For a start, there is scope for debate over what it means to 'create', 'open', 'build', 'constitute', 'construct' or 'establish' a market.[8] That much is obvious from the history of European integration. The Treaty of Paris of 1951 establishing a European Coal and Steel Community adopts a different approach from the Treaty of Rome of 1957 establishing a European Economic Community. Within the EEC, the Common Agricultural Policy was based on a fundamentally different understanding of the workings of markets from most of the rest of the Treaty; and EMU has once again altered established thinking. Some economists see an opposition between the market and the state, and view regulation as an exogenous interference with the market mechanism. Others challenge the idea that markets are a separate realm, arguing that they are social constructs, embedded in social relations, constituted by law and social norms.[9] As for the creation of markets, there are those who argue that it is possible, and desirable, for market order to emerge spontaneously, but others who suggest that it is prudent, even necessary, for political institutions to intervene so as to ensure that markets are constituted and organised in particular ways.[10]

---

[8] 'The legal-economic philosophies of European market-building have witnessed seismic shifts from positive to negative integration, and back again, to novel and varied means of "European" re-regulation such as (national) mutual recognition and conjoined (supranational) standard-setting via ad hoc secondary vehicles of market governance such as committees and agencies': Everson, M (2002), 'Adjudicating the Market', 8 *European Law Journal* 152 at 156.

[9] See Polanyi, K (1944), *The Great Transformation* (Beacon Press).

[10] See Egan, M (2001), *Constructing a European Market* (OUP). See also Supiot, A (2000), 'The dogmatic foundations of the market', 29 *Industrial Law Journal* 321.

For the framers of the Treaty it was seen as axiomatic that, through the establishment of a common market, social and economic benefits would result. The Treaty of Rome was premised on theories which claimed that free international trade would bring about a removal of economic and social disparities between different regions.[11] The expectation, following the Spaak and Ohlin reports of the 1950s,[12] was that social advantages would flow from the establishment and functioning of the common market, and that EU level action in the social field would not be required in order to achieve social benefits. There now seems to be less faith in the operation of the market, and more of an acceptance of the need for intervention at the European level in the course of the market building endeavour. But there is still profound disagreement over the nature of the intervention which might be required, and, of particular relevance to the present enquiry, no consensus over the need for harmonisation at European level in the social field. There are advocates of the total harmonisation of national social policies – and there is a certain instinctive appeal to the argument that the internal market either requires, or at least is well served by, the elimination of the differences between the laws of the Member States. But, these arguments for harmonisation have not gone unchallenged. There are, for example, those who argue that the cause of integration calls for no intervention in the social sphere; for many of these it is axiomatic that social advantages will flow automatically from the completion of the common or internal market, perhaps via the process of regulatory competition, without the need for intervention at the European level. In between, there are many other positions, with calls for minimum standard setting, for coordination, and for various forms of 'managed diversity'.

The arguments for harmonisation under the integrationist rationale are reflected not only in the case law of the Court of Justice (as we shall see in the next section below), but also in the text of the Treaty. Under what was, under the Treaty of Rome, Article 100 EEC, for example, the Council is given the power to 'issue directives for the approximation of such laws, regulations or administrative provisions of the Member States as directly affect the establishment or functioning of the common market'. The fact that the institutions are afforded the specific power to *approximate* laws suggests, first, a clear preference for the approximation of laws as a strategy for the establishment and functioning of the market and, second, that measures which do not approximate, or harmonise,

---

[11]   See Giubboni, S (2006) *Social Rights and Market Freedom in the European Constitution – A Labour Law Perspective* (CUP) at 42, commenting in particular on the Ohlin Report. Giubboni argues that the economic constitution of the EC expresses and reflects 'embedded liberalism'.

[12]   The Spaak Report is summarised in (1956) Political and Economic Planning, *Planning* number 405. The Ohlin Report is summarised in (1956) 74 *International Labour Review* 99.

the laws of the Member States cannot be properly based on legal bases such as Article 115 TFEU (exactly the same point can be made in relation to Article 114 TFEU, the old Article 95 EC). However, what has been termed 'minimum harmonisation' has been a feature of European policy under Article 94 EC since the 1970s, including in the labour law arena, and it now seems impossible to question the legality of minimum standard setting (under this method of intervention, the EU institutions set a floor, but permit the Member States to set their own higher standards and to apply them to all those operating within their territory), or of some other flexible forms of EU legislation, under these Articles, on the grounds that 'approximation' or 'harmonisation' *stricto sensu* is not involved.

The Economic and the Social Rationales

The two other plausible rationales for EU intervention in domestic labour law – what I term the 'economic' and the 'social' rationales – appear to have less of a connection with harmonisation. Since Maastricht, it has become clear that the EU has competence to advance economic and social goals, and to do so independently of its core integrationist mission. Under the economic rationale, the EU takes action to improve the performance of the European economy, for example by reducing unemployment, enhancing efficiency or improving Europe's international competitiveness. Combating unemployment and encouraging non-inflationary growth have become central aims of the European Union, and under the so-called 'Lisbon Strategy', launched in 2000, action has been taken at both the Member State and the European level to realise those aims. Interventions based on the social rationale aim to improve the position of workers. While the economic rationale calls for measures which improve the performance of the European economy, the social rationale is concerned with the distribution of the benefits derived from improved economic performance.[13] The social rationale can be conceptualised in a variety of ways. It may, for example, be argued that workers should be protected either from employers or from the vagaries of the market, or that they should be afforded certain rights, perhaps stemming from their status as human beings or EU citizens.

It is worth reflecting a little on the circumstances in which the economic and the social rationales might be thought to call for harmonisation in the labour law

---

[13] 'While everyone would like to have a larger pie, everyone would also like to have a larger share of that pie': Langille, B (1997), 'Eight Ways to think about International Labour Standards', 31 *Journal of World Trade* 27 at 33. The economic rationale is concerned with the size of the pie; the social with ensuring that workers get to eat it. To pursue the analogy too far, integrationist policies are those which bind the pie together.

field. The argument for harmonisation under either of these heads is dependent on showing that a particular labour law standard is required throughout Europe in order to improve economic performance or social welfare. Under the economic rationale, such arguments are unlikely to be successful. The economies of the EU Member States diverge significantly, and, given this, it is likely that a different balance of measures is required in each state to generate improved economic performance. Economic and monetary union may be changing the picture here – in particular for the eurozone Member States – but even within the eurozone, the most appropriate monetary and fiscal policy mix differs from one state to the next. It is somewhat easier to make the case for harmonisation under the social rationale. If social measures are based on workers' status as EU citizens, or indeed on their dignity or humanity, then it may be thought that there would be arguments for similar standards to apply across the EU, or least for a floor of standards to apply across the continent. To the extent that action under the social rationale is linked to the distribution of the benefits of improved economic performance, it is of course likely that different Member States will have different capacities to act.

These intuitions are reflected in the Treaties. While successive Treaty revisions indicate that the economic and the social rationales can legitimately form the foundations for EU intervention, economic and social legal bases are not couched in the same language as, for example, Articles 114 and 115 TFEU. It is clear that there is no competence to harmonise the laws of the Member States under the economic legal bases which have been used in the labour law field, and at least arguable that there is no competence to harmonise under the social provisions of the Treaty.

Since the adoption of the Treaty on European Union in 1992, the EU has acquired the competence to act to improve the performance of the European economy.[14] Typical of the legal bases which have been used in the labour law arena in pursuit of economic objectives are those in the Employment Title of the Treaty (Articles 145–150 TFEU). It is under these legal bases that the European Employment Strategy (EES) has operated since 1997.[15] It is obvious even

---

[14] The Commission endeavours to ensure that 'we do not rely on market forces to resolve the highly complex problems of achieving higher economic and employment performance': Commission White Paper (1993), 'Growth, Competitiveness, Employment: The challenges and ways forward into the 21st century', COM(93)700 at 16.

[15] The Employment Title was introduced by the Treaty of Amsterdam, which came into force only in 1999. In December 1997, the European Council 'decided that the relevant provisions of the new Title on employment in the Treaty of Amsterdam are to be put into effect immediately'; ensuring that the EES would come into being before the ratification of the Treaty of Amsterdam. See Luxembourg European Council, Presidency Conclusions, 12 and 13 December 1997, paragraph 3.

from a cursory reading of these provisions that the competence to intervene is tightly constrained. The institutions are not afforded the competence to harmonise national laws;[16] they are in fact not even afforded the competence to enact binding legislation. Instead, their role is to coordinate the employment policies of the Member States under what has come to be known as the open method of coordination (or OMC).[17]

The key point is that the OMC does not result in the elimination of differences between the laws and practices of the Member States. Within the confines of the guidelines set at European level, the Member States retain the freedom to pursue their own policies. Indeed, the method relies on differences in approach, explicitly seeking to learn lessons from the variety of strategies adopted by different Member States.

The need for European level action in the social field was first acknowledged in the 1970s.[18] But it was only in the mid to late 1980s that the tide turned decisively. This section discusses the uneven way in which this competence has developed, focusing on Articles 151 and 153 TFEU. These Articles reflect a profound uncertainty as to the modalities of intervention best suited to the realisation of social objectives.

Article 151 TFEU outlines the objectives of the EU and the Member States in the social field. It provides that the Union and the Member States:

> **having in mind fundamental social rights such as those set out in the European Social Charter signed at Turin on 18 October 1961** and in the 1989 Community Charter of the Fundamental Rights of Workers, shall have as their objectives the promotion of employment, improved living and working conditions, *so as to make possible their harmonisation while the improvement is being maintained*, proper social protection, dialogue between management and labour, the development of human resources with a view to lasting high employment and the combating of exclusion.
>
> To this end the Union and the Member States shall implement measures which take account of the diverse forms of national practices, in particular in the field of contractual relations, and the need to maintain the competitiveness of the Community economy.
>
> *They believe that such a development will ensue not only from the functioning of the common market, which will favour the harmonisation of social systems, but also from*

---

[16] Article 129 EC specifically excludes 'harmonisation of the laws and regulations of the Member States'.

[17] Lisbon European Council, Presidency Conclusions, 23 and 24 March 2000, paragraph 37.

[18] See Hepple, B (1987), 'The Crisis in EEC Labour Law', 16 *Industrial Law Journal* 77 at 79: 'the official turning point was the declaration of Heads of Governments in October 1972'.

the procedures provided for in the Treaties and from the approximation of provisions laid down by law, regulation or administrative action.[19]

In the sections which are based on the old Article 117 EEC, Article 151 TFEU refers to the harmonisation of living and working conditions, even the harmonisation of social systems. These references to harmonisation were not included in the Agreement on Social Policy attached to the Treaty on European Union, and they do not appear to be consistent either with the requirement, also in Article 151 TFEU, that the Union and the Member States take account of the diverse forms of national practices, or with the statement that provisions adopted under Article 153 TFEU 'shall not prevent Member States from maintaining or introducing more stringent protective measures compatible with the Treaties'.[20] This confusion between harmonisation and minimum standard-setting – and the text of Article 151 TFEU is an illustration of an all too common tendency – is unwelcome. It points to difficulties both in conceptualising the social rationale, and also in reconciling the social and integrationist rationales. These are issues to which I return below.

With a view to achieving the objectives of Article 151 TFEU, the Community is given specific competences in Article 153 TFEU. Article 153 TFEU describes the types of EU intervention which are permitted in particular policy areas, and lays down the accompanying policy-making procedures. Under Article 153(2) TFEU, the Council may act in one of two ways. First, under Article 153(2)(a) TFEU, added only in 2000 at Nice, it 'may adopt measures designed to encourage cooperation between Member States through initiatives aimed at improving knowledge, developing exchanges of information and best practices, promoting innovative approaches and evaluating experiences, excluding any harmonisation of the laws and regulations of the Member States'. This provision has paved the way for the development of OMC processes in the social field.[21]

Second, under Article 153(2)(b) TFEU, it may adopt 'by means of directives, minimum requirements for gradual implementation, having regard to the conditions and technical rules obtaining in each of the Member States'. In some areas, the 'codecision' procedure applies, while in others the Council can only act unanimously, after consulting the European Parliament and the relevant committees.[22] The final paragraphs of Article 153 TFEU place some restrictions on the competence of the institutions. Article 153(4) TFEU states that provisions adopted

---

[19]   The section in bold was introduced at Amsterdam. The sections in italics are from the old Article 117 EC. The remaining sections are from the Agreement on Social Policy.

[20]   Article 137(4) EC.

[21]   See Szyszczak, E (2006), 'Experimental Governance: The Open Method of Co-ordination', 12 *European Law Journal* 486.

[22]   See Article 137(1) and (2) EC.

pursuant to Article 153 'shall not affect the right of Member States to define the fundamental principles of their social security systems and must not significantly affect the financial equilibrium thereof',[23] and also, as mentioned above, that they 'shall not prevent Member States from maintaining or introducing more stringent protective measures compatible with the Treaties'. Finally, Article 153(5) TFEU provides that 'the provisions of this Article shall not apply to pay, the right of association, the right to strike or the right to impose lock-outs'.

To summarise, the EU's competence to act in the labour law field is restricted. The subsidiarity and proportionality principles invite the institutions to consider carefully whether they should use the competences allocated to them in the Treaties. The three most plausible rationales for EU intervention in the labour law field point in different directions. Under the integrationist rationale, the EU has the competence to harmonise in order to assist in the establishment and functioning of the market; though there is a lively debate on the need for harmonisation in the labour law field. Many argue that harmonisation is un-necessary, and that the operation of the market mechanism will lead to desired improvements in social provision across Europe. Under the economic and social rationales, the preferred modalities of intervention are more flexible, and more tolerant of, even embracing of, diversity. The Treaties provide authority for both coordination strategies and minimum standard setting, and arguably goes so far as to rule out harmonisation. Thus, it appears that if one is to make a case for the harmonisation of national systems of labour law, it will be one which is, at least principally, based on the integrationist rationale.

This perhaps invites a closer consideration of the relationship between the integrationist and the economic and the social rationales. The key point is that the integrationist rationale is of a different order from the economic and social rationales. The Treaties make it clear that integration is pursued, not as an end in itself, but rather as a means through which other – essentially economic or social – ends are to be realised. The ultimate objectives of intervention under the integrationist rationale are economic and/or social. Thus, the distinction between, on the one hand, the integrationist and, on the other, the economic and social rationales is rather subtle. The distinction is between the achievement of economic and social objectives through the pursuit of European integration (such intervention is termed integrationist), and the achievement of the same objectives through other means (such intervention is termed economic and/or social). This insight leaves the competence to harmonise in the labour law field looking rather precarious. While competence to harmonise clearly exists under the integrationist rationale, there are strong arguments against the exercise of that competence. First, the principles of subsidiarity and proportionality appear

---

[23]   Article 137(4) EC as amended by the Treaty of Nice.

to counsel caution; and, second, to the extent that integration is pursued not for its own sake but for what are ultimately economic and social objectives, there are questions about whether we should be heading towards harmonisation.

In fact, the legislative institutions have shown that, at least in the labour law arena, they favour a strategy based not on harmonisation, but on much more flexible intervention. The legislative institutions have not sought to intervene in domestic labour law in order to eliminate disparities between the various national regimes. In fact, the Commission has stated that 'the total harmonisation of social policies is not an objective of the Community or the Union';[24] and there were no proposals for the harmonisation of any aspect of labour law in the Social Policy Agenda of either 2000 or 2005.[25]

One account of this suggests that, contrary to appearances, the EU institutions retain the desire or aspiration to harmonise the labour law rules of the Member States. Harmonisation has not, however, occurred, quite simply because the relevant actors have gradually come to appreciate that there is no realistic chance of attaining political consensus on a harmonised system of labour law, in particular as Europe has evolved from a Community of six relatively homogeneous Member States, towards today's much more heterogeneous Union of 27. According to this account, today's more flexible approaches are the product of irreconcilable differences between the Member States, and represent no more than second-best solutions to the problems facing the Union. Those pointing to the advantages of diversity, and seeking to promote differentiation within the framework of the EU, are simply doing their best to make a virtue out of political necessity.

An alternative account shifts attention to the institutions' views of the market building endeavour. As has already been noted, the creation of a single European market is not straightforward.

> At its highest level of abstraction, the question is surely whether the objective of economic integration, as first pronounced in 1957 and subsequently reaffirmed, really requires an approximation of national provisions in the social sphere in particular, to the point where the regulatory structure of the Community resembles that of a single State.[26]

---

[24] See Commission (1995), 'Medium Term Social Action Programme 1995–97', COM(95)134 at 2.

[25] Commission Communication (2000), 'Social Policy Agenda', COM(2000)379, and Commission (2005), 'Communication on the Social Agenda', COM(2005)33. See also the more recent Commission Green Paper (2006), 'Modernising Labour Law to Meet the Challenges of the 21st Century', COM(2006)708; and Commission Communication (2007), 'Towards Common Principles of Flexicurity: More and Better Jobs through Flexibility and Security', COM(2007)359.

[26] Simitis, S and Lyon-Caen, A (1996), 'Community Labour Law: A Critical Introduction to its History' in Davies, P *et al.* (eds), *European Community Labour Law: Principles and Perspectives; Liber Amicorum Lord Wedderburn* (Clarendon Press) at 5.

Simitis and Lyon-Caen, writing in 1996, argued that 'Community experience to date supports the thesis that no such approximation is necessary'.[27] It may be that the political institutions share this view of the integrationist rationale and that they are prepared to countenance the maintenance of diversity between national labour law systems, confident that the differences do not put the functioning of the internal market at risk.

THE CASE LAW OF THE COURT OF JUSTICE

In the first section, there was no mention of the case law of the Court of Justice. What will become apparent in this section is that the approach adopted by the Court of Justice in its internal market case law is inconsistent with the Spaak and Ohlin reports' understanding of the integrationist rationale, which, as we saw above, was endorsed by Simitis and Lyon-Caen. The Court's view appears to be that differences between national labour laws *are* problematic, in that the differences create barriers to free movement. Once a barrier to free movement has been identified – and the argument advanced here is that the logic of the Court's approach means that any difference between the laws and practices of the various Member States may be characterised as a barrier in the relevant sense – Member States and trade unions are forced to justify their interventions in the labour law arena according to EU law criteria. As a result of the case law of the Court, it is also clear that justifying laws and practices which are capable of having a chilling effect on trade is no straightforward task. The Court's recent case law has provoked an angry reaction, in particular among trade unionists in the EU-15. This section explains the Court's approach to differences between national labour laws and practices. The concluding section of this chapter explores the ramifications for harmonisation.

In *Dassonville*, the Court of Justice held that 'all trading rules enacted by Member States which are capable of hindering, directly or indirectly, actually or potentially, intra-Community trade' fall within the scope of what is now Article 34 TFEU.[28] Under the *Dassonville* line of authority, which applies not only to the free movement of goods but also to the other freedoms,[29] the key question appears to be whether the trading rules in question affect access to markets in other Member States.

If enterprises may elect not to move to Member States in which corporate and labour laws and practices may put an extra burden on their cost structures, or

---

[27]   Ibid.

[28]   Case 8/74 *Dassonville* [1974] ECR 837, paragraph 5.

[29]   See e.g. Case C–5594 *Gebhard* [1995] ECR I–4565, paragraph 37; Case C–415/93 *Bosman* [1995] ECR I–4921, paragraph 103; and Case C–384/93 *Alpine Investments* [1995] ECR I–1141, paragraph 38.

(and this is an option which has not been canvassed before the Court as much as it might) if workers may elect not to move to Member States in which their rights are not protected to the same extent or in the same way as in their home state – and note that under *Dassonville*, potential and indirect effects on trade suffice – the relevant national rules will be held to be capable of amounting to barriers to free movement. Given that both enterprises (in the context of the free establishment and the freedom to provide services) and workers (in the context of the free movement of workers) are able to challenge the legality of national labour law rules, it is not only states with low labour standards, but also those with high labour standards, which may find that their rules are challenged.

Under the case law of the Court, once they are classified as barriers to free movement, national labour law rules are vulnerable. There is an onus on Member States to justify the rules according to EU law criteria. The states must show that domestic rules serve legitimate objectives, and that they satisfy a proportionality test (i.e. they must show that they do not impose any greater restriction on free movement than is necessary for the achievement of the legitimate objectives).

Notwithstanding this line of authority, for many years the Court was able to avoid conflicts between internal market norms and national labour laws. In *Rush Portuguesa*, it felt able to hold that 'Community law does not preclude Member States from extending their legislation, or collective labour agreements entered into by both sides of industry, to any person who is employed, even temporarily, within their territory, no matter in which country the employer is established'.[30] In *Albany International*, in similar vein, it held that collective negotiations between management and labour must 'by virtue of their nature and purpose' be regarded as falling outside the scope of the competition law provisions of the Treaties.[31] While the precise rationales for these holdings is much debated, one is surely entitled to draw the inference that the Court was reluctant to expose national labour laws to scrutiny at the behest of those exploiting the opportunities for movement within the internal market.[32] However, the *Viking* and *Laval* cases,[33] especially when taken together with the later cases of *Rüffert*

---

[30] Case C–113/89 *Rush Portuguesa* [1990] ECR I–1417, paragraph 18.

[31] Case C–67/96 *Albany International* [1999] ECR I–5751, paragraph 60. For a fuller discussion of the Court's approach to 'distortions of competition' see Syrpis, P, *supra* n. 2, Chapters 2 and 4.

[32] See also Case C–190/98 *Graf* [2000] ECR I–493, paragraph 25, in which the Court held that the effect of the legislation at issue in the case, which related to entitlements to compensation on termination of employment, was 'too uncertain and indirect', and was therefore able to conclude that Article 39 EC did not preclude the application of the national provisions in question.

[33] Case C–438/05 *Viking* [2007] ECR I–10779, and Case C–341/05 *Laval* [2007] ECR I–11767. For full analyses of the two cases see Syrpis, P and Novitz, T (2008),

and *Luxembourg*,[34] destroy any cosy assumptions to the effect that labour law may in some way be insulated from the internal market case law of the Court.

In principle, both workers and employers benefit from the free movement provisions of the Treaties. EU law allows both workers and employers to invite judicial scrutiny of practices which restrict their free movement rights. However, as part of the political compromise surrounding the enlargements of 2004 and 2007, the rights of migrant workers from Eastern Europe were, on a transitional basis, restricted by many EU-15 Member States.[35] No similar restrictions applied to the free movement rights of employers; and, predictably, many of the leading cases have been brought at the behest of employers from Eastern Europe, in which labour law standards are typically much lower than those in the EU-15, who have sought to benefit from the freedoms afforded by the Treaties and who have challenged various aspects of the labour law systems of the EU-15.

Let me use the *Laval* case as the central example. The *Laval* case (like *Rüffert* and *Luxembourg*) was made more interesting because of the impact of the Posted Workers Directive 96/71EC.[36] Laval, a company incorporated under Latvian law, posted workers to a construction site at Vaxholm in Sweden.[37] Laval had signed a collective agreement with the Latvian building sector's trade union in Latvia, which entailed lower terms and conditions than those prevailing in Sweden. Swedish trade unions responded by taking industrial action, including boycotts of supplies to the Vaxholm site. Laval brought an action in the Swedish courts in order to obtain a declaration that this action was unlawful, and orders that such action should cease and that compensation be paid. The questions referred to the Court of Justice concerned the implementation of the Posted Workers Direc-

---

'Economic and social rights in conflict: Political and judicial approaches to their reconciliation', 33 *European Law Review* 411, and Davies, A (2008), 'One Step Forward, Two Steps Back? The *Viking* and *Laval* Cases in the ECJ', 37 *Industrial Law Journal* 126.

[34]   Case C–346/06 (2008) ECR I–1989 *Rüffert*, judgment of 3 April 2008, and Case C–319/06 (2008) ECR I–4323 *Commission v. Luxembourg*, judgment of 19 June 2008. On Case C–346/06 *Rüffert* see Davies, P (2008), 37 *Industrial Law Journal* 293.

[35]   See Carrera, S (2005), 'What Does Free Movement Mean in Theory and Practice in an Enlarged EU?', 11 *European Law Journal* 699; Novitz, T (2006–07), 'Labour Rights as Human Rights: Implications for Employers' Free Movement in an Enlarged European Union', 9 *The Cambridge Yearbook of European Legal Studies* 357; and Ryan, B (2008), 'The Accession (Immigration and Worker Authorisation) Regulations 2006', 37 *Industrial Law Journal* 111.

[36]   Directive 96/71/EC of the European Parliament and of the Council of 16 December 1996 concerning the posting of workers in the framework of the provision of services [1997] OJ L18/1.

[37]   See Deakin, S (2007–08), 'Regulatory Competition after *Laval*', 10 *Cambridge Yearbook of European Legal Studies* 711. He (at 723) makes the point that 'the transnational element is marginal or tangential to the dispute at issue'.

tive in Sweden and the scope of the right to take industrial action to attempt to force a service provider to grant posted workers better terms and conditions of employment under Article 49 EC (now Article 56 TFEU).

As explained above, the main thrust of the Court's case law catches all measures which are liable to restrict trade, or, to put this in different ways, to render the exercise of free movement rights less attractive, or to affect market access. This is the orthodox approach, applied by the Court in the *Laval* case; what was innovative and hugely controversial was the Court's decision to apply Article 49 EC to the actions of trade unions as well as the actions of states.[38] The Court held that the right of trade unions to take collective action 'is liable to make it less attractive, or more difficult, for such undertakings to carry out construction work in Sweden, and therefore constitutes a restriction on the freedom to provide services within the meaning of Article 49 EC'.[39] Given that it is difficult, if not impossible, to conceive of labour law rules and practices which would not be caught by this formulation, the breadth of the approach is startling.

It is perhaps worth pointing out that there are other cases, discussed below, in which the Court has, albeit unsystematically, shown a readiness not to apply the full force of the *Dassonville* reasoning. In these cases, the Court must have calculated that it is best not to subject particular practices to scrutiny, presumably on the ground that the impact on freedom of movement is not substantial enough to merit judicial involvement.

First, in the *Keck* case, in the specific context of national provisions restricting or prohibiting certain selling arrangements, the Court held that national rules fall outside the scope of the free movement provisions because their application to the sale of products from other Member States 'is not by nature such as to prevent their access to the market or to impede access any more than it impedes the access of domestic products'.[40] Were the *Keck* test to be used to assess whether labour law rules or trade union action constitute barriers to free movement, the Court would have to determine whether they either (i) 'prevent' access to markets, or (ii) impede the access of imported factors of production in a discriminatory way. The first limb of the *Keck* test is straightforward in this context. While labour law rules and trade union action are capable of 'affecting' market access, they do not ordinarily 'prevent' the market access of enterprises, service providers or workers. Thus, were the *Keck* test to be employed in the labour law field, the key question would be whether the application of labour law rules or the exercise of a trade union's rights to take collective action had

---

[38] Syrpis, P and Novitz, T, *supra* n. 33 at 420–22.
[39] Case C–341/05 *Laval, supra* n. 33, paragraph 99.
[40] Cases C–267 and 268/91 *Keck and Mithouard* [1993] ECR I–6097, paragraph 17.

resulted in discrimination against enterprises seeking to establish themselves, or to provide services, in another Member State.

An alternative 'solution' (i.e. means of holding that there is no barrier to free movement as a result of the trade union action, or the application of host State labour law rules to foreign employers) is the *de minimis* test used in the *Graf* case in relation to Article 39 EC. In the *Graf* case, the Court held, in line with *Dassonville*, that in order to be capable of constituting an obstacle to the free movement of workers, national provisions 'must affect access of workers to the labour market'.[41] However, it went on to hold that the effect of the legislation at issue in the case, which related to entitlements to compensation on termination of employment, was 'too uncertain and indirect'.[42] It was therefore able to conclude that Article 39 EC (now Article 45 TFEU) did not preclude the application of the national provisions in question. In this context, what is in effect a *de minimis* test enables the Court to give primacy to the legitimate interests of states in those cases in which there are only small negative effects on the integration project.

Thus far, we have seen that differentials between national labour law regimes were, according to the Court, capable of amounting to barriers to free movement. But, it would still, of course, be open to the Court to hold that various aspects of the national labour law regime in question were justifiable. The Court's stance did not, at least on the surface, appear to be overtly hostile to 'the social', or indeed to the position of trade unions. In both the *Viking* and *Laval* cases, it made reference to the aims and objectives of the Community in acknowledging that 'since the Community has thus not only an economic but also a social purpose, the rights under the provisions of the Treaty on the free movement of goods, persons, services and capital must be balanced against the objectives pursued by social policy'.[43] It also felt able to hold that 'the right to take collection action' must 'be recognised as a fundamental right which forms an integral part of the general principles of law the observance of which the Court ensures'.[44] But, in spite of this, the Court held that the collective action of trade unions was liable to restrict the exercise of enterprises' free movement rights, and that while the protection of workers is, in general, able to serve as a justification for restrictions on free movement rights, the legality of industrial action turns on the ability of unions to convince courts that the action does not impose disproportionate limitations on the employer's cross-border activities.

---

[41] Case C–190/98 *Graf, supra* n. 32, paragraph 23.

[42] Ibid., paragraph 25.

[43] Case C–438/05 *Viking, supra* n. 33, paragraph 79; Case C–341/05 *Laval, supra* n. 33, paragraph 105.

[44] Case C–438/05 *Viking, supra* n. 33, paragraph 44; Case C–341/05 *Laval, supra* n. 33, paragraph 91.

In the *Laval* case, the Court made it clear that the trade unions would not be able to justify their action. The Court's approach was based on an extremely restrictive interpretation of the Posted Workers Directive. This Directive, the rationale of which is much debated,[45] requires host states to impose certain aspects of their labour law regime on temporary service providers, and thereby guarantees certain rights to posted workers. The Directive *requires* Member States to apply any standards which they may have relating to the matters listed in Article 3(1) of the Directive to posted workers;[46] and appears to *permit* Member States to go further – Article 3(7) states that the Directive 'shall not prevent application of terms and conditions which are more favourable to workers', and Article 3(10) allows Member States to go beyond Article 3(1) 'in the case of public policy provisions'. The Court however, in the *Laval* case, stated that permitting host Member States to apply standards beyond the mandatory rules for minimum protection listed in Article 3(1) 'would amount to depriving the directive of its effectiveness'; and in *Rüffert* and *Luxembourg* proceeded to empty paragraphs 7 and 10 of Article 3 of all meaningful content.[47]

These cases are extremely controversial. Many aspects could have been decided differently. It is, for example, not at all obvious that the actions of trade unions should be caught by the free movement provisions; nor that the Court should have reached the conclusions it did on the balance between the economic and the social. But the aspect of the decisions which has the greatest implications in the context of the harmonisation of labour law in the EU is one that is often neglected – the seemingly simple question of the definition of the barrier to free movement. The Eastern enlargement of the EU has brought in its wake increasingly large differentials between the labour laws of the Member States. Many undertakings have shown that they are keen to exploit these differentials for commercial advantage; and this has put those Member States and trade unions which are keen to preserve existing labour standards on the defensive. The effect of the Court's case law is that labour standards in the EU-15 are being undermined. To give just one example of the problems which have been created, the trade union movement is now concerned about whether agreements

---

[45]   Davies, P (1997), 'Posted Workers: Single Market or Protection of National Labour Law Systems?', 34 *Common Market Law Review* 571.

[46]   This includes maximum work periods and minimum rest periods; minimum paid annual holidays; minimum rates of pay, including overtime rates; the conditions of hiring-out of workers; health, safety and hygiene at work; protective measures with regard to the terms and conditions of employment of pregnant women or women who have recently given birth, of children and of young people; and equality of treatment between men and women and other provisions on non-discrimination.

[47]   See, in particular, Case C–346/06 *Rüffert*, *supra* n. 34, paragraphs 32–36, and Case C–319/06 *Commission v. Luxembourg*, *supra* n. 34, paragraphs 48–55.

which are being negotiated over terms and conditions of employment relating to the construction of the sites of the London Olympics in 2012 will, in so far as they relate to terms and conditions of employment which go beyond what is provided for in Article 3(1) of the Posted Workers Directive, be capable of binding foreign service providers who are posting workers to the UK. The real fear is that they will not; and that injunctions and damages will be sought by employers if there is any attempt by trade unions to insist on higher standards.[48]

HARMONISATION IN THE LABOUR LAW FIELD – FUTURE PROSPECTS

The internal market case law of the Court, the far-reaching implications of which are only becoming clear to labour lawyers in the course of 2008, presents a challenge to the pre-existing approach of the legislative institutions in the labour law field. Service providers are prepared to challenge what they see as the overly restrictive labour standards which states and trade unions in Western Europe seek to impose on them, and have found a willing ally in the Court of Justice. Unless there is a change in the approach adopted by the Court, it appears from the judgments in *Laval*, *Rüffert* and *Luxembourg* that host states may not be able to insist that foreign service providers comply with labour standards in areas beyond those listed in Article 3(1) of the Posted Workers Directive.

The previous section was critical of the Court's approach. However, it may be that trade unions, political activists and academic lawyers fail in the task of persuading the Court to change tack. This concluding section considers what the possible responses of the legislative institutions may be on the assumption that the case law of the Court is taken as a given; with a particular focus on the desirability of a strategy based on harmonisation.

Let us recall once again that the Treaties are based on the assumption, reflected in the Ohlin and Spaak reports, that integration does not call for elimination of differences between the labour law regimes of the Member States. The Ohlin report argues that 'the notion that a *general* harmonisation of social policy is justified by reference to "distortions of competition" brought about by differences between the labour law regimes of Member States is a delusion'.[49] And, according to Spaak, there is a need for harmonisation of laws to assist in the establishment and functioning of the market only where there are specific

---

[48]   See K Apps, 'Damages Claims against Trade Unions after *Viking* and *Laval*' (2009) 34 *European Law Review* 141.

[49]   See Deakin, S (1996), 'Labour Law as Market Regulation: the Economic Foundations of European Social Policy', in Davies, P *et al.* (eds), *supra* n. 26 at 92.

distortions which favour or handicap certain branches of economic activity.[50] Notwithstanding this, the case law of the Court suggests that differences between labour law regimes are, in and of themselves, problematic. Differences are liable to make it less attractive, or more difficult, for undertakings to carry out activities in other Member States, and therefore lead to restrictions on the freedoms guaranteed by the Treaties. High-standard Member States (and trade unions within those states seeking to defend those high standards) have been called upon to justify their high labour standards with reference to EU law criteria, and have been subjected to intense scrutiny before the courts.

If one accepts that differences between labour law regimes in the various Member States are problematic from the point of view of the internal market, then there is surely an integrationist argument that the legislative institutions should be attempting to take steps to eliminate, or at least reduce, these problems. Legislative intervention would enable the internal market to work better, helping to protect national labour law systems aimed at the protection of workers from the threat of litigation from employers exploiting the opportunities available to them in the enlarged EU market. Intervention may also be seen to be serving broader pan-European goals – for example, reducing xenophobic protests against both migrant workers and the EU itself – and may thereby contribute towards the legitimacy of the EU.

One is left with questions surrounding the nature of the intervention which may be called for in order to deal with the problems which the expansive case law of the Court has brought in its wake. Is harmonisation of national systems of labour law the solution, or are there better alternatives? Alternatives may be thought of as better if they are, in line with the principle of proportionality, less burdensome for the Member States, or, using a very different line of argumentation, if they have a more realistic chance of being adopted in the prevailing political climate.

One solution, which falls far short of harmonisation, is premised on seeing the problem as one linked intrinsically and exclusively with the exercise of free movement rights. The Union could adopt what may be thought of as a 'conflicts of laws' or 'jurisdictional' approach based explicitly on the assumption that in principle it should be either the 'home' or the 'host' state – but not both – which should regulate undertakings, including in relation to terms and conditions of employment, provided that the rules it seeks to apply are not discriminatory. This approach has a number of advantages over a strategy based on harmonisation. It does not rely on a top-down, command-and-control style of governance involving the creation of supranational standards which are then imposed on the states. Instead it appears to legitimise and safeguard a substantial degree of autonomy for states.

---

[50] This was the basis for the inclusion of Article 141 (formerly 119) EC in the Treaty.

This sort of approach could be developed and applied by the Court. Equally, it could be premised on intervention by the legislature. In relation to the free movement of goods, it is the Court which makes it clear that goods are only able to benefit from the free movement provisions if they are lawfully produced or marketed in one of the Member States of the European Union.[51] While producers are therefore able to challenge restrictive 'host' state rules, they are bound by the rules in their 'home' state (and, of course, they have the freedom to relocate and to produce their goods in another 'home' state the regulatory regime of which is seen to be preferable). In contrast, the message from the *Viking* and *Laval* cases, and indeed from many earlier cases relating to the free movement of persons, free establishment and the freedom to provide services,[52] is that as far as the Court is concerned the restrictive rules of both the 'home' and the 'host' state are challengeable. In relation to the free movement of workers and free establishment, it seems clear that the Court's approach is misguided. Workers and enterprises benefiting from the Treaties provisions on the free movement of persons and free establishment sever their connections with the 'home' state, and acquire new connections with the 'host' state. The argument advanced here is that they should therefore be bound by the rules of the 'host' state – retaining the ability only to challenge those aspects of the host state's regulatory regime which are discriminatory.

In relation to the freedom to provide services, the situation is rather less clear cut. An enterprise which takes advantage of the freedom to provide services retains connections with both the 'home' and the 'host' state. It is not immediately obvious that one or other is better placed to regulate. Given this, it is perhaps unsurprising that the legislature has intervened. The Posted Workers Directive and the Directive on Services in the Internal Market are both relevant here, as are the conflicts of law rules recently adopted in the form of the Rome I Regulation.[53] As we have seen, the Posted Workers Directive has been interpreted by the Court so that it requires host states to impose certain aspects of their labour law regime, on a non-discriminatory basis, on temporary service providers; but it is now clear that it insists that, other than in extreme circumstances, 'host' states cannot seek to apply terms and conditions beyond those listed in Article 3(1) of the Directive.[54] The rest is left to the 'home' state.

---

[51]   See e.g. Case 120/78 *Rewe-Zentral v. Bundesmonopolverwaltung für Branntwein* (*Cassis de Dijon*) [1979] ECR 649.

[52]   See e.g. Case C–384/93 *Alpine Investments, supra* n. 29.

[53]   Regulation 593/20008 of the European Parliament and of the Council of 17 June 2008 on the law applicable to contractual obligations (Rome I) [2008] OJ L 177/6.

[54]   See Case C–319/06 *Commission v. Luxembourg, supra* n. 34, paragraph 26: 'Article 3(1) sets out an exhaustive list of the matters in respect of which the Member States may give priority to the rules in force in the host Member State'.

The negotiations leading to the adoption of the Services Directive can be seen as providing an opportunity for the legislative institutions to give some guidance to the Court on the relationship between the rights of 'home' and 'host' state in the context of the cross-border provisions of services. Early drafts of the Services Directive were premised on the application of a 'country of origin' principle, the effect of which would be that service providers would be subject only to the laws applying in the country in which they were based.[55] The European Parliament's amendments included a provision that the Directive would 'not apply to or affect labour law',[56] seeming to give a green light to 'host' state regulation of labour law matters. Had such a text been adopted, it would have remained open to the Court to apply the free movement provisions, and, notwithstanding the intervention of the legislature, to decide that the application of particular labour law rules or the exercise of a right to strike might, in particular circumstances, be unlawful; but nevertheless, the Member States would have sent a strong signal to the Court. In the Directive which was finally adopted in December 2006,[57] the clauses inserted by the European Parliament were diluted. Article 1(6) provides that the Directive 'does not affect labour law... which Member States apply in accordance with national law *which respects Community law*' (emphasis added). Similarly Article 1(7) provides that the Directive 'does not affect the exercise of fundamental rights as recognised in the Member States and *by Community law*. Nor does it affect the right to negotiate, conclude and enforce collective agreements and to take industrial action in accordance with national law and practices *which respect Community law*' (emphasis again added). Article 3(3) confirms that 'Member States shall apply the provisions of this Directive in compliance with the rules of the Treaty on the right of establishment and the free movement of services'. The Services Directive thus ducks the question of what to do in the event of conflicts between 'home' and 'host' states, merely delegating the difficult decisions to the Court.

The Rome I Regulation adopts a similar approach. Article 8 of the Regulation provides that individual employment contracts 'shall be covered by the law of the country in which or, failing that, from which the employee habitually carries out his work in performance of the contract. The country where the work is habitually carried out shall not be deemed to have changed if he is temporarily employed in another country'. Article 9 does however permit a country to

---

[55]   See Commission proposal for a Directive of the European Parliament and of the Council on services in the internal market, COM(2004)2, 5 March 2004, Article 16.

[56]   European Parliament legislative resolution on the proposal for a directive of the European Parliament and of the Council on services in the internal market, 16 February 2006.

[57]   Directive 2006/123/EC of the European Parliament and of the Council of 12 December 2006 on services in the internal market [2006] OJ L 376/36.

adopt 'overriding mandatory provisions' 'regarded as crucial by a country for safeguarding its public interests, such as its political, social or economic organisation.' The wording of Article 8 reinforces the territorial scope of labour law, and may have implications relating to the case law of the Court on persons and establishment. In relation to services, the position is similar to that under the Posted Workers Directive and the Directive on Services in the Internal Market. It is clear that much depends on the interpretation of the terms 'temporary employment' and 'overriding mandatory provisions'.

Fundamentally, however, these various attempts to demarcate the spheres of influence of 'home' and 'host' states are, even if done well, likely to take us only so far. Enterprises seem to be unable to resist the temptation of using their free movement rights so as to gain the benefit of what are substantially more permissive legal regimes, and are prepared to litigate to ensure that they are able to cut costs (arguably at the expense of their workforce).

A more comprehensive solution to the problems raised by the internal market case law of the Court may depend not just on an attempt to delineate the situations in which particular states can apply their own very different labour law regimes to particular workers and employers, but on an altogether more ambitious attempt to bring these very different systems into closer alignment. This may even go so far as to encompass harmonisation of various aspects of national labour law and practice.

The case for harmonisation is this. As a first step, it is necessary to take the case law of the Court as a given. This involves an acceptance that differences between the labour law regimes are problematic and that Member States are likely to encounter problems in their attempts to justify aspects of national employment law and practice before the courts. Harmonisation (unlike coordination strategies based on the OMC, and unlike minimum standard setting which does not prevent Member States from maintaining or introducing more stringent protective measures) provides a way to eliminate these differences and, thereby to eliminate the strain which the very existence of differences is said to place on the fabric of the internal market.

The case against harmonisation may be considered more compelling. With the many critics of top-down command-and-control governance, one may wonder about the wisdom of attempting to find pan-European solutions to social questions better settled at the national or local level. One may alternatively, as the first section of this chapter demonstrates, couch one's objections in the language of legal basis, subsidiarity or proportionality. One should also reflect on the fact that, even if legitimacy problems could be overcome, it may not be possible to reach agreement on common standards. For legislation to be adopted, political agreement would need to be reached between at least a qualified majority of Member States; and that does not appear to be foreseeable in the current political climate.

Ultimately, the key question is that posed by Simitis and Lyon Caen: does the objective of economic integration really require an approximation of national provisions in the social sphere? Their answer was that it is does not. However, if the Court continues to see diversity and difference as hindrances to the operation of the internal market, it may be that we have to reconsider this answer, and begin to make an integrationist case for the harmonisation of national systems of labour law.

24. The *acquis* principles: an insider's critical reflections on the drafting process*

Christian Twigg-Flesner[1]

INTRODUCTION

The theme of this book is the theory and practice of harmonisation, with this contribution focusing primarily on the latter. Its purpose is to consider the work of the Acquis Group and its output, the *Principles of Existing EC Contract Law*, better known as the Acquis Principles (abbreviated to ACQP).[2] The ACQP have a dual purpose: on the one hand, they are intended to survey and re-state the body of contract law rules which have already been adopted through EU legislation; on the other, they are supplying provisions for the Draft Common Frame of Reference (DCFR), which, in turn, could be used to consolidate and make more coherent EU legislation in this field. This contribution is intended to be a critical reflection on the process of drafting the ACQP, from the perspective of one member of the Acquis Group involved in both the drafting of particular provisions, as well as the compilation of individual provisions to form the ACQP. It will begin by setting the overall context within which the ACQP have been drafted, followed by a more detailed examination of the drafting process itself. There will be a discussion of the challenges associated with the insertion of the ACQP into the DCFR. It will be argued that the conflation of two separate projects has resulted in methodological shortcomings which, with the benefit of more time, could have been avoided.

---

   *   Editor's note: This contribution has been affected by rapid developments in the field, see the Preface on p. xi for details.

   [1]   Professor of Commercial Law at the University of Hull, UK, and Member of Acquis Group Redaction Committee. Views expressed in this chapter represent the personal views of the author only. Contact: c.twigg-flesner@hull.ac.uk.

   [2]   Research Group on Existing EC Private Law (Acquis Group), *Principles of the Existing EC Contract Law – Contract I. Pre-contractual Obligations, Conclusion of Contract, Unfair Terms* (Munich: Sellier, 2007) and Contract II (2009). These volumes are referred to throughout this chapter as *Contract I* and *Contract II*.

BACKGROUND – TOWARDS A EUROPEAN CONTRACT LAW?

Three Commission documents, published in 2001, 2003 and 2004 respectively, launched the current activities in the field of European Contract Law.[3] The starting shot was fired with the *Communication on European Contract Law*,[4] which the Commission published to start a debate and invite evidence for the need to take further EC action in the field of contract law. A particular focus was on the identified shortcomings in both the quality of the existing *acquis communautaire* affecting contract law[5] and its transposition into the national laws of the Member States. In its follow-up documents,[6] the Commission announced plans to develop a Common Frame of Reference (CFR) on European Contract Law, which would, in the first instance, be utilised in reviewing the consumer *acquis*.[7]

The CFR, as originally conceived by the Commission, would be a kind of toolbox to be used in revising existing legislation as well as for the adoption of further measures in the future.[8] It should contain definitions of relevant legal terms, state the key fundamental principles on which European contract law is based, and provide coherent model rules. As far as the sources on which the CFR is to be based are concerned, domestic legislation and case law, as well as the existing *acquis* and international instruments such as the United Nations Convention on the International Sale of Goods (CISG), were all regarded as relevant. The CFR should therefore be some sort of mixture of *acquis* and best solutions derived from the domestic laws of the Member States.

Including provisions based on the *acquis* was crucial in ensuring that the CFR could fulfil its toolbox function, although how one could arrive at tools

---

[3]   For a general overview see Twigg-Flesner, C (2008), *The Europeanisation of Contract Law* (Routledge-Cavendish).

[4]   COM(2001)398 final, 11 July 2001. See also 'On the way to a European contract code?' (editorial comments) (2002) 39 *Common Market Law Review* 219–55.

[5]   The Annex to the *Communication* contains a long list of measures which arguably have some effect on contract law, or even private law generally, although quite what that relationship might be is not always apparent (see Reich, N (2002), 'Critical Comments on the Commission Communication "On European Contract Law" in Grundmann, S and Stuyck, J (eds), *An Academic Green Paper on European Contract Law* (Kluwer Law International).

[6]   *A More Coherent European Contract Law – An Action Plan* (COM(2003)68 final) and *European Contract Law and the revision of the acquis: the way forward* (COM(2004)651 final) respectively.

[7]   See *First Annual Progress Report on European Contract Law and the Acquis Review* (COM(2005)456 final) and *Second Progress Report on the Common Frame of Reference* (COM(2007)447 final).

[8]   *The Way Forward*, at 3.

for improving the *acquis* by starting from the *acquis* was not addressed in the Commission documents. However, it is obvious that provisions covering the topics already addressed in the *acquis* needed to be included if the CFR were to be utilised for improving the legislation already in place.

From a political perspective, the *acquis* reflects solutions that have generally been accepted by the Member States, conferring on these an inherent degree of 'European' legitimacy.[9] The *acquis* effectively comprises the core of European contract law, as well as having However, as the *acquis* predominantly deals with consumer contract law issues, the CFR will have to contain specific rules on consumer contracts. What was not explored in the Commission's documents was whether such provisions could be based directly on the *acquis*. Of course, the *acquis* in its present state could not simply be restated in the CFR, because one of the main reasons for the CFR is to provide a mechanism for creating a more coherent *acquis*.[10] This correctly implies that the existing *acquis* was insufficiently coherent to be retained in its current state.

Contrary to the Commission' view, one could argue that there was no obvious need for *acquis*-based provisions – just because agreement was reached on something in the past should not mean that it is suitable for the future.[11] Such a view may sound surprising, but ought to be given serious consideration: for example, if empirical research demonstrated that current legislation was ineffective, then it would be entirely legitimate to question whether it should be retained.

The draft CFR (DCFR) has been produced by the 'CoPECL Research Network' which was established under the FP6-research programme.[12] The CoPECL network comprised many research groups working in the field of European contract law, first and foremost the Study Group on a European Civil Code and the Research Group on the Existing EC Private Law (Acquis Group).

---

[9] Grundmann, S (2004), 'The Optional European Code on the Basis of the Acquis Communautaire', 10 *European Law Journal* 678–711; Wilhelmsson, T and Twigg-Flesner, C (2006), 'Pre-contractual information duties in the *acquis communautaire*', 2 *European Review of Contract Law* 441–70, at 444.

[10] A further difficulty is that it is far from clear what 'coherence', and, indeed the concept of a 'principle', might mean: see Wilhelmsson, T (2008), 'The Contract Law Acquis: Towards More Coherence Through Generalisation?' in *Proceedings of the 4th European Jurists' Forum* (Manzsche Verlags- und Universitätsbuchhandlung).

[11] Gómez, F (2008), 'The Harmonization of Contract Law through European Rules: a Law and Economics Perspective', 4 *European Review of Contract Law* 89–118, at 105.

[12] Cf. Study Group on a European Civil Code/Research Group on the Existing EC Private Law (Acquis Group) (2009), *Principles, Definitions and Model Rules on European Private Law – Draft Common Frame of Reference* (Sellier) ('DCFR'), at 48–9. See Collins, H (2008), 'Review', 71 *Modern Law Review* 840–44.

Other groups in the network were the Project Group on a Restatement of Insurance Contract Law, the French Association Henri Capitant, the Common Core (Trento) Group, the Database Group, the Tilburg Group of economists who will prepare an impact assessment of the DCFR, and the European Academy of Law in Trier.[13] A preliminary draft version was published in early 2008,[14] and a final version in 2009. The European Commission will then use the DCFR as a basis for preparing its own CFR.

THE ACQUIS PRINCIPLES

The task of providing *acquis*-based provisions for the DFCR fell to the Acquis Group. The group evolved from earlier research networks on EU private law, and was formed in 2002 with the specific objective of identifying the common principles of the existing EC private law.[15] Since 2005, the Acquis Group, which comprises around 50 scholars from most of the EU Member States, has met in half-yearly plenary meetings[16] to consider draft provisions which restate aspects of the *acquis*.

In terms of output, the main achievement was the publication of the first volume of the ACQP as *Contract I*.[17] In addition there have been several articles in leading journals addressing particular topics, as well as a number of edited collections. A second volume was published in 2009.

It may be useful to explain, briefly, how the ACQP have been presented in *Contract I*.[18] There are seven chapters in this volume: (1) General Provisions;

---

[13] For a critical comment on this approach see Grundmann, S (2005), 'European Contract Law(s) of What Colour?', 1 *European Review of Contract Law* 184–210.

[14] For a critical analysis (in German) see Eidenmüller, H, Faust, F, Grigoleit, HC, Jansen, N, Wagner, G and Zimmermann, R (2008), 'Der gemeinsame Referenzrahmen für das Europäische Privatrecht – Wertungsfragen und Kodifikationsprobleme', 63 *Juristenzeitung* 529–50.

[15] On the importance of surveying what is already in the *acquis* before moving on to consider how it needs to develop see Schulze, R (2005), 'European Private Law and Existing EC Law', 13 *European Review of Private Law* 3–19.

[16] Meetings have been held in Helsinki (March 2005), Tier (November 2005), Hull (March 2006), Barcelona (November 2006), Paris (March 2007), Krakow (October 2007), Copenhagen (April 2008), Leuven (November 2008), Prague (February 2009), Brno (November 2009), Krakow (February 2010), Ljubljana (October 2010) and Hull (February 2011).

[17] *Contract I* (2007).

[18] For a detailed and rather critical analysis see Jansen, N and Zimmermann, R (2008), 'Restating the *Acquis Communautaire*? A Critical Examination of the "Principles of Existing EC Contract Law"', 71 *Modern Law Review* 505–34. A response (to the earlier German version of their article) can be found in Zoll, F (2008), 'Die Grundregeln

(2) Pre-conctractual Duties; (3) Non-discrimination;[19] (4) Formation; (5) Withdrawal; (6) Non-negotiated Terms; and (7) Performance of Obligations. A further chapter ((8) Remedies) was published separately.[20] Each chapter is divided into sections, and these sections then contain individual 'principles' (understood in its European meaning, i.e., 'model rule'). The presentation of each principle starts with the text of the principle itself, followed first by a description of its foundations in the *acquis* (considering both relevant sources and the development towards a single principle, together with any relevant 'political issues') and secondly a commentary which sets out the meaning and purpose of the principle, its context (i.e., relationship with other principles), an explanation, and a number of illustrative examples.

These 'principles' were all developed on the basis of the *acquis communautaire*. In the following sections, the sources and methodology of the Acquis Group will be discussed, highlighting in particular the challenges with had to be addressed.

Sources and Methodology

The purpose of the ACQP is to state the common principles of existing EC Contract Law. Thus, through synthesising what can be found in the fragmented *acquis communautaire*, an attempt is made to provide a coherent restatement of the *acquis*. The idea of tackling the *acquis*, much criticised for its lack of coherence, invites a number of concerns which are considered in this section, before considering the precise methodology adopted by the Acquis Group.

Sources: several challenges
The first step for the Acquis Group was to identify the sources that would be harvested in order to develop the ACQP, i.e., what is the *acquis* that would be analysed with a view to identifying relevant principles? It will come as no surprise that the central focus was the key directives adopted by the EU, primarily those in the field of consumer contract law, but not exclusively so. In addition to the text of the directives themselves, decisions by the European Court of Justice (ECJ) which interpret, clarify, and occasionally even expand, these directives were also rightly included within the field of enquiry.

---

der Acquis-Gruppe im Spannungsverhältnis zwischen acquis commun und acquis communautaire', *Gemeinschaftsprivatrecht* 106–17.

[19] This is clearly one of the most significant contributions by the Acquis Group, reflecting the evolving *acquis* on preventing discrimination on a number of grounds.

[20] See Schulze, R (2008), *Common Frame of Reference and Existing EC Contract Law* (Sellier), Appendix.

More controversially, it was felt that the UN Convention on the International Sale of Goods 1980 (CISG) should be regarded as part of the *acquis*, too, because it had been adopted by almost all of the EU Member States. There are two immediate concerns about this: first, the CISG is not an EU measure, nor has the EU as a whole signed and ratified the convention. Treating this as part of the *acquis communautaire* therefore invites the obvious objection that the CISG is not European at all. Secondly, the CISG has not been ratified by all the Member States; notable exceptions are Ireland and the United Kingdom, representing the EU's key common law jurisdictions, as well as Portugal. So to regard this as part of the *acquis* is tenuous, at best. One reason why this might have been favoured is that – unlike much of the *acquis* – the CISG deals with B2B contracts, and therefore offers a basis for developing rules which are of general application (more on this below).

Leaving aside the controversy of including the CISG within the *acquis*, the measures which stem from EU law also pose a number of challenges. Most significantly, it is the nature of the *acquis* that any legislation is adopted to deal with specific problems that have been identified, and, as such, directives deal with fairly discrete topics. For example, there are directives on distance selling,[21] package travel[22] and timeshare[23] (all in the consumer field), late payment of commercial debts[24] and commercial agency[25] (non-consumer). Only the directives on unfair terms in consumer contracts[26] and consumer sales[27] are of broader application. Indeed, its largely problem-specific nature is one of the cause of the incoherence for which the *acquis* has been criticised, and which the work on the CFR is designed to alleviate.

Moreover, the bulk of the EU legislation in this field is based on directives. These need to be transposed into the national laws of each of the Member States before they can take full effect, a process which brings with it its own challenges

---

[21]   Directive 97/7/EC of the European Parliament and of the Council on the protection of consumers in respect of distance contracts (1997) OJ L 144/19.
[22]   Directive 90/314/EEC on package travel, package holidays and package tours (1990) OJ L 158/90.
[23]   Directive 94/47/EC of the European Parliament and Council on the protection of purchasers in respect of certain aspects of contracts relating to the purchase of the right to use immovable properties on a timeshare basis (1994) OJ L280/94.
[24]   Directive 2000/35/EC of the European Parliament and of the Council of 29 June 2000 on combating late payment in commercial transactions (2000) OJ L200/35.
[25]   Directive 86/653/EEC on the co-ordination of the laws of the Member States relating to self-employed commercial agents (1986) OJ L382/86.
[26]   Directive 93/13/EEC of 5 April 1993 on unfair terms in consumer contracts (1993) OJ L95/29.
[27]   Directive 99/44/EC on certain aspects of the sale of consumer goods and associated guarantees (1999) OJ L 171/12.

with regard to the effectiveness of EU-based legislation on contract law, because this process can, and often does, result in shortcomings in the way a directive is implemented into national law.[28]

More pertinently, the implementation should anchor provisions based on a directive within the national legislative framework on contract law. However, the nature of these directives creates a significant problem: directives provide an incomplete solution to an identified problem only, and do not cover one particular aspect of the law exhaustively. Morevoer, directives contain gaps, and depend on national law to fill these gaps. This interdependence between a directive and national law(s) can be seen in two particular aspects.

First, much of the legislation adopted to date is based on a minimum harmonisation standard. This means that whilst a directive mandates a minimum standard to be met by all national laws, it leaves some room to the Member States for introducing or retaining rules which offer a higher level of protection. This has been used widely in directives dealing with consumer protection, for example.[29] The minimum harmonisation character of much of the *acquis* means that it could be dangerous to state as a firm principle something which is only supported by minimum harmonisation measures. Of course, the minimum standard might be a reflection of what could be achieved during the negotiation process and what was therefore politically acceptable at the time of adoption, giving it a degree of legitimacy that will put any principle developed purely on this basis on a firm footing. On the other hand, there may be more commonality to the Member States than the minimum standard adopted in a directive might suggest, e.g., because in transposing a particular provision, most (or even all) of the Member States may have chosen to exceed the minimum standard mandated by a directive in a specific manner, although such instances appear to be rare.[30]

Secondly, as already mentioned, directives need to be implemented into national law to take full effect. But even directly applicable measures, such as Regulations and even some Treaty Articles, are part of the national laws of the Member States, and these, too, rely on their full effectiveness on related areas of national law. So the *acquis communautaire* cannot even begin to offer a complete resource for developing a full set of principles, because so much is left to national law. Indeed, some directives and regulations explicitly state that certain

---

[28]   Cf. Schulte-Nölke, H, Twigg-Flesner, C and Ebers, M (2008), *EC Consumer Law Compendium* (Sellier), for an analysis of how eight consumer *acquis* directives have been transposed into the national laws of the Member States and the resulting variations.

[29]   Although this practice appears to be coming to an end: see *Green Paper on the Review of the Consumer Acquis* (COM(2006)744 final) and the *Proposal for A Directive on Consumer Rights* (COM(2008)614 final).

[30]   There are many divergent instance of exceeding the minimum standards, though: see *EC Consumer Law Compendium.*

matters are to be determined by national law, with only a very general outcome specified. For example, Article 4 of the Door-Step Selling Directive[31] provides that 'the consumer shall have the right to renounce the effects of his undertaking [i.e., withdraw from a contract] in accordance with the procedure laid down by national law'. So whilst the Directive establishes a right of withdrawal from a contract concluded at the consumer's door-step, the mechanism for doing so and the consequences are largely to be determined by national law.[32]

The fragmentation of the *acquis* and the close inter-relationship between *acquis* and national law therefore make it very difficult to define precisely the sources on the basis of which the ACQP could be developed. This has a significant implication: the attempt to state the principles of existing EC contract law could be a very short endeavour, resulting in a few loose and unconnected provisions which essentially repeat the existing directives. Whilst that might be an accurate reflection of the state of the *acquis*, it would be a somewhat unsatisfactory result if work stopped there. Ultimately, producing something more coherent, i.e., systematic, should be the objective, whilst remaining faithful to what is in the *acquis*. That, however, creates the risk that what is eventually produced may have little to do with the *acquis*. There might be a temptation to develop a particular principle because that would ensure greater coherence and perhaps even completeness in the overall system of the ACQP. Where this has no clear basis, it might be objected that the particular principle is invented and has nothing much to do with the *acquis* at all.

In this context, it must be noted that the *acquis* itself has developed the general principle of *effet utile*, i.e., the 'effectiveness' principle as a tool for dealing with gaps in the legislative *acquis*. This has been deployed by the ECJ as a basis for creating entirely new doctrines of EC law, such as the principle of Member State liability for breaches of EC law,[33] the need for effective remedies in the context of equal treatment,[34] and the possibility for private law remedies for breach of the competition provisions in the EC Treaty.[35] As this is a recognised principle for dealing with lacunae in the *acquis communautaire*, it might be tempting to rely on this principle in order to fill in gaps which have been

---

[31] Directive 85/577/EEC to protect the consumer in respect of contracts negotiated away from business premises (1985) OJ L 372/8.

[32] If the proposed Consumer Contractual Rights Directive is adopted, there will be a standardised EU-wide procedure. However, even in this proposal, there are matters left to national law, e.g., with regard to the effect of exercising a right of withdrawal on so-called 'ancillary contracts': see Art.18 of the proposal.

[33] Case C–6 & 9/90 *Francovich v. Italy* [1991] ECR I–5357 and C–46 & 48/93 *Brasserie du Pêcheur SA v. Germany (Factortame v. UK)* [1996] ECR I–1029.

[34] See the line of cases starting with Case 14/83 *von Colson v Land Nordrhein–Westfalen* [1984] ECR 1891.

[35] Case C–453/99 *Courage Ltd v. Crehan* [2001] ECR I–6297.

identified in the *acquis*. Whether this really offers a sufficiently valid justification in these circumstances is certainly debatable.

A further problem is that those involved in drafting ACQP provisions are not reporting on how a specific matter is addressed in their legal system, but on a separate legal system altogether.[36] However, EC law is not a neutral system, but often viewed by individual scholars through the lens of their domestic law. This can have the effect that a particular rule found in the *acquis* is regarded differently by scholars from different jurisdictions, making it more difficult to reach a consensus. Indeed, the desire to find a system in the *acquis* might be shaped by the relevant national experience of those involved in drafting particular provisions, and the resulting provision might have more to do with particular national laws than what is truly in the *acquis*.

Finally, but just as important as the previous points, the predominant share of the *acquis* can be found in the field of consumer contract law, rather than general contract law. This means that these are rules adopted because there was a perceived shortcoming not only in the existing consumer laws of the Member States, but also in general contract law, necessitating the adoption of consumer-specific provisions. However, if the objective of the ACQP is to state principles of general contract law, rather than consumer contract law, then some considerable detective work is required. As noted by Dannemann,[37] one can then debate whether a particular provision in the *acquis* reflects a general rule which can be used as a basis for drafting a more wide-ranging (i.e., non-consumer specific) measure, or whether that provision is, in fact, a derogation from an unexpressed general rule. Either way, a level of judgement is required as to how much support can be found in the *acquis*, be it for a restatement of consumer-specific rules, or even rules of general contract law.

Drafting the ACQP

As already mentioned, drafts were discussed at plenary meetings of the Acquis Group. These drafts were prepared by small drafting teams who assumed the responsibility of dealing with particular sections of the *acquis*.

In the light of all the reservations set out above, how did the Acquis Group manage to pursue its objectives? The methodology of the group is explained in detail by Gerhard Dannemann in an introductory chapter to *Contract I*.[38] The Group was, of course, well aware of the pitfalls it had to avoid. In particular,

---

[36]   Contrast this with the comparative law approach used by the Lando Commission and the Study Group. See e.g., von Bar, C (2007), 'Coverage and Structure of the Academic Common Frame of Reference', 3 *European Review of Contract Law* 350–61.

[37]   Dannemann, G (2007), 'Consolidating EC Contract Law: An introduction to the work of the Acquis Group' in *Contract I*, at XXVIII.

[38]   Ibid.

he notes (i) that the *acquis* is not limited to the text of legislation and relevant jurisprudence by the ECJ, but there is something in them 'which transcends those statutes and is capable of being formulated at a more general level',[39] and (ii) that one cannot 'construct a comprehensive EC contract law by generalising consumer protection rules to general rules of contract law'[40] so as to avoid overstretching what is really there. These are important *caveats*. Nevertheless, a brief look at the contents of *Contract I* shows that the central focus of the Acquis Group's work has been to analyse the substance of the legislative and judicial *acquis* and develop fairly broad generalisation on the basis of its findings.

How did the process of generalisation operate specifically? At one level, diverse provisions were examined for what they had in common, resulting in a rule of wide application elevated to a general level from the more specific contexts in which the *acquis* currently applies them. A good example is the area of pre-contractual information duties. At present, there are pre-contractual information duties e.g., in the directives on distance selling, timeshare, package travel, distance selling of financial services[41] and payment services.[42] These are generally not particularly well-structured, and there are inconsistencies between the various directives.[43] Nevertheless, it is possible to find sufficient common ground between all these rules to suggest a principle which attempts to generalise these duties, and this was done in Article 2:203 (1) ACQP as follows:

> In the case of transactions that place the consumer at a significant informational disadvantage because of the technical medium used for contracting, the physical distance between business and consumer, or the nature of the transaction, the business must, as appropriate in the circumstances, provide clear information about the main characteristics of the goods or services, the price including delivery charges, taxes and other costs, the address and identity of the business with whom the consumer is transacting, the terms of the contract, the rights and obligations of both contracting parties, and any available redress procedures. This information must be provided at the latest at the time of conclusion of the contract.

This Article restates in general terms the conditions for imposing pre-contractual information duties on a business when dealing with a consumer, as well as the categories of information which are generally referred to. It does not replace the detailed lists of information items developed for particular transactions such as

---

[39] Ibid., at XXVII

[40] Ibid.

[41] Directive 2002/65 of the European Parliament and Council concerning the distance marketing of consumer financial services (2002) OJ L 271/16.

[42] Directive 2007/64/EC on payment services in the internal market (2007) OJ L 319/1.

[43] See *EC Consumer Compendium*, at 482–96; Twigg-Flesner, *Europeanisation of Contract Law*, at 63–71.

time-share or package travel, but it adopts a general principle which can then be applied in reviewing existing provisions.[44]

A principle such as this could easily be open to challenge for its lack of precision, and its consequent negative impact on legal certainty – just when are consumers placed at an informational disadvantage? If one were seeking a very precise legal rule (and, as will be explained below, this is what the DCFR essentially seems to concentrate on), then this is a fair objection to raise;[45] however, if one were much more concerned with a *principle* as the term might ordinarily be understood (i.e., as a basis on which more specific rules could be developed), then this is exactly the kind of provision one can derive from the specific rules found in the *acquis*. Indeed, it is arguable that establishing such common principles would be a much more fruitful endeavour than what appears to be the current focus on a detailed set of rules.[46]

Secondly, some provisions were regarded as specific instantiations of a more general principle, and that general principle was therefore stated expressly in the ACQP. The provisions on the right of withdrawal in consumer contracts can serve as an example.[47] A right of withdrawal is provided for in the directives on door-step selling, distance selling, distance selling of financial services, consumer credit,[48] and life assurance.[49] However, there are inconsistencies e.g., with regard to the length of the withdrawal period, the consequences of exercising this right, as well as the consequences of a failure to inform a consumer about the existence of the right of withdrawal. Again, the ACQP contain one set of principles on the right of withdrawal in Articles 5:101–5:106 ACQP, which seek to generalise the specific examples of the use of the right of withdrawal in the *acquis*.[50]

A further example is the treatment of public statements made by third parties. Both the Consumer Sales Directive (Article 2(2)(d)) and the Package Travel Directive (Article 3(2)) contain provisions which can render statements made by third parties (e.g., a producer or tour organiser respectively) binding. A more

---

[44]   For details see Twigg-Flesner, C (2008), 'Pre-contractual duties – from the *Acquis* to the Common Frame of Reference' in Schulze, R (ed.), *Common Frame of Reference and Existing EC Contract Law* (Sellier).

[45]   Cf. the objections raised by Grundmann, S (2008), 'The structure of the DCFR – which approach for today's Contract Law?', 4 *European Review of Contract Law* 225–47, at 239.

[46]   See the argument developed in Collins, H (2008), *The European Civil Code: The Way Forward* (Cambridge University Press).

[47]   Dannemann, 'Consolidating EC Contract Law', at XXIX.

[48]   Directive 2008/48/EC on credit agreements for consumers (2008) OJ L133/66.

[49]   Directive 2002/83/EC concerning life assurance (2002) OJ L 345/27.

[50]   See Terryn, E (2008), 'The Right of Withdrawal, the Acquis Principles and the Draft Common Frame of Reference' in Schulze, *CFR and Existing EC Contract Law*.

generalised set of principles in Articles 4:105–106 ACQP therefore provides that public statements are regarded as becoming terms of the contract.[51]

Thirdly, certain provisions in the *acquis* have been treated as a derogation from an unexpressed general principle, and that hidden principle has been made explicit within the ACQP. One example is the provisions on form: here, the assumption is that the *acquis* does not presuppose particular rules on form, except where this has been stated explicitly.[52] This assumption has been criticised by Jansen and Zimmermann as contradicting the 'profusion of form requirements'[53] in the *acquis* and lacking a sound basis in the *acquis* itself. Criticism such as this shows that identifying unexpressed principles is a difficult – and controversial – task.

Finally, the doctrine of *effet utile* has been utilised in order to develop principles to fill gaps which have been left by the *acquis*. Of course, these gaps exist only in the *acquis* but not in the national law into which the *acquis* has had to be implemented, but, as explored further below, national law has largely not been taken into account in drafting the ACQP.

For example, the *acquis* does not provide remedies for breach of the precontractual information duties. Nevertheless, one can easily imagine that there might be circumstances when a remedy such as damages should be made available for a failure to provide correct information, including where no contract has been concluded. In some Member States, there will be a basis for imposing liability in damages.[54] But whilst the *acquis* contains no specific provision that could be developed into a general principle on damages for breach of precontractual information duties, there is ECJ case law based on the principle of effectiveness which has permitted the award of damages for a failure to comply with an obligation under European law. In *Courage v. Crehan*,[55] the Court established an entitlement to damages where there has been a breach of Article 81 EC, and in *Antonio Munoz Cia SA v. Frumar Limited*,[56] the ECJ held that regulations could also be enforced in civil proceedings where there had been a contravention of the rules, even where a claimant had no specific right under the particular regulation. It seems possible that this approach might one day evolve beyond the realm of directly applicable provision to encompass claims

---

[51]   The present author disagrees with this generalisation, both as a matter of reading the *acquis* and of substance. See Twigg-Flesner, C (2008), 'Review of Felix R. Stamer, "Die Bindung an öffentliche Äusserungen Dritter im vertragsrechtlichen Acquis communautaire"', 16 *European Review of Private Law* 645–9.

[52]   Dannemann, at XXIX.

[53]   Jansen and Zimmermann, 'Restating the *Acquis Communautaire*', at 517.

[54]   In German law: *culpa in contrahendo*.

[55]   Case C–453/99 [2001] ECR I–6297.

[56]   Case C–253/00 [2002] ECR I–7289.

for damages for a breach of domestic legislation implementing a directive.[57] Article 2:207(2) ACQP consequently provides that '[e]ven if no contract has been concluded, breach of the duties under Art. 2:201 to 2:206 entitles the other party to reliance damages'.[58]

This is an example of how extensively the principle of *effet utile* could be deployed, and caution needs to be exercised, lest *effet utile* becomes a *carte blanche* for creating rules that might seem desirable to particular drafting teams, but have no foundation in the *acquis*.

The process of generalisation is the one aspect of the Acquis Group's work that is most likely to invite intense critical scrutiny. As should already be apparent from the discussion regarding the sources for the ACQP, there is a need for a degree of judgement by the Group in generalising detailed provisions from the *acquis* to form a suitable principle. Wilhelmsson rightly emphasises that there needs to be awareness of the 'legal-political decision making',[59] i.e., the fact that this undertaking is more than a 'pure academic or "technical" exercise'.[60] This observation reflects the wider academic debate about the perceived inadequacies in considering the political issues associated with the creation of the CFR, notably the fact that contract law appears to have been regarded as value-neutral,[61] and that issues such as the role of social justice seem to have been sidelined.[62] The comments to individual principles endeavour to explain at least some of the political issues associated with the generalisation to alleviate some of these concerns.

The Tension between Consumer and General Contract Law

As noted above, the bulk of the present *acquis* can be found in the field of consumer contract law, and it might therefore be thought that the ACQP would, predominantly, deal with consumer-specific issues. However, many provisions are not so limited. There are two reasons for this: first, the *acquis* itself does

---

[57]   Cf. Betlem, G (2005), 'Torts, a European *Ius Commune* and the private enforcement of Community law', *Cambridge Law Journal* 126–48.

[58]   See Twigg-Flesner, C and Wilhelmsson, T (2007), 'Comments to Article 2:207' in *Contract I*, at 98–101.

[59]   Wilhelmsson, 'Coherence Through Generalisation?', at 114.

[60]   Ibid.

[61]   Kennedy, D (2001), 'The Political Stakes in "Merely Technical" Issues of Contract Law', 9 *European Review of Prviate Law* 7–28.

[62]   Study Group on Social Justice in European Private Law (2004), 'Social Justice In European Contract Law: A Manifesto', 10 *European Law Journal* 653–74. For an even more critical view see Mattei, U and Nicola, F (2006), 'A "Social Dimension" in European Private Law? The call for setting a progressive agenda', 41 *New England Law Review* 1–66.

contain non-consumer provisions; and, secondly, some consumer-specific rules reflect a wider general contract law principle which is not specific to the consumer context.

One somewhat controversial example is the principle of good faith, which can be found in many *acquis* provisions. It is also a notion found in most national jurisdictions, although the common law remains reluctant to admit a general 'good faith' principle.[63] The *acquis* refers to this principle e.g., in the directives on Distance Selling (Article 4(2)) and Distance Selling of Financial Services (Article 3(2)). Moreover, the Unfair Commercial Practices Directive (UCPD),[64] although not a contract law measure, regulates the behaviour of traders dealing with consumers on the basis of a good faith standard (Article 2(h)). This has resulted in the development of the following general pre-contractual duty in Article 2:101 ACQP: '[i]n pre-contractual dealings, parties must act in accordance with good faith.' As can be seen, this Article is not limited to consumer contracts, but applies to all contracts. However, the *acquis* foundations for this provision appear to be consumer-specific measures,[65] with the Commercial Agents Directive as the sole exception.[66] It is bluntly conceded that this extension 'may raise a political issue',[67] with what might seem like an almost apologetic justification that 'it should, however, be kept in mind that ... many Member States recognise a general duty of pre-contractual faith'.[68] Such a generalisation could be difficult to justify, particularly beyond the consumer context into the sphere of commercial contracts, where there appears to be a significant common–civil law divide which the *acquis* in its present state has not yet bridged.[69] So in this respect, the Acquis Group may have overshot its target.

A further example of providing a general rule applicable to both consumer and commercial contracts is Article 2:201 ACQP. This states that:

> before the conclusion of a contract, a party has a duty to give to the other party such information concerning the goods or services to be provided as the other party can

---

[63] See e.g., Brownsword, R (2006), *Contract Law – Themes for the twenty-first century* (2nd edn) Oxford University Press), ch.6.

[64] Directive 2005/29/EC concerning unfair business-to-consumer commercial practices in the internal market (2005) OJ L149/22.

[65] See Pfeiffer, T and Ebers, M (2007), 'Comments to Art. 2:101' in *Contract I*, at 61–2.

[66] Directive 86/653/EEC. Note that Arts. 3(1) and 4(1) appear to be concerned with contractual dealings ('in performing his activities' and 'in his relations with his commercial agent' respectively), rather than *pre-contractual* dealings.

[67] Pfeiffer and Ebers, 'Comments to Art. 2:101' in *Contract I*, at 65.

[68] Ibid.

[69] See Cordero-Moss, G (2008), 'Contracts between Consumer Protection and Trade Usages: Some Observations on the Importance of State Contract Law' in Schulze, R (ed.), *CFR and Existing Contract Law*.

reasonably expect, taking into account the standards of quality and performance which would be normal under the circumstances.

In terms of sources in the *acquis*, the commentary[70] refers to Article 2 of the Consumer Sales Directive, which states that goods are presumed to be in conformity with the contract if they are fit for the purposes for which goods of the same type are normally used, and if they show the quality and performance which are normal in goods of the same type and which the consumer can reasonably expect. These reasonable expectations, and therefore the conformity standard itself, can be shaped by specific information given about the goods, and a seller can reduce his exposure for non-conformities by drawing existing defects to the attention of the consumer prior to concluding the contract. This is reflected in Article 2(3), according to which there shall be deemed not to be a lack of conformity if, at the time the contract was concluded, the consumer was aware, or could not reasonably be unaware, of the lack of conformity. Giving information about the quality of the goods therefore affects the degree of conformity required by the Directive,[71] and liability for a lack of conformity can be avoided by giving precise information about the specific defect. This could be characterised as a 'liability without disclosure' approach, which has effectively been reversed in Article 2:201 ACQP to a 'disclosure or liability' approach, although the practical significance seems to be limited.

In addition, this provision is an instance where recourse has been had to the CISG to justify the extension to the commercial sphere. The corresponding provision is Article 35 CISG. This is a provision on non-conformity, which is in very similar terms to Article 2 of the Directive. Although using the CISG can be controversial because it is not common to all the Member States, in this instance the problem is less severe: even British sales law contains provisions very similar to those found in the CISG.[72] As far as the substance of the provision is concerned, therefore, there seems to be a sufficient basis in the *acquis*. Jansen and Zimmermann, on the other hand, are critical of this provision, observing that 'from the mere fact that a rule can be read in a particular way, it does not follow that such interpretation is appropriate and meaningful'.[73] However, in this particular instance, the interpretation does seem appropriate.

---

[70] Twigg-Flesner, C and Wilhelmsson, T, 'Comments to Article 2:201' in *Contract I*, at 76–80.

[71] See also Twigg-Flesner, C (2005), 'Information Disclosure about the quality of goods – duty or encouragement?' in Howells, G, Janssen, A and Schulze, R (eds), *Information rights and obligations: a challenge for party autonomy and transactional fairness* (Ashgate).

[72] Sale of Goods Act 1979, ss.13, 14(2) and 14(3), as well as s.14(2C).

[73] Jansen and Zimmermann, 'Restating the *Acquis Communautaire*', at 533.

The decision to limit a particular provision to the consumer context can also give rise to the objection that a provision that could be generalised has not been so widened. Jansen and Zimmermann have argued that the restriction of Article 2:103 ACQP to consumer contracts is, in fact, an unexpressed political decision *against* a generalisation to least to some commercial contracts, which they regard as 'hardly convincing'.[74] But there seems to be no support in the *acquis* for such a wide-ranging pre-contractual information duty, and the use of pre-contractual information duties in consumer contracts does have a particular rationale.[75]

The Common Frame of Reference and the Acquis Principles

The ACQP have been incorporated into the DCFR, together with the broader outputs of the work undertaken by the Study Group which develops and extends the PECL. So the DCFR is effectively an amalgam of Study Group texts which seek to present best solutions based on comparative research of the various national laws, and the ACQP which are based on an analysis of the *acquis*.

It is against the backdrop of inserting the ACQP into the DCFR that one can identify a potentially rather serious shortcoming in the methodology of the Acquis Group caused, presumably, by the need to contribute *acquis*-based provisions to the DCFR within a short period of time. As will be explained below, in this author's view, a two-stage development of the ACQP would have been essential prior to their insertion into the DCFR to ensure, on the one hand, that the ACQP serve a good purpose as a free-standing exercise and, on the other, that the DCFR can properly fulfil its toolbox function. In fact, it is arguable that a third stage was also necessary, as will be explained below.

The first stage, which was not undertaken as a separate exercise, should have been to survey the *acquis communautaire* with a view to identifying three matters: first, are there any general principles of contract law (such as *pacta sunt servanda*) that can be recognised; secondly, which aspects of contract law are regulated and to what extent can one identify commonalities in the various measures; and thirdly, where are the main gaps in the *acquis* (for gaps there will be, as explained earlier)?

To an extent, the first issue has been addressed implicitly, but not yet been presented comprehensively in the ACQP – in *Contract I*, there are, as yet, no general principles of contract law. The second aspect is, of course, reflected in the output presented by the Acquis Group in *Contract I*.

---

74   Ibid., at 522.
75   Mankowski, P (2006), 'Formation of Contract and Pre-contractual duties to inform in a comparative perspective' in Grundmann, S and Schauer, M (eds), *The Architecture of European Codes and Contract Law* (Kluwer Law International).

It is with respect to the third that a useful opportunity has been missed. As already explained above, the *acquis communautaire* is pointillist, in that it deals with specific problems, and the solutions provided are incomplete: generally, contract law measures are directive-based and require implementation into national law, and, moreover, some matters are usually left to domestic law to resolve, with only a general objective specified. It would have been valuable to identify where there are regulatory gaps, in particular in respect of matters left to national law. Whilst there was some recognition in the ACQP as published, there was also a concern to avoid any gaps. Consequently, as explained earlier, the principle of effectiveness became a justification for some gap-filling principles. In other instances, a so-called 'grey rule' taken from the *Principles of European Contract Law* was used to complete the picture. It is regrettable that there has not been a separate version of the ACQP with such gaps, because this would have offered valuable insights into the extent of coverage within the *acquis* and the areas where there are significant gaps.

The foregoing assumes that it is possible to regard the *acquis* as an entirely autonomous system, free from national influences. Whilst this may be debatable – it is certainly the case that different national provisions may have shaped particular aspects of the *acquis* – it does seem possible to avoid any reference to national laws at this stage, particularly if any attempts to state principles without a clear foundation in the *acquis* are avoided.[76]

The second stage, which would have had to be completed prior to the insertion of ACQP provisions into the DCFR, should have been to examine how the different national laws have filled the various gaps identified at the first stage. This would have meant that the 'second stage ACQP' added to the DCFR would have dealt with matters already in the *acquis*, but taken a much fuller account of (a) what is clearly in the legislative and judicial *acquis*, and (b) how national law complements *acquis*-based rules in order to fill regulatory gaps. Such an exercise would have added to the value of the 'first stage ACQP' by providing an authoritative analysis of how EU and national laws have interacted to provide a new form of contract law.

The possibility of detailed analysis of this interaction is demonstrated by a separate, but related project undertaken by members of the Acquis Group for the European Commission which provides significant insights into the national implementation of six consumer contract law directives (as well as two further non-contract consumer directives): the *EC Consumer Law Compendium*. This

---

[76]   For a contrary view see Jansen and Zimmermann, 'Restating the *Acquis Communautaire*', at 516–20, who take issue with Arts. 1:303 (freedom of form) and 2:101 (contract formation) ACQP for lacking a suitable basis in the *acquis*. Zoll concedes that the Acquis Group may not have adhered to its methodology in respect of the provisions on formation: Zoll, 'Die Grundregeln der Acquis-Gruppe', at 109.

gives a detailed account of how national legislation has supplemented EC-based regulation, e.g., in respect of the consequences of exercising a right of withdrawal. This would be a good starting point for considering how to fill gaps in the *acquis*, and might offer more solid foundations than reliance on *effet utile* (cf. the example on remedies for breach of pre-contractual information duties, mentioned earlier). Whilst some of the findings have, of course, been taken on board in drafting the ACQP, as is evident from the notes and comments to individual principles, there has not been a concerted attempt to undertake this research into how national legislation has dealt with regulatory gaps for all the key directives (and, where relevant, regulations) on contract law. To my mind, this is regrettable, as this could, in itself, both have provided valuable knowledge about the state of the *acquis communautaire*, and offered possible solutions that could have been utilised in drafting the DCFR. However, such research work would have required a huge investment in time and manpower – the *EC Consumer Law Compendium* involved more than 40 researchers and took more than two years to complete, so this is obviously a task that could not have been tackled in the timescale envisaged by the Commission for the preparation of the DCFR.

It is argued here that a third stage should have followed the two stages outlined above. At that point, it would also have been appropriate to consider more carefully the value judgement and underlying political decisions inherent in creating a particular principle, and perhaps also to develop alternatives to provide the legislator with a choice e.g., between a provision that is protective of a weaker party such as a consumer and one that is less interventionist and based on party freedom.[77]

Furthermore, it would also then have been appropriate to cast the net of relevant source material wider, reaching beyond legal texts to consider any available empirical research findings, as well as related theoretical literature.[78] This would have been particularly important, e.g., with regard to the effectiveness of information duties in the context of consumer protection, or the practical utility of a right of withdrawal.[79] It might have revealed that such provisions, whilst reflecting the present *acquis*, have limited practical value, thereby raising as a policy issue whether such provisions ought to be retained in the DCFR and any future legislation based on it.

---

[77]   Schulze, R and Wilhelmsson, T (2008), 'From the Draft Common Frame of Reference towards European Contract Law Rules', 4 *European Review of Contract Law* 154–68 argue that the *acquis* already contains '"social" elements' (at 168), e.g., in respect of non-discrimination provisions.

[78]   See e.g., the discussion by Gómez, 'The Harmonization of Contract Law through European Rules'.

[79]   This is a point well made by Eidenmüller *et al.*, 'Der gemeinsame Referenzrahmen', at 535 and further at 544–5.

As will be apparent from the foregoing, the difference in sources and methodology for drafting the ACQP and Study Group provisions respectively has the potential for 'transplantation'[80] problems: combining comparative-based provisions with *acquis*-based provisions is a difficult tasks. This was taken on by a small group comprising representatives from the Study Group and the Acquis Group, known as the 'Compilation and Redaction Team', whose work has primarily been a technical exercise of ensuring terminological consistency within the DCFR, rather than to consider the wider challenges.

The fact that provisions dealing with *acquis*-based matters (notably on pre-contractual information duties, right of withdrawal, unfair terms and non-discrimination) have not been developed by taking full account of how national laws have supplemented *acquis*-derived provisions, but instead primarily restate what is in the *acquis* as such, could limit their usefulness in deploying the (D) CFR as a toolbox at a later stage. On the one hand, the *acquis*-based DCFR provisions will provide a more logical and coherent solution than the provisions currently found in individual directives. On the other, one can question whether they really provide the 'best solution' for these issues. For example, as noted earlier, the existing *acquis* on the right of withdrawal contains gaps with respect to the consequences of exercising the right of withdrawal, as well as the sanctions that might be imposed for failing to comply with pre-contractual information duties (whether limited to information about the existence of a right of withdrawal, or pre-contractual information duties generally). National laws have had to fill these gaps, but this is not fully reflected in the ACQP, and consequently the DCFR, for the reasons already given. It seems that even the *acquis*-based provisions required comparative research into national laws to identify how those matters not subject to concrete *acquis* rules were addressed. This might have revealed that the Member States have adopted very similar sanctions, for example, or it might have offered several different possibilities for regulating the consequences of exercising a right of withdrawal. Indeed, an examination of how national laws have filled gaps would have provided a rich source of material for something else which the DCFR is lacking: a choice between several possible regulatory responses. Indeed, the DCFR is designed almost entirely as a single code, which does not offer a choice of different legislative options.[81] This appears to conflict with its objective of providing a toolbox for the improvement of existing laws, and the adoption of new measures. In fact, the only discernible instance in the DCFR where there is any kind of choice (or rather, disagreement between the contributing research groups)

---

[80]   Borrowing, and possibly distorting, the concept developed in Watson, A (1993), *Legal Transplants* (2nd ed, University of Georgia Press).
[81]   Cf. Collins, *The European Civil Code*, at 77, on the 'paradox' of the DCFR.

is Article II.-9:404 on unfair terms: here, it is left open whether a term can be challenged only where it has not been individually negotiated, or whether this extends to negotiated terms.

The point is that the drive towards a single 'best solution' has meant that competing, or even complementary, alternatives which are equally worthwhile have not been presented as such in the DCFR. Moreover, if a high degree of commonality between the national laws had been identified, then this could have become a clear 'best solution' provided in the DCFR, but even where there are variations, it might have been possible to present several choices.[82]

None of the foregoing should be taken as suggesting that the ACQP in their present form are not valuable – quite the opposite is the case. However, writing with the benefit of active involvement in the drafting process, it seems to me that, had there been more time, it would have been possible to take better account of the complex interaction between national and European legislation within the field of the contract law *acquis*.

Not everyone would agree with this analysis. Zoll, for example, argues that the ACQP should not be understood as a separate set of principles, but rather be considered within the context of the DCFR.[83] In his view, the main purpose of the ACQP is to supplement the purely comparative work undertaken initially in drafting PECL and subsequently developed in the work of the Study Group. He would agree that the transposition of EU rules into national laws has to be taken into account, and – rightly – notes that this has been done in drafting several of the principles.[84] This is not disputed in this chapter; rather, it is argued that a more cautious approach, with clearly distinct stages, would have produced an altogether better result. In particular, the DCFR-driven approach to drafting the ACQP, and the attending pressures on time, has proven to be a disadvantage.

Use and Application of the Acquis Principles

Although, as already discussed, the immediate use for the ACQP will be to provide the *acquis*-based provisions for the DCFR, there are other instances where the ACQP may be of assistance. For example, as part of the review of the consumer *acquis*, the ACQP themselves, rather than their DCFR version, may provide the model provisions which could be utilised in developing a 'more coherent' *acquis*. The output which has been published to date has also given

---

[82] The absence of real regulatory alternatives in the interim DCFR is regrettable; it seems that the only 'alternative' is whether the provisions on unfair terms should be limited to non-negotiated terms only, or also extend to negotiated terms.

[83] Zoll, 'Die Grundregeln der Acquis-Gruppe', at 107.

[84] Ibid., at 108.

rise to scholarly debate, and *Contract I* was referred to by an Advocate-General
of the European Court of Justice.[85]

The review of the consumer acquis
Although one can justifiably have reservations about the suitability of the ACQP
in their present form for inclusion in the DCFR, the Acquis Group has succeeded
in providing a blueprint for recasting the existing *acquis communautaire* in a
simpler – and arguably more coherent – fashion. Take as an example the area of
pre-contractual information duties: the various directives which contain PCIDs
are often criticised for presenting long lists of information that needs to be provided without any logic attached to these lists. Whilst the ACQP cannot offer
any guidance as to which particular items of information are really essential,
they can – and do – suggest a better way of presenting this information in order
to increase the likelihood that consumers might actually be able to digest that
information. Similarly, in respect of the right of withdrawal, the ACQP offer
one coherent set of rules which synthesises the rather divergent approaches that
have evolved through several directives, as well as ECJ case law, over time, and
thereby provide a possible model that could be utilised in the on-going review
of the consumer *acquis*.

In the autumn of 2008, the European Commission presented a proposal for
a new directive on consumer contractual rights.[86] This contains a chapter on
general pre-contractual information duties which reflects, at least in part, shades
of influence by the corresponding provisions in the ACQP, although they are
not referred to expressly. Admittedly, the draft provision on pre-contractual
information is still a very general one, and, unlike the ACQP, there are no
specific remedies for consumers where these duties have been violated. More
significantly, there is also a chapter on the right of withdrawal, which will introduce a standardised procedure for exercising the right of withdrawal. Again,
however, some of the provisions from the ACQP have not found their way into
the proposed directive, notably those dealing with 'linked contracts'. The proposed directive will undoubtedly prompt an intense scholarly debate, not least
because of its shift towards full harmonisation. The main surprise, however, is
that the proposal does not seem to take proper account of the corresponding
DCFR provisions (nor all of the ACQP provisions), which must raise the question whether both are likely to find any form of concrete application in the near
future.

---

[85] Case C–412/06 *Hamilton v. Volksbank Filder eG* [2008] ECR I–n.y.r., at para 24
(n. 8).
[86] COM(2008)614 final.

CONCLUSIONS

This chapter has been a critical reflection by the author on the process of developing the ACQP. The critical tone to the foregoing should be understood as one of constructive criticism from a single insider within the Group, and one that, it is hoped, might chart the way forward for the years to come. There is clearly a lot more work the Acquis Group could do in strengthening its *Principles of Existing EC Contract Law*, particularly with regard to the interaction between national laws and European legislation.

It seems conceivable that the ACQP might, in time, become of more immediate relevance than the much more extensive DCFR. It remains uncertain what, if anything, will become of the DCFR, but the *acquis* is already there and being added to, and the ACQP can help in promoting a better understanding of how far EU legislation already affects contract law.

Overall, the ACQP are a significant development in the story of harmonisation, and whilst there are aspects of them which are far from perfect, they are an important milestone in the Europeanisation of contract law.

25. Harmonisation of competition law in multilateral trade framework: China's WTO membership and its Anti-monopoly Law*

Qianlan Wu**

I. INTRODUCTION

The debate on economic globalization mainly centres on whether it is defined as a global economy in the making or as increasing internationalization of economies.[1] The two conceptualizations of economic globalization seem to correspond to respective understandings on global law development. The concept of one global economy can provide justification for the development of a uniform law to govern the global market, while the internalization of different economies can provide economic foundations for the legal pluralism in global law.[2]

Nevertheless, amid the complexity of economic globalization and global law development, domestic markets have transcended national borders and become increasingly interconnected. Consequently, market regulations in different economies have become more interconnected and domestic and international market regulation rules have intertwined.[3]

The development of competition laws in different economies serves as one good example. Domestic competition laws can have spill over effects on

---

* Editor's note: This chapter is based on the development of Anti-monopoly Law of China until 2010.

** Lecturer, School of Contemporary Chinese Studies, University of Nottingham, UK.

[1] Manuel Castells (2000), 'Global Information Capitalism' in David Held and Anthony McGrew (eds), *The Global Transformation Reader*, (Polity) at 303.

[2] Wener Menski (2006), *Comparative Law in a global context: the legal system of Asia and Africa* (Cambridge University Press) at 3–25.

[3] Francis Snyder (2004), 'Economic Globalization and the Law in the Twenty First Century', in Austin Sarat (ed.) *Blackwell Companion to Law and Society* (Blackwell Publishing) 624–34.

markets out of their own jurisdictions when the law has extra-territorial effect. Overlapping regulation by different competition laws on players in global markets may increase the cost of operation and decrease the certainty of legal protection. Furthermore, discriminatory application of competition laws may constitute a hidden barrier to restrict liberalization of trade on global markets.[4] Based on the grounds of efficiency and market access, competition laws have been called to be harmonised and to be harmonised with international trade norms such as non-discrimination.[5]

However, harmonising competition laws in international trade fora such as the World Trade Organization has experienced a set-back in the WTO Doha Round due to resistance from the developing countries and the US.[6] Nevertheless, an increasing number of economies have adopted competition laws following the Doha Round. Their competition laws have shown to a certain extent convergence in the following aspects: firstly the structure of competition regulation mainly includes regulating anti-competitive agreements, dominance and mergers. Secondly, competition law has been enforced by one independent regulator or increasingly enforced by private litigation. Thirdly, the competition laws in these countries show shifting of values between social and economical goals, such as fairness, are pure economic concerns. In recent years, more competition authorities have chosen to emphasize the efficiency concerns and converged to adopt a more economics based approach in enforcing competition laws. This voluntary harmonisation of competition laws has been promoted through regional or bilateral trade agreements, dialogues or technical assistance.[7] International trade therefore continues to play a role in the harmonisation of competition laws. Questions can therefore be asked to what extent can international trade norms be internalized into competition law harmonisations?

China acceded to the WTO in 2001 and adopted its first comprehensive competition law, the Anti Monopoly Law (AML), in 2007. This chapter uses

---

[4]   Petersmann, E.U. (1998), 'The Need for Integrating Trade and Competition Rules in the WTO World Trade and Legal System', in G. Parry, A. Qureshi and H. Steiner (eds), *The Legal and Moral Aspects of International Trade* (London and New York, Routledge) and Bacchetta, M., H. Horn and P. Mavroidis (1997), 'Do Negative Spillovers from Nationally Pursued Competition Policies Provide a Case for Multilateral Competition Rules?', Working paper, 14 August.

[5]   Ignacio Garcia Bercero and Stefan D. Amarasinh (2001), 'Moving the Trade and Competition Debate Forward', *Journal of International Economic Law* at 481–506.

[6]   D.J. Gerber (1999), 'The US–European Conflict Over the Globalization of Antitrust Law', 34 *New England Law Review* 123.

[7]   For example, as a result of the EU–Mediterranean Partnership in 1995, 13 Mediterranean states developed competition laws based on EU competition law principles: http://ec.europa.eu/external_relations/euromed/index_en.htm. In 2003, the EU and China established the EU China Competition Policy Dialogue, available at www.euchinawto.org.

China's development of AML after its WTO membership as a case study and attempts to evaluate the impact of WTO membership on AML development and to what extent international trade norms can be internalized into the Chinese AML.

The results of the evaluation include firstly that WTO membership has an impact on AML development. China's WTO membership provides the government with an opportunity to push forward difficult market governance reform and complete the task of building up competition regulation. Secondly, the non-discrimination principle is internalized into the AML to a certain degree as the AML provides regulation to both private and public restrictions of competition on the market. However, the internalization of the non-discrimination principle can be *de facto* limited as the AML has the possibility to exempt the key state-owned sector from its regulation and it provides broad and lax exemption for regulation in anti-competitive agreements, abuse of dominance and mergers. Thirdly, the AML is to be enforced by multiple government agents jointly and may suffer from overly intrusive enforcement caused by possible overlapping regulation. Furthermore, the effectiveness of the enforcement of the AML with respect to administrative abuse may be restricted, given the features of administrative law in China. However, the WTO Trade Policy Review Mechanism lacks legally binding force and the dispute settlement mechanism can be costly and time consuming. As a result, the supervisory role played by the WTO in the enforcement of AML can be limited.

The results of the evaluation require us to rethink what is the role played by international trade norms in competition laws development. In particular, it raises questions as to whether the non-discrimination principle remains the optimal choice to develop and harmonise competition laws. The chapter argues that the non-discrimination principle aiming at improving market access contributes to improving contestability of the market, which is one of the important economic rationales for competition law. However, market contestability in competition law goes beyond market access and aims to achieve maximization of potential competition, which would involve economic analysis, and in some cases positive action to protect disadvantaged players on the market. Partially or overly to emphasize the non-discrimination principle in competition law may deprive the economy of the right to carry out economic analysis or to provide substantive protection to competition on the market, which inevitably would cause resistance from these economies. The chapter therefore calls for international trade organizations wishing to harmonise competition law to listen more to the voice of the economies adopting competition law and strike a balance between international trade liberalization and market specific competition protection in an individual economy.

II. ECONOMIC GLOBALIZATION AND HARMONISATION OF COMPETITION LAW

1. Economic Globalization and Law

Although globalization is not a new phenomenon, its definition remains contested.[8] Held argues that globalization means the entrenched and enduring pattern of worldwide interconnectedness and denotes expanding scale, growing magnitude, speeding up and deepening impact of interregional flows and patterns of social interaction.[9]

Economic globalization can be regarded as one important reason, result and aspect of the complex globalization phenomenon. Economic globalization has been defined as internationalization of capital and cross-border flows.[10] However, it involves more than market integration.[11] The increasing interconnectedness of economic activities on the part of all private, public or hybrid forms of players has raised the question whether a single borderless global economy exists today.[12] Nevertheless, the centre of the argument remains whether economic globalization means increasingly interconnectedness of national economies or the emergence of a universal global economy.[13]

Economic globalization has a direct impact on global law development. Snyder argues that in economic globalization national rules have been increasingly influenced by external factors and domestic decisions are conditions, shaped or made elsewhere as transnational legal regimes penetrated national legal fields.[14] In other words, economic globalization has witnessed the increasing intertwining of international and domestic rules. This intertwining effect has been particularly obvious in some fields such as competition law than in other.[15]

---

[8] Globalization has been defined as action at a distance in Giddens (1999), *The Third Way* (Cambridge: Polity Press) and as time space compression in Harvey, D (1989), *The Condition of Postmodernity* (Oxford: Wiley Blackwell).

[9] David Held and Anthony McGrew (2000), *The Global Transformation Reader* (Polity), at 3.

[10] Saskia Sassen (2002), 'From Globalization and its discontents' in Gary Bridge and Sophie Watson (eds), *The Blackwell City Reader* (Blackwell Publishing) at161.

[11] Francis Snyder (2004), 'Economic Globalization and the Law in the Twenty First Century', in Austin Sarat (ed.), *Blackwell Companion to Law and Society* (Blackwell Publishing) 624–34.

[12] David Held and Anthony McGrew (2000), *The Global Transformation Reader* (Polity) at 250.

[13] Ibid., at 300.

[14] Francis Snyder (2004), 'Economic Globalization and the Law in the Twenty First Century', in Austin Sarat (ed.), *Blackwell Companion to Law and Society* (Blackwell Publishing) 624–34.

[15] Ibid.

In the field of competition law, although norms on international competition law have been underdeveloped, the norms of international trade have impacted on the development of competition law in different economies including competition regulation. Questions therefore can be asked as to what extent can the norms for international trade impact on the harmonisation of competition law in different economies.

It should be noted that the intertwining of international rules and domestic rules in economic globalization is not a one-way process. Risse argues that the internalization and implementation of international norms into the domestic system can be viewed as a socialization process. This socialization process is not straightforward, but experiences – in a spiral order – different stages including instrumental adaptation, moral consciousness raising, augmentation, dialogue and persuasion and institutionalization and habitulization, in which various agents including the state have participated.[16] According to Risse's model, it can be seen that the state that oversees each stage has an important role in the socialization of international norms. It is argued that economic globalization has not undermined national economic sovereignty in any significant way and states and national politics may play an important role, if not more than before.[17]

However, it should also be noted that competition law is a highly technocratic subject and its design and enforcement demand a high level of expertise and resource, which often make it out of reach for developing countries. Furthermore, competition law has been held as *sui generis*. It has its substance relying mostly, if not excessively, compared with other legal subjects, on economic theories chosen by the regulator and is also subject to the doctrines of the legal system it is embedded in.[18] The choice of underpinning economic theories is subject to the political economy of different market economies and the development and application of the law is subject to the legal doctrines, which vary from jurisdiction to jurisdiction. Therefore, on top of the social embeddedness of market economies, the nature of competition law may also constrain the socialization of international trade norms into the competition laws of different economies.

---

[16]   Thomas Risse (1999), *The Power of Human Rights:International Norms and Domestic Change* (Cambridge University Press) at 10.

[17]   Garret, Geoffrey (2000), 'Global Markets and National Politics', in David Held and Anthony McGrew (eds), *The Global Transformation Reader* (Polity), at 384.

[18]   Maher, Imelda (2004), 'Regulating Competition', in C Parker, C Scott, N Lacey and J Braithwaite (eds), *Regulating Law* (Oxford University Press) at 192.

2.   Economic Globalization and Harmonisation of Competition Law

The reasons for harmonising competition laws in economic globalization have mainly included the following.

In the context of economic globalization market players, in particular multinational companies, can find a way to get away with their competition restrictive agreements or merger or acquisition activities in jurisdictions where competition law is not adopted. This is argued to be likely to lead to restriction of efficiency and reduction of welfare on the global market.[19] Secondly, the cross-border competition restriction on the part of international players may fall under multiple regulations of competition laws of different economies, given the extraterritorial application of competition laws. This may sometimes cause overlapping applications of competition regulation and increases the cost of players and decreases efficiency in the global economy.[20] Furthermore, some economies or private parties are concerned that the lack of competition law in one economy may hinder that economy from being liberalized and fair, thus putting foreign competitors at a disadvantage even after trade tariffs are reduced.[21] In fact, governments and private parties in trade liberalization are concerned that the discriminatory application of competition rules by importing countries may be used as an instrument to protect the domestic industry of the latter against foreign competitors and consequently constitute trade barriers and restrict market access.[22] Therefore, the main grounds underpinning the harmonisation of competition laws have centered on the protection of efficiency, non-discrimination treatment and market access, and it is argued that competition regulation worldwide should move forward in line with international trade norms.[23]

International organizations such as the United Nations Conference on Trade and Development (UNCTAD), the OECD (Organization of Economic

---

[19]   Bacchetta, M., H. Horn and P. Mavroidis (1997), 'Do Negative Spillovers from Nationally Pursued Competition Policies Provide a Case for Multilateral Competition Rules?', working paper, 14 August 1997.

[20]   Petersmann, E.U. (1998), 'The Need for Integrating Trade and Competition Rules in the WTO World Trade and Legal System', in G. Parry, A. Qureshi and H. Steiner (eds), *The Legal and Moral Aspects of International Trade* (London and New York: Routledge), 7–26.

[21]   For example, this was one main concern of the EU. See 'Working Group on the Interaction between Trade and Competition Policy – Communication from the European Community and its Member States', WT/WGTCP/W178 7 July 1998 (98-2702).

[22]   Bernard Hoekman and Peter Holmes (2002), 'Competition Policy, Developing Countries and WTO', 22 *World Economy* 875–93.

[23]   Ignacio Garcia Bercero and Stefan D. Amarasinha (2001), 'Moving the Trade and Competition Debate Forward', *Journal of International Economic Law* 481–506.

Cooperation and Development) and the World Trade Organization (WTO) have all actively participated in the harmonisation of competition law. Of these organizations, the WTO was regarded as an appropriate forum to harmonise competition law worldwide because of its wide membership, its adjudicative dispute settlement regime, and past experience in harmonising trade related regulation such as anti-dumping rules.[24]

In 1996 at the WTO Ministerial Conference in Singapore, a working group on interaction between Trade and Competition Policy (WGTCP) was set up. In the 2001 WTO Doha Ministerial Declaration it was provided that the focus of WGTCP would be to clarify core principles and provisions on hardcore cartel, modalities on voluntary cooperation and support for competition law development and capacity building in developing countries under the international trade norms of transparency, non-discrimination and fairness.[25]

However, the harmonisation of competition laws in WGTCP experienced a deadlock because of resistance from developing countries and the lukewarm welcome by the US. By the time competition policy was put on the agenda under the WGTCP, the European Union (EU) had been an active advocator of the harmonisation of competition laws,[26] however most developing countries do not have competition laws. The developing countries are opposed to the idea of giving competence to harmonised competition rules of the WTO, as they claim this would restrict their space for industrial development and competitiveness building.[27] Similarly, the US was reluctant to welcome harmonisation of competition rules because it is reluctant to subject its robust and well developed antitrust regime to harmonised international core principles.[28] In the WTO July decision in 2004, the WTO General Council decided that the issue of competition law would not be one part of the programme set out in the WTO Doha Declaration.

Nevertheless, the current WTO framework provides regulation on trade related competition issues in the following ways.

Under the WTO framework, the GATT agreement does not contain explicit provision regarding competition regulation except the Non-Discrimination and National Treatment Principles provided in Article III.4 of GATT. The

[24]   Taylor Martyn (2006), *International Competition Law: A New Dimension for the WTO* (Cambridge University Press) 147–83.

[25]   Paragraph 25 of the Doha Ministerial Declaration.

[26]   DJ Gerber (1999), 'The US–European Conflict Over the Globalization of Antitrust Law', 34 *New England Law Review* 123.

[27]   Frederic Jenny (2006), 'Cartels and Collusion in Developing Countries: Lessons from Empirical Evidence', 29 *World Competition*, 109–37.

[28]   DJ Gerber (1999), 'The US–European Conflict Over the Globalization of Antitrust Law', 34 *New England Law Review* 123.

WTO Dispute Settlement appellate body has confirmed in the case law that the term affecting in Article III.4 has a broad scope of application. Therefore, as proved in case law, members' economic policies, including competition policy, competition laws and regulations fall within this category and can be subject to scrutiny within the WTO framework.[29]

It is the GATS and the Annex on Telecommunication that touch upon competition regulation in the domestic markets of members. GATS Article VIII provides regulation in relation to monopolies and exclusive service suppliers. Members of the WTO are required to ascertain that a domestic monopoly supplier of a service complies with most favoured nation treatment obligations. The member must ensure that the domestic monopoly service supplier does not abuse its monopoly when it competes outside the scope of its monopoly, either directly or through an affiliated company. In the case of exclusive service suppliers, the member is furthermore prohibited from either formally or in effect fixing the number of suppliers or preventing competition among those suppliers. In areas where market access commitments are made, members are prohibited from taking measures to limit the number of service suppliers, limit the total value of service transaction and limit the total number of service operations.[30]

The same spirit is reflected in the Annex on Telecommunication and the case of *US–Mexico*.[31] Member states must ensure that a service provider from any other territory has access to and usage of public telecommunication transport networks on a reasonable basis and must accord national treatment to service provider from any other territory.[32]

In addition to WTO agreements, competition policies of members are subject to the trade policy review mechanism under the WTO, and some members, like China, may be subject to particular review mechanisms provided by the accession protocols as a result of multilateral negotiations.

In recent years, in spite of the deadlock in competition law harmonisation in the WTO Doha round, many jurisdictions have adopted competition laws or considered doing so. More interestingly, many developing countries have introduced competition regulation as a result of bilateral trade agreements. In some cases, developing countries choose to model their competition law on that

---

[29]   *Japan – Measures Affecting Consumer Photographic Film and Paper*, WT/DS44, WTO Panel Report 1998, available at www.wto.org/english/tratop_e/dispu_e/cases_e/ds44_e.htm.

[30]   Art. VIII, General Agreements on Trade in Services.

[31]   *Mexico – Measures Affecting Telecommunications Services*, WT/DS204/R 2004, available at www.wto.org/english/tratop_e/dispu_e/cases_e/ds204_e.htm.

[32]   Wellenius, Björn, Galarza Tohen, Juan, Manuel and Guermazi, Boutheina (2005), 'Telecommunications and the WTO: The Case of Mexico', World Bank Policy Research Working Paper No. 3759.

of their main trading partner such as the EU or US in bilateral or regional trade agreements.[33] The reasons behind this voluntary convergence of competition regulation worldwide are various. One of the possible explanations could be that strong trade players like the EU or US actively export their competition rules and values through technical assistance programmes, with an aim to facilitate trade originating from their markets into the markets of targeted developing economy. For example, the European Commssion sets out a market access strategy for European businesses to face the global challenge of international trade in 1996.[34] In the strategy, the EC emphasizes that in order to promote the development of European business in internatonal trade, the Community should focus on third country market opening.[35] The EC must, among others, act against non-traditional trade barriers including the lack or ineffective enforcement of competition law in trading economies and actively promote the establishment of these rules.[36] Strong trade partners may use competition regulation as leverage in bilateral trade agreements to guarantee increased market access in developing countries' markets. Based on this, the power a developing country has in international trade negotiations seems to have an important impact on the extent of harmonisation of its competition law with its dominant trade partner. Therefore it is fair to say that international trade does to a certain extent have an influential role to play in the harmonisation of competition laws in different economies.

III.   CHINA'S DEVELOPMENT OF COMPETITION LAW AFTER ITS WTO MEMBERSHIP

1.   State, Law and Market Economy in China in the Era of Globalization

China started its market oriented economic reform in 1978 and established a socialist market economy in 1993. From 1978 to 2007, China achieved continuous economic growth. The government has declared in its latest five-year development plan that China should transform its development model from

---

[33]   United Nations University (2003), *Regionalism, Multilateralism and Economic Integration: The Recent Experience* (United Nations University Press) at 117.

[34]   Communication From the Commission, 'The Challenge of International Trade: A Market Access Strategy for the European Union', Brussels, 14 February 1996, COM(96)53 final, available at http://trade.ec.europa.eu/doclib/docs/2003/june/tradoc_113175.pdf.

[35]   See above at 4.

[36]   See above at 5.

relying on export and foreign investment to developing a recycling economy, high technology and key industries, which named the new industrialization strategy.[37]

The development of a market economy in China forces the state to transform from an all-party state to a modern regulator based on an emerging legal system. A modern legal system is developing quickly as China, like any other market economy, requires legal rules to be installed to provide certainty for transactions, to define property and provide market governance.[38] However, the state maintains its leading role in creating and developing a market economy.[39] In fact, compared with the state administrative system and social customs and kinship, which have strong links with the economic system, the legal system is relatively loosely coupled with market development in China.[40]

The legal system in China is a hybrid of the Soviet Union legal system legacy emphasizing social control and the European Continental Civil Law tradition of hierarchy of rules and codification.[41] Though new legislation has been adopted speedily to support the Socialist Market Economy development, the development of the Chinese legal system contains the following characteristics.

Firstly, the development of new legislation reflects or conforms to the Constitution of China.[42] With respect to the development of a socialist market economy, the 2004 Constitution amendment provides that the state will strive to establish a socialist market economy and a socialist legal system.[43] The Constitution provides that in developing the socialist market economy, the foundation of the economic system is public ownership.[44] The state-owned sector is the leading force of the national economy and the state guarantees the consolidation and development of this sector.[45] The private sector is one important component

---

[37] For a brief summary of the 11th five-year plan of China in English, see www.china.org.cn/english/2006lh/160403.htm.

[38] Neil Fligstein and Iona Mara-Drita (1996), 'To Make a Market: Reflections on the Attempt to Create a Single Market in the European Union', 102 *American Journal of Sociology* 1.

[39] Wu, Qianlan (2007), 'The Making of a Market Economy in China: Transformation of Government Regulation of Market Development', 13 *European Law Journal* 750–71.

[40] Ruskola, Teemu (2000), 'Conceptualizing Corporations and Kinship: Comparative Law and Development Theory in a Chinese Perspective', 52 *Stanford Law Review* 1599–729.

[41] Donovan, Dolores A. (1987), 'The Structure of the Chinese Criminal Justice System: A Comparative Perspective', 21 *University of San Francisco Law Review* 229–316.

[42] Since China's Constitution in 1982, the Constitution has been amended in 1994, 1999 and 2004.

[43] Art. 18 Constitution 2004.

[44] Art. 6 Constitution 2004.

[45] Art. 7 Constitution 1993.

of a socialist market economy and the state protect lawful rights and interest held by the private sector. The state encourages, supports and leads the development of the private sector and supervises and administers the private sector.[46]

In other words, it is China's constitutional principle that the socialist market economy regards the state-owned sector as the dominant and priority part, while acknowledging the private sector as one lawful component. This spirit of the socialist market economy has been reflected in various government policies, measures and legislations. As a result, most of the laws adopted to support the market economy development contain the support of the development of a socialist market economic order as one of their main goals.[47]

Secondly, the development of the Chinese legal system, in particular its economic laws, has in a large part been developed based on legal transplantation of foreign laws. However, China rarely transplants foreign rules *per se*, but often examines the foreign rules based on China's own political, social, economic and legal conditions and necessities before determining which part and to what extent foreign rules will be transplanted into its own system.[48]

Based on the foregoing, it can be seen that in line with the development of a socialist market economy, the legal system has begun to be more closely coupled with the economic system than before. The legal system has also started to build the protection of individual rights and stresses the importance of private law development by fostering a complete civil code in China. However, in this process, the role of law within the society remains largely instrumental and centres on achieving state policies.

## 2.		China's WTO Membership and Anti-Monopoly Law Development

### 2.1		China's WTO membership and competition regulation
China acceded to the WTO in 2001. Its accession to the WTO has had a substantial effect on the liberalization of trade in goods and services on the Chinese market and the administrative framework of the Chinese market.[49] In terms of competition law development, China is subject to the following WTO requirements.

---

[46]		Art. 11 Constitution 2004.
[47]		See preamble to the Company Law 2005, the Contract Law 1999, the Property Law 2007.
[48]		This legal borrowing strategy is clearly confirmed in the speech addressed by the head of the National People's Congress on 16 April 2008, available at http://theory.people.com.cn/GB/49169/49171/7127323.html.
[49]		Cross, Karen Halverson (2004), 'China's WTO Accession: Economic, Legal, and Political Implications', 27 *Boston College International and Comparative Law Review* at 319.

Firstly, pursuant to China's Accession Protocol, China has made commitments in the fields of different economic policies, including policies on the non-discrimination principle, monetary and fiscal policy, foreign exchange, foreign investment policy, pricing policy and state-owned enterprises.[50]

Secondly, China is subject to the transitional review mechanism under its WTO commitments. In the transitional review, China must notify the above-mentioned macroeconomics polices to the relevant committees under the WTO. The Chinese government must submit its annual economic development programmes, China's five-year development plan and any industrial or sectoral programmes or policies promulgated by central and sub-central government entities. Thirdly, China's enforcement of its WTO commitment is subject to the WTO trade policy review, and competition policy is one economic policy subject to the scrutiny of the Trade Policy Review.[51]

However, neither WTO agreements nor China's accession protocol explicitly require China to adopt a competition law as one part of China's WTO obligations. The WTO has provided soft law guidelines on China's competition law development in its Trade Policy Review.

The 2006 WTO Trade Policy Review for China provides that competition law is important to China's transformation from a planned economy into a market economy.[52] However, China faces particular concerns in its development of competition law against a backdrop of economic transition. China's economy is featured with its duality, namely that public ownership remains a mainstay of the economy with the private sector developing alongside, with administrative and state monopolies, and with barriers to internal trade. However, the review states that the complexity of ownership structure in China's economy should not prevent China from adopting a competition law.[53] In other words, China's 'socialist' feature for its market economy should not prevent it from adopting a competition law.

The Trade Policy Review provides advice on both the design and enforcement of competition law in China. It provides the targets to be regulated by China's competition law and states that administrative restrictions of competition in the Chinese market should be dealt with in China's enforcement of competition law.[54]

The Trade Policy Review then emphasizes that enforcement of competition law in China is of great importance. The review recommends China to avoid an

---

[50]   Annex 1A II, Accession of the People's Republic of China, WT/L/432, 23 November 2000.

[51]   Art. 18 of ibid.

[52]   Para. 44, WTO Trade Policy Review on China, WT/TPR/S/161.

[53]   Para. 244, of ibid.

[54]   Para. 245, of ibid.

overly intrusive or discriminatory approach. Transparency and non-discrimination principles must be upheld in the application of competition law.[55]

The Trade Policy Review also touches upon competition regulation and industrialization, which is one common concern for many developing countries. It states that when a developing country wishes to achieve industrialization, possible tensions may arise between development and industrial policies of fostering national champions. However, the Review did not offer any practical solutions for solving this tension, but stressed that 'a well tailored competition law will lead to efficiencies while helping to prevent accumulation of market power and possible related abuses'.[56]

2.2 The Anti-Monopoly Law

Against this backdrop, China's first comprehensive competition law, the Anti-Monopoly Law (AML), was adopted in 2007. The AML sets out its goal to prevent and prohibit monopolistic behaviour, protect fair competition, improve market efficiency, protect consumer interests and public interests and promote the healthy development of China's socialist market economy.[57] The AML includes:

Regulation on Anti Competitive Agreements (Articles 13–16)
Regulation on Abuse of Dominance (Articles 17–18)
Regulation on Concentration (Articles 20–31)
Regulation on Administrative Abuse (Articles 31–37)
Enforcement (Articles 38–45)
Legal Liability (Articles 46–54)

In terms of regulation on anti-competitive Agreements, the AML mirrors Article 101 of EU competition law. It regulates both horizontal and vertical restraints.[58] It sets out that horizontal agreements which fix or change product price, restrict output, divide the sales market or the raw material procurement market, restrict new technological development, boycott transactions or which are defined by a competition authority as restricting competition, must be prohibited.[59] Furthermore, the AML provides clearance of anti-competitive agreements on the ground of *de minimis*[60] and provides an exemption clause similar to Article 101(3) EU competition law.

---

[55]   Para. 246, of ibid.
[56]   Para. 247, of ibid.
[57]   The Preamble to the AML.
[58]   Art. 14 AML.
[59]   Art. 13 AML.
[60]   Art. 15 AML.

However, the AML regulation on anti-competitive agreements does not contain a market integration imperative like that of EU competition law. Furthermore, the AML regulation on anti competitive agreements provides broader and laxer grounds for exemption than Article 101(3) of EU competition law. The AML exemption clause contains similar grounds to what is provided by legal provisions and case law under Article 103(3), which include, among others, promoting technological and research development, increasing efficiency, environmental protection and consumer benefits.[61] On top of this, the AML exemption clause provides that anti-competitive agreements can be exempted on the grounds of protecting China's interests in international trade and international economic cooperation and alleviating over- or reduced production caused by an economy slump.[62] Unlike Article 101(3) that requires the undertakings to prove satisfaction of all exemption grounds cumulatively in order to be exempted, the AML provides that anti-competitive agreements can be exempted as long as the undertaking can prove it satisfies any one of the grounds.[63]

The AML regulation of abuse of dominance mirrors Article 102 of EU competition law. It regulates the abuse of dominance but not dominance *per se*.[64] The AML regulates both exclusive and exploitative abuse of dominance including predatory pricing, refusal to deal, tie-in sales, discriminatory pricing and other abuse of dominance defined by the competition authority.[65] Furthermore, the AML endorses a market share approach to define dominance on the market.[66]

Unlike Article 102 EU, which keeps a close eye on undertakings with dominant positions on the market, the AML provides that undertakings with dominant positions based on market share analysis can be treated as not dominant if the undertaking in question can prove it.[67] It remains to be seen what evidence the undertakings must provide to satisfy this condition. However, the design of the provision shows that the regulation has provided a *de jure* exemption clause for regulation of abuse of dominance in the AML.

The AML regulation on mergers mirrors in general that of the EU Merger Regulation. The AML provides that concentration includes merger, acquisition, taking over and joint ventures.[68] Concentrations are required to be notified to relevant competition authorities.[69]

---

[61] Art. 81(3) Treaty of European Union.
[62] Art. 15 AML.
[63] Art. 15 AML.
[64] Art. 17 AML.
[65] Art. 17 AML.
[66] Arts 17–19 AML.
[67] Art. 19 AML.
[68] Art. 20 AML.
[69] Arts 21 to 26 AML.

The AML merger control has not stated clear criteria for what kind of merger should be prohibited, but provided that in regulating mergers the following factors should be taken into consideration, namely the market power of the undertakings party to the merger, market concentration ratio, the impact of the merger on market access and technological progress, the impact of the merger on consumers and the impact of the merger on the national economy.[70] The AML provides that if undertakings can prove that the concentration can bring about a positive impact which outweighs restriction of competition or which is compatible with public interests, the competition authority can give clearance to the concentration.[71] AML merger control differs from the dominance test as provided by EU Council regulation 4064/89 on the control of concentration.[72] The AML merger clearance approach mirrors the efficiency-oriented market analysis endorsed by US merger control[73] and the substantive test used by EC merger control in 2004.[74]

In terms of regulation of administrative abuse, the AML provides that industrial associations, which are semi-governmental organizations in the Chinese administrative system,[75] are prohibited from organizing anti-competitive agreements.[76] Most importantly, the AML has provided that the government administrative authorities are prohibited from abusing their power to restrict operation or purchase on the part of undertakings. Administrative authorities must not restrict free movement of goods in the Chinese market by setting discriminatory charges for products originating from other regions in China, set up technical standard barriers to prevent products from other regions entering local markets, set up administrative licences exclusive for products from other regions, set up obstacles to free transportation of products from other regions entering or exiting local markets, prevent the free movement of products between local and other regional markets.[77]

---

[70] Art. 27 AML.

[71] Art. 28 AML.

[72] Council Regulation No 4064/89, 21 December 1989, OJ (1989) L 395 at 1–12.

[73] US Horizontal Merger Guidelines 1997 Section 1 provides requirement on market analysis in merger regulation, available at www.usdoj.gov./atr/public/guideline/horiz_book/toc.html.

[74] Council Regulation 139/2004, 20 January 2004, OJ (2004) L24 1–22 , Lars-Hendrick Roller and Miguel de la Mano, 'The Impact of the New Substantive Test in European Merger Control', available at http://ec.europa.eu/dgs/competition/economist/new_substantive_test.pdf.

[75] Wu, Qianlan (2007), 'The Making of a Market Economy in China: Transformation of Government Regulation of Market Development', 13 *European Law Journal* 750–71.

[76] Art. 16 AML.

[77] Arts 32–37 AML.

In terms of enforcement, the AML provides that a Competition Coordination Council will be set up under the State Council (the central government) to be responsible for setting out competition policy, publishing market evaluation reports, issuing enforcement guidelines, coordinating enforcement by different government authorities and other responsibilities imposed by the State Council.[78]

The AML is enforced by different government agents jointly, and these possible agents include the National Development and Reform Committee (NDRC), the Ministry of Commerce (MOFCOM) and the State Administration of Industry and Commerce (SAIC) under the coordination of the State Council Competition Coordination Council.

The three competition authorities engaged in competition regulation to various extents before the birth of the AML. The NDRC is the main regulator for pricing and responsible for regulating price fixing agreements provided by the Price Law.[79] The SAIC is responsible for enforcing the Unfair Competition Law, which involves the regulation of abuse of monopoly by the state-owned sector and the abuse of administrative power by the governments.[80] The MOFCOM is the main regulator for mergers and acquisitions on the part of foreign invested companies and the Chinese companies in Chinese market prior to the merger regulation provided by the AML.[81]

In terms of liability, the AML provides that undertakings caught by the law will face administrative fines though leniency treatment is provided for.[82] Though the law does not state explicitly the validity of the agreements caught by law but not exempted on any grounds, the law provides the possibility for claiming damages incurred by any restriction or prohibition of competition.[83]

In general, the AML shows convergence with advice provided by WTO Trade Policy Review mechanism, in that it sets out to regulate state administrative abuse as well as private restrictions of competition under the law. Furthermore, the AML has chosen to internalize values and principles enshrined in EU competition law and US antitrust laws, and the EU competition law seems to have had a stronger influence.[84] However, the lax and broader exemption clause with

---

[78]   Art. 9 AML.

[79]   Art. 14 of the Price Law provides that operators on the market are prohibited from conspiring to fix prices or engage in any other activities that would harm consumer benefits.

[80]   Arts 6 and 7 Law on Unfair Competition.

[81]   Art. 32 Regulation on Merger and Acquisition of Chinese Enterprises by Foreign Investors, 10 August 2006.

[82]   Art. 46 AML.

[83]   Art. 50 AML.

[84]   Francis Snyder (2009), *The EU and China: 1949–2008 Basic Documents and Commentary*, Hart 807.

respect to anti-competitive agreements regulation, the exemption clause with respect to the abuse of dominance and the efficiency-oriented, market-analysis based merger control provided by the AML provide the necessary space for China to develop its own competitiveness of economy. This shows that the values borrowed from external regulatory systems are internalized only to the degree that they fit with the current economic development needs of China.

Against this backdrop, it would be interesting to observe what impact the WTO as the multilateral trade framework has exerted on the AML and to what extent the international trade norms have been internalized into the AML leading to harmonisation of competition laws.

IV IMPACT OF WTO MEMBERSHIP ON CHINA'S ANTI-MONOPOLY LAW: HARMONISATION AND REALITY

1. The Political Weight of WTO Membership in China's AML

As mentioned before, neither WTO agreements nor China's WTO accession protocol have required China to adopt a competition law. When China started the drafting of its first comprehensive competition law, namely the Anti-Monopoly Law (AML), in the 1990s, questions arose as to why China needed to adopt a competition law now rather than at any other time. Some Chinese scholars argue that it is the administrative restriction on the part of governments rather than private restrictions that constitute the main threat to competition on the market, and administrative restriction in China requires fundamental political reforms, which goes beyond the scope of competition law. As a result, China's AML was promulgated in 2007 thirteen years after it was first put on the legislative agenda of the National People's Congress.

In China's access to the WTO, discussions on the competition law of China can be found in China's WTO Accession Working Group discussions, which were recorded in the Group meeting minutes.

> The representative of China noted that the Government of China encouraged fair competition and was against acts of unfair competition of all kinds. The Law of the People's Republic of China on Combating Unfair Competition, promulgated on 2 September 1993 and implemented on 1 December 1993, was the basic law to maintain the order of competition in the market. In addition, the Price Law, the Law on Tendering and Bidding, the Criminal Law and other relevant laws also contained provisions on anti-monopoly and unfair competition. China was now formulating the Law on Anti-Monopoly.[85]

---

[85]   Para. 65 of WTO Report of the Working Group on the Accession of China, WT/MIN(01)/3/Add.1.

It can be seen that the Chinese government has been keen to adopt a competition law and emphasized the value of fairness in its competition regulation. It is difficult to find the exact reasons explaining China's enthusiasm for a competition law based on fairness in its WTO accession negotiations. One explanation could be that China wishes to develop a comprehensive competition law based on fairness so as to establish a fairer market environment more attractive to foreign investment in international trade. However, it is hard to evaluate the impact of the AML on the market environment in China at this very early stage. Furthermore, although there has been a link between competition law, competition law enforcement and foreign direct investment, their relationship has remained an open question.[86] More interestingly, although the Chinese government has stated that the AML is not to be used to restrict foreign direct investment in the Chinese market,[87] foreign investors have expressed concerns rather than been welcoming to the newly adopted Anti-Monopoly Law in China, as they fear the law will be subject to China's economic patriotism.[88]

Another possible explanation for the Chinese government embracing a competition law is that by committing to a fairness-based competition law, the Chinese government also shows its determination to create a level playing field on its domestic market, which further promotes trade liberalization. This may lend some political support to China in its pre-accession negotiations and even increase its bargaining power in the process. More importantly, the fact that the AML took 13 years to be adopted has proved that the development process has faced resistance from different sectors and interest groups. By justifying the adoption of the AML on the grounds of its WTO obligations, the Chinese government has seized the opportunity to push forward some of its deadlocked domestic reforms. To use the WTO as leverage to push forward deadlocks in its domestic reforms has also been argued to be one of the motivations for China to join the WTO even with WTO-plus conditions.[89]

---

[86]   John Clarke (2003), 'Competition Policy and Foreign Direct Investment', World Trade Institute available at www.etsg.org/ETSG2003/papers/clarke.pdf.

[87]   Francis Snyder (2009), *The EU and China: 1949–2008 Basic Documents and Commentary*, Hart 807.

[88]   Wu Zhenguo (2008), 'Perspectives on the Chinese Anti-Monopoly Law', 75 *Antitrust Law Journal*, 73–116.

[89]   Qin, Julia Ya (2003), '"WTO-Plus" Obligations and Their Implications for the World Trade Organization Legal System – An Appraisal of the China Accession Protocol', 37 *Journal of World Trade* 483–522.

2. The Non-discrimination Principle and AML

The WTO Trade Policy Review for China provides that China's competition law needs to set its regulatory target on a non-discriminatory basis, namely that all undertakings, private or public, should fall under the regulation of the law. Secondly, enforcement of competition law should be undertaken in an equal and non-discriminatory way. In other words, competition law in China should not constitute a hidden local protection for the domestic market. However, the analysis on AML can show that the non-discrimination principle may be restrictively applied in China's AML.

Firstly, Article 7 of the AML provides that the state-owned sector, which is of crucial importance to the national economy and national security and which engages in exclusive dealing provided by other laws, is protected by the state for its lawful activities on the market. The state supervises and adjusts the behaviour on the part of the players and the price of goods and services in this sector, protects consumer benefits and promotes technological progress.

The enterprises in these sectors must operate lawfully and honestly with self-discipline and must be subject to supervision by the public. The enterprises should not use their dominant positions to impair consumer benefits.[90]

The debate on Article 7 of AML is heated in and outside China, and centres on whether this means that the AML applies to the state-owned sector of significance to the national economy and national security but is applied on a particular basis taking into consideration public policies, or the AML provides a legal basis for the state to exempt the regulation of this state-owned sector from the regulation of AML.[91] And what kind of regulatory framework should be established to coordinate among the regulation of state-owned sectors and that of competition protection in both scenarios?

In the past 20 years of economic reform, China has successfully transformed the large scale state-owned enterprises (SOEs) to become the leaders in sectors of significance to the national economy, by allowing small and medium-sized SOEs running in deficit to be privatized or leave the market. The State Assets Supervision and Administration Commission (SASAC), the main regulator of the state-owned sector reform set up under the central government, was in charge of 147 large scale SOEs in 2007.[92] Although the number of large scale SOEs has reduced substantially, these SOEs engage in a wide range of sectors covering energy, infrastructure building, food to investment, tourism

---

[90] Art. 7 AML.

[91] Until 23 September 2008, the Chinese government had not set out secondary enforcement legislation on this aspect.

[92] www.sasac.gov.cn/n1180/n1226/n2425/index.html. See the list of SOEs.

or consultancy,[93] which contribute around 42% of the industrial revenue of the national economy in 2007.[94]

Nevertheless, the sectors of significance to the national economy and national security have not been officially defined by the state. In 2006, the SASAC issued the Opinion on Promoting the Readjustment of State Owned Assets and Reorganization of State Owned Enterprises (Opinion). The Opinion provides that state assets should concentrate in the sectors of significance to the national economy and national champions should be established.[95] However, the head of SASAC, Mr Li Rongrong, has stated that the SOES must keep absolute control in sectors of military engineering, electricity, petroleum, telecommunications, coal, aviation and shipping, and relative control in machinery, automobile, electronic information, construction, steel, chemical products, non ferrous metal, construction survey and design and science and technology.[96]

Nonetheless, the provision of Article 7 shows that the design of competition law in China is subject to and compatible with its own legal doctrine, namely to support and safeguard the socialist market economy order in which the state-owned sector accounts for a leading role.

However, if the sectors of significance to the national economy and national security were subject to the regulation of the AML, it remains to be seen to what extent the AML's regulation of these sectors based on public policy grounds can be consistent with the WTO principles. If the sectors of significance to the national economy and national security were exempted from the AML and subjected to other state regulation, it would substantially limit the application of the AML in the Chinese economy. It is the second scenario that raises the need to scrutinize the limits of the non-discrimination principle being internalized into competition laws of WTO members. To achieve this, the relationship between the non-discrimination principle as one international trade norm and the economic rationale for competition regulation requires to be examined.

Neo-liberal economists have strongly advocated that free international trade based on the non-discrimination principle would lead to ultimate efficiency and growth for the world economy. The same rationale can be applied to a domestic economy, where barriers to internal trade should be broken down and equal

---

[93]   For the business sphere of SOEs see www.sasac.gov.cn/n1180/n1226/n2440/index.html.

[94]   From January to July 2007, the industrial revenue of the SOEs has been 966.2 Billion RMB and that of the national economy has been 2295.1 billion RMB. For more details see the 2007 report on national economy and social development by the National Bureau of Statistics, available at www.stats.gov.cn/tjgb/ndtjgb/qgndtjgb/t20080228_402464933.htm.

[95]   www.sasac.gov.cn/n1180/n1566/n258252/n258644/1727614.html.

[96]   http://finance.people.com.cn/GB/67543/5574923.html.

treatment on a rules-based system must be accorded to players on the market irrespective of their origin or size, with an aim of promoting competition.[97]

However, the non-discrimination principle and national treatment principle in international trade liberalization constitute a value of fairness aiming to guarantee equal treatment in terms of design and enforcement of regulation to all players on the market. In other words, this fairness value allows for equally bad or good treatment to take place and therefore remains mainly formal in nature.

This formal fairness value embodied in the non-discrimination principle is to a certain extent compatible with the market contestability principle, as one economic rationale underpinning competition regulation. A contestable market is a market that is free to enter and exit.[98] The non-discrimination principle contributes to removing entry barrier to markets and thus improves the contestability of markets. However, market contestability in competition regulation goes beyond market access and further requires the maximumization of potential competition on the market.[99] To achieve this end, some competition regulation regimes, such as the EU, have provided positive protection to disadvantaged undertakings on the market with the aim to preserve rivalry and promote competition.[100] In this case, the fairness pursued by these competition laws can be more substantive in nature. Furthermore, in recent years there has been an increasing trend for competition regulation to base its enforcement on comprehensive economic analysis in order to achieve the maximization of efficiency of markets. For example, in the European Commission's 2005 discussion paper on the application of abuse of dominance, it emphasizes a more economic analysis based enforcement approach.[101] Therefore competition regulation, if underpinned by market contestability theory, may uphold a more substantive fairness value and is increasingly more dependent on economic analysis.

Thus, although the non-discrimination principle contributes to guaranteeing market access which is one important aspect of market contestability, it is unable to cover all aspects of the social and economic rationale required by competition laws. To over-emphasize the non-discrimination principle in competition

---

[97] M Taylor (2006), *International Competition Law: A New Dimension for WTO* (Cambridge University Press) at 470.

[98] Van den Bergh, Roger and Camesasca Peter(2006), *European Competition Law and Economics: A Comparative Perspective* (Sweet & Maxwell) at 91.

[99] DG Competition Discussion Paper on the application of Article 82 of the Treaty to exclusionary abuses for public consultation, Brussels, December 2005, available at http://ec.europa.eu/comm/competition/antitrust/art82/discpaper2005.pdf.

[100] Niels, Gunnar and Ten Kate, Adriann (2004), 'Introduction: Antitrust in the U.S. and the EU – Converging or Diverging Paths?', *Antitrust Bulletin* 49 1–27.

[101] Commission DG Competition Discussion Paper on the application of Art. 82 of the Treaty of exclusionary abuses, available at http://ec.europa.eu/competition/antitrust/art82/index.html.

law design may face resistance from countries which pursue the substantive fairness value in their competition laws or which fear that the formal fairness value would deprive them of the opportunity to develop their own national competitiveness. Furthermore, to over-emphasize the non-discrimination principle in enforcement may compromise the role played by economic analysis in achieving effectiveness of competition laws. In the case of China, the market economy development is not in full-fledged and the marketization level varies. The application of competition law calls for case-specific economic analysis. However, the WTO non-discrimination principle seems to leave little space for developing countries like China to apply solid economic analysis and tailor the competition regulation to the markets in these economies.

3.   Enforcement of China's AML

In line with the recommendation of a non-discriminatory application of competition law to all sectors in China's economy, the Trade Policy Review recommends that the enforcement of China's competition law should not be overly intrusive or discriminatory.

The WTO may be concerned that any arbitrary enforcement of competition law without adhering to the rule of law may cause uncertainty in or even a negative impact on the premature market development in developing countries. This would consequently exert a negative impact on the liberalization of trade in a broad sense. This has particularly important implications for developing countries like China where the market economy is premature and a legal system is emerging.

Nevertheless, the AML is to be enforced jointly by NDRC, MOFCOM and SAIC under the chapeau of the State Council Anti-Monopoly Commission in China. The enforcement of the law thus depends on coordination among the different powerful regulators. Consequently, there exist possibilities of overlapping regulation on players in the market. However, the WTO guideline remains unclear on the definition of 'over-intrusiveness' in China's enforcement of competition law. It remains unclear whether the over-intrusiveness should be measured on the basis of protection of individual rights or of economic analysis.

Furthermore, in line with the advice provided by the Trade Policy Review, the AML sets out detailed provisions on administrative abuse, which restrict or prohibit competition on the Chinese market.[102] However, in terms of enforcement, the competition authorities have only the discretion to make suggestions to the superior government authorities in charge of the authorities in question. It is up to the superior government authorities to demand that the authorities

---

[102]   Arts 32–37 AML.

correct its abuse.[103] This shows that the competition authority's competence in regulating abuse by government authorities is limited.

However, the WTO regimes can provide a limited supervision role in this respect. Firstly, the Trade Policy Review Mechanisms as an extra audit of members' trade policies remain mainly political and contains no legal effect, and are detached from the WTO dispute settlement mechanism.[104] Secondly, to use the WTO dispute settlement mechanism to scrutinize the trade-related prohibition or restriction of competition caused by administrative abuse is in theory workable,[105] but could be time consuming.

From the enforcement pattern of AML by joint regulators under central government and the limited effect of AML regulation on administrative abuse, it can be seen that though China harmonises its AML with WTO guidelines in appearance, it has intentionally chosen to adjust the competition regulation to its current market regulatory pattern and to reduce or reverse the impact brought by harmonisation on the internal structure of society. Taking into consideration the political nature of the WTO Trade Policy Review Body and the time-consuming nature of the WTO dispute settlement mechanism procedure, it can also be said that the WTO's supervision role of competition law enforcement in China can be limited.

V   CONCLUSION

Economic globalization has provided grounds for competition law to be harmonised in order to safeguard efficiency and market access in international trade. As the international norms on competition law remain largely underdeveloped, the international trade norms have served as the main guiding norms in the harmonisation of the competition laws of different economies.

The harmonisation of competition laws under the lens of international trade had mainly been undertaken by the WTO. However, the harmonisation of competition law was dropped from the WTO agenda in the Doha round due to resistance from developing countries and the US. Nevertheless, competition laws adopted by countries following the Doha round continue to show certain degrees of harmonisation. It is argued that the competition laws in these countries have

---

[103]   Art. 51 AML.

[104]   Donald B Keesing (1998) *Improving Trade Policy Review in the World Trade Organization*, Institute of International Economics.

[105]   Prof. Dr. Dr. h.c.Claus-Dieter Ehlermann and Lothar Ehring (2002), 'Dispute Settlement and Competition Law : Views from the Perspective of the Appellate Body's Experience', Policy paper (Robert Schuman Centre), No. 02/12, European University Institute.

been products of bilateral trade agreements, bilateral dialogues or technical assistance. It can be said that international trade continues to play an important role in the development of competition law worldwide.

When China acceded to the WTO in 2001, international trade norms began to have an impact on its domestic competition law development. Furthermore, the WTO Trade Policy Review sets out particular advice on competition law in China, in that the law should be applied to all players on the market and enforced in a non-discriminatory manner.

However, the above analysis shows that international trade norms have an impact on China's first comprehensive competition law – the Anti-Monopoly Law – but the impact can be limited. WTO membership has provided the Chinese government with an opportunity to push forward the difficult task of adopting competition law, which had faced resistance in the past 13 years. However, it remains to be seen how the relationship between AML and the competition regulation in sectors of significance to the national economy and national security will develop and how the broad exemptions provided by the law will be enforced. Furthermore, the political nature of the WTO Trade Policy Review mechanism and the cost of time in the WTO dispute settlement mechanism restrict the WTO's role in supervising the enforcement of competition law by the joint regulators and the enforcement of competition law against the government agents which abuse their power.

The limits of the role played by international trade norms in China's AML development require reconsideration concerning the appropriateness of harmonising competition laws purely based on trade norms. In particular, the fairness value based on the non-discrimination and national treatment principles upheld by international trade contains fundamental difference from substantive fairness values and economic analysis upheld by competition law regimes. To over-emphasize the role that the non-discrimination principle based on formal fairness plays in competition regulation risks facing resistance from these economies if market governance is based on substantive fairness values and risks depriving the individual competition regulation regime of the chance to develop its own economic analysis for competition law enforcement.

Therefore should the international trade organizations wish to continue the harmonisation of competition law in the multilateral trade fora, they must pay attention to the difference between the formal and substantive fairness values in trade regulation and competition regulation emanating from the nature of competition law itself. They should also provide space or even assistance for new competition regimes to develop their own economic analysis for competition law enforcement. Most importantly, if the international trade organizations choose to listen to what developing countries really are concerned about, communication and even harmonisation among competition laws may become easier.

26. Harmonised legal framework for carbon trading

Bruno Zeller*

INTRODUCTION

As a result of global warming the question of reducing greenhouse gases has become a focal point of discussion. The result is that industry will be judged by its emissions as either a polluter at one end of the spectrum or as a 'green' business at the other end. It appears inevitable that countries will impose national caps on emission and issue tradable permits or introduce carbon taxes (cap and trade) modelled on the Kyoto Protocol.[1] In addition the Bali Road Map agreed on at the 2007 conference of the Parties of the United Nations Framework Convention on Climate Change (UNFCCC) suggested world wide targets.[2]

In order to comply with the Kyoto Treaty each country will need to introduce emissions targets, a time frame to implement the targets as well as a carbon trading scheme. Whether the practical aspects of reducing greenhouse gases is driven by international conventions, left to individual contracting parties or unilateral decisions by individual countries is not yet absolutely clear. In line with the Kyoto Treaty, Australia and other countries are setting targets and timeframes as national bench marks. However such endeavours are not universally followed. Furthermore the **Party Quantified Emission Limitation or Reduction Commitment** (percentage of base year or period) varies between countries. Australia has set a target of 108 which is at the top scale, whereas others and notably the EU look at a figure of 92 which is at the bottom end of the commitment scale.[3]

Australia has also proposed a system of trading in carbon credits, namely the Carbon Pollution Reduction Scheme (CPRS). In the proposal the big polluters

---

* Associate Professor, Victoria Law School, Melbourne; Adjunct Professor, Murdoch Law School, Perth; Associate, Institute for Logistics and Supply Chain Management, Australia.

[1] For the text of the protocol see http://unfccc.int/resource/docs/convkp/kpeng.html.

[2] Carbon Pollution Reduction Scheme, Green Power, Australian Government July 2008, Summary, available at www.climatechange.gov.au.

[3] See annex B, available at http://unfccc.int/resource/docs/convkp/kpeng.html, at 9.

are required to buy a pollution permit for each tonne of carbon. Such declarations will inevitable produce their own problems to business as the purchase of permits can translate into a question of economic viability if it creates cost variants between competing economies. The Australian Government has recognised that adjustment cost for business must be cushioned by government policies such as providing free permits for the most emission intensive activities, with direct assistance via two industry adjustments funds, namely the Climate Change Action Fund and the Electricity Sector Adjustment Scheme.[4] One fact is clear, namely that it appears a settled conclusion that reducing pollution does come at a cost to the country and to business. Especially in Australia it has been recognised that our emission-intensive economy, the transport needs of a vast continent and the growing population will inevitably increase the adjustment costs compared to other economies.[5]

In the end – whatever is discussed globally or domestically – industries must reduce their carbon emission. At the same time it is also apparent that businesses which are below the emissions targets and have spare capacity will have a commodity which can be traded.

The issue of cap and trade can usefully be divided into two problems, namely the capping of carbon emission and the trading of carbon via permits. Within these two categories several levels of treatment must be distinguished, each with possible different solutions.

The first level is a treaty – and in this case the Kyoto Protocol – which in essence is aspirational in character. This is so as it is a political document, and hence a compromise between the various participating sovereign states. The driving force at this level is the individual governments constrained by their own political and economic reality. Compromises in essence are dictated by the pressure one state can influence on the other participants at the time of negotiations. The importance of domestic pressure groups and political aspirations is a reality in the drafting stages. The Kyoto Protocol in essence is not drafted in a mandatory way and leaves signatory states to vary their responses.[6]

The second level of dealing with greenhouse gas reduction is in essence domestic in nature. The capping of carbon emission that is to set the targets is an issue which arguably will be dealt with by each country on an individual basis and domestic laws will deal with this issue. Australia currently is of the view that excess polluters after acquiring a permit can reduce their costs by purchasing 'carbon pollution credits' either at auctions or in a secondary trading market.[7] It can be confidently stated – and history bears it out – that the world cannot

---

[4] Government Green Paper, above n. 2, at Chapter IV.
[5] Ibid. at 7.
[6] Ibid.
[7] Government Green Paper, above n. 2, at 12.

come up with a unified response, and it will be left to each country to implement suggestions contained within the Kyoto Protocol. The EU and Australia[8] as an example have already stated their intentions, which are not the same. Arguably the debate will be driven by the political, economic and environmental reasons of each individual country.

In each country a sub-level can be detected as individual businesses will take on a necessary but voluntary role in reducing carbon emissions. The driving force is the reduction of costs, and hence influences directly the economic viability of each business. Within this level a further development can be observed, namely a different take on supply chain management. The dominant partner – whether an emitter or saver – within the supply chain will forge backward and forward linkages where the contract will include the trade of carbon. This whole sub-level will be largely self-sustaining, that is decisions will rest with individual businesses or chains of businesses and are therefore of no interest in this discussion.

The third level is the trade of carbon credits,[9] which is the focus of this chapter. The reason is that the topic of trading in carbon has not yet received the required attention. It is the contention of this chapter that a carbon trading law could and should be regulated on an international and not only on a domestic level.

TRADING IN CARBON

The first observation is that trading is impossible if the trader does not own the source of carbon. It would not matter whether carbon trading is classed as a service or a good; the fact that ownership is important remains the same. A service consideration only appears to be appropriate if a business with excess carbon merely provides the service to link the two businesses together in a carbon set-off. In general though, a business with excess emission would be required to buy permits. In Australia it has been assumed that more than 99% of firms would not need to purchase permits as they are not targeted emitters.[10] However the question is whether the excess to trade is dependent on geography

---

[8]   It is interesting to note that the Government commissioned a report which was written by Professor Garnaut but then issued its own Green Paper. See www.climatechange.gov.au/greenpaper/index.html. Professor Garnaut published his own report. See http://www.garnautreport.org.au/.

[9]   Carbon obviously cannot be traded and throughout the chapter it must be understood that it is the permits which are traded. How these permits are issued and on what basis is not discussed in this chapter.

[10]   Government Green Paper, above n. 2, at 13.

or incorporation. That is, does the conflict of laws rule invoke the law of the seat of the business or where the goods that are the carbon are situated?

It follows that any law dealing with carbon trading needs to take proprietary rights, questions of conflict of laws and risk allocation associated with trade into consideration and supply corresponding solutions. Already partnerships between individual land owners and the Victorian State Government are creating pools of carbon credits which – once the trees are planted and the trading system is in place – can be sold. Contracts as to the share of the credits have already been signed. The Australian Government already has indicated that pollution permits would be personal property and that ownership would be tracked in a national registry.[11] This overcomes the problem that 'carbon trading' is merely a book entry as carbon cannot be physically moved. This does not pose an obstacle as many goods are traded as book entries, such as commodities on the futures market. Of course the question needs to be asked whether carbon trading can be viewed as a trade in securities or negotiable instruments or actual goods. The Australian solution is to create a financial market in which permits can be traded. Whether this will be a universal solution needs to be seen as undoubtedly economic, environmental and legal interests will drive the debate.

As stated above, it is obvious that every well run business has already thought about the cap and trade of carbon and has taken steps to minimise emission levels either by reducing emissions or by acquiring a carbon credit scheme in order to remain competitive. Whatever the outcome, in the end a legal framework needs to be constructed to facilitate carbon trading in an efficient and effective way, as an ineffective system will add to costs. This is specifically pertinent for a country if trading is limited within its borders and trading can only be undertaken either via an auction system or a secondary trading market. Simply put, business needs certainty in its dealings and an effective legal system needs to operate using easy to understand laws. A specific point needs to be addressed, namely is the value of carbon sufficient to create an elaborate system of trade? The answer would arguably have to be no. The most important reason is the fact that every business will be preoccupied with conforming to government regulations as well as trying to stay competitive. There is no need to force business also to grapple with a complicated trading system which will only add more costs. A simple reading of current news will show that many aspects of carbon trading have not yet been thought through. Visy, a recycling company – one of Australia's greenest companies – 'has slammed the proposed scheme's cost of $20 on a tonne of emissions, in its response to the Government's green paper'.[12] The company noted that:

---

[11]   Ibid. at 20.
[12]   *The Australian*, Monday, 29 September 2008, at page 1.

> The Carbon Pollution Reduction Scheme does not recognise the carbon benefits from recycling, leading to severe collateral impact on Australia's domestic recycling/manufacturing industries. Full action of permits will unnecessarily damage the economy and constrain business capacity to invest in reducing emissions.[13]

It appears obvious that a system based on domestic criteria is not the best solution and can lead to companies reassessing their situations to either stay in a country or move to one with a more appropriate system of dealing in the reduction of greenhouse gases. The problem is linked to the issue of permits, as in Australia the proposal is to issue only a limited number of permits within a given time period[14] which would no doubt determine prices. From a cost point of view alone it appears to be obvious that a global problem must be resolved on a global level. It is therefore suggested that the trading scheme should also be a global system of law. Indeed the Australian government has indicated that opportunities to link with international carbon markets are also envisaged, and the Green Paper notes:

> Under the Kyoto Protocol, national emission targets are calculated taking account of the flexible mechanism that allow for the transfer of Kyoto unis between parties. ... The purchase of international units will tend to lower the price of carbon pollution permits in Australia.[15]

It is clear that eventually Australia envisages that an international trading scheme will be in operation, despite the fact that initially the Government scheme does not allow the export of 'Australia's own Kyoto Protocol compliance units'.[16] The point is that all proposals elaborate on what system is expected to be implemented, but it has not been made clear under what legal system such trading will take place.

This chapter therefore will simply focus on what would be the appropriate and most efficient laws dealing with carbon trading, given the present international legal framework. A caveat needs to be taken into consideration. This chapter does not attempt to give specific solutions; it rather explores the problems and hints at possible paths which can be taken to implement a viable and effective legal framework for carbon trading. In other words it touches on areas which need to be explored further in order to produce a model of international unified laws for consideration.

Three types of transactions arguably will dominate this trade. The first obvious way to trade is within a domestic system only. The second type – as

---

[13] Ibid.
[14] Government Green Paper, above n. 2, at 21.
[15] Ibid. at 23 to 24.
[16] Ibid. at 24.

already stated above – is within a defined supply chain which can be domestically or internationally based. The dominant partner – most like the emitter – will attempt to trade within the supply chain, taking into consideration either the purchase or sale of carbon emission as one of the contractual condition. This is a purely multiparty contractual matter and no doubt will be conducted by introducing relevant terms into the head contracts. Government interference may influence what contractual terms are allowable or can possibly be used which would not be conducive to competitiveness if trade extends beyond domestic borders.

The third and perhaps dominant aspect is the trade by unrelated businesses which need to trade in carbon credits on the open market. This aspect – being the key feature of this chapter – will be further explored.

It is obvious that carbon trading will rely heavily on contractual obligations, and furthermore that such trades will not respect borders – that is, it will be international in character. To that extent three possible solutions are immediately discernable. First UNICITRAL or any other relevant body could construct a carbon trading convention which would be open to ratification by individual nations. This of course will be a long-drawn-out process judging by the 'birth' of many, if not all, of the international conventions.

The second solution would be for individual countries to enact their own laws in relation to carbon trading. The problem here is that conflict of laws would lead to the application of a governing law which could be radically different as municipal governments would seek their own solutions to carbon trading. An example at hand is the Australian government which proposes that a carbon tax is levied on businesses emitting above the level which has been allocated. At the end carbon credits can be bought in an auction system, which unfortunately does not take stock of international developments. On the other hand, if carbon trading follows the lead of other commodities and trade on the stock exchange, the matter is further complicated as carbon credits can be sold several times over before they reach the end purchaser.

The third possibility is to use existing international uniform laws such as the UNIDROIT Principles and the CISG. This potential solution has the advantage that at least the core units of obligations are known to all and are common to all, hence facilitating the speedy sale of carbon. Within the third option dispute resolution mechanism would also require to be investigated. The question would need to be asked whether private arbitrations or state courts can resolve the disputes or a system like ICSID is required.

A further problem which needs to be resolved initially on a domestic level – and is not the focus of this chapter – is the question whether carbon sales are classed as providing a service or as an actual sale of goods. Such a distinction is of importance for several reasons. First if carbon is a 'good', implications of stock accounting need to be resolved, and hence tax issues will need to be looked at. Secondly the question would need to be asked whether carbon can be a capital item. If that were so questions of capital gains tax and related problems would need to be considered.

A tax on high emitters will certainly encourage investment into lower levels of emissions. Arguably therefore a cap and trade regime will at first glance control the quantity of emission and a carbon tax has the potential to influence the price of carbon. The question inevitably will be asked whether taxes are an efficient way to control carbon emission. It can be confidently argued that a carbon tax is like any other tax; it will drive prices up unless it is offset by productivity gains. In other words high carbon emitters within any industry are driven out of business or they radically change their production techniques.

The systems will not work if 'clean' businesses are not rewarded for their efforts, for instance by being given tax credits. Arguably therefore trade in carbon – nationally or internationally – will not be encouraged unless tax differentials make it economically interesting. However once the international mix is introduced different tax regimes – if any – make trade difficult, as no uniformity exists. Tax differentiation between countries can easily lead to a relocation of industries as cost differentiation and, indeed, the availability of carbon between one country and the next may be so steep that reallocation is the only available option for a business to stay afloat.

A preliminary conclusion is that taxes are not a suitable solution as differentiations of tax regimes amongst countries make harmonisation attempts in the area of tax law impossible. Trade appears to be the only option to harmonise and stabilise world trade as – as with any other commodity – business will source the best available deal without the need to relocate.

WHAT HAVE WE LEARNED IN THE PAST 20 YEARS?

The simple answer is: it depends who is asked. Academics and unfortunately only the minority of businesses have recognised that the application of uniform laws is providing advantages which are not available to those who simply rely on a domestic system. At the same time it must be recognised that domestic laws can never be completely ignored unless a world law is introduced, which appears to be most unlikely. If it took more than 20 years to introduce a sales convention, how long would it take for a diplomatic conference to agree on the creation of a world law? It is instructive to examine the current endeavour of the EU to create a uniform contract law. Despite the fact that the Commission is relying on the work of Ole Lando and having the benefit of the work done on the CISG and the UNIDROIT Principles, the uniform contract law is still – after several years – not very close to completion. However on the positive side several 'think tanks' have taken up work, and the 'soft law codification' in form of the Principles of European Contract Law (1995/1999/2003) shows that the sceptics of a unified, 'Europeanised' contract law are wrong.[17]

It can therefore be argued that the application of an existing uniform law would supply the best and quickest solution. The reluctance of domestic courts and the legal profession to turn to international sources is slowly eroding. The development is being observed in the area of contract interpretation. Significantly in the United Kingdom – the last bastion of clinging to domestic law – the CISG and UNIDROIT Principles have taken a tentative foothold. Lady Justice Ashton in *Proforce Recruit Ltd v. The Rugby Group Ltd*,[18] criticised the parole evidence rule and in an obiter suggested 'a possible change in approach and in support of it made express reference to the [CISG and UNIDROIT Principles]'.[19]

Given the increased awareness of the advantages of international uniform laws two approaches can be isolated. First a uniform law which is currently widely available can be used to resolve carbon trading disputes within the court system. The alternative is that carbon trade is regulated by arbitration. As stated earlier, whatever system is chosen it will be contractual in nature; hence terms in contracts must reflect the desire to adopt a particular system. Looking at the most successful sales law, namely the CISG, leaving it to business does not tend to produce the desired uniform results. Anecdotally more businesses specifically exclude the CISG than include it.[20]

The next option is to look at arbitration. Again the problem is that a clause in the contract has to stipulate that arbitration is the preferred dispute resolution process. A further problem is that arbitral rules would need to be drawn up which reflect not only the procedural aspect but also the substantive law, which would have to be mandatory in character in order to achieve a uniform system of law. Lessons from sports arbitration with the seat in Lausanne should be adopted. A further solution is to entrust a body such as the International Chamber of Commerce (ICC) with the drawing up of the relevant procedural rules. Considering the success ICC had with the UCP600 and the Incoterms 2000 this project would not be beyond its capability. The advantage of arbitration indeed is the fact that government influence is limited and it would not require accession to a treaty. Whether it is realistic that a body like the ICC can draw up specific procedural laws is questionable – but not impossible. A further consideration is that it appears obvious that private international law and public international law dissect

---

[17] Zeller, B (2007), *CISG and the Unification of International Trade Law* (Routledge-Cavendish), at 15.

[18] [2006] EWCA Civ 69.

[19] Bonell, M (2006), 'The UNIDROIT Principles and the CISG – Sources of Inspiration for English Courts?', (2006–2) *Uniform Law Review* 305 at 306.

[20] Not that a specific inclusion is necessary as the CISG is self-inclusive, hence a specific exclusion is required.

the carbon trade model. No doubt Free Trade Agreements and the rules of origin as well as Bilateral Investment Treaties are intertwined into the WTO regime, and therefore overlie the private system with government influence guaranteed. The Australian Green Paper confirms this aspect and notes:

> Australia's strong reliance on emissions intensive energy recourses means that we could also be vulnerable to poorly targeted mitigation responses by other countries, such as protectionist responses that impose tariffs on Australia's emissions intensive exports.[21]

Further research in this area is also warranted, but is not within the scope of this chapter.

It appears to be clear that the lesson which has been learned in the past 20 to 30 years is that global problems are best resolved by global or international laws. The efforts of bodies such as UNCITRAL, UNIDROIT and the European Commission in particular, as well as private bodies such as the ICC, speak for themselves.

One fact stands out: whatever laws are chosen, the usage of customary laws is doubtful. Baasch Andersen described customary laws as follows:

> ... they are produced in trade where the rules are needed by the people who apply them. Either in the form of standard business practice or standard form contracts, they may produce similar results for a given legal phenomenon across jurisdictional boundaries, and are argued to be part of the unification process of law because of this attained effect.[22]

As carbon credit trading is a uniquely new concept, standard practices would not have been established and hence a customary law would not be in existence. However, given legal principles such as contract formation – if they can be termed customary –are already embedded in the uniform conventions or model laws as general principles. The result is that customary law would play a minimal role in the creation of an international uniform trading system as – whatever it can offer – has already been taken up in uniform laws. What can be said though is that uniform laws such as the UNIDROIT Principles and the CISG are more than just novelty items; they are considered to be a recognised discipline within the broader aspects of contract law. From this point of view alone international law is the equivalent in standing to domestic law. If a uniform law is chosen – whether from existing sources or specifically drafted – the advantage is that:

---

[21]   Government Green Paper, above n. 2, at 7.

[22]   Baasch Andersen, C. (2007), 'Defining Uniformity in Law', (2007–1) *Uniform Law Review* 5, at 37.

... practitioners ... must recognise that they are sharing it with colleagues in other jurisdictions, and that its development is a communal evolution requiring a unique approach very different from the (differing) applications of domestic law in varying jurisdictions.[23]

It would appear sensible that the trade of carbon credits goes down the same path and is governed by an international regime. It is difficult to understand that trading should be restricted to domestic principles as all activities are integrated on a global scale. One example can illustrate this. If a coal-fired electricity company in, say, Australia needed to buy credits and they were not available locally or were more expensive than in another country, the price of electricity would increase. It would not only affect consumers but also business, hence the competitiveness of Australian businesses on a global scale would be diminished. A global trading scheme would overcome, or at least minimise, the effects of regional bottlenecks. Furthermore it would supply a body of law which is international in character. The advantage of such a 'common law' is that it shares a common jurisprudence, a tool which has been labelled a *jursiconsultorium*.[24] The advantages of a shared jurisprudence are self-evident.

THE CISG AND THE UNIDROIT PRINCIPLES: A READY-MADE SOLUTION

The first question is whether either principle can be applied to the trade of carbon credits. The first observation is that the CISG only applies if either or both parties have ratified the convention or the private international law rules point to the law of a contracting state.[25] Considering that all major trading nations except the United Kingdom have ratified the convention this would make the CISG a *de facto* world law. The UNIDROIT principles on the other hand are considered to be soft law, and hence need to be included in a contractual document or chosen as the governing law in cases of arbitration by the arbitrators.

The application of the UNIDROIT Principles does not pose any problems as they apply to 'international commercial contracts'.[26] However it must also be noted that the UNIDROIT Principles are not only restricted to international

---

[23]   Ibid. at 45.
[24]   For further reading on this matter see Baasch Andersen, C. (2007), *The Uniformity of the International Sales Law: Understanding Uniformity, the Global Jursiconsultorium, and Examination and Notification Provisions of the CISG* (Kluwer).
[25]   Art. 1 CISG.
[26]   UNIDROIT Principles 2004, at 2.

contracts. The definition of the Preamble is written in such a form that 'there is nothing to prevent private persons from agreeing to apply the Principles to a purely domestic contract'.[27] At first glance therefore the UNIDROIT Principles are eminently suitable either to form the basis for the creation of international uniform laws or to be taken over as the governing domestic law.

The CISG on the other hand is restricted to the sale of goods, hence carbon credits must meet the requirements of Article 2. This Article does not define what goods are, but rather what is to be excluded from the regime of the CISG. Of possible interest is subsection (d) which excludes 'stocks, shares, investment securities, negotiable instruments or money' from the sphere of influence of the CISG. Carbon credits certainly do not fall into the category of stocks, shares and investment securities, but could possibly be termed a negotiable instrument. That is so as carbon arguably is not a tangible product at all and must be represented by an instrument which can be traded. Just because a negotiable instrument is traded does not mean that the CISG cannot protect the holder of the negotiable instrument, as the document in effect is the proof of the existence of the goods. The negotiable instrument is merely a convenient way to transfer the ownership of the goods from one person to another, and is in itself – without the existence of the goods – valueless.

FEATURES OF THE CISG

The question could be asked why the CISG would be superior to any domestic law in regulating carbon trade. The first obvious answer is that it is a unified international law and is already part of the domestic law of 71[28] countries and has been the subject of intense academic scrutiny. Furthermore a sizable international jurisprudence is in existence. It is therefore not an untested system.

However the real advantages of applying the CISG are included within the four corners of the convention. First the interpretation of the convention is embedded in Article 7 which could be termed to be mandatory. Article 7 notes:

(1)   In the interpretation of this Convention, regard is to be had to its international character and to the need to promote uniformity in its application and the observance of good faith in international trade.

(2)   Questions concerning matters governed by this Convention which are not expressly settled in it are to be settled in conformity with the general principles on which it is based or, in the absence of such principles, in conformity with the law applicable by virtue of the rules of private international law.

---

[27]   Ibid. at 3.
[28]   As of July 2008.

Article 7(1) notes specifically that any interpretation of this convention must be international in character and uniform. In other words Article 7 clearly recognises that decisions, irrespective of where they are made, are to be uniform; that is the same results need to be achieved irrespective of where the dispute was resolved. A further element or feature of the CISG which is embedded in Article 7 is that all its provisions are 'stand alone' provisions; that is no other convention or treaty needs to be consulted to add or interpret any of its provisions except Article 7 which requires the aid of the Vienna Convention on the Law of Treaties. However the Vienna Convention due to its similarities with Article 7 will not change an interpretation of Article 7.[29]

Furthermore the flexibility of the CISG is enhanced considerably as provisions within the convention cannot be read in isolation. The 'glue' which holds the convention together is the general principles which are embedded within the four corners of the CISG.[30] The opening sentence of Article 7(2) is the first step in the interpretation ladder, as unfortunately the CISG is not a code and gaps in the end must be filled by having recourse to domestic law. The important point to remember is that as far as the interpretation of the convention is concerned, domestic laws of any system may not be used to assist. The CISG is truly an autonomous instrument free from domestic interference. In the case of carbon trading this could be termed an advantage, as many countries arguably could legislate in order to accommodate their specific unique requirements to fill the gaps pursuant to Article 7(2) CISG.

Such legislation would not be a disadvantage as the CISG can also accommodate special provisions. This is achieved if Articles 6 and 8 are combined with Article 7. Article 6 allows the parties to exclude, derogate from or vary the effects of any of its provisions. This means that the parties, if so desired, can enter into a 'tailor made' contract. As an example they may wish to include the UNIDROIT Principles as filling any gaps or supplement the contract or choose the law of a country which supplies the most beneficial rules to either add or supplement the CISG. However the CISG can still be a 'stand alone' governing law if parties so desire. In other words the CISG is the common language international business can converse in and hence is understood by all.

Article 8 is of special interest, and specifically in a new area of law as it assists in the interpretation of the parties' intentions. In common law the parole evidence rule has traditionally been applied, which means that the textual and

---

[29] See Zeller, B (2009), 'The Observance of Good Faith', A Janssen and O Meyer (eds), *Methodology of CISG* (Sellier European Law Publishers).

[30] For an elaboration of the four corner thesis see Zeller, B (2003), *Four-Corners – The Methodology for Interpretation and Application of the UN Convention on Contracts for the International Sale of Goods*, available at: www.cisg.law.pace.edu/cisg/biblio/4corners.html.

not the contextual approach has been applied to interpret the intent of the parties. In recent years this approach has been criticised as not reflecting the bargain of the parties. To that effect the CISG introduced the subjective approach, which means that the pre-contractual, contractual and post-contractual conduct of the parties is to be taken into consideration in interpreting contracts. Furthermore the 'practices which the parties have established between themselves, usage and any subsequent conduct of the parties'[31] are further considerations the courts and tribunals can look at to inform themselves of the true intent of both parties.

Article 8 makes it clear that the intent of the parties must be commonly understood by both parties. The other party must either know 'or could not have been unaware what the intent was'.[32] It is a true meeting of the minds of the two contractual partners. As stated above, the necessity to adopt a more liberal approach in the use of extrinsic material has been 'put in stone'. Bonell in his analysis of recent English cases notes:

> The opinions of Mummery LJ and Arden LJ in *Proforce Recruit Ltd v The Rugby Group Ltd* are just the most recent, though particularly authoritative ones. The references they contain to the UNIDROIT Principles and the CISG are a remarkable demonstration of the increasing openness of the English courts towards foreign and international sources of inspiration [in the interpretation of contracts].[33]

Another feature worth mentioning is the fact that the CISG distinguishes between two types of breach of contract. What may be termed a 'minor breach' will still keep the contract afoot, and suing for damages is one of the options. A 'major' breach will allow the aggrieved party to declare the contract avoided due to a fundamental breach.[34] This could be of great importance in relation to carbon trading.

Two possible areas of dispute immediately come to mind. The first situation is when a company does not or appears to be unlikely to sell carbon credits despite a contractual obligation. In cases like this a fundamental breach can be quickly established by giving the breaching party a '*Nachfrist*' or extra time to perform pursuant to Article 49 CISG. Once the party refuses to perform a fundamental breach is immediately established and the contract can be avoided. If on the other hand a party sells a credit which later proves to be significantly

---

[31] Article 8(3).

[32] Article 8(1).

[33] Bonell, M above n. 19, at 317.

[34] For further elaboration of the principle of Fundamental Breach see Zeller, B (2007), 'The Remedy of Fundamental Breach and the United Nations Convention on the International Sale of goods (CISG) A Principle lacking Certainty?', 11 *Vindobona Journal of International Commercial Law and Arbitration* 131. Also consult www.cisg. law.pace.edu/cisg/text/e-text-49.html for additional material on Fundamental Breach.

less than previously established, the contract will still remain on foot but the aggrieved party can claim damages. The reason this is of importance is that once carbon credits are locked in – irrespective of whether it is viewed from the seller's or purchaser's point of view – avoidance of a contract can cause more than just an inconvenience. The true consequences of course depend on the domestic regime in relation to carbon caps or the issuing of carbon licences or taxes.

In sum this very brief explanation of the CISG should be sufficient for one to realise that a uniform law which is recognised by all bar one[35] of the major trading nations in the world deserves close examination as to its utility to resolve carbon trading issues.

FEATURES OF THE UNIDROIT PRINCIPLES

The advantage of the UNIDROIT Principles is that the drafters had the benefit of reading the CISG. The first point to understand is that the UNIDROIT Principles are soft law, and secondly they cover contract laws and not only the sale of goods. Furthermore the UNIDROIT Principles have improved on some of the features of the CISG, but in general most, if not all, of the general principles embedded within the CISG have been included. Importantly the regime of interpretation of the CISG has found its way into the UNIDROIT Principles as well. The real asset of the UNIDROIT Principles is that they complement the CISG and can be used as a guide in cases where the CISG is unclear but the subject matter is still covered by general principles contained within the CISG. A further advantage of the UNIDROIT Principles is that they can be used as the governing law in arbitration.

THE CASE FOR ARBITRATION

An investigation of possible international regimes to regulate carbon trading would not be complete without looking briefly at models of arbitration. It is assumed that an *ad hoc* arbitration would not be attempted, as too many problems can emerge, and instead institutional arbitration would be the norm.

It goes without saying that contractual parties can choose from a multitude of institutional arbitration chambers such as ICC, SIAC, CIETAC or the Swiss Rules, to mention just a few. The problem is that the procedural rules of arbitral bodies are not uniform and allow for a variety of procedures. It would make

---

[35]   The United Kingdom.

more sense if a central arbitration institution could be formed such as prevails in Sports Law.[36]

The creation of a body which specifically arbitrates disputes relating to carbon trading is a solution which should be envisaged by nations. The Kyoto Protocol has not done so, and it is certain that the Protocol will run its course without achieving any real agreements, as was the case with the Doha rounds on agriculture.

The problem of 'cap and trade' is interrelated and therefore without a world agreement on capping of emissions as the first step no real progress on trading can be achieved. It is doubtful whether global businesses will remain in a country which unilaterally puts a cap on carbon, and hence increases the cost of the product. Global competitiveness will always be the focus of business, as otherwise a business cannot survive. Hence when a new Protocol replaces the Kyoto Agreement the time will be ripe to discuss and implement the creation of an arbitration body dealing with trading disputes.

Should that happen, lessons from the WTO in its creation of the dispute resolution mechanism should not be forgotten, as well as the lesson learned in the creation of the Court of Arbitration for Sport. The advantages are immense. First of all a court of arbitration with a permanent seat would overcome the problem of which procedural law is applicable in each case. The law simply would be that of the permanent seat irrespective of where the arbitration takes place. Hence matters of court interference and matters such as interim relief or the granting of a stay of proceedings are automatically unified. It would not be surprising if a country like Switzerland were chosen to fulfil this role, as in commercial arbitration the Swiss Rules are often used and internationally Geneva or Lausanne is also often the seat of organisations such as the WTO and Sports Arbitration.

This is important, as no doubt an intersection between public and private international law is more than likely considering that the foundation stone of any agreement on the reduction of greenhouse gases would be a Protocol or Convention. Furthermore in the area of carbon capping state to state disputes can easily eventuate as well as the question whether a carbon permit matches the actual carbon savings, which would have to be determined by a state authority. If the model of Sports Arbitration were be followed then the Court of Arbitration for Carbon Trading could not only resolve disputes but also give non-binding opinions if requested to do so by an individual state.

As far as the determination of the applicable substantive law is concerned the above suggestion of adopting either the CISG or the UNIDROIT Principles as the governing law should also be considered. The 'neatest' solution is to

---

[36] See www.tas-cas.org/news.

mandate a substantive law. However it is doubtful whether a diplomatic conference or a substantial number of states would subscribe to such a suggestion. To overcome the problem a model clause could be suggested along the above lines of arguments. If commodity trade is any indication, the uptake of a model clause would take place in most cases of contract drafting. It is a matter of convincing the legal profession to insert such a clause, and it would bypass the influence of states, as carbon trading after all should remain a contractual question; hence it would be outside state interference.

CONCLUSION

It appears doubtful whether a country can monitor and maintain an effective domestic system of cap and trade without taking note of international trends and cost structures. A domestic system of auctions or secondary trading markets can easily be too skewed within a global trading system, hence making a domestic economy less cost effective than others.

If the attempts of the last 30 years to create global law in distinct areas are any indication, it should not be too difficult to unite business and governments in the creation of a uniform or harmonised carbon trading law. Considering the importance of reducing carbon emission on a global level, the legislative solutions governing the trade in the carbon credits should reflect global concerns.

The preferred and obviously easiest solution is the creation of a Court of Arbitration for Carbon Trading, as it combines the best of all the various options. It not only creates a framework to resolve disputes but also builds a legal tool which gives business the ability to formulate and assess its risk management strategies. The CISG augmented by the UNIDROIT Principles is especially of value as it allows a business to tailor-make its agreements in building on a system which by now has a vast jurisprudence and has created enormous interest amongst academics.

The time perhaps has come to follow the dream of a global law considering the importance of the subject matter, which in reality goes beyond mere improvement of the bottom line. It is a question of sustainability of the world. Perhaps the law can show the way to a unified approach to the solution of a global problem, at least in the aspect of trade. It appears inevitable at this stage anyway that the capping of emissions – due to political considerations – will unfortunately be dealt with on a national basis.

27. Technical considerations in harmonisation and approximation: legislative drafting techniques for full transposition

Helen Xanthaki*

WHY CONSIDER THE TECHNICALITIES OF TRANSPOSITION?

Legal harmonisation is by no means an easy task. It requires exceptional abilities to follow all aspects and developments of EU law, including the ever increasing and ever dynamic interpretation and application of EU legislation by the ECJ; it requires in-depth understanding of the will of the EU legislator as a means of interpreting the commonly vague and often ambiguous provisions of EU legislative texts; and it requires an excellent understanding of legislation and its functioning at the national level, as a means of making legislative choices which can and will work within the holistic and dynamic sphere that is the national legal system.

Legal harmonisation in the pre-accession era does not require different solutions from legal harmonisation in the post-accession, the membership, era. Admittedly, at the pre-accession time the national authorities of aspiring states are now required to meet the additional requirement of the 1995 Madrid European Council, which demands the introduction of the necessary administrative structures for the ultimate enforceability of the *acquis*. The additional Madrid criterion for accession is interpreted as a command for effective and enforceable transposing legislation,[1] which is a far cry from the past requirement to transpose EU law as and how the aspiring Member State saw fit.

However, the Madrid criterion is by no means another unfair order imposed by the strong EU on the vulnerable aspiring Member States. The Madrid criterion is a mere reflection, or in fact an expression, of the final realisation within

---

* Professor of Law, University of London, UK.
[1] Xanthaki, H. (2005), 'The Route to EU Accession', in Stefanou, C (ed.), *Cyprus and the EU: The Road to Accession* (Ashgate), 11.

the EU that EU legislative texts must be of such a level of quality that they can accommodate their being invoked before the national courts[2] in national judicial proceedings via the principle of direct and indirect effect, their use by EU citizens via their application[3] as they stand in the case of measures of direct applicability,[4] and their operation as instruments of regulation for national enterprises lying at the core of the development of the EU's economy.[5]

It is therefore highly surprising that the new daunting task imposed upon old, new and future Member States has managed to attract so little attention from EU lawyers and drafters. The aim of this chapter is to identify the problems that constitute the backbone of the task, and, in the absence of concrete guidance from the EU institutions, to guide national drafters through the choices that lie before them through the application of existing established principles of law.

On this basis, three main themes emerge in our analysis.[6] First, how does one choose the form of national implementing measure that best meets the requirement for complete transposition and, intimately, harmonisation? Second, how does one achieve quality in the national transposition measures? And, third, which are the main drafting techniques that one must employ in the search for tools for effective and complete transposition and harmonisation?

THE PRINCIPLES OF TECHNICAL CONSIDERATIONS: CRITERIA FOR CHOICE

Despite the novelty of the questions posed by national authorities in their contemporary questions towards complete transposition, there are principles of EU law that can assist them on their way.[7] Subsidiarity, proportionality, adequacy,

---

[2]   Eijlander, P and Voermans, W (2000), *Wetgevingsleer* (Boom Juridische Uitgevers), at 257.

[3]   Zeff, E E and Pirro E B (2001), *The European Union and the member states: cooperation, coordination, and compromise*, (Lynne Rienner Pub).

[4]   Weatherill, S (2007), 'The Challenge of Better Regulation', in Weatherill S (ed.), *Better Regulation* (Hart Publishing), at 3.

[5]   Xanthaki, H. (2001), 'The SLIM initiative', 22 *Statute Law Review* 108, at 108–109; Piris, J-C (1998), 'The quality of Community legislation: the viewpoint of the Council Legal Service' in Kellermann, A, Ciavarini-Azzi, G, Jacobs, S, and Deighton-Smith, R, *Improving the Quality of Legislation in Europe* (Kluwer Law), 25; also Commission Staff Working Paper entitled 'Making Single Market Rules More Effective, Quality in Implementation and Enforcement', 25 May 1998, SEC(1998)903, 3.

[6]   Xanthaki, H. (2005), 'Drafting at the EU Level' in Stefanou, C and Xanthaki, H, *Drafting for EU Approximation* (UK Department for International Development-IALS-Ministry of Justice of Ukraine), 7, at 7–8.

[7]   Xanthaki, H. (2005), 'Transposition Techniques', in Stefanou, C and Xanthaki, H, above n. 6, 9, at 9–10.

synergy, and adaptability are known and established principles of EU law that come to their rescue.[8] The application of these principles does not signify a qualification of the principle of autonomy for national authorities that are still of course entitled to make their own choice in the selection of the transposition means of their choice.[9] However, the choice of national authorities[10] is by no means beyond the scrutiny of EU authorities, in the form of Commission officials in the pre-accession stage and in the form of the ECJ at the post-accession stage.[11] It must therefore be accepted that the principle of autonomy, as qualified by the equally important principles of subsidiarity, proportionality, adequacy, synergy and adaptability, now allows national drafting authorities to make their preferred selection from the pool of choice offered to them after the application of the relevant principles of EU law. After all, accountability is not preserved for the EU alone.

The principle of subsidiarity dictates that the highest level of action is justifiable only when lower levels of legislative action are inefficient for the achievement of the goal.[12] When applied to transposition as a means for harmonisation within the umbrella of EU accession and effective membership,

---

[8]   For a full analysis of this point see Xanthaki, H. (2006), 'Transposition of EC law for EU approximation and accession: the role of national authorities', 4 *European Journal of Law Reform*, 89, at 97–100.

[9]   In fact, the application of these principles to non-member states is questioned by some authors: see Wulf-Henning, R (2002), 'Transposing "Pointillist" EC Guidelines Into Systematic National Codes – Problems And Consequences', 6 *European Review of Private Law* 761.

[10]   Usher, J A (2005), 'The Reception of General Principles of Community Law in the United Kingdom', 16 *European Business Law Review* 489, at 495.

[11]   Case C–107/97, *Criminal Proceedings against Max Rombi and Arkopharma SA, the party liable at civil law, and Union federale des consommateurs 'Que Choisir ?' and Organisation generale des consommateurs (Orgeco), Union departementale O6* [2000] ECR I–3367, para. 65; see also Case 145/88, *Torfaen Borough Council v. B & Q plc.* [1989] ECR 3851; *24 Shrewsbury and Atcham BC v. B & Q* [1990] 3 CMLR 535; Cases C–20/00 and C–64/00, *Booker Aquaculture v. The Scottish Ministers* [2003] ECR I–7411.

[12]   European Commission (2005), 'Report from the Commission "Better Lawmaking 2004" Pursuant to Article 9 of the Protocol on the Application of the Principles of Subsidiarity and Proportionality' (12th report), COM(2005)98 final and SEC(2005)364, Brussels, 21 March 2005, at 2; also Davies, G (2006), 'Subsidiarity: the wrong idea, in the wrong place, at the wrong time', 43 *Common Market Law Review* 63, at 67; Rodger, B and Wylie, S (1997), 'Taking the Community interest line: decentralisation and subsidiarity in competition law enforcement', 18 *European Commission Law Review* 485; Lenaerts, K (1994), 'The principle of subsidiarity and the environment in the European Union: keeping the balance offFederalism', 17 *Fordham International Law Journal* 846; Farnsworth, N (2004), 'Subsidiarity – a conventional industry defence: is the Directive on environmental liability with regard to prevention and remedying of environmental damage justified under the subsidiarity principle?', 13 *European Environmental Law Review* 176.

subsidiarity encompasses two parallel concepts: legal subsidiarity is an economy of approaches, whereas legislative subsidiarity is an economy of measures. Legal subsidiarity signifies that legislation is utilised as a means of harmonisation with the relevant EU policies, if, and only if, all other possible forms of harmonising regulation are deemed to fail in the production of the required results.[13] Legislative subsidiarity demands that, if a choice for legislative action is made, national authorities select the lightest possible form of national legislation for the purposes of harmonisation.

The application of the principle of subsidiarity to its extreme could lead to a Spartan method of transposition, which carries the inherent danger of ineffective harmonisation. This danger is thankfully measured, in view of the application of the principle of proportionality. As the choice of regulatory instrument, and, if necessary, the choice of legislative instrument is made, one has to take account of the additional consideration of balancing the aim to be achieved with the choice made. In its positive sense, proportionality within this concept requires that one selects the form of harmonisation that can achieve the required standard. In its negative sense, and this is where the extreme application of subsidiarity is averted, proportionality rejects all forms of harmonisation that are too light for the achievement of the standards required.[14] Legislative proportionality supplements legislative subsidiarity[15] and demands that the choice of form of the national implementing measure reflect its purpose.[16]

Proportionality in its negative sense as the rejection of ineffective measures for harmonisation is also expressed as the principle of adequacy. Adequacy balances subsidiarity, in that it prevents harmonisation choices that are too light for the purposes of transposition. Adequacy accentuates proportionality by ensuring that policy makers and drafters strike an adequate proportionate balance between the need to harmonise and the choice made: over-regulation and under-regulation are therefore averted. Legal adequacy demands that the chosen means of regulation is capable of achieving the effect pursued. Legislative adequacy secures that the chosen form of legislation is capable of achieving the effect pursued. Although adequacy is a value to aspire to in the legislative

---

[13] O'Keeffe, J (2006), 'Making a silk purse out of a sow's ear', *Law Society's Gazette* 14.

[14] Usher, J A (2005), 'The reception of general principles of Community law in the United Kingdom', 16 *European Business Law Review* 489, at 506; Case 11/70, *Internationale Handelsgesellschaft*, [1970] ECR 1125, at 1148; Report from the Commission, 'Better Lawmaking 2004', above, at 2; The Law Society (2005), 'EU Better Law-Making Charter, Better Law-Making Programme' 5.

[15] Snell, J (2000), 'True Proportionality', 11 *European Business Law Review* 50.

[16] De Bùrca, G (1993), 'The Principle of Proportionality and its Application in EC Law', 13 *Yearbook of European Law* 105; Jans, J (2000), 'Proportionality Revisited', 27 *Legal Issues of Economic Integration* 239.

process, true adequacy in legislative drafting can only be secured *post hoc* through a prospective evaluation of the proposed law,[17] namely through a cost benefit analysis and a retrospective evaluation[18] in the form of monitoring of passed laws.[19]

The principle of synergy promotes a holistic approach to the legal system.[20] Legal synergy promotes coherence and interrelated functioning of diverse fields of law within the national legal system of the aspiring Member State. Legislative synergy promotes a holistic approach of the law on a concrete social phenomenon, thus ensuring that the new instruments falls smoothly into place upon its entry into force and that it combines its forces for the achievement of the aim of legislation on the social phenomenon in question. The role of synergy in achieving effective harmonisation is often underestimated: synergy can *prima facie* be seen as a quality that benefits exclusively the implementing national system. However, effective harmonisation cannot be achieved without effective national implementing legislation; it is therefore crucial to note that synergy is a quality that benefits the national legal system directly and harmonisation indirectly.

The principle of adaptability takes into account the practicalities of the national legislative processes. Legislative practice often requires flexibility in the choice of the appropriate instrument: parliamentary time is valuable[21] and the selection of form may be based on the lighter procedural requirements of a form.[22] When combined with subsidiarity and proportionality, adaptability can

---

[17] Where the legislature is obliged to assess the future effects of rules to be adopted and those effects cannot be accurately foreseen, its assessment is open to criticism only if it appears manifestly incorrect in the light of the information available to it at the time of the adoption of the rules in question: Case C–150/94, *United Kingdom v. Council* [1998] ECR I–7235, para. 49; Case T–54/99, *max.mobil Telekommunikation Service GmbH v. Commission of the European Communities* [2002] ECR II–313, para.84.

[18] Kaufmann, D, Kraay, A and Mastruzzi, M (2007), 'Governance Matters VI: Aggregate and Individual Governance Indicators 1996–2006', World Bank Policy Research Working Paper No. 4280; Centre for European Studies, Bradford University (2004), 'Final Report on Indicators of Regulatory Quality', report for DG Enterprise, European Commission, http://ec.europa/enterprise/newsroom/ifl_getdocument.fcm?doc_id=2742.

[19] See Law Society, above, at 8; also Schaeffer, H (2001), 'Evaluation and assessment of legal effects procedures: towards a more rational and responsible lawmaking process', 22 *Statute Law Review* 132.

[20] See Law Society, above, at 15.

[21] Ciavarini Azzi, G (2000), 'The slow march of European legislation: The implementation of directives' in Neuenreither, K. and Wiener A (eds), *European integration after Amsterdam: Institutional dynamics and prospects for democracy* (Oxford University Press) 52–67.

[22] Factors include the lourdeur of parliamentary procedures and the lack of parliamentary time: Usher, J (1995), 'The Legal Framework for Implementation in the United

reach dangerous extremes of under-regulation or under-authorised regulation produced without resort to parliamentary legitimation. An example of this could be the Irish approach to transposition which is commonly left to delegated legislation with the pretext of urgency.[23] However, when delimited by adequacy and synergy, adaptability can serve national governments to achieve results legitimately but without a waste of resources. Adaptability allows for experimental legislation or legislation in stages.

It would seem therefore that despite the lack of express assistance and guidance from the EU to Member States as to the best means for achieving harmonisation, EU law provides clear parameters that assist and guide to the best choice for the task.

However, EU law is not the only factor that contributes to choices made for the purposes of achieving effective harmonisation. The coin of harmonisation has two sides, the EU and the national side. And so the decision whether the national legal order can indeed borrow the EU legislative solution as a means of achieving harmonisation is by no means to be taken for granted.[24] After all, effective harmonisation can only be achieved if the national legal order can utilise the proposed solution and absorb it in the national legal order seamlessly and painlessly. But is this truly possible? Can national legal orders really borrow from the EU, and, if so, on what basis?[25]

Despite the commonality of the transplant practice,[26] national legislators cannot be expected simply to adopt the EU's legislative solution without falsifying or verifying the relationship between the policy choice under consideration and the results of the application of that policy choice.[27] For the Watsonists

---

Kingdom' in Daintith T (ed.), *Implementing EC Law in the United Kingdom: Structures for Indirect Rule* (Chancery Law Publishing) 101.

[23] Mooney, K (2001), 'The work of the Office of Parliamentary Counsel to the government in Ireland', 22 *Statute Law Society* 133, at 138; also The Supreme Court 1993 No. 127, *John Meagher v The Minister for Agriculture and Food, Ireland and the Attorney General*, 18 November 1993 (Judgment of the Court delivered pursuant to the provisions of Article 34.4.5° by Finlay CJ).

[24] For an analysis of the 'good to fit approach' see Haverland, M (2000), 'National adaptation to European integration: the importance of institutional veto points', 20 *Journal of Public Policy* 83.

[25] Xanthaki, H (2008), 'On transferability of legislative solutions: the functionality test', in Stefanou C. and Xanthaki, H (eds), *Drafting Legislation: A Modern Approach – in Memoriam of Sir William Dale* (Ashgate-Dartmouth), 1.

[26] Watson, A (1991), *Legal Origins and Legal Change* (Hambledon Press), at 73; also Fedtke, J (2006), 'Legal Tranplants' in Smits, J (ed.), *Elgar Encyclopedia of Comparative Law* (Edward Elgar), 434.

[27] Van Erp, J H M (1998), 'The use of comparative law in the legislative process', *Netherlands Reports to the 15th International Congress of Comparative Law*, Bristol, available at www.library.uu.nl/publarchief/jb/congres/01809180/ n15/b3.pdf , 36.

amongst us, borrowing is never a real issue, as one can borrow practically any-thing[28] from anywhere.[29] But the followers of Legrand,[30] Kahn Freund[31] and the Seidmans[32] object rather radically to the utility of borrowing altogether, while Schlesinger concludes that the future belongs to integrative comparative law and puts forward the EU's *ius commune* as an example of integration of similar and different legal systems.[33] Jhering, and Zweigert and Kötz[34] view the question of comparability through the relative prism of functionality,[35] namely of usefulness and need.[36]

It is the theory of functionality that seems to serve borrowing legislative solutions from the EU with an aim to harmonise. As the evident current legal globalisation[37] required global, or at least regional transnational, solutions integrative transnational approaches seem to be no longer a luxury but a realistic response. Does it really matter where these responses are borrowed from? Not in principle. However, a qualifier to Watson's liberal approach can be introduced via Zweigert and Kötz's functionality theory. What matters when deciding if the national legal order can borrow from the EU is not the

---

28   Watson, A (1976), 'Legal Transplants and Law Reform', 92 *Law Quarterly Review*, 79, at 80; also Watson, A (1974), *Legal Transplants: An Approach to Comparative Law* (Scottish Academic Press); Watson, A (4 December 2000) 'Legal transplants and European private law', Ius Commune Lectures on European Private Law, no 2.

29   Örücü, E (1999), 'Critical Comparative Law: considering paradoxes for legal systems in transition', 59 *Nederlandse Vereniging voor Rechtsvergelijking* 59; Örücü, E. (2002), 'Law as Transposition', 51 *International and Comparative Law Quarterly*, 205, at 206.

30   Legrand, P (1997), 'The Impossibility of Legal Transplants', *Maastricht Journal of European and Comparative Law* 111.

31   Kahn-Freund, O (1974), '*On Uses and Misuses of Comparative Law*', 37 *Modern Law Review* 1, at 7.

32   Seidman, A and Seidman, R (1994), *State and Law in the Developing Process: Problem Solving and Institutional Change in the Developing World* (Macmillan Publishers), at 44–6.

33   Schlesinger, R (1961), 'The common core of legal systems: an emerging subject of comparative study', in Nadelmann, K, von Mehren, A and Hazard, J (eds), *XXth Century Comparative and Conflicts Law, Legal Essays in Honour of Hessel E. Yntema* (Leyden: A.W. Sythoff); Schlesinger (1957), 'Research on the general principles of law recognised by civilised nations', 51 *American Journal of International Law* 734.

34   Zweigert, K and Kötz, H (1996), 'Einführung in die Rechtsvergleichung', 3 *neu-bearbeitete Auflage*, (J C B Mohr).

35   Zweigert, K and Sier, K (1971), 'Jhering's influence on the development of comparative legal method', 19 *American Journal of Comparative Law* 215.

36   Jhering, K (1955), *Geist des römischen Rechts*, (Basel: Schurabe) at 8–9.

37   Mistelis, L A (2000), 'Regulatory Aspects: Globalization, Harmonization, Legal Transplants, and Law Reform – Some Fundamental Observations', 34 *International Lawyer* 1059.

similarity of their characteristics, but the functionality of the proposal at the national level. If the policy, concept or legislation of the EU can serve the receiving national system well, then the origin of the transplant is irrelevant to its success.[38]

This line of analysis can be used to justify the seemingly unfair demand upon national governments to implement the same policy and legislative choices irrespective of the nature of legal system, its stage of development, and its national intricacies.[39] For the purposes of this chapter, however, it simply proves that the adoption of whatever policy or legislative solution is required by the EU should not, at least in principle, lead to problems in the national legal orders of the Member States. The functionality of the EU solution is by definition formulated on the basis of common functionalities represented in the negotiations, and subsequent agreement, on EU policies and EU legislative texts. Since the functionality of the EU solution is shared with that of national requirements, harmonisation may not be viewed as a pure transplant exercise with its inherent common dangers for the receiving legal system.

Having established that harmonisation is technically free of the dangers inherent in legal transplants, and having identified the principles which delimit the choices related to national implementing measures, it is time to turn the focus of this analysis to the drafting techniques employed by national drafters as a means of achieving effective harmonisation through national implementing laws of good quality.

TECHNICAL RULES FOR DRAFTING

But what are the parameters of good quality in legislation?[40] The EU has gone a long way in defining the quality of EU and national implementing legislative texts.[41] First, legislation of good quality must comply with the five Sutherland criteria:[42] necessity for action, choice of the most effective course of action,

---

[38]   Zhuang, S (2006), 'Legal Transplantation in the People's Republic of China: A Response to Alan Watson', *European Journal of Law Reform* 215, at 223.

[39]   Maher, I (1998), 'Community Law in the National Legal Order: A Systems Analysis', 36 *Journal of Common Market Studies* 237.

[40]   For a complete survey of the literature and recent analysis of quality in EU legislation see Voermans, W (2009), 'The Quality of EU Legislation: What Kind of Problem, by What Kind of Standards?', available http://ssrn.com/abstract=1113774.

[41]   Commission, 'Better Lawmaking Report 1998: A Shared Responsibility', COM(1998)715 final; also see *Bulletin EU* 11–1997, point 1.1.1.

[42]   'The internal market after 1992: meeting the challenge', Report to the EEC Commission by the High Level Group on the operation of the internal market, SEC(92)2044; also 'Supplement to European Report' no 1808 of 31 October 1992;

proportionality of the measure, consistency with existing measures, and wider consultation of the circles concerned during the preparatory stages.[43] Second, texts must be clearer and simpler.[44] Third, texts must be accessible:[45] the wording must be clear, simple, concise and unambiguous; the same term must be used throughout the act; the preamble must be a means of justification of the enacting provisions in simple terms, the rights and obligations deriving from the act must be clearly determined; the act's date of entry into force must be expressly introduced, and the provisions of the various acts must be consistent. Unnecessary abbreviations, Community jargon, long sentences, imprecise references to other texts, too many cross-references, political statements without legislative character, pointless repetitions of existing provisions, and inconsistencies with existing legislation must be avoided.[46]

Thus the ultimate definition of quality was offered by Jean-Claude Piris, who has stated that there are two aspects in the issue of quality: quality in the substance of the law and quality in the form of the law. Quality in the substance of the law refers mainly to issues of legislative policy and covers tests of subsidiarity and proportionality, choice of the appropriate instrument, duration and intensity of the intended instrument, consistency with previous measures, cost/benefit analysis and analysis of the impact of the proposed instrument on other important areas of policy, such as SMEs, environment, fraud prevention, etc.

'Commission Communication to the Council and the EP, "Follow-up of the Sutherland report"', COM(93)361 final and SEC(92)2227 fin; 'Opinion of the Economic and Social Committee of 5 May 1993 "On the Commission Communication on the operation of the Community's internal market after 1992: follow-up to the Sutherland Report"', OJ (1993) C 201/59; 'Communication from the Commission, "Follow-up to the Sutherland Report: legislative consolidation to enhance the transparency of Community law in the area of the internal market"', 16 December 1993, COM(93)361 fin.; 'Communication from the Commission to the Council, the EP and the ESC "On the handling of urgent situations in the context of implementation of Community rules: follow-up to the Sutherland Report"', COM(93)430 fin.; 'Report of the Group of Independent Experts on legislative and administrative simplification: Summary and Proposals', COM(95)288 final of 21 June 1995; Commission's comments on the report SEC(95) 2121 final of 29 November 1995; and the European Parliament Resolution of 4 July 1996, OJ (1996) C211, 23.

[43]   Also 'Communication from the Commission to the European Parliament and the Council, Making Simple Market Rules More Effective', COM(1998)296 final.

[44]   Edinburgh European Council, 'Conclusions of the Presidency', *Bulletin EC* 12/92, 7–40; also http://europa.eu.int/comm/dg15/en/update/general/camb.htm#1, p. 1.

[45]   'Council Resolution of 8 June 1993 on the quality of drafting Community legislation', OJ (1993) C 166/1, 1.

[46]   'Interinstitutional Agreement of 20 December 1994, "Accelerated working method for official codification of legislative texts"', OJ (1995) C 293/2, OJ (1996) C 102/2. These rules are also included in Council Decision 93/662/EC of 6 December 1993 adopting the Council's Rules of Procedure, OJ (1993) L 304/1.

Quality in the form of the law concerns accessibility, namely transparency in the decision-making process, and dissemination of the law.[47]

I classify the drafting rules provided by the EU into three broad categories: rules concerning the substance of the legislative text, rules related to the legislative process which leads to their passing, and rules relevant to technical drafting issues.[48] As for the substance of the legislative text, legislation must be an essential and effective means of achieving the aim of the law in question: alternative means of regulation, such as inter-trade agreements, must be encouraged, and so is abstinence from regulation in areas which do not fall within priority policy issues.[49] Legislation must be proportional to the aim to be achieved,[50] and consistent with existing legislation. It must take into account the particular needs of the users of the final texts: thus, it must determine the new rights and obligations introduced by it in a manner which can be easily understood by lay persons. Furthermore, legislation must take into account its functioning within a multi-lingual and multi-legal regional environment.

As for the legislative process, institutions must respect the principle of subsidiarity.[51] The policy and legislative process must be open,[52] transparent,[53] with full information of legislative dossiers available to all interested parties,[54] and consultation must be as wide as possible. The legislative process must also be carefully planned and co-ordinated. Furthermore, planned legislation must be subject to cost analysis, and already enacted laws must be monitored and evaluated.

As for the technical side of drafting, legislation must be clear, unambiguous and simple; this is all the more important for texts which are going to be translated

---

[47] Piris, J-C, above, 28.

[48] Xanthaki, H (2001), 'The Problem of Quality in EU legislation: what on earth is really wrong?', 38 *Common Market Law Review* 651.

[49] 'Communication of 9 January 1996 by the President of the Commission', SEC(95)2255.

[50] Case C–84/94 *UK v. Council* [1996] ECR I–5755, at paras 47, 55, 57 and 58.

[51] 'Communication from the Commission on Subsidiarity', SEC(92)1990; also 'Interinstiututional Agreement of 25 October 1993 on the procedures for implementing the principle of subsidiarity', *Bull. EC*, no 12, 1993, 129.

[52] 'Communication of the Council, the Parliament and the Economic and Social Committee, "Openness in the Community"', COM(93)258 fin., OJ (1993) C 166/4.

[53] 'Interinstitutional declaration on democracy, transparency and subsidiarity', *Bulletin EC*, 10/93, 119; also 'Resolution of the European Parliament of 6 May 1994 on the transparency of Community legislation and the need for it to be consolidated', A3-0266/94, OJ (1994) C 205/514.

[54] 'Code of Conduct 93/730/EC concerning public access to Council and Commission documents', OJ (1993) L 340/41; also 'Commission Decision 94/90/ECSC, EC and Euroatom of February 1994 on public access to Commission documents', OJ (1994) L 46/58.

and transposed. Clarity includes the use of plain language,[55] and the avoidance of too many cross-references, and of political statements without legislative character. Unambiguity covers the use of the same term throughout the text, lack of unnecessary abbreviations, and lack of pointless repetition of existing provisions. Simplicity incorporates lack of jargon, long sentences and imprecise references to other legal texts.[56] The title of legislative texts must be a full and clear indication of their subject matter. Preambles must only be used as means of justifying the enacting provisions in simple, non-repetitive terms. Citations (namely the short title within the title) must provide the legal basis of the text, whereas recitals within the preamble must be used as a means of presenting the concise reasons for passing this piece of legislation. Moreover, there must be a very clear reference to the date of entry into force which must be clearly distinguished from the date of the actual text. Furthermore, the practices of consolidation, recasting and informal consolidation must be actively pursued for already existing legislation.

As a result of this analysis, in order to contribute to effective harmonisation national implementing measures must be clear, unambiguous and simple.[57] Clarity, or clearness,[58] is defined as the state or quality of being clear and easily perceived or understood.[59] Clarity depends on the proper selection of words and on the arrangement and the construction of sentences.[60] Clarity in the language of the law enhances the understanding and transparency of legislation.[61] Ambiguity is defined as uncertain or inexact meaning.[62] Ambiguity exists when words can be interpreted in more than one way: for example, is a 'light truck' light in weight or light in colour? Thus, semantic ambiguity occurs when a single word has more than one meaning and is cured by defining any term that people might disagree about.[63] Syntactic ambiguity is the

---

[55] 'Opinion of the Economic and Social Committee of 5 July 1995 on plain language', OJ (1995) C 256/8.

[56] 'Resolution of the EP of 4 July 1996 on the report of independent experts on simplification of Community legislation and administrative provisions', COM(95)288 fin.; also A-4 0201/96, OJ (1996) C 211/23.

[57] For an analysis of these concepts see Xanthaki, H (2008), 'On transferability of legislative solutions: the functionality test', above.

[58] Lord Thring (1902), *Practical Legislation: The Composition and Language of Acts of Parliament and Business Documents* (John Murray), at 61.

[59] *Compact Oxford English Dictionary of Current English* (2005, Oxford University Press).

[60] Lord Thring n. 58, above, at 61.

[61] Wahlgren, P (2007), 'Legislative techniques' in Wintgens, L J (ed.), *Legislation in Context: Essays in Legisprudence* (Ashgate), 77, at 84.

[62] *Compact Oxford English Dictionary of Current English* (2005, Oxford University Press).

[63] MacKaye, J, Levi, A W, and Pepperell Montague, W (1939), *The Logic of Language* (Dartmouth College Publications), chapter 5.

result of unclear sentence structure or poor placement of phrases or clauses.[64] Vagueness exists when there is doubt about where a word's boundaries are, or when a word has an open textured meaning.[65] Precision is defined as exactness of expression or detail.[66]

Having defined the criteria for quality of the national implementing measures, one last point needs to be addressed: which is the form of national legislation that is suitable for transposition and thus harmonisation?

Here a number of factors come into play. First, there are normative criteria. Is this area reserved for a special form of legislation? Minor areas are not considered worthy of legislative intervention and are regulated by administrative acts; internal circulars; or lower forms of regulation. Factors in favour of a primary legislation in the formal sense[67] include special needs of democratic legitimacy, serious compromise of fundamental rights, introduction or attribution of important authority and powers, a wide circle of addressees, significant political, economic and social consequences, or controversial political character of the proposed solutions. In contrast to this, factors in favour of subordinate national legislation include a need for flexibility of regulation, the technical nature of the normative mater, or repetitive acts.[68]

When it comes to transposition in specific, the rule for choice for the appropriate form of national implementation also lies on the nature and form of the EU measure[69] under transposition.[70]

The Treaties are provisions of general character and may be included in the Constitution or general instruments of a higher legal value. Of course the downside of this treatment of Treaties is that their application will then be extended to EU citizens and non–EU citizens alike, unless the field of application of the relevant constitutional provision is clearly reserved for citizens of the

---

[64]   Dickerson, R (1986), *The Fundamentals of Legal Drafting* (Little Brown), at 101 and 104.

[65]   Christie, G C (1963–1964), 'Vagueness and legal language', 48 *Minnesota Law Review*, 885, at 886.

[66]   *Compact Oxford English Dictionary of Current English* (2005, Oxford University Press).

[67]   Xanthaki, H (2003), 'Drafting for Transposition of EU Criminal Laws: the EU Perspective', *European Current Law Review* xi.

[68]   Steunenberg, B and Voermans, W (2006), 'The Transposition of EC Directives: A Comparative Study of Instruments, Techniques and Processes in Six EU Member States', Leiden/ Research and Documentation Centre (WODC) of the Ministry of Justice, http://ssrn.com/abstract=1215542.

[69]   Point 13, 'Interinstitutional Agreement on Better Law-Making of 31 December 2003', OJ (2003) C321/01.

[70]   Stefanou, C and Xanthaki, H (2003), 'National Means of Implementation of Third Pillar Instruments', *European Current Law Review* xi.

country rather than mere residents. Regulations do not have to be transposed, as they are directly applicable. If they require further elaboration, they can be transposed through primary legislation. Directives require a more innovative approach as they are binding solely as to the aims to be achieved, leaving the means to be used to the discretion of national authorities.[71] In principle, due to the technical and detailed nature of their provisions directives may be transposed by delegated legislation, provided that the power to use delegated legislation for the purposes of transposition is included in the ratification of the Accession Act. In practice, however, directives often require transposition via primary legislation, especially if they introduce regulation in a novel area of activity which is not yet provided for by existing national legislation. Decisions lend themselves to national administrative acts that can be addressed to the particular addressees of the decision, or to delegated legislation. Recommendations and Opinions do not require express transposition as they are not binding; however, they can be used as a tool for interpretation of the EU provisions that they may interpret or apply. Similar techniques can be used for instruments in the second and third pillars. It must be noted that judgments of the ECJ and CFI must also be taken into account by national legislators as, either as a tool of authoritative interpretation of EU law or as a source of law in the case of established case law of the ECJ, they may well require transposition at the national level.

THE ULTIMATE DECIDING FACTOR: CONCLUSIONS

At the end of the day the choice of format of the national implementing measure, choices related to context of the national legislative texts, and choices related to the policy and, if necessary, the legislative solution can serve harmonisation only if they are made on the basis of one criterion: that of effectiveness. Effectiveness is the legislator's contribution to the efficacy of national implementing measures. Effective meaning that the norm produces effects, that it does not become a dead letter.[72] Parksinson describes effective legislation as reasonable legislation.[73] Mader defines effectiveness as the extent to which the observable attitudes and behaviours of the target population correspond to the attitudes

---

[71] Prechal, S (1995), *Directives in European Community Law: A Study of Directives and their Enforcement in National Courts* (Clarendon Press), at 15.

[72] See Delnoy, P (2005), *The role of legislative drafters in determining the content of norms* (The International Cooperation Group, Department of Justice of Canada), at 6, available at www.justice.gc.ca/en/ps/inter/delnoy/ index.html at 3.

[73] Parkinson, T I (1930), 'Functions of administration in labour legislation', 20 *American Labor Legislation Review*, 143, at 144.

and behaviours prescribed by the legislator.[74] Effectiveness seems to reflect the relationship between the results produced by the national implementing or transposing measures and the purpose of these measures: consequently, it links national measures to the achievement of harmonisation.

In EU law effectiveness appears to be at the forefront of lawmaking and is linked to minimum consultation standards applied by the Commission's departments: this leads to quality and equity of major political proposals which, in turn, guarantees the feasibility and effectiveness of the lawmaking operation.[75] Effectiveness is not simply the elaboration of legal doctrine.[76] It includes but is not limited to implementation, enforcement, impact and compliance.[77] Thus, effectiveness may include both the effects of legal norms and the following of such norms.[78]

However, one could distinguish in general between two prevailing models of effectiveness, often described as the positivist and the socio-legal models. In his positivist approach Jacobson links effectiveness to implementation and compliance.[79] In his socio-legal model of effectiveness Jenkins relates the statute to the social reform attained.[80] Irrespective of which of the two models one favours, the fact of the matter is that drafters are in pursuit of effectiveness of the measure that they draft. And, although stating that a drafter can single-handedly achieve effectiveness in legislation would signify complete ignorance of the interrelation between actors in the policy process, the truth of the matter is that the drafter can, and must seek to, achieve attainment of the purpose and objectives set in the statute under construction.

Ultimately, effectiveness is the criterion of choice for any dilemma related to transposition. Moreover, effectiveness is the common functionality required for the legal basis of harmonisation. The concept justifies harmonisation while at the same time guaranteeing its success.

---

[74]   Mader, L (2001), 'Legislative procedure and the quality of legislation', in Karpen, U and Delnoy, P (eds), *Contributions to the Methodology of the Creation of Written Law* (Nomos Verlagsgesellshcaft), 62, at 68.

[75]   'Communication from the Commission: European Governance: Better lawmaking', COM(2002)275 final, Brussels, 5 June 2002, at 3.

[76]   Snyder, F (1990), *New Directions in EC Law* (Weidenfeld and Nicholson), at 3.

[77]   Teubner, G (1992), 'Regulatory Law: Chronicle of a Death Foretold', 1 *Soco-Legal Studies* 451.

[78]   Snyder, F (1993), 'The Effectiveness of European Community Law: Institutions, Processes, Tools and Techniques', 56 *Modern Law Review* 19, 19.

[79]   Jacobson, H (1998), 'After word: conceptual, methodological and substantive issues entwined in studying compliance', 19 *Michigan Law Journal*, 569, at 573.

[80]   Jenkins, I (1981), *Social Order and the Limits of the Law: a Theoretical Essay* (Princeton University Press), at 180; also Cranston, R (1978–1979), 'Reform through legislation: the dimension of legislative technique', 73 *Northwestern University Law Review* 873, at 875.

Effectiveness, as expressed by the principles examined in this chapter that in turn are expressed in the technical rules for successful transposition, is at the essence of successful harmonisation. To reverse this thread of thought, the technical rules for drafting national implementing measures are necessary for compliance with the principles that delimit transposition; in turn, the principles ensure effectiveness of the policy and legislative solutions at the national and ultimately at the EU level. This is why drafting rules are not mere letters and clauses in the drafting guidelines of national authorities: they are part of the live and dynamic chain that leads to successful harmonisation.

Think about that next time you ignore them!

28. International harmonisation of credit and security laws: the way forward

Orkun Akseli*

I. INTRODUCTION

The law of credit and security is at the core of commercial law. It has been traditionally regulated by domestic rules and interwoven throughout the law of property, contracts and corporate finance where the capital may be raised through borrowing.[1] However, with increasing market interdependency as a result of globalisation of financial markets, there is a commercial necessity in harmonising credit and security law at the international[2] level. The recent financial crisis clearly demonstrates that globalisation of financial markets must be accompanied by globalisation of the law of credit and security. Harmonisation of credit and security laws could substantially assist in reducing the cost of credit by creating certainty in cross-border financing transactions. Financing techniques such as raising finance against company assets and by assignment of receivables are important and their regulation varies under different jurisdictions which limit access to low cost credit. Facilitated access to low cost credit is said to drive economic growth, according to studies conducted by the World Bank.[3] There is a correlation between the facilitation of credit and lowering the

---

*   Senior Lecturer in Commercial Law, Durham University Law School, UK.

[1]   For a similar statement *see* Dahan, F (2000), 'Secured Transactions Law in Western Advanced Economies: Exposing Myths', *Law in Transition* 37, 39.

[2]   In this chapter international harmonisation is used to express the idea of international or global harmonisation under the auspices of international organisation such as UNCITRAL or Unidroit (as opposed to regional harmonisation) and international activities intended to have a global effect. Therefore, international harmonisation and global harmonisation will be used interchangeably throughout the text. For more detailed treatment of harmonisation of secured transactions laws at the international level see Akseli, O (2011), *International Secured Transactions Law: Facilitation of Credit, International Conventions and Instruments* Routledge, Abingdon.

[3]   One of the observations made by the US delegation during the negotiations of the UNCITRAL Convention was as follows: '[t]he benefits of global economics and trade have not yet been fully realized in many states, and the absence of adequate

cost of credit in the way that facilitated credit by harmonised and predictable rules may reduce the cost of credit for small and medium sized enterprises in emerging markets by minimising the risk of the financier not getting paid as the local secured credit laws may be poor.

What is most striking is that often harmonisation activities take place at regional level[4] rather than on a global level. When efforts on the global and regional levels are considered, conflicts may occur between global, regional and bilateral legislative harmonisation texts. Conflicts may also occur even at the domestic law level when a national legal provision and an international instrument on the same subject conflict. Therefore, there must be cooperation and coordination among these regional and international efforts. This chapter suggests that there is a necessity for harmonisation of credit and security laws at the international level and there should be more support for international harmonisation efforts rather than regional ones.

Section II will look at the harmonisation of secured credit laws in context. Section III will examine the necessity of harmonisation of the law of credit and security. Section IV will compare regional and international harmonisation of the law of credit and security and elaborate on the fact that international harmonisation is a necessity in this area. Section V will briefly examine the idea and concept of European Security Interest. Conclusions will be in Section VI.

---

international commercial finance and credit in this important area is one of the obstacles for achievement of these goals. ... In addition to including substantive uniform rules for the assignment of receivables, the ... Convention provides States with options in order to adapt the ... Convention's provisions to their particular economic needs. On some other matters the ... Convention sets out rules to determine which national legal regime applies, which can also promote finance, provided that the rules reflect transactional practice, serve the needs of commercial efficiency and are not counterproductively premised on general notions of conflict of laws. The combination of these techniques in the ... Convention is aimed at assuring the necessary level of commercial certainty, which is critical to the willingness of capital markets to extend credit to areas previously underserved.' See A/CN.9/472/Add.3, at 3: Compilation of Comments by Governments and International Organizations; see also Murphy S.D. (2004), 'U.S. Signing of UNCITRAL Convention on Assignment of Receivables', 98 *American Journal of International Law* 368, 369 where the US position is demonstrated. See also Levine, R (2004), 'Finance and Growth: Theory and Evidence', National Bureau of Economic Research, Working Paper 10766 at 85; see also Machoka, PM (2006), 'Towards financial sector development – the role of the draft UNCITRAL Legislative Guide on Secured Transactions', 21 *Journal of International Banking Law and Regulation* 529 at 529; see also below, 'Modernisation of secured transactions laws for economic growth and increased foreign investment'.

[4]   E.g. OAS Inter-American Model Law on Secured Transactions or recent discussion regarding the security interests in the draft Common Frame of Reference or the discussion with regard to the European Civil Code and the Principles of European Contract Law.

II. HARMONISATION OF SECURED CREDIT LAWS IN CONTEXT

Harmonisation can take different forms. In certain cases harmonisation can be achieved through international conventions.[5] In other cases this can be achieved by model laws.[6] Legal reforms, directives and legislative guides are also means to achieve harmonisation.[7] While there are different views on the definition of harmonisation,[8] in the author's view, 'harmonisation', in the realm of the law of

---

[5]   Such as the UN Convention on the International Sale of Goods.

[6]   *E.g.* UNCITRAL Model Law on International Commercial Arbitration.

[7]   For more information on the means of harmonisation see Mooney, CW Jr (2001), 'Extraterritorial Impact of Choice of Law Rules for Non-United States Debtors under Revised Uniform Commercial Code Article 9 and a New Proposal for International Harmonization', at 187, 196ff, in Bridge, M and Stevens, S (eds), *Cross Border Security and Insolvency* (Oxford University Press, Oxford); see also Akseli, O (2008), 'On the Methods of International Harmonisation of Secured Transactions Law', in Baasch Andersen, C and Schroeter, U (eds), *Sharing International Commercial Law across National Boundaries Festschrift for Albert H. Kritzer on the Occasion of his Eightieth Birthday* (Wildy, Simmonds & Hill, London), at 1–12; see also Faria, JOE, *Legal Harmonization Through Model Laws: The Experience of the United Nations Commission on International Trade Law (UNCITRAL)*, available at: www.doj.gov.za/alraesa/conferences/papers/s5_faria2.pdf.

[8]   See also Mistelis, L (2001), 'Is Harmonisation a Necessary Evil? The Future of Harmonisation and New Sources of International Trade Law', in I Fletcher, L Mistelis and M Cremona (eds), *Foundations And Perspectives of International Trade Law* (Sweet & Maxwell, London) at 3–4: 'harmonisation is a process which may result in unification of law subject to a number of (often utopian) conditions being fulfilled, such as, … wide or universal geographical acceptance of harmonising instruments, and with wide scope of harmonising instruments which effectively substitute all pre-existing law'; 'harmonisation' can be defined as 'making the regulatory requirements or governmental policies of different jurisdictions identical or at least more similar'. See Leebron, DW (1996), 'Claims for Harmonization: A Theoretical Framework', 27 *Canadian Bussines Law Journal* 63, at 66; for a different definition see Ziegel, J (1997), 'Harmonization of Private Laws in Federal Systems of Government: Canada, the USA and Australia', in Cranston, R (ed.), *Making Commercial Law: Essays in Honour of Roy Goode* (Clarendon Press, Oxford), 131 at 133, where he states in relation to the commercial law that '[h]armonization in this field of law is a word with considerable elasticity [and] [i]n its most complete sense it means absolute uniformity of legislation among the adopting jurisdictions'; for different definitions of 'harmonisation' see Glenn, P (2003), 'Harmony of Laws in the Americas', 34 *University of Miami Inter-American Law Review* 223, 246; Zamora, S (1995), 'NAFTA and the Harmonization of Domestic Legal Systems: The Side effects of Free Trade', 12 *Arizona Journal of International & Comparative Law* 401, 403; Boodman, M (1991), 'The Myth of Harmonization of Laws', 39 *American Journal of Comparative Law* 699 at 707; Gopalan, S (2004), 'The Creation of International Commercial Law: Sovereignty Felled?', 5 *San Diego International Law Journal* 267, 276; Gopalan, S (2004), 'New Trends in the Making of International Commercial Law', 23 *Journal of Law and Commerce* 117, from 120.

secured credit, can be defined as the process whereby the laws of countries to the extent that they are related to secured credit are approximated with each other by certain legislative instruments (such as conventions, model laws and legislative guides) or methods (such as legal reforms). Due to differences in public policies it is almost impossible to unify secured credit laws, but it is possible to harmonise them.[9] Unification can only be achieved by a truly uniform manner of interpretation.[10] Harmonisation leaves an opportunity for experimentation, whereas uniformity does not and can be regarded as the 'imposition of one legal model on all jurisdictions'[11] through indirect influence. Wider participation and encouragement of legal cultures as well as uniform interpretation by national courts are necessary elements for an instrument to lead nations to successful and desirable uniformity.

III.   NECESSITY FOR HARMONISATION OF CREDIT AND SECURITY LAWS

The commercial necessity for the harmonisation of credit and security laws is acutely felt by emerging markets. This is particularly true for small and medium sized enterprises operating and the financiers lending therein who need to access to low cost credit with long term maturities. Harmonisation of the laws governing credit and security is necessary to facilitate the terms of credit for especially small and medium sized enterprises in emerging markets to access lower cost credit and to increase cross border trade. From this perspective harmonisation of the laws of credit and security is critical to create predictability and certainty for lenders, which will in turn provide access to lower cost credit. The lender who is confident about the consequence of his transaction, at this point, will not include the risk calculation in his interest rate and lend with long maturity.[12] Harmonisation is also said to reduce legal conflicts arising out of lending

---

[9]   See Cuming, RC (1986), 'National and International Harmonisation: Personal Property Security Law', in King, DB (ed.), 1986, *Commercial and Consumer Law from an International Perspective* Rothman, Littleton, CO 471, 485–6; for a similar view see also Buxbaum, HL (2002), 'Conflict of Economic Laws: From Sovereignty to Substance', 42 *Virginia Journal of International Law*. 931, 948; see A/CN.9/378/Add.3 where UN-CITRAL concludes that 'worldwide unification of the law of security interests in goods … was in all likelihood unattainable'.

[10]   On a truly uniform manner of interpretation see e.g. Ferrari, F (2001), 'Applying the CISG in a Truly Uniform manner: Tribunale di Vigevano (Italy), 12 July 2000', *Uniform Law Review* 203–15.

[11]   See Zamora, *supra* n. 8, at 405.

[12]   For a similar argument see McCormack, G (2007), 'The UNCITRAL Legislative Guide on Secured Transactions Functionalism and Form', in Foëx, B Thévenoz, L

transactions where both parties are not certain with regard to the consequences of the transaction. Furthermore, the applicable law may be less efficient and not protect the interest of the creditor. With facilitated access to lower cost credit economic growth is said to be maintained. Secured lending is also said to reduce poverty.[13] Facilitated access to low cost credit enables small and medium sized businesses to obtain immediate liquidity, which in turn enables them to invest on further projects. Creditors' confidence may be obtained by virtue of predictable rules governing credit and security law. Finally, as a general proposition, it can be argued that activities on the harmonisation of the law of credit and security demonstrate the importance of intangibles as collateral.[14]

Taking security lowers the cost of credit by reducing the risk of non-payment in the event of the debtor's insolvency.[15] The primary function of international secured transactions law conventions, in general terms, is to modernise and harmonise domestic laws to the extent that they are applied to cross-border secured transactions. There are differences in domestic laws regarding the use of movables and intangibles as collateral. Differences among national secured transactions regimes 'create uncertainty and transaction costs that lower the expected value of a transaction to the creditor'.[16] The same differences are also obstacles to the harmonisation process. In some developed countries the use of intangibles and movables is more attractive, whereas in economically less developed countries the use of immovables as collateral is more attractive or more acceptable by financiers.[17] If there is no harmonisation there may be

---

Bazinas SV (eds) (2007) *Réforme des sûretés mobilières. Les enseignements du Guide législatif de la CNUDCI / Reforming secured transactions. The UNCITRAL legislative guide as an inspiration* Schulthess, Geneva 214.

[13]   For the poverty reduction effect of the harmonised law of credit and security see Kozolchyk, B (2007), 'Secured Lending and Its Poverty Reduction Effect', 42 *Texas International Law Journal* 727.

[14]   E.g. UN Convention on the Assignment of Receivables in International Trade http://www.uncitral.org/uncitral/en/uncitral_texts/payments/2001Convention_receivables.html; Hague Conferences Convention on the Law Applicable to Certain Rights in respect of Securities Held with an Intermediary http://www.hcch.net/index_en.php?act=conventions.text&cid=72. But cf. in a study conducted in 60 countries World Bank studies demonstrate that immovables are preferred mainly as collateral: Safavian, M, H Fleisig and J Steinbuks (2006) 'Unlocking Dead Capital', *Viewpoint*, Note Number 307 (March) at 2 and Figure 3.

[15]   See generally McCormack, G (2003), 'The Priority of Secured Credit: an Anglo-American Perspective', *Journal of Business Law* 389, 402; McCormack, G (2002), 'The Nature of Security over Receivables', 23 *Company Lawyer* 84, 85.

[16]   Cohen, N B (1998), 'Harmonizing the Law Governing Secured Credit: The Next Frontier', 33 *Texas International Law Journal* 173, 176.

[17]   See e.g. Safavian, M (2006), 'Firm Level Evidence on Collateral and Access to Finance', 'Presentation made at the International Workshop on Collateral Reform and

uncertainty, which can mean in this context 'credit at a high cost, less or no credit, depending on whether the risk can be reasonably estimated'.[18] Cuming and van Erp argue that these differences arise out of the fact that the secured transactions laws of states 'are grounded in property concepts some of which are peculiar to particular families of law'.[19] Differences may be eliminated by virtue of harmonisation of secured transactions laws and creating certainty and predictability in cross-border credit transactions. International secured transactions conventions present various solutions to these problems arising in the context of cross-border credit transactions. Thus, these projects are supported by international financial organisations.

Access to lower cost credit requires an efficient and modern secured lending regime supported by a prudent supervision regime.[20] Modernisation or modernised harmonisation of credit and security laws can successfully be achieved by either legal reform or international instruments. The former has the risk of imposing rules from top to bottom if it is presented by a foreign national insti-

---

Access to Credit', EBRD, London on 8–9 June 2006; see generally World Bank FDP Forum (2007) 'Making Finance Work for Africa: What Role for Collateral Reform?' (Washington, DC: World Bank); IFC?MPDF (2007) 'Vietnam Increasing Access to Credit through Collateral (Secured Transactions) Reform' (Washington, DC: IFC); FIAS/ IFC PEP China (2007) 'Reforming Collateral Laws and Registries: International Best Practices and the Case of China' (Washington, DC: World Bank).

[18]   See Bazinas, SV (2006), 'Modernising and Harmonising Secured Credit Law: The Example of the UNCITRAL Draft Legislative Guide on Secured Transactions Part 1', 01 *Journal of International Banking and Finance* 20.

[19]   For more information see *infra* n. 42 et seq and the accompanying text. See also Cuming, RCC (1997), 'The Internationalization of Secured Financing Law: The Spreading Influence of the Concepts of UCC, Article 9 and its Progeny', in Cranston, R. (ed.) (1997) *Making Commercial Law Essays in Honour of Roy Goode* (Clarendon Press, Oxford) 499 at 499; for a discussion of harmonisation from the legal-historical and comparative perspectives see Erp, SV (2003), 'Civil and Common Property law: Caveat Comparator – The Value of Legal Historical-Comparative Analysis', *European Review of Private Law* 394.

[20]   The recent financial crisis has clearly demonstrated that banks and financial institutions must be supervised in especially their credit transactions which are open to abusive usage. Capital must be maintained at all times and must be prudently supervised. Securitisation transactions are perfect examples of this. Securitisation technique has been used by banks over and over again on recycled receivables. One can argue that the soundness of the securitisation technique has nothing to do with the crisis, but it is those financiers who used the technique without any safeguards and without taking into account the risk they are passing onto other clients on the recycled receivables. See also Sigman, HC and Kieninger, EM (2007), *Cross Border Security over Tangibles* 1 (Sellier, Munich, 2007), where they state that '[u]nder the Basel II requirements, financial institutions require a clear and certain legal structure to support the efficient supply of credit, generating an immediate need for modernisation of the law governing security in movables'.

tution, and thus creating more difficulty to that economy than being useful.[21] The latter, on the other hand, is more effective in creating modernisation and harmonisation in the medium to long term. However, it also has a risk. That is to say that if the international instrument has been influenced by a particular legal system, then it may be argued that the instrument may not be easily adopted as it does not reflect the recipient jurisdiction's legal and economic structure and imposes one legal system on all jurisdictions. This is critical in the field of credit and security; more so, it has particular relationship with insolvency law and the law of property which are deeply rooted to the legal culture of a jurisdiction. From another perspective it can also be argued that if a particular international instrument does not contain a vital feature of the credit and security law regime, then it may not be efficient and acceptable.[22]

In order to achieve access to lower cost credit for small and medium sized businesses in emerging markets apart from adopting relevant international instruments, it is necessary to build appropriate infrastructure, judiciary and enforcement mechanisms.[23] Furthermore, legal systems must have predictable and comprehensive rules that fit that infrastructure in order to promote secured credit.[24]

During the process of harmonisation both international and national law reform institutions may encounter certain problems. These include difficulty in reaching a compromise between certain major states, the complexity of national laws on certain areas, resistance to changing traditional national legal approaches on certain points of law and the multiplicity of international instruments or activities on similar topics.[25] However, it can be argued that the main problem seems to be experienced between regional and international harmonisation activities.

---

[21]   See below for more information on legal reform activities.

[22]   Such as the Unidroit Convention on International Factoring which does not contain priority of claims and formal validity features, thus leaving these unsolved.

[23]   Bazinas rightly argues 'such an economic result [cannot be achieved immediately and] automatically through the enactment of appropriate legislation but depends largely on the relevant infrastructure, judiciary and enforcement mechanisms': see Bazinas, S (2004), 'UNCITRAL's Work in the field of Secured Transactions' 36 *Uniform Commercial Code Law Journal* 67.

[24]   For a discussion of some best practices and policy options see Welsh, A (2003), 'Secured Transactions Law: Best Practices and Policy Options', *IRIS Discussion Paper No. 03/06* (The IRIS Discussion Papers on Institutions and Development, Center of Institutional Reform and the informal Sector at the University of Maryland, August 2003).

[25]   E.g. the overlap between the Unidroit Convention on International Factoring and the UNCITRAL Convention on the Assignment of Receivables in International Trade.

IV. REGIONAL VERSUS INTERNATIONAL HARMONISATION FROM THE LAW OF CREDIT AND SECURITY PERSPECTIVE

There is a tension between regional and international harmonisation.[26] The issue has political aspects. The tension stems from both whether regional or international harmonisation efforts in the field of secured credit be given preference and the competition between the international and regional organisations. The issue becomes extremely critical when the link, which is traditionally deeply rooted to national legal cultures, between the law of credit and security, insolvency and the law of property, is considered.

Mistelis observes as follows:

> Inevitably there are at least two competing strategies in the harmonization of international commercial law on a worldwide basis: (i) the 'global' conventions proposed by international organizations and (ii) the regional agreements drafted by regional organizations. The goals of such regional conventions often derive from quite different motivations, but often produce agreements that concern the same subject matter as the global conventions. In principle, the conflict between harmonization initiated by intergovernmental organizations and nongovernmental organizations may not be as acute, provided that lobbyists from one side and state functionaries on the other side communicate clearly the interests they represent and that the necessary compromises are made.[27]

As a general proposition one can argue that regional harmonisation activities may undermine international harmonisation activities.[28] Firstly, regional harmonisation activities deal with only regional financial and legal problems with limited or no contribution from extra-regional cultures and legal systems. Expanded contribution from all legal cultures and continents enhances the acceptability of an instrument and makes it more comprehensive and useful.

---

[26]   For a historical relationship between the regional and international efforts of harmonisation of private law see Basedow, J (2003), 'Worldwide harmonisation of Private Law and Regional Economic Integration-General Report', *Uniform Law Review* 31; for a similar view see also Bazinas, S (2003), 'Harmonisation of International and Regional Trade Law: The UNICTRAL Experience', *Uniform Law Review* 53 where he states that '[s]ince the 1997 Treaty of Amsterdam gave the European Union (EU) a mandate in the field of private international law, the relationship between international and regional harmonisation of private law is increasingly being described as one of tension'.

[27]   Mistelis, L (2000), 'Regulatory Aspects: Globalization, Harmonization, Legal Transplants and Law reform – Some Fundamental Observations', 34 *International Law* 1055, 1062–3.

[28]   Drobnig, U (2003), 'Brief Considerations on Coordinating Developments in the Field of Secured Transactions Law', *Uniform Law Review* 353 where he argues that 'various regional efforts will produce instruments with differing regimes'.

Secondly, as Drobnig rightly suggests there is still 'differing levels of development [and] the need for credit may not everywhere be as pressing as it is in certain highly developed countries'.[29] This is equally true even within regional organisations and even 'national and regional legislators may place different degrees of emphasis on the protection of the secured creditor ... and... of the debtor's unsecured creditors....'[30] With regard to the EU, for instance, as McCormack correctly states, trade within the EU functions properly and there is no necessity for a common law of proprietary securities[31] within the framework of the Common Frame of Reference.[32] On the other hand, for other regions there may be a need for a regional approach. For instance, Garro makes a pragmatic argument for harmonising national attitudes to secured transactions at a regional level.[33] His arguments are based on the harmonisation experience of Latin American countries which have strong commercial ties, a common legal tradition and similar social and economic approaches to credit and security transactions.[34] Furthermore, the argument is that developed economies' secured transactions systems cannot easily be adopted by the Latin American countries which have developing economies with a shortage of capital, lack of a conceptual framework (mainly based on Roman law concepts which are not similar to Anglo-American concepts[35]) and lack of experience in secured lending.[36] Thus it seems that regional harmonisation within Latin American countries may be a reasonable step for that particular example.[37] However, the same argument may

---

[29]   Ibid., at 354.

[30]   Ibid., at 354.

[31]   McCormack, G (2008), 'The CFR and Credit Securities – a suitable case for treatment?', *WG Hart Workshop Paper*, at 6 (University of London, 24 June 2008).

[32]   But cf. European Parliament Committee on Legal Affairs and the Internal Market Report which prompts harmonisation on security rights in movables: see Kieninger, EM (2004), 'Introduction' in Kieninger, EM (ed.), *Security Rights in Movable Property in European Private Law* (Cambridge University Press) at 21.

[33]   Garro, A (1990), 'The Reform and Harmonisation of Personal Property Security law in Latin America', 59 *Revista Juridica Universidad de Puerto Rico* 1, at 14–16.

[34]   Ibid., at 16.

[35]   But cf. Kozolchyk, B and Wilson, JM (2002), 'The Organization of American States: The New Model Inter-American Law on Secured Transactions', *Uniform Law Review* 69, 74ff where they argued that Roman legal institutions were more compatible with Anglo-American secured transactions law than the Latin American law they influenced.

[36]   See Garro, *supra* n. 33, at 15;

[37]   However, since the early 1990s, there have been three model laws and reforms none of which had been enacted in Latin America. These model law texts were prepared by the Centre for Economic Analysis of Law, Central Bank of Argentina and the National Centre for Inter-American Trade Law. See Mistelis, L (1998), 'The EBRD Model Law on Secured Transactions and Its Impact on Collateral Law Reform in Central and Eastern Europe and the Former Soviet Union', 5 *The Parker School Journal of East European Law* 455, at 459 and n. 13.

not be equally applicable to the European Union or its efforts.[38] The divergence between the Civil and Common law approaches to credit and security[39] inherent among the EU member States cannot be found in Latin American countries although there is an established common market in the EU. The EU presents a different picture.[40] Security interest regimes within the EU are fragmented; however, the 'intra community trade seems to function perfectly well without a common law of [credit and security]'.[41] A simple example can be given from England where the law of credit and security is fragmented[42] and different rules apply for hire-purchase, conditional sale, mortgages, equitable charges and pledge.[43] The credit and security law systems of former transition economies, some of which are also members of the EU, have recently been reformed.[44] Civil

---

[38] But cf. Garro, *supra* n. 33, at 15 and n. 34.

[39] Goode, R (1998), 'Security in Cross Border Transactions', 33 *Texas International Law Journal* 47, at 48. Goode suggests that the basic difference between the Common law and Civil law systems on security interests is

[the] philosophy and legal culture concerning the extent to which a security should be recognized at all and the conditions necessary, for the validity of a security interest. Common law jurisdictions, which are generally sympathetic to the concepts of party autonomy and self-help, have a liberal attitude towards security. This attitude allows security interests to be taken with a minimum of formality over both present and future assets to secure existing and future indebtedness. [T]hey allow universal security rather than require specific security. By contrast, civil law jurisdictions have been more cautious in their approach to non-possessory security and have been anxious about the false wealth which such practices are perceived as permitting. [Therefore, one can find in civil law jurisdictions…] requirements of specificity or individualization of collateral, the requirements of notice to the debtor as a condition of the validity (not merely priority) of an assignment of debts, and restrictions on self help remedies such as possession and sale of the collateral.

[40] For a critical study of whether or not the EU should act on security interests see di Luigi, MC (2008), 'Divergences of Security and Property Law in the European Union: The Need for Action', *Journal of Business Law* 526.

[41] McCormack, *supra* n. 31, at 6.

[42] For a similar view see Goode, R (1998), *Commercial Law in the Next Millennium The Hamlyn Lectures Forty-Ninth Series* (Sweet and Maxwell, London) at 64.

[43] Despite this fragmentation in the law of credit and security, the UK is the 5th largest economy in the world with 2,727,806 million US$ gross domestic product according to World Bank ranking in 2007/2008. See http://siteresources.worldbank.org/DATASTATISTICS/Resources/GDP.pdf (last accessed October 2008).

[44] See 'Ten Years of Secured Transaction Reform', available at www.ebrd.com/pubs/legal/lit002b.pdf#page=2 (last accessed on 10 September 2008); the EBRD's Legal Reform Work: Contributing to Transition www.ebrd.com/pubs/legal/lit022.pdf#page=39 (last accessed on 10 September 2008); see also Dahan, F and Simpson, J (2004), 'Secured Transactions in Central and Eastern Europe: European Bank for Reconstruction and Development (EBRD) Assessment', 36 *UCCLJ* 77.

law jurisdictions have historically been hesitant about non-possessory personal property security.[45] In some civil law systems within the EU, such as Germany, pledge over receivables and assignment of receivables for security are regulated by different rules[46] and the Civil Code is 'patchy, non-uniform and inconsistent [and] [f]or different types of assets, different security devices are used'.[47] In certain countries non-possessory security arrangements in personal property have been frowned upon on the ground that 'devices which [allow] the debtor to possess and enjoy its assets while purporting to shield from the claims of its common creditors [are] considered immoral and misleading'.[48] However, for instance, the recent reform in France has demonstrated the fact that a civilian law jurisdiction 'can move towards more efficient and credit oriented secured transactions law without [losing] its civilian heritage'.[49] A better view to avoid fragmentation could be stronger participation by the EU in international harmonisation activities on the law of credit and security, where as an important economic power it can obtain workable results rather than attempting to create a binding or non-binding set of rules from new on the law of credit and security which may or may not be acceptable to all member jurisdictions. Thus, the necessity of international harmonisation that encompasses all regional activities under one instrument is once again evident.

Thirdly, there will still be problems of the influence of developed economies in a particular regional organisation and on a particular legislative text. Although the idea is to modernise the law while at the same time harmonising it, this may go against the idea of lowering the cost of credit, as the law of a developed economy influencing the structure of the regional harmonisation instrument may not be compatible with other credit and security regimes.

---

[45]   See Moglia Claps, GA and McDonnell, JB (2002), 'Secured Credit and Insolvency Law in Argentina and the US: Gaining Insight from a Comparative Perspective', 30 *Georgia Journal of International and Comparative Law* 393 at 396. However, recently, for instance, France has reformed her security interest laws. See below for more information on the reform of French credit and security law.

[46]   See generally Hausmann, J (1996), 'The Value of Public-Notice Filing Under Uniform Commercial Code Article 9: A Comparison with the German Legal System of Securities in Personal Property', 25 *Georgia Journal of International and Comparative Law* 427ff; Rakob, J (2007), 'Germany' in Sigman, HC and Kieninger EM (eds), *Cross Border Security over Tangibles* (Sellier, Munich) at 64; see also Haag, H and Peglow, O (2008), 'Germany' in Johnston, W (ed.), *Security over Receivables An International Handbook* (OUP) at 193ff.

[47]   See Rakob, *supra*, n. 46 at 65.

[48]   See Moglia Claps and McDonnell, *supra* n. 45, at 396.

[49]   Ancel, ME (2006), 'Recent Reform in France: the Renaissance of a Civilian Collateral Regime?', in *Collateral Reform and Access to Credit*, EBRD–World Bank Seminar, London, 9 June, at 3.

Fourthly, although the idea is that with complete regional harmonisation under different regional organisations[50] there may be fewer systems to deal with during international harmonisation efforts,[51] this may have conflicting results. Regional organisations' regimes will act as divergent regimes during international harmonisation activities. Furthermore, as a result of a regional harmonisation process there may well be notional conflicts or overlaps within regionally harmonised rules and between international and regional legislative texts. Conflicts may occur on critical issues, for instance as to whether there should be a functional approach in the way that the domestic law should treat all devices that perform security functions as secured transactions, and thus registration is required. The UNCITRAL Legislative Guide on Secured Transactions, like the UCC Article 9, has a functional approach and treats all devices that perform security functions as secured transactions. This may not be compatible with a particular regional harmonisation activity. Basedow argues that '[c]onflicts between the regional instruments and the existing universal treaties are ... not at all different compared to traditional conflicts of conventions'.[52] For instance, the Unidroit Convention on International Interests in Mobile Equipment clearly avoids any conflicts with the UN Convention on the Assignment of Receivables.[53] A similar cross-reference can be found in the UN Convention on the Assignment of Receivables with regard to the Unidroit International Factoring Convention.[54]

Finally, regional harmonisation activities may take binding and non-binding forms[55] which affect the adoption decisions of member states and the fate of the

---

[50]   Such as NAFTA and the EU.

[51]   For this view see Bazinas, *supra* n. 26, at 54ff. where he states that 'national or regional harmonisation promotes national or regional trade, ... and facilitates international harmonisation at least to the extent that it enhances certainty, helps to reduce the number of legal systems and provides a basis for international harmonisation ... [and] [t]his is why UNCITRAL from its inception has encouraged unification and harmonisation efforts at the national or regional level.'; for examples from regional attempts see generally Garro, A (2003), 'Harmonization of Personal Property Security Law: National, Regional and Global Initiatives', *Uniform Law Review* 357ff.

[52]   Basedow, *supra* n. 26, at 35.

[53]   The Unidroit Convention on International Interests in Mobile Equipment makes a clear reference to the UN Convention in article 45bis. Article 45bis of the Cape Town Convention reads as follows: '*Relationship with the United Nations Convention on the Assignment of Receivables in International Trade* This Convention shall prevail over the United Nations Convention on the Assignment of Receivables in International Trade, opened for signature in New York on 12 December 2001, as it relates to the assignment of receivables which are associated rights related to international interests in aircraft objects, railway rolling stock and space assets.'

[54]   The UN Convention, by virtue of Article 38(2) prevails over the Unidroit Convention on International Factoring and the latter, by virtue of Article 15, already acknowledges that it will not prevail over any treaty that may be entered into.

[55]   For these possibilities see Drobnig, *supra* n. 28, at 354.

harmonisation activity. When there is an international harmonisation activity, regions as well as member states will, again, have to reform their systems, which will result in loss of time, efficiency and efforts. Furthermore, that international instrument may not be compatible with the regional system and there may be unnecessary overlaps or critical contradictions. In addition, with a non-binding type of instrument member states may wish not to reform their systems, as it is optional[56] and this may cause conflicting results within a regional organisation and increase the cost of credit as well as of transactions.[57] Even if they wish to reform their laws, a new instrument creating a new terminology and a new system, especially for Common Law jurisdictions in relation to the latter, will create uncertainties. With respect to the Common Frame of Reference, McCormack correctly argues that it 'may straightjacket States into an unpromising and unprofitable uniformity'.[58] In addition, even though Drobnig points out that 'competition is fertile',[59] this type of competition where a regional organisation attempts to harmonise an area of law through an optional text where there is no necessity to do so in intra-community trade and where there is a newly adopted and comprehensive Legislative Guide prepared by an international formulating organisation in which member states of that regional organisation are also full members, may create infertility.

International efforts are generally promoted by UNCITRAL or Unidroit. These organisations, together with others,[60] coordinate the scope of their activities. Harmonisation activities conducted under the auspices of UNCITRAL and Unidroit take into account and target global problems, as opposed to regional ones, and receive global cooperation and assistance during the preparation phase. These organisations' efforts and products are more comprehensive and inclusive of global legal cultures and systems.

Organisations such as the Organisation of American States (OAS), the European Union (EU) and the OHADA[61] are regional organisations and mainly deal

---

[56]   With regards to the Common Frame of Reference/European Civil Code which seems to serve as an optional instrument and supplement national law see Grundmann, S and Stuyck, J (2002), *An Academic Green Paper on European Contract Law* Kluwer Law International, The Hague, Part IV.

[57]   For an opposition view to optional form from the transaction cost perspective see Collins, H (2002), 'Transaction Costs and Subsidiarity in European Contract Law' in ibid., at 277 and 281.

[58]   McCormack, *supra* n. 31, at 34.

[59]   See Drobnig, *supra* n. 28, at 354.

[60]   E.g. the Hague Conferences on Private International Law, another international organisation working on the unification and harmonisation of private law, has prepared a Convention on the Law Applicable to Certain rights in respect of Securities Held with an Intermediary. For further information see http://www.hcch.net/index_en.php?act=conventions.textlcid=72.

[61]   Organization for the Harmonisation of Business Law in Africa.

with regional harmonisation issues.[62] Financial organisations have legitimate financial concerns[63] in initiating and participating in individual and independent harmonisation activities.[64] Thus, in the regional and financial organisations example, the impact of those efforts on possible future international harmonisation may be limited to a particular region, country or organisation.[65] Drobnig rightly states that 'financing will and should not be limited to regional scopes'.[66] Regional organisations should focus their activities on either coordinating regional positions or implementing international instruments,[67] thus assisting

---

[62]   E.g. OAS Inter-American Model Law on Secured Transactions. The OWS Model law has been prepared for lenders to provide credit at competitive rates in their region as well as all around the world. The Model law has a uniform security interest mechanism. OAS Model Law article 1 reads as follows: 'The objective of this of the Model Inter-American Law on Secured Transactions (hereinafter, the 'Law') is to regulate security interest in movable property securing the performance of any obligations whatsoever, of any nature, present, future, determined or determinable. A State may declare that this Law does not apply to the types of collateral expressly specified in this text. A State adopting this Law shall create a unitary and uniform registration system applicable to all existing movable property security devices in the local legal framework, in order to give effect to this law.' UCC §1-201(37) defines security interest as 'an interest in personal property or fixtures that secures payment or performance of an obligation'.

[63]   For example, the World Bank subjects the extension of credit to appropriate legal reform in the law of credit and security. The investment clients of the IMF lend to developing countries and hence the pressure to modernise the law of credit and security in those countries. See www.ifc.org/ifcext/about.nsf/content/About_IFC_Financing (last accessed 18 September 2008). For an example of the World Bank's role in harmonisation efforts see e.g. World Bank Working Group Paper on 'Building Effective Insolvency Systems: Debtor–Creditor Regimes' at 2; see also The World Bank Principles and Guidelines for Effective Insolvency and Creditor Rights Systems, April 2001.

[64]   For example 'EBRD's objective is to act as a ... catalyst of change in the region by facilitating credit for other investors'. See Dahan, F and McCormack, G (2002), 'International Influences and the Polish Law on Secured Transactions: Harmonisation, Unification or What?', *Uniform Law Review* at 715; see also Simpson, J and Röver, JHM (1998), 'An Introduction to the European Bank's Model Law on Secured Transactions', in Norton, JJ and Andenas, M (eds), *Emerging Financial Markets and Secured Transactions* (Kluwer) at 165.

[65]   Berkowitz, D et al. (2003), 'The Transplant Effect', 51 *American Journal of Comparative Law* 163, 164 where it was stated that 'newly designed model laws for secured transactions marketed the value of Western law to their counterparts in the East, backing their campaign to transplant their home legal system with financial aid promises and/or the prospect of joining the European Union'.

[66]   Drobnig, *supra* n. 28, at 354.

[67]   For those views and similar expressions indicated in the Questionnaire of the Inter-American Juridical Committee of the Organisation of American States see Vazquez, CM (2003), 'Regionalism versus Globalism: A View from the Americas', *Uniform Law Review* 63, at 66–7. But he also argues that 'there are fewer legal systems at the regional level than at the global level and because the legal systems within any given region are

international harmonisation activities. Nonetheless, one may also argue that these activities may have the value of serving as a model or inspiration for future international reform activities provided that they do not jeopardise international efforts.

The critical point in every harmonisation type is the risk of overall hegemony of a legal system. In other words, a particular legal system may be taken as an example or as a catalyst in a particular harmonisation instrument.[68] This is equally applicable in regional and international harmonisation activities. This presents problems of enforcement and implementation. Put in another way, a well established system or a concept may not easily be adopted by another system. Concepts, methodology, terminology and business practices and usages may be totally different. The rationale is that if a legal system (which may be called the 'donor' system) has been developed by existing business practices rather than through imposed rules from above[69] there is the possibility that the same legal system may not fit the business practices, culture or financial level of the recipient country. Legal transplants, as Kronke correctly points out, 'rarely work'.[70] For a successful legal transplant or legal reform, precedents and academic opinions of the donor country as well as the black letter must be adopted

---

less diverse, it is possible to tackle a problem in greater depth at the regional level than at the global level'.

[68] For example, the exportability of UCC Article 9 as a model has been debated in the last few decades. See e.g. Cuming, RCC (1995), 'Harmonisation of the Secured Financing Laws of the NAFTA Partners', 39 *St. Louis University Law Journal* 809; Gabriel, HD (2000), 'The New Zealand Personal Property Securities Act: A Comparison with the North American Model for Personal Property Security', 34 *International Law* 1123; Davies, I (1988), 'The Reform of Personal Property Security Law: Can Article 9 of the US Uniform Commercial Code be a Precedent?', 37 *International & Comparative Law Quarterly* 465; McCormack, G (2003), 'Rewriting the English Law of Personal Property Securities and Article 9 of the US Uniform Commercial Code' 24 *Comparative Law* 69; Davies, I (2004), 'The Reform of English personal property security law: functionalism and Article 9 of the Uniform Commercial Code', 24 *Legal Studies* 295ff.; Bridge, M (1996), 'How Far is Article 9 Exportable? The English Experience', 27 *Canadian Business Law Journal* 196.
[69] For a similar statement see Cooter, R (1998), 'Normative Failure Theory of Law', 82 *Cornell Law Review* 947, at 948.
[70] Kronke, H (2008), 'Why Transplants Rarely work – why convergence is insufficient in Commercial Law – methodical changes in paradigm in the harmonisation of commercial law', Presentation made at 'Commercial Law – Where from and Where to' Conference held at Queen Mary University of London, Centre for Commercial Law Studies, 7 February. He gives successful examples of transplantation through imperialism (e.g. Rome and England to colonies etc.) and invitation (e.g. Switzerland to Turkey, France to Latin America, Germany to Greece) and doubtful/failed examples of transplantation which are invited or solicited by scholars, donor countries or business interests (e.g. USA and other to Central Asia, USA to Rwanda).

for a successful reform.[71] This must also be supplemented by appropriate infrastructure.[72] In the last few decades developing economies have experienced problems in the process of harmonised modernisation of credit and security laws. Modernisation activities have been in the form of legal reform where rules were imposed from above without any concerns as to their compatibility with the recipient or host jurisdiction.[73]

In relation to the question whether guidance can be drawn from the UNCITRAL Legislative Guide for the Common Frame of Reference, McCormack submits that '[the Guide is] too prescriptive in tone and too American in orientation to be much of a model'.[74] That may equally be applicable to the UN

---

[71]   See also Watson, A (2000), 'Legal Transplants and European Private Law', 4 *Electronic Journal of Comparative Law Ius Commune Lectures on European Private Law* www.ejcl.org/44/art44-2.html.

[72]   See Bazinas, *supra* n. 23 and the text thereof.

[73]   For more information on legal reforms and problems during that process see Mistelis, L (2000), 'Regulatory Aspects: Globalization, Harmonization, Legal Transplants and Law reform-Some Fundamental Observations', 34 *International Law* 1055, 1064–1065. Mistelis correctly argues that

> [r]egrettably, … many emerging states have occasionally experienced the services of opinionated and expensive foreign experts who attempted to export their legal system or their understanding of it without any concerns as to its compatibility with the system of the host country. Incidents of competition between foreign experts from different countries or from different agencies of the same country have also been seen in the recent years. This is often due to lack of international or local coordination. Hence, confusion of the host country experts is the natural result. Experts from the same country or from different countries who speak, however, diametrically different views as to what is 'right' or 'wrong' with respect to one legal issue can be of questionable assistance to their host countries. Further, foreign experts usually have little or no knowledge of the existing legal system of the host state and so give inappropriate or unhelpful advice. As a result of either competition between foreign experts, lack of knowledge, or academic arrogance, voices against reform were strengthened and little or no reform was motivated by foreign presence. Recipients of technical assistance are interested in the conceptual framework and some statutory variants; they are able to choose and produce their own national variation that meets better their domestic needs. It seems appropriate that such coordination is left to international organizations, provided that they will do it effectively, rather than to a potential self-constraint or willingness of foreign technical assistance.

[74]   McCormack, *supra* n. 31, at 9, 34 and 35. Similar arguments have also been made by Civil law jurisdictions with regard to the guidance of the UN Convention on the Assignment of Receivables on certain provisions of the Rome I Regulation (former Rome I Convention): see generally Flessner, A and Verhagen, H (2006), *Assignment in European Private International Law* (Sellier); see also Verhagen, H (2006), 'Assignment in the Commission's "Rome I Proposal"', *Lloyds Maritime and Commercial Law Quarterly* 270; Steffens, L (2006), 'The New Rule on the Assignment of Rights in Rome I – The Solution to all our Proprietary Problems? Determination of the Conflict of Laws Rule in

Convention on the Assignment of Receivables[75] as it contains a particular bit of UCC Article 9 legislation,[76] or the Organisation of American States' Model Inter-American Law on Secured Transactions.[77] Certainly guidance from the EBRD Core Principles on Secured Transactions Law for EU Member States may be more appropriate for the Common Frame of Reference, given the fact they drew upon the EBRD Model Law which attracted criticism from North American lawyers.[78] Furthermore, the EBRD Core Principles are less prescriptive.[79] However, at least when these Principles are converted into a legislative instrument it should be left to Member States to decide how and whether they will incorporate them in to their systems and what type of reform needs to be made in their credit and security laws, rather than a regional organisation prescribing what needs to be done which may carry the risk of influencing and pressurising a country to adopt another developed legal and financial system or indeed something totally new and untested. This argument in no way suggests an optional

---

Respect of the Proprietary Aspects of Assignment', 4 *European Review of Private Law* 543. See also reports of the Financial Markets Law Committee, Issue 121 – European Commission Final Proposal for a Regulation on the Law Applicable to Contractual Obligations ('Rome I') October 2006 and April 2006.

[75]   The text of the UN Assignment of Receivables Convention can be found at www. uncitral.org/pdf/english/texts/payments/receivables/ctc-assignment-convention-e.pdf (last accessed on 10 September 2008). For instance the United States is considering the ratification of the UN Convention on the Assignment of Receivables. www.law.upenn. edu/bll/archives/ulc/aor/2007june_proposeddraft.htm (last accessed on 10 September 2008). Furthermore, in 2005 the National Conference of Commissioners on Uniform State Laws initiated a project with the Uniform Law Conference of Canada and Uniform Law Centre of Mexico to harmonise the domestic laws in North America to conform to the rules of the UN Convention on the Assignment of Receivables in order to benefit the provisions from the provisions of the Convention in cross-border receivables financing among the three countries. See www.law.upenn.edu/bll/archives/ulc/aor/2007june_am-report.htm (last accessed 10 September 2008).

[76]   E.g. there is a uniform security interest concept under the UCC Article 9 and the UN Convention does not make any distinction between legal and equitable assignments or floating or fixed security interests, and an assignment will be valid as against third parties notwithstanding an anti-assignment clause.

[77]   For more information on the OAS Model Inter-American Law on Secured Transactions see e.g. Kozolchyk B and Wilson, JM (2002), 'The Organization of American States: The New Model Inter-American Law on Secured Transactions', *Uniform Law Review* 69ff.

[78]   E.g. Spanogle, J (1998), 'A Functional Analysis of the EBRD Model Law on Secured Transactions', in Norton, JJ and Andenas, M (eds), *Emerging Financial Markets and Secured Transactions* (Kluwer), 157, at 171–3; Sigman, HC (1998), 'The Case for Worldwide Reform of the Law Governing Secured Transactions in Movable Property', in Ziegel, J (ed.), *New Developments in International Commercial and Consumer Law* (Oxford, Hart), at 229–34. For further information see Mistelis, *supra* n. 37, at 463ff.

[79]   McCormack, *supra* n. 31, at 33.

set of rules, but it suggests an international or national reform rather than a regional reform. The decision should also be left to Member States whether the UNCITRAL Legislative Guide and the UN Convention on the Assignment of Receivables are better options. In any case since the Common Frame of Reference is planned to be an optional text this seems more appropriate, though one can still argue that there is no need to have another regional harmonisation text in the field of the law of credit and security. However, in this approach there may be different possibilities (i.e. some member states may wish to choose the UNCITRAL Legislative Guide type of law of credit and security, some may choose the EBRD Core Principles and some may prefer the rules prescribed in the Common Frame of Reference). This would be against the concept of harmonisation and create more divergence. Thus, one can argue that the best strategy should be to follow the international harmonisation efforts, be more active and adopt international instruments.

In relation to the above argument, it is submitted that the fact that the UNCITRAL texts contain certain UCC Article 9 type secured credit concepts which may or may not be suitable for other systems should not be a resistance point or ground to look for other avenues. Firstly, the relevant UNCITRAL texts have been prepared with great effort by a multinational working group and adopted by a multinational Commission which consists of states representing both civil and common law jurisdictions including some of the EU Member States.[80] In any case, the EU's point of view is also presented at both the Working Group and Commission meetings.[81] Secondly, decisions are taken by consensus and not by majority voting.[82] Thus it seems axiomatic that states present at the UNCITRAL meetings during the deliberations (some of which are also EU Member States) could have intervened and have non-UCC Article 9 concepts incorporated into these texts. In addition, the EU has the power to intervene in international

---

[80]   There are currently 60 member states elected by the General Assembly representing various geographic regions, economic and legal cultures: see www.uncitral.org/uncitral/en/about/origin.html (accessed 23 July 2008).

[81]   For a detailed discussion of EU, difficulties and consequences of international law making see Basedow, *supra* n. 26, at 41 and 43ff. The main difficulty arises out of the fact that the EU as well as other regional organisations is not a member of any international formulating agencies and a position as an observer is not sufficient for regional organisations. This also presents the conflicting problem of becoming a contracting party to international conventions and, for instance, within the context of the law of credit and security the UN Convention on the Assignment of Receivables does not allow the participation of entities other than states. On the other hand, the Unidroit Convention on International Interests in Mobile Equipment Article 48 allows regional organisations to become contracting parties.

[82]   See www.uncitral.org/uncitral/en/about/methods_faq.html (accessed 23 July 2008) where it is stated that '[t]he basis of consensus is that efforts are made to address all concerns raised so that the final text is acceptable to all'.

negotiations[83] and it could have achieved that result. In that connection, it can be submitted that it is not the Guide or the Receivables Convention itself which creates this divergence in the law and proves itself more 'American in tone', but it is the delegations who hesitated to contribute actively to the process and to the substance of these international instruments to make them more generally acceptable by the majority of countries. This contribution could have been in the form of either active lobbying or presenting opposing views to the UCC Article 9 type legislation. In any case, the UNCITRAL Legislative Guide presents solutions to problems acutely felt by small and medium sized businesses in emerging markets (i.e. access to low cost credit) and financiers (i.e. certainty and predictability in the law of credit and security) with a comprehensive set of rules. Arguments opposing UNCITRAL texts and instruments do not assist harmonisation activities within the framework of the law of credit and security but rather pave the way for future inefficiency, overlap, sometimes confusion and loss of time in harmonisation activities and cause every regional organisation to come up with differing regimes. More than a decade ago, Goode rightly argued that the legal literature was full of international instruments which had never been ratified and which overlapped with each other.[84] One can argue that this argument still keeps its freshness and will seem to do so within the next decade.

V. EUROPEAN SECURITY INTEREST?

The European Security Interest[85] is a novel concept which may reduce conflicts that may occur during intra-Community security and credit transactions and which may present a harmonised picture of EU credit and security law. However,

---

[83] See Basedow, *supra* n. 26, at 35 and 36.

[84] For a similar statement see Goode, R (1997), 'International Restatements of Contract and English Contract Law', *Uniform Law Review* 231, 232 where he states that 'the treaty collections are littered with Conventions that have never come into force, for want of the number of required ratifications, or have been eschewed by the major trading States. There are several reasons for this: failure to establish from potential interest groups at the outset that there is a serious problem, which the proposed Convention will help to resolve; hostility from powerful pressure groups; lack of sufficient interest of, or pressure on, Governments to induce them to burden still further an already over-crowded legislative timetable; mutual hold-backs, each State waiting to see what others will do, so that in the end none of them does anything.'

[85] For a similar argument see also Kieninger, EM and Sigman, HC (2007), *Cross Border Security Over Tangibles* (Sellier, Munich), at 34ff. where it is argued that the European Security Right could be introduced through regulation issued pursuant to EC Treaty Article 308 or through a European Model Law.

this concept may conflict with the UNCITRAL Legislative Guide or other international efforts. The concept is similar to the *international interest* concept of the Unidroit Convention on International Interests in Mobile Equipment. Firstly, it may be argued that it is necessary for EU Member States to have a consensus on the concept of 'European Security Interest'. Some of the Member States may not be familiar with or due to technical or sociological reasons prefer to retain their traditional security interest concept[86] or prefer to adopt the UNCITRAL Legislative Guide. In addition, the scope of applicability of this concept must be well drawn and any potential conflicts with already prepared conventions and instruments must be addressed. In other words, it should be made clear whether it would apply to credit transactions in intra-Community or external trade. Furthermore, it may not be beneficial to adopt a European Security Interest if there are future plans to adopt the UNCITRAL Legislative Guide's rules unless the European Security Interest is developed along the lines of the UNCITRAL Guide, which would in the future ease the efforts on harmonisation and be more efficient. Traditional hostility of civil law jurisdictions towards non-possessory security interests and the tension between common and civil law in that area must also be taken into consideration.[87]

The European Security Interest concept may instigate diverse results, as all other regional organisations may wish to create a similar concept but with differences, and this may postpone the chance to have overall harmonisation at international level. It would be more desirable to have an international effort to create an international security interest under the auspices of international formulating agencies and with the full participation of the EU. When one considers the fact that even within the EU there are already multiple projects relating to the law of contracts[88] competing and conflicting with each other, it is not

---

[86]   For European doubts, for example, on public filing system see e.g. Krupski, J (2007), 'Cross Border Receivables Financing at the Cross roads of Legal Traditions, Capital Markets, Uniform Law and Modernity', *Uniform Law Review* 57, at 77ff.

[87]   However, it should also be noted that recently reforms have been made in certain civil law jurisdictions. See e.g. Ancel, ME (2006), 'Recent Reform in France: the Renaissance of a Civilian Collateral Regime?', in 'Collateral Reform and Access to Credit', EBRD – World Bank Seminar, London, 9 June; see also Krupski, *supra* n. 86, at 78ff.; Kieninger, EM and Sigman, HC (2006), 'The Rome-I Proposed Regulation and the Assignment of Receivables', *The European Legal Forum/Forum iuris communis Europae*, issue 1, at 1 and fn. 7.

[88]   The notable ones are the the Principles of European Contract Law (PECL), the Common Frame of Reference, the Acquis Group working on the Principles of the existing EC Contract Law, the Insurance Group. None of these study groups is backed by an international formulating agency to my knowledge and yet they work within the EU (although their framework may be different). Nevertheless there must be clear coordination and cooperation, rather than having multiple fragmentation.

therefore difficult to see the necessity of international harmonisation through coordination and cooperation under one international formulating organisation.

VI. CONCLUSION

In conclusion, it can be argued that for a comprehensive, harmonised and predictable regime of credit and security there is a commercial necessity to proceed with international harmonisation. Regionalism presents issues of multiplicity, fragmentation and lack of legal cultural pluralism. International harmonisation presents comprehensiveness, pragmatism and the participation of different legal cultures. There are studies on the ratification of the UN Convention on the Assignment of Receivables within the framework of harmonising the assignment of receivables rules in cross-border trade in North America. Similar legislative activities may be undertaken within the EU to be part of international harmonisation. Certainly, the North American activity should not be seen as a regional harmonisation effort but an effort to be a part of the international harmonisation.[89] This is also a clear indication of the values of the UN Convention on the Assignment of Receivables and possibly the Legislative Guide.

Efforts to harmonise the law of credit and security may get quite confusing if it is left just to regional organisations or member states of regional organisations or academics of certain regional institutions. New ideas and cooperation should be sought from other jurisdictions, legal cultures and countries in order to create comprehensive and international harmonisation.[90] Furthermore, previous law reform or regional harmonisation efforts have proved that lack of local or international coordination, competition among groups or even experts may lead to unsuccessful results. Thus coordination should be left to experienced international formulating agencies or, indeed, any international harmonisation of secured transactions law should be pursued under the auspices of international organisations.[91]

---

[89] See *supra* n. 75.

[90] Mistelis rightly suggests that '[e]very legal system, even the most sophisticated and developed Western one, can be improved and the impetus in newly independent or emerging markets can offer remarkable ideas to traditional systems. Both the reform impetus and the reception of diverse foreign legal concepts and ideas can be beneficial to any system in need of reform.' See *supra* n. 27, at 1065.

[91] For similar views see ibid., at 1064ff.

29. Towards a theory of harmonisation

Mads Andenas,* Camilla Baasch Andersen** and Ross Ashcroft[†]

I. INTRODUCTION – THE MANY FACES OF HARMONISATION

The concept of harmonisation of legal phenomena[1] can be traced back to early legal history, as far back as Roman law or early colonial law.[2] However, in modern times, we must distinguish modern (and arguably voluntary) harmonisation from that of the imposed laws of military and colonial conquests. Modern harmonisation, however we define it, is an important feature of the modern legal system, which does not exist in a vacuum in today's globalised markets and economy.

Formally, UNIDROIT laid the foundations for legal harmonisation projects as long ago as the 1920s. Although the projects which it aimed at establishing subsequently failed due to lack of international support,[3] other significant projects in the UNCITRAL (United Nations Commission for International Trade Law) and other UN regimes have successfully built on many of the UNIDROIT concepts. Informally, the various trade practices have developed rules for trade

---

*   MA, DPhil(Oxford), PhD(Cambridge); Professor, University of Oslo, Norway. Former Director, British Institute of International and Comparative Law, London and Centre of European Law, King's College, University of London. Senior Research Fellow, IALS, University of London, UK. Research was undertaken with support from the Norwegian Finance Market Fund.

**   Cand.Jur. (Copenhagen), PhD (Aarhus School of Business). Fellow, Institute of International Commercial Law, Pace University Law School, New York, USA and Senior Lecturer in Law, University of Leicester, UK.

†   BA/LLB (Hons) GDLP LLM (*Griffith*), MCL (*Adelaide/Mannheim*), Grad. Cert. of Arts (*UNE*), Law Lecturer, Charles Darwin University, Australia.

[1]   This chapter has chosen to operate with the concept of a 'legal phenomenon' to side-step the difficult task of defining law in this context. See Camilla Baasch Andersen, with reference to William Twining.

[2]   Cicero can be mentioned as an early Roman harmoniser of law, as can King James VI of Scotland, Camilla Baasch Andersen.

[3]   René-Franz Henschel, *Creation of Rules in National and International Business Law: A Non-national, Analytical-Synthetic Comparative Method*, 1.

and traders by the participants of the trading market for even longer, creating common ground for international transactions. Increased globalisation, which has been defined by sociologists as 'a flow of people and services',[4] has naturally increased the need for more formal shared rules and common ground as we share communication, markets, trade sectors and even economy on a global scale. But we must exercise caution in pointing to globalisation as the sole rationale for harmonising laws, as it may lead to broad generalisations similar to the word 'universal', which in usage 'all too often will reflect a particular way of thinking, neither universally held nor applicable throughout the world'.[5] This is possibly the foundation of why some authors suggest wider reasons for harmonisation.[6]

Harmonisation has been an important feature of modern legal systems. Examples exist in both regional and international contexts. For example, harmonisation has been a core instrument of the European Union and Council of Europe, whilst at the international global level, there has been a long and established tradition of harmonisation of commercial law which provides yet another field of emerging scholarship. The examples include, for instance, the United Nations Convention on Contracts for the International Sale of Goods 1980, the UNCITRAL Model Law on International Commercial Arbitration 1985, UNIDROIT's Principles of International Commercial Contracts, the EBRD's Secured Transactions Project, and the ICC's Uniform Customs and Practice for Documentary Credits, to name but a few.

In different regional contexts, further systems and models for harmonisation have been developed outside any global scope. The development of the Internal Market and European Union law is arguably the most extensive and ambitious harmonisation project ever attempted, itself offering a wide array of models and concepts on harmonisation for 27 different countries. Heath has previously suggested that harmonisation within Europe can be broken down into three distinct patterns: harmonisation in part, harmonisation of procedures and 'freeze-plus'.[7]

Nor does harmonisation have to concern the laws of different countries – it merely has to concern the harmonisation of different legal jurisdictions or areas. In the United States of America, harmonisation attempts like the Uniform Commercial Code (UCC), which offer model laws to unify state laws, perpetually

---

[4]   Heather Eggins, 'Globalization and Reform: Necessary Conjunctions in Higher Education', in Heather Eggins (ed.) *Globalization in Higher Education* (2003).

[5]   David B. Goldman, *Globalisation and the Western Legal Tradition – Recurring Patterns of Law and Authority* (Cambridge University Press, 2007), 14.

[6]   Jurgita Malinauskaite, *International Competition Law Harmonisation and the WTO: Past, Present and Future*, 1.

[7]   Christopher Heath, 'Methods of Industrial Property Harmonisation – The Example of Europe' in Christoph Antons, Michael Blakeney and Christopher Heath (eds), *Intellectual Property Harmonisation Within ASEAN and APEC* (Aspen Publishers, 2004), 39 at 46–7.

remind us of the multijurisdictional nature of one single country. And in the development of unified states like Italy or Germany, harmonisation of regions of law in creating a single entity is a very interesting field of study, which has been highly overlooked in the context of modern harmonisation. Similar issues have been expressed in relation to 'federalism'[8] and comparative law.[9]

Moreover, despite the fact that modern harmonised law has its origins in commercial law, we would err to think of harmonised law as the sole property of a globalised commercial market. Public international law offers several extensive treaty systems where harmonisation of national laws plays an important role. The different human rights treaties illustrate this, with their regional rules with counterparts in Africa, America and Europe. Moreover, unique international institutions are based on national legal harmonisation. For example, the Statute of the International Criminal Court requires harmonised international agreement on both substantive criminal law and criminal procedure. In short, harmonisation permeates all areas of law – arguably some more than others – but it is prevalent everywhere.

Finally, it must also be remembered that harmonisation (with or without globalisation) is not a phenomenon limited to legal science. Contributions to understanding harmonisation are made in integration studies, international relations, European studies, sociology and political theory. In short, modern harmonisation presents a very varied and interesting phenomenon in legal development. While it has far-reaching effects on almost all aspect of jurisprudence and sociology, it is a difficult phenomenon to study, because of its many faces outlined above, and because of a lack of overarching jurisprudential theory which can allow cohesive study of this varied field. There is no overall conceptual framework from which lawyers in this field are working,[10] despite the wealth of scholarship and literature in the area. Moving freely over the boundaries that divide the law, and the fragmented scholarly disciplines, may usefully combine perspectives in interdisciplinary and multidisciplinary scholarship and practice to provide models for, and improve, the understanding of the harmonisation process.

It was on this basis that Professor Mads Andenas and Dr Camilla Baasch Andersen organised the W G Hart Workshop 2008 at the Institute of Advanced Legal Studies, London, on a 'Theory and Practice of Harmonisation', which brought together legal scholars from around the world to spark discussion on the topic, and facilitated the dialogue necessary to encourage the development

---

[8]   Anna Gamper, 'A "Global Theory of Federalism": The Nature and Challenges of a Federal State', (2005) 6 *German Law Journal*, 1297.

[9]   Gabriël A Moens and Rodolphe Biffot (eds), *The Convergence of Legal Systems in the 21st Century: An Australian Approach* (Routledge-Cavendish, 2002).

[10]   Jarrod Weiner, *Globalization and the Harmonization of Law* (Cassell, 1999), ix.

of a theory of harmonisation. Due to constraints, the organisers did not engage people from other disciplines, but remain aware of their great contributions to the scholarly activities in the area, as outlined above.[11] Thus, although this project hopes to contribute to the development of the theory and practice of harmonisation, the editors note that this could be achieved even more success-fully in the bringing together not merely of legal scholars, but also scholars from a range of other disciplines in the social sciences and humanities. The lack of a conceptual framework or overarching theory of harmonisation is felt strongly in the jurisprudential fragmentation in the scholarship in which issues of harmonisation are dealt with.

It is self-evident that a more cohesive study of harmonisation as a whole would benefit greatly from the establishment of such an overarching theory, both conceptually and in terms of terminology. It is very desirable – and arguably necessary – to establish a 'common core' for any discipline subject to study, but is harmonisation a legal discipline in which it can be done? The multijurisdictional nature and the many varied forms and degrees of harmonisation make this very challenging. Moreover, even if a perfect model for harmonisation theory could be developed, a universal acceptance of it at this stage would seem unlikely as multi-faceted legal research and develop-ment has been underway for decades. Metaphorically speaking, there is little scope to reinvent the wheel while the car is on the road. However, without the conceptual foundations being fully explored and captured, the notion of harmonisation may well get obscured.

Nevertheless, despite the difficulties in seeing a model theory of harmo-nisation developed or applied, the attempt itself brings about many helpful observations and discussions, which may spark further debate. This book has presented a variety of contributions throughout multiple areas of law, and from the perspective of scholars from many different legal backgrounds, both from attendants at the 2008 W G Hart Workshop, but also solicited from other experts in the field. This concluding chapter aims to sum up some of the observations made during the workshop, and at the concluding round table discussion. As such, the first point to address is the concept of harmonisation itself, and the development of a common reference point or foundation of analysis for harmo-nisation jurisprudence and practice to continue.[12]

---

[11] Mads Andenas, Introductory Speech at the Workshop.
[12] Ibid.

II. THE MEANING OF HARMONISATION

In attempting to create a cohesive theory of harmonisation, the first necessary step is the definition of the concept. And it is in this first important step that the first important problem surfaces. It is not easy, even within the single discipline of legal theory, to specify what is meant by harmonisation, or even to pinpoint its characteristics.

A. Similar but Differentiated Concepts

In broader terms, 'harmonisation' labels the basic notion of the bringing together of legal ideas to allow a functioning in unison. However, one of the problems with the terminological understanding of 'harmonisation' is that it is often used interchangeably with other terms by some scholars and legislators, and often in contexts where different meanings are implied. As a whole, this is an area of law where there are a whole host of terms used to define harmonisation, or used interchangeably with harmonisation, which can confuse research, debates and discussion on the topic.

Some of these other terms include *integration*[13] or *homogenisation*[14] or *convergence*[15] or *unification*[16] or *parallelism*.[17] Linguistically,[18] these concepts have similar meanings. Convergence means to come together, either in a single unit or to a point in which there is an overlap. Uniformity means the creation of

---

[13]   Anne Lise Kjær, 'A Common Legal Language in Europe' in Mark van Hoecke (eds), *Epistemology and Methodology of Comparative Law* (2004), 377 at 378.

[14]   Gerrit Betlem, *Beyond Francovich: Completing the Unified Member State and EU Liability Regime – A Comment on the Jan Jans Contribution*, 305.

[15]   Stelios Andreadakis, *Regulatory Competition or Harmonization: The dilemma, the alternatives and the prospect of Reflexive Harmonization*, 10–11.

[16]   Bruno Zeller, *CISG and the Unification of International Trade Law* (Routledge-Cavendish 2007); see also Clive M Schmitthoff, 'The unification or harmonisation of law by means of standard contracts and general conditions' 17 *International Comparative Law Quarterly* 557 (1968) and John Goodright, 'Unification and harmonisation of the rules of law' 9 *Federal Law Review* 284 (1978).

[17]   Christian Twigg-Flesner, *Pre-contractual Duties – from the Acquis to the Draft Common Frame of Reference*, 9–10.

[18]   It must be noted that language plays a major part within the role of law and harmonisation of 'law'. As such, the authors would also recommend looking at potential issues of languages. Suggested publications included: Anne Lise Kjaer, 'A common legal language in Europe?', in Mark Van Hoecke (ed.), *Epistemology and Methodology of Comparative Law* (Hart Publishing, Oxford and Portland 2004), 377–98; see also Mala Tabory, *Multilingualism in International Law and Institutions* (Sijthoff and Noordhoff, New York, 1980); Ruth Sullivan, 'The challenges of interpreting multilingual, multijural legislation', 29 *Brooklyn Journal of International Law* (2004) and Deborah Cao, *Translating Law*, Multilingual Matters, Clevedon (2007).

something identical. Homogenisation is generally defined in terms of uniformity. Parallelism is slightly different as there need not be uniformity, but the processes may be aiming in the same direction.

In this linguistic context, harmonisation can be defined as bringing two things into accordance or agreement with each other. The term originates from musical composition, where it defines the (aesthetically pleasant) co-existence of notes which are in accordance with one another, but not necessarily the same or even similar.[19] But this linguistic analysis of terms does not prove overly useful once the terms are placed in the context of legal analysis. In this context, they take on their own meaning, both in scholarship and legislature. And that meaning is by no means fixed.

Some authors argue that there are distinct differences in their meanings, whilst others use the terms interchangeably,[20] and the subject quickly becomes a minefield of intellectual discourse which must be navigated carefully. This may be partially caused by the fact that the words are so similar in colloquial language, but not in legal academic discourse.

Zeller suggests that harmonisation is 'the process of making rules similar, whereas unification aims at the sameness of rules'.[21] Furthermore, and relying on the CISG as his example, Zeller suggests that there is necessity for 'uniformity of application and interpretation'.[22] Such application would most likely be assisted with consistent terminology. As Baasch Andersen has pointed out, it is not sufficient to create uniform laws, but to apply them uniformly. This creates a distinction between textual uniformity and applied uniformity.[23]

Parallelism is, in the eyes of Christian Twigg-Flesner, a process in which a provision which may be applied in one jurisdiction in a certain context may be extended in application into another jurisdiction with a similar term via flexible interpretation methods.[24] In other words, parallelism could be viewed as a form of interpretation of texts, possibly by way of analogy.[25]

---

[19]   Stelios Andreadakis, *Regulatory Competition or Harmonization: The dilemma, the alternatives and the prospect of Reflexive Harmonization*, 7.

[20]   Jurgita Malinauskaite, *International Competition Law Harmonisation and the WTO: Past, Present and Future*, 8–9.

[21]   Bruno Zeller, *CISG and the Unification of International Trade Law* (Routledge-Cavendish, 2007), 12 and L Mistelis, 'Is Harmonisation a Necessary Evil?', in L Mistelis, M Cremona & I Fletcher (eds), *Foundations and Perspectives of International Trade Law* (Sweet & Maxwell, 2001).

[22]   Bruno Zeller, *CISG and the Unification of International Trade Law* (2007), 16.

[23]   Camilla Baasch Anderson, 'Furthering the Uniform Application of the CISG, Sources of Law on the Internet', (1998) 10 *Pace International Law Review* 403, 404.

[24]   Christian Twigg-Fleisner, *Pre-contractual Duties – from the Acquis to the Draft Common Frame of Reference*, 9.

[25]   Ibid., 11.

Approximation is another similar notion which is discussed with issues relating to harmonisation of legal phenomena.[26] Heath suggests that approximation differs from 'complete harmonisation' on the basis that it merely aims at reaching a minimum level of common agreement between what people are seeking to make similar.[27]

But it is not just scholarship which confuses the issue. It is also the policies of certain legislatures which apply the more palatable labels to their regional lawmaking. For instance, if we rely on the definitions above to label uniform law as the most identical results obtainable in multi-jurisdictional lawmaking, then the Regulations of the EU are the closest thing to truly uniform law which can be produced. Developed in a shared parliament, with a Court monitoring the application and the autonomy of terms, and with no margin for application or public policy, the EU creates laws which are uniform. But they are labelled 'harmonised law' – presumably to render them more palatable to the wider European audience, some of which may resist the notion of uniform laws stomping across borders. Conversely, in the USA where model laws are created for states to harmonise their approaches to certain aspects of law in the form of restatements, the label 'Uniform' is freely used to indicate the similarity. In such a terminologically confused environment, the task of determining a correct and widely acceptable framework of theory is frustrated.

But, if we are to achieve a common core in the relationship between the theories discussed, it would be wise to make suggestions so a general debate in this field can be encouraged.

B. A Clear Distinction or Matter of Fuzzy Conceptual Borders?

The discussion above highlights several problems faced by scholars in the field. The language we use to discuss 'harmonisation' may be quickly obfuscated by other words which have a similar meaning in our everyday lives. Likewise, in application of the term by the judiciary or politicians, different terms are adopted to describe the same outcome – either 'sameness' of outcome or 'sameness' of method – creating a more difficult environment to research and work within, and thus a necessity to reconceive the boundaries of 'harmonisation' and what it is we are discussing.

---

[26]   Christopher Heath, 'Methods of Industrial Property Harmonisation – The Example of Europe', in Christoph Antons, Michael Blakeney and Christopher Heath (eds), *Intellectual Property Harmonisation Within ASEAN and APEC* (Aspen Publishers, 2004), 39 at 46.

[27]   Ibid.

III. RECONCEIVING HARMONISATION: A SUGGESTED FRAMEWORK

The preceding discussion highlights the overlap harmonisation shares with similar concepts. This next section tries to move harmonisation away from the problems of association with similar concepts by reconceiving the framework of how we deal with harmonisation.

A. Consequential Harmonisation

The first suggested concept we propose predominates round the notion that substantive legal phenomenon are harmonised.[28] As such, harmonisation is being defined as the consequence of a process. This we could term 'consequential harmonisation'.

If harmonisation is consequential, we must determine what exactly it is we wish to achieve through harmonisation.[29] Does consequential harmonisation require the achievement of a 'common legal language'?[30] Or is it wisest to aim for an approximation[31] of terms or substantial correspondence between the terms adopted?[32] Additionally, is the outcome we seek a consequential harmonisation of two discrete areas of law (e.g. contract law for commercial purposes and contract law for consumer purposes[33] or property law and environmental law[34]), or is it harmonisation between jurisdictions of an identical area of law (e.g. areas of contract law)?[35]

---

[28]   Ibid., at 53.
[29]   Christian Twigg-Fleisner, *Pre-contractual Duties – from the Acquis to the Draft Common Frame of Reference*, 1.
[30]   Anne Lise Kjær, 'A Common Legal Language in Europe' in Mark van Hoecke (eds), *Epistemology and Methodology of Comparative Law* (2004), 377; see Christian Twigg-Fleisner, *Pre-contractual Duties – from the Acquis to the Draft Common Frame of Reference*, 4.
[31]   See Christopher Heath, 'Methods of Industrial Property Harmonisation – The Example of Europe' in Christoph Antons, Michael Blakeney and Christopher Heath (eds), *Intellectual Property Harmonisation Within ASEAN and APEC* (Aspen Publishers, 2004), 39–57.
[32]   René-Franz Henschel, *Creation of Rules in National and International Business Law: A Non-national, Analytical-Synthetic Comparative Method*, 10.
[33]   Ibid., at 15.
[34]   Ross Ashcroft, *Harmonisation of Substantive Legal Principles and Structures: Lessons from the Australian Federal Legal System with Respect to Environment & Resource Laws.*
[35]   Christian Twigg-Fleisner, *Pre-contractual Duties – from the Acquis to the Draft Common Frame of Reference*, 7–9.

Alternatively, does consequential harmonisation relate to the jurisdictional capabilities of the institutions? Here we could look towards the learned discussions put forward in relation to jurisdictions:

- jurisdiction to *prescribe* such as the method of prescription (market 'cultures', legislation, regulation, judicial decision) and whether these are of immediate application (*règles d'application immediate*);
- jurisdiction to *adjudicate* including determining how disputes will be resolved; and
- jurisdiction to *enforce*, including whether there be criminal, administrative or executive sanctions for non-compliance of the law.[36]

Another method of perceiving consequential harmonisation is as trying to achieve either a 'core rule' or a 'core principle', without necessarily achieving a harmonised terminology dictionary. This, Betlem explains, is exemplified by the 'principle of state liability' within the European Union construct.[37] As a core principle, there is still room for further development of more specific duties, but the core lays down the foundations upon which this development must be based.[38] This is not unlike the 'draft Common Frame of Reference' (DCFR) which is discussed by Hugh Beale QC and Christian Twigg-Flesner elsewhere in this volume. The DCFR is a 'series of articles or model rules, together with a list of definitions'.[39] However, the DCFR is not merely about finding and explaining the common principles; it is also about acting as a 'toolbox' by defining key concepts and the like, with definitions being a fundamental aspect of harmonised law,[40] or, as we suggest, consequential harmonisation.

A real problem with the issue of finding common terminology or principles also arises in terms of how these are incorporated into the actual legal systems or laws we seek actually to harmonise. For example, Ashcroft discusses the difference in effect if one has a principle as a broad overarching principle of a legal system, or whether it is placed as a 'goal' or 'objective' or 'recital'[41]

---

[36] Piet Jan Slot and Mielle Bulterman (eds), *Globalisation and Jurisdiction* (2004), 2.

[37] Gerrit Betlem, *Beyond Francovich: Completing the Unified Member State and EU Liability Regime – A Comment on the Jan Jans Contribution*, 299.

[38] Ibid.

[39] Hugh Beale QC, *The Draft Common Frame of Reference*, 1.

[40] Ibid., 2.

[41] Christian Twigg-Fleisner, *Pre-contractual Duties – from the Acquis to the Draft Common Frame of Reference*, 5–6; see also Ross Ashcroft 'Harmonisation of Substantive Legal Principles and Structures: Lessons from the Australian Federal Legal System with Respect to Environment & Resource Laws', 14–15 (129/130) and 35 (150).

of a specific piece of legislation or whether a principle is placed as an actual enforceable substantive legal provision within legislation. Alternatively, there may be consequences if a principle or provision is there to guide civil servants in the application of the legislation generally. This analysis is also in line with Christian Twigg-Flesner's discussion in relation to a principle of good faith and whether it is merely applicable to pre-contractual circumstances or whether the application should indeed apply to more circumstances beyond this[42] and the terms of package travel contracts.[43]

This consequential harmonisation however does not always create satisfaction, as the result which is produced may appear artificial, or synthetic,[44] rather than an actual harmonisation of the actual legal phenomenon it sought to harmonise. Others question whether harmonisation, which may lead to a 'one size fits all' model developing, could actually impede developing more effective regulatory mechanisms for novel situations which may arise as globalisation progresses.[45]

In summation, consequential harmonisation is about trying to achieve a defined outcome. But the starting point for consequential harmonisation is necessarily determining what it is one seeks to harmonise.[46] For example, there are several areas where harmonisation is sought:

- institutions;
- mechanisms and forms;
- terms;
- principles and where the principle fits within the overall framework;[47] and
- processes (e.g. how the law is actually implemented and interpreted[48]).

---

[42]   Christian Twigg-Fleisner, *Pre-contractual Duties – from the Acquis to the Draft Common Frame of Reference*, 4.

[43]   Ibid., at 15.

[44]   René-Franz Henschel, *Creation of Rules in National and International Business Law: A Non-national, Analytical-Synthetic Comparative Method*, 1.

[45]   Jurgita Malinauskaite, *International Competition Law Harmonisation and the WTO: Past, Present and Future*, 2.

[46]   Hugh Beale QC, *The Draft Common Frame of Reference*, 6–8; Ross Ashcroft, 'Harmonisation of Substantive Legal Principles and Structures: Lessons from the Australian Federal Legal System with Respect to Environment & Resource Laws', 14–15 (129/130) and 35 (150).

[47]   Jurgita Malinauskaite, *International Competition Law Harmonisation and the WTO: Past, Present and Future*, 6.

[48]   René-Franz Henschel, *Creation of Rules in National and International Business Law: A Non-national, Analytical-Synthetic Comparative Method*, 12.

Viewing harmonisation through this lens however will of course encounter certain problems. Harmonisation of the consequences may indeed lead to a so-called 'race to the bottom' or 'minimal harmonisation',[49] as the only manner to achieve agreement is having a bare minimum.[50] Thus, we must consider harmonisation from a different angle also – the processes used to reach harmonised law – or, as we conceive it, procedural harmonisation. Furthermore, harmonisation of legal phenomenon without taking a comprehensive approach may lead to contradictions of the application of different phenomena within the same law,[51] or scholarly analysis about that legal phenomenon. On the other hand, it may well be argued that a minimal harmonisation is a natural first step in longer evolution of legal diffusion.

There are several suggested benefits of consequential harmonisation. First, laws which are harmonised will minimises our reliance on 'conflicts of laws', although some states may feel as though this is a violation of their territorial sovereignty,[52] a key element even in a post-Westphalian world. Furthermore, harmonised instruments and mechanisms within specialist fields often offer great variety and innovations. This is because they are able to lead to cross-pollination between jurisdictions where a major legal or technological advancement has been made. For example, in recent years, there has been great reliance between jurisdictions on the issue of climate change policy, with different states looking towards each other's developments in order to determine how we can tackle this problem. Where several states have shifted towards similar policy, it may lead to a foundation document which could then be addressed in the international legal arena.

Problems in conceptual harmonisation

The ideal of conceptual harmonisation however is not without its problems. For example, it has been suggested that sometimes there may be a terminological problem, whilst, theoretically, harmonisation of principles may not be so problematic.[53]

A second problem relating to terminology relates to jurisdictional issues. Some authors appear to view harmonisation as a regional consequence, others global, and yet another group as a national issue. There may be a sense of crossover, but the delineation guidelines are not clearly laid down.

---

[49]   Hugh Beale QC, *The Draft Common Frame of Reference*, 3.

[50]   Christian Twigg-Fleisner, *Pre-contractual Duties – from the Acquis to the Draft Common Frame of Reference*, 2.

[51]   Ibid., 16–17.

[52]   Jurgita Malinauskaite, *International Competition Law Harmonisation and the WTO: Past, Present and Future*, 8.

[53]   Gerrit Betlem, *Beyond Francovich: Completing the Unified Member State and EU Liability Regime – A Comment on the Jan Jans Contribution*, 301.

A third issue relating to terminology is ensuring both the 'scientific accuracy' of the legal terms,[54] whilst also making it possible to achieve understanding within the general community.[55]

An example of such problems can be found with the Articles of DCRF, as discussed in the works of Beale and Twigg-Fleisner. According to those authors, the 'Articles' or model rules in the DCRF, together with commentary, would set out the underlying or foundation principles upon which harmonised laws could be based. However, it could be suggested that creating 'fixed' rules, rather than a 'toolbox' of rules within a common core within a rule book would demonstrate an ineffectual conceptualisation.

B. Procedural Harmonisation

A different interpretation of harmonisation appears to subscribe to the theory that harmonisation is not a consequence of a process, but rather it is the process which itself drives the consequence.[56] This could be termed 'procedural harmonisation'. Procedural harmonisation is thus the manner in which the process is undertaken, and relates substantially to the techniques used for adoption of harmonised law or adaptation towards a harmonised law. This differs from Heath's notion of harmonisation of procedures, which appears to be the harmonisation of legislative procedures.[57] According to the definitions adopted in this chapter, Heath's description would be best considered a consequential harmonisation, as it is the implementation and enforcement processes within the legislation which are indeed harmonised, rather than the method adopted to reach this final consequence. 'Procedural harmonisation', as conceived, not only concerns the processes of harmonisation, but indeed aims at adopting the process likely to achieve the 'best solutions'.[58] As such, the authors suggest a range of procedural tools which could be used to harmonise legal phenomenon. Each shall be dealt with below.

---

[54] Hugh Beale QC, *The Draft Common Frame of Reference*, 10.

[55] Ross Ashcroft, *Harmonisation of Substantive Legal Principles and Structures: Lessons from the Australian Federal Legal System with Respect to Environment & Resource Laws*, 13–14.

[56] René-Franz Henschel, *Creation of Rules in National and International Business Law: A Non-national, Analytical-Synthetic Comparative Method*, 3.

[57] Christopher Heath, 'Methods of Industrial Property Harmonisation – The Example of Europe' in Christoph Antons, Michael Blakeney and Christopher Heath (eds), *Intellectual Property Harmonisation Within ASEAN and APEC* (Aspen Publishers, 2004), 39 at 47.

[58] Hugh Beale QC, *The Draft Common Frame of Reference*, 4.

Methods used for harmonisation – comparative law; transplantations?[59]

Boodman has a different perspective on harmonisation, suggesting that harmonisation is indeed a construct of comparative law.[60] This is similar to Sir Francis Jacobs, who refers to comparative law as the 'academic constribution' of harmonisation, although Sir Francis also considered extra-academic contributions to harmonisation through the likes of multi-national law practices which develop solutions through cross-jurisdictional dialogue.[61]

Another consideration at the level of comparative law is the methods by which practitioners, scholars and courts deal with different jurisdictions' laws. In introducing the laws for harmonisation, if one takes purely a national perspective, without engaging in understanding the processes and substantive nature of other jurisdictions' laws, it will merely reinforce the national law, rather than harmonise the legal phenomenon aimed at being harmonised.[62]

Formal vs informal and the debate as to a creation of model rules:

Another aspect of procedural harmonisation which arises is in relation to whether there should be formal methods of harmonisation or whether harmonisation should be undertaken on an information basis,[63] such as whether model rules should be adopted. Mads Andenas classifies informal harmonisation into two predominant streams – the intergovernmental processes and the informal engagement by non-governmental organisations,[64] be they lobby groups or businesses.

Henschel questions the notion of whether, during the harmonisation process, the intent is to consolidate the legal phenomenon (synthetic modelling) or actually codify law into a formal document (analytical approach).[65] His article expresses the view that earlier authors, such as Schmitthoff,[66] were correct in asserting the harmonisation method would be a key feature of modern legal processes in the twenty-first century.

---

[59] René-Franz Henschel, *Creation of Rules in National and International Business Law: A Non-national, Analytical-Synthetic Comparative Method*, 21; see also Christian Twigg-Fleisner, *Pre-contractual Duties – from the Acquis to the Draft Common Frame of Reference*, 4, in respect of transplanting the *acquis* into the DCFR.

[60] Bruno Zeller, *CISG and the Unification of International Trade Law* (Routledge-Cavendish, 2007), 12.

[61] Sir Francis Jacobs QC, Opening Address at the Workshop.

[62] Mads Andenas, Introductory Speech at the Workshop.

[63] Ibid.

[64] Ibid.

[65] René-Franz Henschel, *Creation of Rules in National and International Business Law: A Non-national, Analytical-Synthetic Comparative Method*, 2.

[66] C M Schmitthoff, 'The Unification or Harmonisation of Law' (1968) 17 *International & Comparative Law Quarterly* 551.

A secondary issue arises with formalised laws. In the globalised world, many multi-national corporations wield far more power than some states,[67] especially micro-states or so-called developing states. As such, we may find that corporations will develop their own modern day trade practices to regulate their relations and practices. One must consider whether such informal practices, which may lead to harmonisation in practice, are indeed what we seek to achieve and, if not, whether formal legal structures are necessary to be created with agreements among states. Of course, this then needs the harmonised approach to ensure 'forum shopping' is minimised.

On the other hand, formalised rules can create difficulties for dealing with emerging novel areas or technologies. At present, several jurisdictions are struggling with issues relating to legal frameworks to govern carbon capture and storage (or geosequestration, as it is also known), despite having a very good policy framework in place for developing such technologies and industries. The WTO has experienced difficulties with regulating public–private corporations, as opposed to purely private or public organisations which would normally fall within its jurisdictions.[68]

Cross-pollination

One system which has created some level of harmonisation regionally in Europe has been the European Court of Justice's (ECJ) approach to determining trademark disputes. Whilst the TRIPS agreement is not necessarily incorporated into the national laws of Member States of the EC, the ECJ has often relied on the TRIPS agreement to conclude a form of harmonised laws across the Community.[69] The basis of the ECJ decisions appears to be that such harmonisation is necessary on the ground of intra-Community trade.[70] Although interpreting national legislation in a consistent manner with international treaties is not seen as problematic, but rather a necessity, it is questionable whether such processes would be legitimate for a court invoking international law as its predominant jurisdiction.[71]

A predominant criticism of cross-pollination however is the possibility that it will become regionalised rather than internationalised, as often is a criticism of

---

[67]   Jurgita Malinauskaite, *International Competition Law Harmonisation and the WTO: Past, Present and Future*, 2.

[68]   Ibid., at 10.

[69]   Gail Evans, *The Impact of WTO Appellate Body Jurisprudence on the Harmonization of Trademark Law in the European Union* (2008), 9.

[70]   See *Silhouette International v Hartlauser* 29 IIC 920 (1998) in Christopher Heath, 'Methods of Industrial Property Harmonisation – The Example of Europe' in Christoph Antons, Michael Blakeney and Christopher Heath (eds), *Intellectual Property Harmonisation Within ASEAN and APEC* (2004), 39 at 46.

[71]   Gail Evans, *The Impact of WTO Appellate Body Jurisprudence on the Harmonization of Trademark Law in the European Union* (2008), 10.

comparative literature from Europe.[72] To overcome such problems in procedural harmonisation on a global scale, a project should conceivably, and usually does, include individuals from a variety of legal backgrounds and legal families.

Consistent interpretation principle ('interprétation conforme')[73]

Ability to seek advisory opinions.   Many international and regional attempts to harmonise legal phenomenon come about by setting up supranational institutions, such as the World Trade Organisation, the International Court of Justice, the European Commission, the European Parliament and European Court of Justice, to name just a few.[74]

The manner in which these bodies are able to assist usually comes in the form of providing definitive or, at least, expert opinions as to what words or policies of particular treaties and practices mean. These may be referred to as advisory opinions.[75] As illustrated in the previous paragraph, the advisory opinions may be delivered from judicial bodies, ombudsman bodies or academics.[76]

A global example of advisory opinions is found for international sales law in the CISG Advisory Council, which is composed of private scholars, and which Baasch Andersen includes in the scholarly branch of what she labels the 'global jurisconsultorium'.

Regional harmonisation efforts   Another form of procedural harmonisation relates to the use of cooperative government bodies or representations to achieve a desired outcome through intergovernmental agreements, both within federal

---

[72]   René-Franz Henschel, *Creation of Rules in National and International Business Law: A Non-national, Analytical-Synthetic Comparative Method*, 5.

[73]   Gerrit Betlem, *Beyond Francovich: Completing the Unified Member State and EU Liability Regime – A Comment on the Jan Jans Contribution*, 302.

[74]   Christopher Heath, 'Methods of Industrial Property Harmonisation – The Example of Europe', in Christoph Antons, Michael Blakeney and Christopher Heath (eds), *Intellectual Property Harmonisation Within ASEAN and APEC* (Aspen Publishers, 2004), 39 at 51–2; see also specific treaties, including Statute of the International Court of Justice, Article 65; International Tribunal for the Law of the Sea, Article 191, United Nations Convention on the Law of the Sea (1982).

[75]   Gerrit Betlem, *Beyond Francovich: Completing the Unified Member State and EU Liability Regime – A Comment on the Jan Jans Contribution*, 305 on the ability of state courts to seek a preliminary ruling on the interpretation of a particular section of the Treaties.

[76]   Hugh Beale QC, *The Draft Common Frame of Reference*, 4. Beale QC is rightly concerned with the lack of democratic legitimacy of such a process, although such advice should not necessarily be conceived as the only advice sought, but rather, a range of advice sought. As such, it should not undermine the democratic legitimacy any more than an interest group (e.g. environmental or business) lobbying government on an issue at hand.

states and also between countries. For an example in a federated jurisdiction such as Australia, the Council of Australian Governments (COAG), meets on a regular basis to discuss and formulate ideas of law and policy. This body includes representatives from state and federal government agencies. These policy issues sometimes include trying to 'harmonise law' so as to bring consistency between jurisdictions, given the proximity of jurisdictions and the ease of crossing borders. However, the process is often fraught with political tension and economic competition, which has been judicially recognised by the High Court of Australia.[77]

Likewise, intergovernmental agreements occur at regional levels to 'harmonise laws' between countries. Europe provides some excellent examples of such attempts to create intergovernmental agreements, and they are discussed extensively in chapters of this book. However, like many regional efforts to 'harmonise', the European 'harmonisation' has become problematic in its inconsistent use of fuzzy terminology between 'harmonisation', 'approximation' and 'uniformity'.

IV.   IS HARMONISATION DESIRABLE OR POSSIBLE?

Whether harmonisation is desirable or possible may depend on the form of harmonisation one is discussing – consequential or procedural. For example, Kritikos, in discussing European discourse around genetically modified organisms, suggested that procedural harmonisation in and of itself is not sufficient, but, rather, it is important to ensure that the technical term and grounds are covered also.[78] This implies that both consequential and procedural harmonisations may be necessary and desirable.

Outright harmonisation is very rare in international law and, contrary to popular belief, is also rare in the European context.[79] This is supported by Zeller, who has suggested that due to municipal interests, it is unlikely that uniformity of all laws is possible, though he argues it would be desirable in the contemporary context of globalisation.[80] Zeller asserts that unification in discrete areas

---

[77]   Ross Ashcroft, *Harmonisation of Substantive Legal Principles and Structures: Lessons from the Australian Federal Legal System with Respect to Environment & Resource Laws*, 3.

[78]   Michail Kritikos, *Procedural Harmonization in the EU's GMO Authorization Framework* (2008).

[79]   Christopher Heath, 'Methods of Industrial Property Harmonisation – The Example of Europe' in Christoph Antons, Michael Blakeney and Christopher Heath (eds), *Intellectual Property Harmonisation Within ASEAN and APEC* (2004), 39 at 48.

[80]   Bruno Zeller, *CISG and the Unification of International Trade Law* (Routledge-Cavendish 2007) 1.

of law is however the 'next best thing',[81] although he notes that these ideas are controversial.[82] Harmonisation, to Zeller, is a step along the way to uniformity of law, and as such is desirable.[83] Similarly, many international adjudicating bodies have been set up with similar goals. Whilst it is not necessarily 'harmonisation' *per se*, these bodies recognise the importance of harmonisation in creating 'conditions of stability and well-being' in world and regional legal orders.[84] The same could easily be said within national legal systems themselves. Such stability is also important from a democratic point of view which underpins modern human rights jurisprudence – that is, the notion of *foreseeability* and *predictability* of the way the law will operate.[85] Such certainty and foreseeability are also credited with reducing burdensome costs created by parochial legal differences as well as increasing economic efficiency for compliance.[86] In practice, the rationalisation of a harmonisation of legal phenomenon is unlikely to be made on legal grounds, but rather economic and trade considerations are going to be the most important considerations.[87] Such reasons advanced by Sir Francis include the ability to reduce transaction costs, ability for access to courts and justice and the chance to ensure that new remedies can be made to meet the changing needs of society.[88]

Boodman suggests that harmonisation does not actually add anything to the discourse about interjurisdictional legal transactions.[89] This can be compared with Merryman, who suggests that harmonisation is desirable, not because it is an inevitable consequence of social structures, or today 'globalisation', but rather because those who have control over the law making powers are able to view the benefits which are derived from harmonisation.[90]

---

[81]   Ibid.

[82]   Ibid., 2.

[83]   Ibid., 12.

[84]   Gail Evans, *The Impact of WTO Appellate Body Jurisprudence on the Harmonization of Trademark Law in the European Union* (2008), 4.

[85]   Haim Sandberg, 'Three-Dimensional Partition and Registration of Subsurface Land Space', (2003/2004) 37 *Israel Law Review* 119–30.

[86]   Jurgita Malinauskaite, *International Competition Law Harmonisation and the WTO: Past, Present and Future*, 7.

[87]   Christopher Heath, 'Methods of Industrial Property Harmonisation – The Example of Europe' in Christoph Antons, Michael Blakeney and Christopher Heath (eds), *Intellectual Property Harmonisation Within ASEAN and APEC* (Aspen Publishers, 2004), 39 at 46. See also Stelios Andreadakis' parallel point on reflexive harmonisation, in *Regulatory Competition or Harmonization: The dilemma, the alternatives and the prospect of Reflexive Harmonization*, reproduced in chapter 3 of this volume.

[88]   Sir Francis Jacobs, Opening Address.

[89]   Bruno Zeller, *CISG and the Unification of International Trade Law* (2007), 12.

[90]   Ibid., 14.

Whether one views harmonisation as important may also depend on which area of law one works in. For example, many areas of corporate or trade law seem clearly to benefit from harmonising legal phenomenon. But what about harmonisation in the fields of criminal law or environmental law? Weeramantry J of the International Court of Justice has asserted that

> The problem of steering a course between the needs of development and the necessity to protect the environment is a problem alike of the law of development and of the law of the environment. Both these vital and developing areas of law require, and indeed assume, the existence of a principle which harmonizes both needs.[91]

Others have considered the problems of failing to achieve 'consequential harmonisation' at different levels, whether national or international. Henschel analyses the debate about the functionality of consequential harmonisation where the results are 'synthetic' rather than organic.[92] One of the most problematic issues arising is the inability effectively to enforce rights or obligations of states or persons, be they juristic or natural. Evans, for example, has recognised that the development of a so-called 'international trademark' based on a 'bundle of national or regional trademarks' will only be able to be enforced in particular jurisdictions, and not all jurisdictions as initially hoped for.[93] Evans suggests that without harmonisation of the substance of the laws, it is highly unlikely that courts of different jurisdictions will reach analogous conclusions to one another.[94] Likewise, Ashcroft notes similar issues in the domestic context of a federalised state. The concern expressed recognises that whilst a broad principle may be evident through different jurisdictions, courts are obliged to interpret the law as it immediately stands in a particular jurisdiction.[95] This must be done in a way which detaches the generalisations of harmonisation which could be fraught with difficulties in interpretation and application.

Whilst debate is being had about the desirability of harmonisation, the authors would suggest that empirical research may assist more greatly in understanding whether harmonisation can be considered 'successful'. In approaching such research, it would assist not only to have a clear concept of harmonisation, but

---

[91] *Gabcikovo-Nagymaros Project* (Danube Dam case), Separate Opinion of Weeramantry J, at 90.

[92] René-Franz Henschel, *Creation of Rules in National and International Business Law: A Non-national, Analytical-Synthetic Comparative Method*, 2.

[93] Gail Evans, *The Impact of WTO Appellate Body Jurisprudence on the Harmonization of Trademark Law in the European Union* (2008), 3.

[94] Ibid., 4.

[95] Ross Ashcroft, *Harmonisation of Substantive Legal Principles and Structures: Lessons from the Australian Federal Legal System with Respect to Environment & Resource Laws*, 12–13.

also a set of clear and consistent criteria against which this 'success' could be measured. These criteria may have to be adjusted to reflect the real needs of different areas of law or even specific forms of harmonised law.[96]

A. Problems with Procedural Harmonisation as a Sole Concept?

A significant problem with harmonisation being a process rather than a consequence is that there is no guarantee that a formal set of institutions may arise in which to enforce rules and obligations, which may remain at the level of 'soft law' rather than substantive legal phenomenon.

Additionally, as it is the process which is harmonised, as opposed to the outcome, we may find that the certainty of the legal systems is undermined. Certainty may be undermined as processes may be slow, as well as subject to the fluctuations of government policy shifts when changes in governing parties occur.

A further problem recognised by Christian Twigg-Flesner, especially in the context of international laws or regional laws, such as the European projects, relates to language.[97] It is quite problematic when trying to reach consensus in relation to legal phenomenon across different cultures, and this is magnified when extra languages are involved. Indeed, even where only one language may exist within a federal state such issues can arise, as was recognised in the context of Australian environmental laws.[98]

B. Who Decides whether Harmonisation should Occur?

Whether laws are harmonised is controversial, partly because of a perception that there is a possibility of democratic deficit. Many, particularly those in the English-speaking world, would prefer to leave regulation to markets rather than attempt to find a harmonised law.[99] However, the problem with leaving the harmonisation of laws and regulation to markets is that these organisations have neither been

---

[96] See, for example, the approach for measuring the success of the uniformity of the International Sales Law (CISG) in Camilla Baasch Andersen, *Uniform Application of the International Sales Law: Understanding Uniformity, the Global Jurisconsultorium and Examination and Notification Provisions of the CISG* (Kluwer Law International, 2007) by accepting various degrees of uniformity and different aims of producing harmonised law.

[97] Christian Twigg-Fleisner, *Pre-contractual Duties – from the Acquis to the Draft Common Frame of Reference*, 26.

[98] Ross Ashcroft, *Harmonisation of Substantive Legal Principles and Structures: Lessons from the Australian Federal Legal System with Respect to Environment & Resource Laws*, 8–12.

[99] Bruno Zeller, *CISG and the Unification of International Trade Law* (Routledge-Cavendish 2007), 13.

democratically elected, nor guaranteed to remain in the same jurisdiction. Rather, economic conditions often factor in on the day to day and long term aspirations of companies within the market system, which are there to profit.

Arai has evaluated the issue of harmonisation through the framework of the European Convention on Human Rights and queries whether or not a central court, such as the Strasbourg Court, is equipped to undertake such a role, given the propensity to rely on its own level of discretionary powers,[100] as well as a feeling of 'judicial arbitrariness'[101] and potential subjectiveness.[102] Arai also expresses concern that the judges may shift away from the 'legislative intent' of the Convention's drafters.[103]

By contrast, the works of Beale and Twigg-Fleisner describing the DCRF are indicative of harmonisation efforts through academic and practitioner channels, albeit funded by a supra-national body within the European governance framework.[104] Whilst the drivers behind the DCRF are governing bodies, by providing funding, the work behind the scenes is undertaken through other bodies.

As such, it is appropriate to ask questions about who will decide the fate of harmonisation – be it procedural harmonisation or consequential harmonisation – and even, indeed, which form of harmonisation should be undertaken. The authors throughout this book give different opinions, all of which are equally valid, and all form evidence of how difficult this question is to answer.

C. Economic and Sociological Considerations

Regardless of whether one subcribes to the theory that harmonisation is indeed procedure, or the other side, that is it consequential, there are extra-legal issues which need to be considered by those who seek to either enhance, or deny, harmonisation.

The first of these categories could be classified as *socio-economic considerations*. The second category could be deemed *political considerations*. The considerations are raised by a number of contributors to this book. One must note however that the lines do blur considerably between these considerations.

D. The Applied Practice of Harmonisation

Whilst the debate continues, it could be useful to consider pragmatic issues of applied harmonised law.

---

[100] Yutaka Arai-Takahashi, chapter 5 of this volume.
[101] Ibid., 19.
[102] Ibid., 23.
[103] Ibid., 18–19.
[104] Hugh Beale QC, *The Draft Common Frame of Reference*, 1.

The *application* of harmonised law, or uniform law, is a separate issue from the *creation* of uniform or harmonised rules, which is in need of further attention in academic discourse and debate. The W G Hart workshop sought to bring further focus to this area by also highlighting the practice of harmonised law.

One issue raised by the practical application is the pragmatic and realistic approach which needs to be taken in allowing a certain flexibility in the application of so-called uniform laws. The 'homeward trend' of domestic applications of international law, in any field or area of law, is not a new phenomenon, and is compounding the application of uniform laws. When discussing the practical implications of applying harmonised law, there is a significant distinction to be made between regional and global harmonisation, especially where regional harmonisation allows for the surrender of sovereignty and/or the introduction of systems which can monitor the harmonised law.

Monitored harmonised law, like most EU law, has the potential to attain very high levels of uniform application due to the monitoring of the Court and Commission, as well as the concept of immediately applicable regulations. The vast majority of shared law, however, is self-executing and not monitored for its uniform application. This is especially true for harmonised private law outside any monitored regional framework. This lack of true uniformity in application was addressed by Baasch Andersen regarding sales law, and also by Goldby with respect to shared rules for carriage – it presents a real problem for the enacted globally shared rules, especially in private law, when they present themselves as similar rules but are dis-similar in their applications.

Aside from EU law, the example of the European Convention on Human Rights (ECHR), discussed by Dr Arai, represents another form of regional harmonised law which has included a deliberate safety-valve in the so-called 'margin of appreciation' which allows member states certain discretion in deciding specific issues under specific provisions.[105]

This deliberate decision to allow flexibility in shared rules based on public policies, moral and cultural views and the overall consideration that states are 'better placed' to decide issues for themselves in some cases may well present a blueprint for a solution to applying harmonised or uniform laws in many other contexts. It is worth noting that the ECHR does not set out to unify law, but solely to select standards.[106]

However, it is also worth noting that overly ambitious uniform laws, which attempt to unify law without corresponding transnational practice having reached a similar level of uniformity, tend to fail in any event, because domestic states

---

[105]   Yutaka Arai-Takahashi, ibid.
[106]   Ibid.

will not compromise certain principles when applying shared law. There is a lot of scope for arguing that since a sort of 'margin of appreciation' is inevitable in the application of uniform laws, we may as well factor such an aspect in their overall methodology to make any differences in application less surprising, and exercise more controlled divergences.

Similarly, it could also be argued that simply because the early years of uniform laws are made difficult by homeward trends, we should not rush to accommodate these difficulties, but rather see them as teething difficulties for a new form of shared law.

It would seem that, for both sides of this argument on accepting domestic law divergences in applying shared laws, the area of law involved is instrumental. At least in theory, commercial law lends itself better to the notion of a non-interventionist uniform law application, due to many of the common cores of transnational commercial activities. Suppressing homeward trends and attaining higher degrees of applied uniformity may well be – at the moment – an illusion for shared commercial law, but it may be realisable if the notions of shared law and global jurisconsultorium win greater favour with national courts.[107]

Conversely, any attempts at unifying or harmonising laws which are more closely connected to domestic legal cultures and moral norms – such as family law, inheritance laws, selected forms of liability, and even insolvency – will inevitably require margins for flexible application. The 'margin of application' may thus well form a model or starting blueprint for the methodology of allowing such controlled margins in many other areas of law where unified solutions are sought, but uniform application is – and remains – utopian.

Another issue is ensuring that the legal and regulatory systems as a whole do not suffer tremendous effects by harmonisation methods. Andreadakis discusses the notion of reflexive harmonisation as a possible solution between two polar opposites of complete harmonisation and regulatory competition.

V. CONCLUDING COMMENTS

The preceding discussion has attempted to start the development of a clear 'common core' in the manner in which we consider harmonisation of law, especially within the legal profession. There are two frameworks, sometimes overlapping, from which we advocate that the discipline of harmonisation of laws should be considered: consequential harmonisation and procedural harmonisation. Each of these comes with a unique set of considerations, which we have tried to highlight in a concise and precise manner.

---

[107] Compare Camilla Baasch Andersen's argument in her conference paper.

The preceding chapters each make individual contributions to the literature and debate about harmonisation. The contributions assist in the development of the discipline of harmonisation – a discipline which is growing and will continue to grow only through scholarly discourse and debate. It is recognisable that there is no settled agreement as to whether harmonisation is indeed the best solution, or merely one among many possibilities. Those who engage in harmonisation processes, whether global or regional, must also keep in mind that harmonisation can never be an absolute. Some form of tolerance for divergent application is needed within the system for most laws, as well as a way to work towards minimising these divergences. It may well be a technical disharmony to allow for such homeward discrepancies in applied laws, but it is arguably a disharmony which is necessary.

Whatever the way forward, it is asserted that if these prolific efforts at harmonising law are to make useful contributions to the development of jurisprudence, either consequentially or procedurally, this must be done, in the words of Basil Markesinis QC, in a manner which is pragmatic and flexible and not dogmatic and rigid.[108] Moreover, to ensure that harmonisation is not illusory, and carries with it the intended degree of similarity in legal rules, we must focus on how to sustain similar application of harmonised laws throughout different jurisdictions.

The intermediary goal for ensuring these two aims is ensuring that there is an engagement in the educational processes,[109] as well as within the profession. The authors hope that this chapter and this book, and the conference from which the work evolved, can spark the beginning of a more structured debate in the field of harmonisation theory and practice.

---

[108]   Markesinis is quoted in Bruno Zeller, 'CISG and the Unification of International Trade Law' (2007, Routledge-Cavendish), 14.

[109]   A statement made in the introductory/opening speech by Mads Andenas on the first day of the workshop.

Index